CONTEMPORARY ART

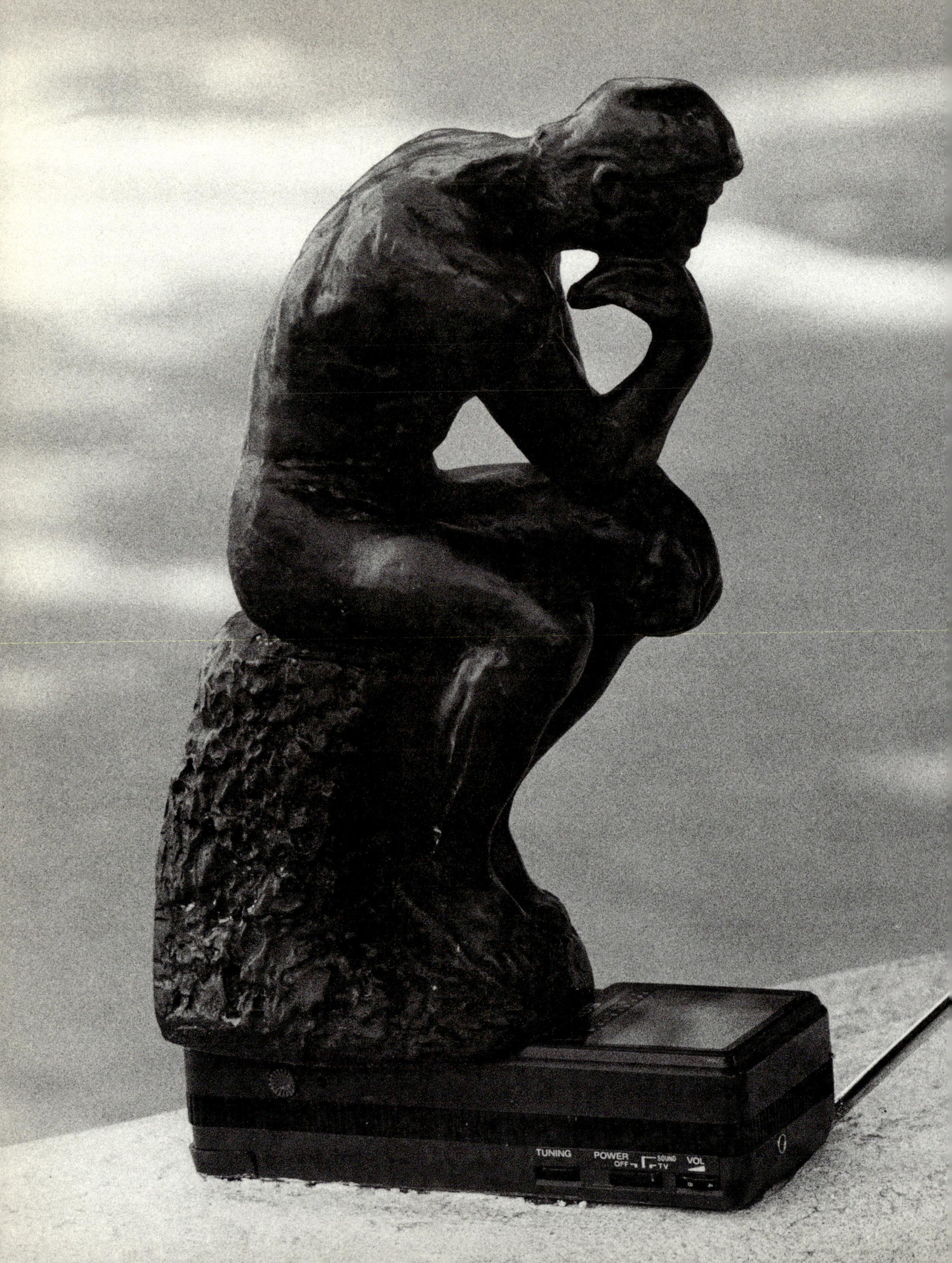

TUNING
POWER
OFF
SOUND
TV
VOL

CONTEMPORARY ART
1965-1990

BRUCE D. KURTZ
Phoenix Art Museum

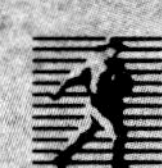

PRENTICE HALL
Englewood Cliffs, N.J. 07632

To ACT UP
AIDS Coalition to Unleash Power
and
To All of the People Who Have Died,
and Will Die, of AIDS

ISBN 0-13-173022-3

This book was designed and produced by
JOHN CALMANN AND KING LTD, LONDON

Designed by Richard Foenander
Picture research by Carrie Haines

Typeset by Fakenham Photosetting Limited
Printed in Hong Kong

Frontispiece: NAM JUNE PAIK
Something Pacific 1986
(Detail, one of seven elements)
Bronze, Sony TV
Courtesy Stuart Collection, University of California, San
Diego
Photo Mathieu Gregoire

Cover (detail): ANSELM KIEFER
Die Meistersinger 1981
Oil, acrylic, emulsion and straw on canvas
72½ × 130 ins
(184 × 330 cm)
Collection Linda and Harry Macklowe, New York

ACKNOWLEDGEMENTS

The most substantial debt the author owes to those
who helped create this volume is due the artists
whose works are represented here, for their coopera-
tion in providing information, for their assistance in
obtaining photographs of their work and permission
to reproduce them, and for making the art which is
this book's subject.

Foremost among those who assisted in the writing are Christopher Knight and Professor Betsy Fahl-
man, both of whom read sections and perceptively
advised me how to improve them. Adrienne Whitaker
resourcefully assisted with research during the editing process. Cate Spencer offered valuable help at a
time when it was keenly needed and much appreci-
ated.

Norwell Therien, my editor at Prentice Hall,
guided and advised me from the development of this
book's concept through the completion of the manuscript and its editing. Melanie White of John Calmann
and King Ltd was a model of patience and attention to
detail during the editing process. The picture resear-
cher Carrie Haines skillfully ferreted out the many
photographs of artworks.

James K. Ballinger, Director of the Phoenix Art
Museum, encouraged and supported me throughout
the entire four year process from the beginning of the
manuscript to this book's publication.

Contents

3. EARTHWORKS AND SITE-SPECIFIC SCULPTURE *79*

4. POST-MINIMALISM *109*

SOCIAL AND POLITICAL BACKGROUND 1970s *142*

5. PLURALISM *145*

SOCIAL AND POLITICAL BACKGROUND 1980s *164*

6. NEO-EXPRESSIONISM *167*

7. POST-MODERNISM   *189*

8. SCULPTURE OF THE 1980s   *211*

9. SIMULATIONISM   *227*

EPILOGUE   *239*

Preface

Art historians define contemporary art as the art made by artists who produced their first mature work after 1945. Many contemporary art courses cover the time period of 1945–1990. Because of the sheer volume of art produced since 1945, most modern art texts give scanty treatment to the art of the last two decades. To permit thorough discussion of the most recent contemporary art, this book has subdivided 1945–1990 into the shorter time period of 1965–1990.

American contemporary art became world-dominant after 1945, when the art capital of the western world shifted from Paris to New York City. Though many significant contemporary art developments have occurred in other countries, American contemporary art remains the most influential in the world. Neo-Expressionists in Germany, Italy, and other European countries have produced art on the same level of quality as in America—perhaps even better in the case of the German, Anselm Kiefer—but no country has consistently produced art equal to American art throughout the time period of 1965–1990.

Why begin with Conceptual Art or with 1965? With Conceptual Art there began a period in American contemporary art during which artists dematerialized their art objects into untraditional, fragile, and often temporary forms. Video, Film, and Performance Art employ the fourth dimension of time or duration, also characteristic of some Conceptual Art and Earthworks. In all these cases, Minimal Art played a seminal role.

Minimal artists' preoccupation with reductivism, with paring down the artwork to its most essential and unembellished core, informs Conceptual Art, Video, Film, and Performance Art, Earthworks, and site-specific sculpture. So too do many of the Minimalists' formal concerns: horizontality in sculpture, interaction between the artwork and the surrounding space, assertion of the medium's inherent structure as the artwork's subject, and utilization of the minimum of artistic means. All of these characteristics find some form in the subjects of the first three chapters. Hence, Conceptual Art makes an appropriate beginning.

Why not begin with Minimal Art? Minimal Art first came into being in the late 1950s, at about the same time as Pop Art and Color Field Painting. To begin with Minimal Art—other than in the Introduction—would be chronologically misleading unless these other two movements were also discussed, but doing so would expand the scope of this book beyond what could successfully be accomplished in this amount of space.

Post-Minimalists employ the Minimalists' formalist visual vocabulary to create an anti-formalist art indebted to the precedents of Conceptual Art and Earthworks. Many of them emphasize the process of the making of the artwork as part of its subject, unlike the Minimalists' insistence on static art objects. Post-Minimalists' incorporation of the fourth dimension of time or duration—in temporary or process artworks—parallels the use of the fourth dimension by many artists in the first three chapters.

Conceptual Art, Video, Film, and Performance Art, Earthworks, site-specific sculpture, and Post-Minimalism all began in the second half of the 1960s and extended into the 1970s. The 1970s was more a decade of assimilation and elaboration than the 1960s. Pop Art, Color Field Painting, Minimalism, Conceptual Art, Video, Film, and Performance Art, Earthworks, site-specific sculpture, and Post-Minimalism all came to fruition in the 1960s—an extraordinary decade in American art history.

Pluralism is a term often used to describe the 1970s. Not only did all of the earlier named movements continue to develop during the 1970s, but several new tendencies emerged: Photo Realism, Super Realism, Pattern and Decoration, and New Image Painting. Compared with the radically transformational impact of the earlier movements, the influence of all but the last of these developments is not as great.

During the late 1970s with New Image Painting, then the early 1980s with Neo-Expressionism, there occurs a re-emergence of representational imagery in traditional art media like oil paint and bronze, as well as a return to story-telling, narrative, metaphor, and allegory. Topics from literature reappear after several decades of having been considered retrograde, outside the purely visual realm of art.

A great deal of important figurative and non-figurative sculpture has been produced in the 1980s, growing in part out of the large body of exceptional sculpture produced in America during the preceding two decades. Some characteristics carry over from one artist to another, such as story-telling related to that of the Neo-Expressionists, or an interest in hollow forms revealing voids, or in anthropomorphism which was shunned by the Minimalists. But for the most part, sculpture of the 1980s was made more by an array of individuals than by artists working within the context of a coherent movement.

With the advent of Post-Modernism in the 1980s, complex references to social, economic, linguistic, and political systems take center stage, often in the form of images borrowed or "appropriated' from the mass-media. Artists take cues from Pop Art's mass-media imagery and from Conceptual Art's emphasis on the artwork's intellectual strategies more than its formal properties. Post-Modernists critique the Modernist concept of the artist as a lone individual heroically creating a unique new personal reality. Instead, Post-Modernists place the artist within a socio-economic and political system with its own overriding reality which subsumes the individual. With the Post-Modernists, imagery shared by the culture as a whole takes precedence over individualistic forms. Thus the opposition between art and the majority culture, or the concept of the avant-garde (which originated in about 1860), comes at least to a temporary end with Post-Modernism.

Simulationists appropriate styles and concepts from Minimalism and Conceptual Art, respectively, but treat their fine art borrowings with the same casualness as their appropriations of commodity merchandising techniques. They carry the Post-Modernists' preoccupation with a populist audience a step further into equating, essentially, art's audience with the same audience for any other commodity. Simulationists equate newness in art with the supreme value of newness in consumer products. They aim their art toward the newly dominant managerial class in our post-industrial commodity culture and underpin it with post-structuralist philosophy, especially that of Jean Baudrillard. They are not as concerned with formal issues as with the meaning and syntax of the objects and images which they use.

And so we return once again to Conceptual Art and to our rationale for beginning there.

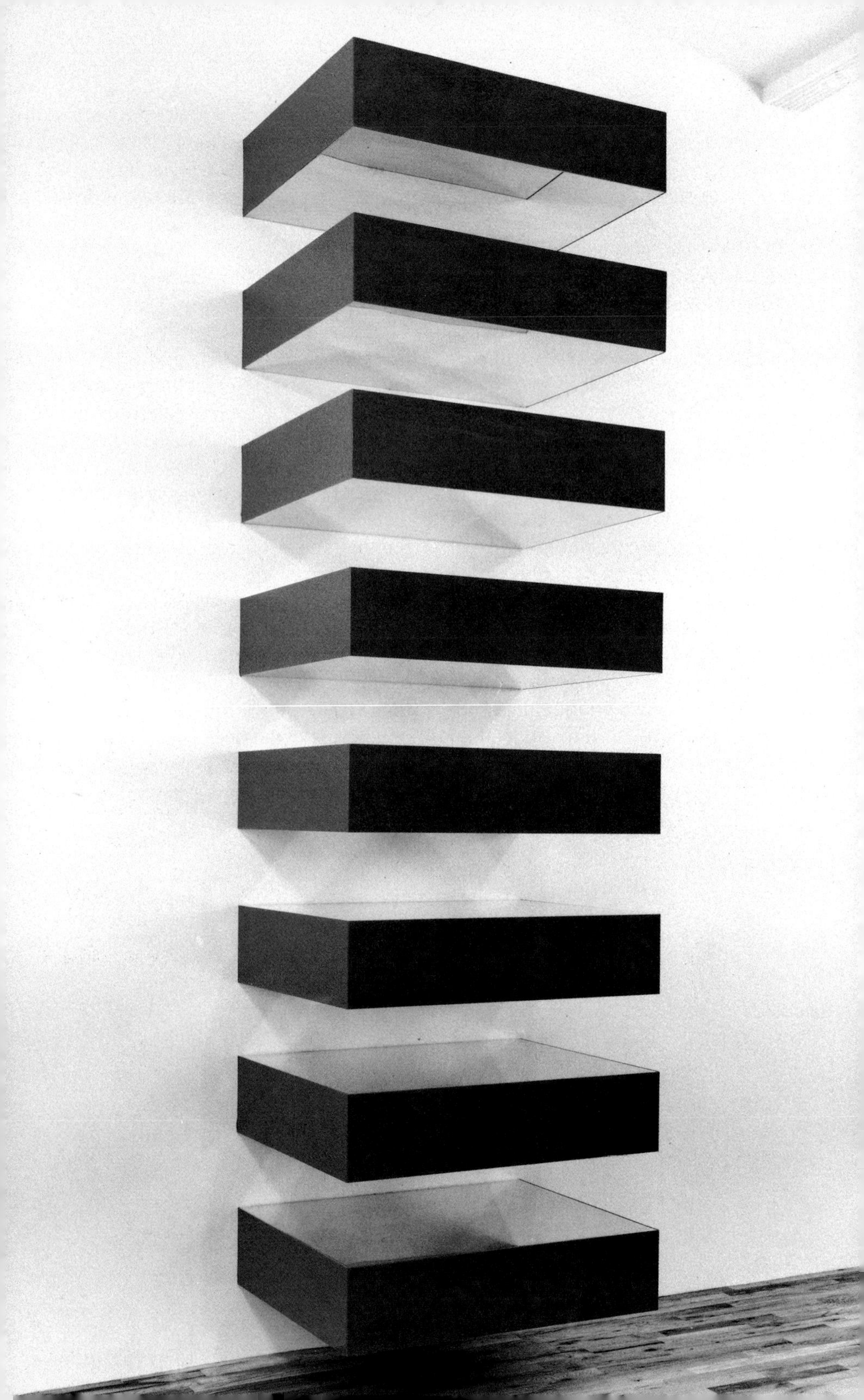

Introduction

"A shape, a volume, a color, a surface is something itself. It shouldn't be concealed as part of a fairly different whole."[1]

—— DONALD JUDD ——

Donald Judd
Untitled 1989
Courtesy Paula Cooper Gallery, New York

Before 1965, two major areas of activity began in American art which have such great significance on the topics discussed in this book that they merit introduction: they are new performance arts and Minimal sculpture. Developments in new performance arts foreshadow the developments in Video, Film, and Performance arts discussed in Chapter 2. Minimal sculpture established sculptural issues and a formal visual vocabulary for addressing them—a vocabulary that Conceptual, Earthwork, and Post-Minimal artists adopted or modified. Understanding the modifica-

tions these latter artists made requires some background discussion of the precedent to which they responded.

A further area of activity which emerged at the same time as Minimal sculpture was Color Field Painting and Pop Art. The influence that Color Field Painting had on the topics discussed in this book was not, however, as great as that of Minimal sculpture. Pop Art was an important precedent to Post-Modernism and will be discussed in the introduction to Chapter 7.

The Avant-Garde

Major shifts occurred in the function and role of artists between the Conceptual Art of the later 1960s and the present, shifts which altered the concept of the avant-garde. The term "avant-garde" originated in the French military where it referred to scouts who ventured into unknown territories ahead of the troops. Hence it was adopted to indicate artists who ventured into new artistic fields far ahead of their audience's experience or their ability to comprehend the innovations.

Avant-gardism originated in the nineteenth century in France, following several centuries of church, aristocratic, royal and government patronage of artists. During this time the norm was, to simplify matters greatly, for art to evolve, more or less, in line with the patron's wishes and within the artistic mainstream sanctioned by the authorities of the time.

Exactly when avant-gardism first appeared remains open to discussion, but it is generally agreed that the spirit of avant-gardism was to oppose the majority culture, to oppose officially sanctioned artistic values in favor of new experimental ones. Some date the avant-garde's beginning at 1819, the year Théodore Géricault (1791–1824) exhibited his *Raft of the Medusa* at the Paris Salon (an official art exhibition, then virtually the only opportunity in France that an artist had to present work to the public). Others use the date 1824, the year of the Salon when the English landscape artist John Constable (1776–

1837) exhibited his *Hay Wain* to the astonishment of the French Romanticist Eugène Delacroix (1798–1863). Others state the avant-garde's advent as 1855, when the French Realist Gustave Courbet (1819–77) installed his Pavilion of Realism, containing his paintings, including *The Painter's Studio: a Real Allegory*, outside the 1855 World's fairgrounds in Paris. That year the Salon at the *Exposition Universelle* offered large selections of paintings by J.A.D. Ingres (1780–1867) (representing officially sanctioned, mainstream art), and Eugène Delacroix (representing the "modern" or experimental approach). Courbet's artistic tendencies were taken by the official arbiters of taste to be completely unacceptable.

I prefer to use the date of 1863 as marking the beginning of the avant-garde, although ultimately it does not really matter what date one uses, as long as the character of the event is clearly understood. The year 1863 was that of the Salon des Refusés, an exhibition of the artworks that had been rejected from that year's officially sanctioned French Salon. It was the year that *Luncheon on the Grass* by Manet (1832–83) created such an outrage and scandal that he became identified by experimental artists—such as Monet, Renoir, and Degas—as the leader of a new school (he eventually earned the name "the father of Impressionism"). Manet's status as *the* renegade artist was secured when, after a loosening of the Salon eligibility rules in 1865, his *Olympia* (Fig. **0.1**)

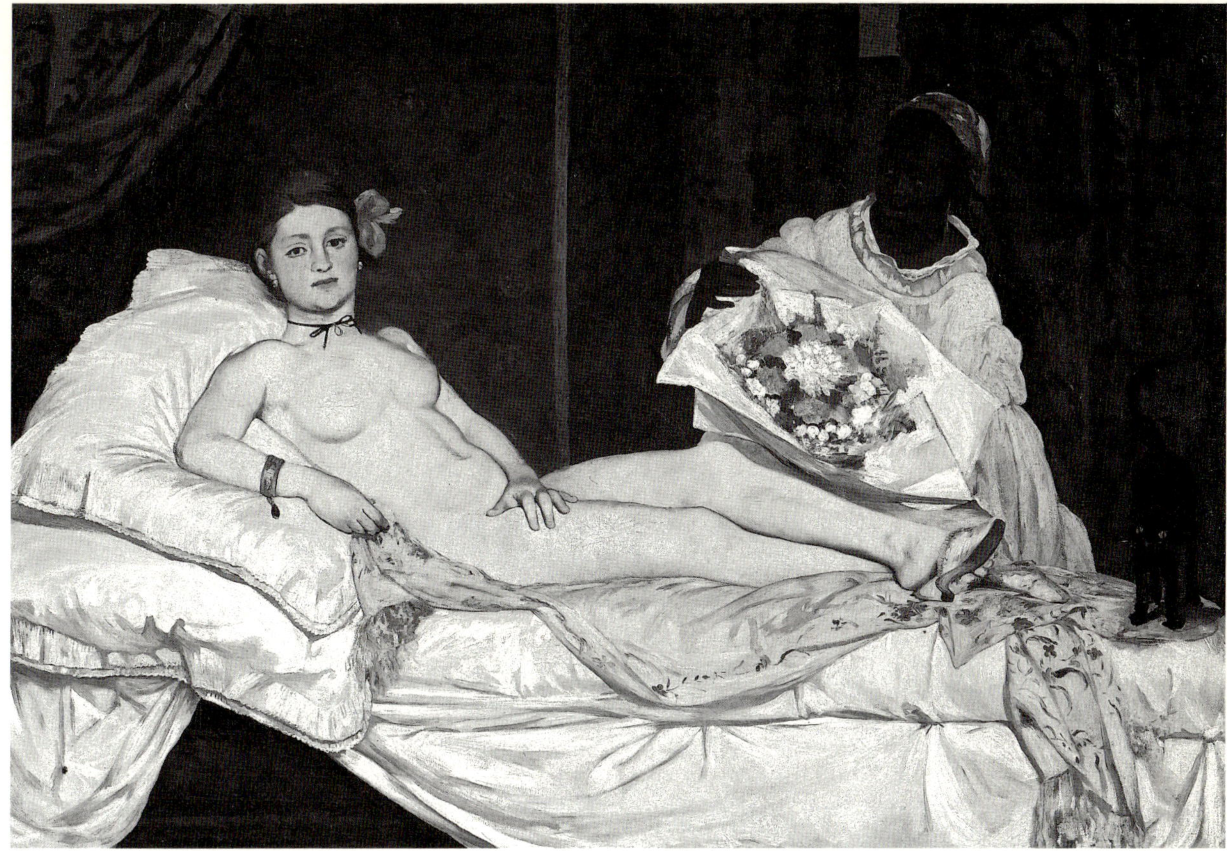

0.1 EDOUARD MANET
Olympia 1863
Oil on canvas
51 × 74¾ins
(129.5 × 189.9cm)
Musée d'Orsay

was accepted and created such a scandal that it became the first artwork in history to require police protection from the crowds that tried to destroy it.

It is difficult to imagine anyone becoming that volatile about an artwork today. The avant-garde has certainly undergone stark changes since the days when artists worked in relative isolation and in small numbers, developing their artistic ideas independently from the marketplace, and often struggling in poverty, with only a small audience of artists and like-minded intellectuals understanding their art. Van Gogh (1853–90), who sold only one painting in his lifetime, is the quintessential avant-garde artist. Yet most of the Impressionists, Post-Impressionists, Expressionists, Fauvists, Cubists, Dadaists, Surrealists, and Abstract Expressionists, at least in the early stages of their mature work, worked in relative obscurity before obtaining recognition, though most to a lesser extent than Van Gogh.

Beginning with Pop Art in the 1960s, the adversarial relationship between mainstream visual culture and the avant-garde began to break down far more radically than it had at any other time since the nineteenth century. Avant-gardism continued well through the 1970s, and even into the 1980s, in the work of certain artists such as Susan Rothenberg, Robert Smithson, Nam June Paik, and Jonathan Borofsky. But by far the majority of artists in the 1980s have aimed their art toward a more populist audience than the initially, at least, narrower one of the traditional avant-garde.

Post-Modernism, which could not have occurred without the advent of Pop Art, is partly defined as self-consciously representing an end to the opposing role of avant-garde art. Modernism and avant-gardism have historically been of the same ilk; both refer to art which is, at its beginning, highly specialized, difficult to understand, and thoroughly comprehensible only by a small, initiate audience knowledgeable about modern art history and theory. At least to some extent, Pop Art is comprehensible by the people who look at comic books; and a great deal of Post-Modernism is deliberately aimed toward the populist audience of the mass media. A sub-theme of this book is therefore, the transformation of the avant-garde to the extent that, according to some contemporary art specialists, it may no longer exist.

Has the period (1965–1990) represented in this book witnessed the end of the avant-garde? Have artists ceased to define their art in opposition to the majority culture, instead embracing it and seeking to enter into it? Will the relationship between artists and the general public typical of earlier avant-garde art ever recur? These are all questions which concern scholars and art-lovers alike.

New Performance Arts

John Cage and Black Mountain College

Performance arts incorporating avant-garde dance, theater, music, poetry, film, and the visual arts developed in the 1950s and 1960s. The key figure in American avant-garde music prior to 1960 was John Cage (born 1912), whose belief that "everything is music," and that a composer's function is to call attention to that fact, led him to use sounds that accidentally occurred at the performance site (using sound like the surrealists used "found" objects—see page 18), and untraditional sound-making (or noise-making) apparatus, like radios or duck calls. In Cage's 1937 manifesto *The Future of Music* (one of his many influential writings), the composer stated that "wherever we are, what we hear is mostly noise ... Whether the sound of a truck at 50 mph, rain, or static between radio stations, we find noise fascinating." He wanted to "capture and control these sounds, to use them, not as sound effects, but as musical instruments."[2]

John Cage's *4'33"*, first performed by David Tudor in 1952, entails the performer, sitting at a piano, closing the keyboard cover for four minutes and 33 seconds while the audience listens to itself fidget, cough, ruminate, and criticize; the chairs squeak; the air conditioning blow; taxis honk outdoors, and so on.

John Cage was an important teacher of the new avant-garde generation which sought alternatives to traditional static objects like painting and sculpture. Beginning in the summer of 1948, Cage and his long-time collaborator, the dancer and choreographer Merce Cunningham, taught at Black Mountain College in Lake Eden, North Carolina (not far from Asheville).

The art of Robert Rauschenberg (born 1925) bridged the gap between Pop Art and the most dominant preceding style, Abstract Expressionism. He was a student at the College in the summer of 1952 when John Cage orchestrated what is regarded as the first avant-garde multi-media event of the postwar period, the forerunner of the "Happening," the Fluxus "Event," and "Performance Art." Art historian Rose Lee Goldberg describes the event:

Spectators took their seats in the square arena forming four triangles created by diagonal aisles, each holding the white cup which had been placed on their chair. White paintings by a visiting student, Robert Rauschenberg, hung overhead. From a step-ladder, Cage, in black suit and tie, read a text on "the relation of music to Zen Buddhism" and excerpts from Meister Eckhart. Then he performed a "composition with a radio," following the prearranged "time brackets." At the same time, Rauschenberg played old records on a hand-wound gramophone and David Tudor played a "prepared piano" [a piano with objects inserted in between the wires and into the sound box]. Later, Tudor turned to two buckets, pouring water from one to the other while, planted in the audience, Charles Olsen and Mary Caroline Richards read poetry. Cunningham and others danced through the aisles chased by an excited dog, Rauschenberg flashed "abstract" slides (created by colored gelatine sandwiched between the glass) and film clips projected onto the ceiling showed first the school cook, and then, as they gradually moved from the ceiling down the wall, the setting sun. In a corner, the composer Jay Watt played exotic musical instruments and "whistles blew, babies screamed and coffee was served by four boys dressed in white."

The country audience was delighted. Only the composer Stefan Wolpe walked out in protest, and Cage proclaimed the evening a success. An "anarchic" event; "purposeless in that we didn't know what was going to happen," it suggested endless possibilities for future collaborations. And it provided Cunningham with a new decor and costume designer for his dance company: Robert Rauschenberg.[3]

HAPPENINGS

Beginning in 1956 in New York City at the New School for Social Research, John Cage taught a small and influential class in the composition of experimental music. Students who attended included Allan Kaprow, Dick Higgins, Jackson MacLow, George Brecht, Al Hansen, and others who were to make important inroads into new art forms. Sometimes the regular students brought friends, like George Segal, Larry Poons, and Jim Dine. "We all felt something terrifically exciting was going on in that class," Kaprow recalled some years later. "I just couldn't wait to get back there every week."[4]

These artists and others—Claes Oldenburg, Lucas Samaras, and Red Grooms, for example—orchestrated and performed in events similar to the 1952 Black Mountain precedent, but mostly for each other and small groups of friends. The year 1959 is usually given for the first "Happening" open to a wider public—Allan Kaprow's *18 Happenings in 6 Parts* (Fig. **0.2**) which took place at the Reuben Gallery in New York. It was scripted, choreographed, and each part was timed to last a total of 90 minutes. *This event took place in three separate rooms (environments) with the audience moving from one to another to watch human and non-human actors (there was a dancing toy and a pair of wheeled constructions) perform activities that varied from performance to performance. Words were spoken, both live and on tape, but there was no plot or story, no development, and no meaning or message. "Happenings," as he [Kaprow]* *explained in a subsequent article, "are events which, put simply, happen ... they appear to go nowhere and do not make any particular literary point."*[5]

The Pop artist Claes Oldenburg's Happenings take their subjects from mundane, everyday life, like his sculptures. Oldenburg's sculpture titled *The Store* (1961), is an imitation of a real-life store with mer-

0.2 ALLAN KAPROW　　　1959
18 Happenings in 6 Parts　　Photo by Fred W. McDarrah

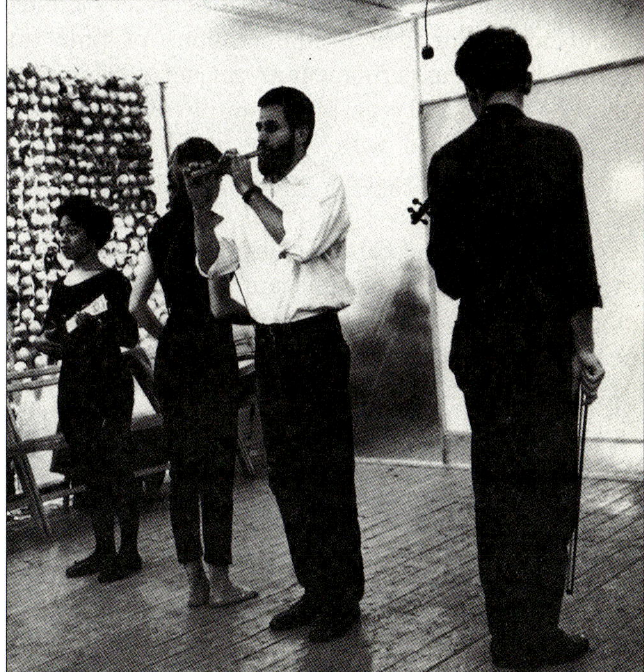

chandise like sneakers, skirts, pies, and other consumer goods made out of plaster painted with enamel. *The Store* manifested Oldenburg's search for an art that "takes its form from the lines of life itself, that twists and extends and accumulates and spits and drips, and is heavy and coarse and blunt and sweet and stupid as life itself."[6]

Oldenburg's 1960 Happening, *Snapshots from the City* was "realistic," with "fragments of action immobilized by instantaneous illuminations," consisting of "a collaged city landscape with built-in street and immobile figures on a stage against a textured wall, flickering lights and found objects on the floor."[7]

None of the "Happenings" artists actually agreed to the use of the term; not even Kaprow, who first used it in the title of his 1959 live event. No manifesto was issued, no magazine or collective statement printed. But the term "Happening," for want of a better one, became used to describe a sometimes scripted, more often improvisatory, live, multi-media event.

Happenings only briefly maintained their radical position. Originally conceived as alternatives to object-oriented artworks which had become, in some artist's views, embodiments of status or money rather than aesthetic concerns, Happenings quickly became chic. "By 1962 the whole thing had become totally commercial," according to Oldenburg. "People were arriving in Cadillacs."[8] But while Happenings artists maintained their edge, they brought new energy to the idea of live art that combined music, dance, painting, sculpture, film, and other art forms. Meanwhile, other artists added momentum to live art.

FLUXUS

A group later identified as Fluxus grew out of the same John Cage class as Happenings but was distinguished from the latter because it put less emphasis on improvization, physicality, and gesture and more emphasis on conceptual clarity and simplicity of actions.

In place of the visually engaging costumes and sets, the Events (so-called to distinguish them from Happenings) were enacted in unadorned settings by performers wearing ordinary street clothes. They usually consisted of a unitary gesture, such as a light going on and off, or a line of performers shuffling across the floor. Typically, a deadpan wit pervaded the disciplined enactment of these isolated, quotidian actions.[9]

George Brecht's *Motor Vehicle Sundown* (1960) consisted of giving an unspecified number of performers differently-shuffled cards with instructions to go to their cars at dusk and turn the headlights or radios on or off, roll the windows up or down, honk the horns, operate the windshield wipers, or switch the glove compartment light on or off. The performers allotted whatever time they wished to each activity and the performance was over when all of them completed their tasks and turned the car motors off. " . . . Such scrupulously annotated performances differed markedly from the improvisatory permissiveness of most Happenings."[10]

In a different way, Dick Higgins' *Winter Carol* (1959) obliterated the distinction between the audience and the performers. The instructions read:

Any number of people may perform this composition. They do so by agreeing in advance on a duration for the composition, then by going out to listen in the falling snow.[11]

George Maciunas was the organizing force behind Fluxus, although it was never more than a loosely knit group of anarchists whose association was motivated as much by their need for mutual support and performance places to share, as much as anything else. In 1962 a Fluxus concert took place in Wiesbaden, West Germany; in 1964 the first New York City Fluxus concert occurred. Both took place thanks to Maciunas's organizational abilities. Scores of other Fluxus events have occurred before and since then, but no one agrees on what artists and events do or do not carry the label of Fluxus, an attitude in keeping with the original artists' free-spiritedness. "The formative years of Fluxus nevertheless proved seminal to the development of a reductivist art which was to find expression in Minimalist sculpture and the Judson Dance Theater," wrote Barbara Haskell.[12]

JUDSON DANCE THEATER

Beginning in 1955, just outside of San Francisco, the dancer Ann Halprin's Dancers' Workshop Company trained artists in a new dance tradition. Freeing itself from the symbolism, metaphor, analogy, and emotionalism of the American modern dance pioneer Martha Graham (1894–1991), this new tradition utilized instead everyday movements and activities, like walking, eating, bathing, and touching. Dancers Simone Forti, Trisha Brown, Yvonne Rainer, and Steve Paxton worked with Halprin, along with musicians Terry Riley, La Monte Young, and Warner Jepson.

In 1960, many of the Dancers' Workshop Company's members arrived in New York City, where they "translated Halprin's obsession for an individual's sense of the straightforward physical movement of their own bodies in space into public performances, in programs of happenings and events held at the Reuben Gallery and the Judson Church."[13] Some of the dancers worked with Merce Cunningham, others with Robert Dunn at Cunningham's studios. Eventually they created enough of a repertory to stage a performance at the Judson Church as "The Judson Dance Group," including pieces by Trisha Brown, Lucinda Childs, Sally Gross, Carolee Schneeman, John McDowell, Philip Corner, and others. Along with Merce Cunningham's troupe, this group gave a focal point to the most experimental dance in New York and energized performance arts with new ideas about movement in space.

By 1963, Robert Rauschenberg and Robert Morris became involved in the Judson Dance Group. Rauschenberg had already made "combines"—combinations of painting and sculpture—evidencing his interest in expanding the boundaries between traditional art mediums. Morris had previously worked in dance with Yvonne Rainer in San Francisco before both artists moved to New York. For the Judson Dance Group, Rauschenberg did the lighting for *Terrain* and used the dancers for his own dance compositions. Morris created *Site* (Fig. **0.3**) in 1965, with Carolee Schneeman posed nude like Manet's *Olympia*. Morris wore a rubber mask "designed by Jasper Johns to reproduce exactly the features of his own face"[14] and rearranged large sheets of plywood into

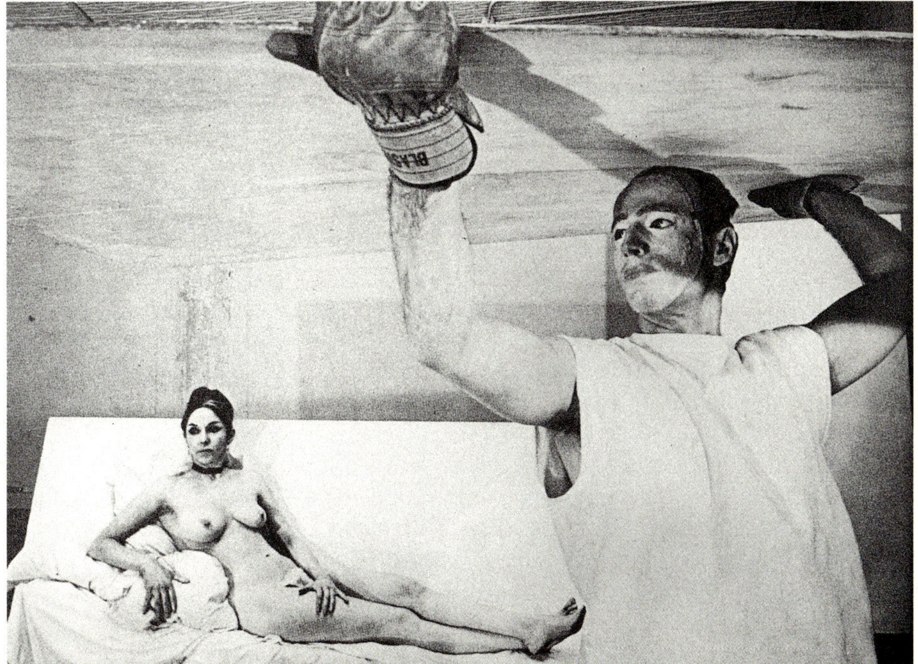

0.3 ROBERT MORRIS
Site 1965
Performance
Courtesy Leo Castelli Gallery,
New York

different configurations which redefined the spatial volumes in relation to the static figure.

Happenings, Fluxus Events, and the Judson Dance Theater all explored new artistic links between art and the activities and objects of everyday life, blurring distinctions between art and life to a greater extent than ever before in American art. The expansion of contemporary art to embrace elements of everyday life that had formerly been considered outside its range typifies many subsequent contemporary art movements such as Pop Art, Post-Modernism, and Simulationism. The use of the fourth dimension of time, and of live performance incorporating avant-garde music, dance, poetry, theater, and visual arts also foreshadowed the development of Video, Film, and Performance Art (see Chapter 2).

Minimal Sculpture

One of the most startling aspects of Minimal sculpture is the artists' use of prefabricated units or their practice of having their sculptures made in factories. In both cases, the end result is that the artwork has not only not been handmade by the artist, but may not even have been touched by him or her. The possibility of an artwork being made without the artist making or even touching the art object was first put forward by Marcel Duchamp (1887–1968).

In Paris in 1914, Duchamp randomly selected a common French hardware store item and designated it a work of art. When he moved from Paris to New York City in 1915, he left the *Bottle Rack* (Fig. **0.4**) behind, replacing it later with another off-the-shelf bottle rack.[15] Duchamp used the term "readymade" for the *Bottle Rack* and other common items he designated as art.

The principle operating in Duchamp's "readymades" is the primacy of the idea in an artwork rather than its visual appearance. Duchamp called Impressionism "retinal art"—art that only addresses the eyes. He wanted to create cerebral art—art that only addresses the mind. How can one make visual art that has no visual interest? Toward the end of seeking the clearest and most essential embodiment of his concept—an attitude affiliated with an urge toward essences that characterizes much of twentieth-century art—Duchamp systematically eliminated everything but the idea from his *Bottle Rack*. Though Duchamp did not change the physical and visual appearance of the bottle rack in any way, by designating it an artwork he changed the idea the object repre-

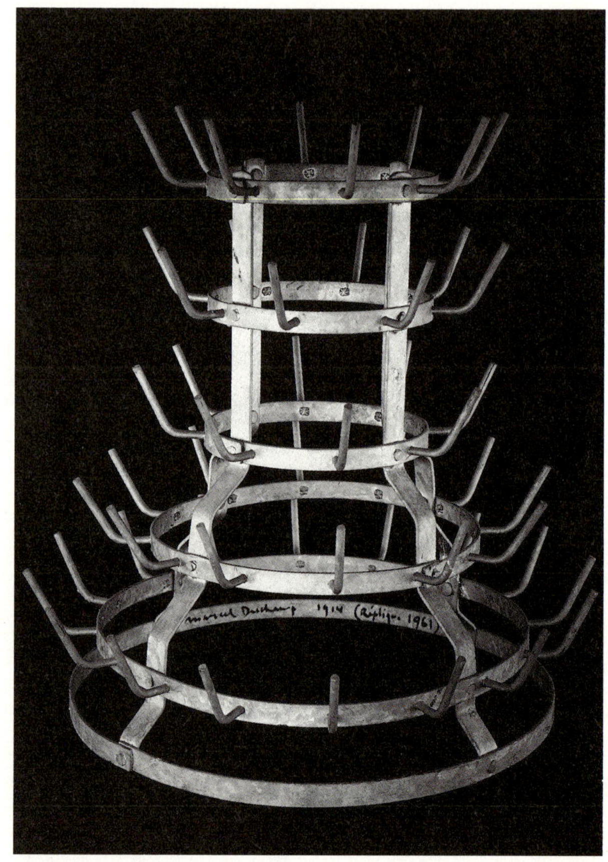

0.4 MARCEL DUCHAMP
Bottle Rack (Bottle Dryer)
1914

Found object
Philadelphia Museum of Art

sents, he changed the way we look at it and think about it. In Duchamp's mind, he changed the most essential art aspect about it. Like few artworks in history, *Bottle Rack* still has the power to provoke art viewers more than any unaltered hardware store item.

Of course, Duchamp hoped that it would. He deliberately situated *Bottle Rack* within the traditional notion of the avant-garde—the idea that art should shock and offend complacent bourgeois sensibilities and require a giant leap of faith from its audience, like Manet's *Olympia* (Fig. **0.1**) had unwittingly done in 1865. Believing that the audience's response is at least half of the artwork, Duchamp deliberately provoked his viewers, posing a completely logical philosophical proposition with an absurd but inarguable conclusion: that *Bottle Rack* is an artwork.

CARL ANDRE

The Minimal sculptor Carl Andre (born 1935) stacked unaltered fire bricks in various configurations called *Equivalents* (1966). Each *Equivalent* (Fig. **0.5**) employs an identical number of firebricks—120 of them—stacked two bricks high and arranged in four different configurations: 3×20 bricks, 4×15, 5×12, and 6×10. (Andre rejected the other two possibilities of 1×60 and 2×20 bricks.) A total of eight variations was obtained by stacking the bricks two different ways for each of the four configurations: on their sides or flat.[16]

Writing in 1984, art critic Peter Schjeldahl described his 1966 response to *Equivalents*:

The lightning of the movement called Minimalism—in retrospect, the dominant aesthetic of the last two decades and one of the most important renovations of the art idea in modern history—struck me in March 1966 when I entered the Tibor de Nagy Gallery and saw some bricks on the floor: eight neat, low-lying arrangements of them. Construction in progress, I thought, and I turned to leave. Then another idea halted me. What if it's art? Scarcely daring to hope for anything so wonderful (I may have held my breath), I asked a person in the gallery and was assured that, yes, this was a show of sculpture by Carl Andre.[17]

Carl Andre makes horizontality the main subject of his sculpture; the subject first became rigorously clear in the *Equivalents*. All of Andre's subsequent art, and much of the best sculpture produced throughout the 1960s, addresses the formal issue of the relationship of sculpture to the horizon.

In Minimal sculpture, the horizon usually takes the form of a floor in an enclosed architectural space. Minimal sculpture reiterates the manmade environment and imitates the mechanized mass production techniques of industrial society. In imitating mass production, Minimal sculpture is affiliated with Pop

0.5 CARL ANDRE
Equivalent VI 1966
120 Firebricks
$5 \times 108\frac{1}{2} \times 22\frac{1}{2}$ins
($12.5 \times 274 \times 57$cm)
Courtesy Saatchi Collection, London

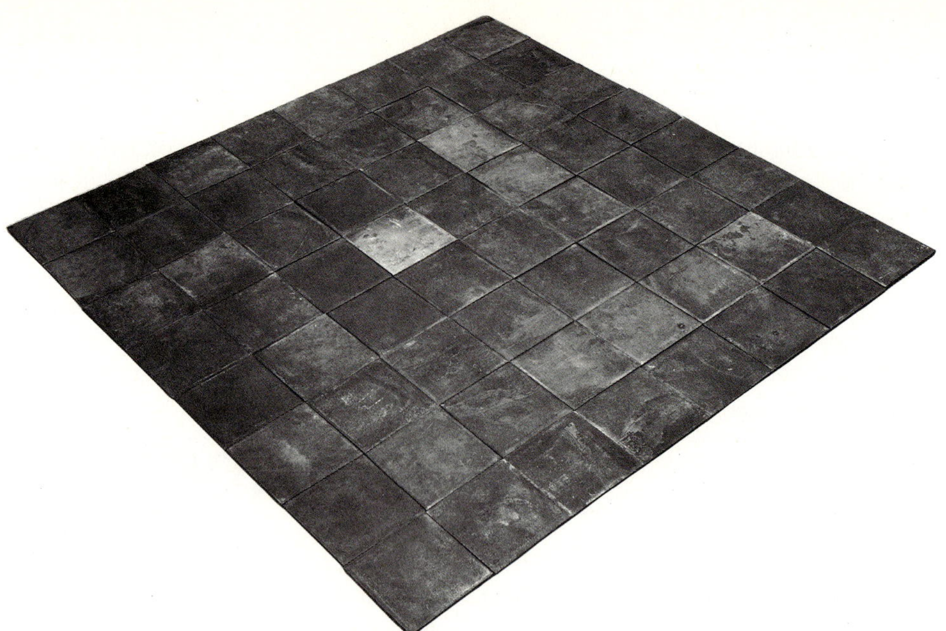

0.6 CARL ANDRE
64 Steel Square 1967
Hot-rolled steel, 64-unit
square (8 × 8)
each ⅜ × 8 × 8ins
(1 × 20.3 × 20.3cm)
overall ⅜ × 64 × 64ins
(1 × 162.6 × 162.6cm)
Collection, Edward R. Broida
Trust

Art, but the latter emphasizes the mass production of images in the mass media while Minimal art emphasizes the industrial mass production of objects.

The Minimalists' avoidance of the human form and its narrative implications parallels their interest in the relationship between sculpture and its base— which in most cases is the floor—a relationship which is often expressed in forms that are more horizontal than vertical and that rest directly on the floor.

No matter how abstract, if a human form is horizontal it appears to be reclining. Why is it reclining? Is it wounded, sleeping, resting, copulating, sunbathing; in other words, is it engaging in any one of a number of narrative actions? And so, if the sculptural form were human, the issue of the relationship of the sculpture to the horizon and to an interior architectural space would become clouded with extraneous narrative information. The purity, simplicity, and concreteness the Minimalists sought would become compromised.

In 1967 Andre made the first of what became a large series of metal plate pieces. He bought the pre-cut metal plates from a salvage store then laid them flat on the floor in a carpetlike arrangement. Usually, the number of plates Andre used in each arrangement was determined by each plate's dimensions: 8 inch (20.3 cm) square metal plates, for example, would be used to make squares that had eight plates on each side, or a total of 64 plates. In each case, Andre used the repeated identical prefabricated units of the purchased metal plates, analogous to the fire bricks

he had used earlier in the *Equivalents*.

Unlike the *Equivalents*, however, the metal plate pieces invite viewers to actually walk on them. Andre's placement of them in interior spaces often required viewers to face what amounted to a moral decision: if this is sculpture, can I walk on it? Viewers were so used to perceiving sculpture as what you "bump into when you back up to see a painting," (as the Abstract Expressionist Barnett Newman had defined it)[18] that they resisted stepping on one. Some viewers step upon Andre's metal plate pieces not even knowing that they are standing on art. Others innocently stroll onto one, then realize they have walked onto a sculpture, and gingerly hot-foot off it.

Whatever the initial response, walking across an Andre metal plate piece changes forever one's concept of sculpture: sculpture is no longer solely vertical, but rests firmly on the horizon. One does not bump into it while backing up to look at a painting. Instead, you walk upon it and physically sense it by touching it with the soles of your feet.

For Andre, and for other Minimal sculptors, it was important to remove from the artwork any attribute extraneous to its central idea, in fact, for the artwork to possess one central idea and only one. Indivisibility and wholeness, unitariness, and inseparability are more radically asserted than ever before—in concrete physical terms—in Minimal Art.

In Andre's metal plate pieces, the physical sensation of touching the metal plates with one's feet impresses viewers with a concrete perception—a perception that is indivisible from the sculpture's meaning. *Steel Square* (Fig. **0.6**) asserts the sculptural concept of horizontality more insistently than any sculpture before it. As such, this and others of Andre's metal plate pieces redefine what sculpture is and where it takes place.

Andre succinctly summed up the concept of indivisibility: FORM = STRUCTURE = PLACE[19]. By this, Andre meant that the *form* of a sculpture is its concrete, physical *structure*, devoid of illusions or allusions, and that both the *form* and *structure* are, in turn, inseparable from the sculpture's *place*—in this case, its horizontality on the floor of an enclosed architectural space, placed in such a way as to frequently require viewers to walk on it.

The concern with indivisibility, concreteness, unitariness, and the question of the place where sculpture is situated preoccupied other Minimal sculptors as well. The latter issue became central to serious sculpture throughout the 1960s and into the 1970s.

DONALD JUDD

Donald Judd (born 1928) attended Columbia University and the Art Students League in New York City from 1949 to 1953, when he graduated from Columbia *cum laude* in philosophy, a field he had an affinity for because of its practical and experience-related theories. He returned to Columbia between 1957 and 1962, earning a master's degree in art history. During the 1950s and early 1960s Judd kept abreast of art exhibitions in New York, and from 1959 until 1965 he was a contributing editor of *Arts Magazine*, writing some of the most insightful art criticism of the period.

Meanwhile, Judd painted during the 1950s, flat, hieratic, mostly unitary compositions very much at odds with the prevailing Abstract Expressionist compositions, although he admired Jackson Pollock's all-over compositions (see page 111). In the early 1960s, Judd renounced painting in favor of sculpture's more concrete and literal qualities. At first he fabricated the sculptures himself, making them out of painted wood and showing them in several group shows at the Green Gallery in 1963; in December of that year he had a solo show at the gallery. In March of 1964, he began having Bernstein Brothers fabricate his sculptures and he shifted from wood to metal.

Several of Judd's sculptures exist in more than one example, sometimes with slight variations from one example to the next. Making more than one of them in a factory does not compromise their artistic values in any way. Like other Minimal sculpture, the manufacturing of Judd's art is completely consistent

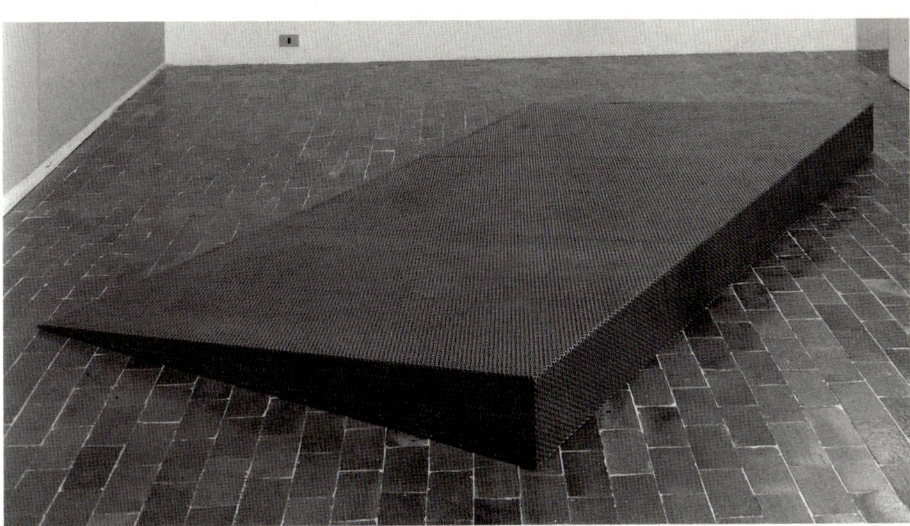

0.7 DONALD JUDD
Untitled (Perforated Steel Ramp) 1965
Perforated steel
119¼ × 8¼ × 65¾ins
(303 × 21 × 167cm)
Collection Giuseppe Panza di Biumo-Varese

with the manufacturing of goods which typify the industrial age. The artist still makes all the aesthetic decisions, including the right to reject an unsuccessful result.

In 1965 Judd had Bernstein Brothers fabricate a wedgelike floor piece out of perforated steel; in 1968 and 1969 he had three identical works made from heavier gauge steel. This untitled work (Fig. **0.7**) rises up in a slope from the horizontal plane of the floor, making us want to walk on it. Yet the perforation of the steel allows us to see through the sculpture and makes it appear somewhat light and perhaps not strong enough to bear our weight. Still, the form occupies space with the insistence and authority of a substantial mass, although we can see right through it. Its dimensions in relation to the enclosed architectural space make it a formidable obstacle; it is not something that can be stepped over or quickly walked around. Rising up from the floor, it affirms the horizontal plane sculpture traditionally rests upon, like André's work, yet it also rises up from that plane. It is a composition which is completely whole and without parts, an indivisible and concrete object. Writing in 1967, Judd stated:

> *A shape, a volume, a color, a surface is something itself. It shouldn't be concealed as part of a fairly different whole.*[20]

Discussing the unitary, non-relational forms Minimal sculptors made, art critic Roberta Smith wrote about Judd's art in 1975:

> *Traditional composition means a balancing of major and minor parts, one against the other, into a hierarchical structure. Parts are not equal and they are not clear. The arrangement reflects a larger idea of order and the acceptance of a scheme which is exterior to the work of art. It is, like illusionistic space, a reference to something else, which dilutes the immediate experience of art.*[21]

Even when separate parts occur in Judd's sculpture, our first impression of the work is of an indivisible, unitary artwork which is secondarily perceived as having several parts. In the mid-1960s, Judd had Bernstein Brothers make the first of what became a large series of "stacked" wall sculptures. An untitled 1989 (Fig. **0.8**) version in copper and red plexiglass typifies the series which Judd began in the mid-1960s and continues to make in various materials to this day.

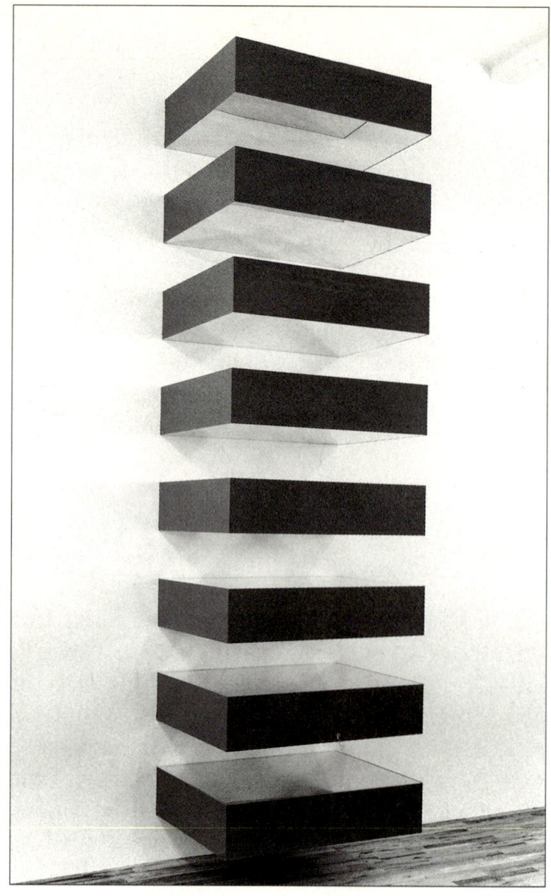

0.8 DONALD JUDD
Untitled 1989
Copper, red plexiglass
each 9 × 40 × 31ins
(23 × 101.6 × 78.7cm)
Courtesy Paula Cooper
Gallery, New York

From floor to ceiling, arranged with spaces the same size as the sculptured units between them, rectangular forms project from the wall. This sculpture depends upon the floor, wall, and ceiling of a room. It shapes the space as much as its own shapes: the spaces between each unit are as tangible and concrete as the rectangular units themselves. Although we may perceive separate parts, all the parts are unified into an indivisible whole. "It is the quality of the space, of the visible static volumes, which each arrangement delineates again and again, that is central to the work."[22]

Art critic Roberta Smith summarized Judd's art:

> *Judd continues to make it clear that art is and always has been an object, and what makes objects art is not the way they mirror the world and mimic men, but the way they separate from the world and involve, through visual perception, access to the artist's ideas and decisions about structuring experience.*[23]

ROBERT MORRIS

After attending colleges in Kansas City, San Francisco, and Oregon, Robert Morris (born 1931) moved to New York City in 1961 where he continued to work in theater and dance with Yvonne Rainer and others. He made his first sculpture in 1961; his first solo show took place at the Green Gallery in 1963.

The engagement of interior architectural space as an integral part of sculpture characterizes Morris's second Green Gallery show in 1964 (Fig. **0.9**). Large unitary geometric forms obstruct the floor, hang from the ceiling, join the floor and the wall, join two walls, or join two walls and the floor in a corner. Each massive painted plywood form shapes the space enclosed by the floor, ceiling, and walls, without which the forms would have little visual impact.

Corner Piece (Fig. **0.10**) is a painted wooden triangle which joins two walls and the floor in a corner, enclosing a four-sided pyramidal volume with a single plane the other three planes of which are two walls and the floor. The hollow volume *Corner Piece* encloses has no literal mass or weight in the traditional sculptural sense, yet the space that cannot be seen behind the single plane of painted plywood is tangible to us because of our extensive familiarity

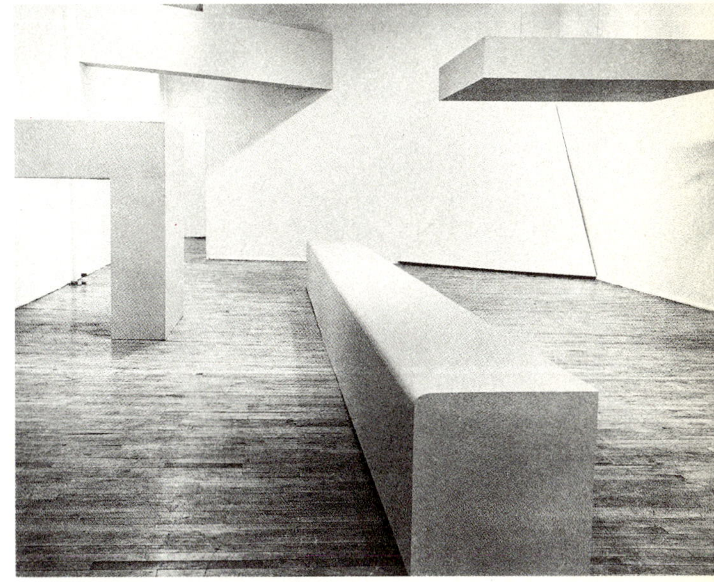

0.9 ROBERT MORRIS
Green Gallery Installation 1964
Painted wood, dimensions variable
Courtesy Leo Castelli Gallery, New York

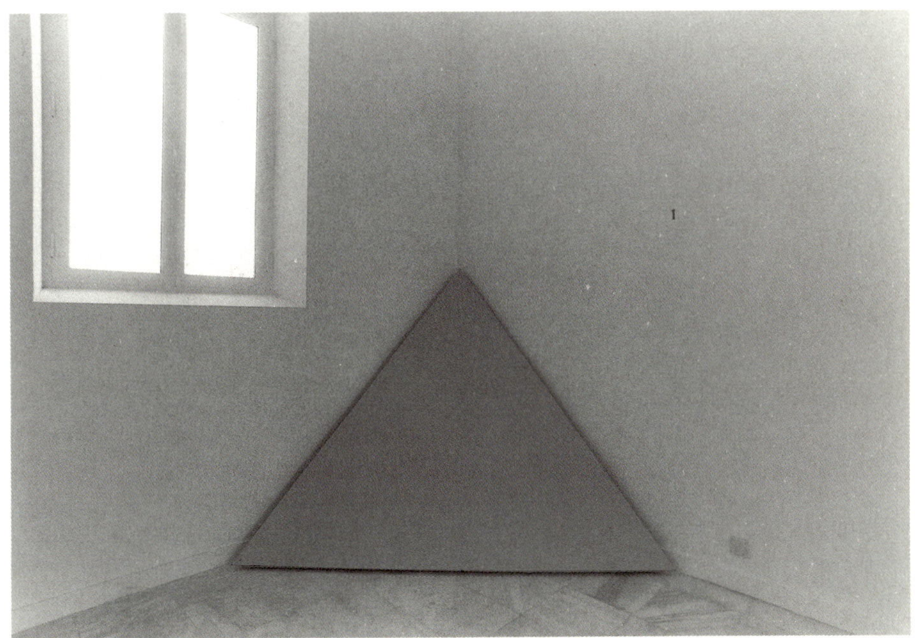

0.10 ROBERT MORRIS
Untitled (Corner Piece)
1964 Grey painted plywood
108 × 78ins
(274.3 × 198.1cm)
Collection Giuseppe Panza
di Biumo-Varese

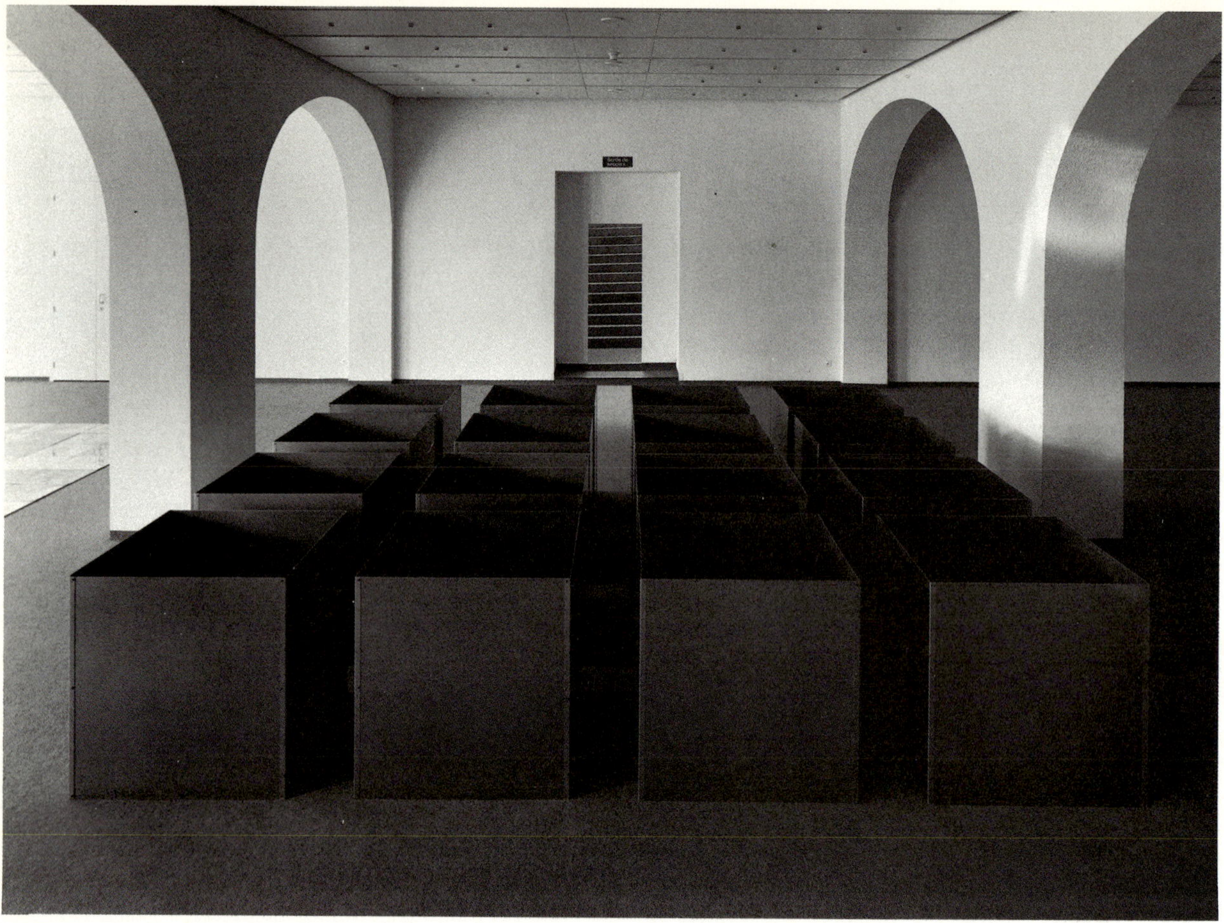

with architectural space. We simply know what is behind the painted plywood plane without having to see it. And so we sense a sculptural volume without any traditional sculptural volume being present, and the existence of that volume is dependent upon the architectural setting.

An *Untitled* work Morris had fabricated in 1967 (Fig. **0.11**) utilizes 16 identical open steel boxes arranged with spaces between them equal to their own dimensions. Being open at the top and bottom, each box encloses a volume of space without having a mass in any traditional sense of sculptural mass. The boxes function as obstructions in a maze and as planes which enclose space. The identicalness of each unit is impressed upon us by their relentless repetition which creates an overall impression of an indivisible whole.

The repetition of identical units occurs frequently in Minimalism and in Pop Art. In 1964, Pop artist Andy Warhol filled the Leo Castelli Gallery in New York with facsimiles of *Brillo Boxes* and other boxes of consumer goods, as though to say that artworks are

0.11 ROBERT MORRIS
Untitled (16 steel open boxes) 1967
16 steel boxes,
each 35⅘ × 35⅘ × 35⅘ins

(91 × 91 × 91cm)
overall 252 × 35⅘ × 252ins
(640 × 91 × 640)
Collection Giuseppe Panza
di Biumo-Varese

just another type of consumer product. The repetition of identical units characteristic of Warhol's art and of Minimal sculpture parallels the mass manufacture of images and objects typical of America's consumer society. Repetition also typifies the serial imagery of the Color Field painters.

If repetition induces a lack of drama in the usual sense of the word—that is of episodes building up to a climax—this is intentional. One manufactured object or image does not vary from others like it; if it did, it would be considered a deviation. If repetition is boring, well, yes, by utilizing an overall composition rather than the drama of individual parts leading up to a whole, the repetition of identical units *is* boring compared to former notions of visual unity. It's intended to be. As Andy Warhol said, "I like boring things."

SOL LeWITT

Sol LeWitt was born in 1928 and grew up in Connecticut. He attended Syracuse University in upstate New York, graduating with a BFA before serving in the army in Japan and Korea in 1951–52. Afterwards, he settled in New York where he worked on his own paintings and on commercial design, including I. M. Pei's project for the Roosevelt Field shopping center in Long Island. Between 1960 and 1965, he worked at the information and sales desk at The Museum of Modern Art.

LeWitt's first solo show of painted wood constructions took place at the short-lived Daniels Gallery in 1965. A year later, LeWitt made his first open cubic forms and first began working in series.

Art critics and art historians have variously claimed LeWitt as a Minimal artist and a Conceptual artist.[24] As long as we accurately interpret his art, it is not so important what "ism" we identify him with. LeWitt's spare, geometric sculptures, based on grids like so much of Minimal art, share many of Minimalism's qualities of immediate comprehensibility, overall unity of form not derived from its parts in summation, emphasis on basic geometric units, rigorous reductivism, singleness of isolation of sculptural phenomenon, and de-emphasis of human form and emotion.

Even so, there is something in LeWitt's sculptures which differentiates his art from other Minimal sculp-

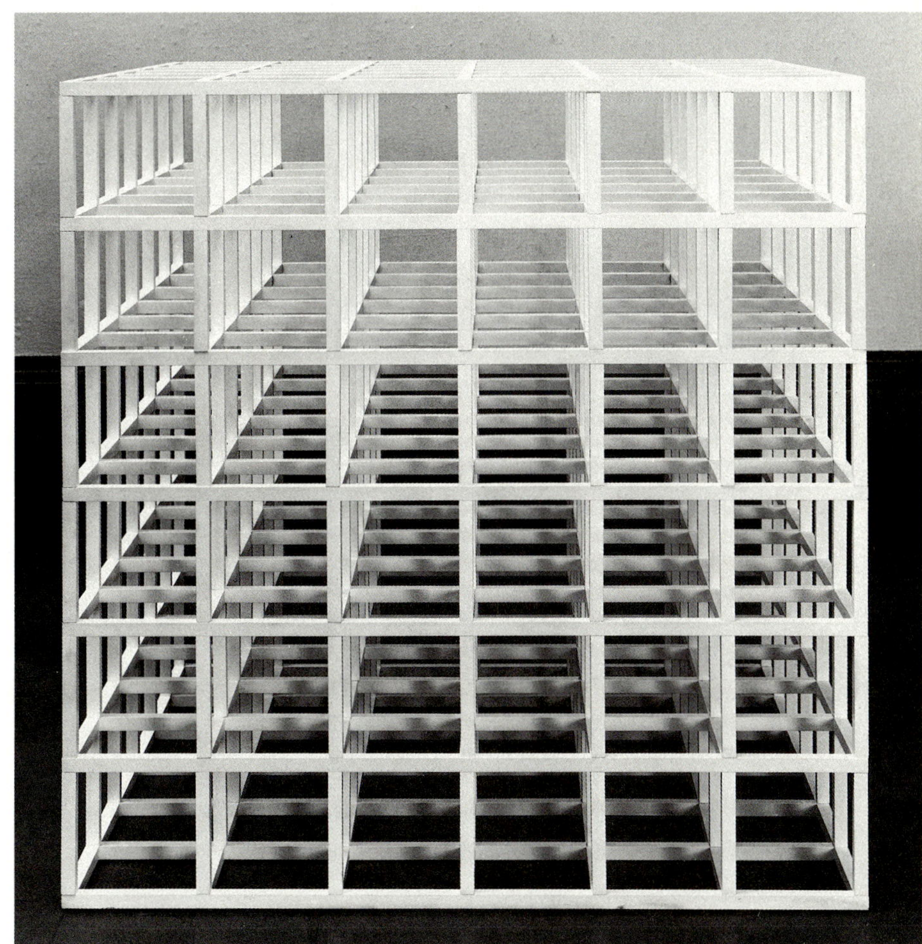

0.12 SOL LeWITT
Open Modular Cube 1966
Painted aluminum
60 × 60 × 60ins
(152.4 × 152.4 × 152.4cm)
Courtesy Art Gallery of
Ontario, Canada

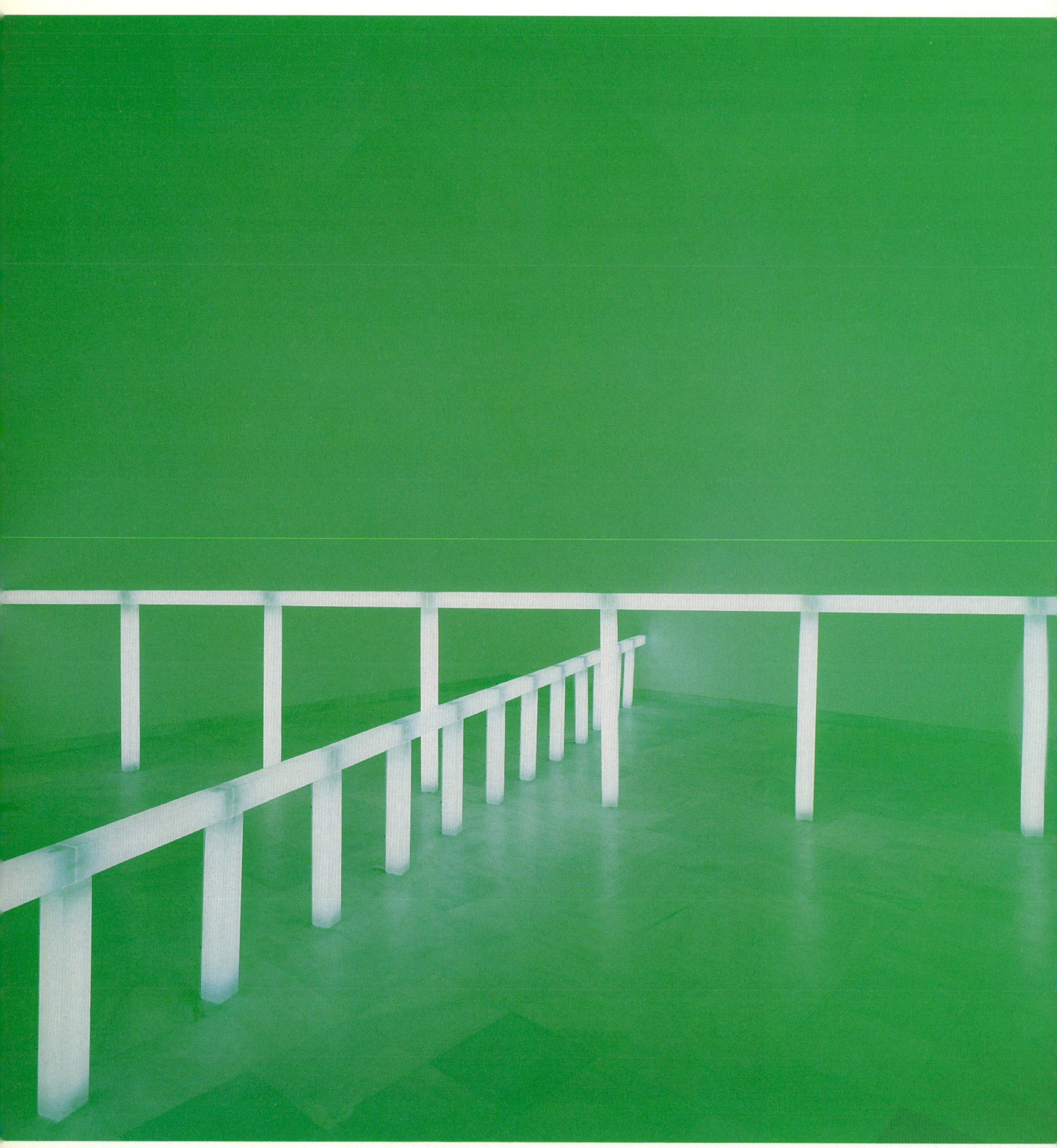

ture. His wall drawings (see pages 30 and 52–53) are so resolutely based on LeWitt's written instructions to the fabricators (which are outside of, and separable from, the visual manifestation itself) that these latter works oppose the Minimalist dictum that all the parts of an artwork be inseparable. "The idea becomes a machine that makes the art,"[25] LeWitt has written.

LeWitt's *Modular Cube* (Fig. **0.12**) is made of repeated modular units which we know to be identical but which we cannot perceive as being so, a discrepancy between what we know and what we see that varies from other Minimal sculpture's literalness. Art critic Robert Rosenblum differentiates LeWitt's art from that of other Minimalists such as Andre, Judd and Morris:

Even the materials of most Minimal art—Andre's bricks, Flavin's flourescent tubes, Judd's Plexiglass and plywood—are somehow, for all their plainness and clarity, too literal, too palpable for LeWitt, who seeks out rather the most abstract looking materials, or ideally, nonmaterials, to render, in Donald Kuspit's felicitous phrase, "the look of thought."[26]

DAN FLAVIN

LeWitt, Andre, and Morris use neutral colors like white and gray in their Minimal sculpture to avoid optical qualities they believe reserved for painting in favor of sensations of touch they believe reserved for sculpture. Judd, however, has used comparatively shining and even vulgar automobile colours, as has the California Minimalist John McCracken. Colored light—the most immaterial of all materials—is Dan Flavin's medium.

Dan Flavin was born in New York in 1933 and studied at the University of Maryland and the New School of Social Research, Columbia University, but he had no formal training in art and only began to seriously make art in 1959. The only material employed in his mature work is flourescent light. Flavin's extreme reductivism and his total reliance upon interior architectural spaces solidly link him with Minimal sculpture, yet his art is much more elusive, immaterial, pictorial, and less concrete than that of other Minimal sculptors. Colored light washing across a wall resembles painted transparent veils, such as those of the Colour Field painter Morris Loüis, for example, who stained large, unprimed canvases with brightly colored acrylic washes.

But Flavin's combination and positioning of flourescent light fixtures in interior spaces gives both the light itself and the fixtures a surprising, physically tangible matter-of-factness despite their poetic blush. Flavin's art's immediate comprehensibility, its indivisibility and unitariness, its singleness of isolation of phenomenon, its absence of emotion, its use of pre-existing materials (related to Andre's use of bricks), all link it with Minimal sculpture.

Flavin's sculptures cease to be art and become hardware the moment they are turned off. They depend entirely upon an art context—an art gallery or museum or other neutral space—for their visual impact. Placed in a home or office space, they become lost in the welter of functional objects. Their dependence upon neutral, contemplative interior spaces parallels the optimum viewing conditions of other Minimal art.

Installed in a neutral space, *Green Crossing Green (to Piet Mondrian who lacked Green)* (Fig. **0.13**), like Flavin's best sculpture, gives light a physical tangibility it never possessed before. Light becomes not two-dimensional or illusionistic, as it is in painting, but volumetric and sculptural.

0.13 DAN FLAVIN
Green Crossing Green (to Piet Mondrian who lacked green) 1966
Green flourescent lights
263¾ × 240⅛ins
(670 × 610cm)
Collection Giuseppe Panza di Biumo-Varese

Social and Political Background

The 1960s was a decade of great changes. In politics, society, science, technology, mass media, popular culture, and the arts, rapidly evolving new developments superseded established norms at an astonishing rate. It seemed as though the whole world, and all of its basic premises, changed in the 1960s.

The 1960s was the first decade to experience the widespread use and appeal of television. President John Fitzgerald Kennedy's funeral, following his assassination in 1963, was probably the first globally-watched television event. Television gave voice to many different political and social factions which discovered the power of public demonstrations reported on the television news. Civil rights protests and anti-Vietnam war demonstrations were frequent nightly television fare.

Martin Luther King's electrifying "I Have a Dream" speech in 1963, heard and seen by over 200,000 people gathered at the Mall in Washington, D.C.—and by uncounted people on television—roused the nation's civil rights movement and created enormous public empathy for the rights of racial minorities. Anti-Vietnam war demonstrations transformed the nation's social fabric and contributed to President Lyndon Johnson's decision not to run for re-election in 1968.

Stereos—which first appeared in the mass market in the early 1960s—spread Rock and Roll music which (as art always does) characterized the times, alarming parents who correctly recognized that the new music glorified promiscuous

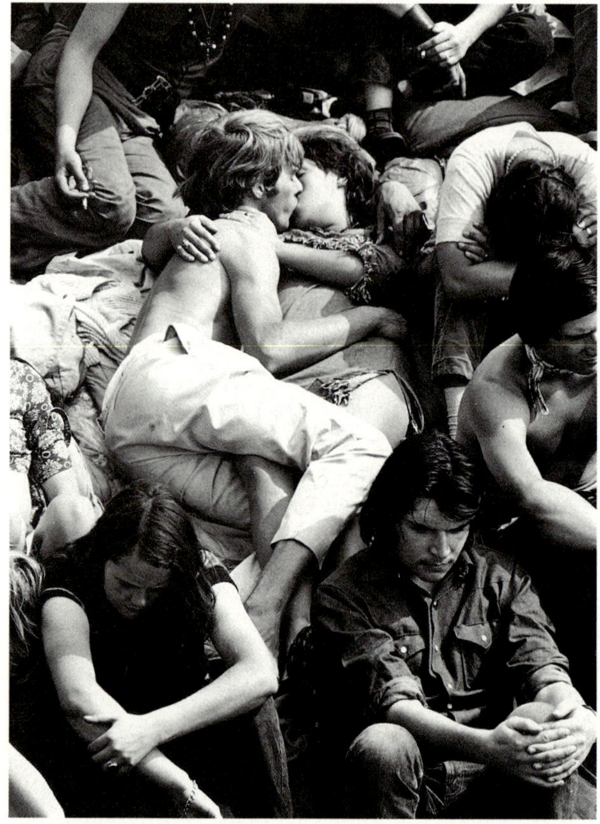

sex, drugs like Marijuana, LSD, amphetamines, peyote, and Quaaludes, and contributed to what they called "juvenile delinquency," by which they meant the failure of their children to conform to old norms.

Drugs certainly entered popular culture in the 1960s, both in the behavior of Rock and Roll stars (Janis Joplin and Jimmi Hendrix died of overdoses) and in that of the fans. The widespread use of drugs and of the newly-available birth control pills (first marketed in 1960) contributed to a loosening of sexual inhibitions and widespread sexual promiscuity, all aspects of the generation gap and the counter-culture. If these social evolutions had their destructive aspects (drug overdoses, unwanted pregnancies, venereal disease) they also brought new awarenesses—through experimentation, role-playing, and lowered inhibitions—that contributed to the emergence of feminist and gay rights activists in the late 1960s, developments which have altered sexual politics in positive ways since.

Many sobering social and political events took place in 1968: the dual assassinations of Martin Luther King and Bobby Kennedy, the Chicago police's brutality against protestors at the 1968 Democratic convention, the continued clashes between Vietnam War protesters and police and the National Guard, and other deepening rifts between the "counter culture" and the "establishment."

A major technological accomplishment in 1969 brought renewed optimism and faith in the future: the first manned voyage to the moon. Reported live on global television, it demonstrated the transformational power of short-lived imagery and contributed to an undermining of artists' confidence in the power of permanent, separate objects. If the moon landing was the great "establishment" event of 1969, the Woodstock festival represented the "counter-culture" equivalent. The weekend-long Rock and Roll festival in Upstate New York was attended by 500,000 fans, one of the largest gatherings of people in one place in history. Concert-goers openly consumed drugs like Marijuana and LSD and participated in promiscuous sex.

Radical social evolution became commonplace in the late 1960s. Against this background, contemporary artists sought both to reflect the conditions of their time and to renew the avant-garde's traditional out-of-the-mainstream stance with even more radical artistic manifestations.

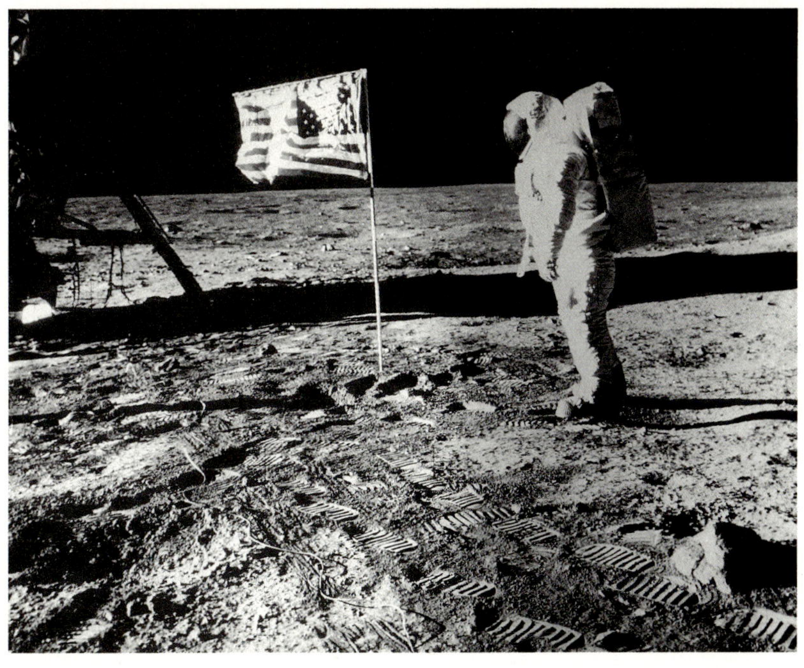

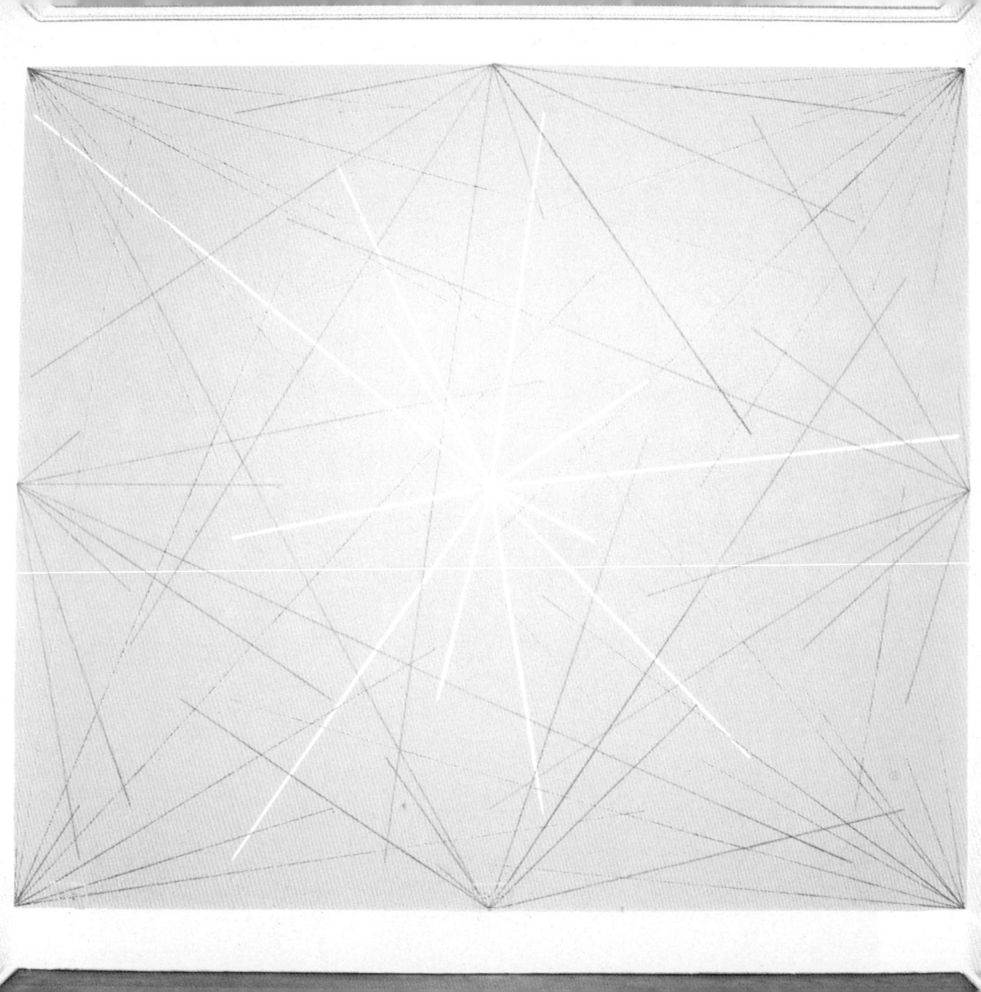

1
Conceptual Art

"Conceptual artists are mystics rather than rationalists. They leap to conclusions that logic cannot reach." [1]

—— SOL LeWITT ——

Sol LeWitt
Wall Drawing #280   1976
Red, blue, and white crayon, black pencil grid, yellow wall
First installation: January 1976
Dimensions variable
Private Collection, San Francisco, California

Dematerialization of the Art Object

Minimal and Color Field artists sought to make art objects which embodied the unique qualities of sculpture and painting as distinct from all other types of objects. Color Field painters like Morris Louis, Jules Olitski, Larry Poons, Ellsworth Kelly, and Kenneth Noland sought to eliminate from painting all experiences that were not inherently visual and derived from the physical properties of painting. They emphasized two-dimensional space, flat shapes, optical (as opposed to tactile) sensations, color, and the relationships between their painted areas and the edge of the canvas (called edge tension). Both Color Field painters and Minimalists were concerned with defining paintings and sculptures as *objects* unlike any other classification of objects.

Conceptual, Video, Performance, Earthwork, and site-specific artists however sought to redefine artworks outside of an object-orientation. They wanted to undermine the concept of artworks as commodities. Conceptual artists emphasized new dimensions of impermanence or temporariness. Video and performance artists emphasized "live" time or filmed, tape-recorded, or videotaped time, incorporating duration and, hence, the short-lived time dimension of television and the movies. Earthworks and site-specific artworks being non-portable, and even sometimes perishable, were therefore less desirable as embodiments of portable monetary wealth than object-oriented Pop, Color Field, and Minimal art.

Marcel Duchamp provided the precedent for Conceptual artists' emphasis of the *idea* of an artwork over its visual appearance.

Like Marcel Duchamp, the Conceptualists believed in ideas more than objects, and their chosen mission was to investigate systems of information and theories of knowledge and perception. Many had political beliefs, forged in the counterculture ethos of the day, that led them to seek ways to avoid producing more "art objects" for consumption; they wanted to "dematerialize" art, to take it away from its traditional dependence on the physical object—or, as Duchamp put it, to free art from the tyranny of the retinal. Among the alternatives used in their attempt to free art from its dependence on the nonstop production of paintings and sculpture was, needless to say, photography.[2]

Conceptual artists used photographs, words, and the medium of artists' books, to dematerialize the art object in favor of emphasizing the ideas it represented. Again, Duchamp provided the art-historical parentage for this position. Duchamp stated about his *Bottle Rack* (1914) (see page 18) and other "Ready-mades":

... the choice of these Ready-mades was never dictated by an esthetic delectation. Such choice was always based on a reflection of visual indifference and at the same time total absence of good taste.[3]

ED RUSCHA

Experimentation with art forms and media other than painting and sculpture characterizes much of Conceptual Art and pertains to the photographic artist's books that the Los Angeles-based artist Ed Ruscha (born 1937) first began making in 1962.

Twenty-Six Gasoline Stations (1962) was Ruscha's first book, consisting of matter-of-fact photographs which he said "Above all, ... are not 'arty' in any sense of the word. I think photography is dead as a fine art; its only place is in the commercial world,

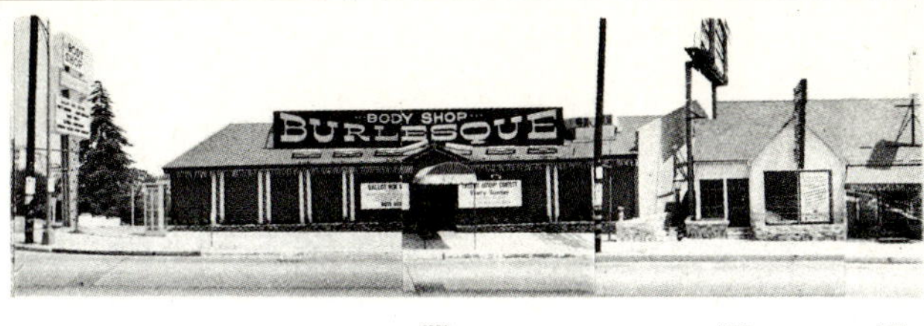

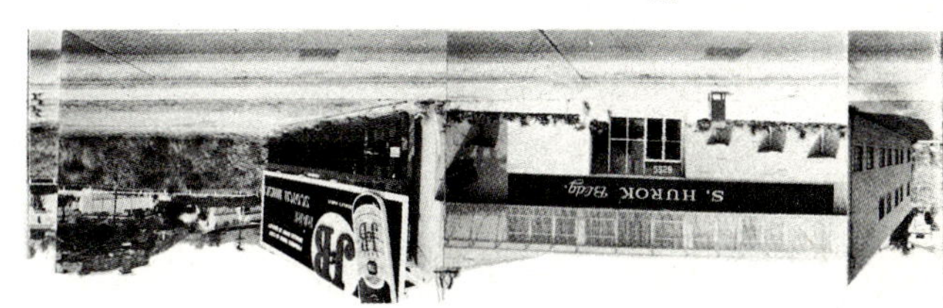

EVERY BUILDING ON THE SUNSET STRIP

EDWARD RUSCHA

1 9 6 6

1.1 ED RUSCHA	Artist's book
Every Building on the	7ins × 24ft 9ins
Sunset Strip 1966	(17.8cm × 7.54m)

for technical or informational purposes."[4] Ruscha revealed another de-aestheticizing aspect of his books when he stated that "One of the purposes of my book has to do with making a mass-produced object."[5] Further, the artist not only chose media—the book and photographs—that were neutral of artistic interest (according to him) but also chose subjects devoid of interest. "I don't have a message about subject matter at all. They are just natural facts, that's all they are," Ruscha commented about his gasoline stations.[6]

Ruscha's subsequent books include *Various Small Fires and Milk* (1964), *Every Building on the Sunset Strip* (1966), and *Thirtyfour Parking Lots in Los Angeles* (1967). All three books feature documentary-style, deadpan photographs of the subjects named in the titles. The Small Fires book shows 16 small fires—a cigarette lighter, a torch, a stove burner, a book of matches, and so forth—and one glass of milk. The Sunset Strip book is an accordion-folded continuous photograph showing both sides of the street, one of them upside down running the length of the photo (Fig. **1.1**). The Parking Lots book shows

aerial views, identifying the company name and the location of each parking lot. For each of Ruschca's books, one is less interested in the visual manifestation than in the reasoning that led to the book's production.

Artists' books frequently take the place of an exhibition. Being portable, an artist's book can easily travel to the viewer and as they are inexpensive because mass-produced, they can easily be purchased by many different people. Devoid of traditional aesthetic interest or subject matter, artists' books also address different audiences than the traditional media of painting and sculpture.

Photography's reproducibility and the artlessness it permits along with its outsider status in the fine art world made it an ideal medium for Conceptual artists' extra-visual, idea orientation. Ed Ruscha is primarily a Pop artist, but his pioneering of the photographic artist's book and his use of words affiliate him with Conceptual Art, in fact make him a forerunner. California-based artists Bruce Nauman and John Baldessari also used photographs and words in Conceptual Art contexts.

BRUCE NAUMAN

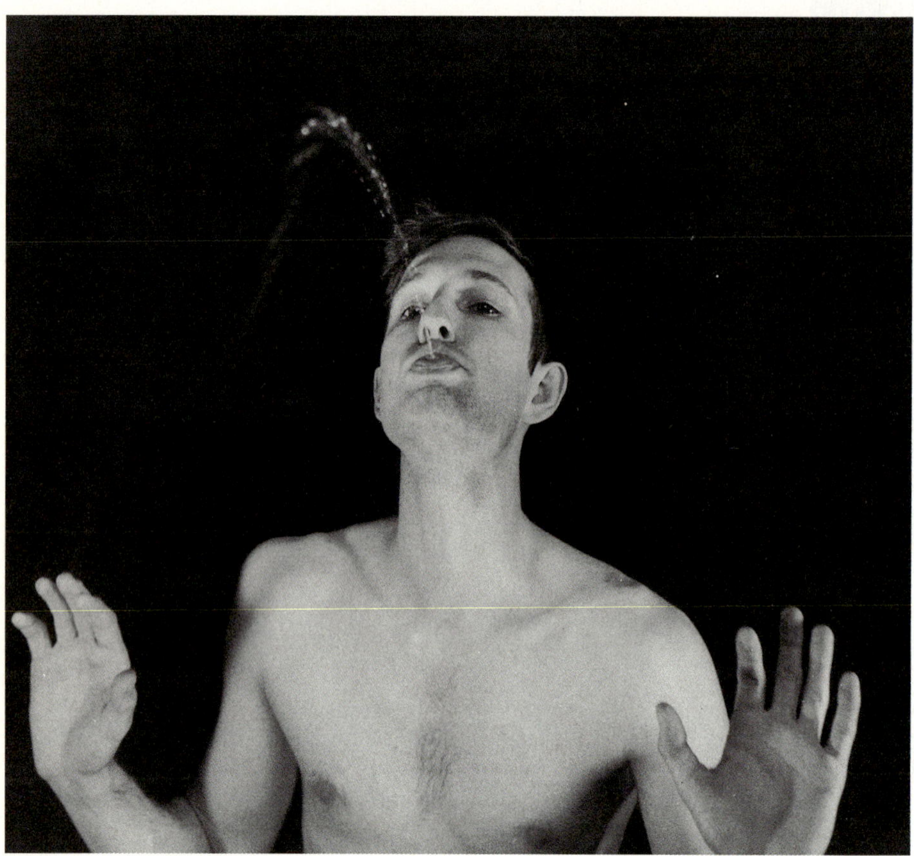

1.2 BRUCE NAUMAN
Self Portrait as a Fountain
1966
Color photograph
Sheet and image
20 1/16 × 23 5/16 ins
(51 × 60.8cm)
Collection of Whitney
Museum of American Art,
New York
Purchase 70.50.9

1.3 MARCEL DUCHAMP
Fountain 1917
Ready-made
height 24ins (61cm)
Collection The Museum of
Modern Art, New York

Although Bruce Nauman (born 1941) came to artistic maturity at the height of Minimalism, perhaps partly because he developed geographically outside the New York mainstream, he was one of the first artists in the United States to make art using media and methods that came to typify Conceptual Art.[7] Beginning with the moment he gave up painting in 1965, Nauman first used untraditional art materials and processes like molding latex and casting fiberglass, then added photographs to his repertoire and used words, punning, and his own body as the subject and/or material of his artworks. Minimalists disliked the use of human form in their art and additional visual devices—in Nauman's case, words—gave meanings which they and Color Field artists considered not to belong to sculpture and painting.

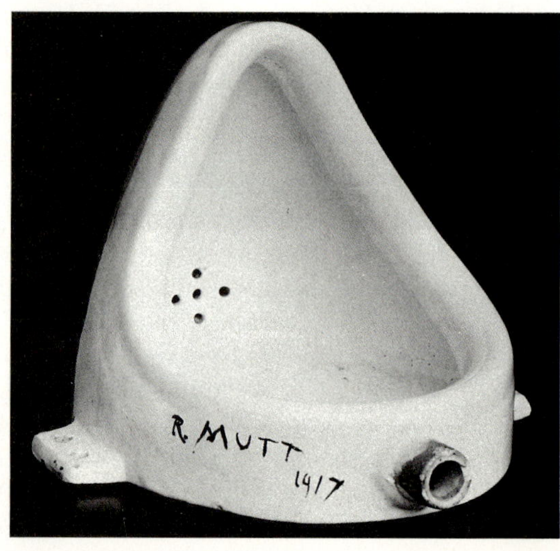

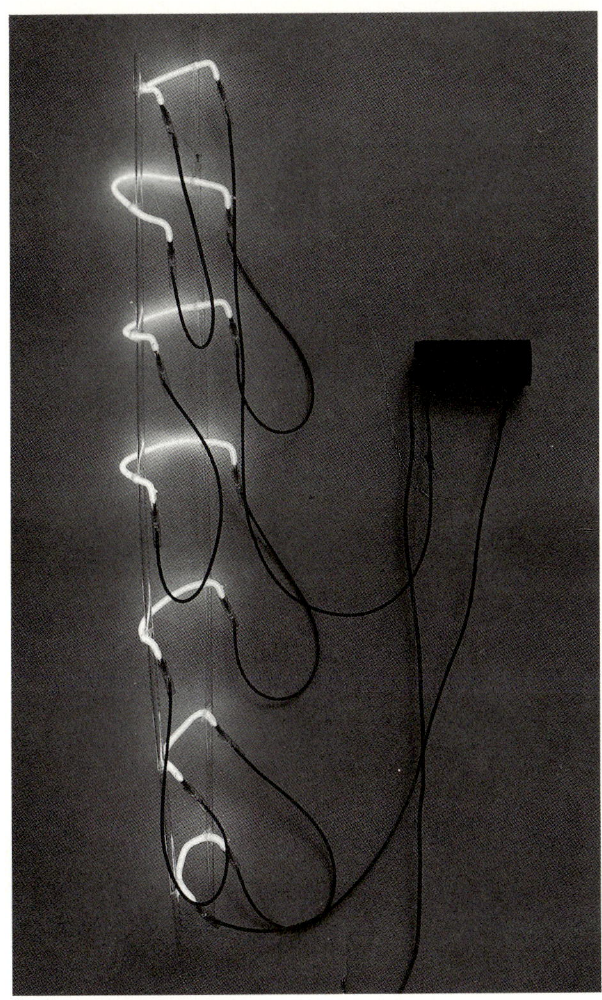

Two types of images typify an *Untitled* set of 11 color photographs Nauman made in 1966–67: images which play on the difference between visual and verbal meaning, and visual images made from the artist's own body. *Feet of Clay*, showing Nauman's own feet swathed in modeling clay, is an example of the former and emphasizes the inability of words and visual images to convey the same meanings. The title gives interest to a bland, documentary photograph which otherwise is devoid of aesthetic interest but which functions simply as a recording device. Thus Nauman minimizes the significance of the art object's classification, as for instance a painting or sculpture, in favor of emphasizing both the unimportance of the art object as object and the importance of words to supply meaning.

An example of the second type of image in the series is *Portrait of the Artist as a Fountain* (Fig. **1.2**), which portrays the shirtless artist from the chest up, with hands raised shoulder-high and head tilted back, spurting a stream of water from his lips. The reference to Duchamp's Ready-made *Fountain* (Fig. **1.3**)—a common American urinal turned on its side—is inescapable. A great deal has been written about the relationship between Nauman's and Duchamp's art, a relationship perhaps best summed up by Nauman himself:

> *Rather than having a 'formal program,' like [Frank] Stella, I always came in from the back door.... I*

1.4 BRUCE NAUMAN
Neon Template of the Left
Half of My Body
Taken at Ten Inch
Intervals 1966

Neon tubing
70 × 9 × 6ins
(177.8 × 22.9 × 15.2cm)
Courtesy Philip Johnson,
Connecticut

1.5 BRUCE NAUMAN
Collection of Various Flex-
ible Materials Separa-
ted by Layers of Grease
with Holes the Size of
My Waist and Wrists

1966, Aluminum foil, plastic
sheet, foam rubber, felt,
grease, 1½ × 90 × 18ins
(4 × 228.6 × 45.7cm)
Courtesy Saatchi Collection,
London

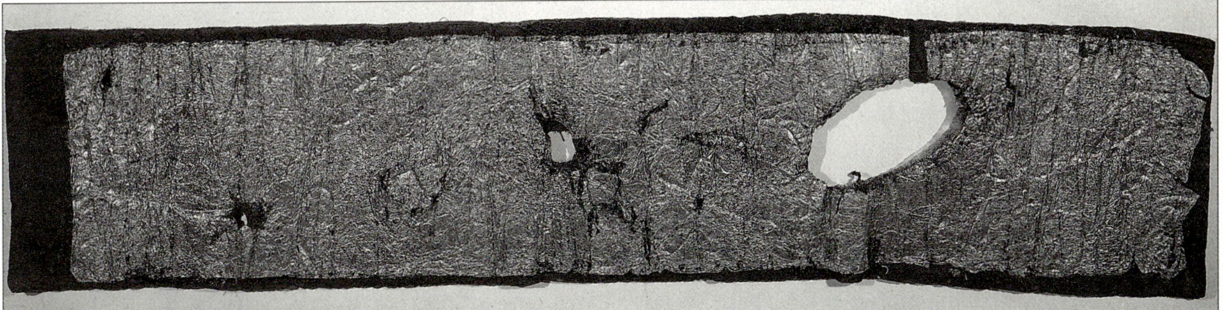

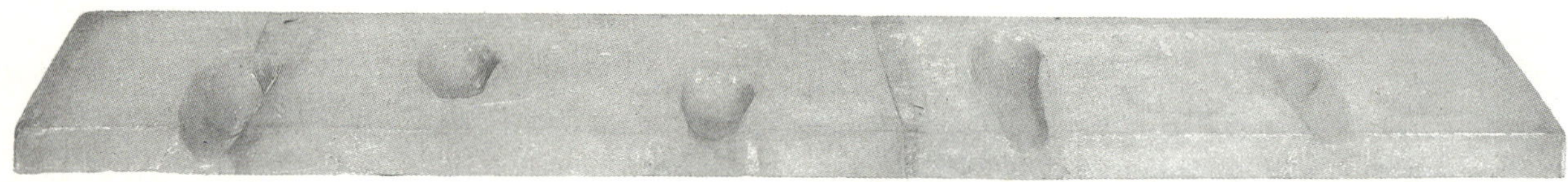

**1.6 BRUCE NAUMAN
Wax Impression of the
Knees of Five Famous
Artists** 1966
Fiberglass
2¾ × 85¼ × 15⅝ins

(7 × 216.5 × 39.5cm)
Courtesy Saatchi Collection,
London
*"I couldn't decide who to get
for artists, so I used my own
knees. Making the*

*impressions of the knees in a
wax block was a way of
having a large rectangular
solid with marks in it. I didn't
want just to make marks in
it, so I had to follow another*

*kind of reasoning. It also had
to do with trying to make the
thing itself less important to
look at."*[9]

*had just a few ideas. But I wanted to put ideas into
the works—mainly to put language into the work. I
would say my interest in Duchamp has to do with
his use of objects to stand for ideas. I like Man Ray
better; there's less 'tied-upness' in his work, more
unreasonableness.*[8]

In four sculptures from 1966 and 1967 Nauman
further explores the dual strategy of using his body
as the subject or object of the artwork and of giving
the art object meaning through its title. Here
Duchamp remains an important precedent, though
Nauman persists in greater perversity and "unreasonableness." *Neon Template of the Left Half of My
Body Taken at Ten Inch Intervals* (Fig. **1.4**) is exactly
what its title states and would be incomprehensible
without the explanatory words. The same is also true
for Nauman's *Collection of Various Flexible Materials Separated by Layers of Grease with Holes the
Size of My Waist and Wrists* (Fig. **1.5**) and *Wax Impressions of the Knees of Five Famous Artists* (Fig.
1.6). In the latter work Nauman pressed his own
knees into the wax, unable to decide which "five
famous artists" to use.

Using untraditional sculpture materials (like
grease, neon, spun fiberglass, and gold leaf) and the
human form as alternatives to Minimalism's rigid
geometries, these works foreshadow, or in some
cases parallel, related "Post-Minimalist" art produced on the East coast of America (see page 110),
but with a major difference: words are integral to
Nauman's art, integral to making "the thing itself less
important to look at," to making the idea that the
artwork represents more important than its visual
form. Thus, while his art from 1966 *formally* antici-
pates Post-Minimalism in the artistic forms he used,
his use of words links his art with Conceptual Art.

From Hand to Mouth (Fig. **1.7**) is a cast of the

artist's right hand, arm, shoulder, throat, jaw, and
lips. The title literally describes the visual image and
humorously alludes to the artist's precarious finan-
cial position while simultaneously summarizing the
last two years of his art by demonstrating the inade-
quacy of verbal language for describing visual art,
and vice versa.

From late 1967 to the present, Nauman has increasingly diversified his approach, working in "films,
videotapes, various kinds of environmental, or
'project' pieces, sculptures, holograms, prints, 'books,'
and of course always drawing."[10] (see chapter 2.)

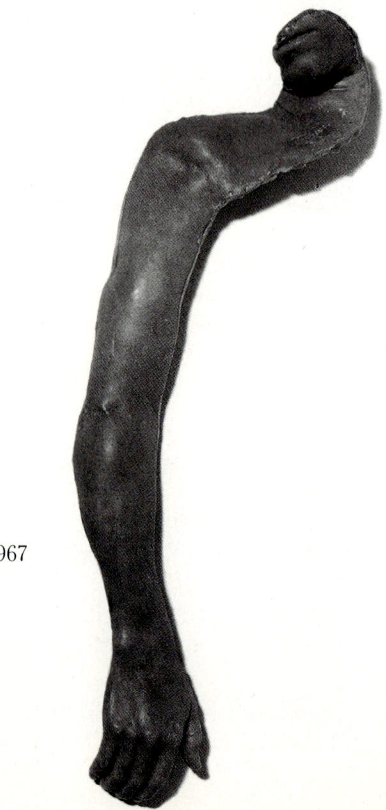

**1.7 BRUCE NAUMAN
From Hand to Mouth** 1967
Wax over cloth
30 × 10 × 4ins
(76.2 × 25.4 × 10.2cm)
The Helman Collection,
New York
Courtesy Blum Helman
Gallery, New York

JOHN BALDESSARI

Photography critic Andy Grundberg wrote, "John Baldessari is probably the most important influence on contemporary, Conceptual-based photography, both as an artist whose use of photography has maintained its originality for more than fifteen years and as an influential teacher on the West Coast."[11]

Baldessari (born 1931) attended the University of California, Berkeley beginning in 1954; then moved to San Diego during the 1960s, where he taught at the University of California. In 1970 he accepted an invitation to join the faculty of the new California Institute of the Arts in Valencia, near Los Angeles, where he was an influential teacher until 1989. "Cal Arts" has become the most important art school in the United States, and Baldessari has nurtured some of its best talents.

During Baldessari's formative years, California was more isolated from the artistic mainstream than it is today (Los Angeles is now the second most important contemporary art center in the Western world, next to New York City). The artist regarded the difference between the two American coasts as an advantage. In a 1980 interview Baldessari stated:

You don't want anyone to say, "You can't do that!" But you do get a lot of that in New York. One of the healthiest things about California is—"Why not?" One of the reasons for this mentality is certainly ignorance of art history. There's less history saying you can't do it, so you do it.[12]

In the mid-1960s Baldessari made a series of "standard size" photographic works on canvas incorporating "photographs [that] were originally taken for non-art use, some [that] were taken to violate then-current photographic norms, and others [that] were taken by pointing the camera blindly out the window while driving."[13] The only "art signal" Baldessari wanted was the canvas; he had someone else stretch and prime the canvases, and their "standard size" of 45 × 59 inches (114.3 × 149.9 cm) was determined by the largest diagonal opening of his van. Each work included text, mostly taken from art books and lettered by a sign painter Baldessari hired. Thus Baldessari physically crafted no part of the artworks, but treated his choosing of what to include as the artist's role; in other words, he removed

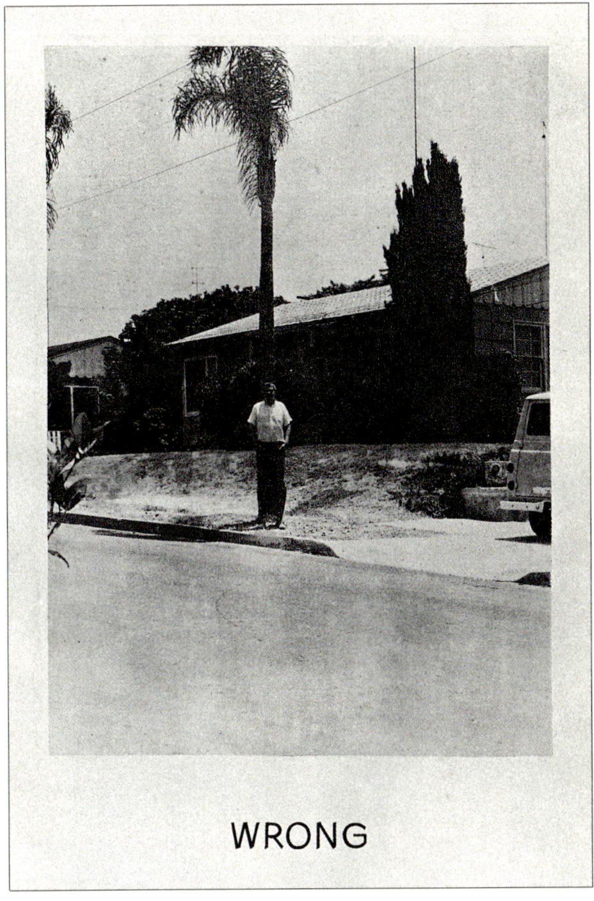

1.8 JOHN BALDESSARI
Wrong 1967
Photo emulsion, acrylic on canvas
59 × 45ins
(149.8 × 114.3cm)
Courtesy Los Angeles County Museum of Art, Los Angeles
New Talent Purchase Award

from his role everything but the ideas the artwork represented.

Having the artist's choices be the content of the artwork derives from Duchamp, of whose art Baldessari first became aware in 1959. He says:

It was as if I had come across a long-lost brother … all of a sudden I felt I had a home, that I wasn't so strange … It probably was partly to do with Duchamp's focus on language … I probably didn't understand it, though, at the time. I talked about getting away from art schools and leaving L.A. to

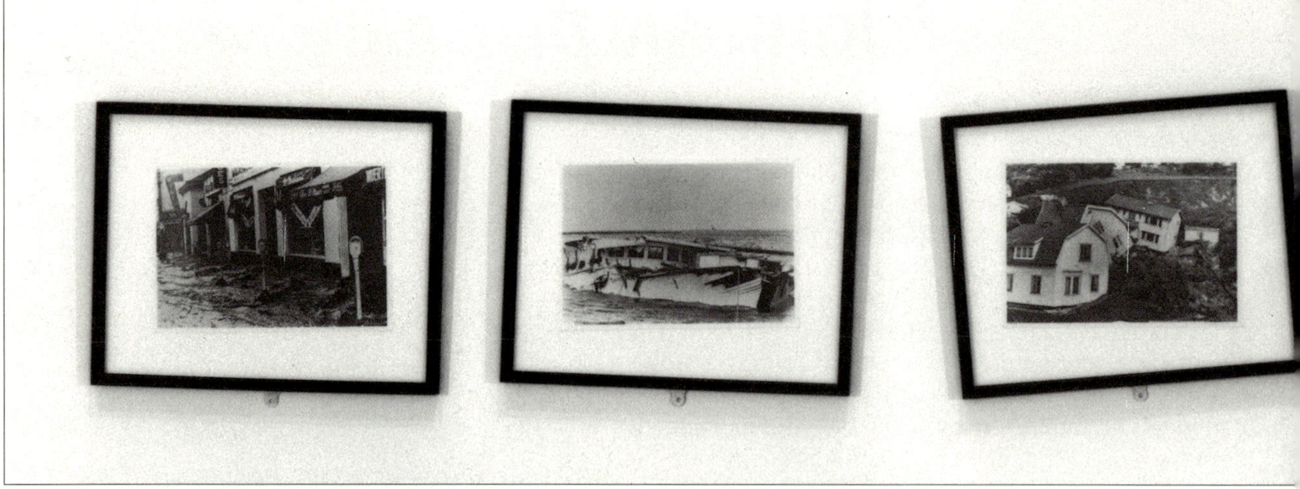

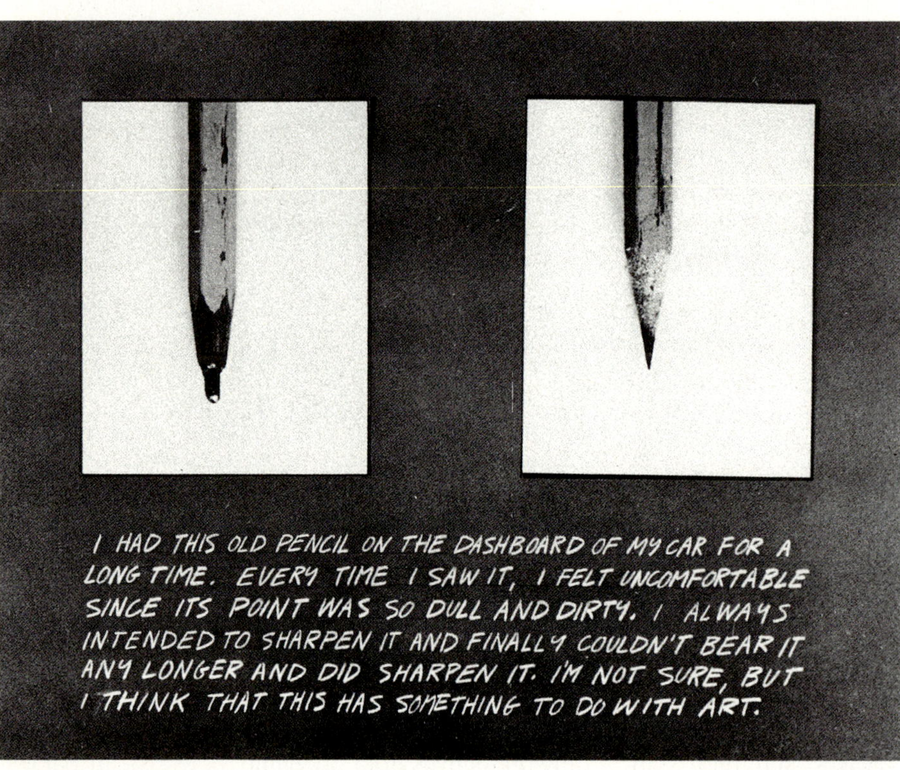

1.9 JOHN BALDESSARI A Different Kind of Order (The Thelonius Monk Story) 1972–73
Five gelatin silver photographs and one typewritten sheet, individually framed
Each image 6⁹⁄₁₆ × 9³⁄₁₆ins (16.7 × 24.9cm)
Each sheet 6¹⁵⁄₁₆ × 10¹³⁄₁₆ins (17.6 × 25.9cm)
Courtesy The Museum of Fine Arts, Houston. Museum purchase with additional funds provided by the National Endowment for the Arts

1.10 JOHN BALDESSARI The Pencil Story 1972–73
2 Type R prints and white pencil on board
22 × 27¼ins (55.9 × 69.2cm)
Collection of Mr. and Mrs. Nicola Bulgari, New York

work through a lot of things, to find out what I was about, rather than following certain models. And it came out that I was more interested in language than in painting.[14]

Wrong (Fig. **1.8**) is from Baldessari's series of "standard size" canvases which include photographs he made to "violate then-current photographic norms." Baldessari's art is typically suffused with clear but subtle intellectual wit; the funniness of each image is immediately clear, but why it is funny is not always so apparent. The multi-level meanings of the relationship between language and visual im-

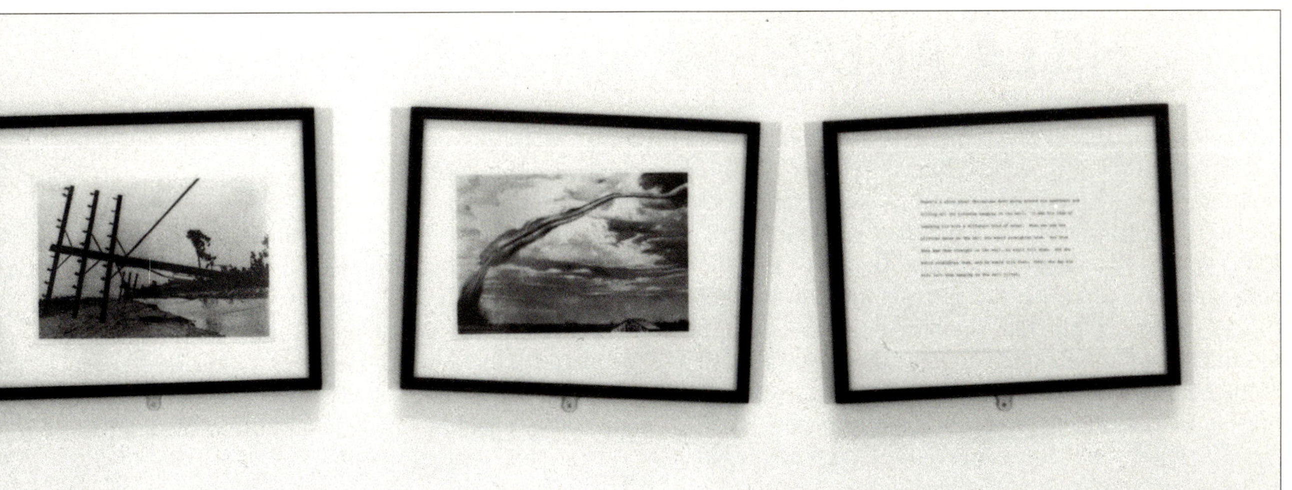

ages in Baldessari's work derive in part from his wide-ranging reading. By itself neither the word nor the image would make sense in an art context. The use of context as an important ingredient of an artwork is another attribute of Duchamp's art which many Conceptual, Minimal, Pop, and other contemporary artists borrowed as a point of departure. *Wrong* is a basic lesson in aesthetics. A clearer statement of an error in conventional artistic composition would be difficult to imagine, yet Baldessari makes the "wrong" right by suffusing it with provocative originality.

Information theory (part of the intellectual currency of the early 1970s) makes distinctions between two different kinds of meanings: *semantic*, which is logical, explicable, and prepares one for action; and *aesthetic*, which is untranslatable, unforeseeable, and shapes states of mind.[15] Baldessari's series *A Different Kind of Order* (1972–73) relates to both kinds of meaning but embodies the semantic meaning in the images and the aesthetic meaning in the words. Baldessari accompanied "found" press photographs of disasters with a text of his own writing.

For *A Different Kind of Order (The Thelonius Monk Story)* (Fig. **1.9**), Baldessari mounted five photographs in frames a little bit larger than the photographs themselves. Each photograph is crooked in relation to the frame; but Baldessari hung the works with the photographs straight and the frames crooked. The question is: are the photographs or the frames crooked, or are both crooked? A typed text mounted crookedly in the sixth frame explains:

There's a story about Thelonius Monk going around his apartment tilting all the pictures hanging on the wall. It was his idea of teaching his wife a different kind of order. When she saw the pictures askew on the wall she would straighten them. And when Monk saw them straightened on the wall, he would tilt them. Until one day his wife left them hanging on the wall tilted.[16]

One last example of Baldessari's photograph and text combinations: *The Pencil Story* (Fig. **1.10**) shows two side-by-side photographs of the same pencil, one depicting the pencil badly in need of sharpening, the other depicting it freshly sharpened. This "before and after" imagery parodies the sculptural concern of many Post-Minimalists with transforming materials from one state to another and making that transformation the subject of the artwork (see page 110). The text written beneath the photographs explains:

I had this old pencil on the dashboard of my car for a long time. Every time I saw it, I felt uncomfortable since its point was so dull and dirty. I always intended to sharpen it and finally couldn't bear it any longer and did sharpen it. I'm not sure, but I think that this has something to do with art.[17]

Once again, through language, Baldessari has given aesthetic meaning to semantic photographs, not only extending the range of meaning that art—and photographs—can embody but at once identifying and parodying other current aesthetic concerns.

HILLA AND BERNHARD BECHER

Since the late 1950s, the German artists Hilla (born 1934) and Bernhard Becher (born 1931) have made documentary photographs of domestic and industrial architectural structures in Germany, Holland, Scotland, Wales, France, Luxembourg, Belgium, and the United States. Grouping the photographs in the grid format favored by Minimalists like André, and LeWitt, the Bechers combine many images of structures with similar functions, such as cooling towers, ore preparation plants, water towers, or blast furnaces.

The results are large-scale photographic collages with an underlying organizational principle that is completely consistent with other Conceptual artists' use of photography as an aesthetically neutral documentation device. "Their grid format 'typologies' focus our attention on the uniformity of certain functional motifs; at the same time they display the diversity possible within a given set form" photography critic Andy Grundberg wrote, but continued later in the same paragraph, "But as much as their work is allied with Conceptual Art's interest in the line between order and disorder, the Bechers function more like cultural anthropologists, sifting the visual shards of a vestigialized industrial culture."[18] When their work was first shown in the United States in the late 1960s, it immediately caught the attention of Conceptual artists.

Wherever one situates *Cooling Towers* (Fig. **1.11**)—as cultural anthropology, Conceptual Art, or "between the established categories"—the Bechers' work extends the roles of photography in particular, and visual imagery in general, into challenging new territories, goals consistent with Conceptual Art.

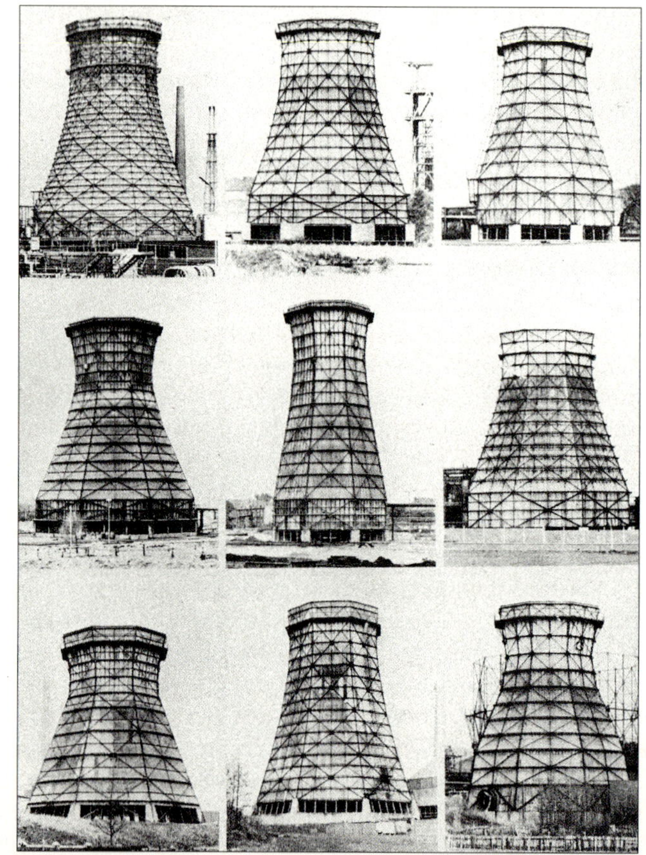

1.11 HILLA AND BERNHARD BECHER
Cooling Towers 1959–72
Black and white photographs
60 × 40ins
(152.4 × 101.6cm)
Courtesy Sonnabend Gallery, New York
"The question if this is a work of art or not is not very interesting to us. Probably it is situated in between the established categories. Anyway the audience which is interested in art would be the most open-minded and willing to think about it."[19]

GILBERT AND GEORGE

1.12 GILBERT AND GEORGE
The Total Mystery of Each Man-Layed Brick 1971
Charcoal on paper
110¼ × 88⅝ins
(280 × 225cm)
Courtesy Sonnabend Gallery, New York

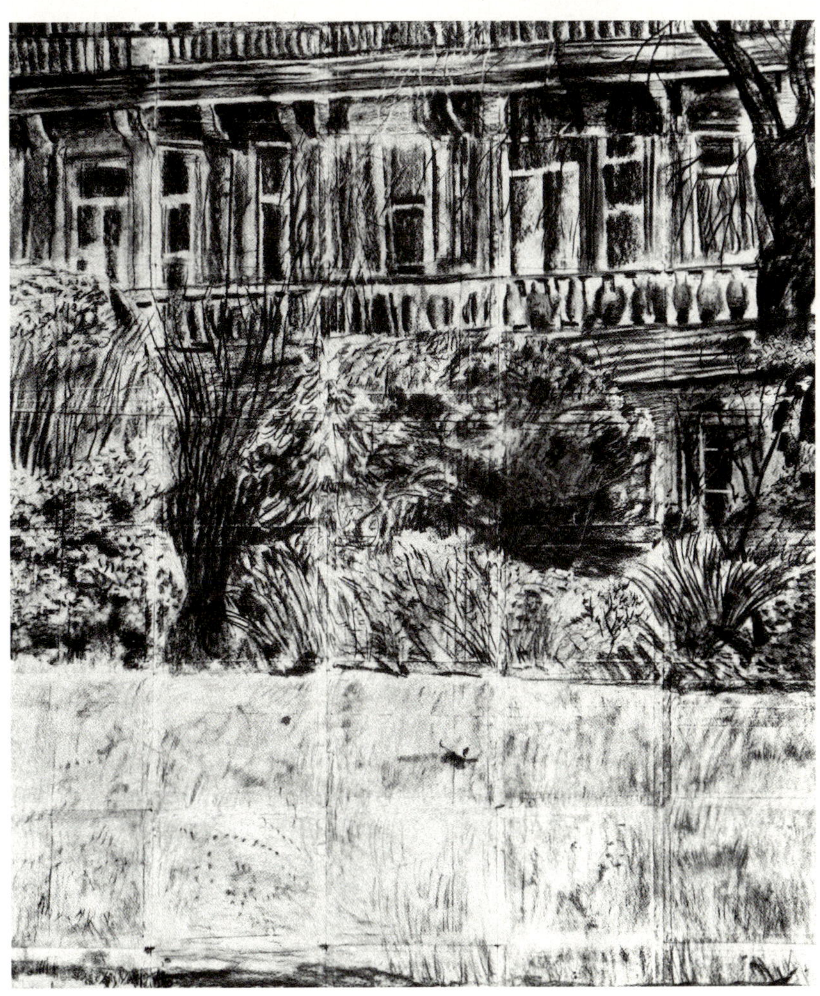

Like the Bechers, the British artists Gilbert (born 1943) and George (born 1942) (they use only their first names) work together as a team. They began their collaboration in 1967 while students at St. Martin's School of Art in London. They have systematically formalized and claimed all of their daily activities as art, turning themselves into "living sculptures" or into lifelong, real-time performance artworks. "They approached such a prospect as if they were entering a religious order and accordingly created a life in which mundane details require virtually no deliberation and suffer little alteration from day to day. . . . In order to eliminate issues of choice and vanity, they adopted a uniform (what they call 'the responsibility-suits of our art') comprised of white nylon shirts (George's cuff-linked and Gilbert's button-cuffed), loud or often emblematic ties, and worsted suits."[20]

Gilbert and George document some of their "living sculptor" activities in books, photographs, and collaborative drawings. An artist's book titled *George and Gilbert: the Living Sculptors, London—Catalogue for their 1973 Australian Visit* contains photographs of the artists along with reproductions of their drawings and their texts. One of the latter reads:

| *London 1970. Gilbert and George, the sculptors, say—*

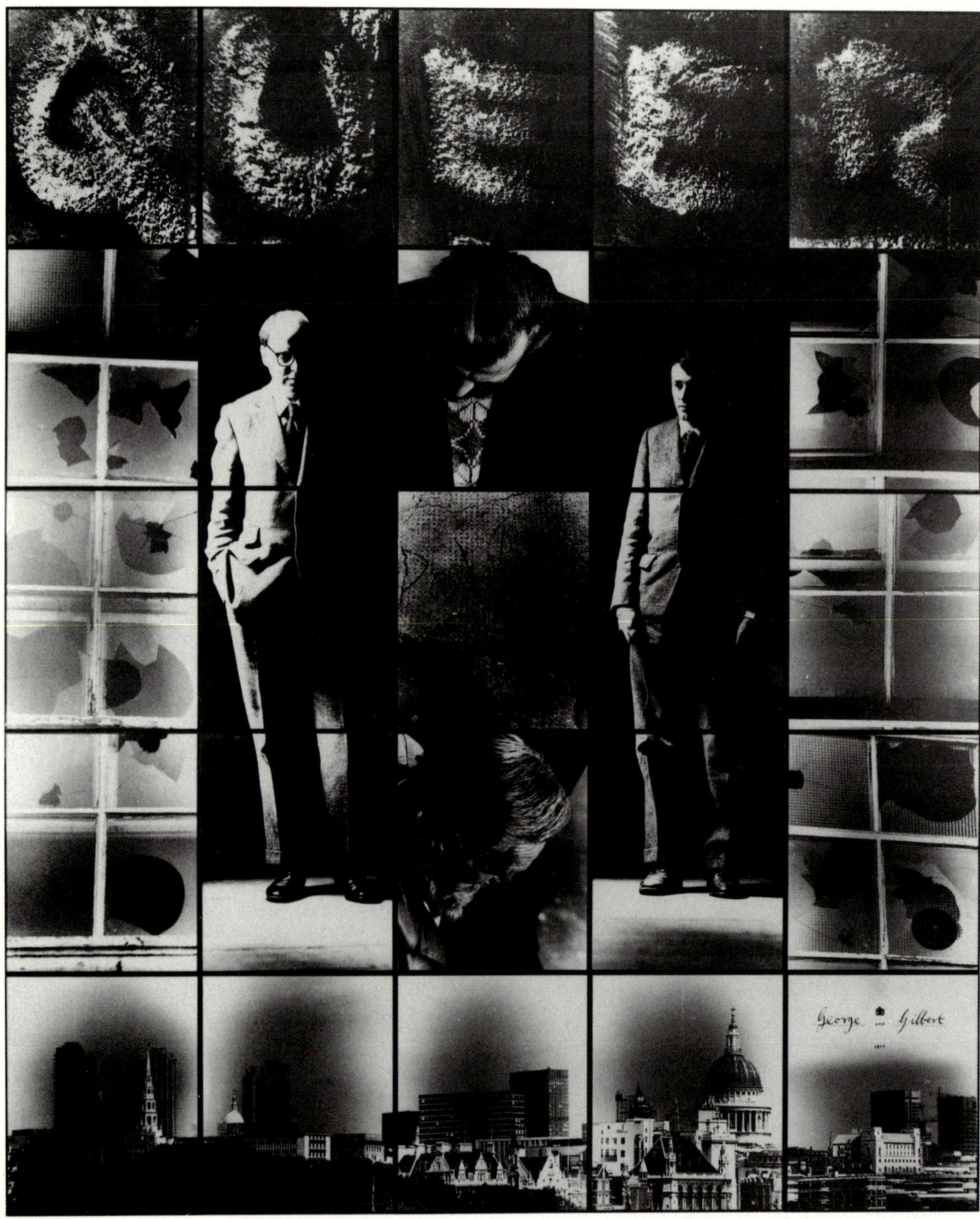

1.13 GILBERT AND GEORGE
Queer 1977

Black and white photograph
118¾ × 98¾ins
(301.6 × 250.8cm)

Courtesy Museum Boymans-
Van Beuningen, Rotterdam,
Holland

"WE ARE ONLY HUMAN SCULPTORS"
We are only human sculptors in that we get up
every day, walking sometimes, reading rarely,
eating often, thinking always, smoking moderately,
enjoying enjoyment, looking, relaxing to see, loving
nightly, finding amusement, encouraging life,
fighting boredom, being natural, daydreaming,
travelling along, drawing occasionally, talking
lightly, tea drinking, feeling tired, dancing
sometimes, philosophising a lot, criticising never,
whistling tunefully, dying very slowly, laughing
nervously, greeting politely and waiting till the day
breaks.

Another artist's book titled *"The Paintings" (with Us in the Nature) of Gilbert & George the Human Sculptors*, Amsterdam, Autumn 1971, and emblazoned with ART FOR ALL (their corporate name) and their London address reads in part:

SIX POINTS
toward a better understanding

Essentially a sculpture we carve
our desires in the air
Together with you this sculpture presents
as much contact for experiencing as is possible
Human sculpture makes available every
feeling you can think of
It is significant that this sculpture is
able to paint its message with colour and form
The sculptors, in their sculpture
are given over to feeling the life of the
world of art
It is intended that this sculpture brings
to us all a more light generous and
general art feeling

Some semblance of the page's layout has been retained to impress readers with the importance of the typography in this and other artists' books. Conceptual artists used the artist's book medium as a means of dematerializing the object-status of artworks, as a means of making artworks inexpensive and readily available in more than one example (unlike a one-of-a-kind painting or sculpture), and as a means of emphasizing the information contained in words and photographs over the purely visual appearance of the artwork. Working as a team in which the contributions of neither artist can be differentiated from the other, Gilbert and George further de-aestheticize or "anesthetize" visual art's traditional aesthetic content. Their aesthetic concept is their art.

Drawing was Gilbert and George's preferred medium between 1970 and 1975; huge, mural-sized charcoal drawings on paper. Both artists worked on all parts of each drawing, but the neutral, anesthetized styles they used makes each artist's marks indistinguishable. *The Total Mystery of Each Man-Layed Brick* (Fig. **1.12**) from *the General Jungle* series (1971) is subtly gridded into separate sheets of paper taped together, the artists' solution to a technical problem with aesthetic ramifications. The practical solution allowed for the handling and shipping of the huge drawings by folding them along the grid lines. Aesthetically, the result is a bending of the static Minimalist grid, similar to the Bechers' homage to and subversion of Minimalist geometry. Typically, Gilbert and George worked the grid into their aesthetic philosophy. Brenda Richardson wrote:

The artists view the world as having universal, natural divisions: they see life as evolving serially, step by step, year by year, almost as a house is built brick by brick [reference to the title, The Total Mystery of Each Man-Layed Brick*]. They see everything, both natural and constructed, as being composed of sections based on discipline and order. They wanted to produce their pieces at large scale and in conjoined units to reflect their "driven sense of sectioning."*[21]

In two 1977 photograph series, *Red Morning* and *Dirty Words*, Gilbert and George turned overtly political. *Red Morning* began the artists' use of black frames for each section of the large photo murals; butting the frames against each other creates a grid similar to folding the drawings. Framing the large photos in sections also facilitates their handling—a method they continue to use.

Like each work in the *Dirty Words* photograph series, *Queer* (Fig. **1.13**) shows the title scrawled in graffiti upon a wall. Gilbert and George are present everywhere, but in this series they are for the first time amidst the squalor of their working-class London neighborhood rather than living a fantasized Victorian life. Their subsequent photographic works even more overtly embrace contemporary social problems and make references to their homosexuality.

DOUGLAS HUEBLER

Working in New York and Massachusetts, Douglas Huebler (born 1924) evolved from painting (which he gave up in 1962) into Minimalist sculpture (which occupied him from 1962–67), and then into Conceptual Art from 1967 until the present. "Art is not necessarily about painting or sculpture," Huebler wrote in 1969, "and a conceptual artist who gets involved in making things that begin to look like painting or sculpture weakens his position and confuses the issues."[22]

Huebler uses photographs and texts. The photographs are as devoid of aesthetic interest as possible. Art critic April Kingsley wrote that, "Huebler avoids this natural temptation to take 'good' photographs by stratagems which are based on choice-negating procedures or by having others (non-artists) take his photographs."[23] The texts are as purely descriptive as possible, maintaining the ambiguity of everyday experience and avoiding both poetic connotations and philosophizing (though the work has sturdy philo-sophical underpinnings). In Huebler's words, "I'm really posing the question of renegotiation of experience, rather than saying take my experience, you see."[24]

An artwork Huebler began in 1971, titled *Variable Piece #70—Global*, is a plan to eventually photograph all of the people in the world. It is a lifelong artwork which will never be finished. Huebler set up sub-categories like "at least one person the artist may know personally," and "look-alikes". *Represented Above is at Least One Person Whose Life is an Open Book* (Fig. **1.14**) is a photograph from another of the sub-categories and has all the hallmarks of a slipshod amateur snapshot.

The language (the words) provides the images' meaning rather than their aesthetic content (since they have none). The relationship between the words and images—since neither by itself has aesthetic interest—creates a third reality, which is the change in the "normal sensory experience." According to

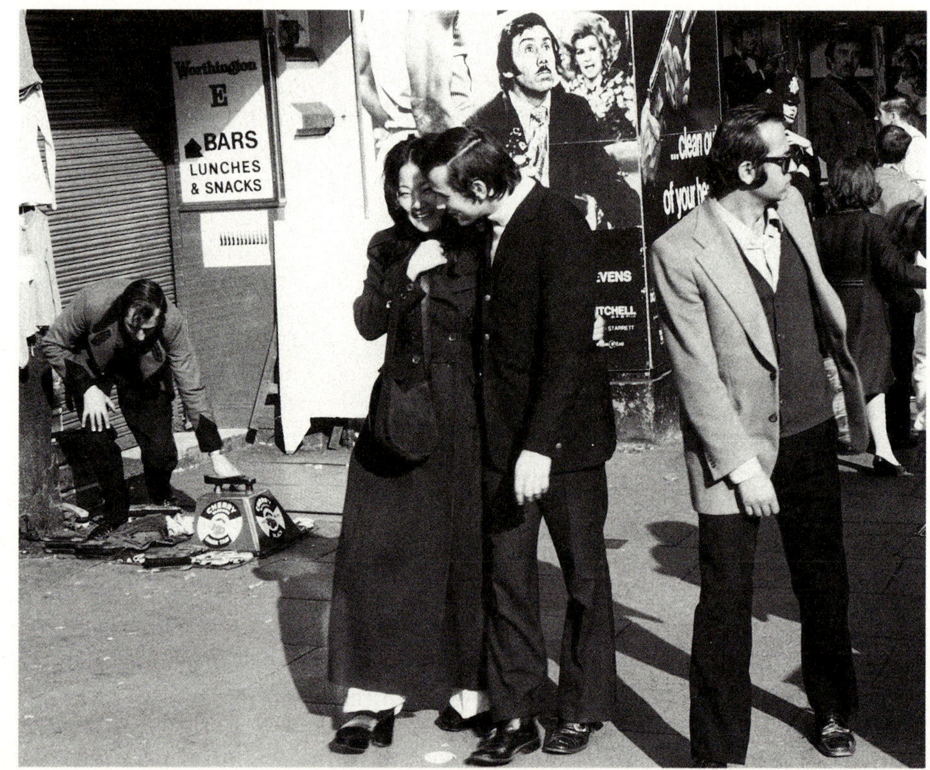

1.14 DOUGLAS HUEBLER Represented Above is at Least One Person Whose Life is an Open Book 1972
Black and white photograph
Courtesy of the artist
"I use language within the work to release the photographs or drawings from carrying the burden of being anything about aesthetics. The words allow the visual signs, which are always the least possible, to return as themselves to the world, as only some things that were appropriated mechanically. That way they can be fresh again, and the people who see them can see them freshly again, too."[25]

Huebler, "You can change the normal sensory experience, change the conceptual model, by changing the language."[26]

Huebler and other Conceptual artists whose work incorporates language have been liberally quoted because their language is part of their art. Quoting their language is like reproducing a photograph of a primarily visual artist's work. Another aspect of Conceptual artists' use of language and photography is its inbuilt art criticism, as Huebler noted in 1969:

*The world is full of objects, more or less
interesting;
I do not wish to add any more.*

*I prefer, simply, to state the existence of things in
terms of time and/or place.*

*More specifically, the work concerns itself with
things whose interrelationship is beyond direct
perceptual experience.*

*Because the work is beyond direct perceptual
experience, awareness of the work depends on a
system of documentation.*

*This documentation takes the form of
photography, maps, drawings, and descriptive
language.*

*What I say is part of the artwork. I don't look to
critics to say things about my work. I tell them
what it's about.*

*People deny words have anything to do with art.
I don't accept that. They do. Art is a source of
information.*[27]

HANS HAACKE

The German artist, Hans Haacke (born 1939), first came to the United States in the early 1960s. By the 1970s he was living in New York. His work in the 1960s typically dealt with physical and biological systems, but in the 1970s his primary subject became social systems. An example of a physical system is Haacke's *Condensation Cube* (1963–65), a clear plexiglass cube containing a small amount of water which condenses on the plexi in constantly changing patterns. An example of a biological system is Haacke's *Ten Turtles Set Free* (1970), which took place in St. Paul de Vence, France, when the artist did exactly what the title states. All three types of Haacke's systems break down boundaries between art and "non-art," but his social systems artworks became the most controversial because they interacted with art institutions in what were perceived to be threatening ways.

For his piece in The Museum of Modern Art's (MoMA's) *Information* show in 1970 (one of the first major Conceptual Art museum shows), Haacke stated a question on the wall and invited the museum audience to vote. The question was: "Would the fact that Governor Rockefeller had not denounced President Nixon's Indo-China policy be a reason for you not to vote for him in November?" Viewers were asked to place a ballot in a box on the left if their answer was "yes," or in a box on the right if "no." Each clear plexi-

glass box contained an automatic counter. Museum visitors voted "yes" approximately two to one.[28]

Governor Nelson Rockefeller had been the chairman of MoMA's board of trustees. His mother was a founder of the museum, and his brother David was the current board chairman. MoMA had been supported by Rockefeller money and art since its beginning. Haacke's *MoMA Poll* (1970) tested the boundaries between art and non-art, between art and socio-economic politics. It is very much to MoMA's credit, therefore, that no attempt was made to stifle Haacke's implicit criticism of Rockefeller.

One cannot say the same, however, for the Solomon R. Guggenheim Museum. Haacke's most well known exhibition never took place. The exhibition was canceled by the museum's director and board of trustees shortly before it was scheduled to open on April 30, 1971. The museum felt that exhibiting Haacke's social systems pieces would have placed it in a libelous position. The works in question included photographs of slum tenements accompanied by the buildings' addresses and the information contained in public records about the current owners, the previous owners, the sale price, and the mortgage holder. *Shapolsky et al.* (Fig. **1.15**) was to have been in the show.

The issue that Haacke raised was, "What are the boundaries between art and life?" an issue central to

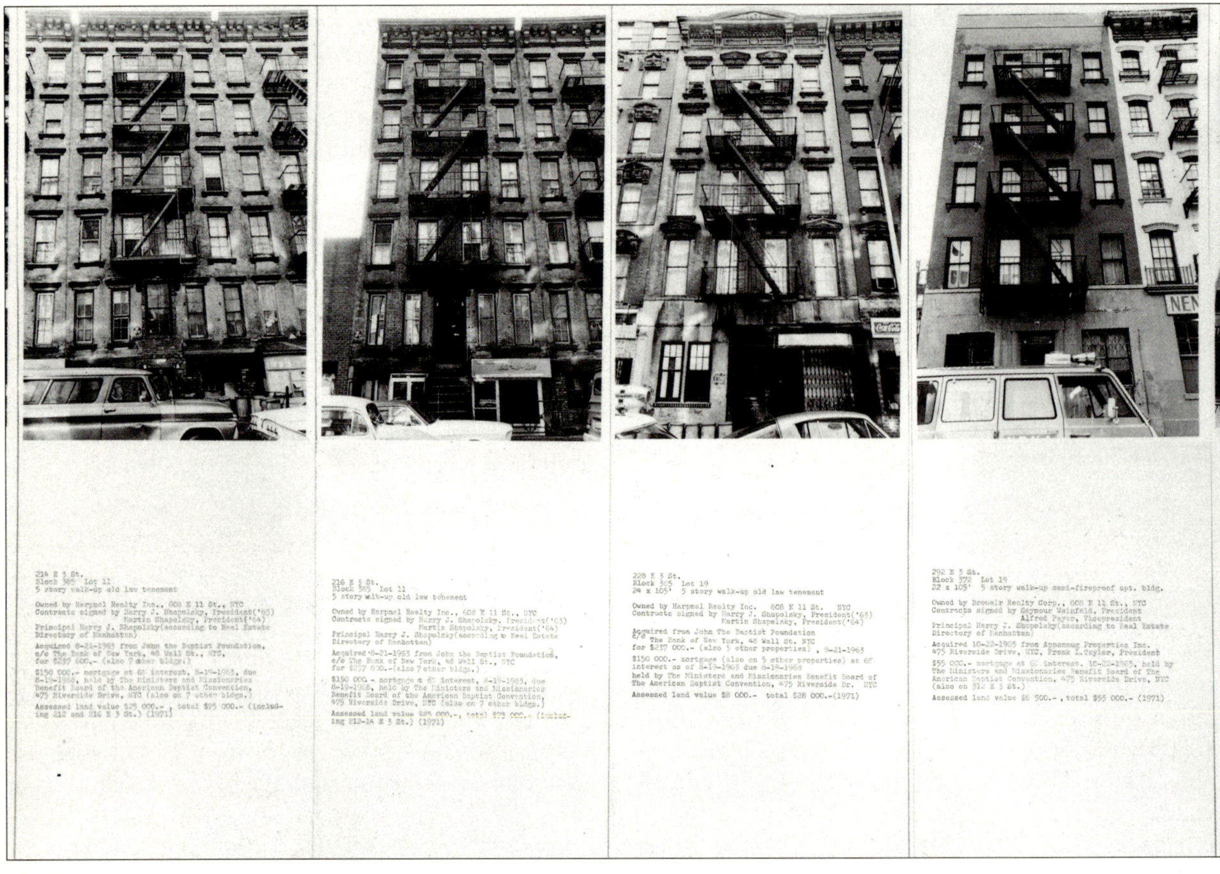

**1.15 HANS HAACKE
Shapolsky et al.
Manhattan Real Estate
Holdings, A Real Time
Social System, as of
May 1, 1971**
Two maps (photo-enlargements), one of the Lower East Side and one of Harlem, each 24 × 20ins (61 × 50.8cm). 142 photos of building facades empty lots, each 10 × 8 ins (25.4 × 20.3cm). 142 typewritten data sheets, attached to the photos and giving the property's address, block and lot number, lot size, building code, the corporation's address and its officers. The date of acquisition, prior owner, mortgage and assessed tax value, each 10 × 8ins (25.4 × 20.3cm), 6 charts on business transactions, each 24 × 20ins (61 × 50.8cm). First exhibited at Galleria Françoise Lambert, Milan, Jan. 1972. Courtesy John Weber Gallery, New York

art of the twentieth century. Various boundaries had been extended by many artists, but none had been as overtly political as Haacke.

In a "Guest Editorial" in *Arts Magazine*, the Guggenheim's director Thomas Messer wrote that " . . . we foresaw procedural complications of many kinds if the museum were to be propelled into extra-artistic situations beyond its natural scope," and "Should social malpractices be exposed if the evidence is dependable and verifiable? Certainly, but not through the auspices of an art museum." Messer continued, "The issue has other, more deeply situated levels which are related, though not identical, to the preceding discussion. I am referring to the blurred and ever-elusive limits of art."[29]

Key phrases in Messer's editorial include "extra-artistic situations," "not through the auspices of an art museum," and "limits of art," all of which were issues Haacke intentionally raised in his art. The exhibition's cancellation, therefore, could be taken as a measurement of the art's success. Haacke here set the limits for dematerializing an artwork and extending art beyond traditional aesthetic boundaries into political territories.

WILLIAM WEGMAN

William Wegman's first characteristic work was made while he was teaching at the University of Wisconsin in Madison in 1970. There Wegman (born 1942) realized that the photographs he had been making to document temporary installation "pieces" (he said he was a member of the "piece movement") could be conceived as ends in themselves.

Cotto (Fig. **1.16**) makes a visual joke out of the surrealistic wandering of the round, sliced peppercorns in the salami onto Wegman's hand and the table as well as the visual correspondence between the round stone in his ring and the various circles. Visual jokes became Wegman's *forte*, in photographs, videotapes (see page 68), and drawings.

1.16 WILLIAM WEGMAN
Cotto 1970
Black and white photograph
10⅝ × 10⅝ins
(26.9 × 26.9cm)
Courtesy of the artist
"I was going to a party one night and so I decided to decorate myself a bit—after all, it was the era for that sort of thing. So I put on my favorite ring and then drew some little circles on my hand. Later at the party I reached for a piece of cotto salami on a white plate and saw that the circles on my hand looked [like] the circles in the salami. I was struck by the magic of the coincidence. I got very excited, rushed home early to recreate the scene on my kitchen table and photographed it."[30]

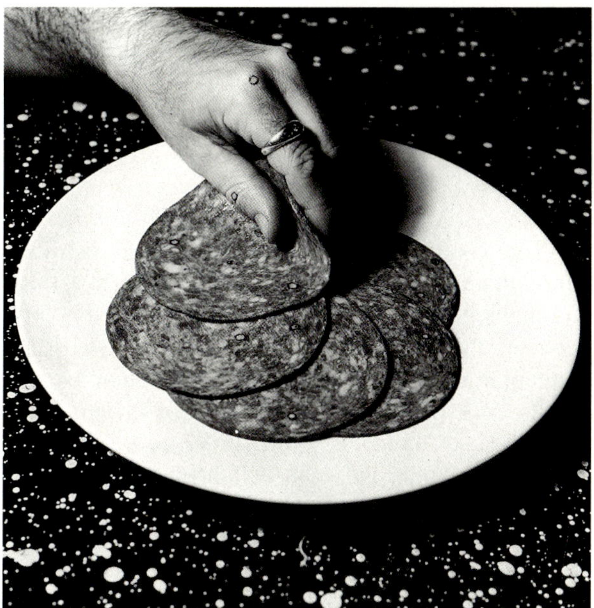

Later in 1970, Wegman moved to Long Beach, California to teach at California State College, eventually settling in Santa Monica, near Los Angeles (where John Baldessari lived) in 1971. Wegman continued to make photographs using props and titles which explained otherwise nonsensical situations. For example, one photo shows a sheet of masonite leaning against a wall with two shoes protruding from beneath it. The title explains: "To hide his deformity he wore special clothing." The image and text combine to make the meaning; either without the other would be even more nonsensical than their combination. Even so, the good-natured ridiculousness of Wegman's art makes him an odd Conceptual artist, unlike any other (though closer to Baldessari than to anyone), and difficult to categorize. His reliance upon language and use of strange differences between visual and verbal information link him more with Conceptual Art than with any other current movement.

Shortly after moving to Santa Monica in 1971, Wegman gave in to his wife's request for a dog, choosing a male Weimaraner they named Man Ray after the American Dadaist. Man Ray demanded a lot of attention, finally becoming such a pest that he wandered into the camera's range when Wegman was making videotapes. There was only one thing to do: put Man Ray on camera, and there began an artistic collaboration that lasted Man Ray's lifetime, until he died of cancer at the age of 12 in 1982.

In 1972, Wegman moved to New York where he made *Before/On/After: Permutations* (Fig. **1.17**) in collaboration with Man Ray, parodying the current preoccupation of performance and process-oriented Post-Minimalist artists with permutations (see pages 110–11). Lisa Lyons describes:

Here seven photographs set in a grid show Man Ray responding to geometric symbols on a chart by assuming different positions in relation to a wooden box. In the first row of pictures the symbols are presented to him one at a time: seeing a circle, he stands behind the box; seeing a triangle, he mounts the box; seeing a square, he stands in front of the box. In the second row, the symbols are presented to him in pairs and he

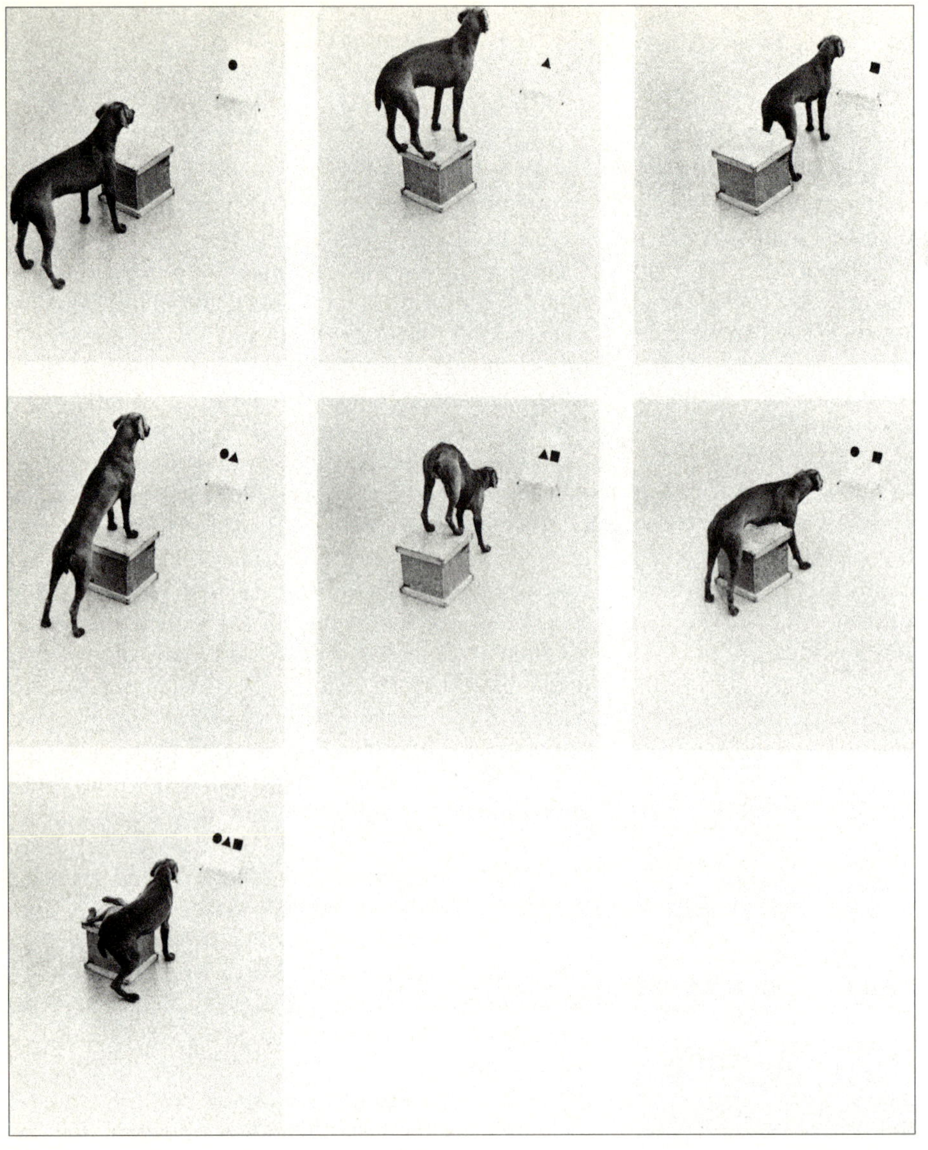

responds by placing first his front paws, then his back paws on the box and finally by straddling the box. Up to this point, Ray's performance, impressive as it is, could be interpreted as that of an extraordinarily well-trained Pavlovian specimen. Then comes the last picture where all three symbols are presented to him on the chart and he responds by placing just his left front and back paws on the box. His contorted pose is funny in and of itself. But it's all the more comical because, if only for a moment, we catch ourselves thinking it is the result of a decision-making process—one that involves imagination and creativity. Of course, to interpret Ray's behavior in such human terms is absurd; dogs just don't think that way. The performance is sheer sleight of paw and we know that Wegman has manipulated us, just as surely as he has manipulated Man Ray.[31]

The geometric symbols and the grid parodies Minimalism, the permutations parody Post-Minimalism and Performance Art, and the link between the images, the title, and the overriding concept that joins them parodies Conceptual Art.

In 1979 the Polaroid Corporation invited Wegman to use their large-format camera. Wegman traveled to Cambridge, Massachussets with Man Ray and various props from his "fun trunk." *Fey Ray* (1979), featuring Man Ray extending a fingernail-polished paw, is one image from this first Polaroid shooting session. It is typical of Wegman to word-

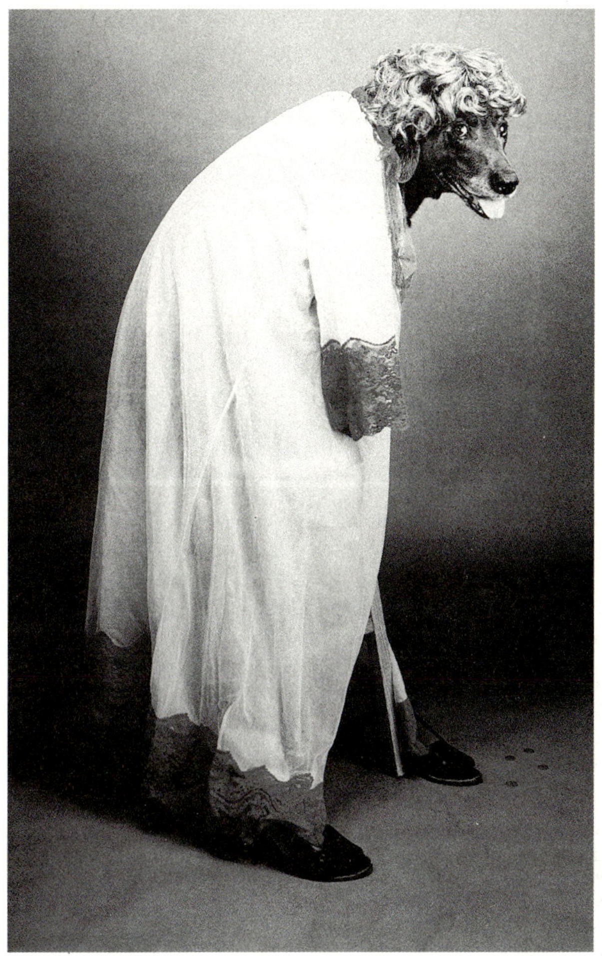

1.18 WILLIAM WEGMAN
Tall Dog 1982
Color Polaroid Polarcolor II film
24 × 20ins
(61 × 50.8cm)
Courtesy Holly Solomon Gallery, New York

play, this time with the name of the female movie star who was the first King Kong's love interest, Fay Wray. Between 1979 and Man Ray's death in 1982, Wegman made hundreds of 20 × 24 inches (50.8 × 60.9 cm) Polaroids of the art world's most famous canine.

Tall Dog (Fig. **1.18**) shows Man Ray sitting on a drafting stool wearing a frumpy gray woman's wig and draped in a filmy negligee. Clunky shoes peep out from beneath the negligee's hem, recalling *To Hide His Deformity He Wore Special Clothing*. Just as the latter parodied the artistic movement called "distribution sculpture" that Wegman flirted with during his "piece movement" period, *Tall Dog* and many of the Man Ray images parody Pop Art's and Post-Modernism's adoption of advertising imagery. Wegman takes the ridiculous situations and banal cuteness of advertising to the borderline of lunacy, thus stripping the advertisements of their manipulativeness—or, to use Post-Modernist language, "deconstructing" and "recontextualizing" them. Though *Tall Dog* and other current work grow out of Wegman's early 1970s concerns, his comments on current aesthetics are so highly original that they ultimately defy categorization.

JOSEPH KOSUTH

Joseph Kosuth (born 1945) is one of the most abstract of all the Conceptual artists, theoretically placing art in the realm of ideas: "It is impossible to see my work. What is seen is the presentation of the information. The art exits only as an invisible, ethereal idea."[32] Stated another way, "All my work exists when it is conceived because the execution is irrelevant to the art . . . the art is for an art context only . . ."[33]

One and Three Chairs (Fig. **1.19**) shows three different chairs: an actual chair, a photograph of the chair, and an enlarged dictionary definition of a chair. Each of the three chairs is a chair, but each is a completely different way of defining "chair". Present-

ing the same thing in such different ways makes us realize how unable we are to precisely define even the simplest objects. All three chairs are both abstract and representational, both symbolic and actual, both images and objects.

Self-Defined (Fig. **1.20**) uses words alone. The words in neon are exactly what they state themselves to be, and more. The ability or inability of human beings to comprehend the "nature and grounds of knowledge," or the "nature and relations of being"—called "epistemology" and "ontology" by philosophers—frequently concerned Conceptual artists. Kosuth focuses almost exclusively on such issues.

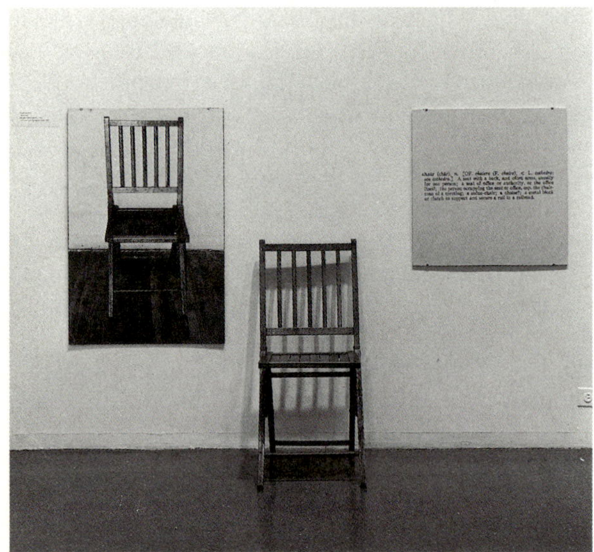

Self-Defined refers not only to itself alone, but also to the mandate of Color Field and Minimalist artists that art be solely about attributes which belong only to whatever particular traditional form, painting or sculpture, the artist uses. And so, it both is and is not self-defined, making it a contradiction and a clear statement of our inability to define anything precisely.

1.19 JOSEPH KOSUTH
One and Three Chairs
1965
Wooden folding chair, photograph of chair, and photographic enlargement of dictionary definition of chair: chair, $32\frac{3}{8} \times 14\frac{7}{8} \times 20\frac{7}{8}$ins ($82 \times 37.8 \times 53$cm); photo panel, $36 \times 24\frac{1}{8}$ins (91.5×61.1cm); text panel, $24 \times 24\frac{1}{8}$ins (61×61.3cm). Collection The Museum of Modern Art, New York. Larry Aldrich Foundation Fund

1.20 JOSEPH KOSUTH
Self-defined 1966
White Neon
Collection Giuseppe Panza di Biumo-Varese

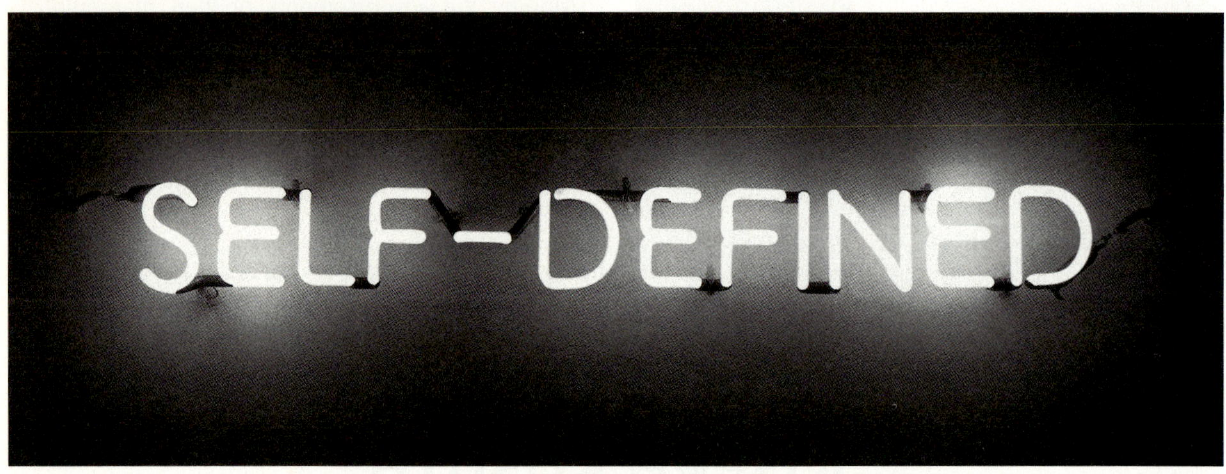

LAWRENCE WEINER

Lawrence Weiner (born 1940) works exclusively with words, sometimes placing them on paper, sometimes applying them directly to the wall. He treats the words as objects and as signifiers of meaning, albeit ambiguous meaning, but not as literature. Words function in Weiner's art more like art theories and philosophy than anything else, consistent with Kosuth's epistemological and ontological discourses.

To the Sea, on the Sea, from the Sea, and *At the Sea* (1970) consist of each of the four sets of words on a page. The most important Conceptual Art collector, Guiseppe Panza di Biumo, explains:

The word in a Weiner doesn't belong to speech, to a logical development, to a relationship between speech and reality. Words are taken out of reality and used as objects. It is very interesting to see the meaning each word could have, but they are separated from representation. They are not literature, because in literature every word represents something. This is not the case with

Weiner. He uses the word as a potential for meaning, but unconnected in speech.... It is a printed word and can be copied any time we want. But it is a very nominal kind of ownership, very conceptual, because we own something immaterial ... Anyway Weiner found an intelligent solution because we get a statement from his attorney that we are the owner of a particular piece. This is a kind of guarantee that we are the owner of this word as object.[34]

Weiner dematerializes the artwork to an extraordinary degree. *To the Sea* and others in the series need not even be seen to be experienced.

MEL BOCHNER

Like Kosuth and Weiner, Mel Bochner (born 1940) lived in New York City during the 1960s, keeping abreast of the most current art developments. In 1967 Bochner applied black tape in a gridded pattern on a wall, then photographed the result, but "He at length abandoned photography since ... the photograph itself became an object in the world."[35] In 1972 the art critic Robert Pincus-Witten wrote that:

As early as 1967 then, Bochner had recognized that art may be, but need no longer be embodied in some kind of here and now sensuous object, like those things conventionally called paintings or sculptures. The feature that made art of certain activities was the integrity of the thinking that the work entailed. This is not the central focus of Minimalism—though it is implicit in the style —since, whatever else it may be, Minimalism was primarily realized in the fabrication of autonomous objects. At this point Bochner had come to personify what by now is self-evident—that whatever else art may be, it is the best thinking of any given moment.... [Later in the same essay] ... physicality or materiality is not his work's core and indeed it may be only an ancillary consideration of the information projected.[36]

Bochner intentionally used inexpensive, intrinsically valueless material for *Theory of Sculpture #6* (Fig. **1.21**). The sculpture is about different ways of structuring—of structuring anything, including ideas—not necessarily about ways of structuring materials, and especially not about ways of structuring sculptural materials. The clarity of Bochner's

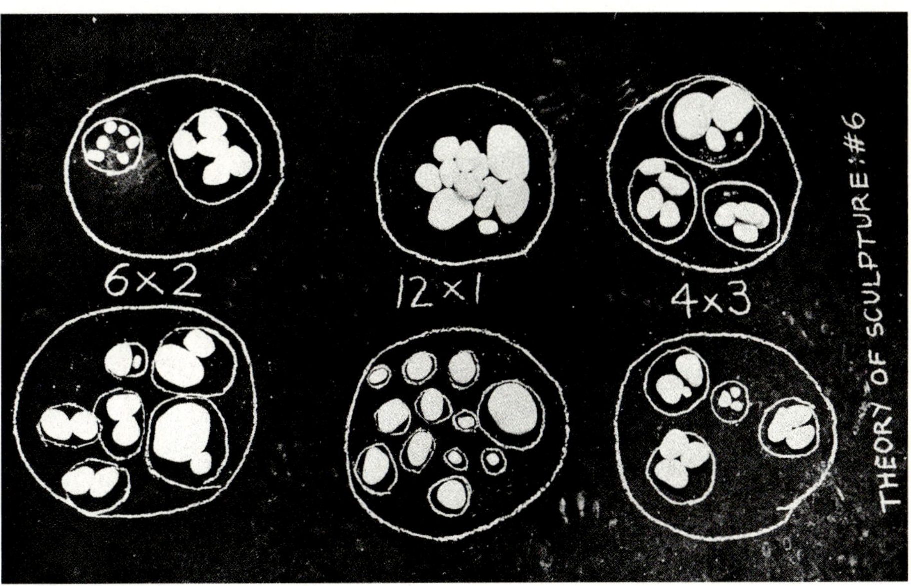

1.21 MEL BOCHNER
Theory of Sculpture #6
1972
Chalk and stones on floor, installation at Lisson Gallery, London
Courtesy Sonnabend Gallery, New York

thought process determines the sculpture's success, not the manipulation of materials. The materials this sculpture is made of have no bearing on what the sculpture is or means.

Incorporating into his art what had formerly been the critic's and art historian's role, Bochner wrote:

Parenthetical Reflections on Five Earlier Statements

1. My primary interest is with methodology.
   (Why my art is is not its meaning)
2. Individual demonstrations should be seen simply as a determinant of place and convenience.
   (Where my art occurs is not its meaning.)
3. Given an alternative set of circumstances, the same idea may take a radically different form.
   (How my art looks is not its meaning.)
4. My art exists only when it is asked for ... there is nothing "between" exhibitions.
   (When my art happens to be done is not its meaning.)
5. For me, all a work of art needs to be is uninteresting.
   (The condition of my art is its avoidance of attributed meanings.)[37]

SOL LeWITT

Sol LeWitt's first "wall drawing" dates from 1968; he drew it himself directly on the wall of the Paula Cooper Gallery in New York City. When the exhibition closed, the wall drawing was painted over. LeWitt wrote in 1970, "The wall drawing is a permanent installation, until destroyed. Once something is done, it cannot be undone."[38] Since 1968, LeWitt has continued to make wall drawings; most are executed by draftsmen following his written instructions; usually, the artist himself does not make the drawing on the wall but furnishes verbal instructions and an ink drawing. "The ink drawing is a plan for but not a reproduction of the wall drawing; the wall drawing is not a reproduction of the ink drawing. Each is equally important," wrote the artist.[39]

For an exhibition in Amsterdam in 1971, LeWitt instructed draftsmen to draw: "Ten thousand straight lines at random."[40] For a show in Boston that same year he instructed draftsmen to draw: "Fifty randomly placed points connected by straight lines."[41] Four people, including LeWitt, drew the first wall drawing; five people without the artist drew the second. "Whether or not the artist himself works on the wall makes no difference," wrote art critic Lawrence Alloway.[42]

The instructions for *Lines to Points on a 6" Grid* (Fig. **1.22**) are as follows: "A six-inch (15 cm) grid covering each of the four black walls. White lines to points on the grids. 1st wall: 24 lines from the center; 2nd wall: 12 lines from the midpoint of each of the sides; 3rd wall: 12 lines from each corner; 4th wall: 24

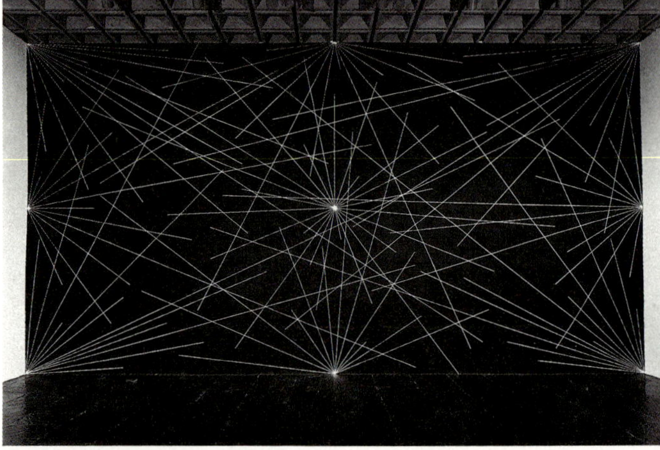

1.22 SOL LeWITT
Lines to Points on a 6″ Grid 1979
White crayon lines and black pencil grid on black walls

Courtesy Whitney Museum of American Art, New York Purchase, with funds from the Gilman Foundation, Inc. 78.1.1–4

lines from the center, 12 lines from the midpoint of each of the sides; 3rd wall: 12 lines from each corner; 4th wall: 24 lines from the center, 12 lines from the midpoint of each of the sides, 12 lines from the corner. (The length of the lines and their placement are determined by the draftsman.)"[43]

For an exhibition in 1977 at the Art Gallery of New South Wales, Australia, LeWitt published a brochure documenting all possible combinations of five different kinds of lines within a grid drawn upon the wall. The five types of lines are: *Arcs from Four Corners,*

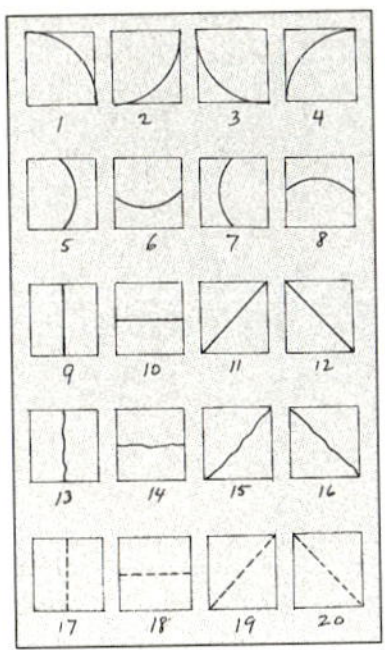

1.23 SOL LeWITT
Arcs from Four Corners,
from Four Sides, Straight
Lines, Not Straight Lines,
Broken Lines 1977
Wall drawing
Dimensions variable
Courtesy John Weber Gallery,
New York

1/2	1/6	1/10	1/14	1/18	2/8	2/16	3/7	3/15	4/7	4/15	4/19	5/8	5/12	5/20	6/14	7/9	7/17	8/13	9/10	9/14	9/18	10/12	10/20	11/19	12/19	13/20	15/17	17/18
1/3	1/7	1/11	1/15	1/19	2/9	2/17	3/8	3/16	4/8	4/16	4/20	5/9	5/13	6/7	6/15	7/10	7/18	8/14	9/11	9/15	9/19	10/13	11/12	11/20	12/20	14/15	15/18	17/19
1/4	1/8	1/12	1/16	1/20	2/10	2/18	3/9	3/17	4/9	4/17	5/6	5/10	5/14	6/8	6/16	7/11	7/19	8/15	9/12	9/16	9/20	10/14	11/13	12/13	13/14	14/16	15/19	17/20
1/5	1/9	1/13	1/17	2/3	2/11	2/19	3/10	3/18	4/10	4/18	5/7	5/11	5/15	6/9	6/17	7/12	7/20	8/16	9/13	9/17	10/11	10/15	11/14	12/14	13/15	14/17	15/20	18/19
				2/4	2/12	2/20	3/11	3/19	4/11			5/16	6/10	6/18	7/13	8/9	8/17					10/16	11/15	12/15	13/16	14/18	16/17	18/20
				2/5	2/13	3/4	3/12	3/20	4/12			5/17	6/11	6/19	7/14	8/10	8/18					10/17	11/16	12/16	13/17	14/19	16/18	19/20
				2/6	2/14	3/5	3/13	4/5	4/13			5/18	6/12	6/20	7/15	8/11	8/19					10/18	11/17	12/17	13/18	14/20	16/19	
				2/7	2/15	3/6	3/14	4/6	4/14			5/19	6/13	7/8	7/16	8/12	8/20					10/19	11/18	12/18	13/19	15/16	16/20	

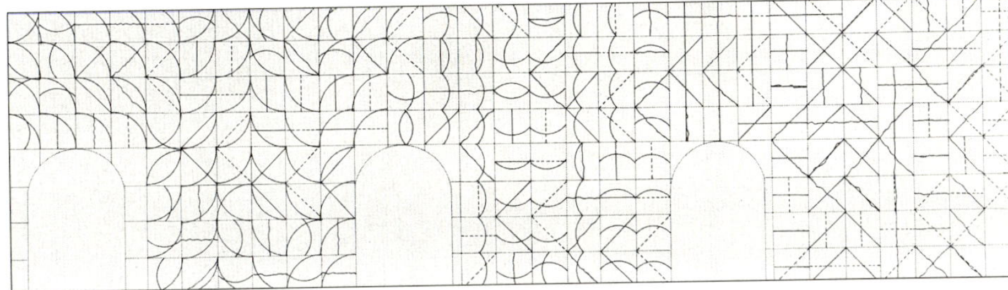

from Four Sides, Straight Lines, Not-Straight Lines, Broken Lines (Fig. **1.23**). The brochure includes both a diagram of the gridded wall with the placement of each combination (indicated by numbers) and a drawing of the different line combinations as they would appear within the grid. Even the schematic drawing is surprisingly sensuous, recalling LeWitt's first of 35 "Sentences on Conceptual Art" published in 1969: "Conceptual artists are mystics rather than rationalists. They leap to conclusions that logic cannot reach."[44]

LeWitt's wall drawings elegantly reconcile logical order and irrational randomness: the artist instructs the draftsmen in detail, but differences in each draftsman's manual touch and conceptual choices (for example, how a draftsman draws a "not-straight line") affect the final result. The wall drawings also reconcile the personal and impersonal: while reflecting LeWitt's completely unique artistic concepts, they are executed by anonymous hands.[45] And, although Lewitt balances the traditional polarities of Western art between the eye and the mind—or between the visual and the conceptual—in favor of the conceptual, the results are "stunningly beautiful."[46] The wall drawings are remarkable for their conceptual clarity and visual complexity.

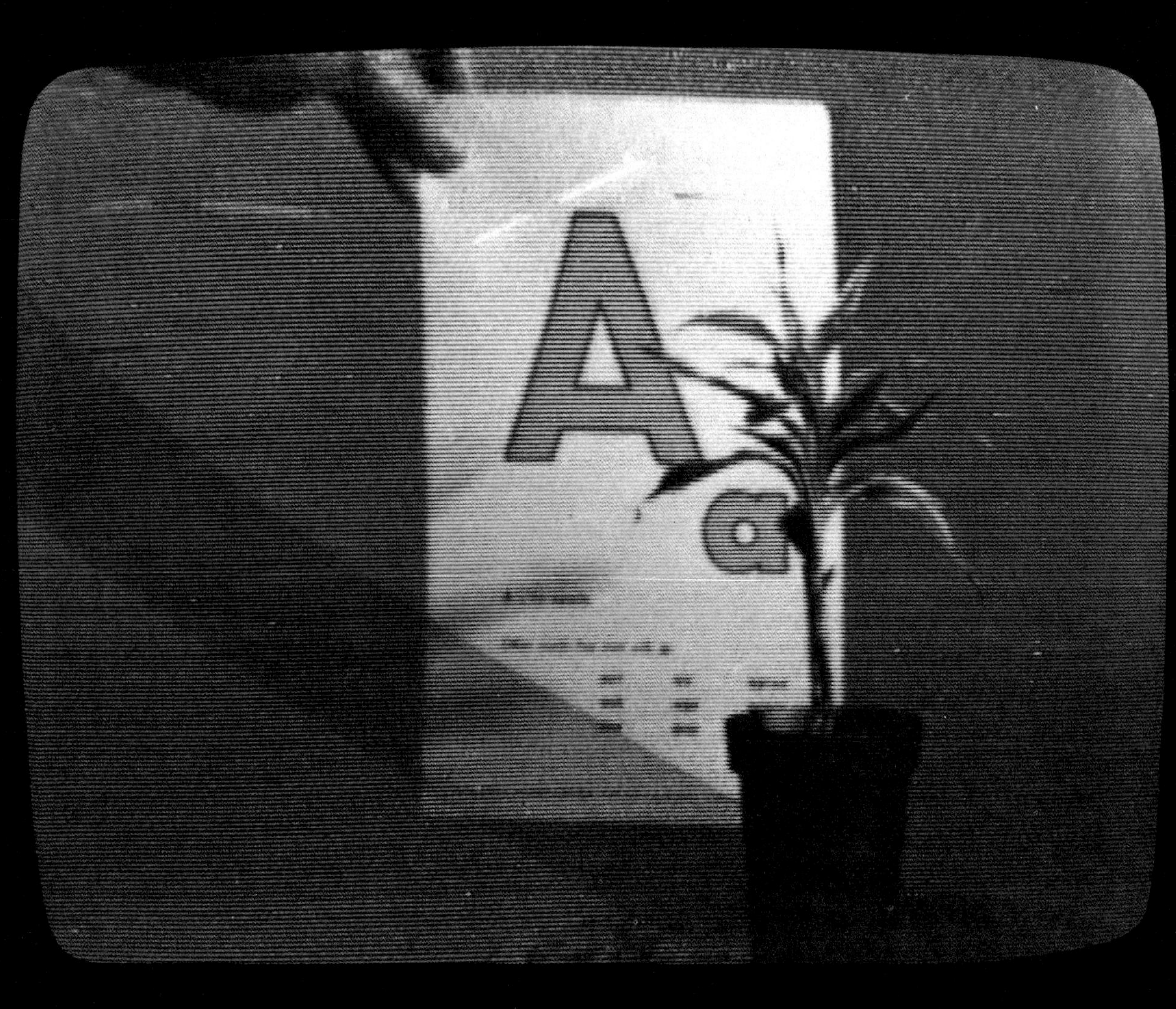

2
Video, Film, and Performance Art

"... for there to be progress in TV, the medium must be as neutral as a pencil. Just one more tool in the artist's toolbox. Another tool to have around, like a pencil ..." [1]

—— JOHN BALDESSARI ——

John Baldessari
Teaching a Plant the Alphabet   1972
Courtesy of the artist

The Fourth Dimension

Like Conceptual Art, Video, Film, and Performance Art offer artists alternatives to object-oriented art media like painting and sculpture. Many Conceptual artists work in video, film and performance. Many of the same goals motivate Conceptual artists and Video, Film, and Performance artists: evading the marketplace, taking art out of galleries and museums, using language and other extra visual elements, shifting the focus from the art object to the artist or the spectator, and minimizing the monetary value of art.

But the major difference between the artworks discussed in this chapter and those discussed in the preceding chapter on Conceptual Art is that every artwork in this chapter employs the fourth dimension—time. Video, Film, and Performance Art begin and end; they have duration, whereas most paintings, sculptures, and even photographs are static objects.

The Dynamics of Electronic Media

"The medium is the message," (or the "massage") said the popular sociologist Marshall McLuhan, the first widely-read chronicler of mass-media's effects on perception and behavior.[2] McLuhan believed that hidden messages underly the subject matter of media, messages based more on the method of *structuring* information and on the *sensory balance* of the medium in question than on the explicit information.

Print media—books, magazines, newspapers, essays, poems—are primarily visual, and perceived in a sequential structure, one word after another. Reading both isolates one of the senses—the sense of sight—and makes the reader focus on one thing at a time in a structured sequence.

Audio media—radio, television, music—address the sense of hearing, which lacks a "point of view."[3] Sound surrounds the listener from all directions. With the introduction of portable stereo "ghetto blasters" or "boxes," then the "Walkman," listeners can carry their own enveloping environment with them.

Television adds the sense of touch to sound's appeal to the sense of hearing. Comprised of thousands of constantly changing dots of colored light projected from behind the screen, television images wash over us in a massage of glowing color.

Being omnidirectional, television lacks the fixed "point of view" of print media. Film, television, and stereo also lack a fixed point of view in another respect. Cameras and microphones are media equivalents to our eyes and ears; they can be moved from one location to another, or electronic editors can switch from one to another, thus changing our point of view while we remain stationary. Switching from "live" television coverage of man's first steps on the moon to "mission control" at NASA in Houston instantly changed our "live" point of view by a distance of 250,000 miles (402,325 km).

The "live" dimension of television and radio have radically changed our perception of the world and, hence, our perceptual patterns in general. Any event that television choses to broadcast can be perceived by millions of people at the same time as it happens. For example, an estimated 700 million people worldwide watched the Royal Wedding of Britain's Prince Charles and Lady Diana Spencer in 1981. Radio also possesses this live dimension, but while radio is only audio, television appeals to our senses of hearing, touch, and sight. McLuhan believed that because color television and stereo became so widely used in the 1960s, many people became sensorily reoriented from the visual, linear sequentiality of the formerly dominant media—print—to the omnidirectional sound and touch of stereo and television.

Incorporating the senses of hearing, touch, taste, and smell—as well as the more traditional one of sight—Video, Film, and Performance artists reflect the reintegration of the senses characteristic of the new mass-media environment. They employ not only the three dimensions of height, width, and depth, but also the fourth dimension of duration. And like some Conceptual artists and some Earthwork and site-specific artists, they sometimes make artworks as impermanent as the live television coverage of man's first step on the moon.

ANDY WARHOL'S FILMS

Independent cinema flourished in the United States in the late 1950s and 1960s, growing out of its origins in the early 1940s with the invention of the Bolex 16 mm camera which made filmmaking less costly than Hollywood's 35 mm format. The Bolex was for independent cinema what the Sony Portapack (the first portable video equipment) was for Video Art in the mid-1960s.

American independent cinema of the late 1950s and 1960s characteristically differentiated itself from Hollywood products by using complex editing strategies, new locations and actors, found footage and soundtracks, elaborate narratives, suggestive montage, satires of commercial film genres, and taboo subjects. Andy Warhol (1928–87) employed only the last of these.

Jonas Mekas, the director of the Filmmaker's Cooperative (the most influential independent film institution) wrote in the citation when Warhol received *Film Culture's* sixth Independent Film Award in 1964 for *Sleep, Eat, Haircut, Kiss,* and *Empire*:

> *Andy Warhol is taking cinema back to its origins, to the days of Lumière, for a rejuvenation and cleansing. In his work, he has abandoned all the "cinematic" form and subject adornments that cinema had gathered around itself until now.*[4]

Sleep (Fig. **2.1**) is a six-hour long black-and-white silent film shown at the silent-film speed of 16 frames per second (fps) rather than the standard sound film speed of 24 fps. Slowing down the projection speed further slows down the already endlessly slow action: John Giorno sleeping. The camera only changes position when the 30-minute long roll of film runs out and the camera has to be reloaded.

2.1 ANDY WARHOL
Sleep 1963
Black and white film, 6 hours
Courtesy Andy Warhol
Foundation, New York

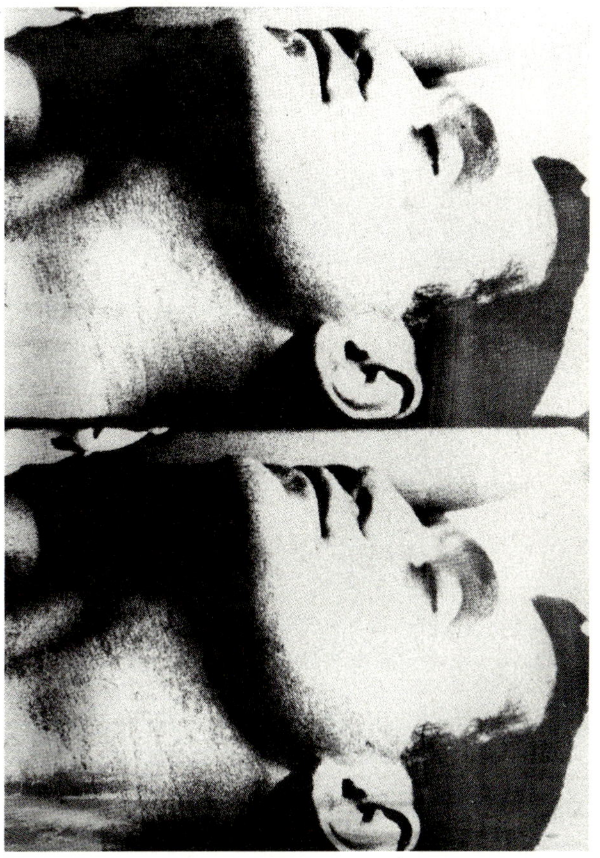

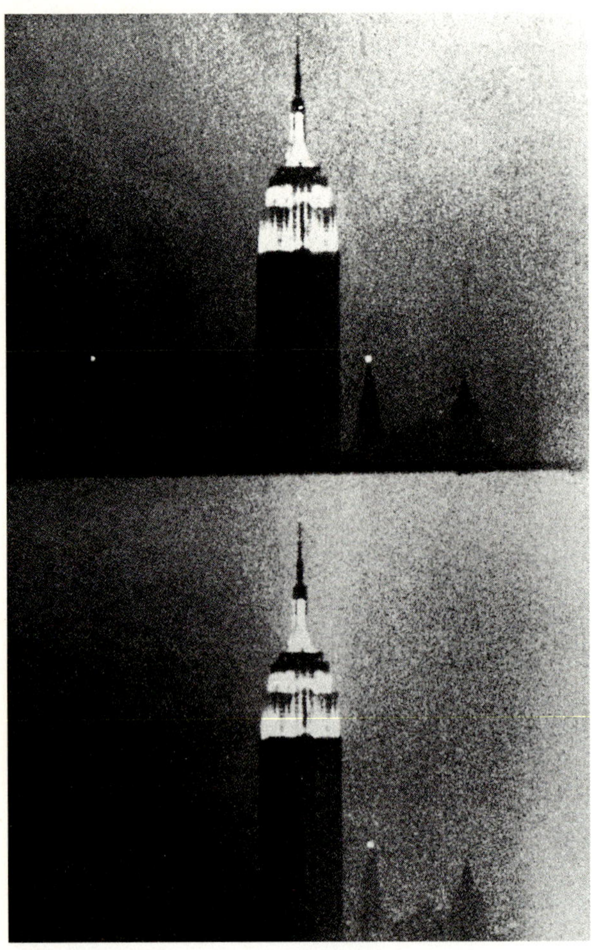

2.2 ANDY WARHOL
Empire 1964
Black and white film,
8 hours

Courtesy Andy Warhol
Foundation, New York

Warhol spliced all the film rolls together, including the brilliant white flash at each reel's end (where it was exposed to light on loading and unloading the camera). Thus each reel of film records "real time" rather than the manipulated time characteristic of edited films. Opposing the narrative conventions of previous films, while also presenting film's ability to make even the most mundane events interesting, are Warhol's subjects in *Sleep*.

For *Empire* (Fig. **2.2**), Warhol set up his camera on a tripod, focused it on the upper two-thirds of the Empire State Building in New York City, and never moved the camera or changed the field of vision for the entire eight hours of the film's length. Like *Sleep*, *Empire* links "reel" and "real" time. Clouds pass by, the sky's light changes, eventually darkness comes, lights start to be turned on in some windows, the outdoor lighting on the building comes on: that summarizes the entire action, shot from the 44th floor of the Time-Life building. "The Empire State Building is a star!," Warhol exclaimed during the shooting, identifying the ability of "movies" to make anything seem important.[5] "In the future, everybody will be world famous for at least fifteen minutes," Warhol said in another brilliant statement.[6]

Warhol takes film back to its most abstract—most "filmic"—and fundamental condition, a filmmaker's equivalent to the Color Field and Minimal artist's concern with essentially painterly or sculptural qualities, but without either their visual radiance or intellectualism; instead, with brilliant dumbness. With his insistence on film's most fundamental qualities, Warhol influenced the best subsequent independent American cinema.

JOSEPH BEUYS

The German Joseph Beuys (1921–86) set himself the task of renewing German art after its depletion by the Nazis in the 1930s and 1940s, and to his enormous credit he succeeded, not only with his own art but by providing new foundations for subsequent generations of German artists. Beuys's artistic materials are his own life, mixed with the deeply rooted myths and cultural traditions of the German people.

Beuys was a Nazi Luftwaffe pilot during World War II when he was shot down over the Crimean. According to the legend he built around this experience—however true or mythical it might be—Tartars looking through his plane's wreckage for spoils found Beuys buried in snow and half-frozen. They nursed him back to health by wrapping him in fat and covering him with felt to gradually restore his body's natural heat. Since then, felt and fat have figured prominently in Beuys's art as symbols of regen-

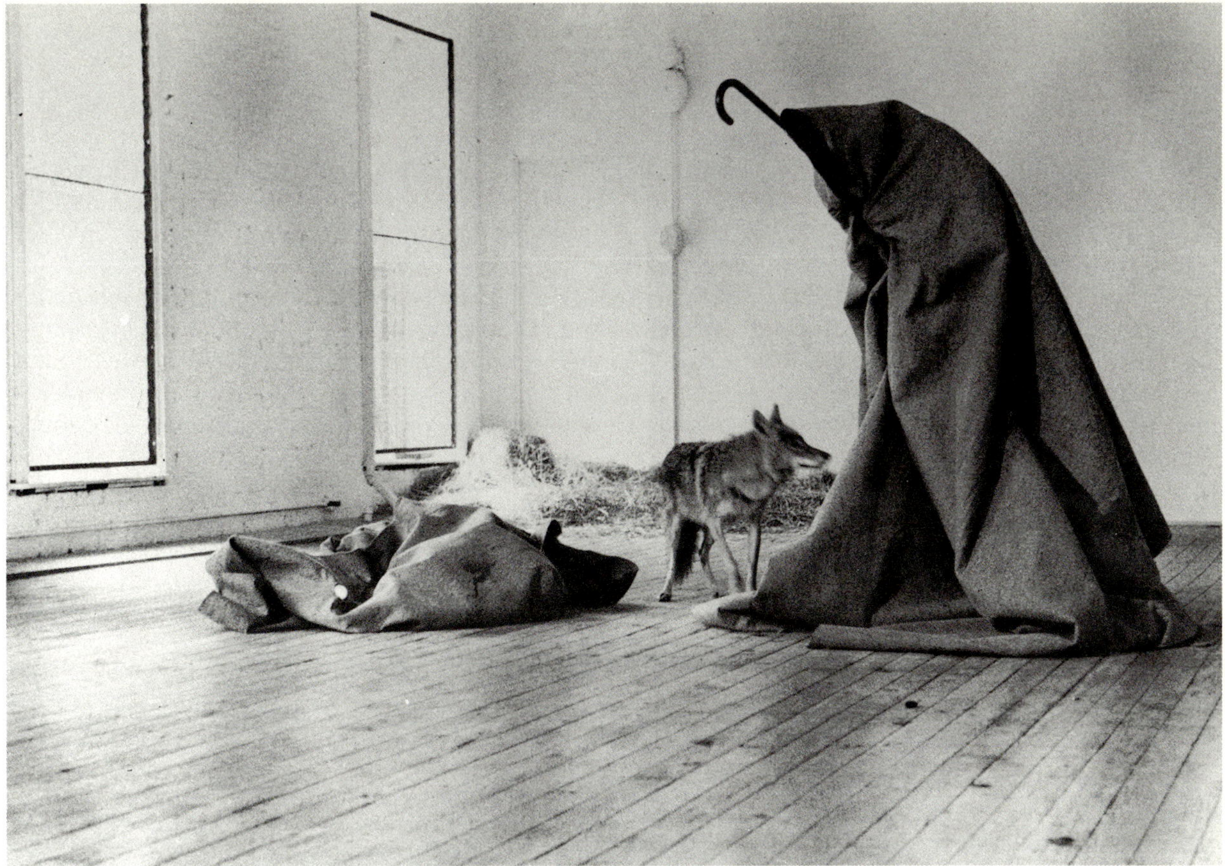

2.3 JOSEPH BEUYS
**Coyote: I Like America
and America Likes Me**
1974
Performance at the Rene
Block Gallery, New York
Courtesy Ronald Feldman
Gallery, New York

eration and renewal, both for Beuys personally and for Germany after Nazism.

Beuys performed *How to Explain Pictures to a Dead Hare* at the Galerie Schmela in Düsseldorf, West Germany, in 1965. With his head covered in honey, then gold leaf, one foot swathed in felt, and with fat under his chair, Beuys first walked around the gallery cradling in his arms a dead hare whose paws he touched to his paintings while explaining them. He then sat in the chair and continued the monologue, "because I do not really like explaining them to people" and since "even in death a hare has more sensitivity and instinctive understanding than some men with their stubborn rationality."[7]

The hare is a symbol for the Eurasian planes, the German homeland, because wild hares existed there

in great abundance at one time. The hare symbolizes the profound attachment to the homeland that traditional German culture fosters and that Hitler exploited. Thus the dead hare represents both appeasement and revival. Honey and gold represent ideas, the products of the brain. Felt and fat refer to Beuys's personal rescue in the Crimean and his "rebirth" after Nazism. Drawing upon the earnest Germans' perpetual quest for heroes, in his own person Beuys creates a new mythology of rebirth.

Beuys believed in art as a healing agent and he became equally important as both a teacher and artist. In 1961, at the age of 40, he became a professor of sculpture at the Düsseldorf Art Academy. Here he taught that artists should not be as concerned with their own careers as with making the world a better place to live. Beuys's discussion of politics and other non-art topics led authorities to question the appropriateness of his teaching. But when he was fired in 1972, violent student protest led to his being reinstated. Beuys returned to the academy by being ceremonially rowed across the river like a hero out of a Wagner opera.

Coyote: I Like America and America Likes Me

(Fig. **2.3**) was Beuys's American debut. For his first trip to the United States, Beuys had an ambulance meet him at New York's Kennedy Airport. The artist was swathed head-to-toe in felt. The ambulance drove him to the Rene Block Gallery in New York City's SoHo, where Beuys was conveyed by stretcher to an area enclosed by a cyclone fence and also containing a live coyote. For a week Beuys and the coyote lived in the enclosure. Felt, a walking stick resembling a shepherd's crook, and the *Wall Street Journal* (which was delivered daily and upon which the coyote urinated) were among the few objects in the spartan space. For Beuys, the coyote represented America; the felt, a healing process; himself, Germany and the curative effects of art.

In his teaching and his art, Joseph Beuys renewed and regenerated German visual culture which had been depleted by Nazism. His "Actions" parallel "Happenings" and Fluxus "Events" (see pages 15–16) and foreshadow Performance Art, by integrating sound, objects, movement, the dimension of time, and personal autobiography as well as by extending the boundaries between art and life in completely original ways. For several generations of German artists—such as the Neo-Expressionists Anselm Kiefer, Georg Baselitz, and Sigmar Polke (pages 173, 182, 183)—Beuys became a signpost to German art's reemergence as a credible international presence.

NAM JUNE PAIK

Nam June Paik is the Buddha of Video Art, the first and most brilliant artist to make art from television and video. Irresistibly entertaining, Paik entices us into a web of multi-level meanings woven from communications theories, avant-garde music and visual art, Zen riddles, and Duchampian puns.[8]

Born in Korea in 1932, and after a brief sojourn in Hong Kong, Paik went to Japan, where he first saw commercial television. He lived in Japan from 1950 to 1956, earning a degree in aesthetics and writing a thesis on Arnold Schönberg; he then traveled to Cairo and Calcutta before temporarily settling in Germany, where he knew Beuys and participated in Fluxus concerts. Paik recognized the persuasiveness of entertainment television and, after meeting John Cage in 1958 (a meeting he terms "pivotal"), grafted television's popular appeal to his wide-ranging artistic experiments.

Paik went to New York in 1964 and the following year he bought a Sony Portapack from the first shipment to the United States. Stuck in a traffic jam on the way home from the store, Paik made a videotape after discovering that the traffic jam was created by Pope Paul VI's motorcade. That night he showed the tape at the Café à Go-Go. John Cage, Merce Cunningham, and some important foundation officials were present. "As collage technic [sic] replaced oil-paint, the cathode-ray tube will replace the canvass," [sic] Paik declared.[9]

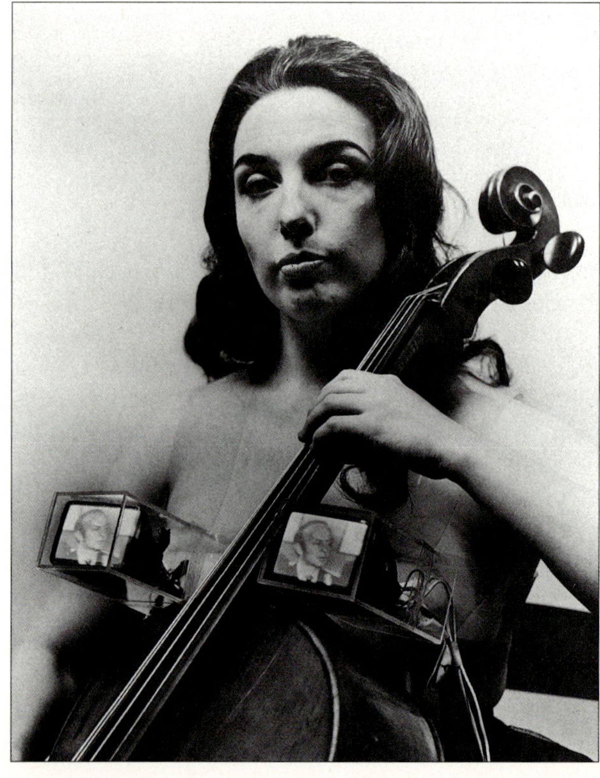

2.4 NAM JUNE PAIK TV Bra for Living Sculpture 1969 Performance by Charlotte Moorman with television sets and cello Photo © 1982 by Peter Moore

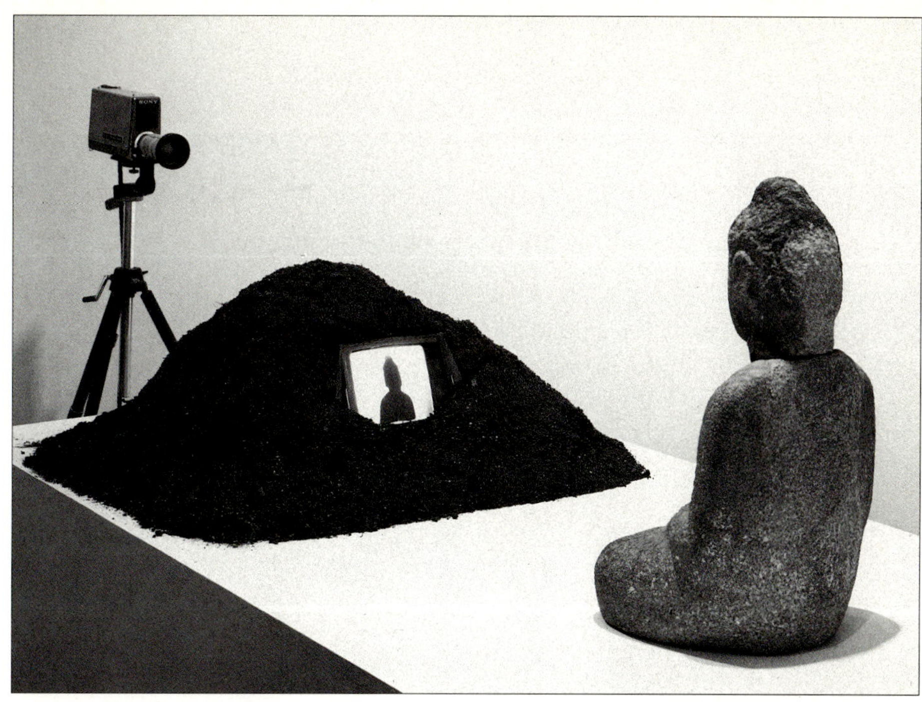

2.5 **NAM JUNE PAIK**
TV Buddha 1974–82
Mixed media,
55 × 115 × 36ins
(139.7 × 292.1 × 91.4cm)
Photo © 1982 by Peter
Moore

Korea, Hong Kong, Japan, Germany, New York, aesthetics, Schönberg, Cage, television—this is a combination unlike that of any other contemporary artist. It combines East and West, entertainment and avant-gardism. The peculiarities of Paik's range, as well as his adoption of entertainment strategies, account for the uniqueness of his art. Paik is a truly global artist.

Throughout Paik's performances, compositions, sculptures, and videotapes from 1959 to the present, four basic characteristics consistently appear in his works: he structures most of them, in whatever medium, as sequences of events in time—using his training in music; he frequently employs puns—drawing on the examples of both Duchamp and popular entertainment; he often alters the image-making apparatus—out of motives parallel to those that led to Cage's altered pianos; and he constantly changes and reworks his art, often allowing free reign to chance—after the model of Fluxus. Being a global artist, he switches from Korean drum music to Native American chants to Japanese television commercials (in his videotape *Global Groove*, 1973) rather than drawing from American media, as Andy Warhol does.

Unlike many early media artists who began as painters or sculptors, Paik understood right from the beginning the dimensions of time and sound. Rather than imitating static art's fixed images, Paik opted for media manipulation combining the short-lived nature of musical performances and throwaway popular culture, a synthesis that was obvious in his Fluxus experience. From his work with audiotape recording for electronic music, he knew how to sequence and structure recorded material, a technique he used later in his videotapes.

There is something hilarious in Paik's smashing a violin (in his composition *One for Violin Solo*, 1962), or toppling a piano (in another composition, *Homage à John Cage: Music for Tape Recorder and Piano*, 1959), or setting a toy piano aflame (in a videotape, *Electronic Opera No. 2*, 1971, also known as "The Boston Symphony"). Of course, Cage's altered pianos preceded Paik's altered instruments, but Paik's smashed violin came before pop singers started smashing their instruments—joining avant-gardism with popular entertainment. Paik adapted Cage's notion that "everything is music" to elicit new sounds from these traditional instruments.

Paik manipulates television's tactility and intimacy. The millions of grainy, flickering phosphor dots, projected at viewers by a cathode-ray tube, literally wash over us as if we were the screen. The close-ups favored by television show faces framed as though seen from a distance of 12 inches (30.5 cm), and television viewing is usually a solitary experience. Paik's *Opera Sextronique* (1967), extends television's intimacy to the experience of hearing and seeing a cello solo, as Charlotte Moorman pauses periodically to

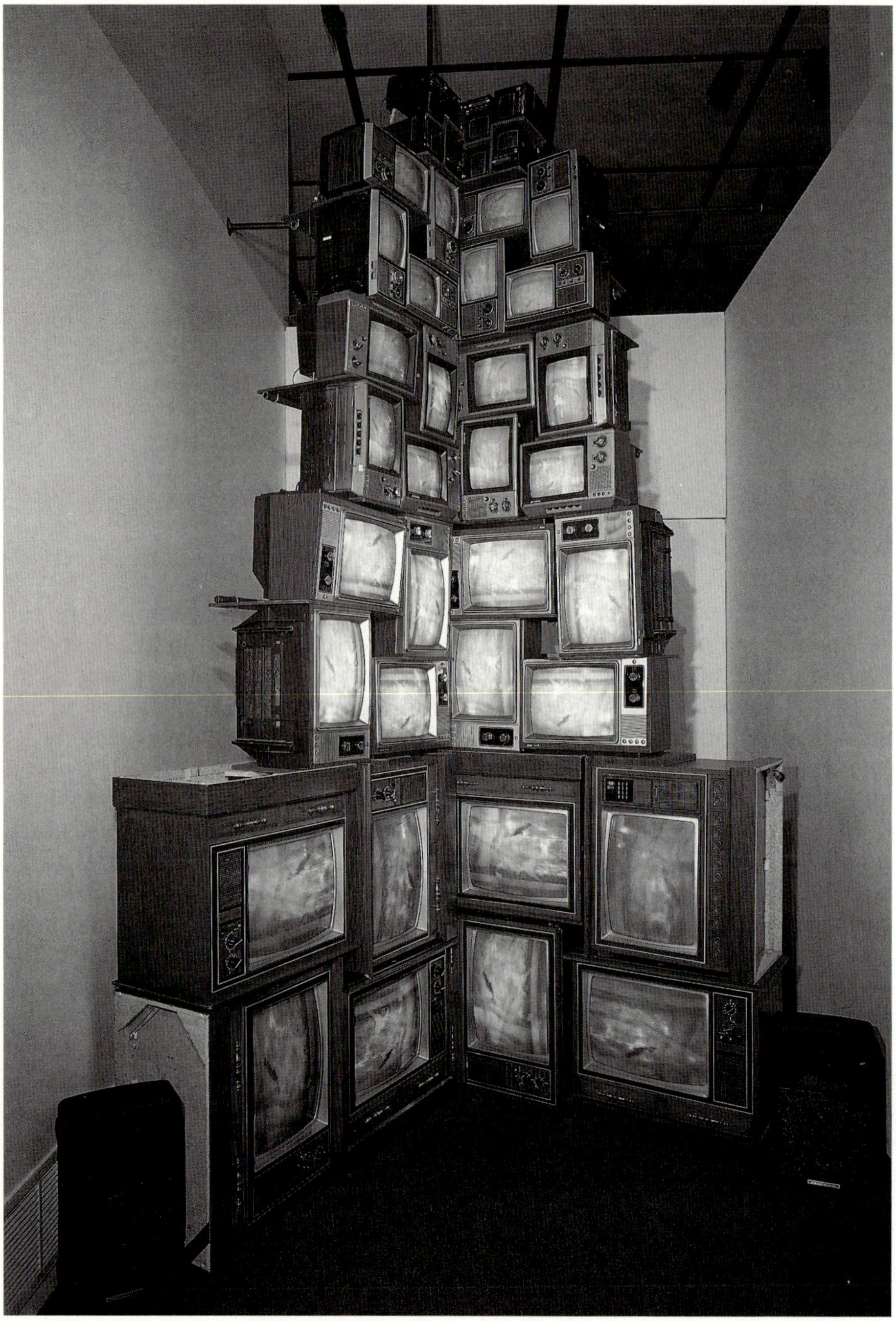

2.6 NAM JUNE PAIK
V-yramid (detail) 1982
40 television sets, 8½ minute
videotape sequence repeated
on minute cassette
(produced with Shridar
Bapot, Jud Yatket, Pamela
Sousa and David Alwood)
186¾ × 74ins
(474.3 × 188cm)
Collection Whitney Museum
of American Art, New York
Purchase with funds from the
Lemberg Foundation, Inc. in
honor of Samuel Lemberg.
82.11a–xx.

remove a piece of clothing, until she is naked. (At a New York performance in 1967, Moorman was arrested for indecent exposure. Las Vegas offers followed.) For Moorman, Paik designed *TV Bra for Living Sculpture* (Fig. **2.4**)—two small televisions were attached to each breast—giving another dimension both to television's intimacy and to the idea of the electronic babysitter, the "boob tube."

Paik explores time dimensions that are unique to television: the "live" time of closed-circuit and the simultaneity of mass broadcast. Gautama Buddha lived at approximately the same time that Periclean Athens flourished (the fifth century BC); but he now exists in the same time dimension as programs such as "Roseanne Barr" in Paik's *TV Buddha* (Fig. **2.5**). A stone Buddha contemplates his own "live" image on a monitor, banked with earth and hooked up to a camera. Ironically, this millennia-old symbol of eternity is contrasted here with television's ability to create instant fame. *Something Pacific* (see page 2) shows a bookend of Auguste Rodin's *Thinker* sitting above a miniature television, whose broadcast programming he contemplates. In Rodin's *Gates of Hell*, the *Thinker* occupies the position (above the doorpost) that during the Romanesque period was reserved for

Christ to sit in judgment. Rather than contemplating the fate of writhing, Dantesque humanity, however, Paik's *Something Pacific* watches the afternoon soaps.

Paik's *V-yramid* (Fig. **2.6**) physically affects the viewer's sensory balance. Unlike purely visual artworks, *V-yramid* primarily addresses the sense of touch and hearing, washing over the viewer in waves of video-synthesized color imagery and sound. (Invented by Paik and Shuya Abe in 1964, the video synthesizer is an electronic device for manipulating video color and form by turning dials and flipping switches.) *V-yramid* is a pyramid of 40 stacked color televisions—on their left, right, bottom, or top sides—forming a right-angle in which the viewer can stand, surrounded by color and sound. The tape, a video-synthesized mix from various Paik videos, switches from Allen Ginsberg chanting "Om" to a stirring disco-dance accompanied by the popular song, *Devil With A Blue Dress On*.

Nam June Paik was the first—and continues to be the most wide-ranging and prolific—artist to work with video and television, revealing the often unpredictable influences that electronic mass media have on our perceptions.

JOAN JONAS

Joan Jonas was born in New York in 1936 and educated at Mount Holyoke College, the Boston Museum School, and Columbia University from which she received an MFA. Jonas makes recorded videotapes that are shown as artworks in themselves and uses both recorded tapes and live feedback (in video projection or on a monitor) in her live performances. With live feedback (the "live" viewing of whatever the camera is focused on) Jonas can magnify and call attention to the details she especially wants the audience to notice, thus using video as a series of live clues to the performance. The camera circulates freely around the performance space, in pre-arranged movements and shots, so even though the audience is seated in front of the performance space, its relationship to the space of the performance is not fixed. The audience relationship to the space is, however, carefully controlled by Jonas, who uses the video

camera as part of the choreography.[10]

Jonas is consistently concerned with space in her live and recorded work; she uses video as one of her tools to flatten, dislocate, attenuate, and otherwise manipulate space.

My own thinking and production has focused on issues of space—ways of dislocating it, attenuating it, flattening it, turning it inside out, always attempting to explore it without ever giving to myself or to others the permission to penetrate it. I have returned again and again to a specific set of formal/material metaphors with which to shape this space. The two most important of these are the mirror—with its capacity to interrupt and therefore to fragment deep space and its property of disorientation through left-right reversal—and the transmission of signals through a dislocating medium, such as a very deep landscape that creates delays and relays of the signal, or the video feedback, which both dislocates and fragments the signal.[11]

In her performance, *Organic Honey's Visual Telepathy* (Fig. **2.7**) Jonas made use of a monitor and a video projector to project an 8 × 12 feet (2.44 × 3.66 m) live image on the wall. Whether a monitor or a projector is used in live performance, the scale is always changed, creating a discrepancy in space perception between the real event and the image of the event. In this case both were used, causing a

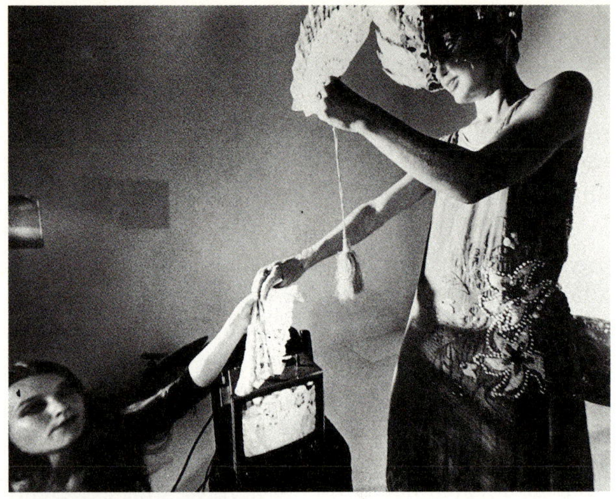

2.7 (above) **JOAN JONAS**
Organic Honey's Visual Telepathy 1972
Performance
Photo Roberta Neiman
Copyright © 1976 Joan Jonas

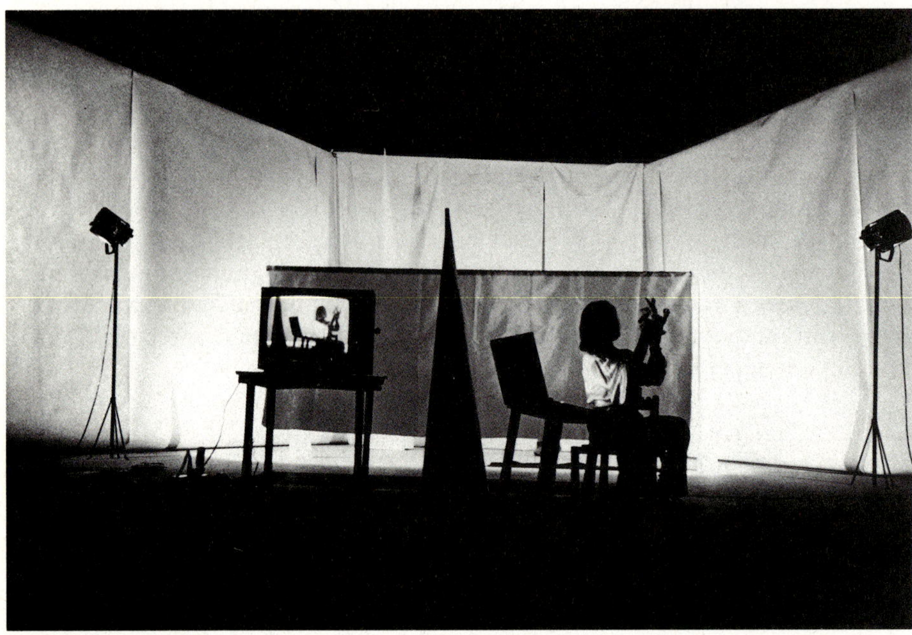

2.8 (left) **JOAN JONAS**
Funnel 1974
Performance
Photo Babette Mengo
Copyright © 1976 Joan Jonas

triple reading of the same event—one image was larger than the event, one smaller. In many cases the image can be seen more clearly than the actual event. Questions arise as to which perceptions are of real events and which are of images: the imagery and the actual event become completely integrated. Controlled in this way, not only the space dislocation but also the parameters of the field of vision affect how the space is perceived. The live dimension is essential to this kind of control.

Funnel (Fig. **2.8**), another performance, makes use of both live and taped video on a single monitor within the space. Jonas uses a large paper funnel as a prop. The set's walls create an exaggerated illusion of perspective. Jonas explores illusions of spatial depth in the videotape *Glass Puzzle* (which is part of the performance) though video normally tends to flatten space. She employs both distortion feedback and live feedback as additional means for manipulating space.

Vertical Roll (Fig. **2.9**), a videotape shown by itself and as part of the performance, *Organic Honey's Vertical Roll* (1973), drastically alters perception of the space of the room in which it is seen. Jonas shot the tape off a monitor with the vertical hold adjusted to make the image roll, then performed on and with the rolling image. Within the vertical roll she carried out actions conforming to the rate of the

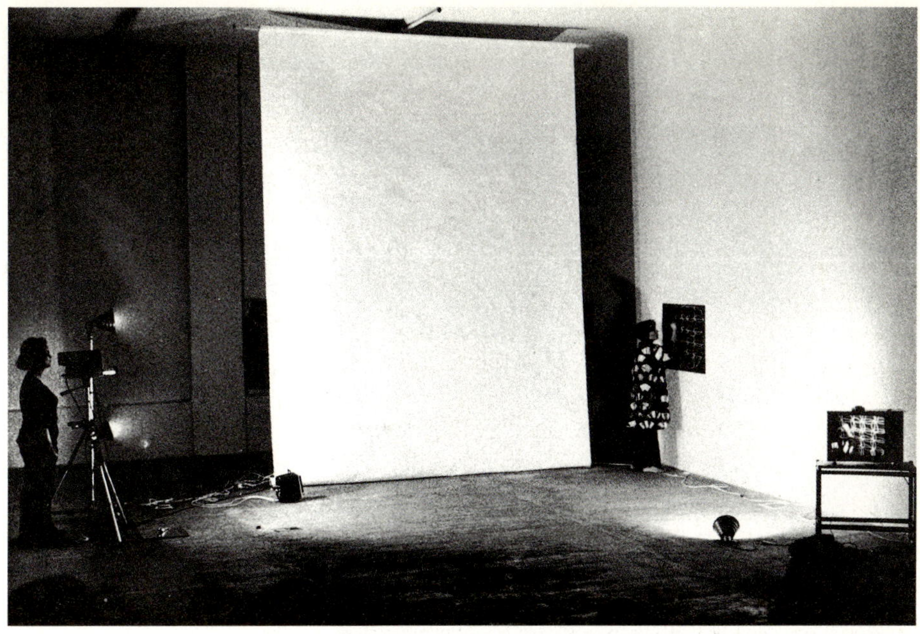

2.9 JOAN JONAS
Vertical Roll 1972
Black and white sound
videotape, 20 minutes
Photo courtesy Castelli/
Sonnabend Tapes and Films,
Inc.

roll. She begins with her face horizontal on the screen, clacking what appears to be spoons together in front of her face at the instant that the black band of the vertical roll reaches the bottom of the monitor. Various activities follow, such as clapping and jumping in keeping with the roll. Jonas jumps with the roll, coming down when the black band reaches the bottom of the monitor; jumps against the roll; and then jumps out of the top of the monitor and does not come back into it. Slowly, Jonas's head reappears in front of the monitor in which she had performed, the monitor still rolling.

The floors, walls, and ceiling of the viewer's actual space appear to undulate, expand, contract, throb, and sway, causing visual disorientation. Even though *Vertical Roll* is recorded, the viewer experiences it in terms of his or her actual space. The subject of *Vertical Roll* is the alteration of space perception outside the monitor.

Of all the artists working with live video, Jonas is the most concerned with purely perceptual experience, dealing with abstract formal relationships. Her work has identified a unique area of activity that is hard to describe because it is so extremely abstract. She has identified a live dimension of space perception linked to the live dimension of video.

FRANK GILLETTE AND IRA SCHNEIDER

Ira Schneider (born 1939) and Frank Gillette (born 1941) have collaborated on Video Art since the early 1970s. Schneider received an AB degree from Brown University in 1960 and an MA degree from the University of Winconsin in 1964. Gillette studied painting at the Pratt Institute. *Wipe Cycle* (Fig. **2.10**) was first shown at the "Television as a Creative Medium" exhibition at the pioneering Howard Wise Gallery in New York City in 1969. Unsuspecting viewers coming off the elevator were confronted with live, eight-second, and 16-second delay images of themselves, plus live broadcast, taped, and tape collage imagery on nine different television sets. Gilette said that part of the artwork's intent was for viewers to experience themselves as being "as much a piece of information as tomorrow morning's headlines." and Schneider stated that "The most important function of *Wipe Cycle* was to integrate the audience into the information."[12]

At that time, with video being such a new medium in an art context, for viewers to experience themselves as being integrated within an information network from which they were normally separated brought about an entirely novel psychological and physical experience of space and time. Not only was the viewer in three places at one time—standing

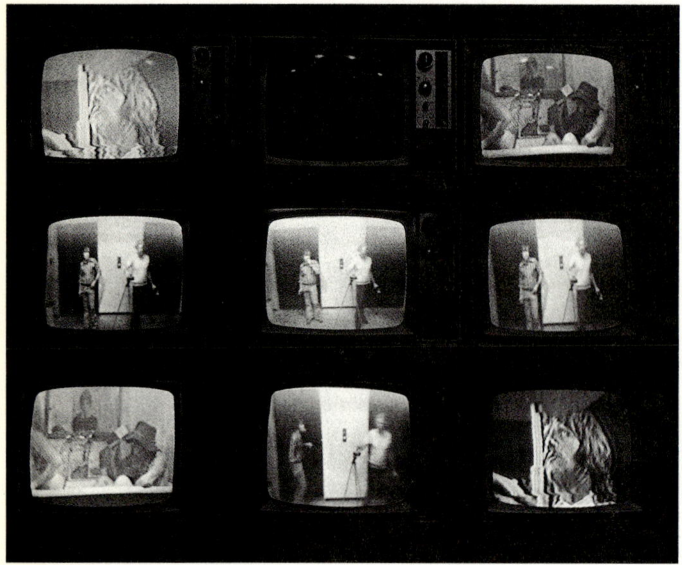

2.10 **SCHNEIDER AND GILLETTE**
Wipe Cycle 1969
Black and white video installation
Photo Allen Frank
Courtesy Ira Schneider

there here and now, and on two monitors there and now—but also on two different monitors there and then, eight seconds ago and 16 seconds ago. This kind of space and time experience can only be achieved with video, and when it was first made available to people who had formerly always experienced television passively the result was a completely new awareness.

JOHN BALDESSARI

Speaking at a conference called "Open Circuits: An International Conference on The Future of Television" at New York's Museum of Modern Art in 1974, John Baldessari said:

> *... for there to be progress in TV, the medium must be as neutral as a pencil. Just one more tool in the artist's toolbox. Another tool to have around, like a pencil ...*[13]

Conceptual artist John Baldessari's use of photography (see pages 37–39) emphasizes the images themselves rather than abstract qualities of the medium. His approach to video is consistent with his other work in this respect: that he is much more interested in how it is used than in its intrinsic qualities. Baldessari uses portable video equipment to make loosely structured but conceptually rigorous videotapes. The inexpensiveness of portable video equipment and of reusable videotape permits casual experimentation compared to the higher cost and unreusable nature of film, but other than that the medium of video itself has little bearing on Baldessari's work.

The exploitation of time and duration are the two most significant qualities that differentiate Baldessari's Video Art from his other work. With

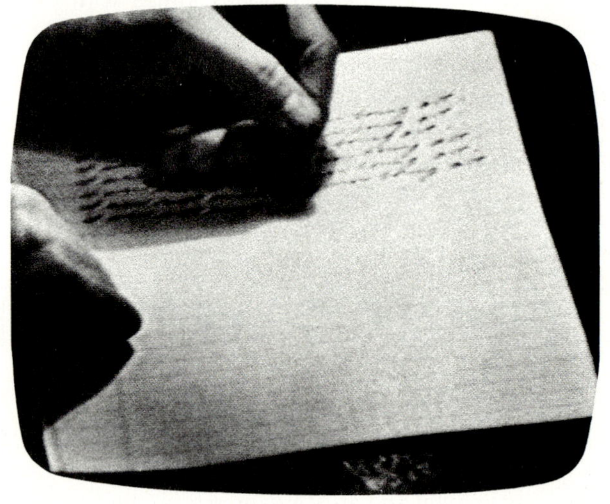

2.11 **JOHN BALDESSARI**
I Will Not Make Any More Boring Art 1971
Black and white sound videotape, 30 minutes
Courtesy Castelli/Sonnabend Tapes and Films, Inc., New York

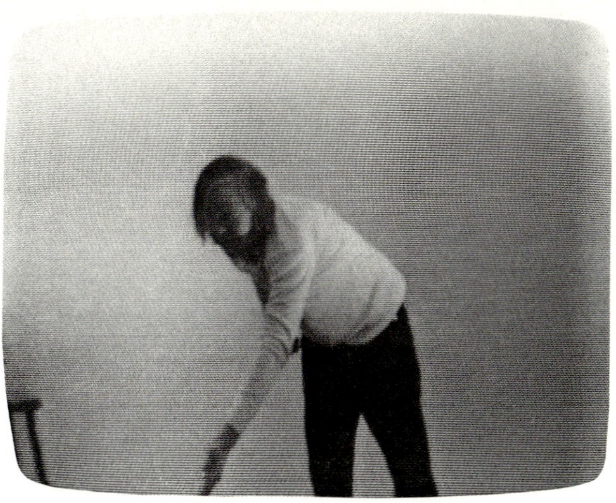

2.12 JOHN BALDESSARI
I Am Making Art 1971
Black and white videotape,
15 minutes
Courtesy of the artist

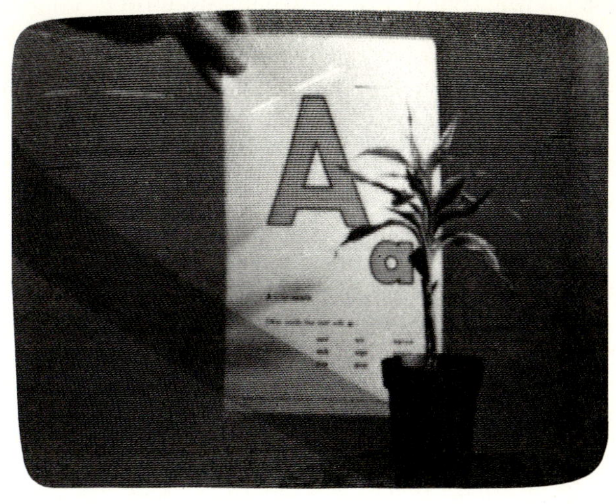

2.13 JOHN BALDESSARI
Teaching a Plant the
Alphabet 1972
Black and white sound
videotape, 30 minutes
Courtesy of the artist

deadpan wit, Baldessari endlessly prolongs ridiculous acts, making them conceptually hilarious if almost unbearably boring. Much early Video Art depicts slow and drawn-out actions, positioning itself as an alternative to the hyped up, accelerated editing of entertainment television. Baldessari stretches time to excruciating lengths.

In his 30-minute, black-and-white sound tape, *I Will Not Make Any More Boring Art* (Fig. **2.11**), Baldessari writes the words of the title over and over on a notebook page as though he—and we—were suffering a student's punishment. Of course it is a self-defeating exercise, because "the experience of the videotape is exactly what the lesson is meant to abolish."[14] The obvious contradiction between the words and their meaning relates to other Conceptual Art.

I Am Making Art (Fig. **2.12**) and *Teaching a Plant the Alphabet* (Fig. **2.13**) likewise repeat ostensibly ridiculous actions which are much more interesting as ideas than experiences. Watching the videotapes is, however, perversely enjoyable. In the former, Baldessari imitates other artists' practice of making art with their own bodies. He makes deadpan poses, holding each one a few seconds while he states "I am making art." In the latter, Baldessari focuses a fixed camera (which he usually uses) on an ordinary houseplant, behind which he places instructional cards printed with each letter of the alphabet, then speaks, for example, "A A A A A A A," "a a a a a a a," "A A A A A A A ," and so on throughout the entire alphabet.

WILLIAM WEGMAN

William Wegman is another Conceptual Art humorist who uses video to lampoon the implausible situations of television commercials, in the process dislocating sensory information and heightening perception.[15] His tapes consist of series of unrelated vignettes which are dialogues between himself and the video camera, sometimes including his dog, the late *Man Ray*. The tapes are always humorous, often personal, and always about a set, acted situation with the camera usually fixed on a tripod. Though Wegman scripts the scenario, the feeling is very casual, loose, experimental. He discovers a range of psychological relationships uniquely exploitable by video, rather than rigidly structuring his works according to the medium's physical properties.

The ease and casualness of Wegman's performances derive from the fact that he can re-record over and over on the same videotape, until he gets it right.

This permits a casualness and experimentation that the costliness and permanence of film do not allow.

In *What's Wrong With Your Eye (Ventriloquism)*, the tape begins with the camera in close range on Wegman's face with one eye closed. He speaks, without moving his lips, "Hey, what's wrong with your eye?," and answers himself, this time moving his lips, "I don't need it right now." "Oh, yeah, what's this?" "A rose." "How did you know it's a rose?" "I could tell by the smell." "What's this?" "A potato chip." "How did you know it's a potato chip?" "I could tell by the taste." "What's this?" "A glass egg." "How did you know it's a glass egg?" "It doesn't sound like a real egg." "What's this?" "A piece of petrified wood." "How did you know it's a piece of petrified wood?" "It's heavier than real wood." "What's this?" "A screwdriver." "How did you know it's a screwdriver?" "I guessed." Wegman deals with six senses in this tape: sight, smell, taste, hearing, feeling, and intuition, each of them with equal time and equal significance. Characteristically, he deals with sensory balances in a lighthearted way, producing both entertainment and serious investigation into how we integrate our various sensory responses to form an overall response.

In *Stomach Song* (Fig. **2.14**), we see the artist seated, framed from the chest to the knees, wearing shorts with his shirt off. He makes humming sounds while at the same time protruding, sucking in, and convoluting his stomach; it looks like the sound is

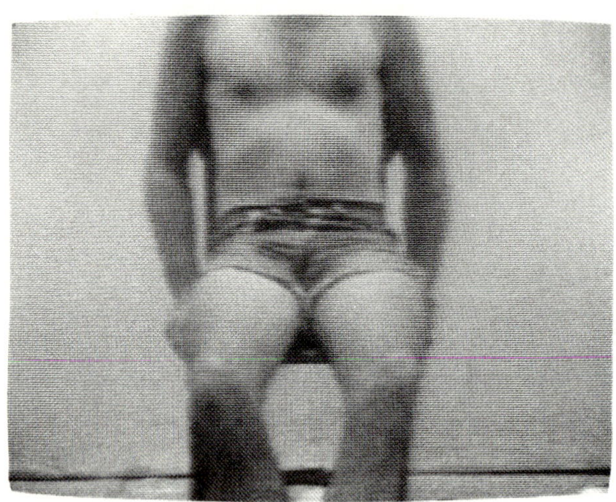

2.14 WILLIAM WEGMAN
Stomach Song 1971
Black and white sound
videotape, one minute
Courtesy of the artist

coming from his navel, and that his nipples are his eyes while his stomach is his cheeks. It's a completely ridiculous situation, like something a demented boy would do with home video, and yet its dislocation of normal sensory responses parodies television commercials' "simulations" and "dramatizations."

PETER CAMPUS

Peter Campus was born in New York in 1937 and received a BSc from Ohio State University in 1960. He returned to New York after serving in the Army from 1960–62. His first solo exhibition was at New York's Bykert Gallery in 1972, where he showed *Interface* (Fig. **2.15**), a live video projection, that is nonexistent until the viewer enters the camera's range.[16] The viewer's presence participates in the artwork's never-completed unfolding. The space does not exist until it is activated by the viewer.

Campus set a large sheet of glass in a metal frame about 6 feet (1.8 m) from the wall, then aimed a video camera from behind the glass's right side to the glass's left side. A video projector hooked up to the camera projects what the camera picks up on to the right front side of the glass. A dynamic field exists in the space, though the field is invisible, vacant, until the viewer enters.

Standing in front of the glass's left side, the viewer's reflection appears in the glass at the same time that his or her live and life-size video-projected image appears on the wall behind the glass. The viewer is confronted with three different live images of him- or herself, all different: one real, one reflected, one projected. The reflected image is reversed left-to-right (like a mirror image), but the projected image is not. Thus, viewers can face themselves in two images, even embrace or shake hands with themselves.

Where does this space exist? In what time dimension does the event take place? One can test the real time occurrence of the event by observing the three images engaged in simultaneous actions, but can one be sure? Which image is the control? If there is a "loop," where does it begin? Does the event occur now or later, or maybe before? It occurs in the time and space of thought. "Our view of objects, other beings, is not a fragmented two- or three-dimensional one, but one in space and time. We can't reproduce it, so we're not aware of it. Its nature is vague in our minds."[17]

Interface's surface is as vague as its space and time. Its actual surface is the glass and the wall, but at the same time it fills the space, occurring between the reflections and projections in the dynamic fields between the images. The images are physically there, but on closer look they are as tangibly present as dynamic fields in the space that they do not occupy as they are within their own boundaries. The images uniquely disperse themselves throughout the space.

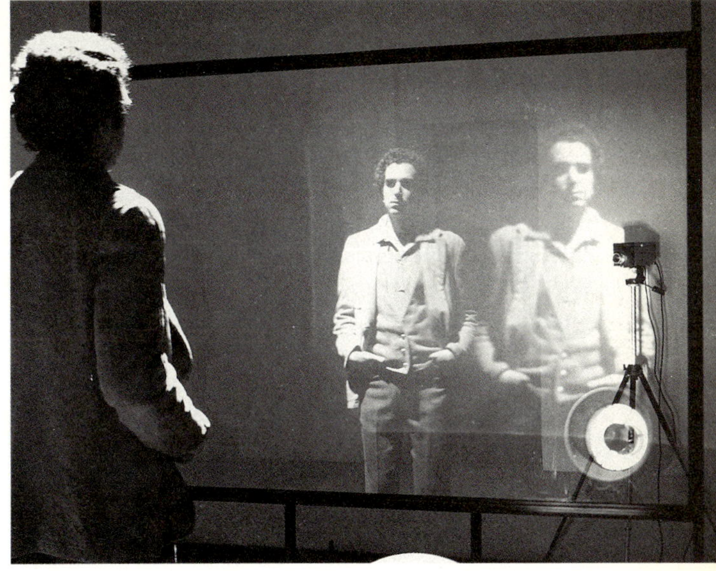

2.15 PETER CAMPUS
Interface 1972
Black and white video
projection and mixed media
installation
Courtesy Paula Cooper
Gallery, New York

BRUCE NAUMAN

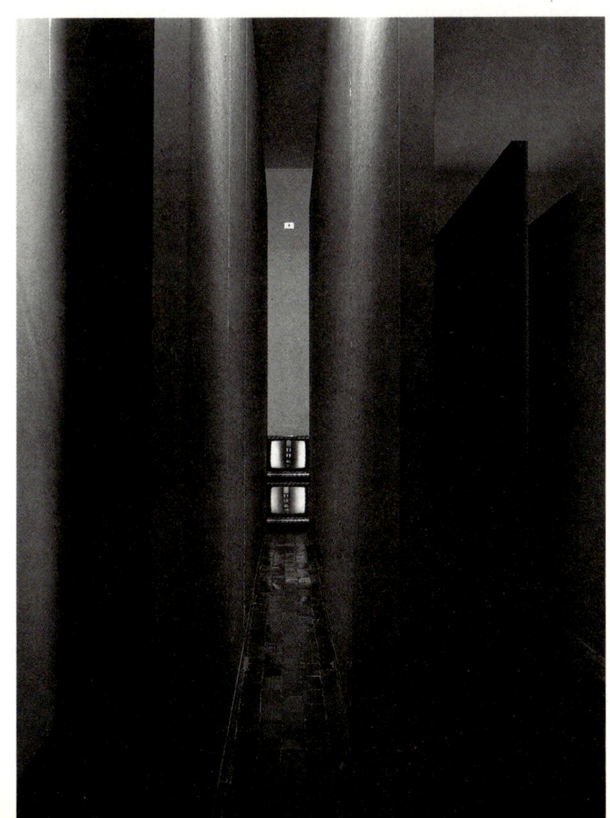

Bruce Nauman makes—and sometimes performs in—videotapes, video installations, and films. He also makes photographs, sculptures, installations, drawings, and prints (see pages 34–36). Nauman's very large body of important work with "time" or "duration" media alone rank him as a major artist.

In *Live/Taped Video Corridor* (Fig. **2.16**) Nauman manipulates the viewer's physical and psychological sensations of time and place as much as the materials that went into the sculpture's making. Nauman mounted a closed-circuit video camera on the ceiling at the entrance to a narrow corridor at the end of which he stacked two television sets on the floor. Viewers enter the corridor after noticing that the camera is aimed at the empty space. The corridor is just narrow enough to make participants aware of the

2.16 BRUCE NAUMAN
Live taped Video Corridor
and Performance Corridor
1968–70

Installation
Collection Giuseppe Panza di
Biumo-Varese

space's narrowness, inducing a slight feeling of claustrophobia. Walking into the corridor while watching the top television, participants look for their images to appear. They do not. A moment of panic occurs: "Where am I?" they ask themselves, not seeing their image on the television screen. They feel suddenly absent and lost. "Will I ever get out of here," they wonder. And then they glance into the lower monitor and see themselves, with relief. A videotape of the empty corridor was playing on the top monitor, while the bottom one was hooked up to the live camera.

The video corridor casts the participant in the role of the performer; Nauman himself performed in his previous work. From being the performer in real time, Nauman evolved to being the performer on film and on videotape, eventually expunging himself from these media as well. As he put it in 1971:

> Originally a lot of the things that turned into videotapes and films were performances. At the time no one was really interested in presenting them, so I made them into films. No one was interested in that either, so the film is really a record of the performance. After I had made a few films I changed to videotape, just because it was easier for me to get at the time. The camera work became a bit more important, although the camera was stationary in the first ones.[18]

In 1969 Nauman made four extremely slow motion films, shot at speeds varying from 1000 to 4000 fps, then projected at the normal silent speed of 16 fps so the action was slowed way down. The camera is extremely close-up on simple actions that use his own body to generate the artwork, as in his sculpture and photography at the time (see pages 34–36). In *Black Balls* Nauman puts black make-up on his testicles; in *Bouncing Balls* he bounces his testicles; in *Pulling Mouth* he pulls at the corners of his mouth; in *Gauze* he slowly pulls gauze strips out of his mouth. Each film runs from eight to nine minutes.

The relationship between the films and Nauman's sculpture is important, because he uses film as just another art-making material, within the context of his other artwork, not within the context of independent cinema or entertainment movies. Manipulating the film's speed, Nauman handles the medium of film like Warhol did earlier in *Sleep* and *Empire* (see pages 57–58). Artists' films in the 1960s and 1970s

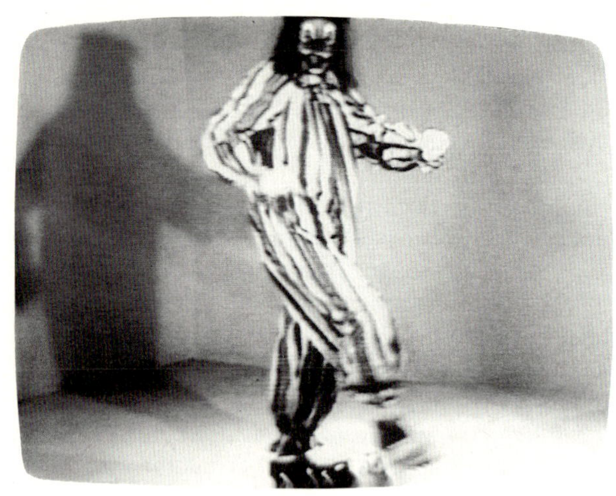

2.17 BRUCE NAUMAN
Clown Torture: A Dark
and Stormy Night with
Laughter 1986
Color videotapes and
installation, 60 minutes
Courtesy Saatchi Collection,
London

typically minimizes plot, narrative, or storyline in favor of more abstract "filmic" qualities. Thus artists' films experiment with completely original possibilities for the film medium.

Nauman's later videotapes, such as *Clown Torture: A Dark and Stormy Night With Laughter* (Fig. **2.17**), entail sculptural setups reminiscent of his earlier corridors. For *Clown Torture*, two color video monitors face each other from a distance of about 20 feet (6.1 m). Each monitor plays a different color videotape sometimes containing similar sequences but not at the same time. For 60 minutes a clown keeps repeating, "It was a dark and stormy night. Some guys were sitting around a campfire. One of them said, 'Hey, tell a story,' so another guy said, 'It was a dark and stormy night' …" and repeats the story, accompanied by endless raucous laughter by a female clown from the other monitor (the clown's action occasionally switches monitors with the laughter, and sometimes the clown laughs, too). The soundtrack's verbal circularity recalls Nauman's earlier punning and use of palindromes (words that read the same backwards or forwards) and anagrams plus his consistent interest in verbal/visual discrepancies. Facing each other, the monitors create a field charged with equal parts of frustration and amusement, magnified sensations related to those induced by commercial broadcast television's cliches and laughtertracks.

Much of the Video, Film, and Performance Art of the 1980s ties in with popular culture's use of these media, whereas during the 1960s and most of the 1970s artists sought more to differentiate the artistic use of these media from popular culture usages. Blurring distinctions between popular culture and fine art typifies Post-Modernism (see Chapter 7). Extended back into the mid-1960s and continuing into the late 1980s, Nauman's extensive and influential work in these media situate him in a central role.

MICHAEL SNOW

The Canadian filmmaker Michael Snow (born 1929) bridges independent cinema with artists' films. Snow makes films solely about the abstract qualities of the medium of film. Perhaps his most widely acclaimed work, *Wavelength* (Fig. **2.18**), a color and sound film, centers on one simple action. To quote the filmmaker, "The film is a continuous zoom which takes 45 minutes to go from its widest field to its smallest and final field. It was shot with a fixed camera from one end of an 80 foot loft, shooting the other end, a row of windows and the street."[19] The zoom ends on a photograph of waves pinned to the wall between the windows. " ... The artist has seized upon a strategy proper to the medium and carried it to ultimate consequences," wrote the art critic Annette Michelson.[20]

Noise from the street outside and off-camera talk make up the sound track, a strategy typical of Warhol's sound films. The sound occurring off-camera emphasizes that the camera records only a portion of the scene; the slow zoom emphasizes how the film camera determines a field of vision, in this case one which so slowly shrinks as the lens zooms in that the incre-

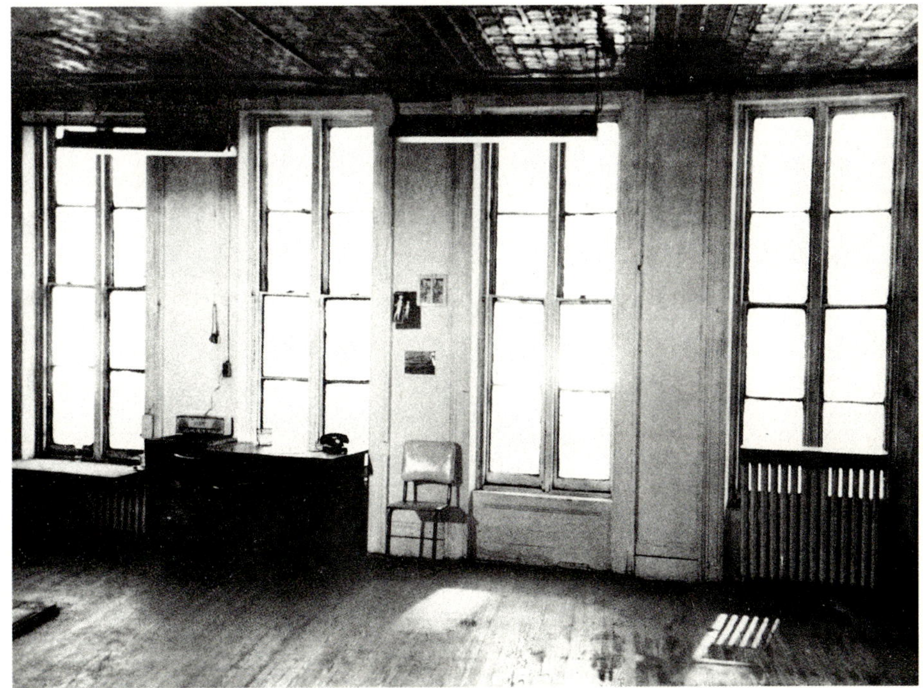

2.18 MICHAEL SNOW
Wavelength 1966–67
Color 16mm sound film, 45 minutes
Courtesy Castelli/Sonnabend Tapes and Films, Inc., New York

ments of its diminuition can barely be perceived. The final frame shows such a radically diminished field of vision that its reduction cannot be denied, yet neither can its gradual shrinking be perceived as it occurs. Thus an awareness of how the camera lens limits the viewer's perception results. Snow's subsequent films—⟵———————⟶ (1968–69), and *La Région Centrale* (1970–71), for instance—explore similar filmic experiences. In these cases Snow employs camera pans and other camera movement as the films' subjects.

RICHARD SERRA

Post-Minimalist Richard Serra (born 1939), is best-known for his sculpture (see pages 130–31), but he has also worked in film and video. Born in San Francisco, Serra attended the University of California at Berkeley from 1959–61, and then earned an MA and an MFA at Yale between 1961 and 1964 before spending a year in Europe. He moved finally to New York City in 1966 where he met Carl Andre, Eva Hesse, Nancy Holt, Jasper Johns, Joan Jonas, Donald Judd, Philip Leider, Bruce Nauman, Robert Smithson, Michael Snow and others. Serra's sculpture in the late 1960s and early 1970s emphasized procedures and processes, like splashing, tearing, rolling, leaning, rather than the static qualities Minimal sculptors favored. In 1967–68, Serra made a *Verb List Compilation* which reads, in part:

TO ROLL
TO CREASE
TO FOLD
TO STORE
TO BEND
TO SHORTEN
TO TWIST
TO TWINE
TO DAPPLE
TO CRUMPLE
TO SHAVE
TO TEAR
TO CHIP
TO SPLIT
TO CUT
TO SEVER
TO DROP[21]

In 1968, Serra made a three-minute black-and-white silent 16 mm film titled *Hand Catching Lead* (Fig. **2.19**), in which a fixed camera records the repeated attempts of a hand to catch lead. Serra uses

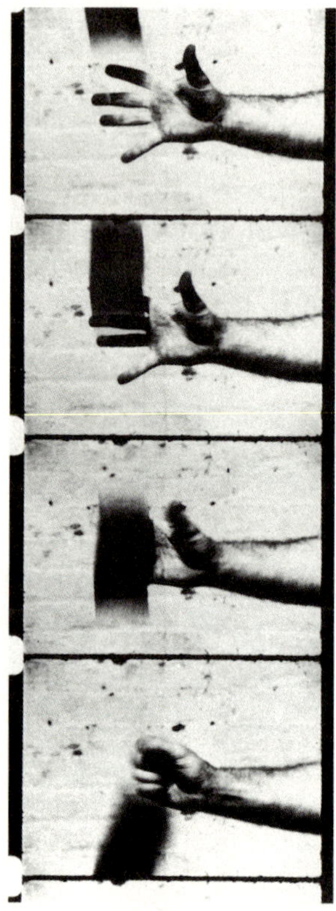

2.19 RICHARD SERRA
Hand Catching Lead 1968
Black and white 16mm film,
3 minutes
Courtesy Castelli/Sonnabend
Tapes and Films Inc., New
York

film as a recording device devoid of plot, narrative, or storyline, simply to record an event in time, using the duration that film possesses as the sole filmic characteristic. In 1976, Serra completed a 19-minute black-and-white silent 16 mm film titled *Railroad Turnbridge* (Fig. **2.20**), consisting of a fixed camera recording an action.

Serra's interest in "movement in filmic structure," or movement in time within a fixed frame, belongs exclusively to film: no other medium could manifest his stated interest. Serra's and other artists'

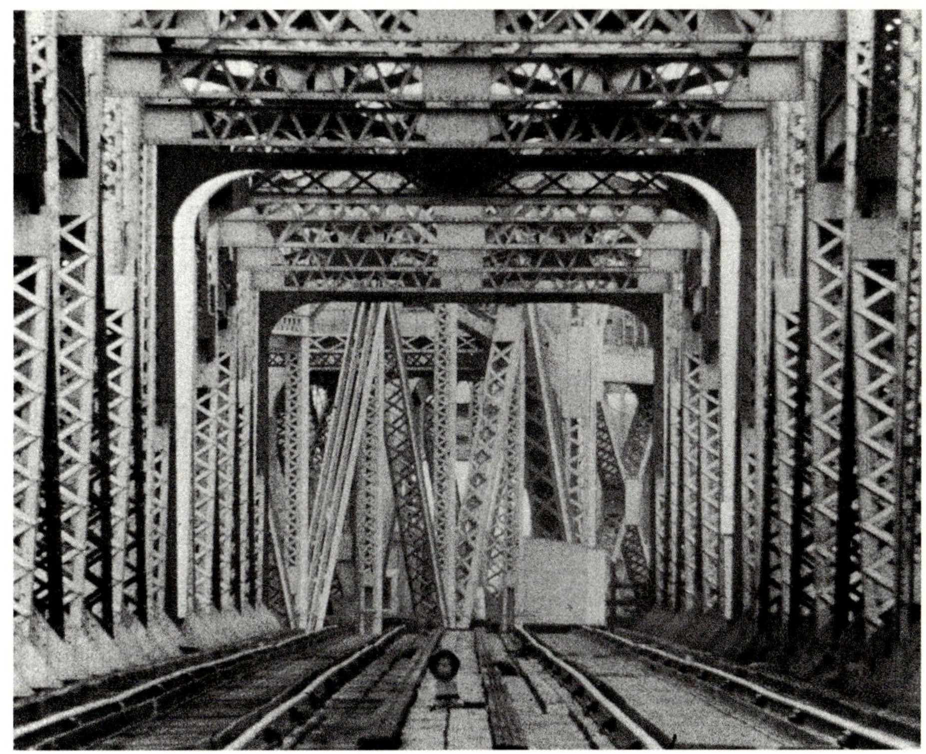

2.20 RICHARD SERRA
Railroad Turnbridge 1976
Black and white silent 16mm
film, 19 minutes
Courtesy Castelli/Sonnabend
Tapes and Films Inc., New
York
"The center section [of the
bridge] ... rotates electrically
on a cylindrical axis. The
bridge opens and allows the
boats to pass through; turns,
closes and locks, carrying the
trains over ... the bridge
enabled me to examine
movement in filmic
structure...."[22]

—like Snow, Campus, Wegman, and Nauman—interest in experiences that can be uniquely formed in a particular medium typifies much of the best art of the late 1960s and early 1970s.

VITO ACCONCI

Conceptual artist Vito Acconci (born 1940) has worked in portable sculpture, Film, Video, Installation, and Performance art. Acconci began as a poet, then transposed his interest in language to Performance Art through verbal instructions, such as his *Step Piece* (Fig. **2.21**).

Step Piece is accompanied by photographs of the artist performing the actions and with a list stating the length of time he was able to sustain the action each day for a month. He was, according to the artist, using his body as an alternative "ground" to the "page ground" of his poems.[23]

But in Acconci's 1971 *Seedbed* (Fig. **2.22**) the artist shifted the "ground" to the spectator's—or should one say the participant's?—body. At the time, the artist had been reading Kurt Lewin's *The Principle of Topological Psychology* in which he found a "description of how each individual radiated a personal power-field which included all possible interaction with other people and objects in a particular physical space."[24] In *Seedbed*, Acconci radiates his "personal power-field" upon the unwitting spectator.

Visitors entered the Sonnabend Gallery in New York City only to conclude that nothing was there. The hardwood floor gently sloped upward toward the back wall; the only object on the ramp was a stereo speaker. A printed text on the wall sketched the artwork's intention, but visitors did not experience the piece until they walked up the ramp. Acconci was under the floor verbalizing his sexual fantasies about the visitor into a microphone (attached to the speaker) while he masturbated. Suddenly the empty space

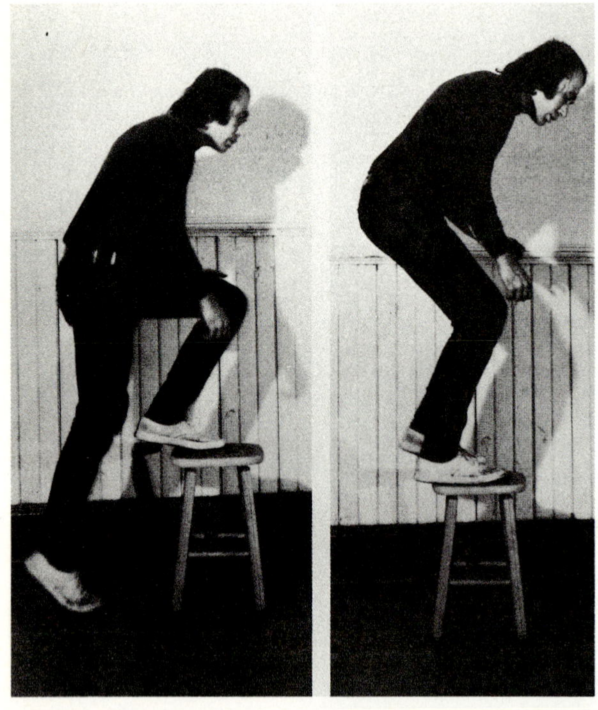

2.21 VITO ACCONCI
Step Piece 1970
Performance
Courtesy Sonnabend Gallery,
New York
*"Project: An eighteen-inch
stool is set up in my
apartment and used as a
step. Each morning, during
the designated months, I step
up and down the stool at the
rate of thirty steps a minute;
each morning, the activity
lasts as long as I can
perform it without
stopping."*[25]

seemed very crowded.

Acconci manipulates visitors' psychological senses and their physical sensations of space, or of that particular place. Rather than manipulating sculptural materials, the artist manipulates viewers' sense of privacy by intruding upon them psychologically and invading their personal space. Conducting publicly what is normally done privately—and certainly not in an art gallery—Acconci fills the empty space.

In *Seedbed*, the visitor (one cannot say "viewer" because there is very little to see) becomes the unwitting accomplice, really more of a participant in the performance than a spectator. Thus the focus of the art experience is shifted from the artwork as an embodiment of the artist's ego to the participant, a shift that also occurs in Bruce Nauman's corridors (see page 69). In the process, the gallery's empty space and the objectless artwork take on terrifying palpability. The dematerialized artwork becomes the participant's psycho-physical sensations.

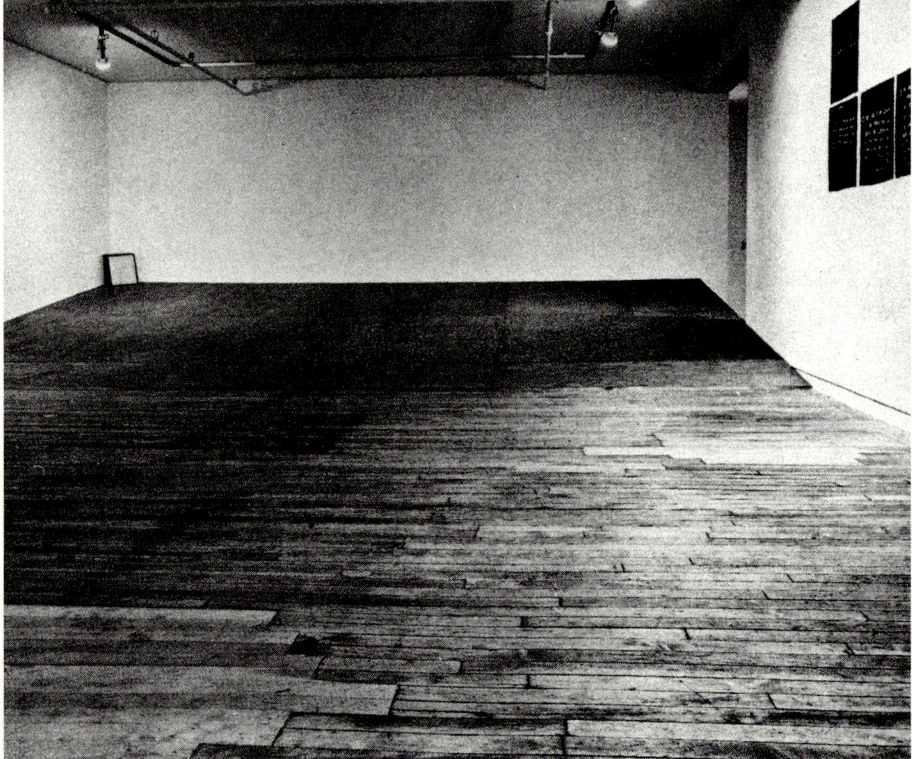

2.22 VITO ACCONCI
Seedbed 1971
Presented at the Sonnabend
Gallery, New York
Courtesy Sonnabend Gallery,
New York

GILBERT AND GEORGE

British Conceptual artists Gilbert and George (see pages 41–43) turned their entire lives into "living sculptures," thus creating a life-long performance. Within that inclusive dimension, though, Gilbert and George have created separate performances.

The first performance of *The Singing Sculpture* (Fig. **2.23**) took place in London in 1969 under the title of *Our New Sculpture* (later it was retitled *Underneath the Arches* before finally being retitled again in 1971). Gilbert and George stand atop a square table wearing their "responsibility suits," with their faces and hands covered with bronze powder. One artist holds a single glove; the other, a walking stick. To the British standard music hall tune, Hardy and Hudson's version of Flanagan and Allan's "Underneath the Arches," they slowly and stiffly act out the lyrics, over and over again. "At the Düsseldorf Kunsthalle in 1970 the presentation lasted eight hours on each of two consecutive days."[26]

Their performance of *The Singing Sculpture* in New York City in 1971 at the opening of the galleries at 420 West Broadway (Sonnabend—where they performed—Castelli, Weber, and Emmerich) announced their presence to the New York art world and stimulated Performance Art in the United States. The timing of their gesture was particularly apt, because the opening of these major galleries in the same building marked an important transition of SoHo from its beginnings to its subsequently central role. The openings—and Gilbert and George's *The Singing Sculpture*—were marked with rapt interest. Since 1977, Gilbert and George have worked in photography as their preferred medium.

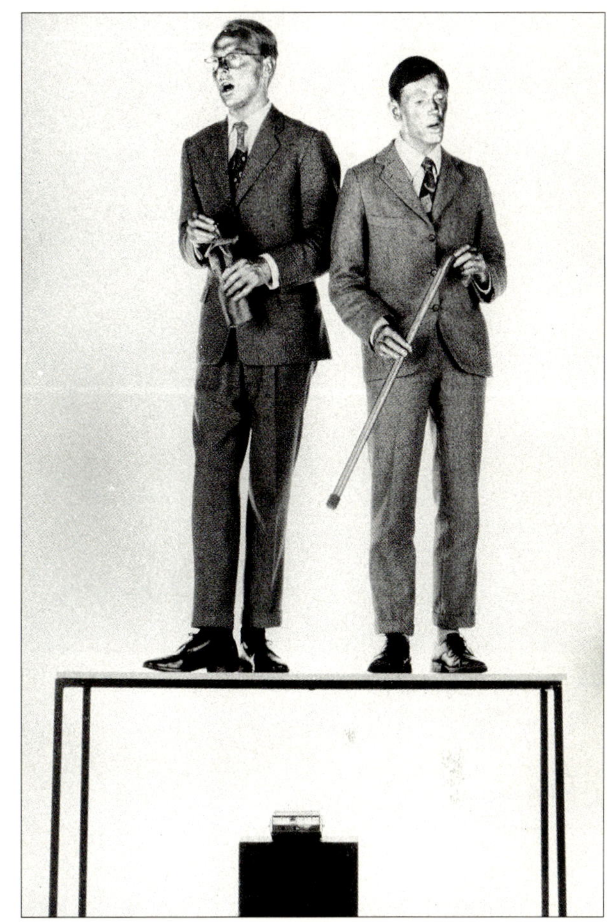

2.23 GILBERT AND GEORGE
The Singing Sculpture
1969

Performance
Courtesy Sonnabend Gallery,
New York

CHRIS BURDEN

California performance artist Chris Burden (born 1946) polarizes issues central to Performance Art in the mid-1970s. His confrontation of the audience with violence and moral dilemmas represents an extreme of dare-devilry compared with artists whose video, film, and performance are based on more perceptual phenomena, like Campus, Nauman and Jonas.

Shoot took place on November 19, 1971, at F Space in Los Angeles. At 7:45 PM Burden had a friend shoot him in the arm with a .22 rifle. He had intended the wound to be a superficial one, but the friend aimed badly and wounded Burden more seriously

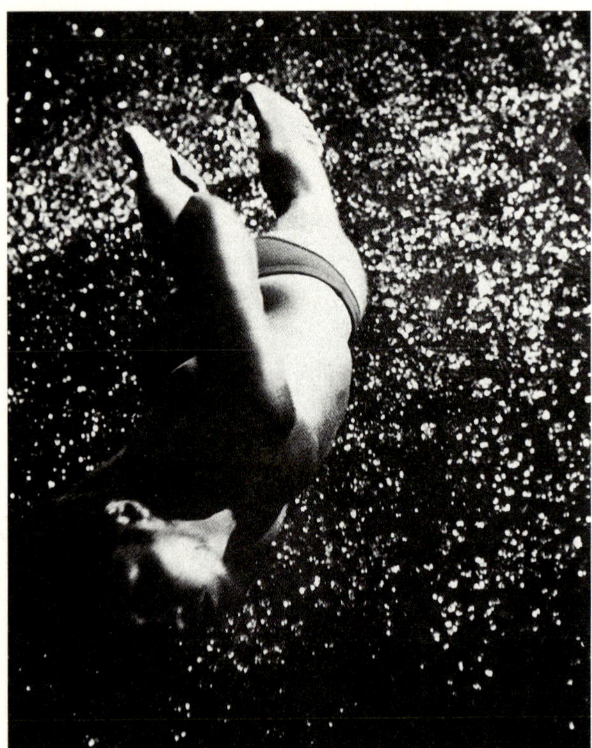

2.24 CHRIS BURDEN
Through the Night Softly
September 12, 1973
Performance in Main Street,
Los Angeles
Courtesy of the artist

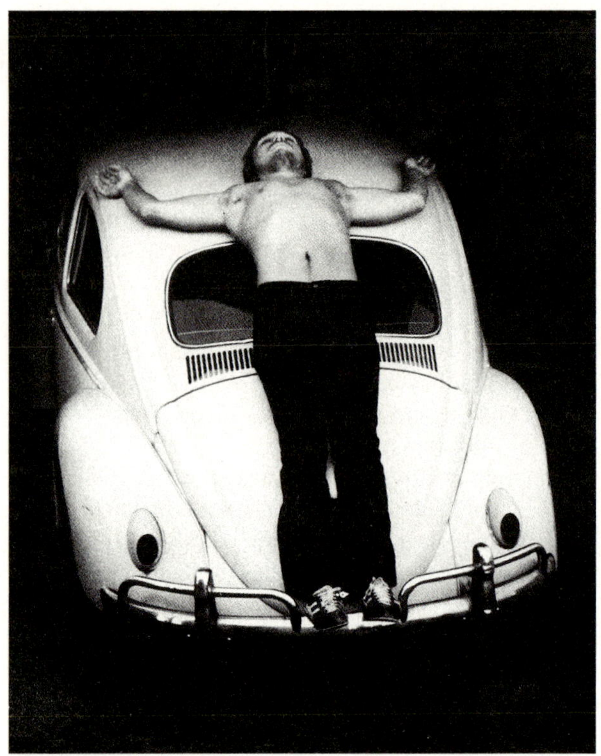

2.25 CHRIS BURDEN
Trans-Fixed
April 23, 1974
Performance in Venice,
California
Courtesy of the artist

than planned. In relation to the violence of the Vietnam War and the assassinations of President John F. Kennedy in 1963, and of Martin Luther King and Robert Kennedy in 1968, *Shoot* could be seen as a naïve and innocent gesture, yet compared to most Performance Art maybe it bordered on the perverse.

Dead Man confronts viewers with another moral dilemma. On November 12, 1972, Burden lay down in the middle of Los Angeles's busy gallery boulevard, La Cienega, and had a friend cover him with a tarpaulin, placing 15-minute flares at either end. Cars had to veer to avoid hitting him. Not knowing what was under the tarp, the drivers probably were motivated more by self-interest than by the desire to avoid killing someone. But Burden often places viewers in non-passive roles where they are forced to make moral decisions affecting the artist's welfare or his life

itself. Can we prevent him from doing this self-destructive act by stopping the performance, or would this amount to interfering with his artistic freedom and destroying his art? Where are the borderlines between commitment to one's art and lunacy, between artistic freedom and moral abandonment?

Through the Night Softly (Fig. **2.24**) was performed on September 12, 1973 on Main Street in Los Angeles. Burden stripped to bikini trunks and, "Holding my hands behind my back, I crawled through 50 feet of broken glass. There were very few spectators, most of them passers-by."[27] It was automobile safety glass, so the resultant cuts and scratches were minor ones but, still, Burden's act was one of martyr-like self-inflicted pain, a sort of contemporary flagellation.

Religious overtones of forgiveness are even more evident in *Transfixed* (Fig. **2.25**) which took place on April 23, 1974, (in Venice, California). Shirtless, Burden stood on the back bumper of a Volkswagen "Bug," leaned backward and stretched his arms up on the roof, then a friend drove sterilized nails through his hands into the roof. With the engine racing, the car and Burden were pushed into a busy street where they obstructed traffic for a few minutes. Burden carefully indicated where the nails were to be driven, studying beforehand how to avoid serious injury. Later, the nails were exhibited as "relics".

Physically pushing himself to the limits of endurance—often at high personal risk—Burden approaches being a daredevil as much as an artist. Certainly, he crosses over boundaries that formerly existed between such activities as flag-pole sitting, marathon dancing, or circus sideshow feats like sword-swallowing or fire-eating—and art. Still, Neo-Expressionism and Post-Modernism reintroduce narrative and populist content to visual art beginning in the late 1970s, so some argue that Burden's newsworthiness foreshadows later art's populist leanings. Another view is that Burden requires viewers to become more than passive spectators, involving them in moral issues, and that to provoke people jaded by mass media requires exaggeration.

Epilogue

By the late 1970s, Video, Film, and Performance art reached a turning point. Certainly the original goals of evading the marketplace by working in uncollectable—even impermanent—art forms were reached with extraordinary success. Very few collectors or museums set about to form complete collections of Video or Film art, and performances are uncollectable. In 1977 I wrote:

… there are few major collections of artists' videotapes, and there seems to be a degree of lingering reluctance on the part of museums and collectors to become involved—probably largely due to the uncertainties which accompany any new medium. (A complicating factor is that few museums have full-time video curators—the job often yokes video and film or even, as at The Museum of Modern Art, video and prints and illustrated books.) Uncertainty over video is centered particularly around considerations of permanence, both in regard to whether or not there will be continued activity in this area, thus meriting the development of a collection, and in regard to the physical stability of videotape itself. Fears of physical impermanence as well haunt institutions dedicated to collecting for posterity, but while we have not had the experience of keeping videotapes for years, we do not know that early predictions of the medium's impermanence have proven exaggerated.[28]

These remarks about artists' video tapes equally refer to artists' films and performances. Early video, film, and performance artists' success in evading the art marketplace ironically contributed to subsequent artists eventually addressing a less initiated, more populist audience, as many Neo-Expressionist painters and sculptors and most Post-Modernist artists do. Annexing more populist audiences, some Post-Modernist artists like Haring, Sherman, Bogosian, and Burton, court the marketplace. In the same essay quoted from above, in 1977 I wrote:

Could it be that, through artists' use of a medium which was first developed as a popular art form and which will probably remain the most widely disseminated and most reproducible medium in history [video], we will witness the closing of that centuries-old gap between high and popular art?[29]

The gap has not been closed by the late 1980s, but it certainly has been narrowed, as we shall see in chapters 6, 7, and 9.

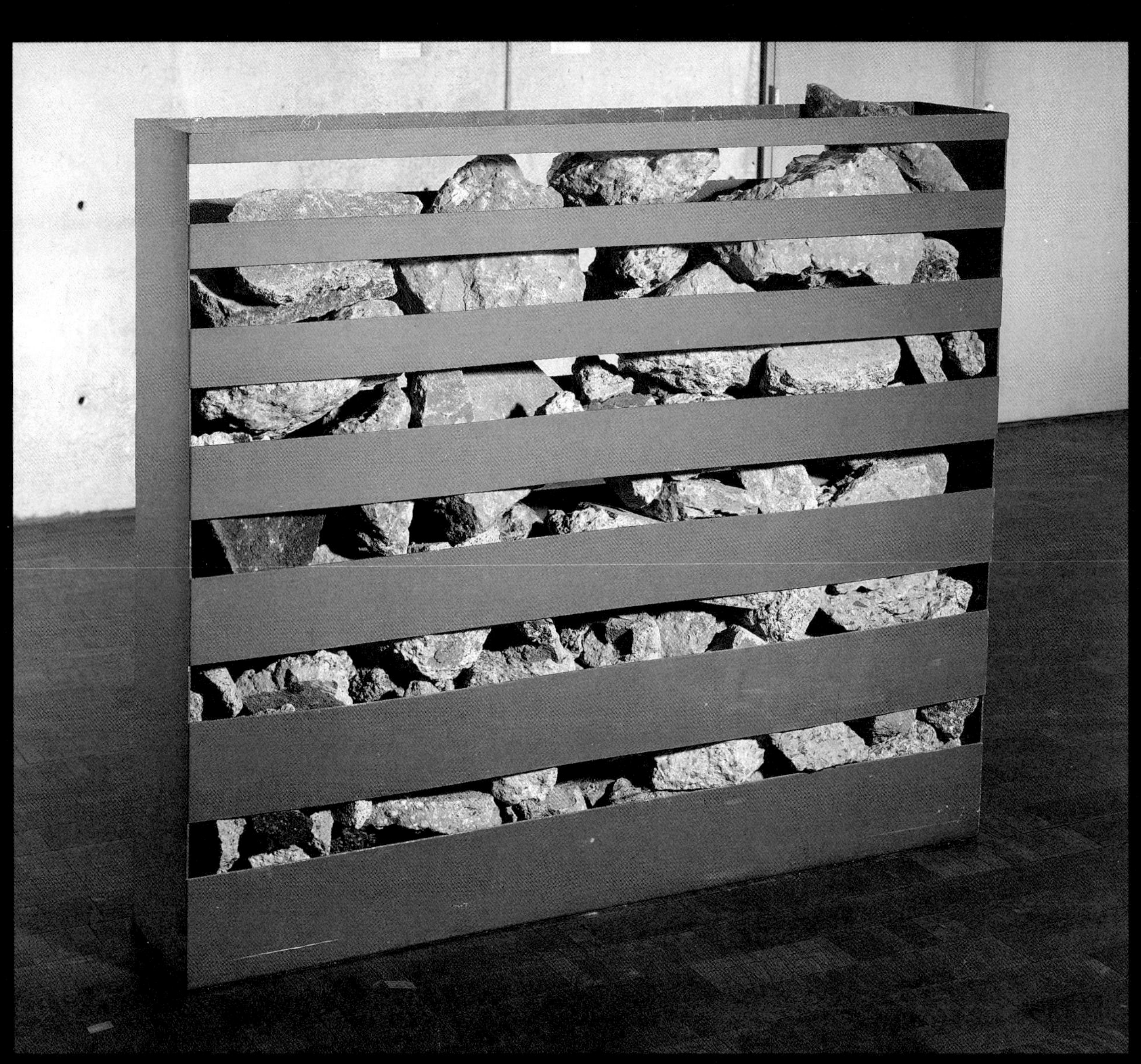

3
Earthworks and Site-Specific Sculpture

"One's mind and the earth are in a constant state of erosion, mental rivers wear away abstract banks, brain waves undermine cliffs of thought, ideas decompose into stones of unknowing, and conceptual crystallizations break apart into deposits of gritty reason."[1]

—— ROBERT SMITHSON ——

Robert Smithson
Nonsite: Line of Wreckage   1968
Courtesy Milwaukee Art Museum

Earthworks and other site-specific sculpture share some characteristics with Conceptual Art and Video, Film, and Performance Art. They all comment upon the art marketplace by overturning what Earthwork artist Michael Heizer called "the position of art as malleable barter-exchange,"[2] often by making short-lived or dematerialized artworks, or, as in the case of Earthworks and other site-specific artworks, by linking artworks so inseparably to their location that they cannot be transported and exchanged. All of these mid- to late-1960s developments responded to the burgeoning monetary values of artworks by exercising various strategies for the artist to maintain control.

Earthworks and other site-specific sculpture are fabricated and permanently located outside galleries and museums, usually in outdoor spaces chosen by the artists. Portable artworks are usually made in the artist's studio (or at a fabricator's work place), then transported to wherever they are exhibited. In the latter case, the dealers who handle the artworks may have as much, or more control, as the artist over where and under what conditions the artworks are seen; once the works are sold to a third party, the artist's control effectively ends.

In the second half of the 1960s artists became more concerned with the politics of the art world than they had been earlier in the postwar period. Issues of power were urgent current concerns within the populace as a whole in the late 1960s. The Vietnam war debate, the civil rights struggle, and the numerous political assassinations kept politics in the daily news. Artists' power—their ability to influence the conditions under which their work is seen and the methods by which it is given value—became an important issue against the backdrop of other power struggles. In 1972, Robert Smithson said:

I'm just interested in exploring the apparatus I'm being threaded through, you know, and to me that's a legitimate interest. I've always been interested in different sites and different kinds of relationships, you know, like the relationship in a white room as opposed to a quarry. I mean there's obviously a difference of intention there, and the whiteness of the room looks like a little neutral cell in heaven and the painting hanging on the wall … you're supposed to not even think of the wall that the painting is hanging on. You're supposed to just respond metaphysically to the painting in terms of color, line, structure, you know, and talk about the framing support, but forget about where you're standing, where you are, and the ambience of the entire space. So I think that actually this is an investigation of some kind of space control that's shot through with all kinds of social, economic, political implications.[3]

In their large scale, which requires viewers to walk around and through them, and in their often temporary nature, Earthworks and other site-specific sculptures employ the dimension of time—like some Conceptual Art and all Video, Film, and Performance- Art. The fourth dimension of time (in addition to height, width, and depth) became increasingly important to artists in the late 1960s, including the Post-Minimalists who emphasized the process of the artwork's own making as an integral part—and sometimes as the only subject—of an artwork (see pages 110–11). Perhaps the element of time became of such great interest to visual artists at this particular moment in American cultural history partly because social and political changes occurred so rapidly during the 1960s, and partly because electronic mass media had a more influential role then.

Many Earthworks share with Minimalism a formal concern with horizontality, although in Earthworks the landscape horizon extends nearly infinitely compared with the enclosed architectural horizons Minimal sculptures affirm. Earthworks also frequently extend beneath the horizon.

Three of the earliest Earthworks exist entirely underground, two of them totally out of view. In 1967 the Pop artist Claes Oldenburg (born 1929) hired a grave-digger to dig a grave in New York City's Central Park, then fill it in. In 1968, the Minimal and Conceptual artist Sol LeWitt created *Buried Cube Containing an Object of Importance but Little Value*, a 10 inch (25.4 cm) steel cube completely buried in the ground. Both of these works share Conceptual artists' belief in the primacy of the idea of the artwork, since they are both invisible. Also in 1967, Michael Heizer created two subterranean voids—one cube, one cone—marking north and south coordinates in the Sierra Nevadas (Fig. **3.1**). (Heizer planned east and west coordinate markings, too.) Heizer's voids were visible, yet below the horizon. All three sculptures manifested radical new ideas

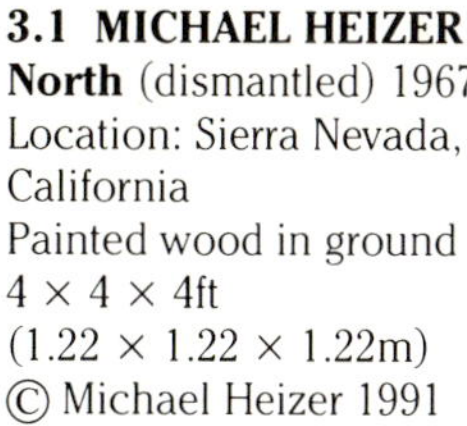

3.1 MICHAEL HEIZER
North (dismantled) 1967
Location: Sierra Nevada,
California
Painted wood in ground
4 × 4 × 4ft
(1.22 × 1.22 × 1.22m)
© Michael Heizer 1991

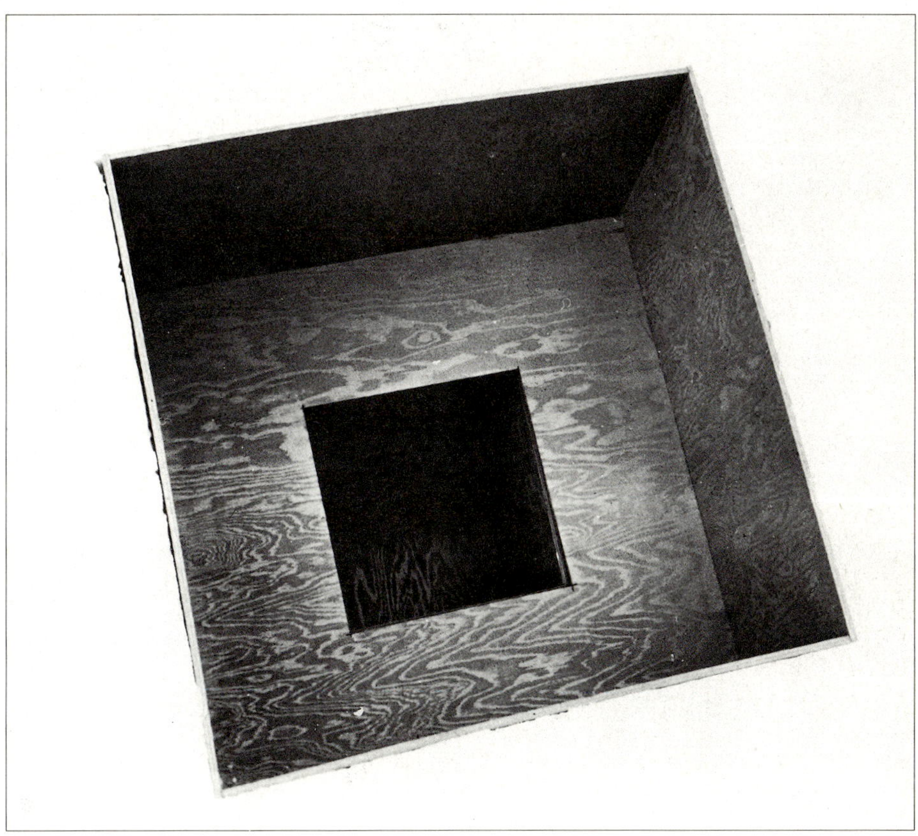

on the relationship of sculpture to the horizontal plane upon which it traditionally rested, furthering a rich dialogue about sculpture and its base or support, which runs throughout modern sculpture from Rodin to the present.

But Earthwork and other site-specific artists sought to escape from European sculptural traditions in other important ways. In locating many of their works in the vast landscape spaces of the western United States, Earthwork artists call attention to the uniquely American experiences of distance and scale, experiences unobtainable in the more populated and more altered landscapes of Europe. Earthworks interact with the western landscape which the Abstract Expressionists, like Jackson Pollock, Franz Kline, and Willem de Kooning, only metaphorically represent. Both, however, underscore uniquely American landscapes: in the case of the abstract Expressionists, at the same time as the destruction of Europe during World War II; in the case of Earthworks, at the same time as American space explora-

tions.

The 1969 American landing on the moon provoked the imaginations of many artists. "Man will never create anything really large in relation to the world—only in relation to himself and his size," Michael Heizer wrote in 1969. "The most formidable objects that man has touched are the earth and the moon. The greatest scale he understands is the distance between them."[4] "I described the moonshot once as a very expensive non-site,"[5] Robert Smithson said in 1972, referring to the moon rocks that astronauts brought back to earth and their relationship to his sculptures, called non-sites, which he began making in 1968.

Late 1960s artists' interest in social and political systems—including the politics of the art world—paralleled many Earthwork artists' interest in natural systems, spurred partly by space exploration and the unitary view of the earth seen from outer space. This latter perception—embodied in the famous NASA photograph of the entire earth—brought about an

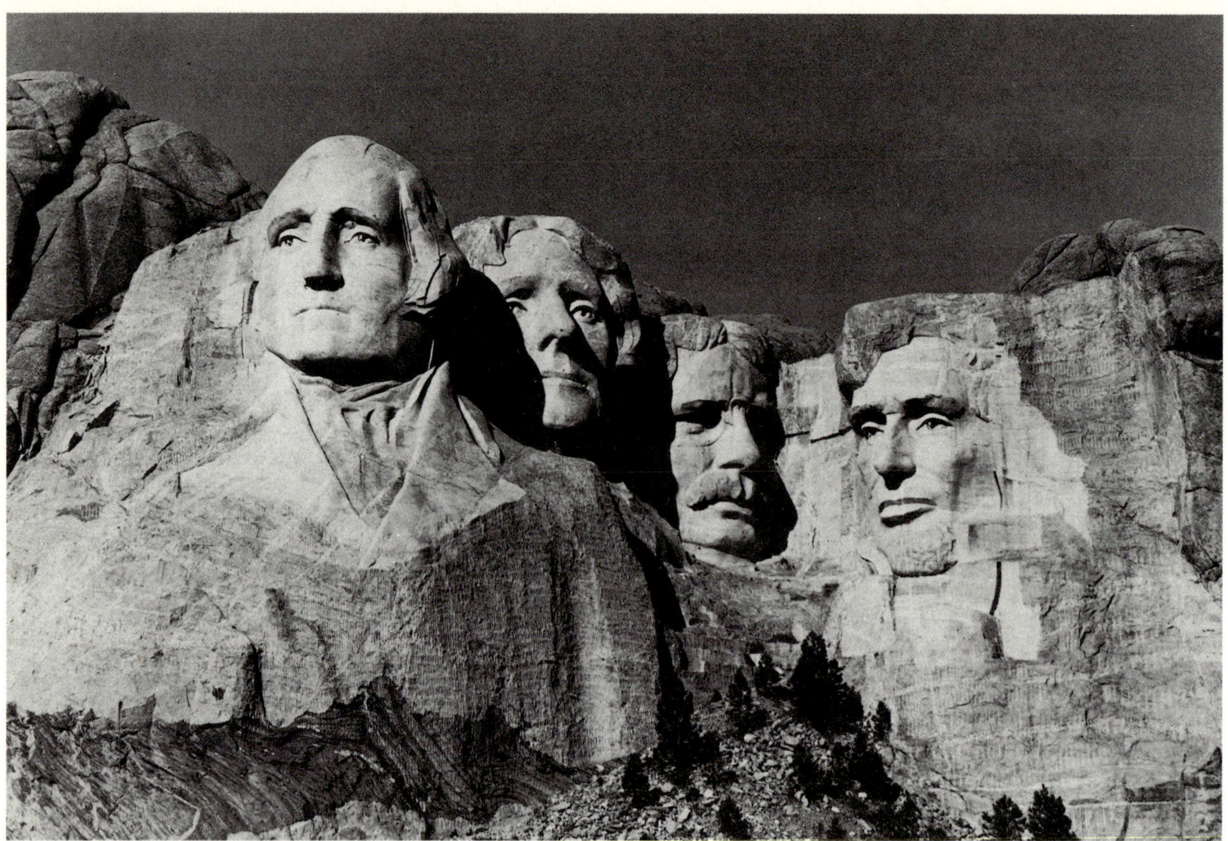

3.2 GUTZON BORGLUM
Mount Rushmore National
Memorial 1927–41
Each face 60ft (18.3m) from
chin to top of forehead
Courtesy National Park
Service, South Dakota

awareness of the earth as a finite planet and fostered widespread thinking about the ecology, or natural system, of the planet earth. Interest in natural and man-made systems also paralleled the mushrooming electronic communications industry—telecommunications, television, computers, satelites—and its lingo of "systems" and "information" theories and emphasis on process. All of these systems indicate networks of variables in flux, in opposition to static art.

Something else uniquely American about Earthworks, in addition to the vastness of their landscape spaces, is the feeling of there being no clear boundary between the artworks and the landscapes that they not so much occupy as possess. Where, for example, does Smithson's *Spiral Jetty* (see page 85) end and the Great Salt Lake begin? Or where does

Michael Heizer's *Double Negative* (see page 90) end and Mormon Mesa—not to mention the space that fills the void—begin? Commensurate with the scale of Mount Rushmore (Fig. **3.2**) another quintessentially American (albeit kitsch) site-specific sculpture, the scale and integration of these Earthworks into the landscape depends upon vast unencumbered spaces.

That many Earthworks are located in the western United States links them to western frontier mythology, including the myth that wide open spaces foster individualism and freedom from conventions. The privations one must endure to visit most remote western Earthworks require a certain degree of endurance, certainly more than going to a museum in a city. Traveling through the ample and engulfing space surrounding most western Earthworks for scores of miles in any direction places one in psychological and physical solitude. Privations, endurance, solitude: these are ingredients of popular western frontier mythology.

When shown in museums and galleries, Earthworks and other site-specific artworks are represented by documentation: studies, drawings, architectural plans, models, films, and especially photographs. As it did for Conceptual Art and to a lesser extent for Performance Art, photography plays a major documentary, non-aesthetic role. Photographs of Earthworks and other site-specific sculptures are not artworks in themselves but documents of artworks. Most Earthworks translate accurately into photography and other documentation, making them well-suited for dissemination through art magazines.

Few people will ever see most of the Earthworks in remote locations. In fact, because of unprecedented high waters in the great Salt Lake, Smithson's *Spiral Jetty* (see page 85) has been under water since 1972, only two years after it was completed. What may be the world's most renowned Earthwork has been virtually invisible during most of its existence—yet it is widely known through photographs.

ROBERT SMITHSON

Robert Smithson (1938–73) was as influential a writer and conversational art theorist as he was an artist.[6] He was a catalyst who focused his and other artists' ideas by challenging them in endless discussions, often at New York City's Max's Kansas City, the artists' bar-restaurant that served as a meeting place for artists, dancers, musicians, actors, photographers, models, and filmmakers during the late 1960s and early 1970s.

… almost every night from 11 or 12 o'clock until closing this [seating area] was Robert Smithson's territory. Carl Andre, Richard Serra, Mel Bochner, Don Judd, Larry Weiner, Joseph Kosuth, Ted Castle, Michael Heizer, Keith Sonnier, Dan Graham and Dorothea Rockburne were also often there, and occasionally Sol LeWitt. LeWitt remembers,

"Smithson was the real catalyst. He had a way of provoking people, of provoking discussion. It was very important because it forced people to defend themselves and to qualify their own ideas." …

This group's art was idea-oriented, and all kinds of ideas were discussed—not just art ideas, but those from other disciplines as well. Various writers were popular at different times—Barthes, Ehrenzweig, Wittgenstein, Levi-Strauss, Robbe-Grillet. Not everyone read the books, but they read the reviews in the New York Times. *Relationships between language and visual images were a major concern of these artists …*[7]

Although Smithson was friends with many of the major Minimalists, and showed with them in the first important museum exhibition of Minimalism—the Jewish Museum's *Primary Structures* in 1966—his art shares fewer similarities with Minimalism than it has differences. *Alogon #1* (Fig. **3.3**) employs Minimalism's geometric forms and straight surfaces, but it differs from Minimalism's unitary compositions by employing a progression: the serial forms gradually diminish (or increase) in size. A Minimalist would have rendered the forms identical—static—whereas Smithson has implied an infinite number of changes.

Contrasting the idealized, static and Classical balance of Minimalist Art, Smithson maintained the possibility for unknowable permutations and

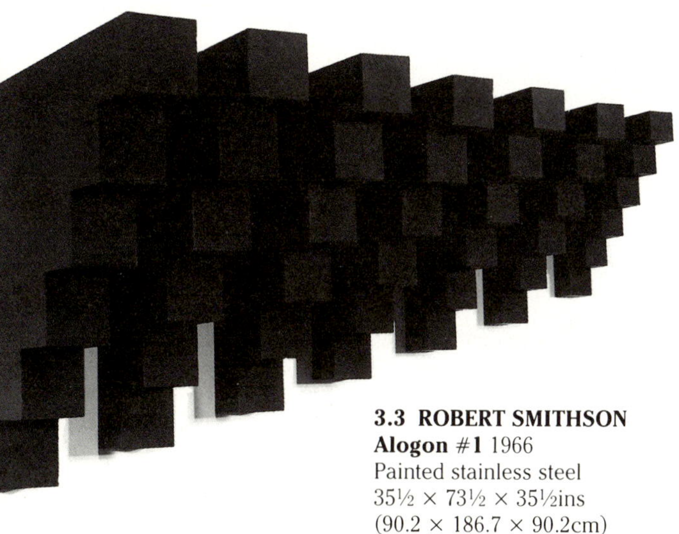

3.3 ROBERT SMITHSON
Alogon #1 1966
Painted stainless steel
35½ × 73½ × 35½ins
(90.2 × 186.7 × 90.2cm)
Collection Whitney Museum
of American Art, New York.

Gift of the Howard and Jean Lipman Foundation Inc. Photograph courtesy Dwan Gallery
"… the title Alogon … comes from the Greek word which refers to the unnameable, the

irrational number …[8] *Ambiguities are admitted rather than rejected, contradictions are increased rather than decreased—the alogos undermines the logos."*[9]

change. He was fascinated by entropy, the law of thermodynamics which states that matter tends toward less and less complex patterns of order, eventually resulting in undifferentiated sameness. In "The Monuments of Passaic," in 1967, he wrote:

I should now like to prove the irreversibility of eternity by using a jejune *experiment for proving entropy. Picture in your mind's eye the sand box divided in half with black sand on one side and white sand on the other. We take a child and have him run hundreds of times clockwise in the box until the sand gets mixed and begins to turn grey; after that we have him run anti-clockwise, but the result will not be restoration of the original division but a greater degree of greyness and an increase of entropy.*[10]

Smithson was fascinated by systems in states of chaos or collapse. He wrote about his first view of the *Spiral Jetty's* site: "A great pleasure arose from seeing all those incoherent structures [referring to various abandoned buildings and equipment]. This site gave evidence of a succession of man-made systems mired in abandoned hopes."[11] John Coplans wrote about the same site: "The site is a terribly lonely place, cut off and remote, conveying the feeling of being completely shunned by man."[12] The "lonely" and "shunned," evidencing "a succession of man-made systems mired in abandoned hopes," gave Smithson "great pleasure." An interest in the impotence of man-made systems in the face of nature's entropy informed Smithson's art. He did not personify nature, nor did he take an apocalyptic view; he simply accepted what he regarded as given.

Smithson had an uncanny ability to incorporate a wide range of interests into his art. Science fiction and B-movies interested him as much as philosophy, geology, and art theory. In the above-mentioned essay, "The Monuments of Passaic," Smithson refers to a science fiction paperback he bought to read on the bus trip to New Jersey. "I bought a copy of the

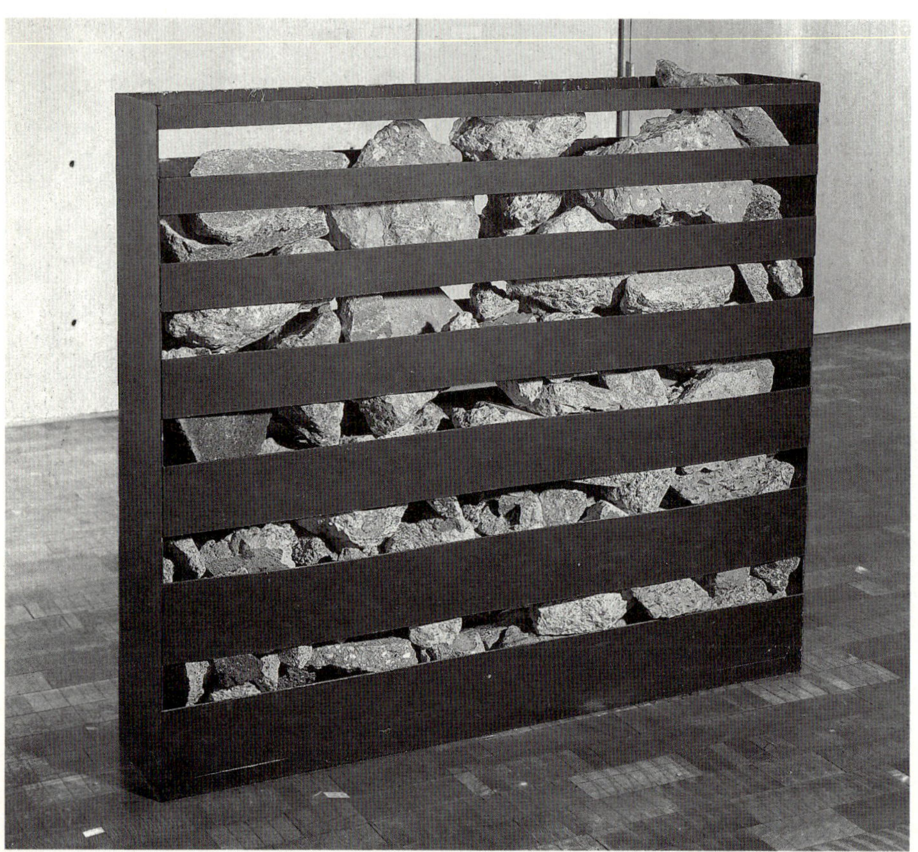

3.4 ROBERT SMITHSON
Non-site: Line of
Wreckage
Location: Bayonne, New Jersey 1968
Painted aluminum cage with chunks of busted concrete, 3 photo panels; 1 map panel
cage: 59 h. × 70 l. × 12½ d. ins
(149.9 × 177.8 × 31.8cm)
all panels: 3¾ h. × 49 l. ins
(9.5 × 124.5cm)
Courtesy Milwaukee Art Museum, Purchase, Milwaukee Art Museum, National Endowment for the Arts Matching Funds
"The land or ground from the Site is placed in the art (Nonsite) … rather than the art placed on the ground."[13]

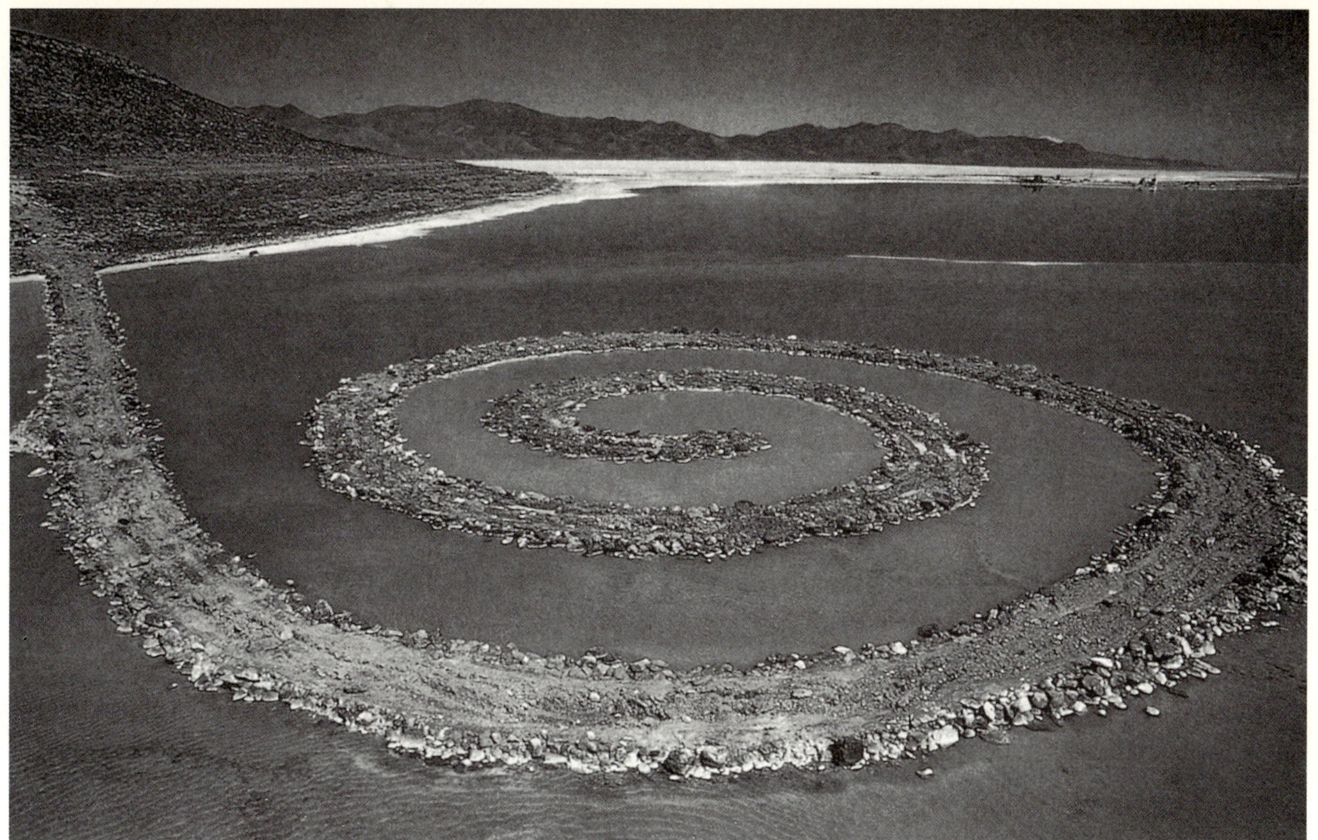

3.5 ROBERT SMITHSON
Spiral Jetty 1970
Earth, mud, water, salt,
volcanic rock
1500ft (457.2m) long
Courtesy John Weber Gallery,
New York

"The Spiral Jetty, located in the lake called 'America's Dead Sea,' is an image of contracted time: the far distant past (the beginning of life in saline solutions symbolized by the lake) is absorbed in the remote past (symbolized by the destructive forces of the legendary whirlpools in the lake) and the no longer valid optimism of the recent past (symbolized by the Golden Spike monument). All these pasts collide with the futility of the near present (the vacated oil rigging)." [16]

New York Times and a Signet paperback called *Earthworks* by Brian W. Aldiss. . . . I read the blurbs and skimmed through *Earthworks*. The first sentence read, 'The dead man drifted along in the breeze.' It seemed the book was about a soil shortage, and the Earthworks referred to the manufacture of artificial soil." [14] This is the origin of the term "Earthworks."

In 1968, Smithson began making his *Non-sites*, sculptures utilizing samples removed from specific documented outdoor sites, then placed in containers resembling Minimal sculpture and exhibited away from the original site. Whereas Minimal sculpture refers primarily to itself and secondly to the interior architectural space it occupies, the *Non-sites* refer to the outdoor landscape locations where Smithson found the samples.

Smithson set up what he called a "dialectic of site and non-site," in which he identified the sites as characterized by "open limits," the non-sites by "closed limits;" the sites by "a series of points," the non-sites by "an array of matter;" the sites by "scattered information," the non-sites by "contained information;" the sites by "some place (physical)," the non-sites by "no place (abstract)." [15]

Non-site: Line of Wreckage, Bayonne, New Jersey (Fig. **3.4**) is a purple-painted metal bin containing chunks of broken concrete coated with asphalt on one side. The concrete was taken from a site identified in an accompanying map and photographs as being a coastal fill area which had formerly been a ship graveyard. On the map the site is identified as a "Foul Area." Apparently the concrete had formerly been a road, then became coastal fill before being recycled again into a non-site. During the same year he made *Line of Wreckage*, Smithson made the following analogy between geological phenomena and thought processes:

| *One's mind and the earth are in a constant state of*

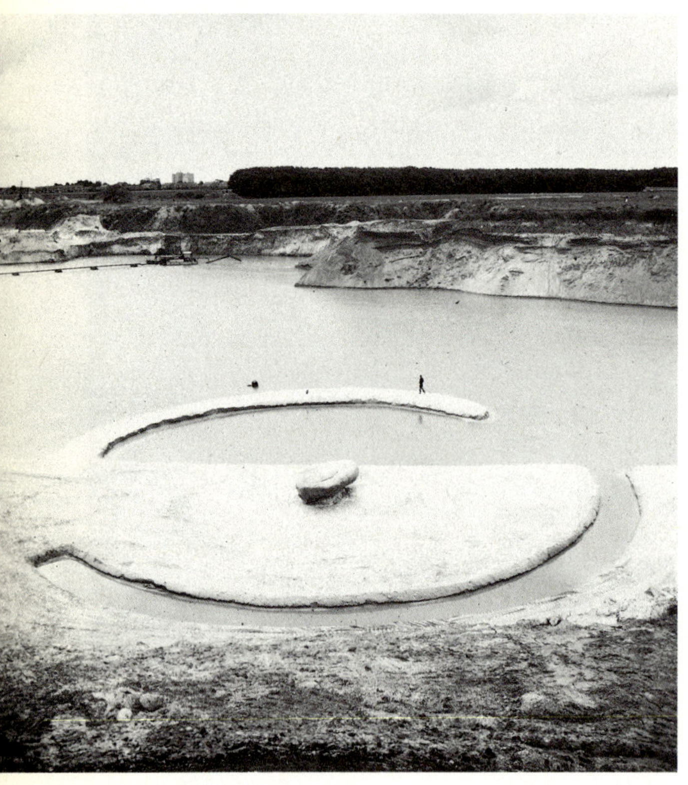

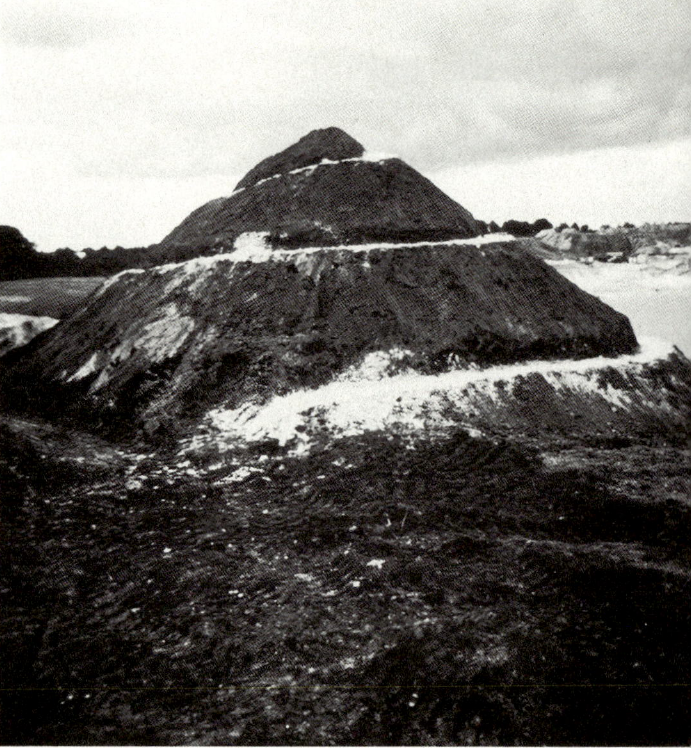

3.6 ROBERT SMITHSON
(left) **Broken Circle** 1971
Location: Emmen, Holland
(right) **Spiral Hill** 1971
Location: Emmen, Holland

Earth, black topsoil, white
sand, 75ft (22.8m) at base
Courtesy John Weber Gallery,
New York

*erosion, mental rivers wear away abstract banks,
brain waves undermine cliffs of thought, ideas
decompose into stones of unknowing, and
conceptual crystallizations break apart into
deposits of gritty reason.*[17]

Here the preoccupation of Minimalism with perceptual phenomena directly perceivable in the artwork gives way to poetic analogies.

It was typical of Smithson to recycle or reclaim materials or sites which had already been despoiled or befouled rather than to disrupt them. An island he bought off the coast of Maine to make an Earthwork upon he eventually decided not to use because it was too picturesque. At the time of his accidental death in 1973, he was negotiating with a mining company to reclaim strip-mined land by recycling it into art.

Reading about red lakes in Bolivia led Smithson to investigate if such salt-water lakes existed in less remote locations. Hearing that the Great Salt Lake in Utah contains red algae that make parts of it the color of tomato soup was incentive enough for Smithson and his wife, Nancy Holt, to travel there. They found a site at Rozel Point on the northern shore of the lake on which Smithson took out a 20-year renewable lease and began constructing the *Spiral Jetty*.

The 1500 feet (457.2 m) coil of the *Spiral Jetty* (Fig. **3.5**) was built by frontloaders and dumptrucks using materials taken from the prehistoric site. Coiling counter-clockwise, the spiral implies going back in time, but the spiral form's open-endedness also implies infinite progression as well as regression, ambiguities Smithson planned. The multi-layered symbol of the spiral includes these latter meanings and refers also to the spiral formation of salt crystals on the jetty's basalt boulders, to a folkloric spiral whirlpool connecting the Great Salt Lake to the ocean through an underground river, and to spiral nebulae, or immense bodies of rarified gas or dust in space. The sun, which reflects off the dead lake in blinding sheets of light, warms the water in the *Spiral Jetty's* center, causing red algae to flourish there. The red salt water symbolizes saline and blood, the origins of life. The *Spiral Jetty* incorporates the elemental materials of earth, air, fire, and water.

In 1971, various artists including Smithson were invited to build artworks at different locations throughout Holland as part of the international art exhibition, Sonsbeek '71. Smithson chose a depleted quarry in Emmen that was slated for conversion into a recreational area. The quarry included materials deposited there by glaciers during the Ice Age (10,000 BC), a time dimension Smithson liked. He also delighted in the fact that the country of Holland itself, having been largely claimed from the wet lowlands by a series of dikes, was itself a man-made Earthwork.

As its title suggests, *Broken Circle/Spiral Hill* (Fig. **3.6**) incorporates two opposing elements: an earthen conical hill with a sandy counter-clockwise spiral path, and a circular sandy plane incorporating water. The circle is partially composed of a sand jetty symbolizing Holland's dikes. From atop the *Spiral Hill*—one of the highest promontories in Holland— one looks down on the *Broken Circle*.

The large boulder at the circle's center was an unanticipated feature: it was uncovered during construction and provided what Smithson regarded as an undesirable center to the Earthwork. However, Smithson discovered that the boulder was one of the largest in Holland, deposited there during the Ice Age, and that only the Dutch army was equipped to move it. Partly because it had links with prehistoric tombs— called "Hun's beds"—made of similar boulders, Smithson decided to leave the boulder where it was.

During the next two years, Smithson negotiated with various companies to create land reclamation projects by recycling disrupted and despoiled sites into Earthworks. He was working in very original artistic territory, defining a role and function for himself that expanded the traditional concept of the avant-garde artist working alone in his or her studio into a role where the artist works with other people and incorporates their ideas into the artwork. Smithson termed this interaction "dialectic." John Coplans wrote, quoting Smithson, "Smithson's overriding concern, especially in the last two years of his life, was to propagate his art as 'a resource that mediates between ecology and industry.'"[18] Unfortunately, none of the projects came to fruition.

The last project Smithson was working on when he died was the *Amarillo Ramp* (Fig. **3.7**) in Amarillo, Texas. He was inspecting it by air when the single-engine plane stalled and crashed, killing Smithson, the pilot, and the photographer. The *Amarillo Ramp* was completed after Smithson's death by his widow, Nancy Holt, and his friend, Richard Serra, who had been present when the *Spiral Jetty* was built. There will always be those who question the *Amarillo Ramp* as a Smithson sculpture, believing that he might have made changes as the Earthwork progressed. Those who support it state that Smithson completely staked-out the work and thoroughly discussed his intentions with Holt before his death. He also typically listened to other peoples' suggestions—especially the construction crew's—and sometimes incorporated them.

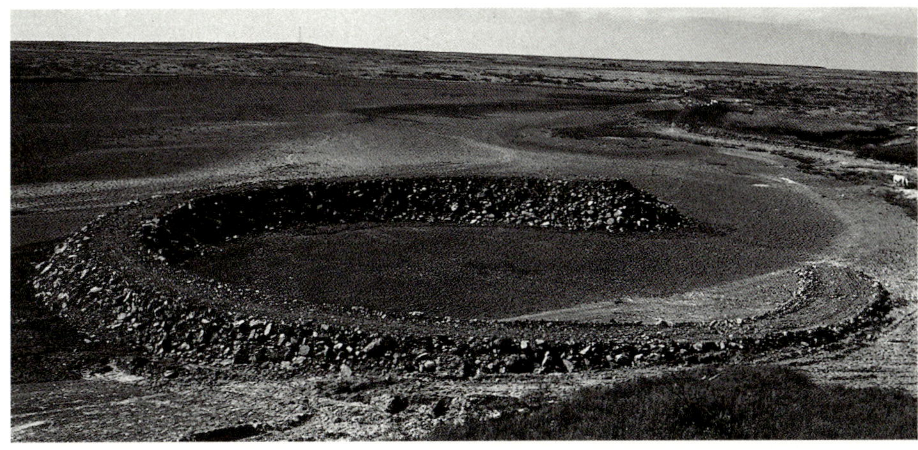

3.7 ROBERT SMITHSON
Amarillo Ramp 1973
Location: Tecovas Lake, Texas
Length 396ft (120.7m)
Diameter: top 150ft (45.7m), base 150–60ft (45.7–48.8m)
Courtesy John Weber Gallery, New York

MICHAEL HEIZER

Michael Heizer (born 1944) grew up in the western United States, though he claims no special attraction to western mythology. Throughout his youth Heizer accompanied his father—the late Dr. Robert F. Heizer, a prominent archaeologist-anthropologist—on expeditions in Central and South America, where he witnessed the remnants of many ancient cultures.

I helped with the field work. I took notes on the measurement and location of objects and did technical drawings of such things as prehistoric gutter systems, potsherds, statues, lithic fragments—whatever they wanted me to do. One of my father's major subjects was massive stone transport. All of this came out in my art fifteen or twenty years later.[19]

In 1966, in his early twenties, Heizer moved to New York City where he continued to paint large geometric abstractions and became acquainted with other artists, such as Smithson and Walter De Maria (see pages 92–95). The summer of 1967 found Heizer in California's Sierra Nevadas installing the North and South coordinates of his NESW (see page 80), one of the earliest outdoor Earthworks. Both were voids dug in the ground below the horizon, one

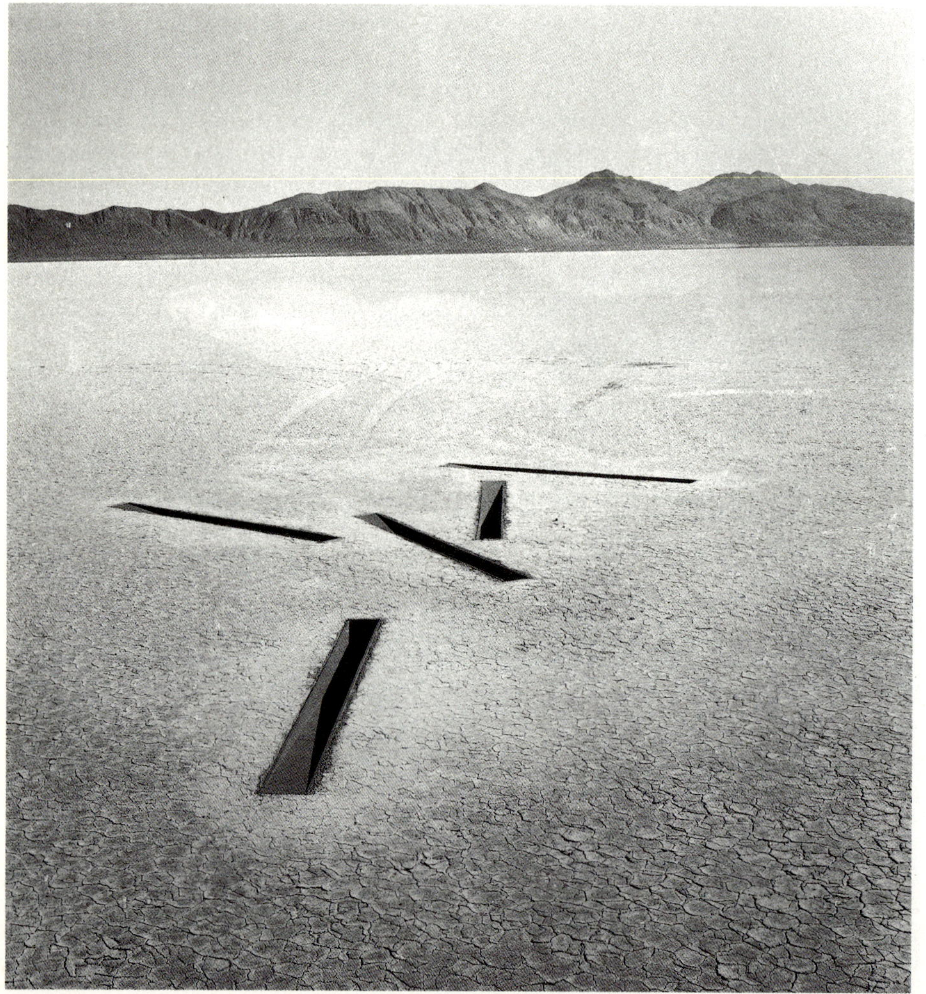

3.8 MICHAEL HEIZER
Dissipate (deteriorated)
1968
#8 of Nine Nevada
Depressions
Location: Black Rock Desert,
Nevada
Wood in playa surface
45 × 50 × 1ft
(13.7 × 15.2 × 0.3m)
Commissioned by Robert
Scull
© Michael Heizer 1991
"Many negative sculptures I built in the late sixties were inundated with water because they were built on dry lakes that flooded in the spring and winter or were eroded by wind. These works were photographed in this condition. They were extended and developed by natural forces, both physically and intellectually, beyond the 'completed' state I had left them. I never planned this change, but I accepted it."[20]

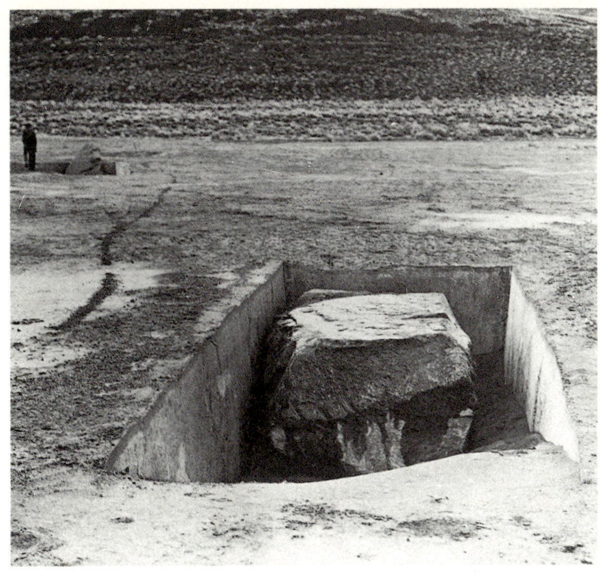

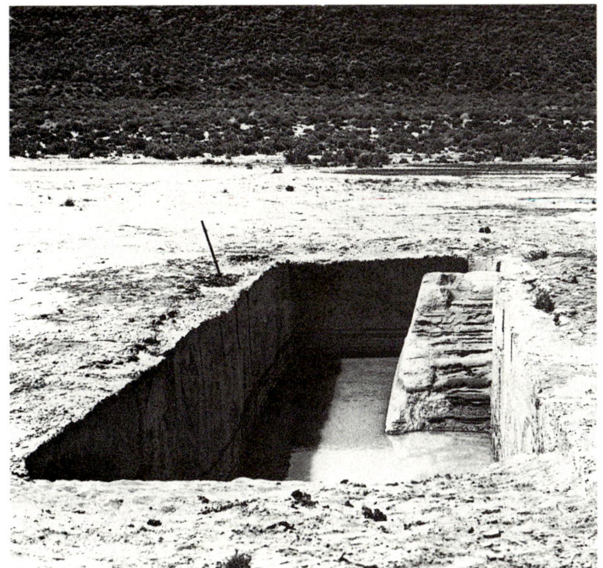

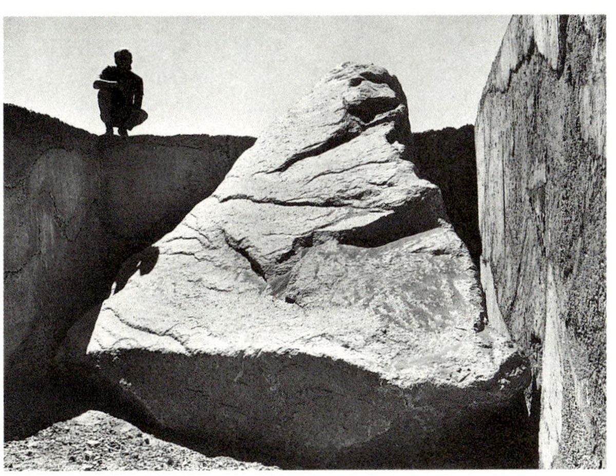

cubic, the other cone-shaped.

During the summer of 1968 Heizer drove west with Walter De Maria, this time to create Earthworks in the Black Rock Desert, the Jean and Massacre Dry Lakes, Nevada, and in the Coyote and El Mirage Dry Lakes, California. Robert Smithson and Nancy Holt visited Heizer that summer; Smithson helped dig a trench for one of Heizer's Earthworks.

Heizer dug a series of voids below the extensive horizontal planes of the dry lakes and desert land-scapes, sometimes reinforcing them with wood, sometimes not. They extended the formal dialogue of modern sculpture with the horizon and with the concept of the base in highly original ways because, in effect, Heizer made sculptures out of voids, or negative spaces, while sculpture had previously been thought of as primarily positive spaces, or forms. Where voids figure prominently in modern sculpture—in works by the Russian Constructivists, Gabo, Pevsner, Tatlin, and Rodchenko, for example—they are voids in portable objects, and certainly voids above ground.

Another important feature of Heizer's Earthworks made that summer is their impermanence. Heizer photographed *Dissipate* (Fig. **3.8**) as it weathered and eventually disintegrated. Reflecting in 1983 about the works he made that year, Heizer said:

I found new materials and new conditions by working outside. I became involved with phenomenological impact rather than interior artifice. I had to contend with the weather and its destructive effects. But the history of sculpture, as we know it, consists mostly of remains and fragments, damaged either by man or by natural phenomena.[21]

In 1969, Heizer moved huge boulders from mountains into which they had been thrust by geological action, placing them in cement-lined depressions in the desert. *Displaced/Replaced Mass* (Fig. **3.9**), Silver Springs, Nevada returned a 68-ton (69,088 kg) boulder from the elevation of 9,000 feet

3.9 MICHAEL HEIZER
Displaced/Replaced Mass
(dismantled) 1969
Location: Silver Springs, Nevada
Granite and concrete in playa surface. Overall 100ft × 800ft × 9ft 6ins (30.5 × 243.8 × 2.9m)
Commissioned by Robert Scull
© Michael Heizer 1991

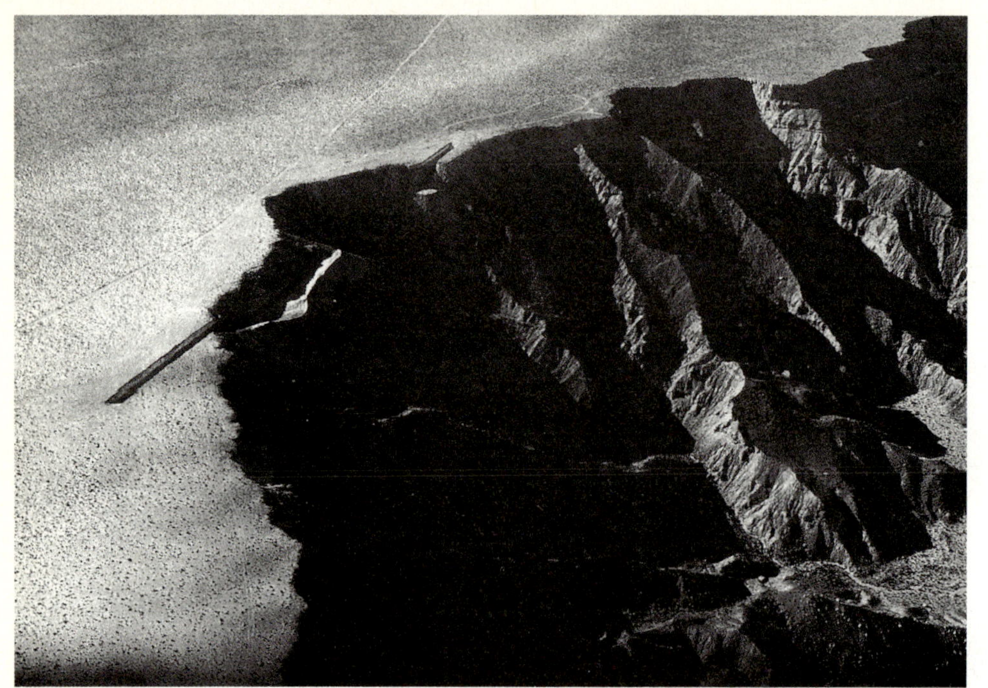

3.10 MICHAEL HEIZER
Double Negative 1969–70
Location: Mormon Mesa,
Nevada
200,000 ton displacement in
rhyolite and sandstone
50 × 500 × 30ft
(15.24 × 152.4 × 9.1m)
Collection Virginia Dwan
*"Double Negative is a cut
into a wall of rock. All it
really is, is absence.
Obviously the open space
between the two cuts is
implicated. This combination
creates the double negative.
If you can visualize the voids
combining, then you
understand the work. What's
interesting is that the center,
almost a third of the
sculpture, is an implied
volume."* [22]

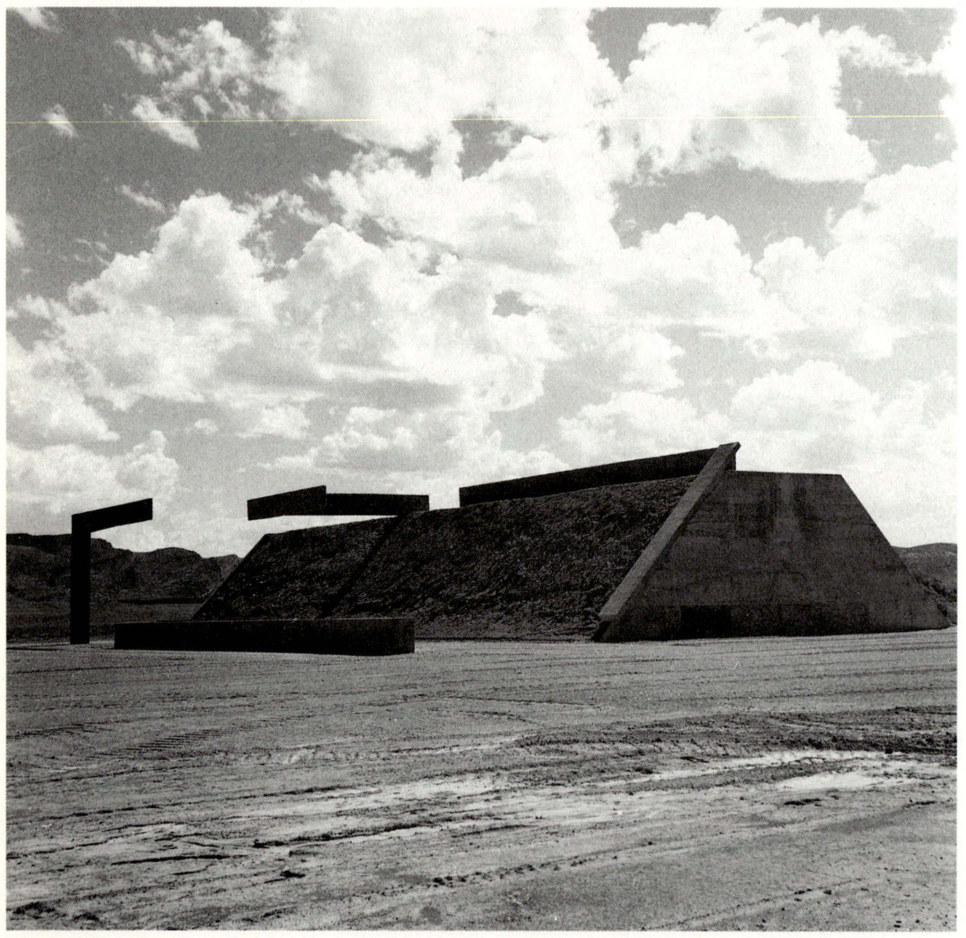

3.11 MICHAEL HEIZER
Complex One 1972–74
Location: Garden Valley,
Nevada
Concrete, steel and
compacted earth
23ft 6ins × 140ft × 110ft
(7.2 × 42.7 × 33.5m)
Collection of the artist and
Virginia Dwan
© Michael Heizer 1991
*"Part of my art is based on
an awareness that we live in
a nuclear era. We're
probably living at the end of
civilization."* [23]

(2,743 m) to 4,000 feet (1,219 m), in effect reversing geological time by returning the boulder to its original position. Eventually, the depression will fill with blowing silt and sand, virtually obliterating the huge mass. But while it is visible, the literal size of the massive boulder gives it a dramatic presence. Hugeness fascinated Heizer at the time; he perceived mammoth size as uniquely American. Jumbo jets, American space travel across 250,000 miles (402,325 km) to touch the moon, and Mount Rushmore (see page 82) were especially current in his thinking at the time. "I wanted to make an American art which was trans-national. . . . It was a question of an American sensibility, things were being done that felt uniquely American—a lot of them had to do with size—size and measurement."[24]

Heizer purchased 60 acres (242,814 sq m) on Mormon Mesa near Overton, Nevada in 1969 and began building *Double Negative* (Fig. **3.10**), completing it the next year. The void he dug out of two opposite walls of the canyon is longer than the Empire State Building is tall. About one-third of the void spans the canyon, yet this literally unbroken void is perceived as continuous with the two massive cut voids in the adjoining canyon walls.

In grammar the title—*Double Negative*—is a contradiction; two negatives make a positive. "The title *Double Negative* is a literal description of two cuts but has metaphysical implications because a double negative is impossible. There is nothing there, yet it is still sculpture."[25]

Between 1972 and 1976 Heizer worked on *Complex One* (Fig. **3.11**), a large architectural sculpture on land he owns adjacent to a Nevada nuclear test site. "When I completed the *Double Negative* in 1970, it was considered an organic structural success, but people said, 'You'll never do that again.' That was a challenge to build another big sculpture. I decided the next one would be high tech. Both are paired in location and time—the one a void in the earth, a negative space, the other a positive, above-ground sculpture—as if *Complex One* evolved from the chasm created by the *Double Negative*."[26] One side of *Complex One* faces the nuclear test site. Heizer built it like a blast shield, using the highest specifications for seismic conditions and even employing laboratory shear tests.

Complex One depends upon the unencumbered distant vistas obtainable in open landscape space. (Heizer sited it so the surrounding mountains are

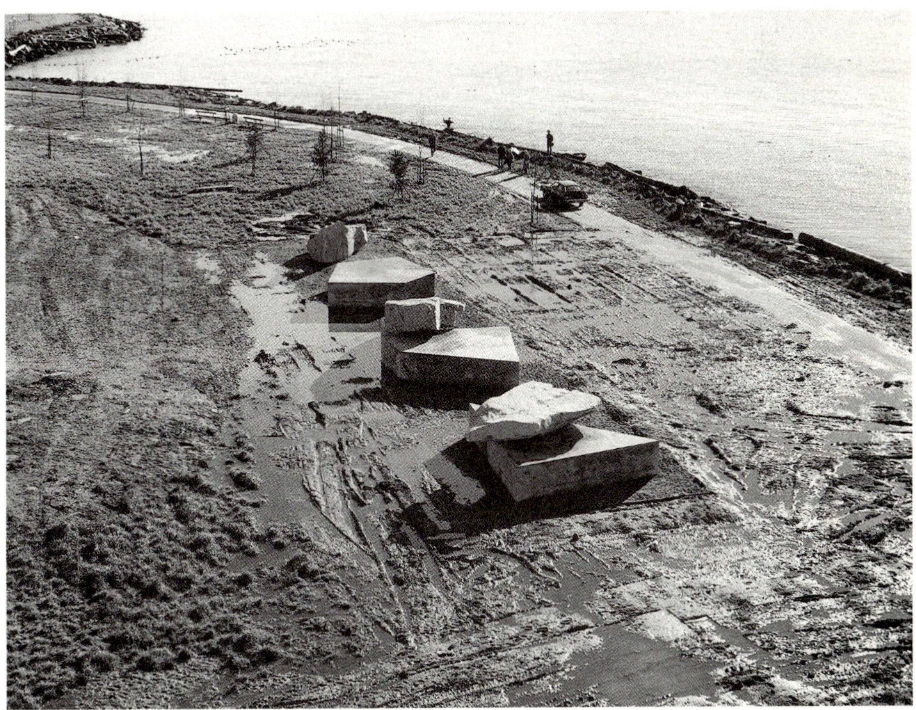

3.12 MICHAEL HEIZER
Adjacent, Against, Upon
#**1/3** 1976
Location: Myrtle Edwards
Park, Seattle, Washington
Granite and concrete
9 × 25 × 130ft
(2.7 × 7.6 × 39.6m)
Commissioned by the City of
Seattle
© Michael Heizer 1991

not too picturesque.) From a distance, the architectural beams appear to form a large, flat rectangle. On approaching *Complex One* the rectangle dissembles into separate elements on different spacial planes. The distance from which a subject is perceived affects our perception of it, along with the object's literal size. Literal size from a distance, especially in a space without boundaries, is difficult to gauge. The perceptual effects of literal size and implied size—scale—plus distance are part of what *Complex One* is about.

Complex One depends upon being surrounded by open space, but it does not necessarily have to be in the particular location where it is sited. Unlike *Double Negative*, whose site could never be duplicated, any open space would suffice. Of course, neither artwork could be transported elsewhere; in that respect both are site-specific. But *Double Negative's* relationship to its site is a more integral aspect of the artwork than *Complex One*. Heizer's views on sites are puzzling in this respect:

> *I really dislike the word 'site' as applied to sculpture. You have to put it somewhere. Do you think Michelangelo's sculpture of Moses is sited well? Portable object sculpture can be made of anything and put anywhere. Only a work such as the Mount Rushmore memorial by Gutzon*

> *Borglum, built into the Black Hills of South Dakota, is really environmental because the mountain is both the material and the place.... My only comment is that I haven't seen a work of art that is referential to its location.*[27]

Heizer's more recent Earthworks, such as *Adjacent, Against, Upon* (Fig. **3.12**), are not site-specific. (Not all Earthworks are site-specific: Robert Smithson's non-sites, for example.) This sculpture employs verbal/visual links to much of Conceptual Art. Heizer continues to displace monolithic natural masses; literal size and mass remain central to his art. *It is interesting to build a sculpture that attempts to create an atmosphere of awe. Small works are said to do this but it is not my experience. Immense, architecturally-sized sculpture creates both the object and the atmosphere. Awe is a state of mind equivalent to religious experience, I think if people feel commitment they feel something has been transcended. To create a transcendent work of art means to go past everything. If you ask about a fundamental and personal sense in relation to larger ideas and memories, I think that large sculptures produced in the sixties and seventies by a number of artists were reminiscent of the time when societies were committed to the construction of massive, significant works of art.*[28]

WALTER DE MARIA

Walter De Maria (born 1935) produced his first western Earthwork (with Heizer's help) in April, 1968: two 1-mile (1.6 km) long parallel chalk lines drawn in the Mojave Desert. The temporary lines provided a visual measurement to the otherwise visually immeasurable space. The lines, like many large-scale Earthworks, were big enough to be visible from an airplane or from outside the Earth's atmosphere. De Maria's *Mile Long Drawing* (Fig. **3.13**) evokes Nazca Indian line drawings in the Peruvian desert, made long before travel by airplanes existed. The Nazca drawings remain a mystery to this day.

That same year De Maria exhibited *Earth Room* (Fig. **3.14**) at the Heiner Friedrich Gallery in Munich. He filled the gallery with 1,600 cubic feet (45.3 cu m) of leveled earth, making an unmistakable formal statement about horizontality in sculpture and about the function of galleries as containers of artworks.

De Maria was in the western desert again in 1969 when he made *Las Vegas Piece* (Fig. **3.15**). For this he used a bulldozer with a 8 feet (2.4 m) wide blade, shallowly scraping the earth's surface just enough to make a relatively erosion-free path. After a visit to the site in 1976, *Art in America's* editor Elizabeth Baker wrote:

> *This piece requires that you walk on it. At ground level (it is a clear form seen from the air), knee-high scrub growth hides it unless one is right on it—its track is shallower than all sorts of natural washes and holes. Ground-level perception seems essential to its full meaning. It provides a 4-mile (6.4 km) walk, and an experience of specific place,*

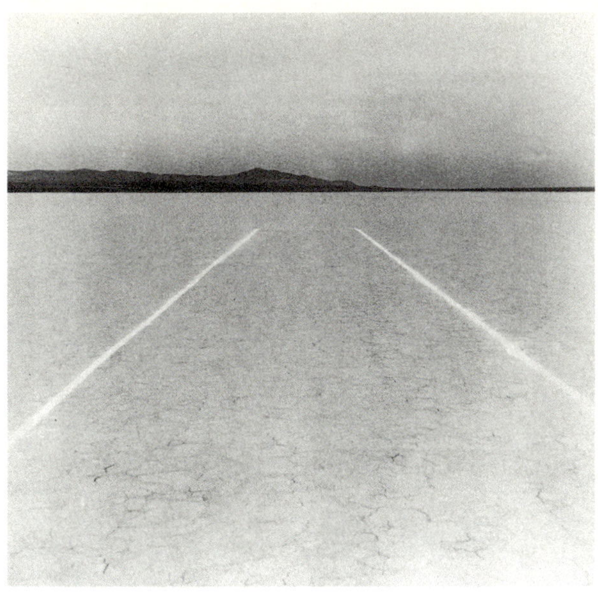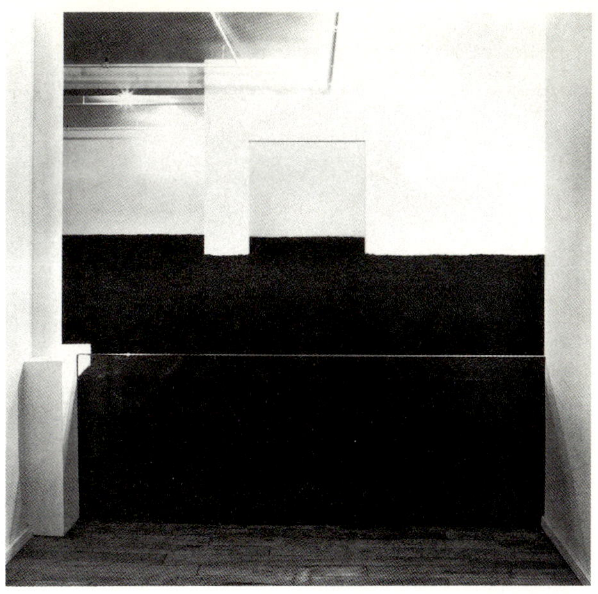

3.13 WALTER De MARIA
Mile Long Drawing 1968
Non extant
Location: Mojave Desert,
California

Chalk, 2 parallel lines 4ins
(10.16cm) wide, 12ft (3.65m)
apart and 1 mile (1.6m) long
© Walter De Maria 1968

3.14 WALTER De MARIA
The New York Earth Room
1977
© Dia Art Foundation, 1980

3.15 WALTER De MARIA
Las Vegas Piece 1969
Location: Tula Desert,
Nevada
Two cuts in the earth
Each cut 1 mile long (1.6km)
× 8ft (2.4m) wide
© Walter De Maria 1968

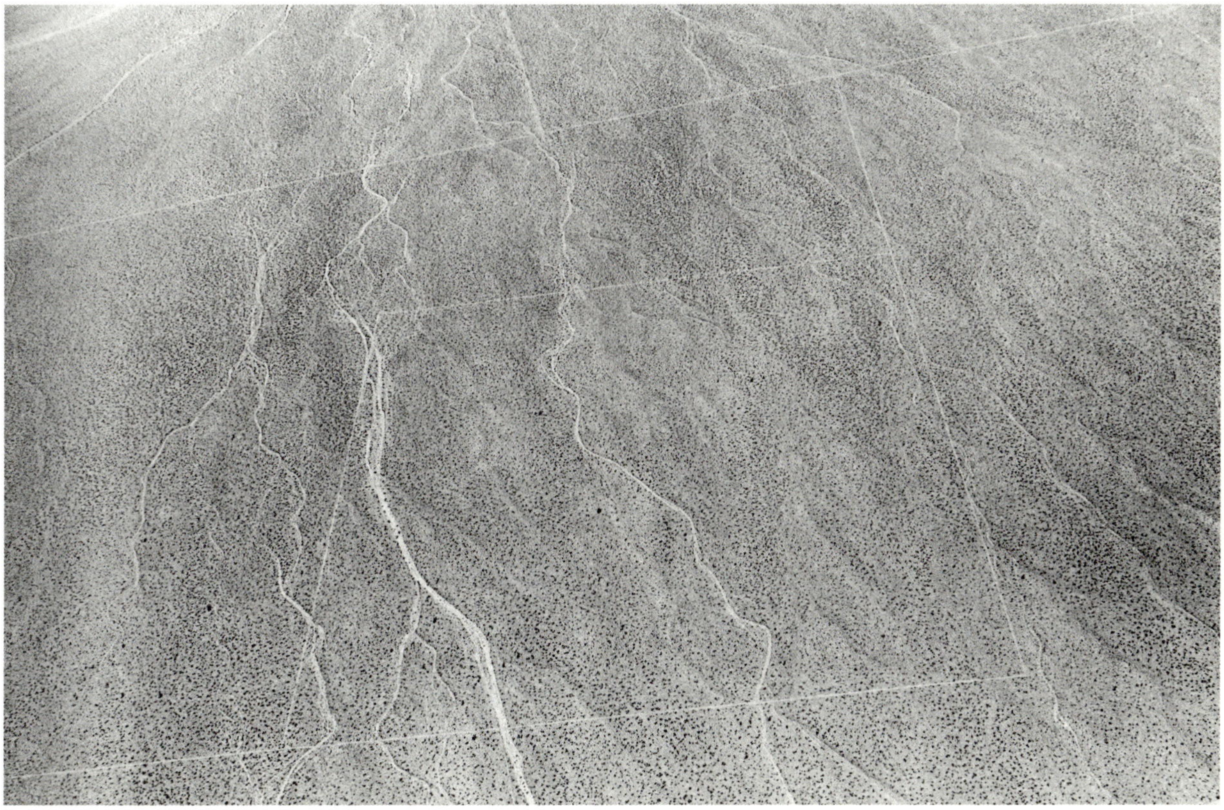

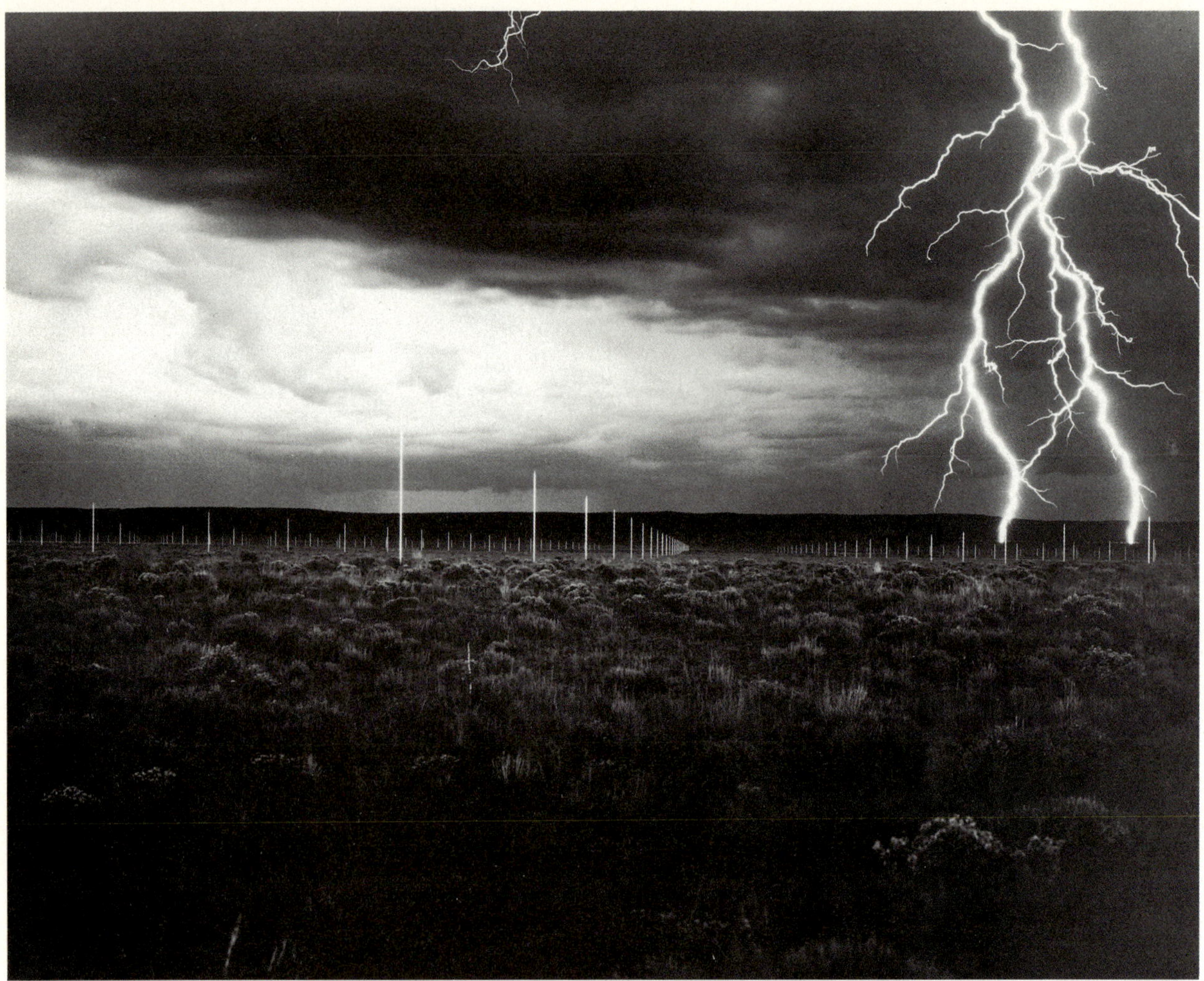

3.16 WALTER De MARIA
The Lightning Field 1977
Location: Quemado, New
Mexico
© Dia Arts Foundation 1980

*random apprehension of surroundings, and an
intensified sense of self which seems to transcend
visual apprehension alone.*[29]

Compare Baker's impression with art critic John
Coplan's comment about Smithson's *Spiral Jetty* and
Amarillo Ramp: "But in both pieces you become unusually aware of the physicality of your body in relation to its surroundings, of temperature, of the movement of wind, of the sounds of nature, and of how
isolated you have been from nature until this
moment."[30] Commentators about Earthworks frequently express their renewed or newly-discovered
awareness of nature, as though in their perception
one of the functions of Earthworks is to call attention
to natural phenomena. This is not always part of the
intent of Earthworks but it is often the result. Most
writers who have this response are city-dwellers who
otherwise would not have visited the remote and isolated landscapes where most western Earthworks are
located, and whose more habitual environment
sharply contrasts the Earthworks' settings. Still, many
Earthwork visitors report being profoundly moved by
their experience of the landscape site, enough of
them to make this response an aspect of these Earthworks. Considering the psychological and physical
response of the viewer as part of the Earthwork is
similar to viewers' psycho-physical responses to
some Conceptual and Performance Art, such as Nauman's *Live/Taped Video Corridor* (see page 69) and
Acconci's *Seedbed* (see page 74).

De Maria temporarily located a smaller version
of his *Lightning Field* about 40 miles (64.4 km) outside of Flagstaff, Arizona, while he searched

throughout Arizona, California, Utah, and Texas before locating a permanent site in West-central New Mexico. Here he constructed the piece (Fig. **3.16**) between 1974 and 1977. *The Lightning Field*, which was commissioned and is maintained for public visiting by the Dia Center for the Arts, consists of a 1-mile (1.6 km) by 3,300 feet (1005.8 m) grid of 2-inch (5 cm) diameter stainless steel poles varying in height from 15 feet (4.6 m) to 26 feet 9 inches (8.2 m) (with their tips level), the poles spaced 220 feet (67 m) apart. Each pole is set into an underground concrete foundation and tipped with a solid stainless-steel cone. An iron bar within the hollow stainless-steel pole grounds the cone through the concrete foundation to the earth. Altogether, there are 400 poles. Their height and spacing conform to tolerances of fractions of an inch.

Desert light has a clarity and subtlety unlike the light of any other landscape. De Maria considers the various natural lighting conditions to be part of *The Lightning Field*. During the mid-day overhead sun the poles seem to nearly disappear; when the sun is low on the horizon, they take on a reddish glow. On very rare occasions when there is a strong electrical current in the air, a glow known as "St. Elmo's Fire" may be emitted from the tips of the poles, according to the artist.[31] During the thunder and lightning season, lightning that comes within 200 feet (61 m) of the poles is attracted to them.

The nearest town to *The Lightning Field* is Quemado, New Mexico. Through the Dia Center for the Arts office in New York, visitors can make arrangements to stay at a cabin on the site, refurbished as guest quarters. Only small groups are admitted, and the preferred visiting time is at least 24 hours, in order to observe a full range of light changes.

DENNIS OPPENHEIM

Dennis Oppenheim (born 1938) participated in the important *Earth Art* exhibition at Cornell University's Andrew Dickson White Museum of Art in 1969, along with Smithson, Morris, and others. Oppenheim's piece *Accumulation Cut* (Fig. **3.17**) was a path cut through ice on the lake, then pushed over the falls. The artwork lasted only as long as it took for the lake water to freeze again. Many of Oppenheim's Earth-

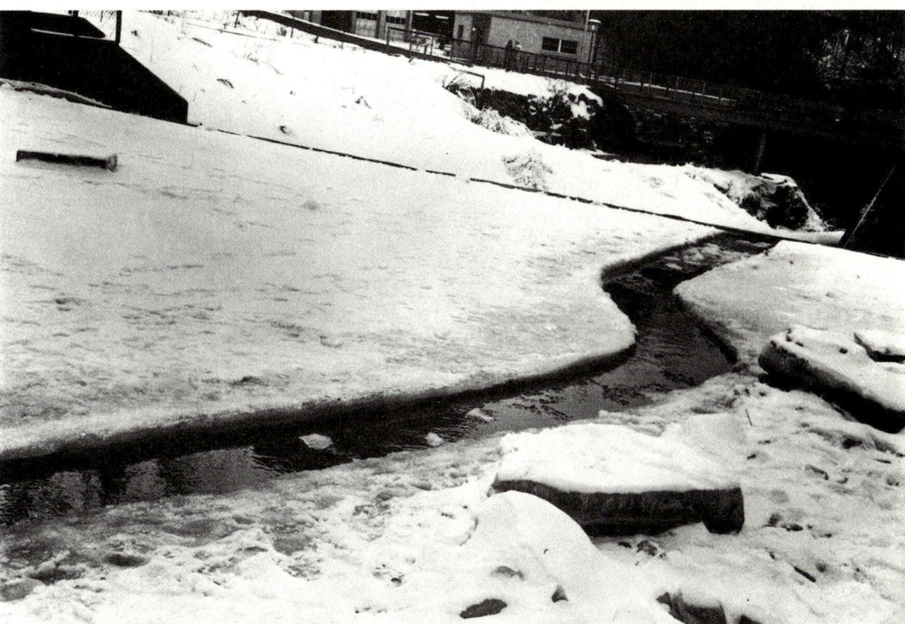

3.17 DENNIS OPPENHEIM
Accumulation Cut 1969
Location: Ithaca, New York
4 × 100ft (1.2 × 30.5m) cut
made perpendicular to
frozen waterfall
Equipment: Gasoline
powered chain saw. 24 hours
required to refreeze
Courtesy of the artist

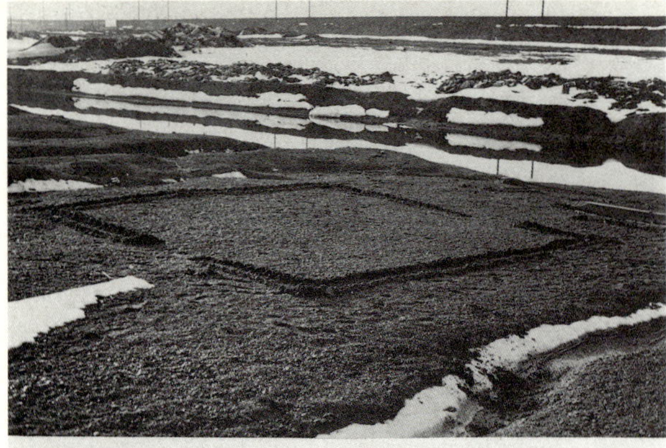

GALLERY TRANSPLANT. 1969.
Floor specifications Gallery #3, Stedelijk Museum, Amsterdam, transplanted to
Jersey City, New Jersey. Surface: Snow, dirt, gravel. Duration: 4 weeks.

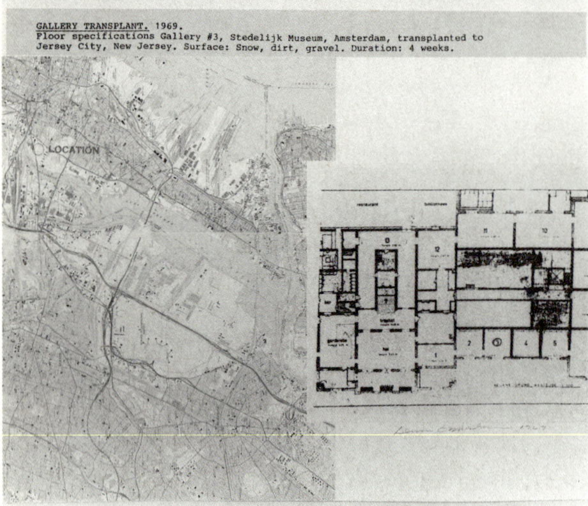

3.18 DENNIS OPPENHEIM
Gallery Transplant 1969
Floor specifications Gallery
#3, Stedelijk Museum,
Amsterdam, transplanted to
Jersey City, New Jersey
Surface: Snow, dirt, gravel
Duration: 4 weeks
Photodocumentation.
Photography and text 60 ×
40ins (152.4 × 101.6cm)
Courtesy of the artist

3.19 DENNIS OPPENHEIM
Directed Seeding
April, 1969
Reduced route to Nieuwe
Schans plotted on a
505ft 3ins × 876ft (154 ×
267m) field and used to
dictate seeding pattern for
common wheat
Courtesy of the artist

works were temporary, taking a more permanent form only in photographs or other documentation.

At the time Oppenheim said, "I'm to the point now where I see the earth as a sculpture—where flying over the earth is like viewing existing painted areas or pictorial, painterly surfaces. While on the ground it is more volumatic (sic). It's like walking through sculpture."[32]

Gallery Transplant (Fig. **3.18**) utilizes a photograph, a map, and an architectural floor plan; three types of documentation, all of which represent locations. Joseph Kosuth's earlier Conceptual Art work, *One and Three Chairs* (1965) (see page 50), represents three different manifestations of the same object, while Oppenheim documents three different locations of the same space: galleries of the Stedelijk Museum in Amsterdam, a map showing the transplant's location, and a photograph of the gallery's floorplan drawn in earth. In this case the documentation functions as the artwork, not merely as a signifier of it.

Directed Seeding—Wheat (Fig. **3.19**) was another temporary Earthwork. Oppenheim instructed the farm equipment operator to seed a field in Holland according to a pattern that reiterates the topography. During the crop's growth period the Earthwork continued to change and evolve; after the harvest, it ceased to exist.

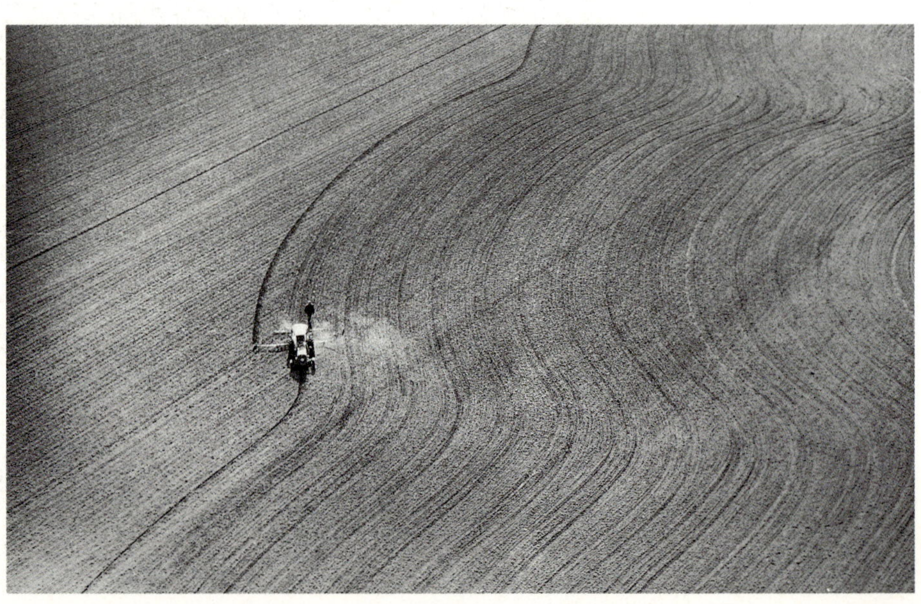

ROBERT MORRIS

Robert Morris's *Observatory* (Fig. **3.20**)—constructed for Sonsbeek '71—aligns with the sunrise on the equinoxes and on the winter and summer solstices. (It was demolished after the exhibition, but recreated in 1977 at a different site in Holland.) *Observatory* consists of two concentric earthen rings. The inner-ring made of earth piled up against a wooden stockade. The outer-ring consists of three embankments and a canal. Entrance to the complex is gained through a triangular opening which aligns with an opening in the inner-ring. Three other openings in the inner-ring face notches in the outer embankment made by two steel plates. These three notches align with the sun's positions.

The alignment with planetary movements of Stonehenge (1800–1400 BC) in England suggests a parallel, though Morris at the time was more interested in South American precedents. Many ancient cultures, such as the Aztecs, Incas, and Egyptians, constructed sculptural/architectural monuments aligned with the sun, the moon, and the stars. Other contemporary artworks deal with astronomical observations, too: Nancy Holt's *Sun Tunnels* (see page 99) and James Turrell's *Roden Crater Project* (see page 105) for example.

3.20 ROBERT MORRIS
Observatory 1970–77
Location: Oostelijk
Flevoland, Holland
View 4, earth, wood
and granite
Diameter 298ft 6ins (91m)
Courtesy Castelli, New York

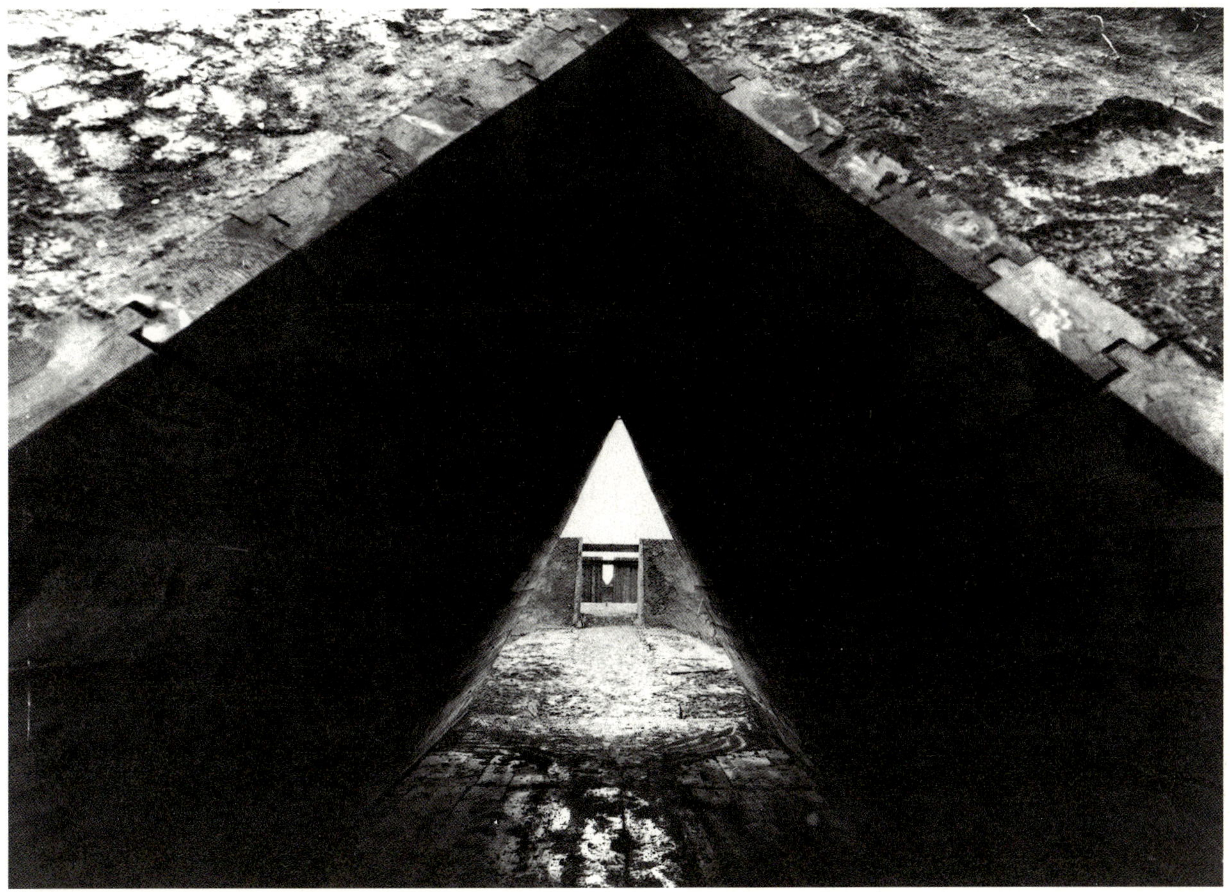

"It seems a truism at this point that the static, portable indoor art object can do no more than carry a decorative load that becomes increasingly uninteresting," Morris wrote in 1971.[33] Writing in 1977 about the Nazca Indian line drawings in the Peruvian coastal desert, Morris stated: "Yet common to this ancient drawing and certain recent work is an obsession with space as a palpable emptiness: for the Indians an indeterminate exterior, and in the 1970s, an interior, a bounded void, a recaptured absence."[34] And "One can speculate that the lines in the desert were spiritual irrigation systems connecting certain places of power in the surrounding sierra to the lower plains."[35] All three statements show Morris searching for transcendent alternatives to Minimalism's concern with perceptual phenomena rooted in the viewer's experience of the art object.

An undercurrent of hesitant longing toward transcendence runs throughout many Earthworks as artists seek to break free of contemporary art's entrenchment in purely visual experiences. Earthwork artists, however, never personified nature, or treated it pantheistically, metaphorically, allegorically, or as a narrative: these avenues were not open to them, having been exhausted for the moment. Instead, in the case of *Observatory* and related Earthworks, an aspect of nature is "framed," isolated for recognition and contemplation. The Earthwork becomes a gateway to a renewed perception of something outside it, if not to that loaded concept "nature," to something resembling it.

RICHARD SERRA

Richard Serra and a companion spent five days walking the two sloping hills of *Shift* (Fig. **3.21**) before deciding where to locate the various elements.

We discovered that two people walking the distance of the field opposite one another, attempting to keep each other in view despite the curvature of the land, would mutually determine a topological definition of the space. The boundaries of the work became the maximum distance two people could occupy and still keep each other in view.... What I wanted was a dialectic between one's perception of the place in totality and one's relation to the field as we walked.... I'm not interested in looking at sculpture which is solely defined by its internal relationships.[36]

Serra determined the direction and length of the six concrete planes according to the slope of the land, following the maximum decline until reaching a 5-feet (1.5 m) drop in elevation. The highest point of each concrete plane is 5 feet (1.5 m), or approx-

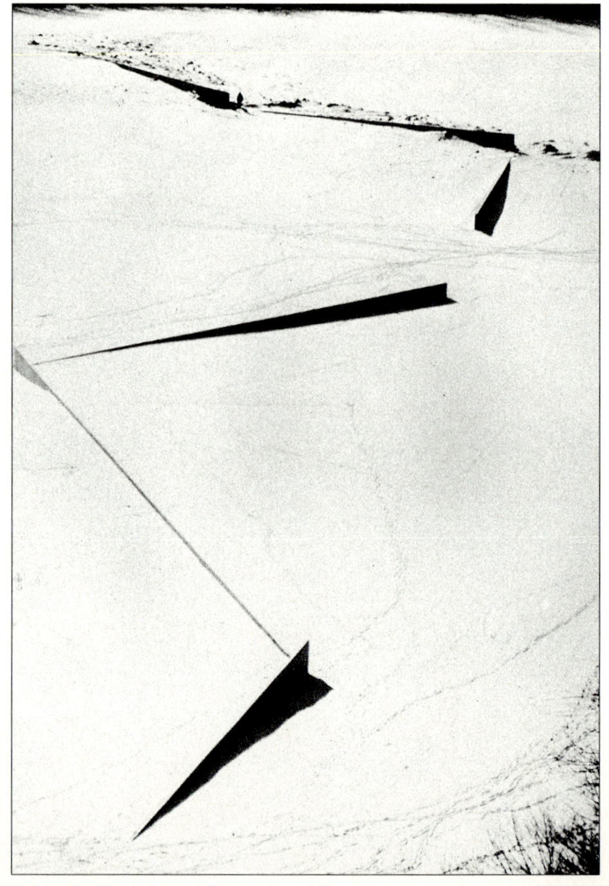

3.21 RICHARD SERRA
Shift 1970–72
Courtesy Leo Castelli Gallery, New York
"What I wanted was a dialectic between one's perception of the place in totality and one's relation to the field as we walked ... I'm not interested in looking at sculpture which is solely defined by its internal relationships."[37]

imately eye-level, so the piece never completely blocks one's view. Altogether, there are six concrete planes, an equal number on each of two hills that slope toward each other. The planes are like markers measuring the hills' topography, guiding one in walking the land. "The intent of this work is an awareness of physicality in time, space and motion," Serra wrote.[38]

Shift parallels Serra's other portable and site-specific sculpture (see pages 72–73) in its concern for space and volume, but its remote rural location (in King City, Canada) and its having been, in effect, deduced from the natural topography, make it unique in his work. It is a site-specific sculpture and an Earthwork in the sense that its configuration was determined by the landscape's topography. The relationship between time, space, and volume also figures prominently in Serra's other work. In *Shift*, the time it takes for one to walk the landscape determines one's experience of space, the cumulative effect of which constitutes the sculpture's volume. In Serra's other art, the element of time has more to do with the process of making the artwork itself than with the viewer's time in experiencing it. Like many Earthworks, the sense of time in *Shift* relates to the time of certain video installation and performance artworks in that the emphasis is on the duration of the viewers' experience rather than the artist's or the artwork's.

NANCY HOLT

Nancy Holt (born 1938) received a BS degree from Tufts University, Massachusetts in 1960 before moving to New York. She has lived and worked there ever since, and it was there that she married Robert Smithson in 1963. She built *Sun Tunnels* (Fig. **3.22**) in a remote desert location outside Lucin, Utah (population ten) near the Nevada border. The local people believed that the land was useless because it did not have enough vegetation either for grazing or for botanical interest, and because it had no minerals or shade, and no water on the site. Like Smithson, Holt liked the idea that she gave a use to land which had been deemed useless. She looked in Arizona, New Mexico, and Utah before finding the appropriate site: flat desert surrounded by low mountains. Another con-

3.22 NANCY HOLT
Sun Tunnels 1973–76
Location: NW Utah Desert
Total length 86ft (26.2m)
Tunnel 18ft (5.5m) aligned
with sunrise and sunset on
solstices (see page 100)
Courtesy John Weber Gallery,
New York
"From the center of the work,
the tunnels extend the
viewer visually into the
*landscape, opening up the
perceived space. But once
inside the tunnels, the work
encloses—surrounds—and
there is a framing of the
landscape through the ends
of the tunnels and through
the holes … I wanted to
bring the vast space of the
desert back to human
scale.*"[39]

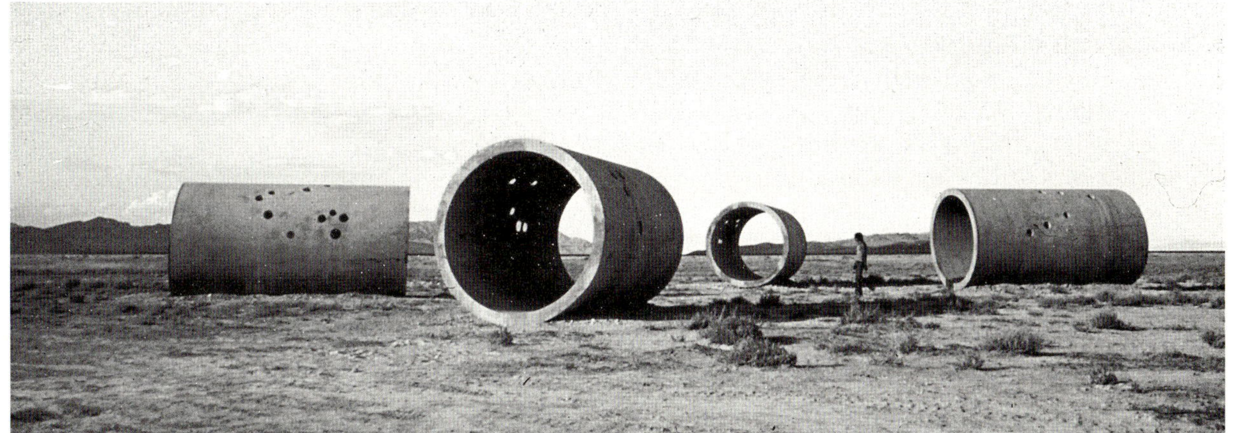

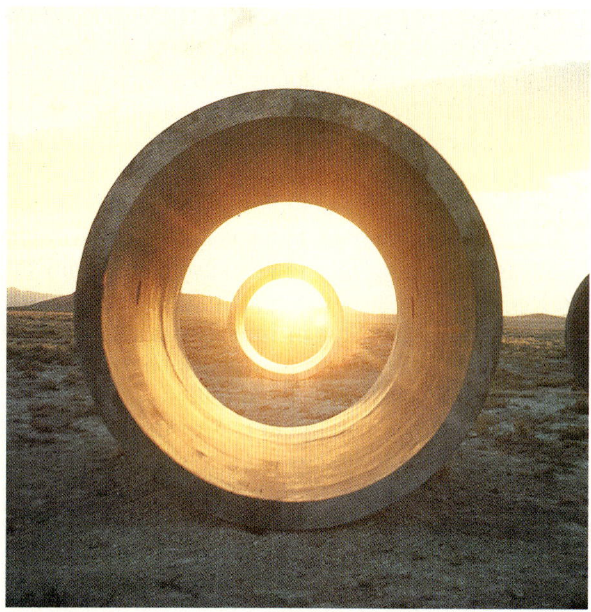

an outside diameter of 9 feet 2½ inches (2.82 m) and an inside diameter of 8 feet (2.44 m). Holes cut in the tunnel's sides correspond to the locations of stars in four constellations: Draco, Perseus, Columba, and Capricorn. Holt aligned two sets of two tunnels each with the winter and summer soltices of the sun—the most northern and most southern positions of the sun on the horizon. The light and temperature inside the tunnels change radically as the sun's and moon's positions go through their cycles. The alignment of the stars in the constellations also goes through alterations according to the season. Holt sought the clear light of the desert and the desert's open spaces in order to isolate the experiences of light and of the planets' and stars' movements, which are the *Sun Tunnels*' subject.

Framing and isolating particular elements of a site figures in Holt's earlier and subsequent work. She describes the framing effect of *Sun Tunnels*:

The panoramic view of the landscape is too overwhelming to take in without visual reference points. The view blurs out rather than sharpens. Through the tunnels, parts of the landscape are framed and come into focus. I chose the diameter, length, and distance between the tunnels based on the proportions of what could be seen of the sky and land, and how long the sun could be seen rising and setting on the solstices.[40]

sideration was the size of the plot, because the usual unit of land sales in the western deserts is one square mile (2.59 sq km). In the Utah deserts Holt found 40 acres (161,876 sq m) of the topography she needed.

Sun Tunnels consists of four steel-reinforced concrete tubes each measuring 18 feet (5.5 m) long with

MARY MISS

Mary Miss was born in New York in 1944, received a BA degree from the University of California, Santa Barbara in 1966 and an MFA degree from the Maryland Institute College of Art in 1968. She lives and works in New York City. Her *Blind* (Fig. **3.23**) may be more of a "sited" sculpture than a "site-specific" one, though the distinction is one that entails subjective judgment. The term, "site-specific" designates sculptures that are not merely "non-portable," but that also derive at least part of their form from their particular site. The configuration of Richard Serra's *Shift* (see page 98), for example, would be different it if were sited at a different location. Nancy Holt claims that the *Sun Tunnels* are site-specific—they certainly depend upon open space and a particular clarity of light, but

whether that space and light could be obtained at a different site is an open question. Mary Miss's *Blind*, however, could be built elsewhere without appreciably changing the artist's intent, as could Alice Aycock's *Low Building with Dirt Roof (for Mary)* 1973 (see facing page) and Christo's *Running Fence* (see page 102) (1976). These latter three works may be more "sited" sculpture than "site-specific."

Mary Miss characterizes her art as, "the experimental fringe of architecture as much as of art,"[41] a description which aptly applies to *Blind*. The title refers to the effect Miss's configuration has on the viewer: as one descends into the various levels of the artwork's underground concentric rings, one's perception of the surrounding landscape is in-

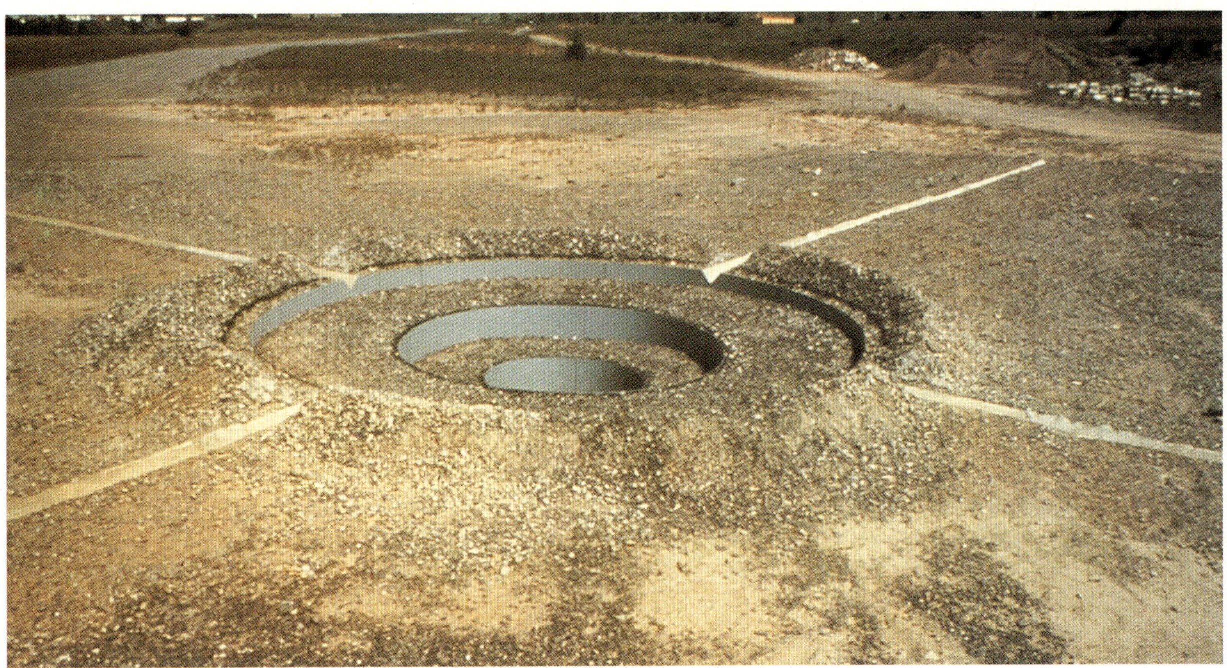

3.23 MARY MISS
Blind 1976
Location: Artpark, Lewiston,
New York
Steel, concrete, crushed rock
140ft (42.7m) across, 81ft
(24.7m) deep
Courtesy of the artist

creasingly "blinded" until it is completely blocked. Four "v"-shaped channels permit views somewhat like looking down a gun-sight. Her work is architectural in that it involves the viewer moving through three-dimensional space and experiencing the work through time, yet it is sculptural in that the space and time articulation have a purely artistic goal rather than the more functional goals of architecture.

ALICE AYCOCK

Like Mary Miss, Alice Aycock (born 1946) combines architecture and sculpture in original ways. *Low Building with Dirt Roof (for Mary)* (Fig. **3.24**) resembles the partially underground dwellings built by frontier settlers in the Midwest, yet it was not built for habitation. It also suggests a less grand version of an architectural memorial like a miniature Greek temple mausoleum. But its function is to embody Aycock's personal experiences from her past and to restructure

3.24 ALICE AYCOCK
Low Building with Dirt
Roof 1973
Location: Gibney Farm, New
Kingston, Pennsylvania

Wood, stone, earth
12 × 20ft
(3.7 × 6.1m)
Courtesy John Weber Gallery,
New York

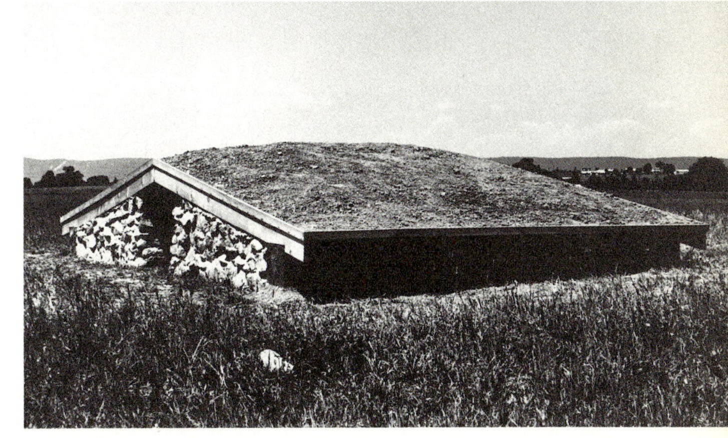

them as myths, thus evoking a narrative out of a particular place and its surrounding circumstances.

Aycock wrote about *Low Building with Dirt Roof (for Mary)*:

About 15 years ago I visited the house in which my great-great grandparents, Benjamin and Serena, lived and where my great grandfather, Francis, was born. It was a small wood-frame house. I climbed alone into the attic where they slept and stood under the rafters. In the yard was the family cemetery. I remember the tombstone of Catherine, who died at age three. Years later I had the dream. My brother Billy came for me and took me to that same wooden house set into the hills of Greece like a tholos tomb. I climbed the stairs again and behind a screen a young girl whose face I could not see lay dead. Then sometime after that I built the Low Building with Dirt Roof (for Mary).[42]

CHRISTO

Christo (born in Bulgaria in 1935 and who uses only his first name) works alone in his studio without assistance an average of 15 hours a day. Unlike Christo many artists, from Minimalism to the present, are "post-studio": in other words, they work in factories or at other sites rather than in studios. Christo considers all the extensive litigation, real estate negotiating, labor management, work force recruitment, and construction supervision involved in building a project like *Running Fence* (Fig. **3.25**) to be part of the artwork.

Running Fence traversed 24–1/2 miles (39.43 km) of rolling Californian countryside north of the Golden Gate Bridge in Sonoma and Marin counties. Made of 18 feet (5.5 m) high nylon panels stretched between steel poles, it crossed the properties of 59 different landowners. The project employed 480 people, cost the artist more than three million dollars to construct, and was in place for only two weeks. Christo financed it through the sale of his drawings. When it was complete, *Running Fence* was discussed on all

3.25 CHRISTO
Running Fence 1972–76
Location: Sonoma and Marin Counties, California
Erected 1976
Woven nylon fabric and steel
cables
height 18ft (5.5m) × 24½ miles (39.43km) long
© Christo 1976
Photo Wolfgang Volz

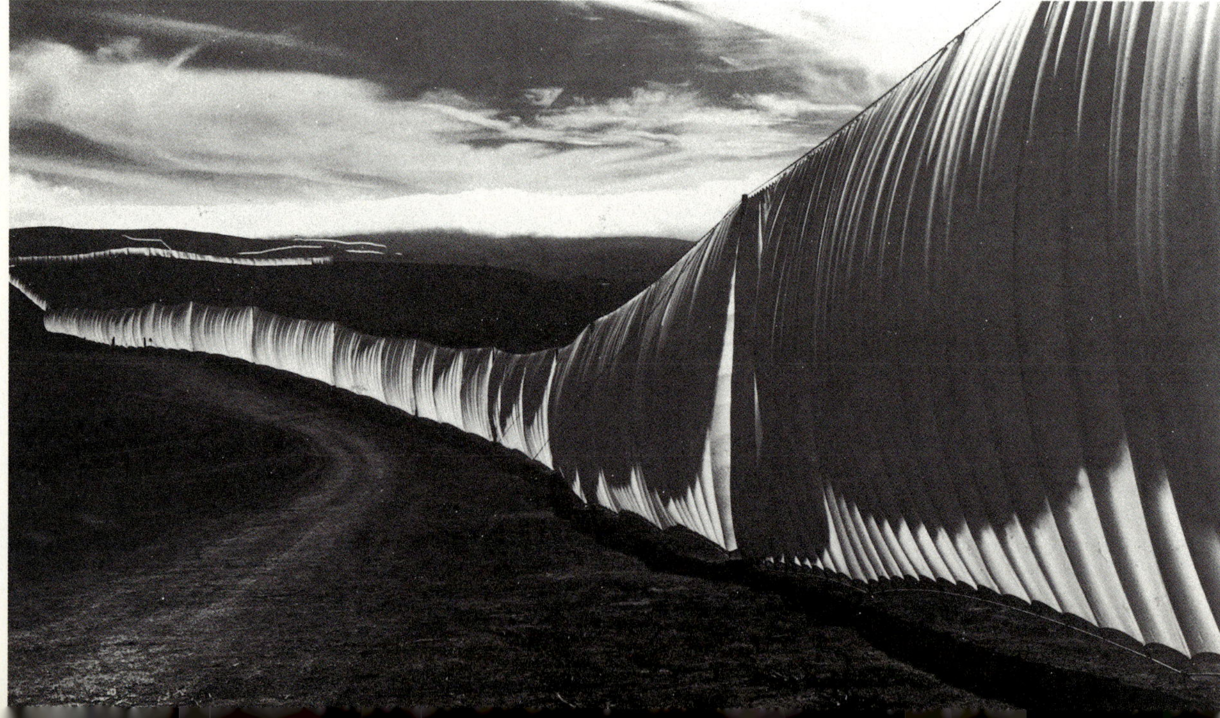

three national television network's nightly news. A local newspaper, the *Tomales Bay Times*, enthused: "A wonderful pandemonium of tourists, press, workers, monitors, passing motorists, cyclists and locals shared the blazing hot sun making this the theater event we all knew it really was."[43]

Populist showmanship pervades Christo's art so much that he has been accused of being more of a theatrical entertainer than serious visual artist. His art is certainly very photo- and telegenic, and it is so easily comprehensible that it appeals to mass audiences. Whether or not this perception is considered a criticism of Christo's art depends upon how flexible one is willing to be. The least that can be said is that Christo defines the role of an artist and his relationship to his audience in a completely original way.

ROBERT IRWIN

Robert Irwin (born 1928) first painted in a style loosely derived from Abstract Expressionism between 1957 and 1961; then gradually reduced his pictorial means to two painted lines on a colored field or a dot pattern between 1961 and 1967; and finally, between 1967 and 1969 painted aluminum or plastic, slightly convex discs held out from the wall on an 18-inch (45.7 cm) plexiglass tube and illuminated by four Sylvania flood lights, two from above and two from below. The positioning of the lights creates clover-leaf-like shadows which Irwin considers part of the artwork; he painted the curving discs in shaded values that make both them and the shadows appear touchable.

Untitled (Fig. **3.26**) is inseparable from the space it occupies. Where does the artwork end and the space begin? Irwin precisely defines the viewing conditions and requires that the space be completely neutralized, with no visual distractions. Given these conditions, his discs possess an extraordinary presence. They elicit acute perception of light and space, directing perception away from the painted objects themselves and into their surrounding conditions.

Art critic John Coplans wrote in the catalogue for an exhibition of Irwin's discs at the Pasadena Art Museum in 1968:

The result of the cross illumination combined with the ambient light is that the shadow, the disc, and the outer area of the illumined wall are seen as an entity. Thus the three elements—wall, shadow, and painted disc—are equally positive; the shadow, in fact, sometimes becomes almost more positive than the disc.[44]

"What happened is that the discs resolved that one simple question—how to paint a painting that doesn't begin or end at the edge—by more or less transcending painting…. After the discs, there was no reason for me to go on being a painter," Irwin explained.[45] And so in 1970 he got rid of his studio and sold his tools and art supplies and thought about what to do next.

Excursions into the Southwest's deserts (Irwin then lived in Los Angeles; he now lives in a highrise in Las Vegas, where he enjoys the desert light) led Irwin to realize that what he was really interested in was light, especially when it could be perceived as palpable, the way it appears under certain desert conditions. Light is more clear and more present in the desert, where there is little else to distract from it, than anywhere else. The perception of light and its relationship to space became Irwin's subjects.

For his 1977 retrospective exhibition at New York's Whitney Museum of American Art, Irwin stretched a scrim (a light woven cloth that captures light) across the center of the huge fourth-floor gallery from about eye-level up, marked the lowest edge of it with a black line and repeated the black line at the same eye-level on the peripheral walls. The scrim made the light appear sometimes as a foggy mass that was difficult to visually locate on a specific visual plane, or from some angles the scrim appeared nearly transparent. Light on the scrim filled the gallery with an atmospheric haze that transformed the space. Combined with the black lines, which gave the false impression of a systematic and objective outline of the space, the result was a strangely affecting heightened perception of that particular light and space. Laurence Weschler wrote in 1982:

As you walked around the space, under the scrim, into the corners, along the walls, the room itself

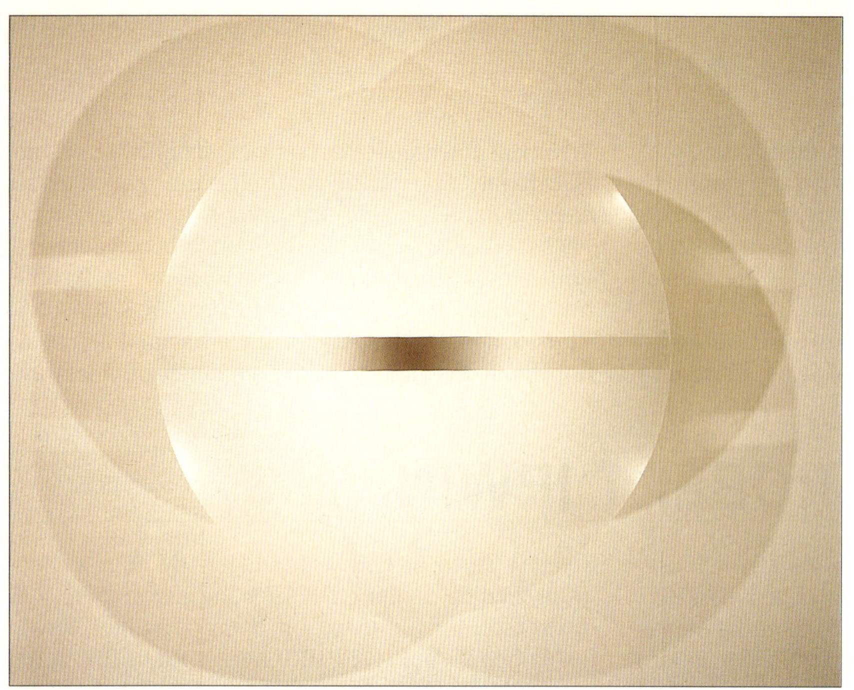

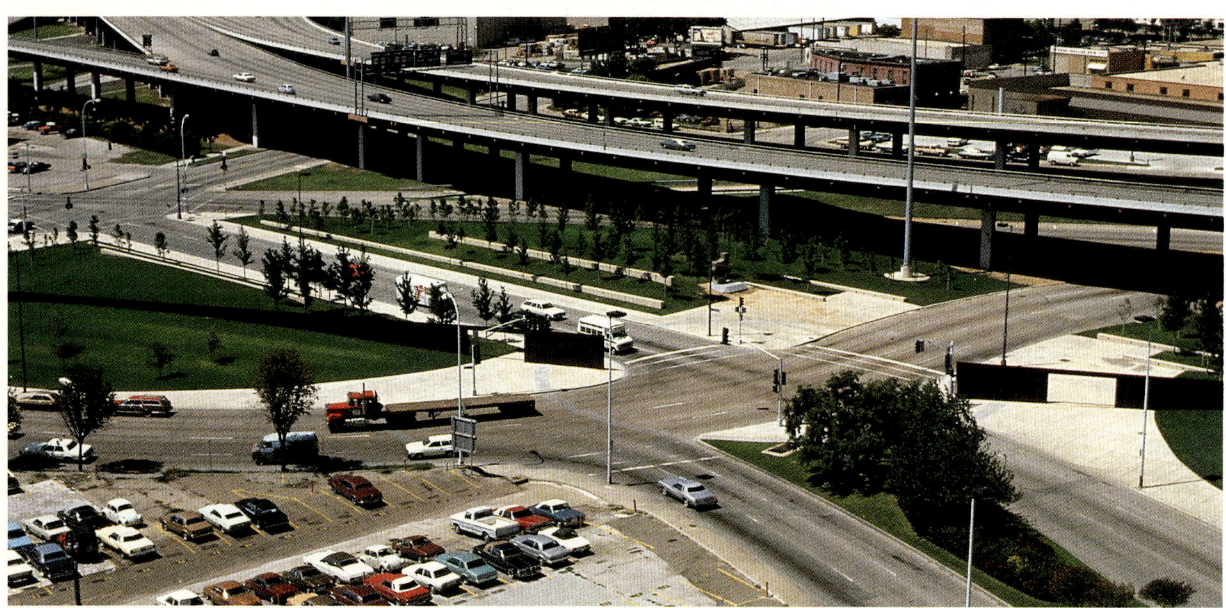

seemed to hum. Things that had always been there—the even, modular hive of the ceiling, the dark rectangular grid of the floor—you noticed as if for the first time. There was a sense of great excitement in all of this, but at the same time an evenness, a lightness, almost a serenity.[47]

Following the Whitney show, Irwin returned to making less ethereal artworks, but he maintained his interest in articulating light and space. Wanting to work outside of the traditional art contexts of galleries and museums, Irwin applied to various public art projects. Writing in 1985, he made four basic distinctions between various site-related artworks:

1. Site dominant. ... *monuments, murals, etc. ... A Henry Moore would be an example of site dominant art.*
2. Site adjusted. ... *Here consideration is given to adjustments of scale, appropriateness,*

placement, etc. But the "work of art" is still either made or conceived in the studio and transported to, or assembled on, the site. . . .

3. Site specific. *Here the "sculpture" is conceived with the site in mind; the site sets the parameters and is, in part, the reason for the sculpture. . . .*

4. Site conditioned/determined. *Here the sculptural response draws all of its cues (reasons for being) from its surroundings. This requires the* process *to begin with an intimate, hands-on reading of the site. This means sitting, watching, and walking through the site, the surrounding areas (where you will enter from and exit to), the city at large or the countryside. . . .*[48]

This latter definition—site conditioned/determined—applies to Irwin's *Portal Park Slice* (Fig. **3.27**) in Dallas. The site included various parcels of vacated land adjoining freeway entrances and exits. Irwin described the site as a "dusty, abandoned jigsaw puzzle" and wrote that "whatever is proposed will need to be visible and effective at 30 miles (48 km) an hour."[49] Working in collaboration with an engineer and landscape architects, Irwin proposed a 700 feet (213.4 m) long Corten steel plane bisecting grassy mounds, interrupted by openings for traffic and pedestrians. Combined with the landscape design, the result is a unification of the complex space into a comprehensible whole.

Here Irwin has overlapped his art so much with the realms of engineering and landscape design that distinctions between them blur. This kind of collaboration that entails a redefinition of the art object and the artist's role characterizes much of the best "public art:" art made for—and conditioned by the mentality of the users of—public spaces. "Isn't the 'art object' actually understood as a distinct and special category of thing?," wrote Irwin. "What actually happens to what was once distinct and special when we fold it into the fabric of its circumstances? Into our daily lives? Gain and loss? Are you intrigued by the possibilities—or put off by the complexities?"[50] The extension of the art object to include the light and space which determines one's perception of it has taken another great leap to include all of the circumstances surrounding its making and its context, in the process redefining what the words "artist" and "artwork" mean.

JAMES TURRELL

James Turrell (born 1943) has been working with light and space since the mid-1960s when he used natural gas to create flat flames. Subsequently, he has used projected light to create perceptions of solid forms, cut openings in walls and ceilings to manifest different conditions of natural light in space, employed artificial light to create various perceptions of light's presence and, since 1975, has been designing and constructing a series of light observation spaces on and in a 500,000-year-old volcanic crater. "I'm interested in the weights, pressures, and feeling of the light inhabiting space itself and in seeing this atmos-

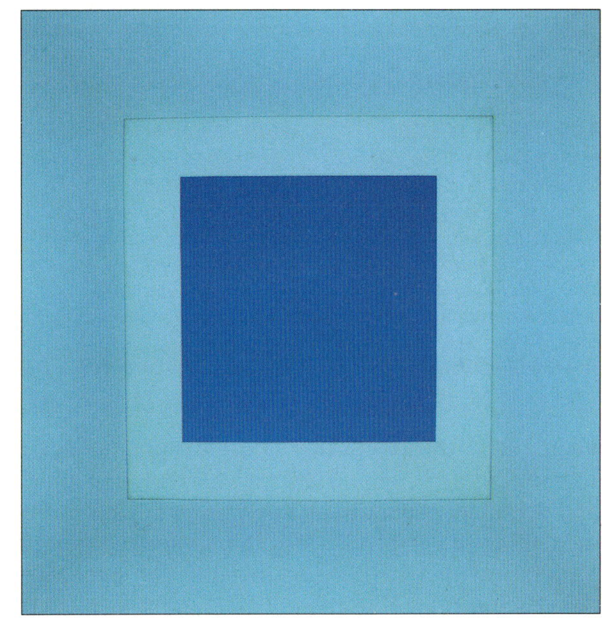

3.28 JAMES TURRELL
Skyspace I (twilight) 1976
Interior light and open sky
Collection Giuseppe Panza di
Biumo-Varese

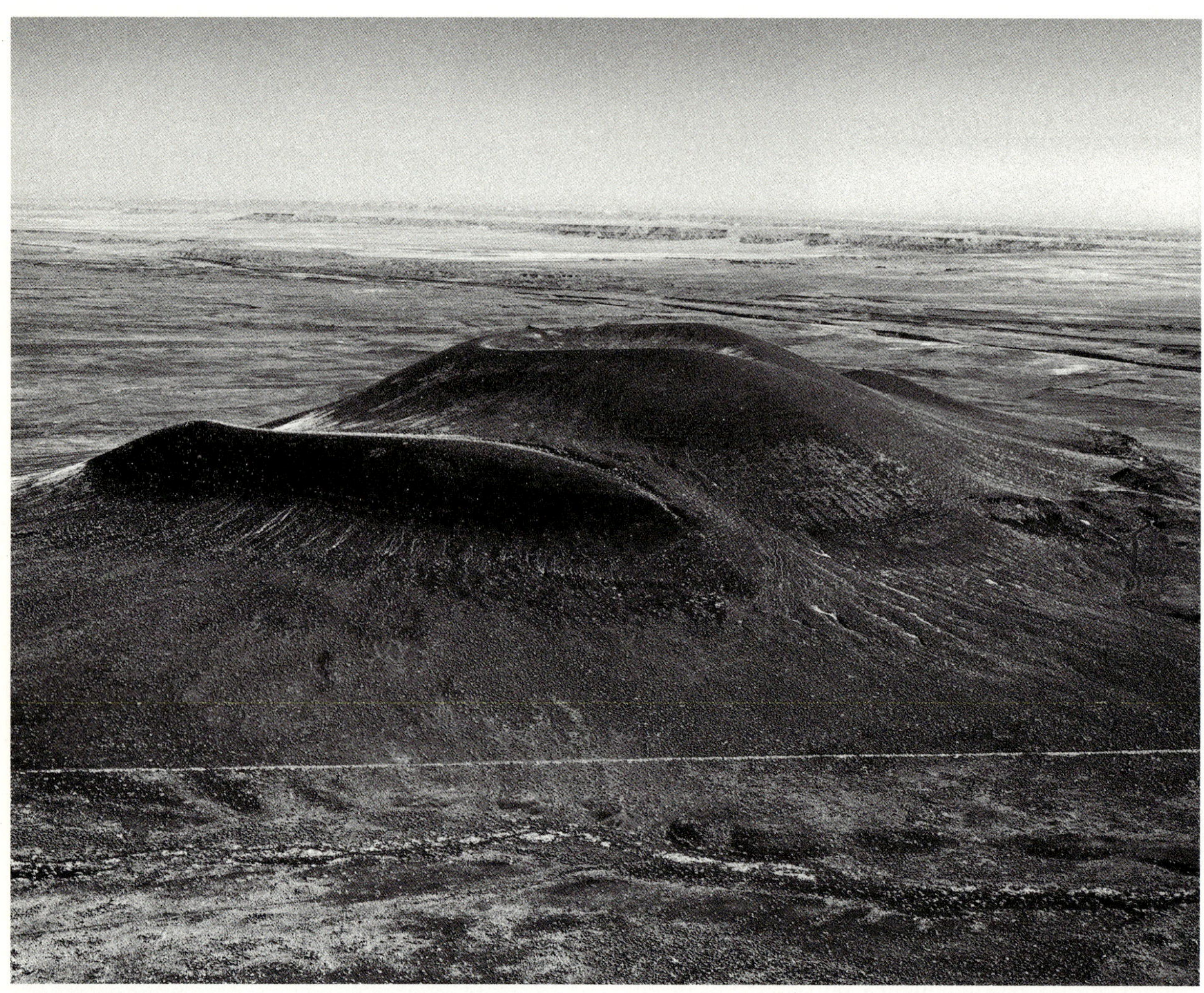

3.29 JAMES TURRELL
Roden Crater 1979
Location: Arizona
Courtesy Skystone
Foundation, Inc., Arizona
"By making something out of light with filling space, I am concerned with issues of how we perceive … In working with light, what is really important to me is to create an experience of wordless thought, to make the quality of sensation of light itself something really quite tactile … Light is not so much something that reveals, as it is itself the revelation."[52]

phere rather than the walls," Turrell explains.[51]

Skyspace I (Fig. **3.28**) is a neutral interior architectural space with an opening to the sky cut in the ceiling (it can be closed with a motorized cover). Turrell designed the opening to gather the light from the sky and bring it to the opening and the space, a description that sounds mysterious and incomprehensible but which, when experienced, is lucid and revelatory. The interior space is so completely neutral that one hardly notices it; the space functions as a container for the light. The light changes constantly in such subtle shifts that the demarcation points of each change are impossible to perceive, yet over a period of time (time is an essential component of Turrell's art) the light totally changes color and value. Light becomes so real that you feel as though you can almost touch it. In fact, in other works by Turrell people have actually leaned against openings and have fallen into them, the light seemed so tangible.

Turrell explains:

Light is a powerful substance. We have a primal connection to it. But, for something so powerful, situations for its felt presence are fragile. I form it as much as the material allows. I like to work with it so that you feel it physically, so you feel the presence of light inhabiting a space. I like the quality of feeling that is felt not only with the eyes. It's always a little bit suspect to look at something really beautiful like an experience in nature and want to make it into art. My desire is to set up a situation to which I take you and let you see. It becomes your experience. I am doing that at Roden Crater. It's not taking from nature as much as placing you in contact with it.[53]

During 1974 and 1975 Turrell flew his small private plane over the entire western United States, criss-crossing the space from the western slopes of the Rockies to the Pacific ocean and from Lake Louise and the Canadian border down into Chihuahua, looking for a suitable landscape site for a large outdoor work. He found what he wanted in northern Arizona, in the Painted Desert, about 50 miles (80.5 km) northeast of Flagstaff: a 500,000-year-old extinct volcanic crater with a base about 2½ miles (4 km) wide and a bowl more than 1200 feet (365.8 m) in diameter. From the Roden Crater one can see for miles into astounding landscapes manifesting geological time. The clear and intense desert light constantly shifts. Because of the clear desert air, the stars and other planets are brighter than perhaps anywhere else on earth. It took two years to convince the owners to sell the Roden Crater to Turrell. When they finally agreed to let him buy it, they were astounded to learn that he had no money. But Turrell subsequently raised the money. He had been working on the design for the *Roden Crater Project* since 1975.

When the *Roden Crater Project* (Fig. **3.29**) is finished some time in the 1990s, it will include numerous spaces designed to disclose aspects of light and space. The spaces will all be open to the exterior but will possess a sense of visual closure and will be of neutral design so as to manifest the light and space without distracting from them. Visitors will be admitted in groups of no more than four people, for a minimum of 24 hours at a time, so that a range of light and space perceptions over changing lighting conditions can be experienced. Turrell describes how subtle changes in the site can alter perceptions of light and space:

If you're standing on black sand in a moonless starry night, you will probably comprehend the deepest amount of visual space you can take in. But if you then walk to an area of white sand, starlight coming off the white sand will dramatically limit the amount of stars you see and thereby bring the space closer.[54]

Various spaces will align with different celestial events and the cardinal directions of the compass. One space that has been completed is the bowl of the crater, which Turrell spent several years laboriously reshaping with a bulldozer, moving thousands of tons of volcanic material to change the bowl's diameter and to even it out. The changes are barely perceptible in "before" and "after" photographs, but the change in light and space perception is dramatic.

Turrell wanted to maximize "celestial vaulting"—the perception of the sky being a dome or a vault over our heads. To determine the optimum dimensions that would maximize celestial vaulting, he visited many domes and amphitheaters, but none was as big as the crater. So he guessed 1200 feet (365.8 m) in diameter, spent years reshaping the volcano's bowl, and discovered that his hunch was correct. When you lie on your back toward the center of the bowl, where Turrell has built a small narrow ledge, and look at the bowl's rim upside down, it appears as though the entire sky emanates in a huge dome from the edges of the crater's bowl. You feel yourself in the center of an enormous sphere of space and light, a sensation that gives a profound feeling of wholeness.

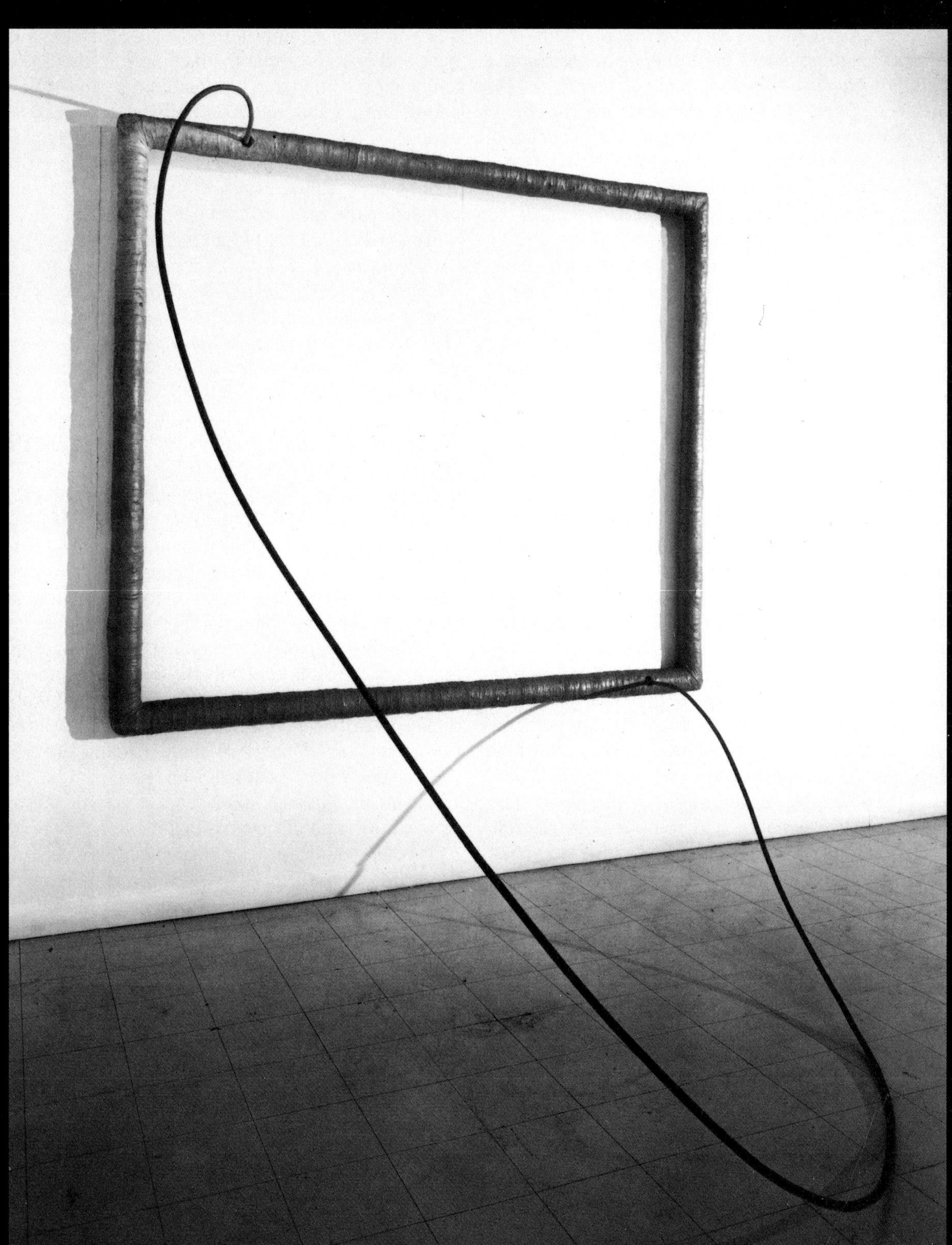

4
Post-Minimalism

"It is the most ridiculous sculpture I have ever made and that is why it is really good. It has a kind of depth or soul or absurdity of life or meaning or feeling or intellect that I want to get."[1]

—— EVA HESSE ——

Eva Hesse
Hang-Up   1966–67
Collection Art Institute of Chicago
Photograph courtesy Robert Miller Gallery, New York

Minimalism and Post-Minimalism

Robert Pincus-Witten—the art critic who invented the term—maintains that Post-Minimalism began in 1966, at almost the same time as Minimalism. An extremely rich decade for contemporary American art, the 1960s also saw the beginning of Color Field painting, Pop Art, Conceptual Art, Video, Performance, and Film Art, Earthworks and site-specific sculpture. Pincus-Witten wrote:

Certain aspects of Post-Minimalism are also readily seen to derive from Minimalism's essential reductive and analytical character, others less immediately so. The term, then, is useful in a broad way … a term covering a multitude of stylistic resolutions preceded and posited by an apparent generative style.[2]

Minimalism dominated the abstract art of the 1960s; Post-Minimalism derived many of its aspects from the parent style of Minimalism. Yet, a painting movement that originated in the 1940s—Abstract Expressionism—which was the antithesis of Minimalism's analytical deliberateness, figured as a prominent precedent to Post-Minimalism's early phases.

Many of the characteristics that Minimalists omitted from their art became central to Post-Minimalism. Where the Minimalists resolutely avoided representations of the human form, narration, allegory, or metaphor, the Post-Minimalists sought links between their artworks and extra-visual content. The Post-Minimalists countered Minimalism's hermeticism, autonomy, and rationalism with less stringent approaches which permitted a fuller range of responses than Minimalism's primarily formal preoccupations.

Two formal interests found parallel—if different—manifestations in both types of art: serial imagery and a concern for the inherent physical properties of materials. Serial imagery—especially from Minimalism but also from Warhol's Pop Art and from Color Field painting—was the most dominant

4.1 RICHARD SERRA
Splashing 1968
Lead, indeterminate dimensions
Courtesy Leo Castelli Gallery, New York

compositional device of the 1960s, which also carried on well into the 1970s. For the Minimalists the repetition of identical units always conformed to non-human-like forms and geometric norms, while the Post-Minimalists frequently favored connotations of human and organic forms. While the density and weight of steel, for example, might have been considered by a Minimalist like Carl Andre as central to a piece's aesthetic; more eccentric and, frequently, soft materials often occur in Post-Minimalism. Robert Morris's and Barry Le Va's felt (see pages 132 and 133), Eva Hesse's string and latex (see page 122), Keith Sonnier's latex and flocking (see page 125), and Richard Tuttle's unstretched canvas (see page 137) exemplify soft materials used by Post-Minimalists. Often, an eccentric material favored by a Post-Minimalist became a "signature" material—Lynda Benglis's poured latex, for example (see page 128).

Narrative content frequently occurs in Post-Minimalist art—not usually the story-telling kind, but narrative content related to a sequence of events in time, whether those events pertain to the artwork's making (such art has been called "process art") or to extra-visual meanings. Richard Serra's *Splashing* (Fig. **4.1**)—for which the artist melted lead and then splashed it against the join of a wall and floor where it cooled and solidified—both narrates its own mak-

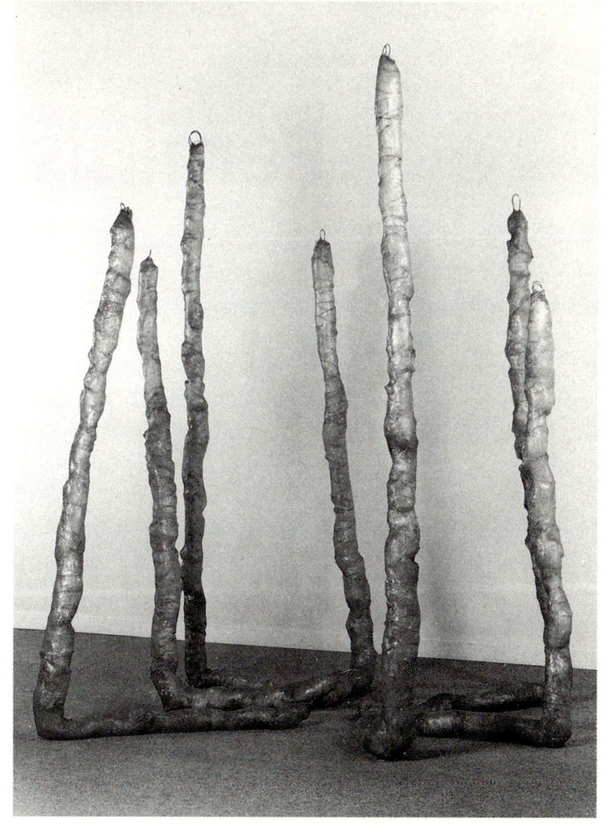

4.2 EVA HESSE
Untitled 1970
Fiberglass over polyethelene over aluminum wire
7 units each 74–111ins high × 10–16ins circumference
(188–282 × 25.4–40.6cm)
Photographie Musée National d'Art Moderne, Centre Georges Pompidou, Paris

4.3 JACKSON POLLOCK
Blue Poles 1952
Oil, enamel, aluminum paint, glass on canvas
6ft 11ins × 16ft
(210.4 × 486.8cm)
Collection Australian National Gallery, Canberra

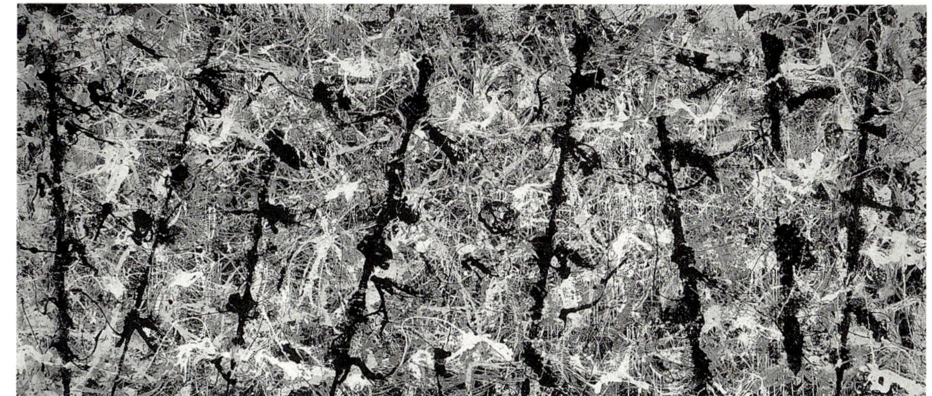

ing and refers to the Abstract Expressionist Jackson Pollock's (1912–56) famous "drip" style. Eva Hesse's *Untitled* (Fig. **4.2**) narrates the process of coiling the wire framework and layering the fiberglass skin on top of it, while also referring to Jackson Pollock. Her seven "poles" derive from the Abstract Expression-ist's huge painting, *Blue Poles* (Fig. **4.3**) made in 1952. Hesse's wormlike organic forms also connect the floor with the ceiling (they hang from above) and seem flexible while they are rigid, furthering sculpture's formal explorations in completely original and foresightful ways.

Feminist Content

The Minimalist's insistence on forms with an overriding unity contrasts another characteristic of Post-Minimalism: the latter artists often constructed artworks through a series of actions resulting in a part-by-part accumulation of elements. Sometimes the series of actions takes on a compulsive/obsessive complexion, such as Jackie Winsor's and Eva Hesse's wrapping of string, twine, wire, or cloth around other forms. The joining of one material or form with another results in an accretion which counters Minimalism's unitariness.

Wrapping also represents another feature of Post-Minimalism—the importance of the women's movement. Feminist issues first came to the fore during the late 1960s. Women, who had long been excluded from the all-male art world, made themselves more welcome than ever before, though they were admitted belatedly. The contemporary art world still however remains predominantly male—and white. From the late 1960s onward, women artists have begun to be recognized. For Eva Hesse, who died in 1970, it was a difficult struggle to gain recognition; in her journal she recorded frustration that her male peers achieved recognition more readily than she did.

Smithson and Mel [Bochner] described and highly praised my work. Necessary because 1) I am relatively unknown and 2) am woman. Am sure that exists for all, however. I must drop that thought as totally meaningless.[3]

Women artists in the late 1960s were acutely aware of their status. Like blacks in the civil rights movement of that time, women sought to make advantages out of their perceived differences from men. Wrapping represents "women's work" and formally narrates a difference between women's and men's roles. Women are usually the care-givers of a family. Wrapping connotes the bandaging involved in caring for the sick, as well as the emotional care-giving of enfolding, encircling, and protecting. While, historically, men's visual imaginations were

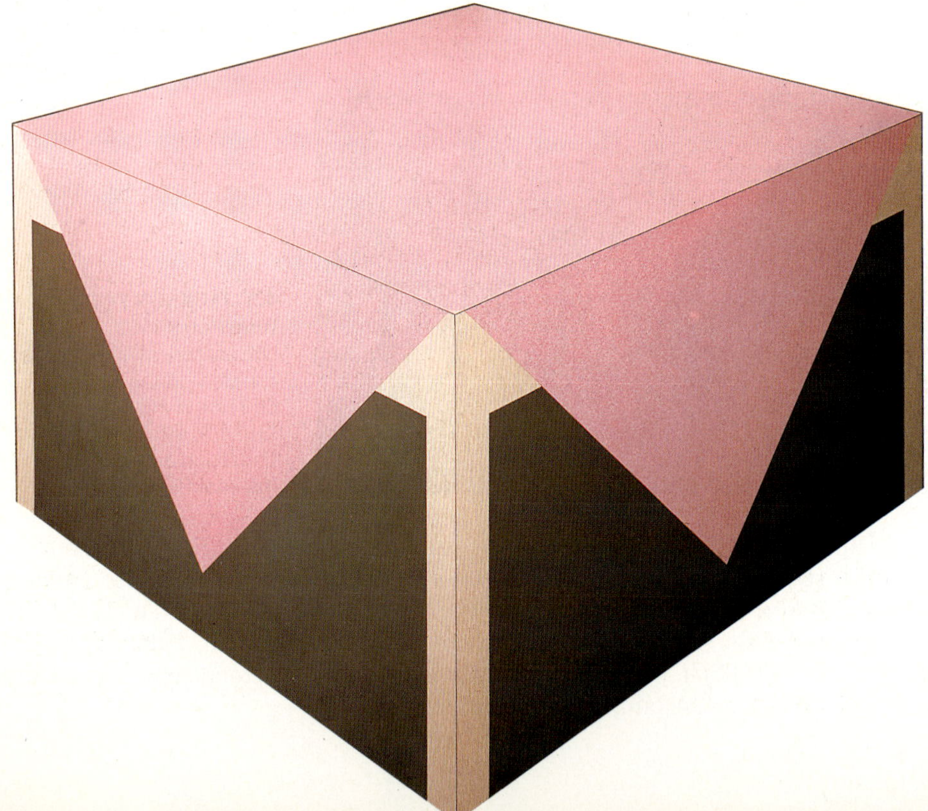

4.4 RICHARD ARTSCHWAGER Table with Pink Tablecloth 1964
Formica on wood
25½ × 44 × 44ins
(64 × 112 × 112cm)
Courtesy Saatchi Collection, London
"It's not sculptural. It's more like a painting pushed into three dimensions. It's a picture of wood. The tablecloth is a picture of a tablecloth. It's a multipicture."[5]

given expression in painting and sculpture, women were permitted expression through sewing, knitting, decorating, and other domestic handicrafts. Wrapping gifts, coiling balls of yarn, threading needles—actions associated with domestic handicrafts—these parallel the use of string, wire and strips of cloth that formed part of the process of artworks by Lynda Benglis and Eva Hesse (see pages 120–24), who deliberately employed the "women's work" connotations these actions and materials possess.

The growing consciousness of women's exclusion from the white male-dominated art world helped men to become more aware of how gender-specific art made by American men was. The macho scale of Jackson Pollock's drip paintings or of David Smith's welded steel sculpture suggests muscular burliness and dominating aggressiveness. Being the frontier culture that America is, America's earlier male artists responded to the threat of being considered over-sensitive or "feminine" by exaggerating the cliched aspects of their "masculinity." This exaggerated machismo could have been one of the features that Europeans perceived as being uniquely American about postwar American art. A greater awareness of this feature led male artists in the late 1960s to consider using materials formerly regarded as "feminine" and to employ a smaller and more delicate scale than they had in the past. Keith Sonnier's use of flocking and Joel Shapiro's dollhouse-like furniture sculptures (see page 140) are examples. The advent of the women's movement, therefore, and its resultant consciousness raising about gender-specific connotations, informed both women's and men's art from the late 1960s onward. This kind of content was frequently a considered and deliberate aspect of Post-Minimalism.

Precursors: Richard Artschwager and Lucas Samaras

Richard Artschwager and Lucas Samaras practiced aspects of Post-Minimalism before Minimalism became a completely mature style. Their adaption of Minimalism at the same time as its emergence was one of those many occasions in the history of art when artists simultaneously manifest ideas that are "in the air." Artschwager and Samaras lived in New York, where they were fully conversant with contemporary art developments. In the early 1960s, both artists charged what was to become Minimalism's "formal jargon" (to use Pincus-Witten's phrase) with highly individualistic, sometimes autobiographical content. Yet neither artist belonged to any group tendency; each was a hybrid, resolute artistic loner.

RICHARD ARTSCHWAGER

Richard Artschwager (born 1924) began his object making career as a furniture designer and craftsman, but when he was commissioned by the Catholic church "around 1960"[4] to design altars for ships, he realized that he was interested in making objects which transcend function. The ceremonial aspect of the altars excited him. He had drawn and painted previously but he had not made any sculptures. In 1965 Artschwager said:

It was formica which touched it off. Formica, the

4.5 RICHARD ARTSCHWAGER
Untitled (Construction)
1967
Formica-covered wood
48 × 72 × 12ins
(121.9 × 182.9 × 30.5cm)
Collection of San Diego
Museum of Contemporary Art

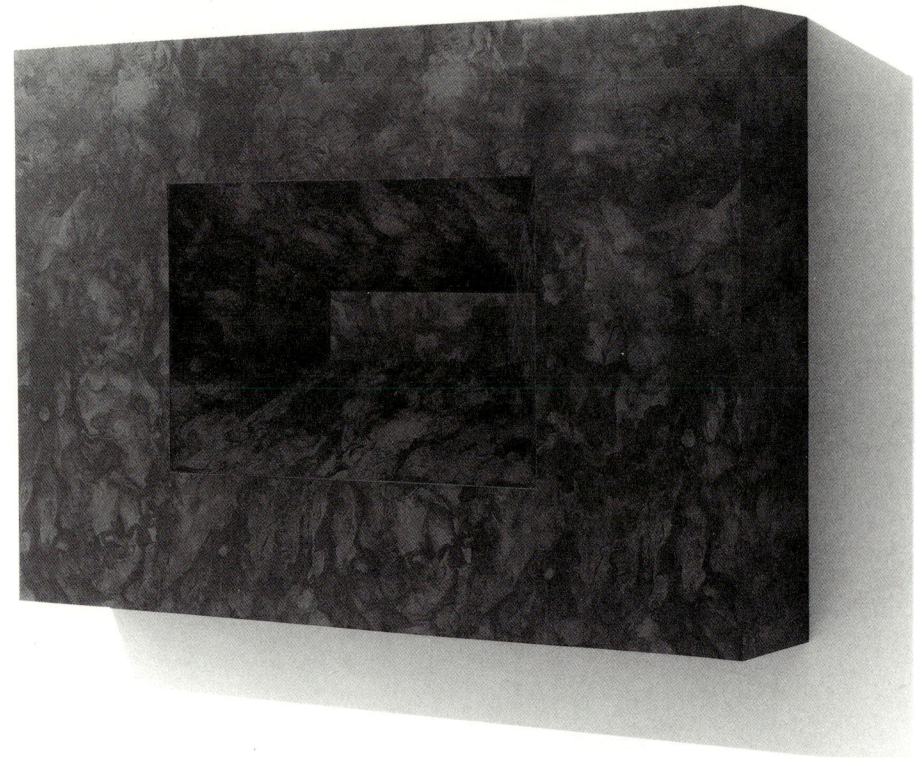

great ugly material, the horror of the age, which I came to like suddenly because I was sick of looking at all this beautiful wood.... So I got hold of a scrap of formica—something called bleached walnut. It worked differently because it looked as if wood had passed through it, as if the thing only half existed. It was all in black and white. There was no color at all, and it was very hard and shiny, so that it was a picture of a piece of wood. If you take that and make something out of it, then you have an object. But it's a picture of something at the same time it's an object.[6]

Artschwager had been using formica for several years before he said this in 1965. Since the late 1950s, Jasper Johns and Robert Rauschenberg, followed by the Pop artists, had been making art out of "picture(s) of something." Formica, being an aesthetically discredited "imitation" material, parallels the vinyl that Oldenburg used. Artschwager knew Oldenburg and each artist was aware of the other's work. (It was falsely rumored that Artschwager built Oldenburg's *Bedroom Ensemble*, 1963.) Making sculptures out of a material that was a "picture of something" is related to the Pop artists' use of imagery that was

twice removed from nature; and portraying everyday objects as sculpture likewise parallels Pop Art's ironic banality.

Artschwager's combination of painting and sculpture as in *Table with Pink Tablecloth* (Fig. **4.4**)—of a picture of something and a three-dimensional object—chronologically follows Rauschenberg's combines from the late 1950s and compares with Andy Warhol's 1964 *Brillo Boxes* (made of plywood silkscreened to look like actual cardboard boxes) and other early 1960s' representational painting/sculpture combinations. Throughout the 1960s there ran a counter-current to the Minimalists' and Color Field painters' preoccupation with strictly defining painting or sculpture, a counter-current which deliberately blurred distinctions between the two. Artschwager's art represents an important blurring of the boundaries between painting and sculpture in the early 1960s. Manifesting in sculpture what had formerly been regarded as qualities more appropriate for paintings became central to Post-Minimalism during its first stages between 1966 and 1970.

Artschwager not only blurs distinctions between

painting and sculpture but also blends aspects of Pop Art and Minimalism in his art. The reductive geometry that relates his sculpture to interior architectural space, which the reference to furniture furthers, ties in with Minimalism. But the use of illusionism, taken from painting, and of representation runs counter to Minimalism. Artschwager's *Untitled* (Fig. **4.5**) overlays formica patterned like burled walnut or tortoise shell onto a form like a window or a frame, but the window does not look out on anything and the frame does not contain a picture. Or do they? The rectangular shape within the "frame" reiterates the frame's proportions. Diagonal lines from each corner of this second rectangle lead to a third and smaller rectangle. The diagonal lines make a reference to the Renaissance painting convention of perspective, which was said to have enhanced illusionism to the extent of making paintings into "windows on the world." The formica, being a pic-

ture of something, is a picture within the frame. So we return to the question in which Artschwager takes perverse delight: What kind of object is this?

A curator at the Whitney Museum of American Art, Richard Armstrong, wrote in 1988: "For twenty-five years, Richard Artschwager has sought to alter the context of viewing by making pictorial sculpture and dimensional, space-occupying paintings."[7] In 1983 the art critic Coosje van Bruggen wrote: "By making visual perception the most important element of his work Artschwager rearranges our habits of seeing and, insidiously and in a paradoxical manner, displaces the visual meanings of his objects, ending up with something that is neither sculpture, nor painting, nor furniture."[8] The furniture aspect of Artschwager's art had a special influence on Post-Modernism in the 1980s, and the blending of painting and sculpture foreshadows this aspect of early Post-Minimalism.

LUCAS SAMARAS

"I find that I need to give others a sharp kick in their head's ass," Lucas Samaras wrote on the occasion of his retrospective at the Whitney Museum of American Art in 1972.[9] That "sharp kick in their head's ass" usually combines autobiography with an array of frequently disconcerting sensual responses—including eccentric eroticism—and the transformation of useful objects into threatening ones.

When he was a student at Rutger's University in the late 1950s Samaras (born 1936) knew Alan Kaprow, who taught there. After graduating, Samaras acted in Kaprow's first Happening (in the fall of 1959) and later also performed in Happenings by Oldenburg and Whitman (who had been a fellow student at Rutgers).

Oldenburg's preoccupation with metamorphosis and eroticism compares with Samaras's art, but with the important difference that autobiography is Samaras's only subject. Richard Bellamy, the owner of the Green Gallery where Samaras first showed his art in 1959, said:

I'd never had the experience before of knowing anyone who was so totally autotelic, self-engendered. That kind of narcissism that being so

extreme and so conscious becomes something else. He's turned all of what might be termed neuroticisms in his behavior to such conscious perfection that it's something quite other than bizarreness. He has made a consistent fabric of his personality; it's quite seamless.[10]

Art critic Kim Levin wrote:

Jars of beads, sequins, springs, lenses, and epoxy fingers are lined up in his studio like jars of dazzling pigments. They are his paints. Instead of turpentine Samaras uses glue, and the substances, finally, are all interchangeable skins that express the multiple alternates and reflections of a single object: himself.[11]

In 1961 Samaras covered 16 plywood squares with the amateur sculpture material, Sculpmetal, in a repulsively lumpy texture. He modeled the corners of four of the panels in higher relief than the rest. Arranging the squares with all four raised corners in the center makes the sculpture look as though it is trying to rise up; arranging the raised corners at the sculpture's edges makes it look as if you could trip over it. The textured surface of *Untitled* (Fig. **4.6**) looks very uncomfortable to walk on in bare feet, and the sculpture conveys an off-putting aggressiveness and argumentativeness that is consistent with Samaras's autobiographical art.

Samaras experimented with placing *Untitled* in various positions, including suspending it from the ceiling or hanging it on the wall, but settled for laying it directly on the floor without a base or pedestal. This arrangement predates Carl Andre's first floor piece by six years (see page 19). In 1972 Samaras wrote: "It was what it was without thinking about what it was and now it has relatives all over the pages of *Artforum*."[12] Yet it is typical of Samaras not to become focused on a formal issue, as Andre brilliantly did, but to remain fixated on manifesting his autobiography.

Other differences from what was to become Minimalism's formal vocabulary also occur in Samaras's art. A 1964 *Untitled* (Pin Cube) (Fig. **4.7**) resembles Minimalist Sol LeWitt's open cubes (see page 25), the

earliest of which dates from the same year. While LeWitt's open cubes are smoothly textured and appear to have been machine-made, Samaras's cube bristles with an obsessive encrustation of threatening pins. Like Artschwager's formica and Beuys's fat and felt, pins are a "signature" material for Samaras. In addition to their threatening and bristling aggressiveness, pins also have autobiographical meanings.

In a story called *Killman* which Samaras began writing while performing in Happenings (he never

4.6 LUCAS SAMARAS
Untitled 1961
Sculpmetal on wood
48 × 48ins
(121.9 × 121.9cm)
Collection of the artist
Courtesy Pace Gallery, New York

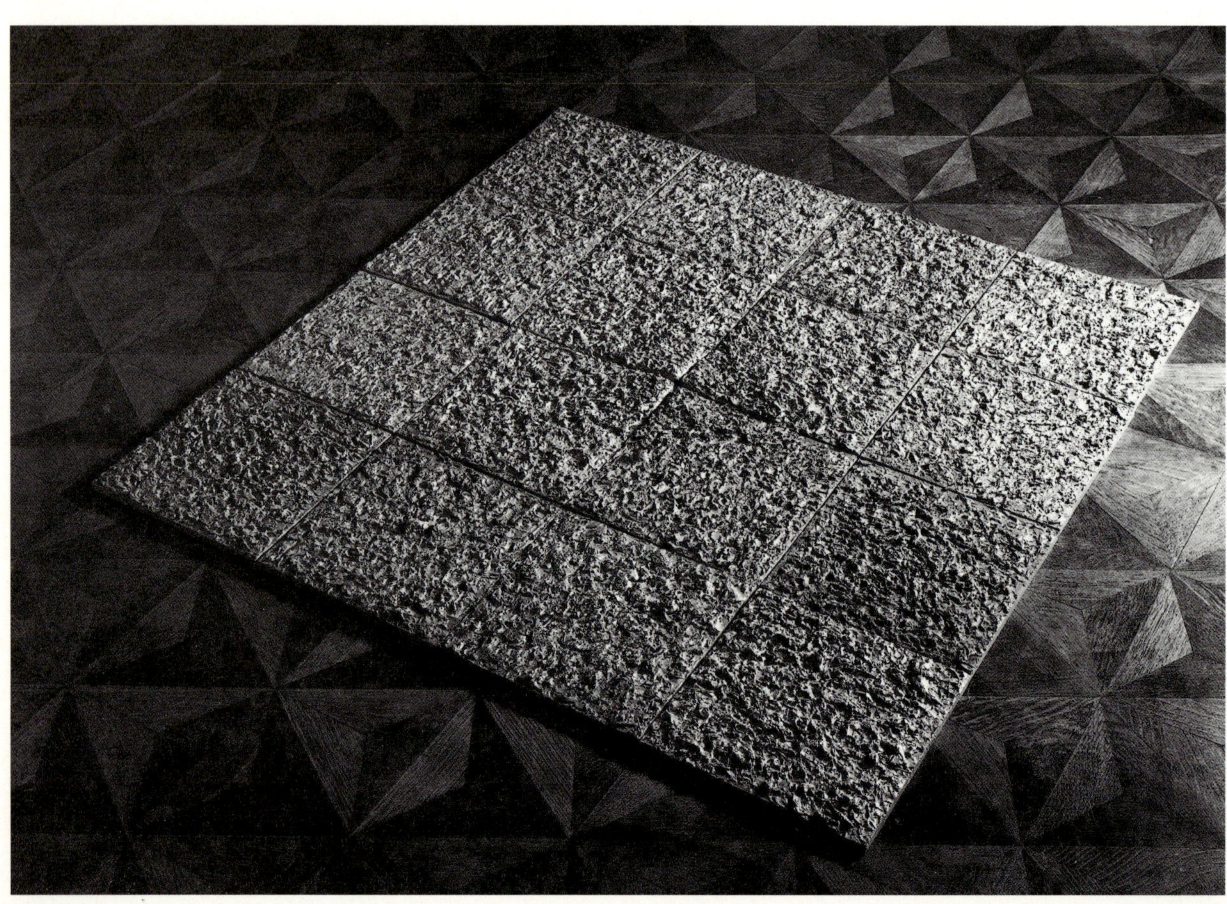

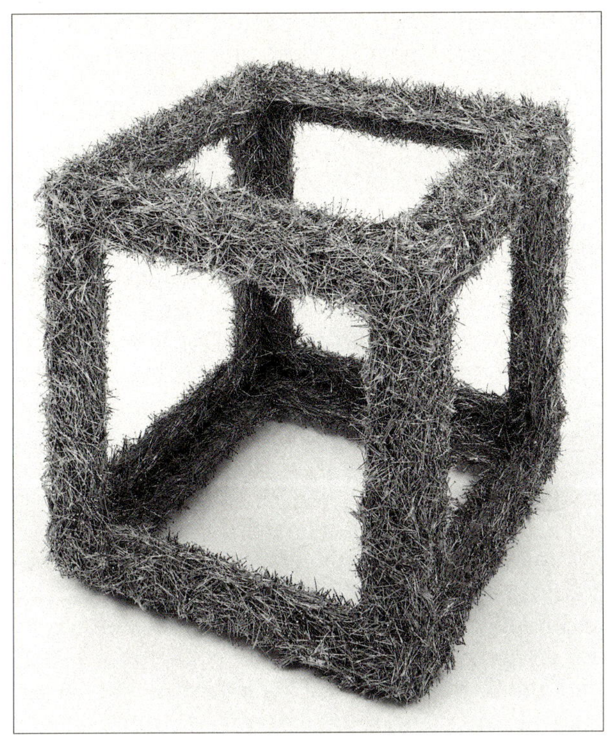

4.7 LUCAS SAMARAS
Untitled (Pin Cube) 1964
Pins on wood
18 × 18 × 18ins
(45.7 × 45.7 × 45.7cm)
Courtesy Pace Gallery, New
York

wrote Happenings of his own), Samaras wrote: "He lived in a huge magnetized pin-covered building. Any living thing passing flying crawling near the structure would be zook pinned to the walls. Birds, kites, cats, people, helicopters, embellished the skyscraper."[13] When he was a child in Greece, "more than anything else, penetration was my favorite occupation," Samaras wrote in his *Autobiographic Preserves*. "To cleave the twigs and leaves from a long skinny branch, transform it into a spear and never to stop thrusting it into the air, earth, or objects ..."[14] In his freshman year at Rutgers, Samaras joined a rifle club and saved a small page of targets in which he had shot perfect holes in each bullseye. The head of the pin Samaras likened to a hole and the pin's sharp end to the idea of penetration. Bullets and their penetration recall Samaras's childhood spent in wartime Greece, where children would throw found bullets into fires to watch them explode, and where one night a raid during which bullets were fired through the family home resulted in his grandmother's death. The relationship between a pin head or point and a hole relates with

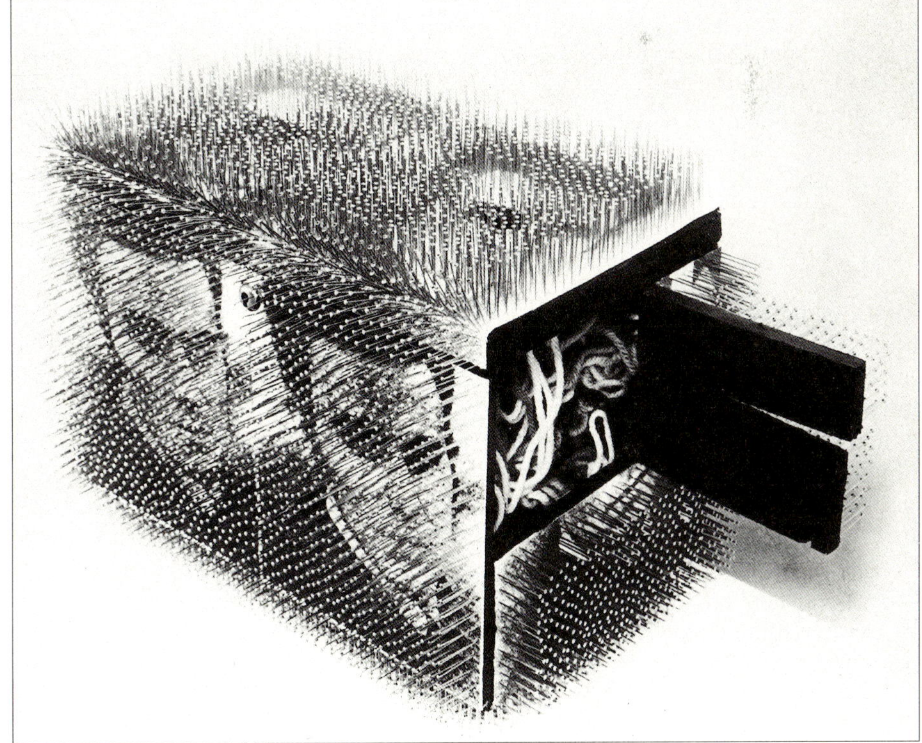

4.8 LUCAS SAMARAS
Untitled (Face Box) 1963
Wood, photograph, pins, and
wool
10½ × 15 × 18½ins
(26.7 × 38.1 × 46.4cm)
Courtesy Pace Gallery, New
York

Samaras's perfect bullseye and his interest in Jasper Johns's targets painted in the late 1950s—an interest, typically, in what Samaras perceived as the possibility for transformation, that "the expansion and contraction of a dot was possible."[15] Samaras made the following comments in a self-interview in 1963:

I mean do pins mean anything to you? Let me find out. (1) When I use them with the flat paintings they create a net pattern which breaks up the flat picture and creates a stranger illusion. (2) Pins are marks, lines, and dots. (3) They are relatives of nails. My father spent some time as a shoemaker. I was raised up by a very religious family. The nailing on the cross. As a child I often played with pins at my aunt's [cousin's] dress shop. Nailing pieces of cloth. My father spent many years in the fur business stretching and nailing furs. The pin is to an extent a part of the family. One of my earliest and strongest memories deals with seeing an Indian Fakir sitting on a bed of nails in a World Book Encyclopedia.[16]

Autobiography in the form of a portrait photograph is pinned to Samaras's *Untitled* (Face Box) (Fig. **4.8**) made in 1963. The box form has autobiographical connotations as well as transforming Minimalism's geometry into smaller scale and narrative content. Samaras's father left the family in Greece and went to America when Samaras was three years old, returning when he was ten. "Yes, I think I am still waiting for him to come in the form of a letter, a package, a party, an explosion, an icon, a natural event," Samaras wrote. "When I am making art I am making a father."[17] The boxes that Samaras made in the 1960s are very small in scale, foreshadowing the interest of Post-Minimalists, like Shapiro and Tuttler, in small scale and paralleling these later artists' reevaluation of male gender connotations in scale. In a comment about the boxes, Samaras elaborates on scale gender connotations and on the notion of combining painting and sculpture: "If they were not taken as paintings or sculptures they did nevertheless contain both and because the international he-man aesthetic went in for big, bold eye spectacles I made it my business not to be sidetracked from my interest in intimate but quite lethal things."[18]

Autobiography reenters the "formal jargon" of Minimalism in Post-Minimalism. Like Artschwager and Beuys, Samaras does not really fit within any of the group artistic tendencies of his time, but his art importantly prefigures Post-Minimalism in relation to autobiography and to his charging of what came to be Minimalism's rigid geometry and anti-narrative content. Sometimes Samaras's relationship to Post-Minimal artists is traceable—Eva Hesse, for example, refers to his art in her journals.[19] More often, Samaras's art functions as a precedent rather than a direct source.

JOSEPH BEUYS

The German artist Joseph Beuys prefigured Post-Minimalism in his use of signature materials and autobiography (see pages 58–60). Chapter 2 discusses Beuys at greater length than this chapter which will concentrate on his relationship to Post-Minimalism. Though Beuys's art was not well known in the United States during Post-Minimalism's formative stages, Beuys was aware of Minimalist art almost from its beginning because it was widely collected in Germany. His strongly autobiographical bent led him to interpret Minimalism's formal ideas into his signature materials.

For his *Fat Chair* (Fig. **4.9**), Beuys mounded fat against the seat and back of a wooden chair, smoothing the mound into a diagonal that forms the apex of a triangle, the other two sides of which are comprised of the chair. Of course the chair is uninviting to sit on. As the fat occupies the position normally assumed by a person, the association of it with Jews reduced to fat and soap in German concentration camps during World War II is inescapable. Beuys did not shy away from the shameful Nazi period of German history, but instead faced it squarely in an effort to comprehend and continue beyond it. The triangle, being a basic geometric form (although here made literally organic and human-like) compares with Minimalist geometry.

Fat Corner (Fig. **4.10**) made in 1969 more expli-

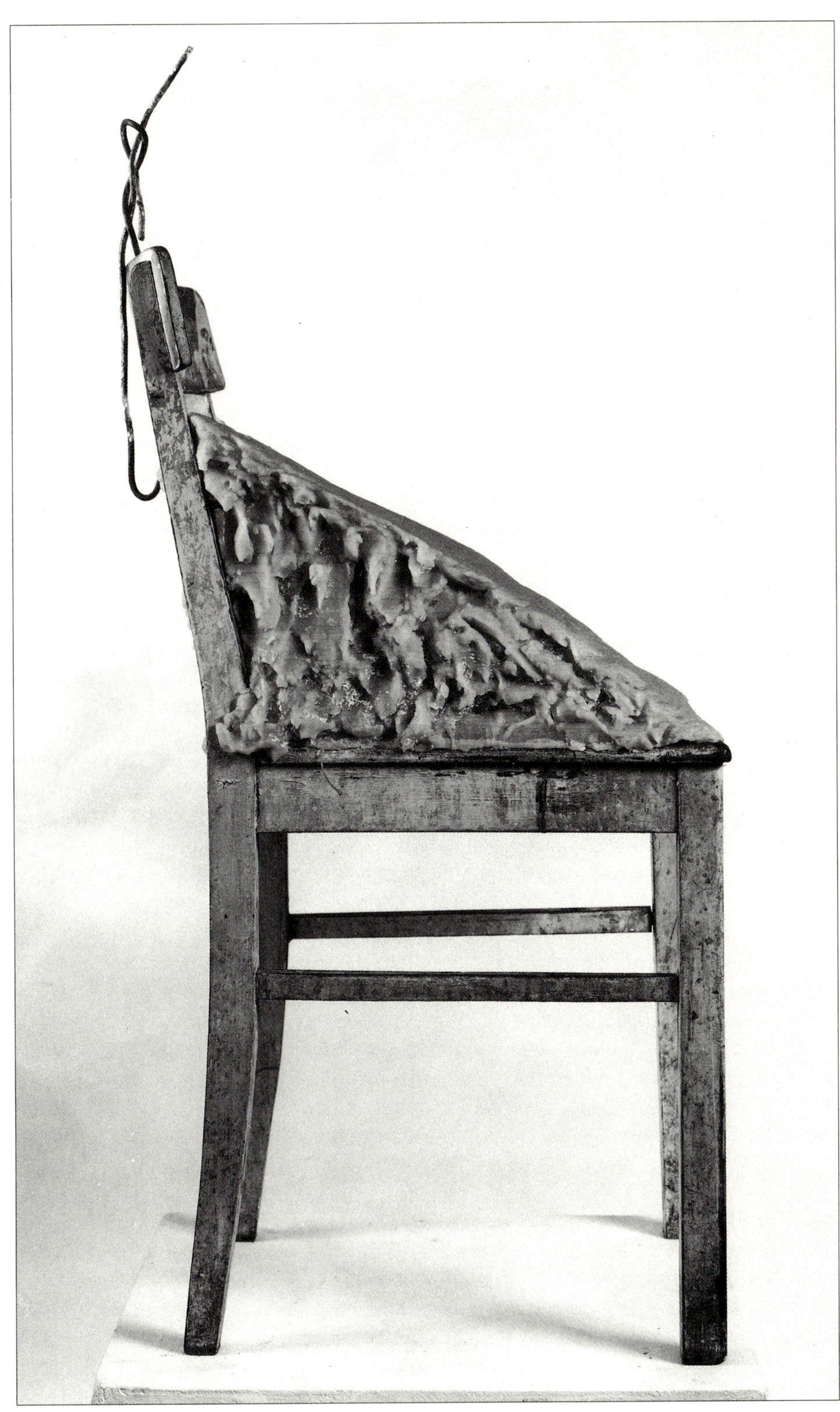

4.9 JOSEPH BEUYS
Fat Chair 1964
Wood chair with fat
35⅜ins (89.9cm) high
Courtesy Hessisches
Landesmuseum, Darmstadt

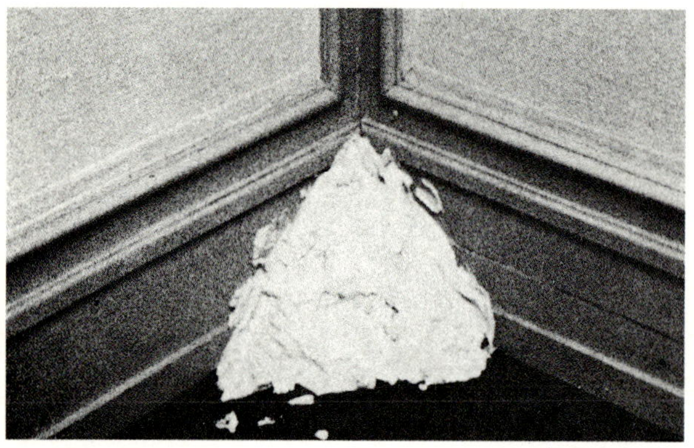

4.10 JOSEPH BEUYS
Fat Corner 1969
Courtesy Marian Goodman
Gallery, New York

citly relies upon interior architectural space, being literally formed by walls and the floor and also resembling Robert Morris's *Corner Piece* from his Green Gallery show in 1963 which was widely known through photographs in art magazines (see page 23). Beuys also made a *Felt Corner* in 1963 and in 1970 made an edition of *Felt Suits*, another autobiographical manifestation of his signature material.

EVA HESSE

Eva Hesse's biography is so filled with tragedy and struggle that the telling of it sometimes overshadows an accurate perception of her art, an art that is original and important despite the very short time span of her mature production—from about 1966 to 1970, when she died of a brain tumor at the age of 34 years. Her art is not directly autobiographical, but the sense of "a presence so tenuous and mortal"[20] which curator Linda Shearer perceived in her late work relates to the events of her life. Though it is not literally narrative, Hesse's art conveys what art critic Lucy Lippard characterized as: "that unconsciously wistful quality which is so much a part of her work."[21]

Because Hesse's biography informs her art, a brief account of it is worthwhile. She was born in 1936 in Hamburg of Jewish German parents from whom she was separated for three months when she was an infant. In 1939 she fled the Nazi holocaust with her mother, father, and sister, and moved to New York City, where she attained American citizenship in 1945, the year her parents divorced and her father remarried. The following year her mother committed suicide. The worst thing about an unhappy childhood, as bad as it is in itself, is that it often comes back to haunt one. Hesse was given to periods of gloom and intense self-doubt exacerbated by her personal background and her struggle to be taken seriously as an artist. A 1965 diary entry reads:

My yearly fall into the pit of darkness is upon me … and as I am working constantly with a great intensity it is mounting inside. The intensity with which I work is translated then into the gloom of despair. All my stakes are in my work. I have given up all else.… I do feel I am an artist—and one of the best. I do deeply … With my work I have one person here and one there, artists who know me and think I am good. Most others don't know me as an artist and give me no credit at all and I can't take this.[22]

Her marriage by this time was almost non-existent; her husband, Tom Doyle, left her the following year for another woman. Her father died the same year. She acutely felt the loss of family by the Holocaust (grandparents), suicide, death, and absence.

But Hesse began to achieve recognition for her art in 1966 when it was included in an exhibition called *Eccentric Abstraction* organized by Lucy Lippard for the Fisbach Gallery in New York City. Her work was supported by artists she respected, like Sol LeWitt, Carl Andre, Robert Smithson, and Mel Bochner, whose review in *Arts Magazine* (November 1966) reads: "Eva Hesse's work was the best in the exhibition."[23] Just the summer before her father had died and she wrote in her dairy: "I feel more helpless, insufficient, stupid … I want to prove myself. My only weapon is art."[24] Hesse's mature production as an artist spans a short four years. In 1969 she physically collapsed from a brain tumor; after several operations she died in 1970.

Hang-Up (Fig. **4.11**) connects the wall with the floor, a frame with a projecting form, thus combining formal concepts of painting and sculpture in a

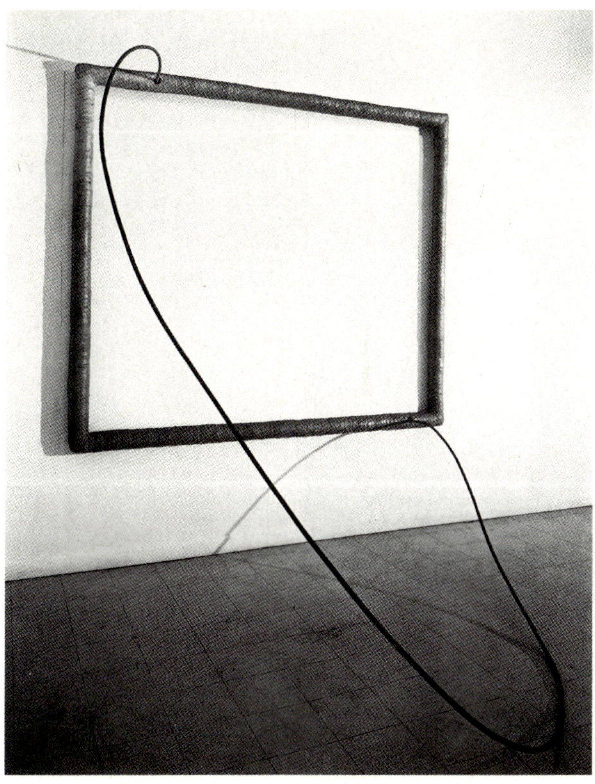

4.11 EVA HESSE
Hang-Up 1966
Acrylic on cloth over wood
and steel
72 × 84 × 78ins
(182.9 × 213.4 × 198.1cm)
Collection Art Institute of
Chicago
Photo courtesy Robert Miller
Gallery, New York
*"It is the most ridiculous
structure I have ever made
and that is why it is really
good. It has a kind of depth
or soul or absurdity or life or
meaning or feeling or
intellect that I want to get …
I know there is nothing
unconnected in this world,
but if art can stand by itself,
these were really alone and
there was no one doing
anything like that at the
time."[25]*

makes it a formal concept parallel to works by Andre, LeWitt, Morris, and Serra, but there is more to it than formal exploration. Hesse described *Hang-Up* as, "the most important early statement I made. It was the first time my idea of absurdity of extreme feeling came through."

It was a huge piece, six feet by seven feet. The construction is really very naïve, it is a frame, ostensibly, and it sits on the wall with a very thin, strong but easily bent, rod that comes out of it. The frame is all cord and rope. It's all tied up like a hospital bandage—as if someone broke an arm. The whole thing is absolutely rigid, neat cord around the entire thing … It is extreme and that is why I like it and don't like it. It's so absurd to have that long thin metal rod coming out of that structure. And it comes out a lot, about ten or eleven feet out, and what is it coming out of? It is coming out of this frame, something and yet nothing and—oh, more absurdity!—it's very, very finely done. The colors on the frame were carefully gradated from light to dark—the whole thing is ludicrous. It is the most ridiculous structure I have ever made and that is why it is really good. It has a kind of depth or soul or absurdity or life or meaning or feeling or intellect that I want to get …[26]

Hesse wrapped the frame in rope and string and covered it with cloth, then wrapped the projecting wire in string, and painted both elements in monochromatic tonal gradations. The obsessive/compulsive wrapping gave *Hang-Up* the bandaged quality Hesse referred to, giving it a feeling of vulnerability as well as reflecting women's issues (see page 112). Lucy Lippard described *Hang-Up* in a review written the year it was first exhibited: "There is a yearning quality of suppression and release as well as pathos and humor to this strange relief that should reach a broad audience."[27]

Repetition 19, III (Fig. **4.12**) changes Minimalism's repetition of identical geometric units into the repetition of similar but irregular, varied forms, resulting in an evocative sense of each form's individuality. Rather than using repetition to emphasize the mass production of identical goods or images—an aspect of Minimalism and Pop Art—Hesse emphasized the individuality of the unique, handmade object. She took great pains to make each of the units different, rejecting one casting of the piece because the units

pictorial/sculptural dialogue which Pincus-Witten identified as central to Post-Minimalism during its first phase from 1966–70. The formal originality of Hesse's sculpture is always very powerful. Color Field painters' notion of painting being a two-dimensional plane hanging on a wall and Minimalist sculptors' idea of sculpture taking place on the horizon are here both expressed in a hybrid object which is neither painting nor sculpture. *Hang-Up* is not an isolated object placed on a base, which

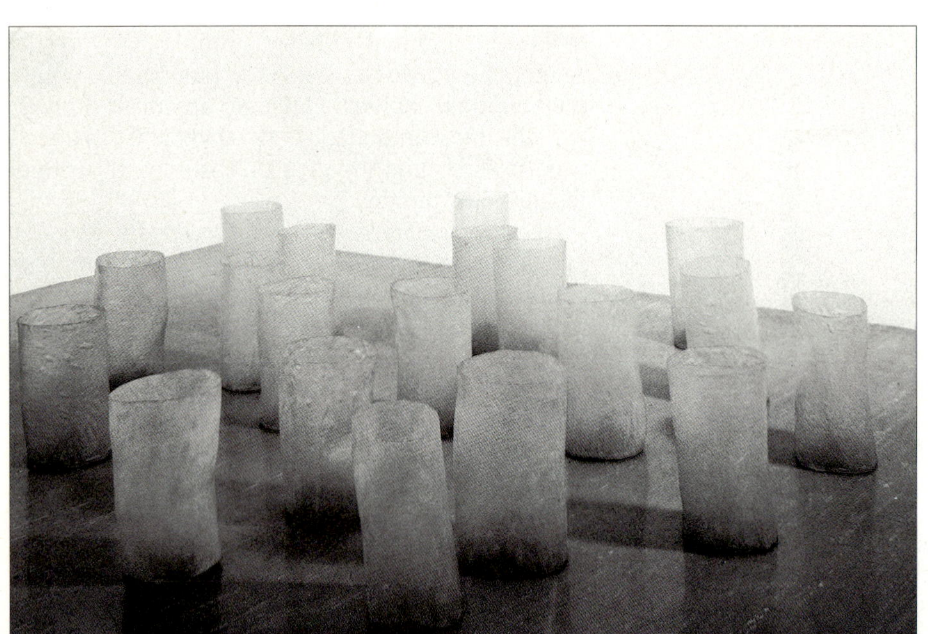

4.12 EVA HESSE
Repetition 19, III 1968
Nineteen tubular fiberglass
units
19 to 20¼ins h. × 11 to
12¾ins diameter
(48 to 51.4cm h. × 27.8 to
32.3cm diameter)
Collection, The Museum of
Modern Art, New York. Gift of
the Eva Hesse Estate

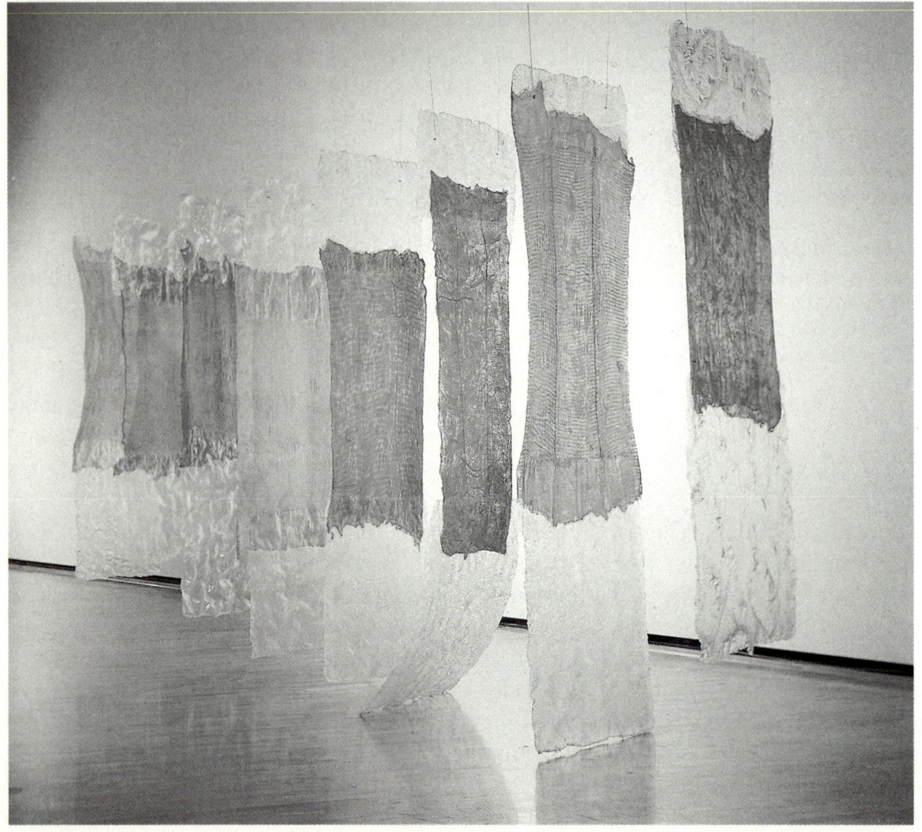

4.13 EVA HESSE
Contingent 1969
Cheesecloth, latex, fiberglass
8 panel installation
137¾ h. × 248 w. × 43 d. ins
350 × 630 × 109cm
Collection Australian
National Gallery, Canberra

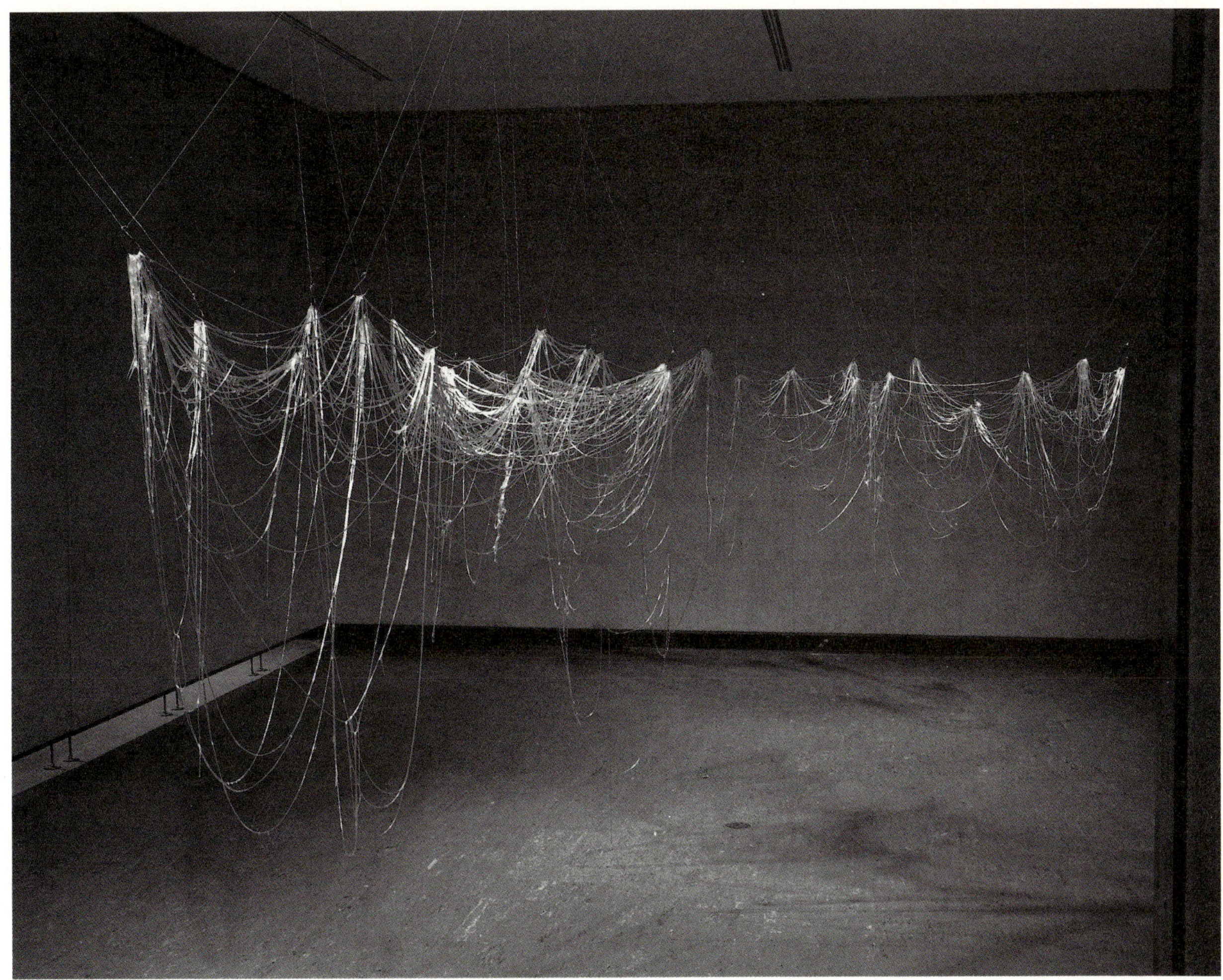

4.14 EVA HESSE
Right After 1969
Fiberglass
c. 5 × 18 × 4ft
(1.52 × 5.48 × 1.22m)
Courtesy Milwaukee Art
Museum, Gift of Friends of
Art

"... this piece is very ordered ... Chaos can be as structured as non-chaos. That we know from Jackson Pollock."[28]

were too identical. Hesse used repetition for express-ive as well as formal purposes. "Series, serial, serial art, is another way of repeating absurdity," she said.[29]

If something is meaningful, maybe it's more meaningful said ten times. It's not just an esthetic choice. If something is absurd, it's much more absurd if it's repeated ... I don't think I always do it, but repetition does enlarge or increase or exaggerate an idea or purpose in a statement.[30]

About the absurd in general Hesse stated:

... absurdity is the key word ... It has to do with contradictions and oppositions. In the forms I use in my work the contradictions are certainly there. I was always aware that I should take order versus chaos, stringy versus mass, huge versus small, and I would try to find the most absurd opposites or extreme opposites—I was always aware of their absurdity and also their formal contradictions and it was always more interesting than making something average, normal, right size, right proportion ...[31]

For *Contingent* (Fig. **4.13**) Hesse impregnated cheesecloth with fiberglass and latex, hanging the eight large sheets from the ceiling to the floor, making the two-dimensional planes of painting into volume-occupying sculpture. *Contingent* clearly establishes a formal concept of painting obtaining sculptural presence. Hesse fully realized the implications of this work; she wrote about it: "The last piece I did really was like paintings that are hung from the ceiling and it could be hung against the wall ... and a lot of my sculpture could be called paintings and a lot of it could be called nothing—a thing or an object or any new word you want to give it because they aren't traditional."[32] Repetition is again used but with individual differences in each unit. Transparency and apparent flimsiness create a wistful, vulnerable feeling.

Both of Hesse's late sculptures *Right After* (Fig. **4.14**) and *Untitled* (informally called *7 Poles*, 1970) resemble spontaneous painting gestures in three dimensions, yet both show precise control. In both, one can tell the processes by which they were made, but the rigid forms solidify the process into unchanging forms. Both manifest painterly gestures related to the Abstract Expressionist Jackson Pollock's drip style, in effect making the skeins and poles of his "all-over" compositions into actual space-occupying, all-over sculpture. This reinvestment of sculpture with expressiveness taken from the gestures and compositions of Abstract Expressionism became one of the most salient features of Post-Minimalism.

Jackson Pollock is frequently mentioned in the literature about Hesse, perhaps partly because both artists died relatively young—she younger than he—cutting short the full development of their talents, and perhaps partly because the lives of both were filled with emotional turbulence, the material of myths. Mainly, however, the artists are often linked for two reasons: because Hesse revived Pollock's gesture and all-over composition, translating it into sculpture at a time when sculpture was becoming more painterly, and because both artists worked in extraordinarily original artistic territory before other Abstract Expressionist and Post-Minimal artists. Pollock was then—as he still is—the great American hero of artistic pioneer loners. Being comparable to Pollock is just about as great as an American artist can be considered to be.

KEITH SONNIER

Keith Sonnier's (born 1941) sculpture creates pictorial visual effects with untraditional sculptural materials such as latex, flocking, gauze, and neon. Several qualities link Sonnier's art with Hesse's: his use of eccentric, "signature" materials and of painting-like gestures made into sculpture; and his breaking out of painting's framing edge—a variation of all-over composition. Sonnier's source for these latter two characteristics (gesture and all-over composition) is Abstract Expressionism, the same one Hesse used.

In 1966 Sonnier moved to New York from Europe to accept a teaching assistantship at Rutgers University. He had been in France since 1963, having moved there from his native Louisiana where he grew up speaking French and English. Robert Morris was at Rutgers when Sonnier arrived in 1966. Through him Sonnier was introduced to the New York art world. Sonnier had been a painter, using lush and dank, evocative colors, but at Rutgers he switched materials to prefabricated plastics like vinyl, then to folded and pleated metal screen and satin-covered rubber lengths tied into links. Works made with these latter materials Sonnier laid directly on the floor.

In 1968 Sonnier began working with latex, flocking, neon, and cloth, configuring them in arrangements which make barely three-dimensional forms. The transluscent latex, painted on in liquid form, solidifies to a thin membrane-like plane resembling a stretched canvas. Flocking—powdered rayon that is used to make velvet effects in wallpaper (as aesthetically discredited a material as one can imagine)—adheres to the latex when applied while it's still wet, creating misty hazes of atmospheric color. The works' fragility, their impermanence, and their veil-like quality give them an affecting feeling of vulnerability despite their use of tacky, lower-class-taste culture materials.

Formally, Sonnier's work from this period embodies important consequences: it undermines Color Field and Minimalist painters' beliefs that painting is

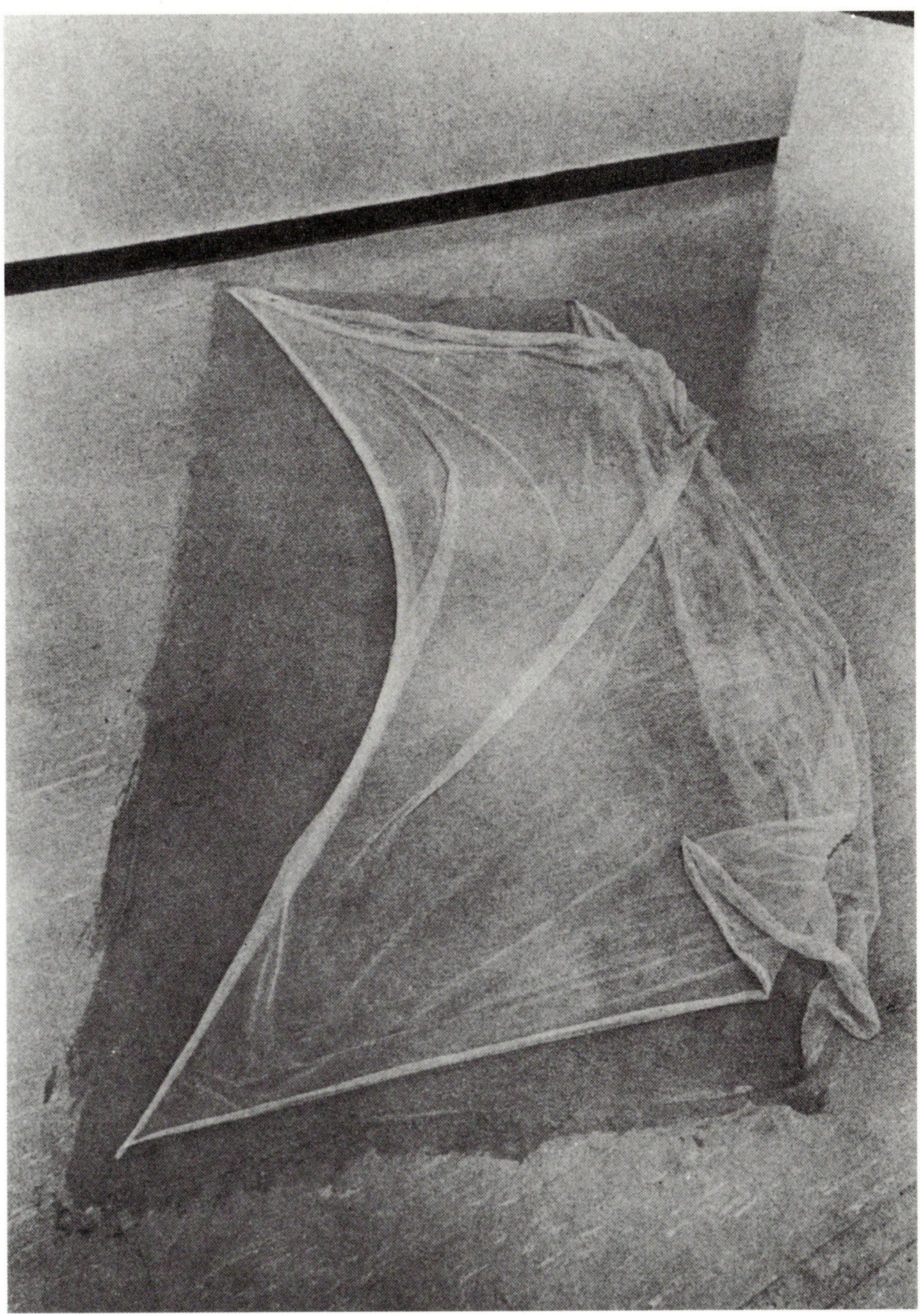

4.15 KEITH SONNIER
Untitled 1969
Dacron, latex, flock
destroyed
Courtesy Castelli, New York

a flat plane of fabric stretched on a wooden support. Not only does Sonnier make "paintings" that are not stretched on a wooden support, but they exist in three-dimensional space. Sonnier peels the latex or fabric planes from the wall or floor, sometimes holding them limply taut with strings: separating, in short, painting's two-dimensional plane from the wall, sometimes even laying it on the floor.

The limp and fragile works—a 1969 *Untitled* (Fig. **4.15**) dacron, latex, and flocking piece installed on the floor, for example—were sometimes temporary when applied directly to the floor or wall. Writing about this latter pink and grey painterly wash-like work, Robert Pincus-Witten said it suggested a "gauzy blanket" and a "funerary site."[33] It was as diaphanous and immaterial a sculpture as any made that year. *Mustee #1* (Fig. **4.16**)—made of latex, flocking, and string—peels off the wall for nearly half of its height, revealing the "painting's" underside that in an ordinary painting would normally face the wall. Holding the peeled-away portion of *Mustee #1* away from the wall with strings attached to the floor turns it into a space-occupying volume (an obstruction) and connects the wall (painting's province) with the floor (sculpture's arena).

4.16 KEITH SONNIER
Mustee #1 1968
Latex, flocking and string
72 × 144ins
(182.8 × 365.7cm)
Courtesy Leo Castelli Gallery,
New York

The Pop artist James Rosenquist uncharacteristically used neon in his important sculpture *Tumbleweed* in 1963–66, and Bruce Nauman began using neon in the mid-1960s, *Neon Template of the Left Half of My Body Taken at 10 inch Intervals* (1966) (see page 35), for example. Nauman's neon works had come to Sonnier's attention prior to his use of this material beginning in 1968. Sonnier's *Ba-o-ba #3* (Fig. **4.17**) floods neon "lines" with colored light "washes" across the wall and a glass plane in painterly three-dimensional effects.

In 1969 Sonnier participated in several important exhibitions chronicling what Pincus-Witten in 1970 and Lippard in 1966 characterized as, respectively, "forms related to . . . painterly issues"[34] and the influence of painters who had "undermined sculptural tradition, producing a non-sculptural or object idiom that looks to formalist painting rather than to previous sculpture for its precedents."[35] Three of the most important of those 1969 exhibitions are *When Attitudes Become Form* at the Kunsthalle in Berne, Switzerland

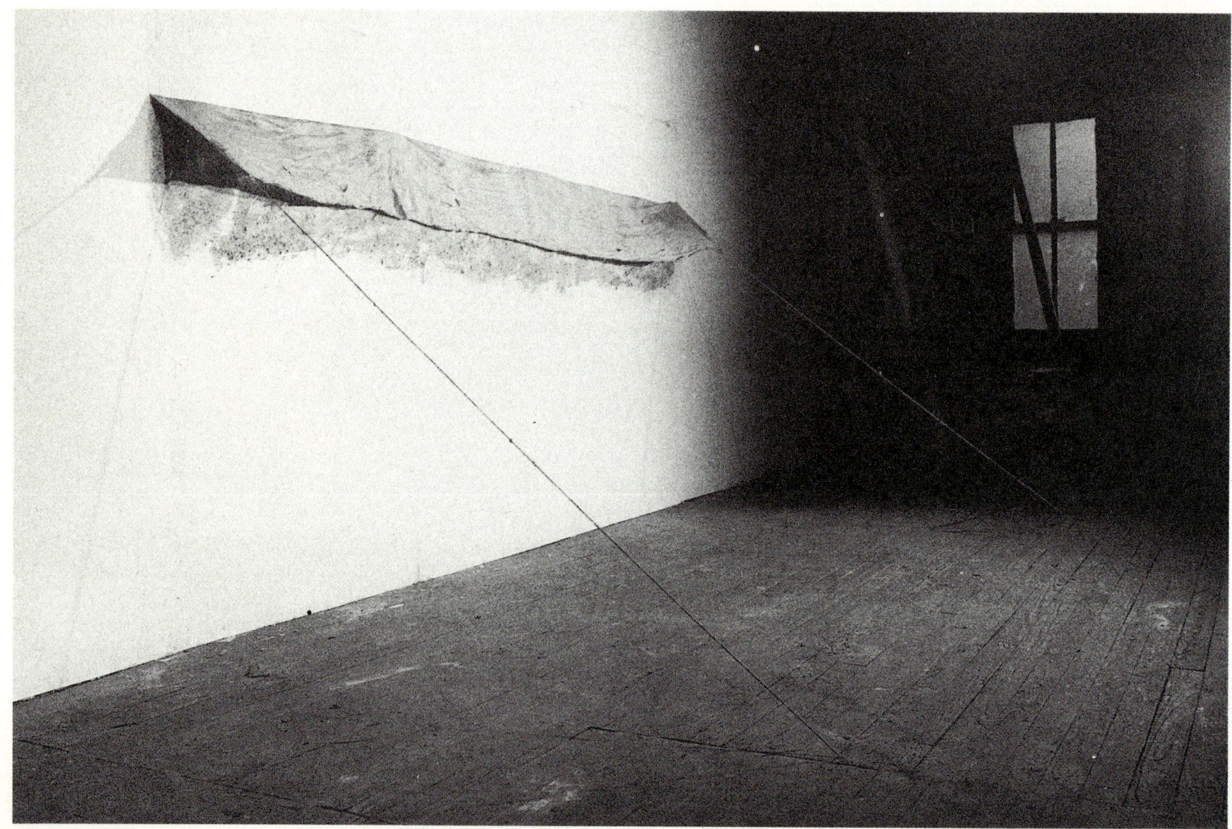

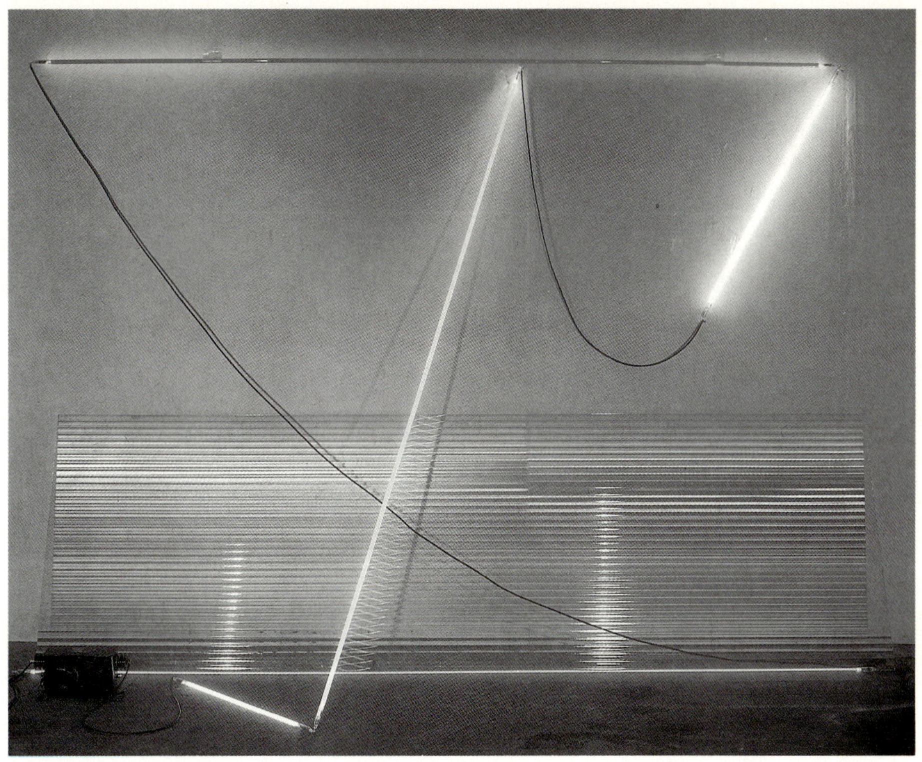

and The Institute for Contemporary Art in London; *Anti-Illusion: Procedures/Materials* at the Whitney Museum of American Art in New York (both of these exhibitions also included Eva Hesse, Lynda Benglis, and other artists in this chapter); and *Here and Now* at Washington University in St. Louis, Missouri. By this time it was clearly apparent in avant-garde art capitals throughout Europe and the United States that a widely practiced pictorial/sculptural sensibility was well underway.

LYNDA BENGLIS

Lynda Benglis (born 1941) received a BFA degree from Newcomb College, in her home state of Louisiana, in 1964. Shortly thereafter she moved to New York where she has lived ever since. Writing in 1969 about Lynda Benglis's *Bounce* (Fig. **4.19**), art critic Emily Wasserman stated:

Miss Benglis spills skeins of liquid rubber in a freely flowing, twining mass directly onto the floor of the exhibition space, mixing flourescent oranges, chartreuse, day-glo pinks, greens, and blues, allowing the accidents and puddlings of the material to harden into a viscous mat. The outer contours trace the natural flow of the latex and define the amoeba-like but self-contained field of this strange and startlingly colored spread. The method by which the piece was (non)formed is thus actually objectified, while the events and timing of its process are congealed.[36]

Later in her review, Wasserman referred to *Bounce* as "a kind of painting entirely freed from an auxiliary ground or armature."[37]

Asserting the process of an artwork's making as part of its subject, and freeing painting both from two dimensions and from its framing support, all typify Post-Minimalism and Benglis's art. But in Benglis there exists a different attitude than in any other Post-Minimalist: an attitude of mocking, particularly of mocking the machismo of Abstract Expressionist gestures. Speaking about her involvement with video Benglis said: "I saw it was a big

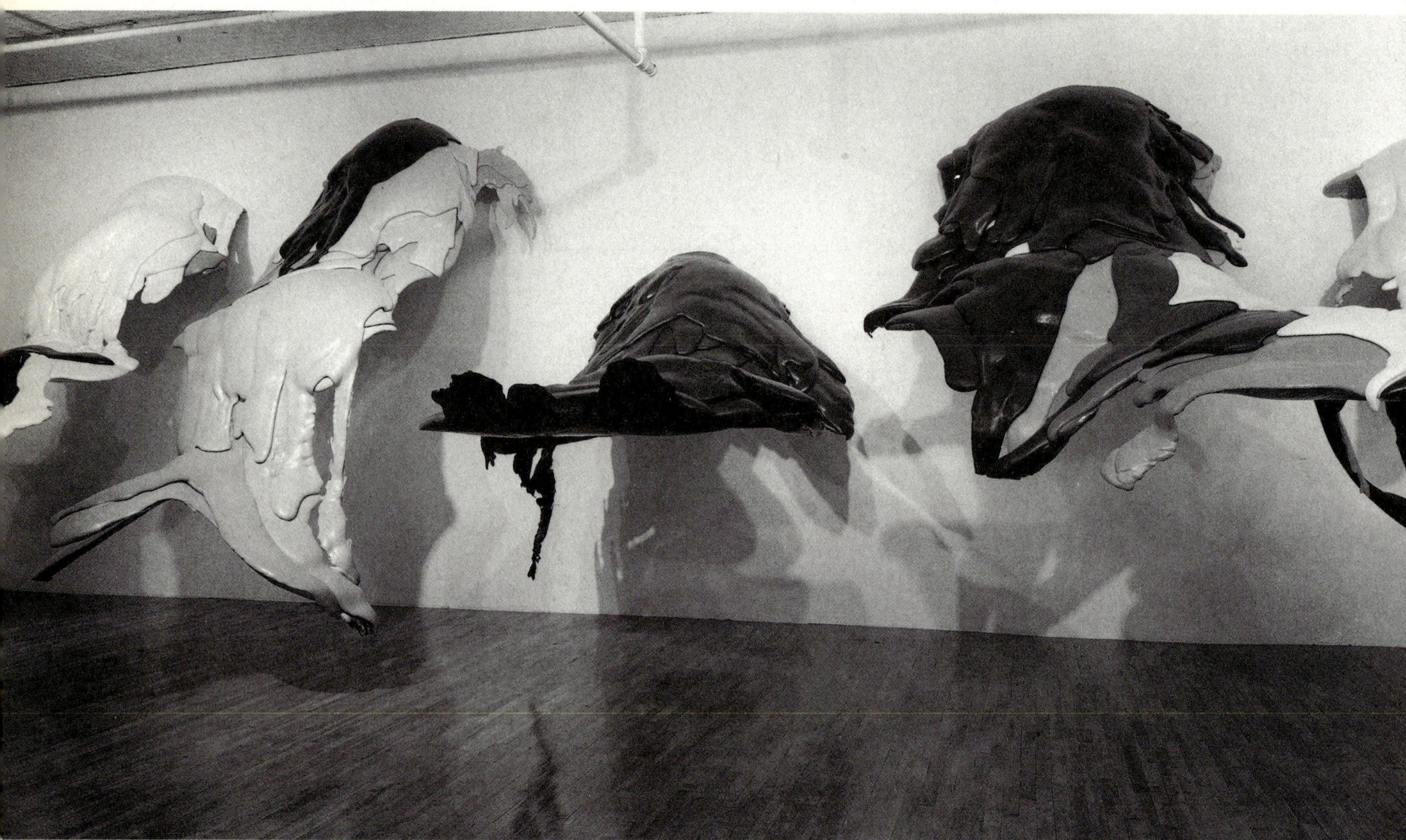

4.18 LYNDA BENGLIS
Pinto 1971
Polyurethane, foam
10½ × 60 × 11ft
(3.2 × 18.29 × 3.35m)
Courtesy Paula Cooper
Gallery, New York

macho game, a big, heroic, Abstract Expressionist, macho sexist game. It's all about territory. How big?"[38] Benglis also mocks popular culture stereotypes of taste by crossing over boundaries of "feminine" behavior and sexual propriety.

Pinto (Fig. **4.18**) made in 1971 leaps off the wall in an expressionist gesture of flowing and puddling. Made by spraying foaming styrofoam over inflated balloon-frameworks, then casting the hardened results, *Pinto* details the process of its own making. It also takes painting off the wall, out of the frame, and into sculptural dimensions.

Two (Fig. **4.20**) manifests Benglis's "frozen ges-

ture" (her words) in plasterized cloth, paints, and sparkles. Built over a chickenwire framework, the expanding and contracting tubes of plasterized cloth suggest figurative gestures. Benglis's use of glitter, sparkles, and "frosted" colors in the "sparkle knots" expresses her mocking fascination with aesthetically discredited popular taste culture.

Gesture in both a physical and a psychological sense—as in "it was a lovely gesture"[39]—figure in Benglis's art. In the psychological sense, Benglis theatricalized her gesture into a kind of frozen performance art for her 1974 exhibition announcement and scandalous *Artforum* ad (November, 1974). In both instances, she posed herself nude or semi-nude with macho assertiveness, either seen from behind with dropped pants and standing on platform shoes (a kind of pedestal) or arrogantly pretending that a giant latex dildo is her own gender equipment. This theatrical, mocking, gender role-playing relates to Benglis's earlier gestural art, bringing to it an insistent and outrageous feminist meaning.

4.19 LYNDA BENGLIS
Bounce 1969
Poured pigmented
polyurethane
161½ × 188ins
(409.4 × 477.5cm)
Courtesy Paula Cooper
Gallery, New York

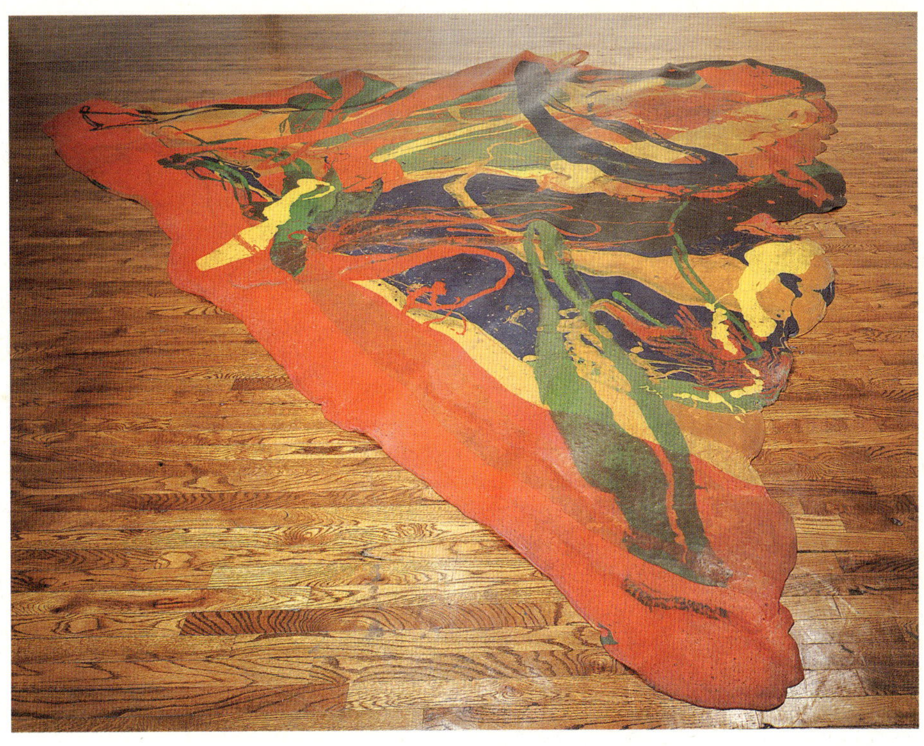

4.20 LYNDA BENGLIS
Two 1973
Mixed media (gauze, paint,
plastic, cellophane, plastic
sequins)
31 × 12¼ × 16½ins
(78.7 × 31.1 × 41.9cm)
Courtesy Solomon R.
Guggenheim Museum, New
York. Gift of Mrs. Andrew P.
Fuller

RICHARD SERRA

Richard Serra made several pictorial/sculptural works in the late 1960s, but by 1969 he renounced painterly issues in favor of more purely sculptural ones. All of his work from the late 1960s, though, manifests his concern with asserting the process of making the artwork as part of its subject.

Belts (Fig. **4.21**) dates from about the same time as Andre's first metal plate "rugs" in 1967 (see page 19), and Eva Hesse's *Hang-Up* (1965–66) (see page 121).

Serra's interest in exploiting gravity parallels Andre's preoccupation with sculptural horizontality (see page 19). Using a flexible material—rubber—which droops when hung vertically allows gravity and the character of the material itself to determine the sculpture's shape, a kind of sculptural equivalent to Pollock's dripping paint on a canvas laid on the floor, exploiting the paint's liquidity, viscosity, and gravity. Serra's gestural neon squiggle reiterates Pollock's skeins of dripped paint. Draping the droopy belts on a single nail submits them to the tug of gravity, creating taut tension in the supporting belt(s) and allowing others to relax, thus forming a structural arrangement that is at once sculptural in its use of physical stresses and strains, yet painterly in its linearity, frontality, and dependence on the wall. Serra's 1980 statement (see caption for Fig. **4.21**) reveals uneasiness with these latter two pictorial attributes.

In 1968 Serra produced the first of a series of splashed lead pieces made by melting lead and flinging it against a rigid surface where it cooled and hardened (see page 110). In an interview made in 1970 Serra expressed reservations about the extension of sculpture into pictorial issues, but *Splashing* remains a clear and important statement of painting and sculpture's union at that particular moment. At the time the interview was recorded, Serra must have been thinking about the options of his then current work which maintained more purely sculptural issues.

Solving the problem of the base has been crucial to the development of sculpture.... if the floor actually functions as a base, there is no need to construct ... surrogate bases within the work to make the floor appear to function structurally. The debt of such solutions to pictorial conventions is

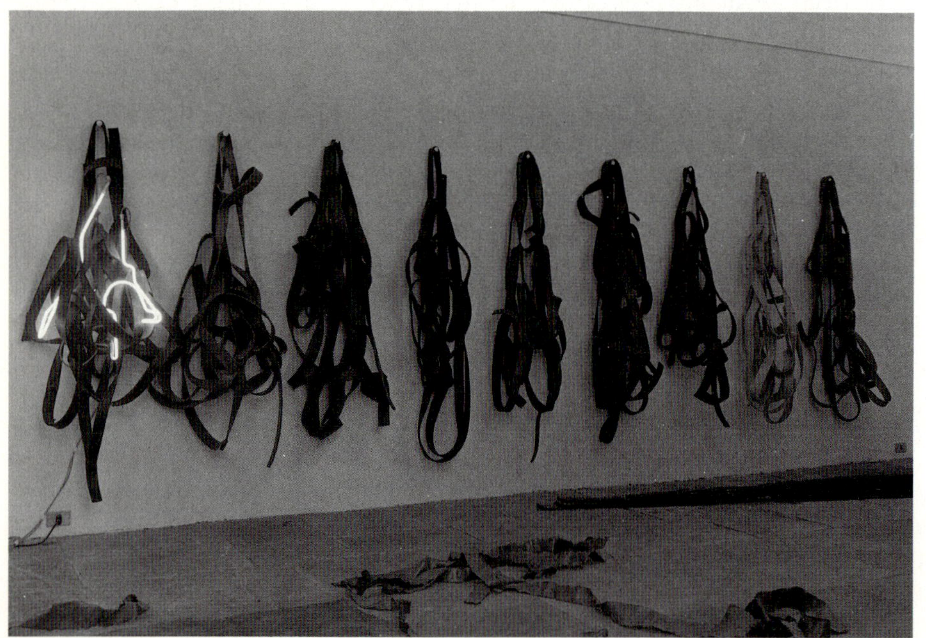

4.21 **RICHARD SERRA**
Belts 1966–67
Vulcanized rubber, blue neon
217¾ × 74⅘ × 17⅓ins
(553 × 190 × 44cm)
Collection Giuseppe Panza di Biumo-Varese
"I made a work with eleven units which was consciously influenced by Pollock's Iowa State Mural. At that point I was dealing with color, plane, line in high relief, i.e., elements of an extended painted space. It left me feeling a little vacant because I have always thought that relief is nothing more than a hybrid, its volume being undercut by the plane of the wall and its perception being reduced to frontality and obliqueness."[40]

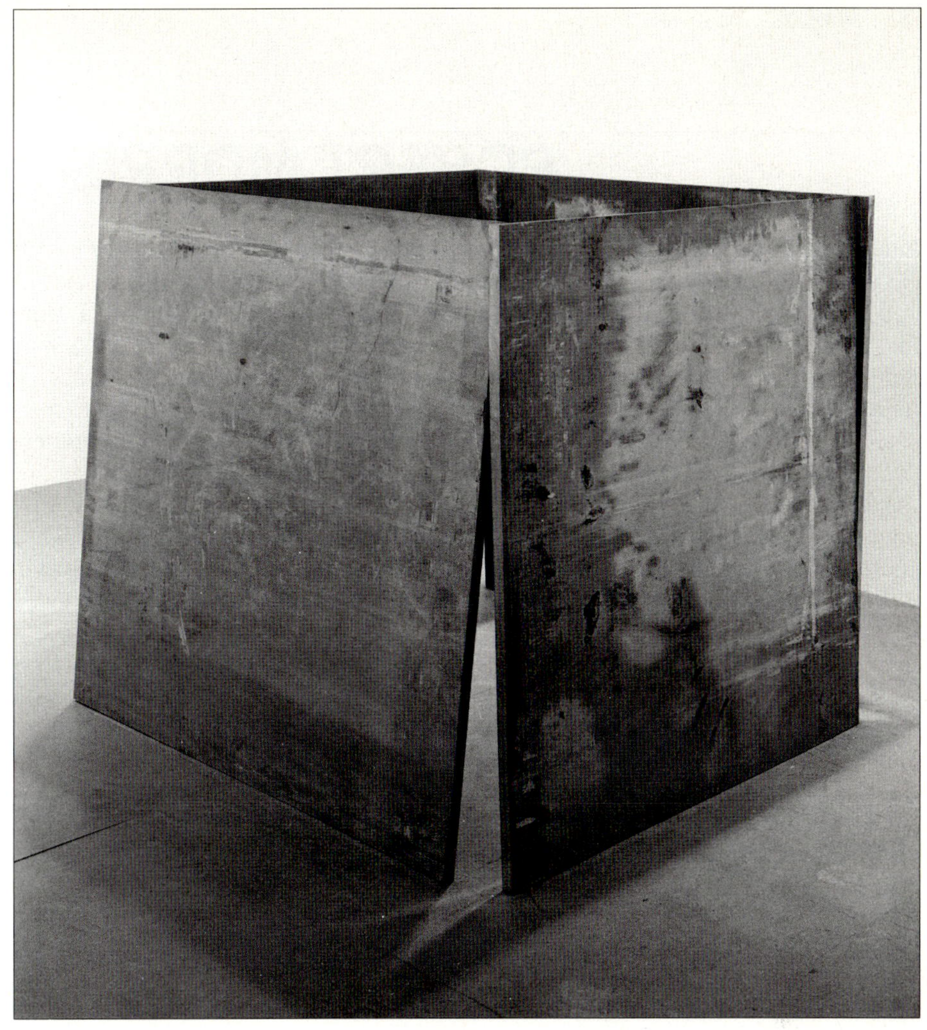

obvious. When pieces are viewed from above, the floor functions as a field or ground for the deployment of decorative linear and planar elements. The concern with horizontality is not so much a concern for lateral extension as it is a concern with painting. Lateral extension in this case allows sculpture to be viewed pictorially— that is, as if the floor were the canvas plane.... The crucial problems confronting sculpture today are the avoidance of the concerns properly belonging to architecture and painting which, as Barbara Rose has indicated, have produced in the name of sculpture so much failed architecture and three-dimensional painting.[41]

The same year Serra made *Splashing*, 1968, he began using lead sheets and plates, sometimes rolling, tearing, or cutting them into shapes and forms that reveal their own making, sometimes propping one element against another, or against a wall or corner.

For *One Ton Prop (House of Cards)* (Fig. **4.22**) Serra leaned four 500-pound (226.8 kg), 48 square inches (309.7 sq cm) lead plates against each other in a configuration which reveals the sequence of steps involved in forming the sculpture. Serra disdained welding, dismissing it as "stitching,"[42] and instead utilized the lead's own weight and density—along with gravity—to hold the structure together. Occupying the same space as the sculpture makes viewers uneasy because of the feeling that it could collapse. Serra so successfully achieves here the sensation of sculptural process that one feels that the work constantly recreates its own making, the outcome of which is forever uncertain. *One Ton Prop (House of Cards)* was included in the Whitney's 1969 exhibition *Anti-Illusion: Procedures/Materials* and has become one of Serra's most widely known sculptures. From that point to the present, Serra has concerned himself with more purely sculptural issues.

ROBERT MORRIS

Beginning in 1967 Robert Morris (see pages 23–24) cut thick industrial felt sheets with parallel incisions and hung them on the wall, allowing them to droop into forms determined by their weight and density. Morris's *Untitled* (Fig. **4.23**) parallels Serra's *Belts*,1966–67 (see page 130), and many other Post-Minimal sculptures, in that it reveals the process of its own making and makes reference to both painterly matters—an articulated flat plane, linearity, dependence on the wall, frontality—and sculptural matters, such as gravity, density, weight, and mass.

The sculptural concept of softness and of indeterminate form originated in the Pop artist Claes Oldenburg's work in the early 1960s. An important art writer as well as artist, Morris acknowledged Oldenburg's role in his short but influential essay, *Anti-Form* in 1968: "Recently, materials other than rigid industrial ones have begun to show up. Oldenburg was one of the first to use such materials. A direct investigation of the properties of these materials is in progress. . . . The focus on matter and gravity as means results in forms which were not projected in advance."[43] Oldenburg's invocation of erotic sensations and of humanlike, metamorphosed soft forms functioned as important precedents for many Post-Minimal artists, including Hesse and Morris. Neither followed Oldenburg's precedent exactly. Hesse's sculpture is much less explicitly human-like than Oldenburg's. In keeping with his earlier Minimal sculpture, Morris's soft sculptures are absolutely free of any allusion to human or animal forms—they are completely formal in their insistence on cutting, hanging, and on the material's inherent properties, along with gravity, as being their subject.

The concept of "truth to materials" is an important factor in Post-Minimalists' uses of eccentric materials. Truth to materials received impetus in the early twentieth century in the sculptures of Constantin Brancusi. In *Anti-Form*, Morris wrote about Pollock's contribution to truth to materials:

Of the Abstract Expressionists only Pollock was able to recover process and hold on to it as part of the end form of the work. Pollock's recovery of process involved a profound re-thinking of the role

4.23 ROBERT MORRIS
Untitled 1970
Heavy industrial felt,
c. 10 × 25ft
(c. 3.1 × 7.62m)
Courtesy Milwaukee Art
Museum, Gift of Friends of
Art

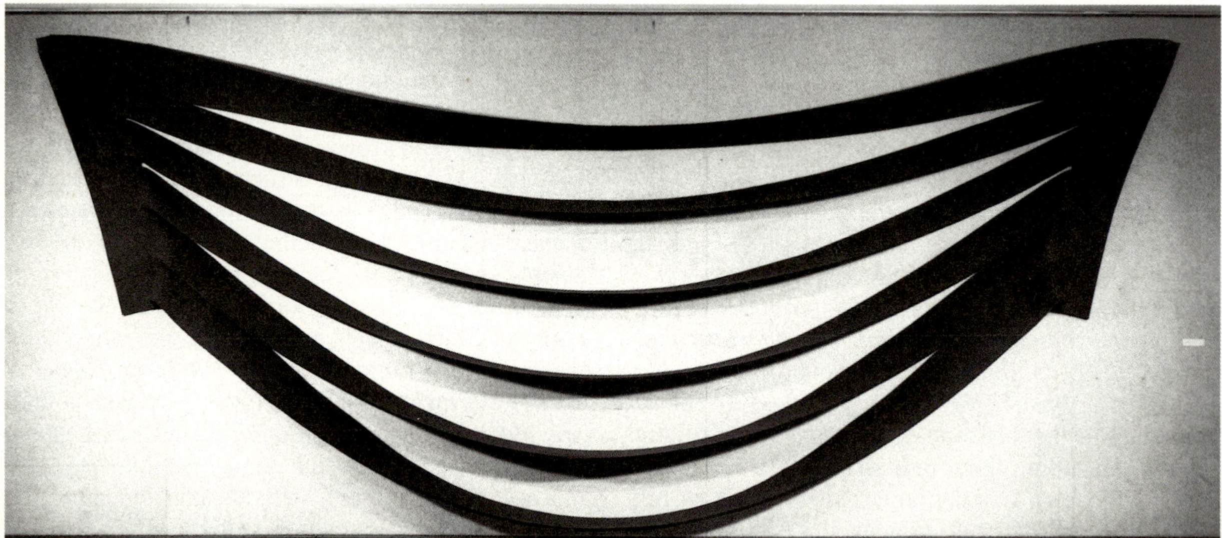

of both material and tools in making. The stick which drips paint is a tool which acknowledges the nature of the fluidity of paint. Like any other tool it is still one that controls and transforms matter. But unlike the brush it is in far greater sympathy with matter because it acknowledges the inherent tendencies and properties of that matter.[44]

The Post-Minimalists' use of eccentric materials which sag, slump, droop, stretch, splay, liquefy, and so on, brings a hallowed twentieth-century sculpture tradition up to date in a pictorial manner. The choice of eccentric materials and the use of their inherent properties gives certain sculptural concepts like horizontality, gravity, or softness a concrete materiality unobtainable in painting while simultaneously making reference to pictorial precedents.

BARRY LE VA

Beginning in 1967 in Los Angeles, Barry Le Va (born 1941) made sculptures by distributing pieces of felt across the floor—using the floor like the ground of a painting and the felt like paint. The artist used a general plan for the arrangement of the elements, but variations within each installation occurred according to the proportions of the site and chance. Le Va was teaching at the Minneapolis School of Art in 1968 when Robert Morris's *Anti-Form* essay came out, yet he regarded Morris's work at the time to be "still tied to an object aesthetic, an art still captured in a single glance."[45]

Untitled (To Disarrange, to Re-Arrange) (Fig. 4.24) employs felt and aluminium lengths in a 35 × 65 feet (10.7 × 19.8 m) scattered configuration. Because the arrangement is largely random, the configuration could theoretically be rearranged infinitely. Viewers walking through the piece can disrupt it without substantially marring its aesthetic, but Le Va did not intend for others to rearrange it.

Le Va's "distribution" sculptures objectify indeterminancy, randomness, and chaos. He once experimented with two different methods: firstly, carefully distributing the elements according to the dictates of taste; secondly, randomly arranging them. The result was that one could not tell the difference.

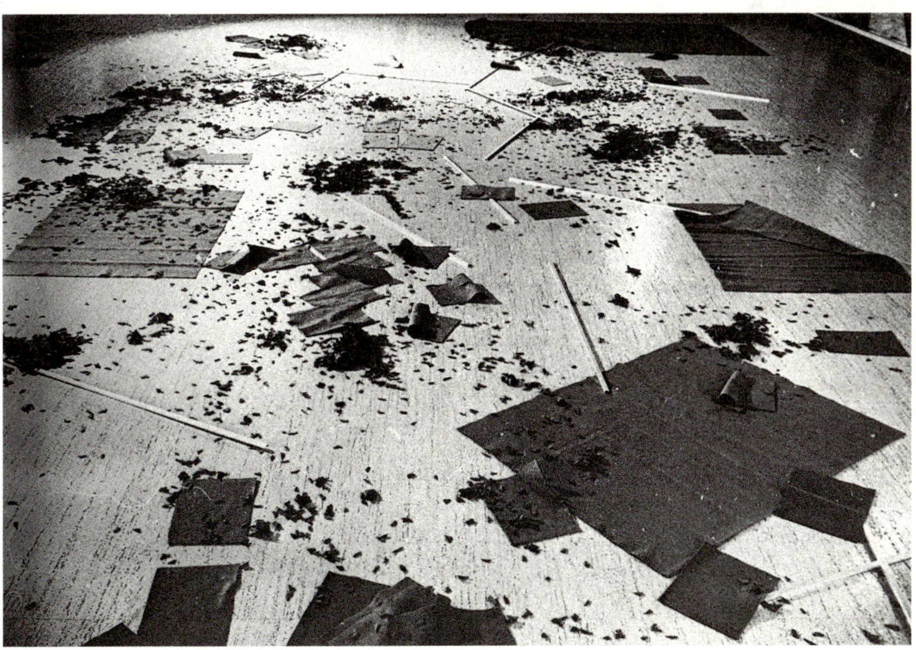

4.24 BARRY LE VA
Untitled (To Disarrange, to Re-arrange) 1967
Black felt and aluminum lengths
35 × 65ft
(10.7 × 19.8m)
Courtesy Whitney Museum of American Art, New York

The notion that sculpture could be composed of at least random-appearing arrangements found its most emphatic expression in Le Va's art in the late 1960s. Other artists, like Morris and Serra for example, experimented with apparently randomly distributing elements across the floor. Le Va's entire art proceeded from the distribution aesthetic. As such, it defines the most extreme position regarding randomness and chaos.

Writing in 1968, art critic Jane Livingston stated that: "In the last analysis, the viability of Le Va's work seems in large part to depend on whether it is enough simply to explore the abstract concept of 'randomness' (chaos), or whether such a concept is by itself aesthetic." She continued:

Jackson Pollock, of course, brought the question of accidental imagery into full esthetic consideration, though his paintings work on other levels to transcend the mere fact of chance procedure in a way that Le Va's distributions don't. The latter's progressive elimination of referential or individually evocative elements (color, sculptural shape, etc.) on the one hand, and over-all expansion and multiplication of parts on the other, tend toward an increasingly specific emphasis on the evocation of chaos. What happens to the spectator's perceived relationship to his environment when it is made to appear chaotic in one degree or another is the essence of what Le Va's recent work is about; all other issues are residual. Whether the experience offered is felicitous or not, it is revelatory.[46]

ALAN SARET

The wire webs and rubber clumps in the art of Alan Saret (born 1944) appear as random and indeterminate as Le Va's felt scatterings, yet more than one art critic has perceived them as having poetic meanings, thus connecting what may appear to be solely formal explorations with metaphorical meaning. Emily Wasserman wrote in 1969 that: "23-year old Saret has ... been working for over a year with ... flimsy materials, creating strangely reticent, though airy, energetic and lyrical webs, clusters, and billows ('sculpture' seems almost too heavy a designation for Saret's work)."[47]

An *Untitled* (Fig. **4.25**) wire work from 1969 suggests Jackson Pollock as a source, but such an exclusive reading would be overly simplistic. Saret dematerializes sculpture into an airy wire web corresponding to drawn lines, but its impenetrable, space-occupying mass is decidedly sculptural. Unlike Le Va's felt distribution pieces, a Saret sculpture cannot

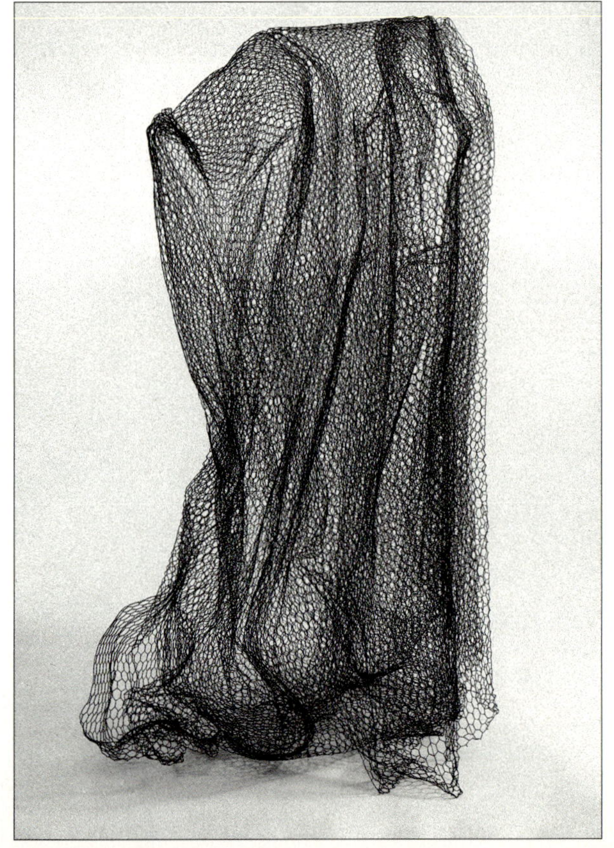

4.25 ALAN SARET
Untitled 1969
Vinyl-coated hexagonal wire netting
7ft 2¾ins × 49 × 41⅝ins
(220.3 × 124.5 × 105.5cm), irregular

Collection, The Museum of Modern Art, New York. Dorothy and Sidney Singer Foundation Fund be walked through. It may be an open form, but it is definitely a sculptural form and not a three-dimensional painting.

Saret's use of gridded materials and his frequent assertion of the horizon link his work with Minimalism, while the apparent randomness of his organic shapes, their indeterminancy, and their bending of Minimalist ideas link it with Post-Minimalism. Saret's elusive art is difficult to characterize in relation to other Post-Minimalists because it is so personal, unique, and so primarily based on intuition and sensibility.

The art critic Richard Armstrong wrote that: *His (Saret's) work embodies an entropic, anti-formal comprehension of art that is common to much of the best work of the generation of sculptors born in the 1940s, from Serra to Benglis. But Saret, in his deliberate turning-away from mass, either in reforming it as art (the Earthworks ethos) or from joining it together in unlikely, effective ways (Constructivism), distinguishes both his method and his product.*[48]

JACKIE WINSOR

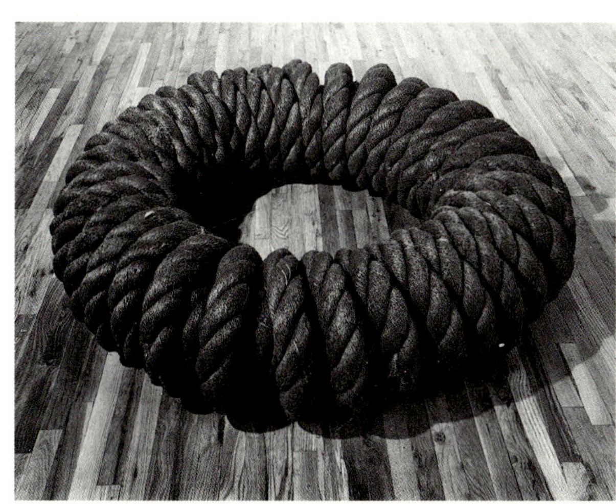

Jackie Winsor's primary concern is with a "highly charged manipulation and transformation of very simple forms—squares, circles, cubes, and spheres. These forms are constructed in a variety of materials, including rope, brick, plywood, twine, pine, nails, and lathing."[49]

Winsor (born 1941) claims that no feminist meaning was intended by the compulsive wrapping and binding that formed *Double Bound Circle* (Fig. **4.26**), nor by the sculpture's form—a circle containing a void (a millennia-old symbol of females, males being symbolized by a shaft, totem, or other long, upright forms). Feminist issues were unavoidable in the late 1960s and early 1970s, and although Winsor was aware of how difficult it was for a woman to break into the art world, and conversant with the

4.26 JACKIE WINSOR
Double Bound Circle 1971
Hemp
16 × 61ins
(40.6 × 154.9cm)
Collection High Museum of
Art, Atlanta

4.27 JACKIE WINSOR
Bound Square 1972
Wood and twine
6ft 3½ins × 6ft 4ins ×
14½ins
(191.8 × 193 × 36.8cm)
Collection, The Museum of
Modern Art, New York
Joseph G. Mayer Foundation,
Inc. in honor of James Thrall
Soby and Grace M. Mayer
Fund in honor of Alfred H.
Barr, Jr.
"I just never feel comfortable unless it takes some time to do. My interest is in slowing everything down, as slow as it can be, so it's imperceivable. To create a one-to-one relationship between 'making time' and 'perceiving time' so that the form grows out of process."[50]

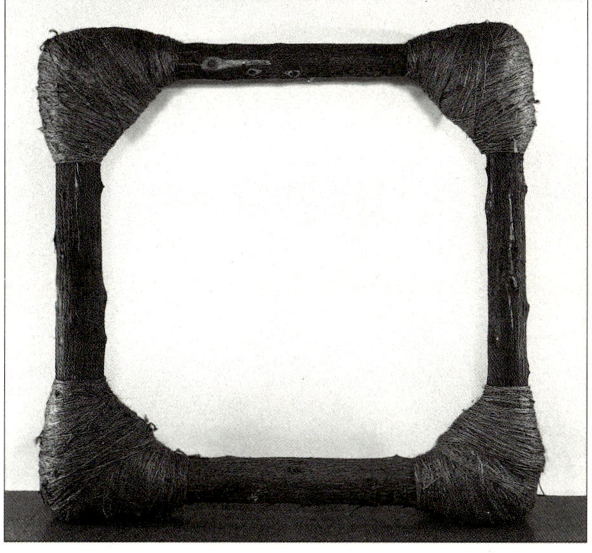

various feminist arguments, she claims no feminist content in her art.

The forming process of wrapping which Winsor frequently uses—as in *Bound Square* (Fig. **4.27**) for example—painstakingly joins various elements through laborious actions. The resulting form visually re-enacts the slow process of its coming into being.

Process is important to Winsor's art, but only in so far as it reveals the form, not as an end in itself. Her work is unique among that of Post-Minimalists because of its feeling of self-containment—as if something were withheld or concealed within her wrapped or boxed forms. "The overall element I seek is self-containment," says Winsor.[51] This attitude toward process leads to something solid and perma-

nent as opposed to the process art of Serra or Sonnier.

Leaning against the wall, *Bound Square* suggests an empty picture frame and evokes Eva Hesse's *Hang-Up* (see page 121). It connects the wall and the floor, encompassing the spheres of painting and sculpture, like *Hang-Up*. Asked about Hesse, Winsor replied:

The way she would finish something was exactly the way I wouldn't have finished it. I would be clearer about the form, how the surface got to be there in the first place. How it reveals itself in the process of its making. She seemed more interested in the material itself. And now since her death she's been blown out of scale by the women's movement—diefied.[52]

JACKIE FERRARA

The wooden pyramids Jackie Ferrara (born 1929) began making in 1972 invite viewers to visually re-enact the laborious process of their construction. To this extent they relate to process art, but like Jackie Winsor's sculptures, Ferrara's work seems more solid and permanent than the process art of Serra or Sonnier. In

the late 1960s, Ferrara employed organic imagery and eccentric materials similar to Hesse's but with more of a link to primitive art. Much of this earlier work has perished by disintegration due to the fragile or unstable materials Ferrara employed.

The term "pyramid" implies an impenetrable,

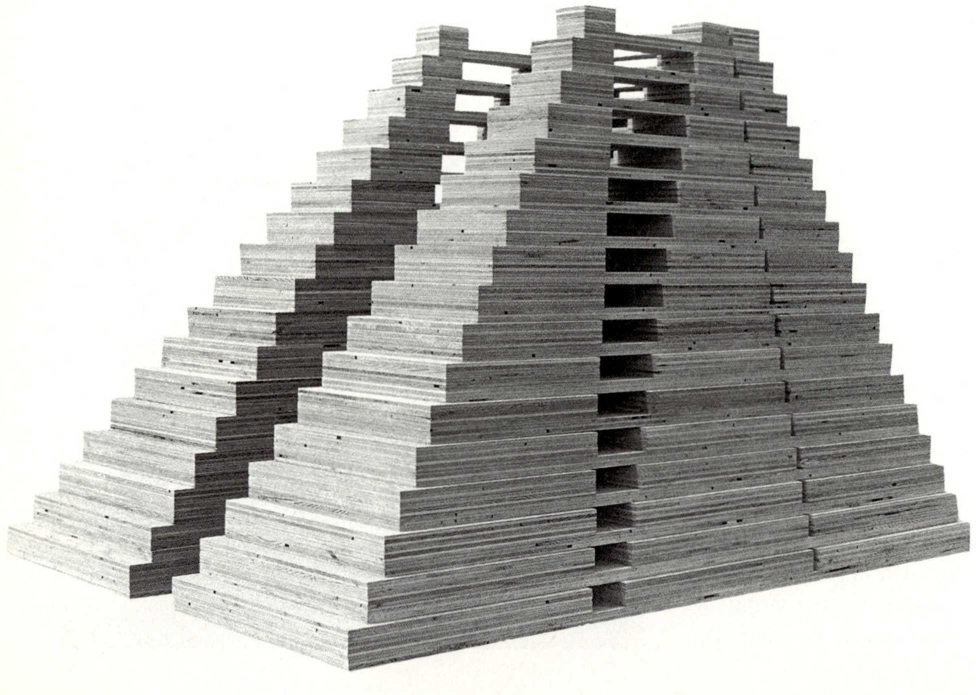

4.28 JACKIE FERRARA
T Pyramid A 148 1975
Plywood
38¼ × 60½ × 43½ins
(97.2 × 153.7 × 110.5cm)
Collection, Wellesley College
Art Museum, Wellesley, MA
Photo courtesy: Michael
Klein Inc., New York

monolithic form, yet many of Ferrara's sculptures are penetrated by openings suggesting visual passageways and rise in steps like ziggurats, or stepped pyramids. The forms of *T Pyramid A148* (Fig. **4.28**) accumulate by increments, unlike Minimalist wholistic forms which are perceivable at a glance. Ferrara's sculptures enact a slow unfolding in a very quiet and reserved, unassertive way. This attitude of modesty and absence of heroics gives the work a unique appeal.

The compulsiveness of Ferrara's meticulous constructions and the obsessive step-by-step careful building of them suggests fragile house-of-cards constructions. Each delicate step builds on the last process and builds to form a whole comprised of many parts and actions. The whole contains the process of its own making yet suggests a concealed mystery.

RICHARD TUTTLE

The diminutive and withdrawn, hermetic sculpture of Richard Tuttle (born 1941) is Post-Minimalist in its departure from Minimalist reductiveness and in its pictorial/sculptural concerns. Sometimes Tuttle's sculpture goes beyond formal issues into associative realms. Art critic Emily Wasserman perceptively identified Tuttle's uniqueness in a 1968 review: "And yet Tuttle distinguishes himself from these others [Novros, Judd, and André] in at least two very important ways—he seems to encompass a concern for the sensuous, and for a kind of chromatic fantasy with an imaginative charm in his dyed fabric shapes, both of which are levelly denied by the work and thinking of his colleagues."[53]

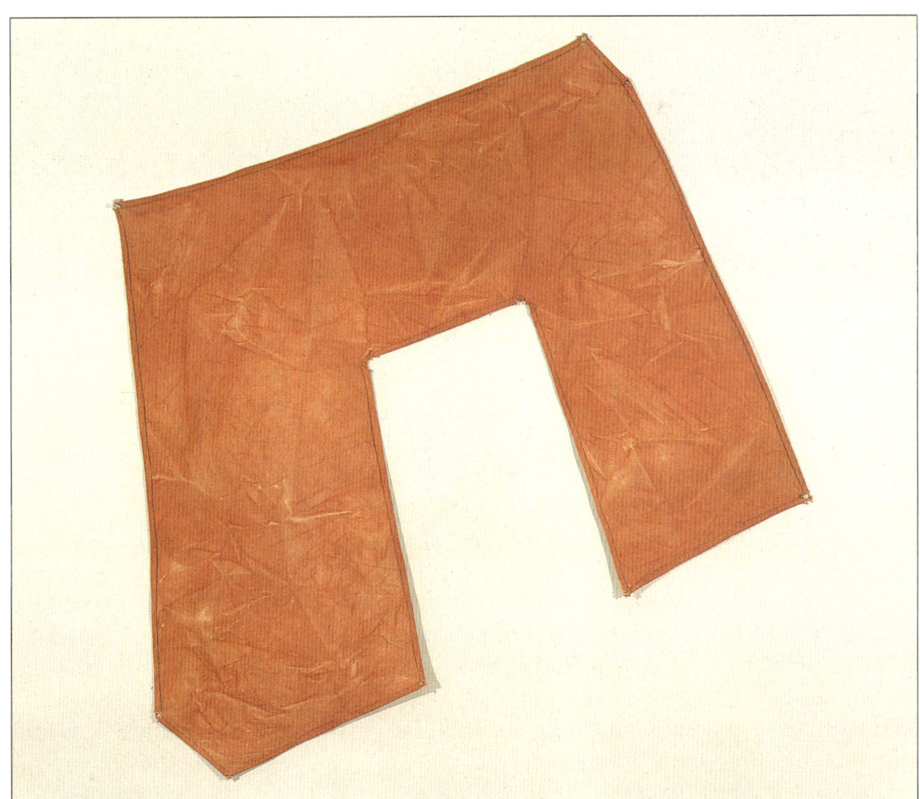

4.29 RICHARD TUTTLE
Untitled 1967
Dyed/sewn canvas
38¾ × 46½ins
(98.4 × 118cm)
Collection Mr. and Mrs.
Ronald K. Greenberg

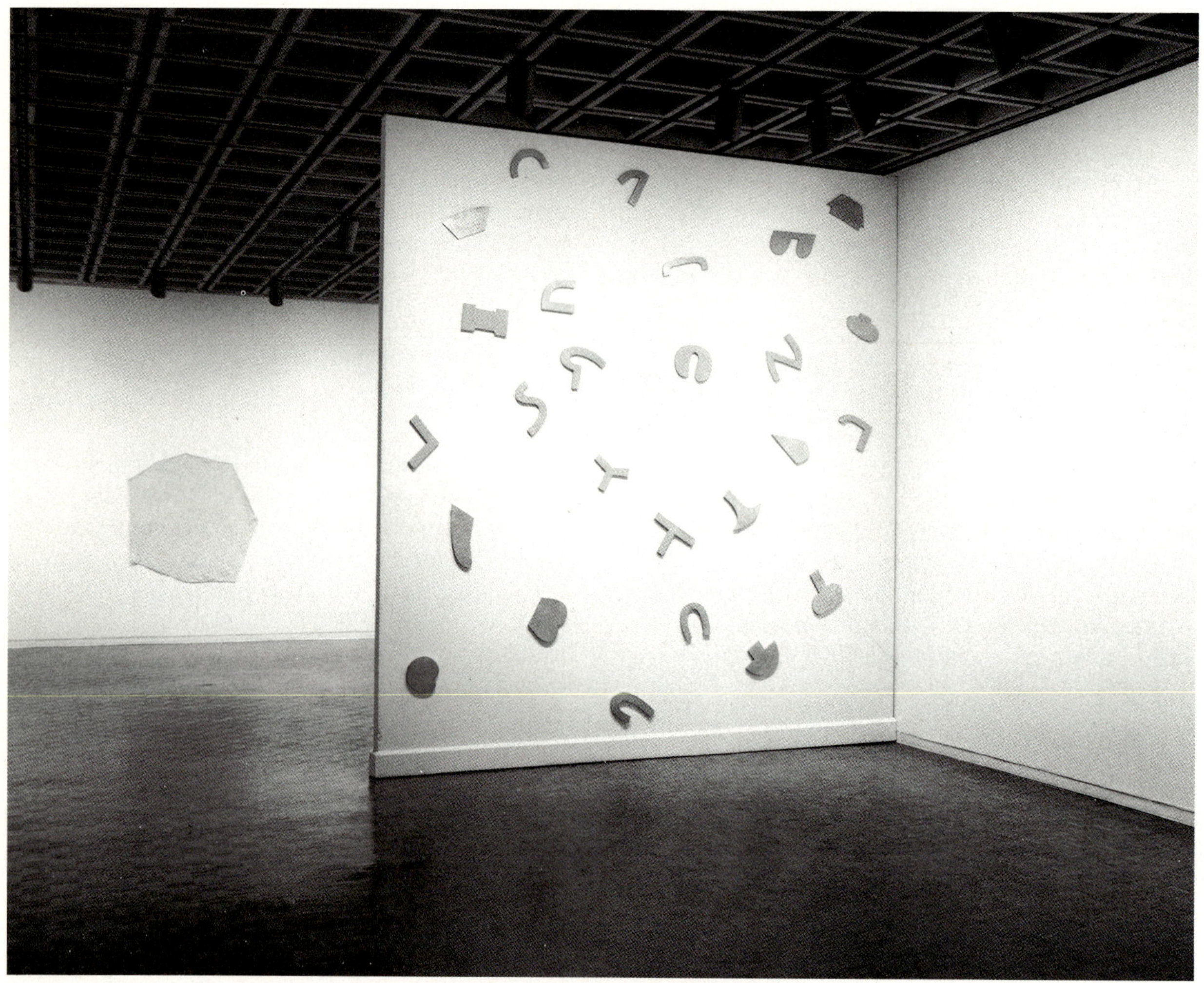

In 1967 Tuttle began making the "dyed fabric shapes" to which Wasserman refers. The eccentrically-shaped canvas polygons were trimmed around the edges in sewn canvas tape, then dyed with fabric dye before being pinned to the wall with push-pins or laid upon the floor. Tuttle's variation of taking painting out of the frame, off the stretcher, out of the rectangle, and of dyeing the color into the resultant object rather than resting it on the surface link his work closely with formal alternatives to formalist painting. But the allusions to representational forms that some of the canvas polygons make introduce representational imagery, perhaps an even more radical position for the time than questioning the criticism of formalist painting. *Untitled* (Fig. **4.29**), a red-dyed

4.30 RICHARD TUTTLE
The Twenty-Six Series
1967
Soldered metal,
each unit 6–10ins
(15.2 – 25.4cm)
Collection of Jost Herbig,
Abholfach, Germany

canvas shape, suggests trousers, an architectural structure, or a piece to a puzzle. At the same time, it conveys visual conviction as a shape with its own reason for being quite independently of any associative meaning.

In Tuttle's childlike representation of the alphabet, *The Twenty-Six Series* (Fig. **4.30**), some letters are more clearly identifiable than others—T, U, and L, for example. Most of the letters are more suggestive than descriptive; they hide more information than they reveal. Tuttle's sculptures often seem to withhold something—a very different attitude from Minimalism's explicitness. Art critic Roberta Smith observed:

Like a number of artists born c. 1940 and who started showing after 1965, Tuttle works with a more clearly emotional, maybe even mystical, approach to abstraction than artists, somewhat older, who emerged 1960–65. While artists like Flavin, Judd and Stella seem concerned with what is literally there, Tuttle, in particular, becomes more and more involved with what is "there" by implication only.[54]

The Twenty-Six Series is meant to be seen either strewn across a spacious wall or scattered haphazardly upon the floor. Like many of Tuttle's works from this period, it cannot be seen either as painting or sculpture, as eloquent or taciturn, simple or complex, present or absent, expressive or mute. Because Tuttle's art requires its viewers to perceive so much of what is "there by implication only," it exists in an expressive realm all of its own.

JOEL SHAPIRO

The art of Joel Shapiro (born 1941) crosses over aesthetic boundaries between Post-Minimalism and the New Image art of the 1970s (see pages 160–63) or the Neo-Expressionism of the 1980s (see pages 167–87). Throughout the 1970s, Shapiro maintained a slightly altered Minimalist geometry and used the spaces his sculptures occupy as part of his artistic means. Unlike Minimalist sculpture's pragmatic and physical articulation of interior architectural spaces, Shapiro treats space as a "void of great emotional power."[55] The art critic Roberta Smith, writing in the catalogue for Shapiro's Whitney Museum of American Art

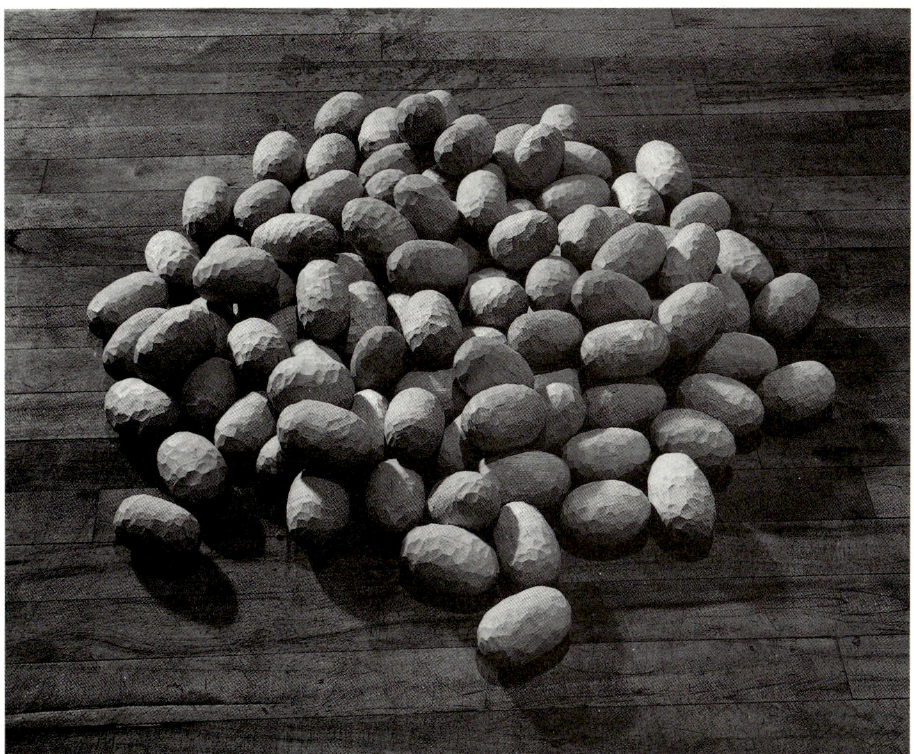

4.31 JOEL SHAPIRO
Untitled 1971
Carved pine
104 units each 2 × 2 × 3ins
(5.1 × 5.1 × 7.6cm)
Courtesy Paula Cooper
Gallery, New York

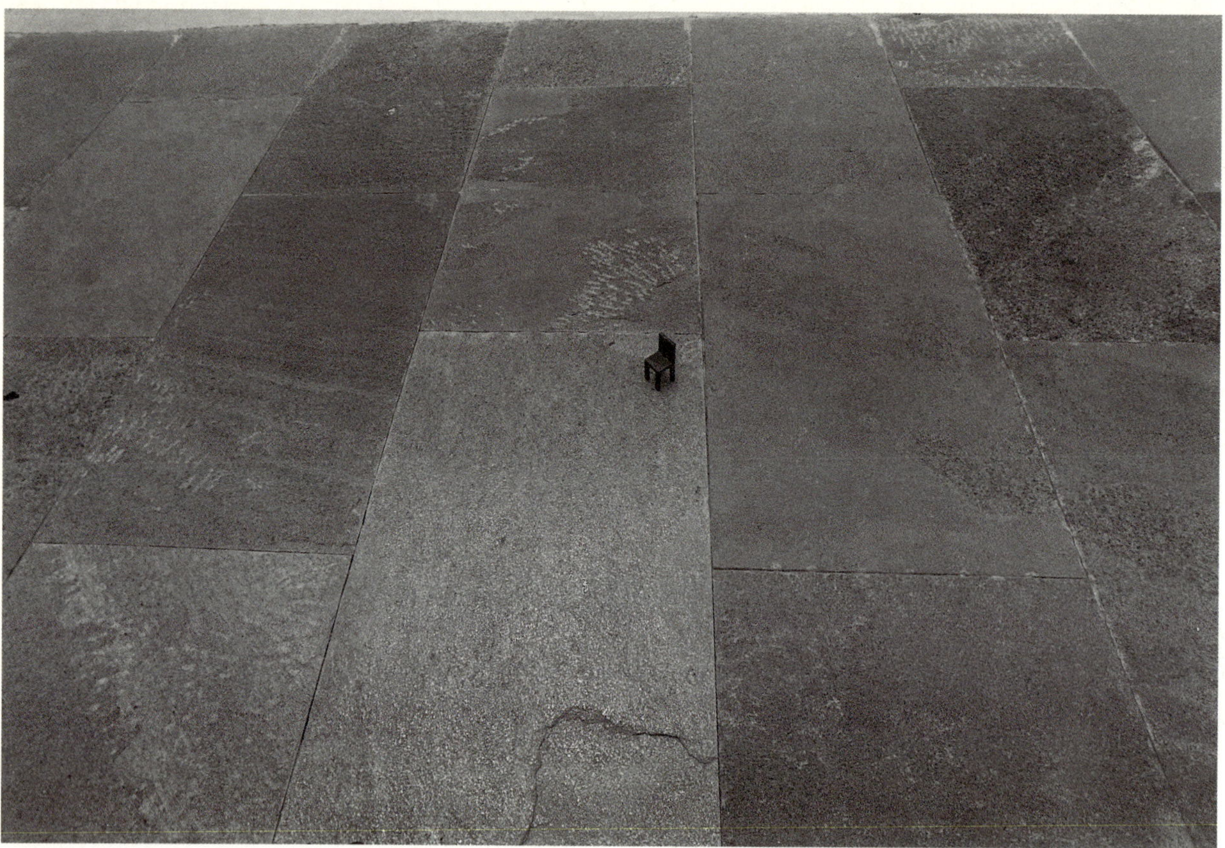

Retrospective in 1982, stated: "This soft, almost schmaltzy underbelly of emotion which weaves in and out of Shapiro's work is one of its great strengths; for the most part it is saved from sentimentality by the purely experiential way it is communicated, through a combination of geometric form and spatial isolation."[56]

Shapiro bridges late Post-Minimalism and early Neo-Expressionism. His earliest mature work dates from 1970, the end of Post-Minimalism's first phase and several years before New Image Art's first appearance. A brief flirtation with Process Art in the early 1970s ended without a romance, and Shapiro never adopted the Neo-Expressionist's *angst*-ridden agitations. Shapiro begins with the Minimalists' assumption that sculptural form should be unencumbered of figurative meanings and associations, then he imbues his pared-down forms with psychological connotations that dramatize and emotionalize them along with the spaces they occupy.

Early forays into process art include a 1971 sculpture titled *One Hand Forming/Two Hands Forming*, a fired-clay sculpture consisting of 170 small nutlike forms, 93 of them made by one hand, 77 of them by

4.32 JOEL SHAPIRO
Untitled (Chair) 1973–74
Cast iron
3⅛ × 1⅜ × 1⅜ins
(8 × 3.4 × 3.4cm)
Courtesy Giuseppe Panza di Biumo-Varese
"The chair evokes physical memory. It seemed to act not only to me, but to other people too. It was perceptually right, and I thought there was no need to make it any bigger. The scale of a piece is its viability in that size, not the size itself. Viability has to do with the fact that it functions as a sculpture."[57]

two hands. It was shown in Shapiro's second exhibition at the Paula Cooper Gallery in New York in 1972, along with an *Untitled* (Fig. **4.31**) pine carving of 104 2 × 2 × 3 inches (5.1 × 5.1 × 7.6 cm) nutlike forms. This latter work contains the kernel of Shapiro's subsequent art. Freed of process connotations, it nonetheless maintains a handmade appearance. The hand-size self-contained forms create witty and intimate encounters with contemporary sculptural issues. Piling the units randomly on the floor suggests process and distribution sculpture and relates to sculpture's vanished base. (By the early 1970s, advanced sculpture took place on the floor or wall or it hung from the ceiling.) Shapiro barely raises parts of his sculpture up from the floor in an apparently casual, witty pile. This modest accumulation in the midst of a large gallery space seems touchingly vulnerable and tentative, without being sentimental because of the "purely experiential way it [the emotion] is communicated, through a combination of geometric form and spatial isolation."[58]

An *Untitled* work from 1973–74 (Fig. **4.32**) miniaturizes the most common man-made occupant of interior architectural space—furniture—in a representational form which evokes both Minimalism's engagement of interior architectural space and rich figurative associations. Artschwager exploited the territory between abstract geometric sculpture and furniture connotations, and much of Minimalist sculpture, in its reiteration of interior architectural spaces, resembles furniture. But Shapiro's sculpture is much more modest than these precedents; for one thing, he engages space less aggressively than the Minimalists, and for another, his diminutive sculpture—it is only 3⅛ inches (8 cm) high—maintains the merest hint of wit and throws the scale way out of our expectations.

> *Controlling negative space is a critical issue in sculpture [Shapiro said].... I described the right-angled space of the seat of a chair, and that is the familiar space of a chair—the space one occupies. Our bodies are in that space in a room, we know that space, and we bring that information to the piece when we see it. Our bodies and our experience become condensed.*[59]

The pared-down, reductivist nature of Shapiro's sculpture parallels Minimalism's bare-bones stance, but Shapiro's extension of this Minimal art characteristic into representational and emotional realms sets his art apart.

A life-size cast bronze figure made from undisguised lumber joined in self-evident ways raises sculpture up from the floor a little bit less tentatively than the chair's diminutive legs. *Untitled* (Fig. **4.33**) still reiterates Minimalist reductive geometry and acknowledges the ground plane, that typical feature of advanced sculpture in the late 1960s and early 1970s. Yet the late 1960s sculptural issues of gravity, weight, and balance here take on connotations of a human figure. While the artist uses geometric rather than organic forms to indicate arms, legs, and other body parts, the figure's weights, balances, and grav-

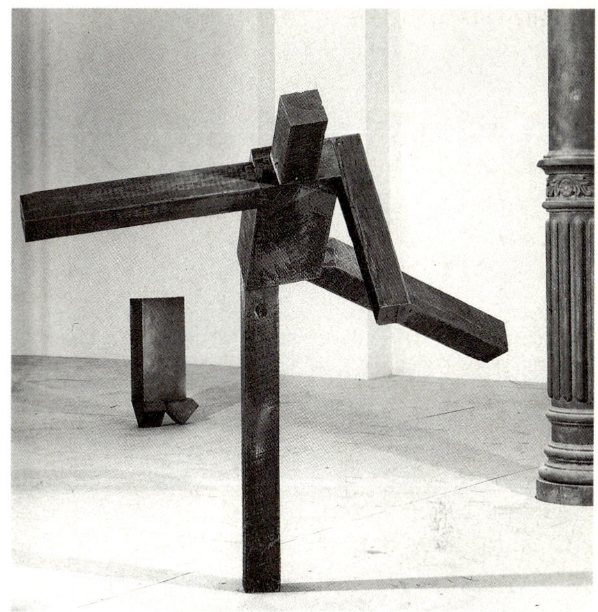

4.33 JOEL SHAPIRO
Untitled 1980–81
Bronze, edition AP/3
52⅞ × 64 × 45½ins
(134.3 × 162.6 × 115.6cm)
Courtesy Paula Cooper
Gallery, New York

ity engage the space around it and activate our psychological/physical bearings.

Throughout the 1970s, many of the artists whose work we have discussed beginning in the 1960s continued to evolve, some maintaining their path, some veering off. Few artistic currents of much consequence originated in the 1970s; it was a decade of assimilation and elaboration. Shapiro maneuvered his way through the complicated terrain and never lost his aesthetic balance, a forerunner of Neo-Expressionism yet a projector of Minimalism and Post-Minimalism into new expressive realms.

> *I'm more interested in how one thinks about something than in what something looks like [Shapiro said]. I am interested in what a house or a figure might mean, or what it means to me. I am interested in my capacity to refer to it in terms of sculpture, but not to illustrate it or describe it.*[60]

Social and Political Background

Many of the protests about social and political issues that typified the 1960s carried over into the 1970s. Demonstrations for the equality of blacks, women, and gays; along with protests against the Vietnam war and the embattled President Nixon were loud and shrill, especially during the first half of the decade. During the second half, despite the worst recession since World War II, worldwide inflation, and the declining United States dollar, Americans' real disposable income rose 28.5%. Consumers purchased from a huge abundance of goods and services and pampered themselves so much that the 1970s came to be called the "Me Decade."

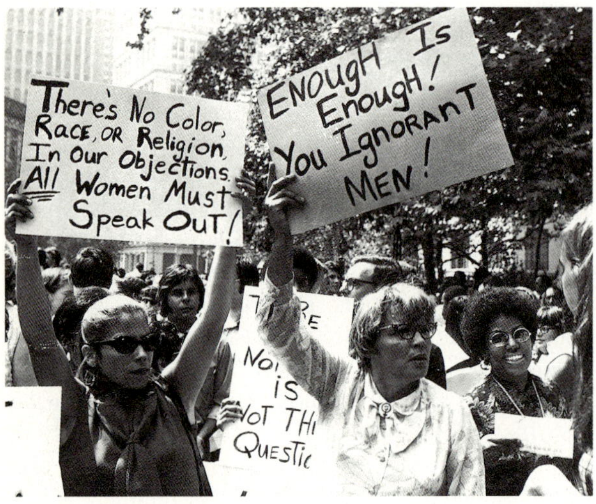

The women's liberation movement demanded equality through marches and strikes. In 1972, the Senate approved the Equal Rights Amendment to the United States Constitution, legally ending discrimination based on sex, but it failed by three states from being ratified and becoming law. Women nonetheless transformed their roles in American life, becoming miners, priests, jockeys, West Point cadets, ship captains, astronauts, and students in medical, law, and business schools. In 1973, the United States Supreme Court legalized abortion during early pregnancy, giving women control over their own bodies. In 1979, Britain elected its first woman Prime Minister, Margaret Thatcher.

Gay liberation came out of the closet, demanding equal rights and society's approval. Gay Pride parades of homosexual men and women took place in cities throughout the world, from New York to San Francisco and Paris. American Blacks endured a turbulent decade. Efforts toward the racial integration of schools provoked opposition and violence as the nation struggled toward desegregation. At Kent State University in 1970, National Guardsmen killed four student anti-war protestors and wounded ten. A Mayday war protest march in Washington, D.C. in 1971 resulted in 13,400 arrests, most of them tear-gassed and herded into an open-air stockade.

After the long, bloody, and divisive Vietnam war, the United States withdrew without a victory in 1973. China's leaders ended two decades of hostility with the United States by welcoming President Nixon to China in 1972. Russia's Politburo exiled the dissident author Aleksandr Solzhenitsyn in 1974 and sentenced dissidents Anatoly Shcharansky and Aleksandr Ginzburg to long prison terms in 1978.

The Arab oil embargo in 1973 jolted the

world—especially the United States which obtained two-thirds of its oil from the Arabs—into a period of short supplies, gasoline lines, and high costs. The worst recession in 40 years occurred in 1974, leading to predictions of worldwide economic collapse and even worse inflation. The year 1975 saw the highest rate of U.S. unemployment since 1941 and the biggest drop in industrial production since 1937. In 1977, the value of the dollar reached a postwar low.

Vice President Spiro Agnew resigned and was convicted of tax evasion in 1973. President Nixon appointed Congressman Gerald Ford in Agnew's place. The Republican Nixon's lying about his involvement in an illegal burglary of the Democratic National Headquarters led to his forced resignation under the threat of impeachment in 1974. Gerald Ford became the first non-elected U.S. President in history and issued a full pardon for Nixon. Ford was defeated in the 1976 Presidential election by the popular Washington outsider Jimmy Carter. The nation celebrated its bicentennial in a national outpouring of pride and healing that same year.

The 1970s also saw the election, by the College of Cardinals, of the first non-Italian Pope in 455 years in 1977: the Polish Cardinal Karol Wojtyla became Pope John Paul II. The new Pope traveled to Mexico, Poland, and America, where he became the first Pope ever to visit the White House. This decade also saw the birth in

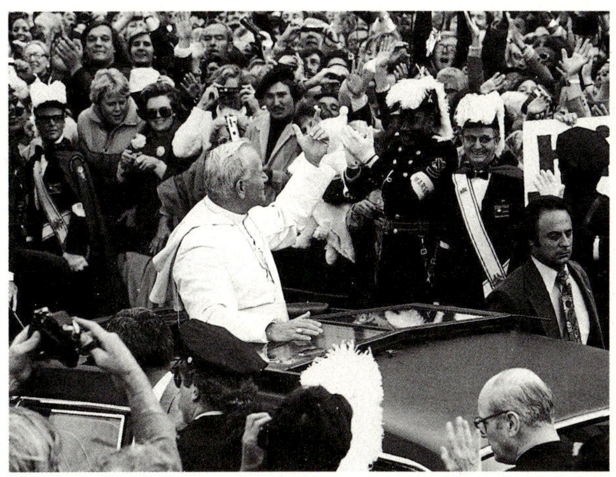

England in 1978 of the first child ever conceived outside her mother's womb—"test-tube baby" Louise Brown.

The 1970s was a fragmented decade of special interests fighting for their own goals rather than a time of widely shared aspirations. The art world did not coalesce around any new major movements. Despite the decade's economic woes, modern art reached higher prices than ever before: in 1970 the American painter Jasper Johns's 30 feet (9.1 m)-long *Map* sold for $200,000, then the highest price ever paid for a work by a living artist. Australia's National Gallery paid $2 million for Jackson Pollock's 1952 painting *Blue Poles* in 1973, setting the record price paid for a work of modern art until then.

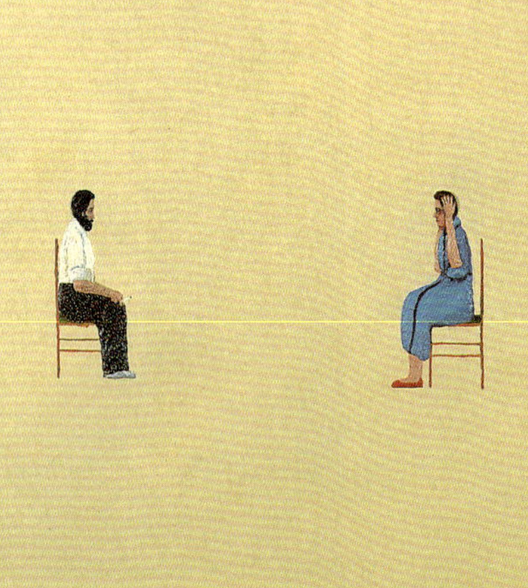

5
Pluralism

"I want my paintings to be about something, as opposed to being about nothing or being about themselves . . . I want something to mean something, in a cogent and revealing way, because I want to be purposeful, even useful. So I regard subject matter as my primary concern as an artist."[1]

—— NICHOLAS AFRICANO ——

Nicholas Africano
The Cruel Discussion   1976–77
Courtesy Holly Solomon Gallery, New York

The 1970s was a decade during which many artistic approaches existed simultaneously without any single style dominating. Pop Art, Minimalism, Conceptual Art, Video Art, Performance Art, Film, Earthworks, site-specific sculpture, and Post-Minimalism—all of which originated in the 1960s—continued to evolve throughout the 1970s. Several new developments originated in the 1970s, though none of them achieved the significance of the earlier styles. Pluralism is the term that has been used to describe this situation in which no single style dominated, but many existed at the same time.

Realism had long been a strong current in American art, but during the first two decades of the twentieth century, American artists increasingly looked to Europe for guidance and adopted European Modernism. Still, many American artists continued to practice realist styles despite Abstraction's dominance during the twentieth century. During the 1930s and 1940s, American Scene and Regionalist artists interpreted the daily life they observed around them. One of the greatest painters America has ever produced—Edward Hopper (1882–1967)—painted his scenes of loneliness and desolation throughout nearly the entire first 60 years of the twentieth century. Alice Neel, Fairfield Porter, Moses Soyer and his brother, Raphael, persisted in their figurative styles throughout the 1960s and beyond.

On the west coast, where Abstract Expressionism never achieved the dominance it had on the east coast, the Bay Area Figurative style reinvigorated representational painting, beginning in the 1950s and continuing to this day. David Park, Richard Diebenkorn, Elmer Bischoff, Nathan Oliveira, James Weeks, and Joan Brown adopted the spontaneous brushwork of the Abstract Expressionists but used it for Edenic, sun-drenched scenes of suburban fulfilment in the same mode as Matisse's Mediterranean idylls. Californians Wayne Thiebaud and Mel Ramos painted representational scenes in a Pop Art style.

Pop artists and their precursors, Jasper Johns and Robert Rauschenberg, used representational imagery in their art beginning in the late 1950s and early 1960s, but with a difference from other realist artists. Pop artists used secondary sources, mostly taken from mass-media or the human-made world, rather than working from direct observation of the outside world. Conceptual artists and artists working in video, film, and performance utilized recognizable images, too, though mostly ones seen through cameras rather than painted, drawn or sculpted.

Cameras came into play in the Realist Art of the 1970s, whether in the photo flash-like lighting, exaggerated reality, or snapshot-like cropping of Realists such as Alfred Leslie, Philip Pearlstein and Duane Hanson; or in the practice of working directly from photographs that typifies the Photo Realists such as Malcolm Morley, Richard Estes, Chuck Close, and Audrey Flack. These artists' styles of Realism acknowledge the role that photography has played in conditioning our perception of the real world, and emphasize the Pop artists' assertion that in a mass-media, consumers' society, our lives are more filled with human-made things than natural ones.

Until the 1970s, "decorative" was the worst insult one could level at any postwar art. "Decorative" stood for everything that was facile, pretty, unserious, unchallenging, too easy to like, and simply not "tough" enough. In short, "decorative" stood for all the wrong things in art. The Pluralism of the 1970s included an art movement called Pattern and Decoration that was intentionally and frankly all of the things that decorative had formerly meant, with several radical purposes. One was to assert that which had formerly been aesthetically discreditable as aesthetically credible. Another was to thereby annex the populist audience that did not know of, or understand, the art theories underlying other abstract painting but that could respond to pattern painting with the same eyes that enjoy beautiful fabrics.

Two New York museum exhibitions that opened in 1978—*New Image Painting* at the Whitney Museum of American Art and *"Bad" Painting* at the New Museum—announced a third kind of representational painting that originated in the 1970s, New Image Painting. Both shows included artists who worked with recognizable imagery and emphasized narrative, associative, and humorous content, foreshadowing the Neo-Expressionism that was shortly to become internationally dominant. All of the artists were highly idiosyncratic, employing very personal imagery and alluding to their narrative content rather than specifying a storyline. Most retained vestiges of Abstract Expressionism's tremulous brushwork, and all conformed to the formalist dictum that painted space be non-illusionistic, flat. Yet their injection of narrative content into modernist painting norms gave their work an accessibility that postwar avant-garde painting hadn't had until then, except with Pop Art.

Growing populism is a strong current in the Pluralism of the 1970s, marking a gradual transition from the avant-garde that began in the 1860s to a lessening of the rift between fine art and the general populace. Incorporating mass-media effects on perception, asserting narrative content, and overthrowing elitist aesthetics made art more comprehensible to a larger audience in the 1970s than the more hermetic approach to art of the 1960s. By the 1980s, hermeticism lessened to the extent that Post-Modern artists openly addressed the same audience as movies and advertising.

Many symptoms indicating changes in fine art's relation to the majority culture took place before the overall condition was evident enough to be identified. Economics often played a role. The 1973 Sotheby Park Bernet auction of works from the Robert and Ethel Scull collection demonstrated that contemporary American art had a strong international market. The number of contemporary art galleries in New York burgeoned from only a few dozen in the 1960s to an estimated 500 by the 1980s. Art and artists attained a mystique and desirability in the 1970s that they had never before had in the United States.

Beginning in the late 1960s, galleries followed artists to SoHo (south of New York's Houston Street), a former neighborhood of light manufacturers and warehouses, where relatively inexpensive large interior spaces could then be obtained. Changes in real estate laws made SoHo essentially an arts district. Boutiques, restaurants, and other services sprang up to thrive on the increased tourist traffic. Then real estate prices rose so sharply that SoHo became and still is, one of New York's most expensive neighborhoods. (New York remained the art capital of the western world throughout the 1970s.) Clearly, art had become a big money-maker and artists no longer occupied the bohemian fringe of society.

These are only a few symptoms of the art world's changed socio-economic conditions, conditions which we will discuss more thoroughly in Chapter 7. Post-Modern and many subsequent artists comment upon art as an embodiment of money and status, as well as upon its links with popular culture and commerce, as part of the artwork's content. That this became important subject-matter for artists in the 1980s indicates the extent to which the formerly adversarial relation of fine art to popular culture—a relationship that 1960s artists assumed—underwent a transformation in the 1970s.

Realism

ALFRED LESLIE

Alfred Leslie (born 1927) vacillated between figurative and abstract expressionistic imagery throughout the 1950s, finally settling on representational painting in the early 1960s. Leslie's *The Killing Cycle—Six: Loading Pier* 1975 is one of seven monumental paintings in a series about the death of the poet Frank O'Hara, killed by a taxicab on Fire Island in 1966. O'Hara was a friend of many of the second generation Abstract Expressionists, including Leslie, who began work on the theme almost immediately and continued working on it during the next 14 years. The seven paintings both starkly record O'Hara's death and allegorize it, making it seem more momentous than an occurrence in the everyday world.

The sixth painting of the series, *Loading Pier* (Fig. **5.1**), derives its composition from the seventeenth-century Italian painter Caravaggio's *Entombment*, which pictures Christ about to be lowered into an abyss from a stone slab which is painted in the lower third of the canvas, much like Leslie's *Loading Pier*. Leslie not only borrowed Caravaggio's composition but his connotations of momentousness as well. He also borrowed the Italian baroque master's use of dramatic lighting to enhance the narrative, a feature Caravaggio was celebrated for all over Baroque Europe and which influenced artists as diverse as Rembrandt, Velazquez, Rubens, La Tour, and Le Nain.

But Leslie combined Caravaggesque lighting with a photo flash-like harshness resembling the lighting in photo-journalist Wegee's grisly infra-red flash photos of murder victims. Wegee was a newspaper photographer whose works are admired by photography enthusiasts for their perception of people on the fringes of society. "Wegee" was a nickname he used professionally, taken from the "Ouija Board," a device used to send messages from the spirit world. Because he arrived at crime scenes before the police, Wegee was believed to be psychic. In reality, he had a police radio. This combination of the exalted and the reviled accounts, along with its huge scale, for *Loading Pier's* visual impact. Once seen, it is hard to forget.

Placing a poet in the position of the Saviour allegorizes art itself, making *Loading Pier* simultaneously a homage to Caravaggio, to O'Hara, and to art, as well as a commentary on the position of artists in contemporary society. Such a traditional, dramatic, narrative approach was very risky to attempt in 1975. Leslie's painting is narrowly saved from being unbelievable by the contemporary clothes and the contemporized photo flash-like lighting, neither of which would have been conceivable without Pop Art's precedent. However, Leslie's strong moralizing, didactic tone differentiates his art from other contemporary Realists and Photo-Realists.

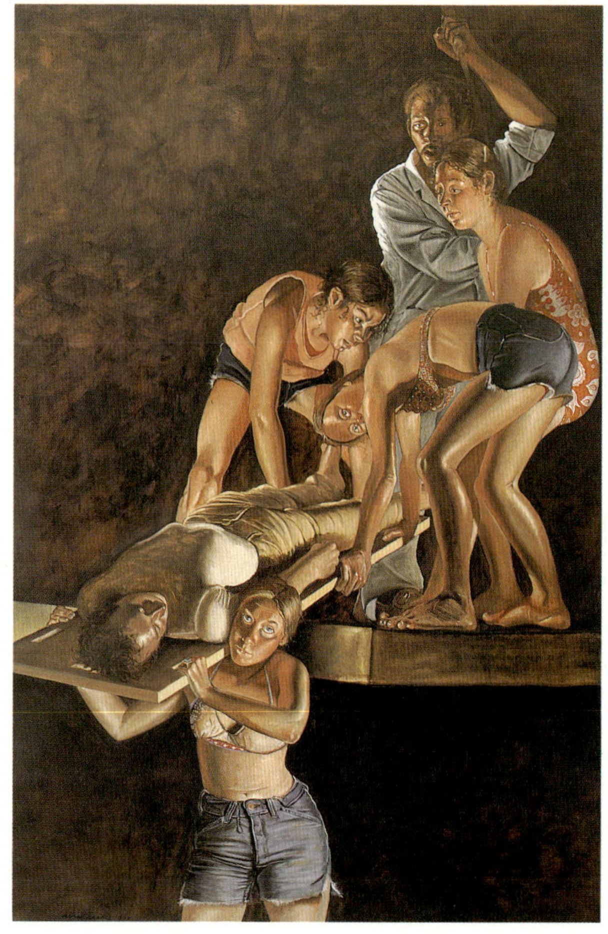

5.1 ALFRED LESLIE
The Killing of Frank
O'Hara: The Loading Pier
1975
Sixth painting of **The**
Killing Cycle

Oil on canvas
108 × 72ins
(274.3 × 182.9cm)
Collection Mr. and Mrs.
Robert H. Orchard

PHILIP PEARLSTEIN

Philip Pearlstein was born in Pittsburgh, Pennsylvania, in 1924, where he received a BFA degree from the Carnegie Institute of Technology in 1949. Andy Warhol was a classmate. Moving to New York, Pearlstein received an MFA from the Institute of Fine Arts, New York University, in 1955. His painted figures hardly ever touch each other or make eye contact. While Leslie deletes everything but the figures and the primary narrative elements, Pearlstein treats everything in his studio set-ups with equal interest and intensity. Figures, chairs, rugs, are all subjected to the same dispassionate gaze. "He renders the naked

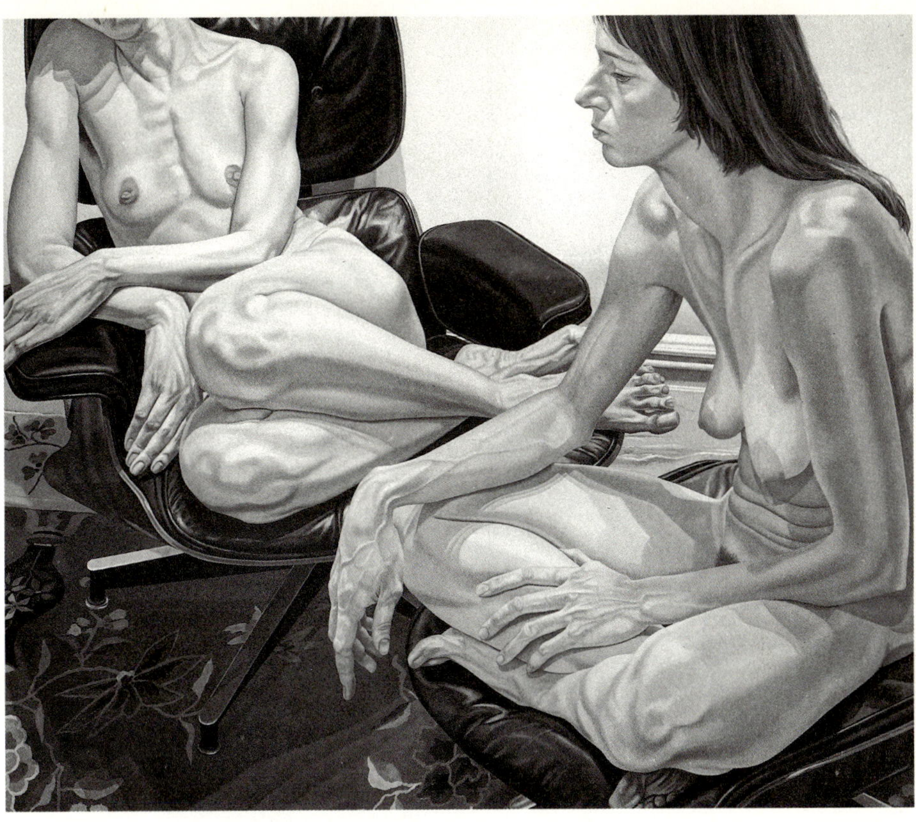

body as visual fact, deliberately distancing himself from its psychological implications," wrote curator Michael Auping.

Pearlstein begins by isolating a visually dominant aspect of the figure, then painting out to the edge of the canvas, allowing the canvas edge to crop out heads or other parts of the figure that would be considered essential to a narrative approach. Using the canvas size as a given aesthetic precondition, like the fixed size of a camera's viewfinder, Pearlstein evades a perception of the figure's placement as intending to convey psychological meaning. This dispassionate attitude is consistent with the Minimalists' interest in perceptual phenomena. It allows Pearlstein to underplay the eroticism of the nude. "I'm not painting people," Pearlstein said. "I'm dealing with what you see, how you see, and how you depict what you see.... I'm concerned with the human figure as a found object."[3]

One of the figures in *Two Female Models on Eames Chair and Stool* (Fig. **5.2**) is cropped at the jaw and hand, while the other is bisected at the head and back. The close-up view that the cropping implies emphasizes surfaces. The reflective surfaces of the leather chair and stool are given the same degree of visual attention as the model's skin. Drained of emotional content, the figures become as inanimate as the objects in the scene. Pearlstein's distanced stance makes it possible to deal with the subject of nudity without lapsing into a conventional treatment.

DUANE HANSON

Duane Hanson (born 1925) began making fiberglass figure sculptures in 1966 with a series of sculptural groups expressing social issues, like a race riot or skid row alcoholics. By the early 1970s, Hanson turned to fleshy middle-class people bent by "the homogenizing oppressiveness of meaningless work and mass-material culture and the wasteful excess of self-indulgence."[4] These latter sculptures achieved a huge popular success despite their scathing criticism of the very people who admired them. Perhaps the novices admired them at least in part for their technical accomplishment; a high degree of realism and

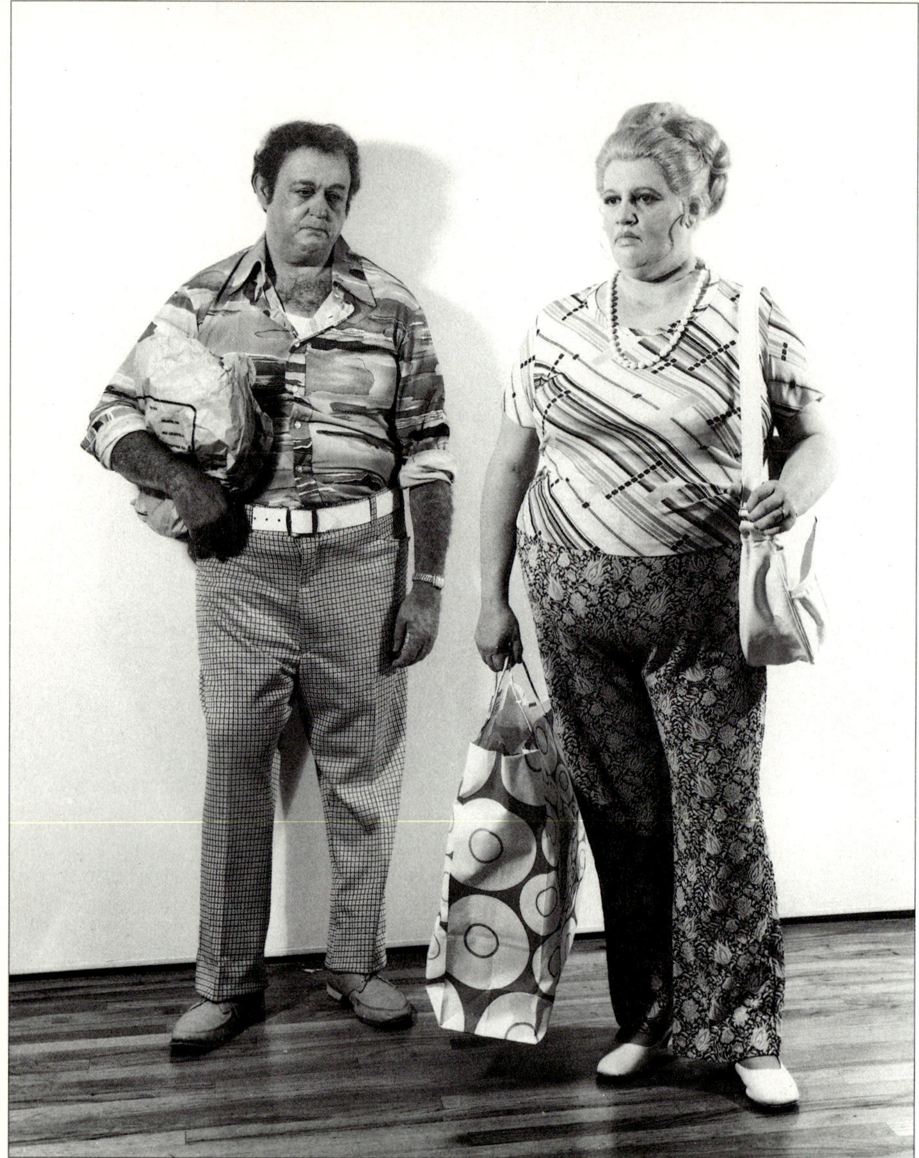

obvious craftsmanship skills appeal to untutored audiences who know no other way to measure artistic achievement. Suspecting this populist stance, art critic Harold Rosenberg wrote that: "The major response to it is curiosity: 'How did he do it?' One admires Hanson's *Businessman* neither as a sculpture nor as a concept but as a technical feat that seems a step in advance of the waxworks museum."[5]

Yet the art historian Kirk Varnedoe wrote that:
He (Hanson) has actively sought an art that is aggressively anti-elitist and non-hermetic, directly accessible to many different viewing publics on widely different levels of understanding. In so doing, he has resigned himself to the contempt of most self-styled 'serious' contemporary art critics, and to the misdirected praise of others for matters of technique that concern him only as means rather than goals.[6]

Shoppers (Fig. **5.3**) depicts two weary suburbanites weighted down by their purchases and excess pounds. They both have all the signs of middle-class material success but no signs of spiritual vitality. We see them here in a photograph, which we expect to be still, but when viewed as sculptures their stillness and lack of life makes them seem even more spiritually bereft.

Photo-Realism

MALCOLM MORLEY

Malcolm Morley (born 1931) briefly painted in a style related to Photo-Realism but did not strictly adhere to the techniques that came to typify the later Photo-Realists. Just as he anticipated Neo-Expressionism in his paintings from 1975, Morley's work beginning in 1965 foreshadowed Photo-Realism. The main difference between Morley and the other Photo-Realists is that he never worked directly from photographs themselves but, rather, from photographic reproductions on tourist postcards and brochures. Using pre-existing secondary sources, Morley's paintings from this period are somewhere between Pop Art and Photo-Realism.

Morley moved to New York from England in 1958, when the proto-Pop paintings of Johns and Rauschenberg were first gaining widespread attention. He continued to paint in an abstract style until 1964, when he painted the ships which he could see docked in the harbor outside his studio window. By 1965, the artist turned to painting postcards of ships in larger scale than the postcards themselves, always surrounding the image with a white border to make it clear that they are images of images. The postcard paintings are smoothly textured, with an absence of expressive brushwork.

Like Chuck Close, Morley gridded the postcard and the canvas in an equal number of squares, then transferred the photographic image to the canvas square-by-square, thus maintaining neutrality toward the subject matter. As with Pearlstein, neutrality toward the subject typifies Photo-Realism. Photo-Realists are more interested in how a photograph records information and how that information looks when translated to a painting. Information theory preoccupied Conceptual artists (in fact, a 1970 Museum of Modern Art Conceptual Art exhibition was titled "Information"); the grid is the primary compositional device of the Minimalists.

"I accept the subject matter as a by-product of surface," Morley said in 1967.[7] The combination of neutrality toward the subject matter, emphasis on surface, and the white border tends to flatten the spatial illusionism; we read *S. S. Amsterdam in Front of Rotterdam* (Fig. **5.4**, see page 152) as a postcard, not a seascape. Absence of spatial illusionism was an important critical principle of avant-garde painting at the time. The critic Clement Greenberg's belief that painting was essentially a two-dimensional art still held sway. Most Photo-Realists emphasize surface in one way or another; in this way, they conform, at least in spirit, to the principles of avant-garde painting.

CHUCK CLOSE

Chuck Close (born 1940) first began painting from photographs in 1966 when he shot black and white photographs of a young woman who was a secretary at the University of Massachusetts (he was teaching at Amherst at the time). First, he attempted a color painting using a traditional brush technique, but reluctantly abandoned the canvas. After moving to New York in 1967, he painted a 22 feet (6.7 m) long black and white reclining nude of the same subject, testing a variety of techniques that resulted in a disunified painting with too much attention attracted by certain areas—the breasts and crotch—though he had tried to treat every part of the figure with equal importance. "It was connected to the notion of all-overness that came out of Jackson Pollock," Close explained. "I had the belief that the essential American image at that point, whether it was Pollock or Stella, had a consistent surface . . . and that every piece was essen-

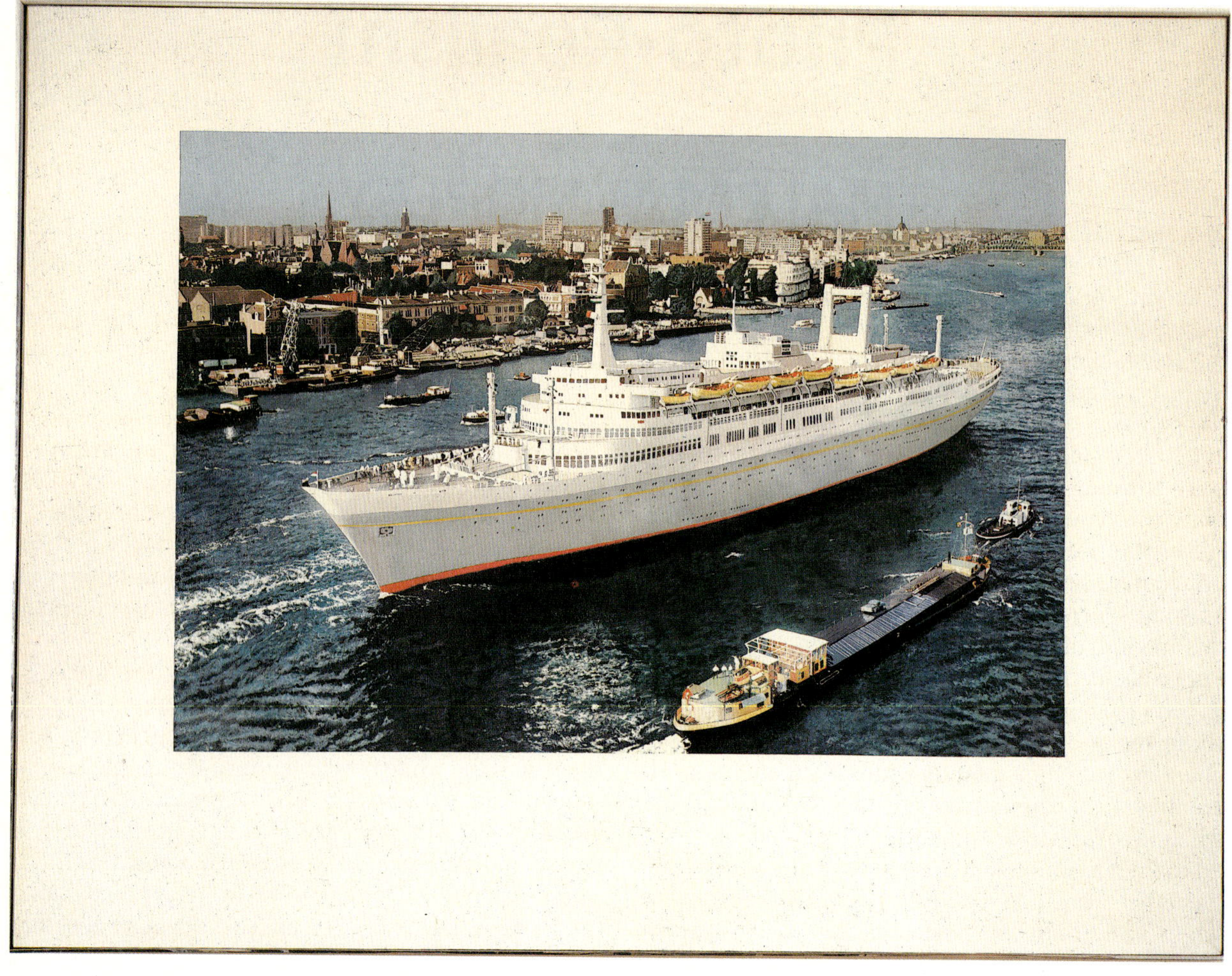

5.4 MALCOLM MORLEY
S.S. *Amsterdam* in front
of Rotterdam 1966
Acrylic on canvas
62 × 84ins
(157.5 × 213.5cm)
Courtesy Saatchi Collection,
London

tially the same. I wanted to approach the nude with that same kind of lack of hierarchy . . . in a deadpan, dumb kind of way."[8]

Some film left over in the camera after photographing the large nude prompted Close to shoot a mug shot of himself. Accidentally, the angle was from slightly below and, having misjudged the lens's focal length, certain areas were out of focus. "That range of focus allowed for a potentially more abstract reading of the image,"[9] Close said. He gessoed and gridded a 9 × 7 feet (2.7 × 2.1 m) canvas, then began laboriously transferring the photograph to the canvas square by square using an airbrush and acrylic paint. He worked for nearly four months on this single painting. "With the self-portrait, Close established the basic elements of his style: large scale, anonymous surface, formula composition, and photographic veracity. He refined and explored these characteristics in a series of enormous black and white portrait heads that occupied him until April 1970."[10]

Big-Self Portrait (1968) (Fig. **5.5**) is so huge in scale that it has a monumental presence, yet when you move close to it the surface is a completely unified topography with an even-handed treatment. Close exactly reproduced the out-of-focus areas. Blown

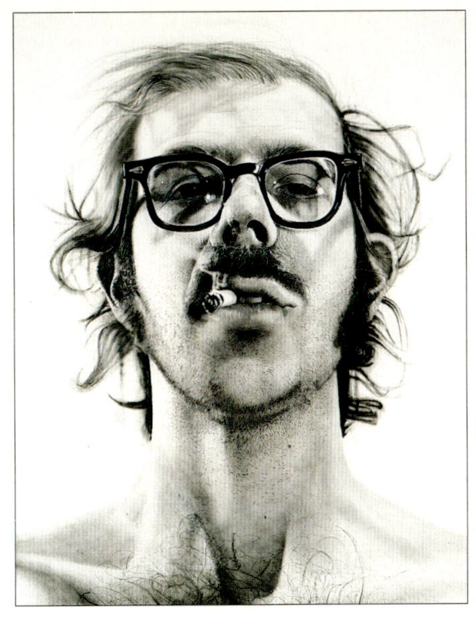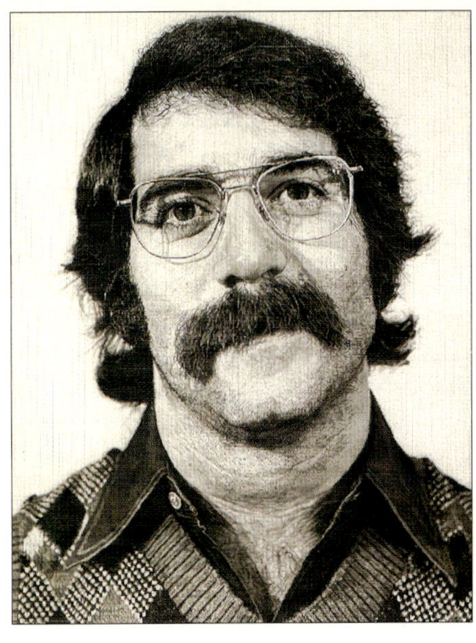

5.5 CHUCK CLOSE
Big-Self Portrait 1968
Acrylic on canvas
107½ins × 83½ins
(273 × 212.1cm)
Collection Walker Art Center,
Minneapolis Art Center
Acquisition Fund, 1969

5.7 CHUCK CLOSE
Robert/104,072 1973–74
Synthetic polymer paint and
ink with graphite on gessoed
canvas
9 × 7ft
(2.74 × 2.13m)
Collection, The Museum of
Modern Art, New York.
Gift of J. Frederic Byers III
and promised gift of an
anonymous donor

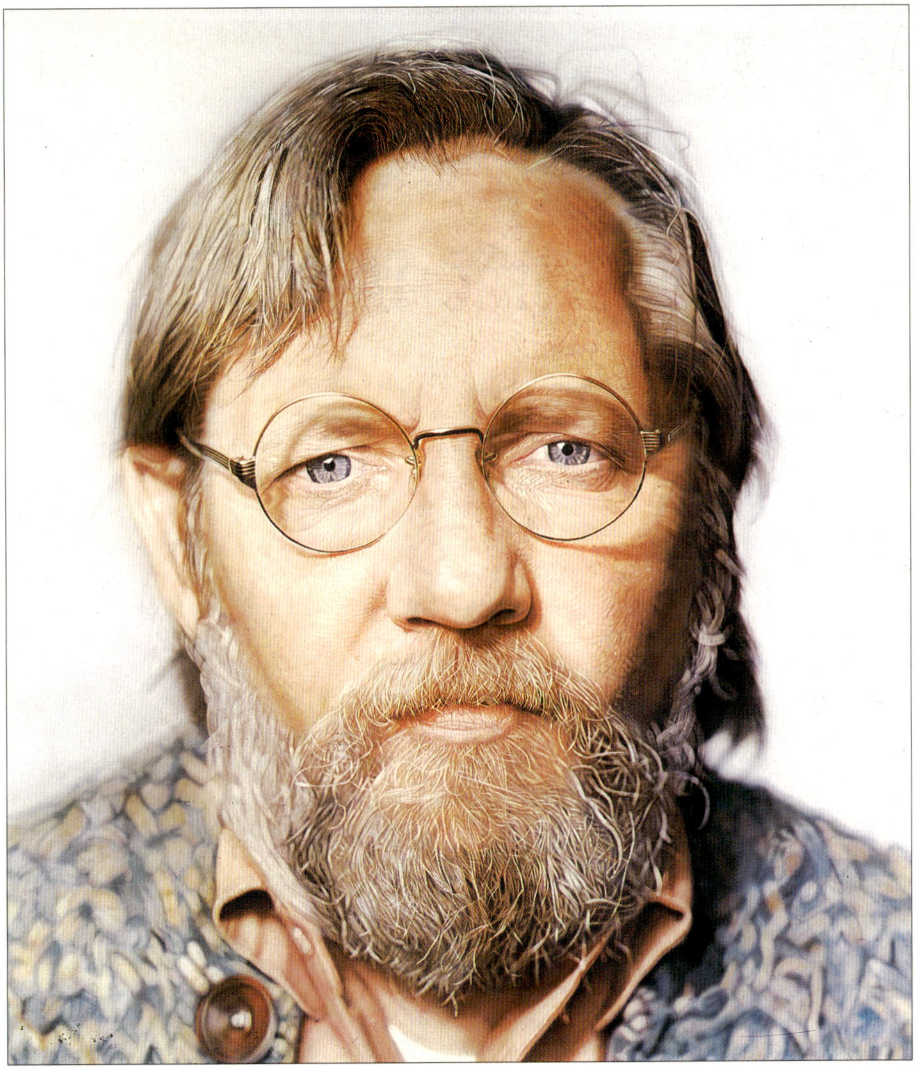

5.6 CHUCK CLOSE
John 1972
Acrylic on canvas
100 × 90ins
(254 × 228.6cm)
Collection of Mrs. Robert B.
Mayer, Chicago

up to 9 × 7 feet (2.7 × 2.1 m), every pore looks like a crater, every whisker a tree trunk. The psychological impact of the monumental portrait head gives way to a surface reading resembling photographs from unmanned spacecraft surveying the lunar surface. Evenness, neutrality of subject matter, emphasis on surface—these are all typical qualities of Photo-Realism.

By 1970, after producing a series of black and white monumental heads of his friends, Close wanted to work in color. Again choosing to transfer photographic information to a painting, he employed the color system of dye transfer prints and photo lithography, reducing the palette to red, blue, and yellow which he applied with an airbrush in successive layers, one layer at a time, staying within boundaries defined by wrinkles, shadows, scars, or edges rather than using a grid. *Big-John* (Fig. **5.6**) is from Close's first series of color paintings.

To this day, Close continues to work with bland mug shots of friends, reusing the same image over and over again, transferring the photographic information from one "mapping" system to another. In a series of "dot" drawings begun in 1973 (Fig. **5.7**), Close reduced the mark he makes to a uniform pattern of dots on a grid. The artist explains his motivation:

Looking at the eye is one thing and looking at the cheek, another, but I have always tried to have the same attitude toward both of them. But because of the nature of things I had to function differently. The act of making an eyelash with one long stroke is not the same as making a cheek. So as much as I was interested in sameness, there was still a need to function differently, depending on what I was doing. But by breaking it down this way I can make the act of painting exactly the same all the way through.[11]

The systematic rigorousness of Close's strategies allies him with Conceptual Art; his use of the grid and concern with reductivism with Minimalism; his interest in neutrality, evenness of surface, and use of photographs with Photo-Realism.

RICHARD ESTES

Richard Estes (born 1932) studied at the Art Institute of Chicago from 1952–56 and moved to New York in 1959. He now lives in New York and Maine. Estes takes multiple colored slides of his subjects, then uses the slides as visual references when painting. For each painting he uses several slides; his paintings are composites of photographs; yet he never projects slides onto the canvas itself. Neither does Estes ever use photographs made by someone else, stating that he needs to be familiar with the subject first-hand in order to interpret the photographs. Estes explains:

A photograph is just values. It doesn't have line. When you use the photograph, you are using the values, but you are adding line and space and movement, coming from your experience. That's why, although I work from photographs, I like the subject to be things I'm familiar with. I don't think I could use someone else's photograph of some place I've never been to and make a painting. Although I could copy the photograph, I really wouldn't have a feeling for the place. You're always remembering, and the photograph is like a reference you use, a sketch.[12]

Estes paints everything in sharp focus; a single photograph could not achieve uniform focus. Neutrality typifies his attitude toward the subject, concentrating instead on reflections and on the myriad details momentarily caught on reflective surfaces. He paints an instant in time during which everything is frozen in eerie stillness. Favoring urban scenes of reflective storefronts, Estes depicts a prolonged moment of calm amidst the turmoil of New York. Time standing still—along with the cleanliness of his scenes (he tried painting the garbage, but it didn't come out right)—classicizes urban clamor into an idealized orderliness. "You take the elements of reality, but you eliminate the chaos," says Estes.[13]

Teleflorist (Fig. **5.8**) captures a whole panorama in its reflections, yet not a single person appears. An unpeopled urban cityscape in the hands of most painters would suggest a neutron bomb attack, but Estes' hyper-real emphasis on the glitzy surface completely captures our attention and diverts us from narrative thoughts.

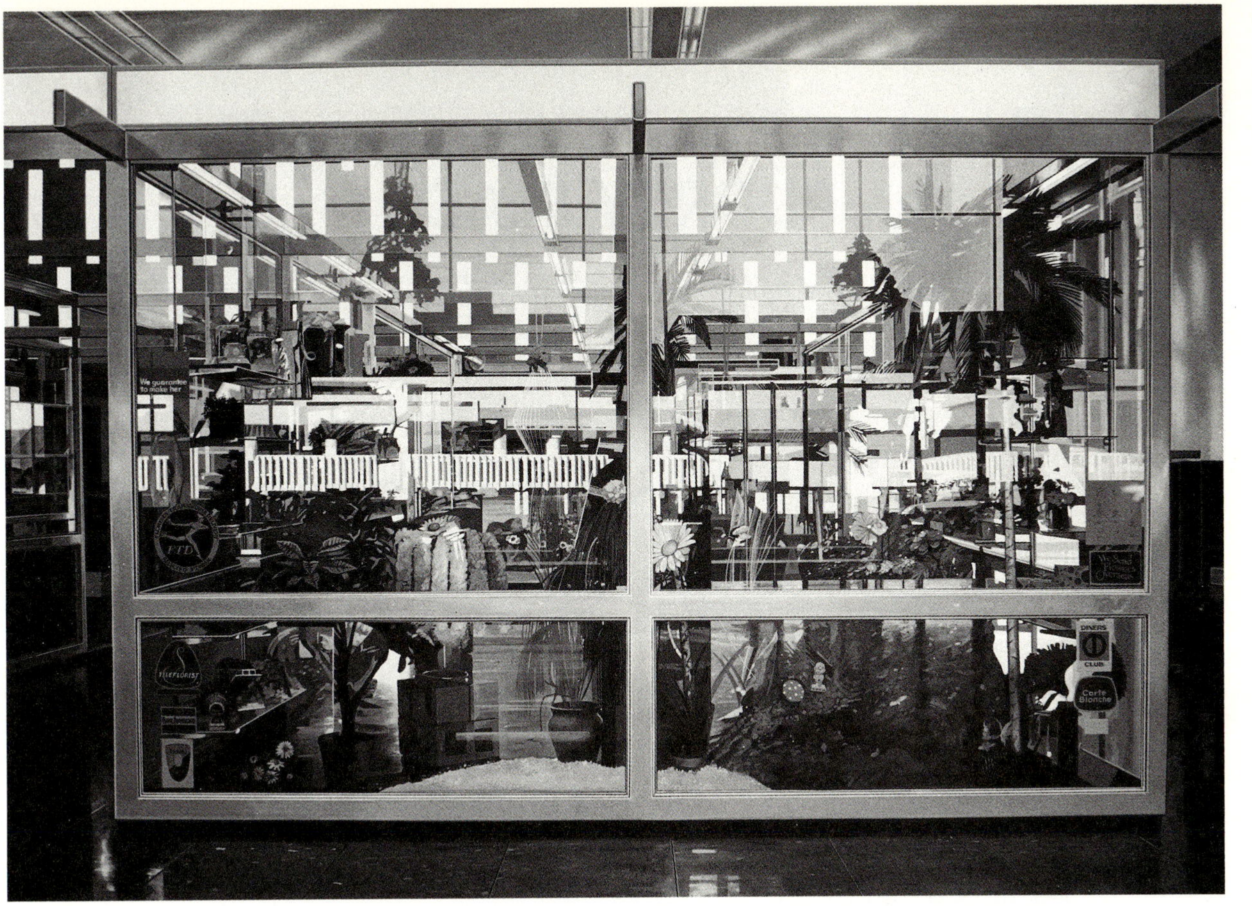

5.8 RICHARD ESTES
Teleflorist 1974
Oil on canvas
36 × 52ins
(91.4 × 132cm)
Courtesy Louis K. Meisel
Gallery, New York

5.9 AUDREY FLACK
Royal Flush 1973
Oil and acrylic on canvas
70 × 96ins
(177.8 × 243.8cm)
Inventory #361
Courtesy Louis K. Meisel
Gallery, New York
*"I have lived with gamblers,
real compulsive gamblers
who play for real money . . .
They play for days on end,
taking out time for a nap, but
they don't sleep. It is not just
a still life—it comes out of
my personal background.
Gambling is related to life—
a Royal Flush is symbolic.
It's the biggest winner; who
wouldn't want it?"*[14]

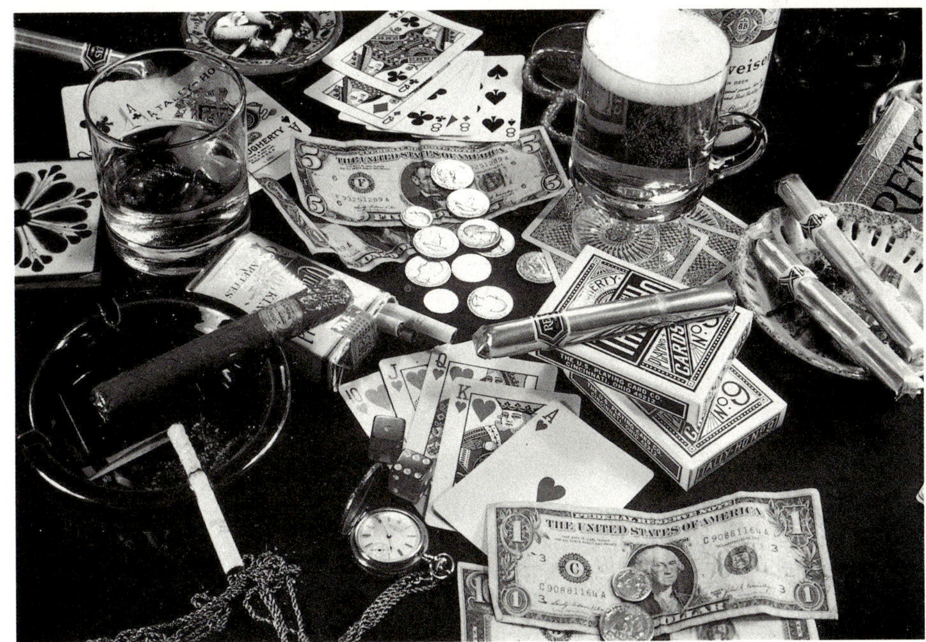

AUDREY FLACK

Audrey Flack was born in New York in 1931. She studied at Cooper Union and then received a BFA degree from Yale University in 1952. She lives and works in New York City.

Flack has a photographer make slides of a subject, selects *the* slide from as many as 150 choices, projects the slide onto a canvas, and airbrushes the colors. Her method requires that she works in darkness. The slides are usually close-up views which Flack then blows up to large scale, drawing the viewer into the scene. Mixing the colors on the canvas—making green by airbrushing blue over yellow, for example—gives them luminosity resembling that of the projected slide. Flack follows the slide precisely, not adding anything that is not in the photographic image, including lines.

Royal Flush (Fig. **5.9**, see page 155) is a still life which Flack set up and rearranged in many different configurations for the photographer, carefully studying the slides before selecting this one. (She always sets up the still life for the photographer, never using a "found" subject.) The symbolic meanings that Flack attaches to her paintings are atypical for Photo-Realists (see Fig. **5.9** caption); so is her interest in a very personal interpretation of her subjects. But her interest in subject matter is equaled by her interest in reflected light as it can only be captured by a photograph. Many of her paintings include beads, perfume bottles, glasses, and other highly reflective and often transparent objects, where the light hovers within the form. Formally, her work emphasizes visual information that is unique to photography.

Pattern and Decoration

The term Pattern and Decoration was first used in the mid-1970s to describe various artists whose paintings, collages, and sculptures are related in their use of extravagant patterning and blatant decoration at a time when the reductivism of Minimalism and Conceptual Art was still the aesthetic norm. Some of the artists—Joyce Kozloff and Miriam Shapiro, most notably—attached feminist content to the formerly insulting connotation of "decorative," believing, to simplify, that in a male-dominated world, women are permitted to decorate while men make art. Pattern and Decoration for them, therefore, acquired the task of righting the wrongly assumed lower artistic status of anything deemed "decorative," believing that the artistic bias revealed a sexist bias.

One of the major people who spoke for Pattern and Decoration, the art critic John Perreault, believed that it also represented an enfranchizement of the third world, where he believed Pattern and Decoration to rank alongside fine art. Equal recognition for women artists and the enfranchizement of third world

art are laudable goals; unfortunately, neither was achieved by Pattern and Decoration Art. As much as I endorse these dual political goals, in my opinion the Pattern and Decoration Art that was overlayed with feminist goals is not good art or effective politics. The art functions too much as illustrations of political agendas rather than as embodiments of original artistic ideas. To quote art critic Corinne Robins on Miriam Shapiro's *Anatomy of a Kimono*, it seemed "a little over-programmed."[15]

On the other hand, John Perreault wrote that:

Pattern painting is non-Minimalist, non-sexist, historically conscious, sensuous, romantic, rational, decorative. Its methods, motifs, and referents cross cultural and class lines. Virtually everyone takes some delight in patterning, the modernist taboo against the decorative notwithstanding. As a new painting style, pattern painting, like patterning itself, is two-dimensional, nonhierarchical, allover, a-centric, and aniconic. It has its roots in modernist art, but contradicts some

5.10 KIM MacCONNEL
Miracle 1980
Acrylic on cotton with
metallic paint
93 × 123ins
(236 × 312.4cm)
Courtesy Holly Solomon
Gallery, New York

5.11 JUDY PFAFF
Deepwater 1980
Mixed media, variable
dimensions
Courtesy Holly Solomon
Gallery, New York

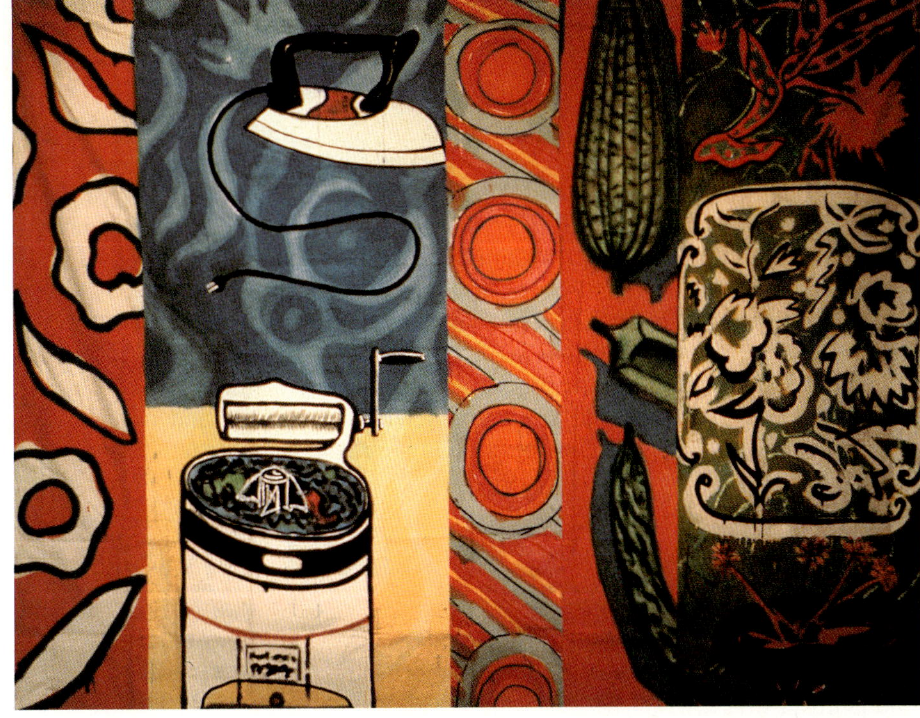

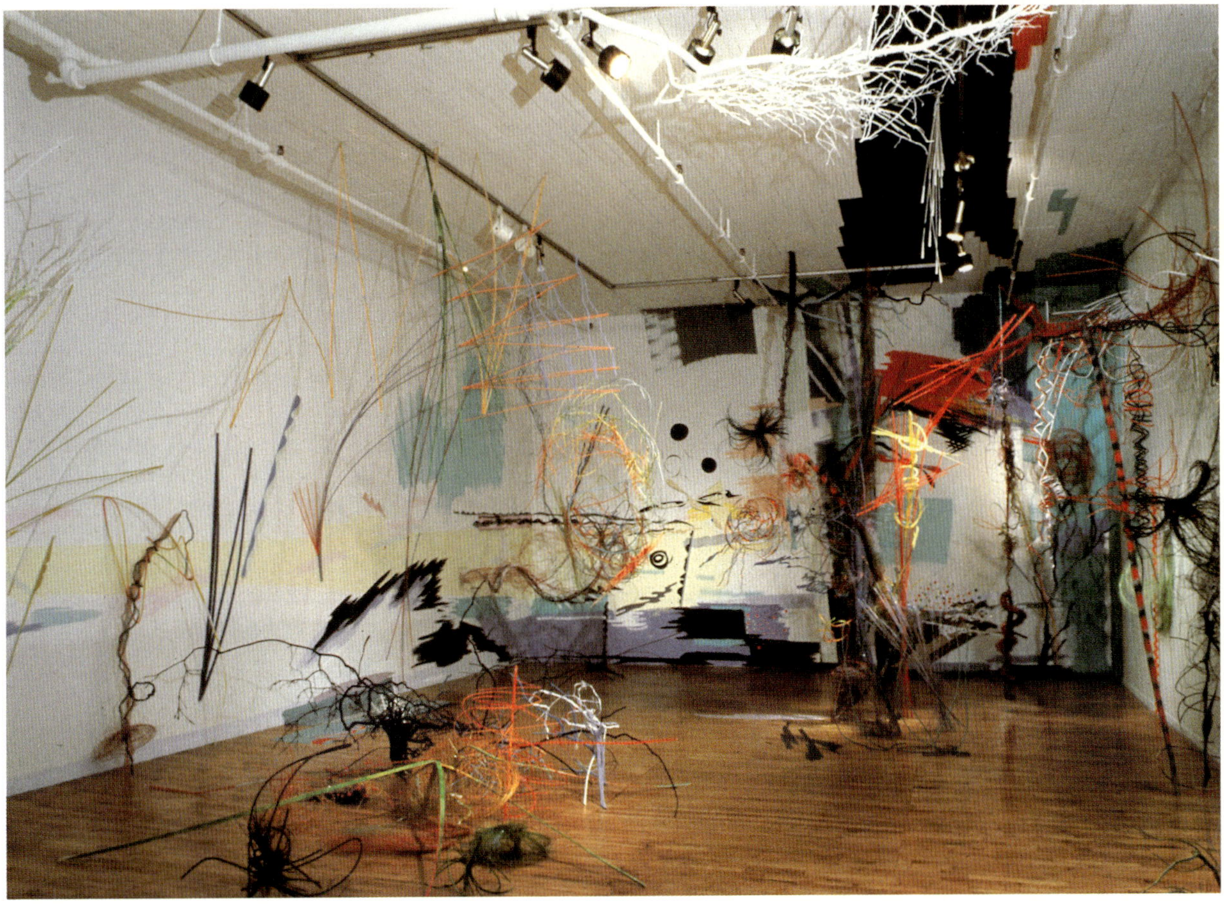

of the basic tenets of the faith, attempting to assimilate aspects of Western and non-Western culture not previously allowed into the realms of high art.[16]

Pattern and Decoration re-examined taboos against the decorative in art—long regarded antithetical to good art—and against materials and themes that had been regarded, until then, as "feminine" in the male-dominated and presumably "masculine" art world. As we discussed in Chapter 4: Post-Minimalism, the sexual politics of the art world underwent changes in the 1970s, thanks to the women's movement, which resulted in the questioning and revising of gender values more than ever before. The machismo of the Abstract Expressionists gave way to the inclusion of art—made by men and women—that is smaller in scale, less assertive, and employs methods formerly regarded as feminine (see pages 112–13). Ironically, in two-dimensional media the male Pattern and Decoration artists challenged and overthrew the taboos more successfully than the females.

KIM MACCONNEL

Kim MacConnel (born 1946) was Kushner's classmate at the University of California at San Diego, graduating in 1972. By 1975 he was living in New York and showing at the Holly Solomon Gallery. MacConnel sewed patterned fabrics together into large crazy-quilt-like hangings attached directly to the wall, sometimes adding painted passages, as Kushner did at the time.

Unlike Kushner, though, MacConnel employs clichés, both in patterns and in painted images. Patterns associated with the 1940s and 1950s frequently recur in MacConnel's art—amoeboid forms borrowed from surrealist-derived patterns, wallpaper designs, and homey prints—either painted or sewn; along with clichéd, cartoon-like images styled like telephone book or product literature illustrations. These common printed sources, which have obtained meaning by their having been reproduced and dispersed so widely, come out as patterns, which are themselves printed. MacConnel uses their connotations like cultural signs, without ironic intent.

Pop artists recycled mass-media imagery for its iconic content; Warhol's *Campbell's Soup Cans* have come to symbolize all that is reassuring and comforting in America. Warhol also meant his appropriation of an advertising image to be ironic, to say that his discredited imagery is art. Post-Pop Art takes the irony for granted: borrowing from mass-media is not ironic any more. Instead of appropriating images for their irony MacConnel appropriates them for their familiarity. They are simply part of the visual landscape, another repeated motif, another pattern.

Miracle (Fig. **5.10**, see page 157), painted in 1980, humorously borrows an image of a 1950s wringer washing machine along with a period iron—objects used to launder and press fabrics like the ones painted on the adjoining strips of cloth. Other patterns mimic corny kitchen wallpaper or pot holders. Altogether, they recreate an idealized domestic scene dating roughly from the artist's childhood, typifying the air of nostalgia that permeates MacConnel's art.

JUDY PFAFF

The sculpture of Judy Pfaff (born 1946) does not neatly fit into any category. As the art critic Roberta Smith wrote:

The elaborate installations which form the basis of Pfaff's reputation combine elements of painting, sculpture, and drawing on an environmental scale via an encyclopedic range of colors, materials, and references to both high and low culture. Not surprisingly, these gesamtkunstwerk *have proven relevant to major art tendencies of both the '70s and the '80s, from late Post-Minimalist installation/performance art, through Pattern and Decoration, to Neo-Expressionism, as well as the ongoing enterprise of abstract art.*[17]

Pfaff's 1980 installation, *Deepwater* (Fig. **5.11**, see page 156), at the Holly Solomon Gallery gave the sensation of scuba diving in a Caribbean reef amongst brightly colored fish and plants. Viewers were completely enmeshed in colored branches, raffia, brushstrokes, and lights. Installed in a specific space, the sculpture could not be replicated anywhere else, so when the exhibition was over it was dismantled and has never been recreated. Since then, Pfaff has made other installations—at the Hirschhorn Museum, the John and Mable Ringling Museum of Art, the Venice Biennale, the University of Massachusetts, the Wacoal Art Center, Tokyo, and other venues—using various brightly-colored materials dispersed throughout the space. All use unlikely materials in chaotic and decorative configurations.

Since the early 1980s, Pfaff has been making permanent sculptures that attach to the wall and project outward, sometimes also resting on the floor. These brightly painted reliefs have the same exuberance of the installations, often repeating forms like circles or grids in irregular patterns. No other artist makes anything like it, but in its celebration of decorativeness and use of pattern, Pfaff's work is more allied to Pattern and Decoration than to any other recent tendency.

ROBERT KUSHNER

Robert Kushner (born 1949) earned an MFA at the University of California, San Diego, in the early 1970s, moving to New York City in 1972, where he continued presenting the Performance Art he began in California, featuring richly patterned costumes which he designed and made. A 1974 trip to Iran with the art critic Amy Goldin excited his already manifested interest in decoration: "On this trip, seeing those incredible works of genius, really master works which exist in almost any city, I really became aware of how intelligent and uplifting decoration can be," Kushner said.[18]

Back in New York, Kushner worked as an Oriental rug restorer and began making calligraphic drawings with India ink. In 1975, the artists Miriam Shapiro and Robert Zakanitch held the first meeting of the Pattern

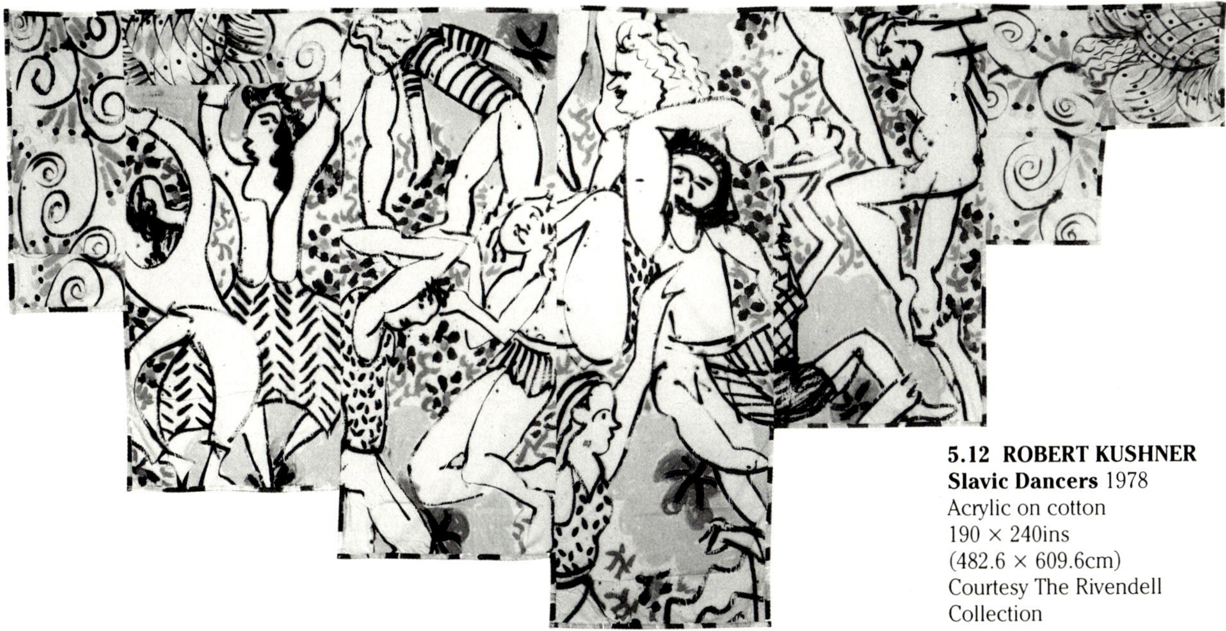

5.12 ROBERT KUSHNER
Slavic Dancers 1978
Acrylic on cotton
190 × 240ins
(482.6 × 609.6cm)
Courtesy The Rivendell
Collection

and Decoration Artists' Group, which led to a public discussion on the topic a month later, and a controversial group show at the Alessandro Gallery in September and October, 1976. Kushner was not in the show. But he became one of the first artists of the Holly Solomon Gallery, which opened in SoHo in 1975, and which became the most prominent showcase for Pattern and Decoration.

Kushner pinned the costumes he made for his performances on the wall, showing them as alternatives to the standard artistic format of a stretched canvas. We have seen that Richard Tuttle made monochromatic abstract canvas shapes pinned directly on the wall without stretchers (see page 137). Both artists conduct a formal dialogue with the Modernist tradition that painting is a two-dimensional medium on canvas—a fabric—but both take the fabric off the standard wooden stretcher. This idea informed Kush-

ner's next series of works, made as unstretched wall hangings.

Slavic Dancers (Fig. **5.12**) measures more than 15 × 20 feet (4.5 × 6.1 m), and is painted in acrylic on an irregularly-shaped canvas to resemble the format of an architectural decoration. The vertical panels hang in bands like banners, furthering their association with decorative formats rather than a traditional painting form. Sensuous rhythms of undulating lines interlace the dancers with decorative patterns, the overall visual effect being more important than the subject matter. As Kushner defined the decorative in relation to his art, it includes:

1. Flatness rather than illusion,
2. expansiveness rather than containment,
3. use of pattern, and
4. subject matter or meaning that is secondary to visual effect.[19]

New Image Painting

New Image painters use images that fluctuate between abstraction and representation. They favor the flat, often monochromatic, space typical of abstract, Minimal painting, but inject associative meanings into the often-silhouetted shapes they place against their flat grounds. Just as the Post-Minimalist sculptors Richard Artschwager and Joel Shapiro only slightly altered Minimalist forms to give them narrative meaning—taboo to the Minimalists—the New Image painters began with Minimalism as their aesthetic starting point, endowing its visual sparseness with suggestion, association, ambiguity.

The Photo-Realists used Pop Art as their aesthetic jumping-off point; in some respects Photo-Realism is

a mannerist phase of Pop Art, with its reliance on secondary images, its cool, neutral stance, emotional detachment, and uniform surfaces. Like Mannerism, future possibilities suggested by Photo-Realism led to a dead end. New Image painters renewed the possibility of narrative content, which had long been absent from American art. They marked the transition from Minimal Painting's hermetic austerity to the gregarious visual utterances of the Neo-Expressionists (see pages 167–87). One of the ways to measure the significance of an art style is to see what came after it, what it engendered. In this respect, New Image Painting is by far the most significant development discussed in this chapter.

NICHOLAS AFRICANO

Figures in Africano's art stand on blank, isolating backgrounds, trapped in and engulfed by space. The uninflected space derives from monochromatic Minimalist painting, but while the Minimalists' intentions

were purely formal, Africano (born 1948) charges the space with psychological connotations—loneliness, alienation, psychological withdrawal. Rendered in high relief with wax and paint, the figures seem

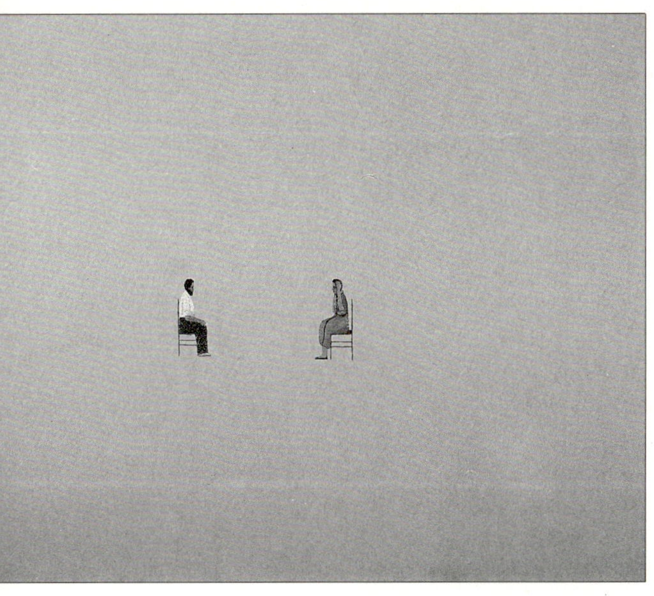

5.13 NICHOLAS AFRICANO
The Cruel Discussion
1976–77
Oil, acrylic and wax on canvas
73 × 90ins
(185.4 × 228.6cm)
Courtesy Holly Solomon Gallery, New York

"Thematically (the works) are related by concerns about emotional paralysis that I have experienced, an inability to make contact, to confront people or situations directly."[21]

leaden, weighted down by their bulky forms. Their awkward, ungainly proportions describe their psychological stresses.

Medieval manuscript illuminations are one of Africano's sources. He especially admires the *Book of Kells* and the *Lindisfarne Gospels* because their imagery is not self-reflective, not about itself or about formal issues, but about moral issues which the figures summarize.

I want my paintings to be about something, as opposed to being about nothing or being about themselves. Their reference is human experience, so they are figurative and narrative. I don't assume a rhetorical posture as a painter and I don't want my work to reiterate rhetorical assumptions—I want something to mean something, in a cogent and revealing way, because I want to be purposeful, even useful. So I regard subject matter as my primary concern as an artist.[20]

Placing his diminutive figures on an imaginary ground line toward the center of the canvas, Africano requires us to step close and when we do, the painting's space engulfs us, too. Close up, the figures make intimate revelations, but because of the voids between and around them, they remain pained and isolated. *The Cruel Discussion* (Fig. **5.13**), for example, depicts an experience all of us have had: the moment when a relationship requires hurtful disclosures. Taking from his personal experience, Africano generalizes psychological archetypes.

NEIL JENNEY

Leapfrogging backwards over Minimalism, Neil Jenney (born 1945) rooted his art in the grandfather, Abstract Expressionism. Minimalism was not a prior style for Jenney to overcome because he rejected it.

Each brushstroke in Neil Jenney's *Here and There* (Fig. **5.14**) contributes to the overall image but is separable from it, as though it has a life of its own as a brushstroke apart from its representational function. The autonomy of painting's formal language— the independence of the brushstroke from having to represent something other than a brushstroke—was one of the accomplishments of Abstract Expressionism. Painted in 1970, nearly a decade before rep-

resentational painting's international resurgence, Jenney's *Here and There* retains links to an earlier painting style while simultaneously announcing the arrival of a new one.

Jenney switched from sculpture to painting in 1969, and created a large body of work within the following two years. All of this series includes autonomous brushwork and heavy frames bearing the painting's title. "This gesture [of placing the titles on the frames] is a crucial reinforcement of the seriousness with which the subjects are to be taken, as if an antidote to the potential irony of Pop and the inherent banality of Photo-Realism," wrote the curator and art

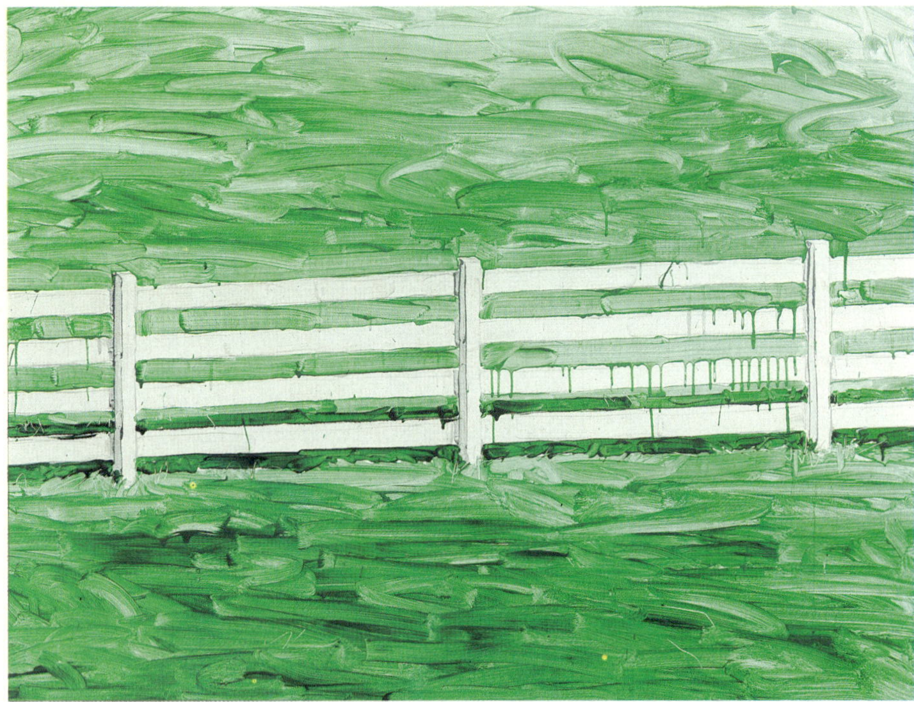

critic Mark Rosenthal.[22] Jenney's subjects in this first series usually represent opposition or conflict between two elements. The artist wrote in the New Image Painting catalogue:

I was more concerned with approaching the viewer with relationships—for instance, a crying girl and a broken vase, birds and jets, or trees and lumber. I'm not interested in narrative; I'm interested in showing objects existing with and relating to other objects because I think that is what realism deals with—objects relating to other objects.[23]

SUSAN ROTHENBERG

Susan Rothenberg (born 1945) began painting her archetypal images of horses in 1973, continuing the series until 1979. She was one of the few artists then painting representational imagery that nonetheless conforms to established abstract painting norms: "It was great. I was able to stick to the philosophy of the day—of keeping the painting flat and anti-illusionistic," she said, "but I also got to use this big, soft, heavy, strong, powerful form to make those ideas visible."[24] The horse image came to Rothenberg one day when she was doodling; it holds no special significance for her. As she tells it: "I drew a line down the middle, and before I knew it there was half a horse on either side. The horse held the space, and the line kept the picture flat."[25]

Rothenberg energized the surface of *United States* (Fig. **5.15**) with undulating brushwork that nervously flickers across its expansive surface—it is 9½ × 15¾ feet (2.89 × 4.8 m). Sensuous fields of color hold the horse's contour on the surface without implying spatial depth. Rothenberg reversed the figure/ground colors on either side of the dividing line. While making reference to Minimalist painting in its flatness, surface, and dual colors, *United States* steps out of the Minimalist mold with provocative associations. "Things rush into empty places and Minimal Art had become an empty place," Rothenberg said.[26]

The title makes a play on words because the two different halves come together to create a whole, making "united states." In the United States, the horse symbolizes unbridled freedom in the open plains of the American west, conjuring up western mythology and folklore. Combined with the painting's title, the horse symbolizes the taming of the west and, hence, the domestication of nature. It is a remarkable achievement that Rothenberg so powerfully treated such a loaded symbol in an artistic climate where cool detachment and psychological neutrality dominated.

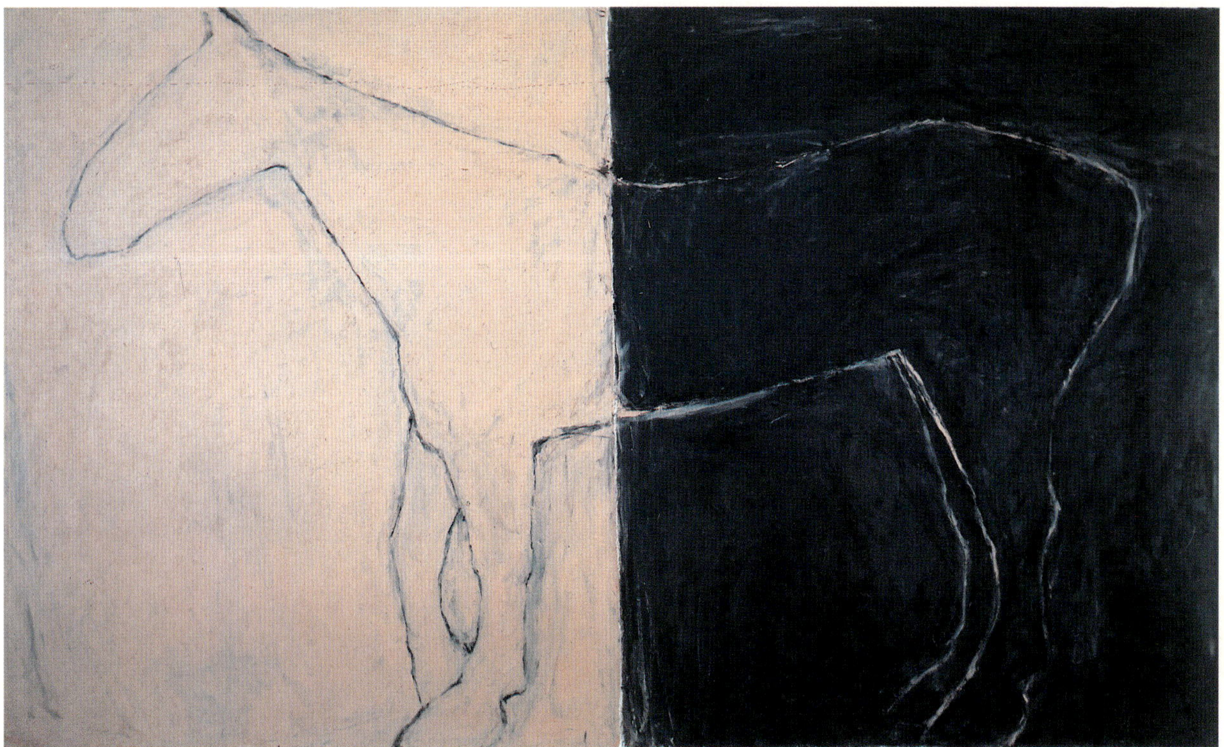

5.15 SUSAN ROTHENBERG
United States 1975
Acrylic and tempera on canvas
114 × 189ins
(289.6 × 480.1cm)
Courtesy Saatchi Collection, London

Social and Political Background

The 1980s was a decade of considerable political change both in the United States and Western and Eastern Europe. In 1980 and 1984 Ronald Reagan enjoyed a landslide victory in the Presidential elections. The conservative Republican increased military spending while decimating social programs and lead the nation out of inflation and into its deepest debt ever with economic reforms that made the rich richer, leading to the introduction of the term "yuppies" for young, upwardly mobile professionals. A period of conspicuous wealth and greed included the immensely popular television series, "Dynasty," a saga of money, glamour, and corruption. Insider Wall Street trading involved billions of dollars in illegal profits.

Modern paintings led the enormous surge in prices paid for art. The American publisher S.I. Newhouse paid $17.05 million for Jasper Johns's *False Start* (1959) at Sotheby's in 1988, the highest price ever paid for a work by a living artist until then. An unidentified buyer paid $47.85 million for Picasso's youthful self portrait, *Yo Picasso* (1901), in 1989. In 1987, the Australian financier Alan Bond paid $53.9 million for Vincent van Gogh's *Irises*. When Bond was unable to make the payments on a $27 million loan from Sotheby's auction house arranged prior to the auction, he sold the painting to the John Paul Getty Museum in Malibu, California for an undisclosed sum. Another van Gogh, *Dr. Gachet*, was bought at auction in May, 1990, for $82.5 million by the Japanese paper company owner Ryoei Saito.

Violence and assassination seemed to mark

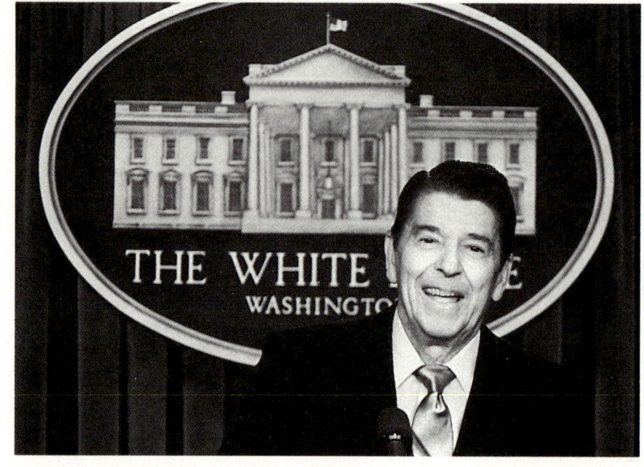

political change in the 1980s. Iraq attacked Iran's oil fields in 1980, beginning an eight-year bloody and brutal war that included Iraq's use of internationally outlawed chemical weapons. In 1981, John Hinkley shot President Reagan in Washington, D.C.; a Turkish terrorist shot Pope John Paul II in St. Peter's Square, Rome; and Muslim militants assassinated Egyptian President Anwar el-Sadat. In 1984, India's Prime Minister, Indira Ghandi, was assassinated by two of her Sikh bodyguards. Two years later, President Ferdinand Marcos was forced to leave the Philippines after he tried to steal the election from Corazon Aquino, the widow of his murdered rival, Benigno Aquino. Marcos died in exile in Hawaii in 1989. Frenzied mourners at the funeral of Iran's political and religious leader, Ayatollah Khomeini that same year created havoc as they tried to kiss his corpse.

Mikhail Gorbachev became the Soviet leader in 1985. The 54-year-old agriculture specialist with no foreign affairs experience initiated a series of sweeping social and political reforms designed to vitalize Russia's economy and introduce new freedoms. Britain's Margaret Thatcher was reelected in 1987, becoming the first Prime Minister in the twentieth century to win three consecutive terms of office. In 1989, Solidarity won a huge victory in Poland's first free election since the Communists took over. In 1990 Communist East Germany opened the Berlin Wall, on

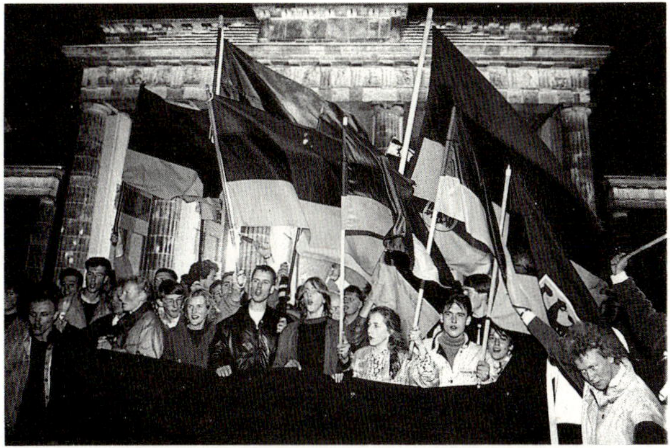

which ecstatic Germans from both East and West danced and drank champagne. Elsewhere in Eastern Europe demonstrators in Czechoslovakia forced the Communist party to cede its absolute power. In Rumania, one of the last holdouts against reform in the Eastern block, angry pro-democracy demonstrators forced the leader, Nicolae Ceausescu, to flee Bucharest.

In the United States, Chicago elected its first black mayor, Harold Washington, in 1983. The black political leader Jesse Jackson became a serious contender for the Democratic Presidential nomination in 1988. In 1989, David N. Dinkins became the first black mayor of New York City. In 1983, Sally Ride became the first American woman in space. The space shuttle Challenger exploded in 1986, killing all seven aboard, including Christa McAuliffe, a teacher.

In 1981, the first cases of what was later recognized as AIDS (Acquired Immune Deficiency Syndrome) were reported in Los Angeles by the Center for Disease Control. The virus that is believed to cause AIDS was not identified until 1985. Political activists accused the government of reacting slowly and inadequately to the AIDS crisis because of bigotry toward its homosexual victims. President Reagan did not publicly mention AIDS until 1986. By 1990, more Americans had died of AIDS than in the Vietnam war and millions of people were infected worldwide.

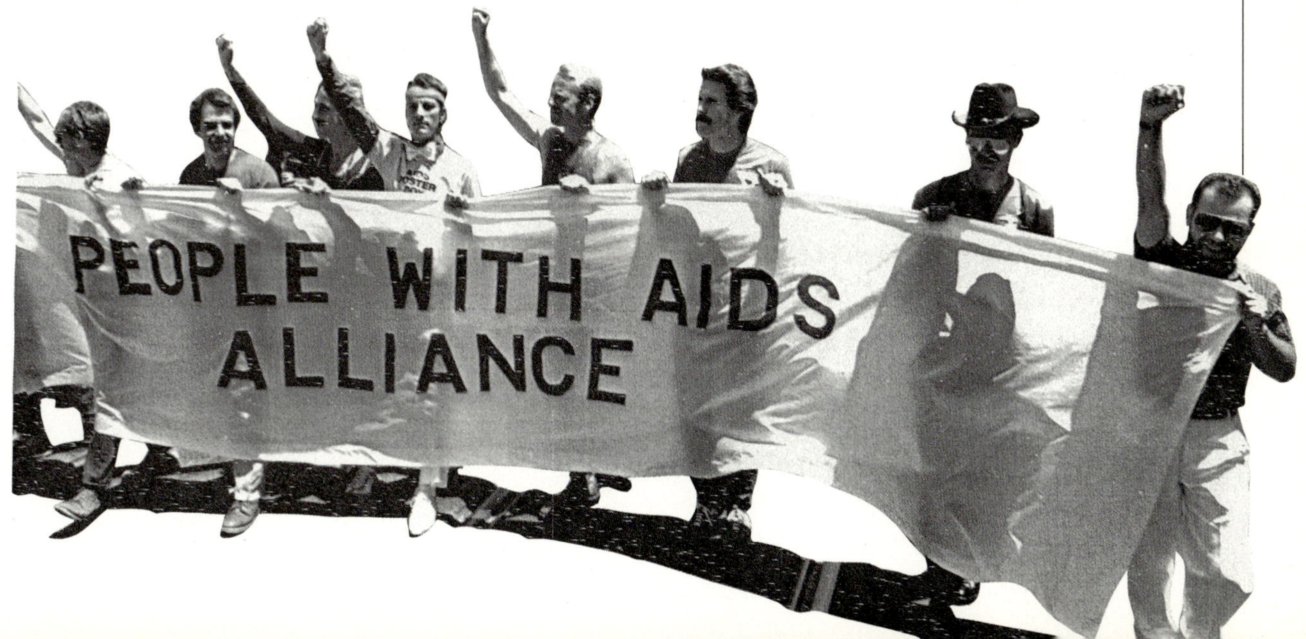

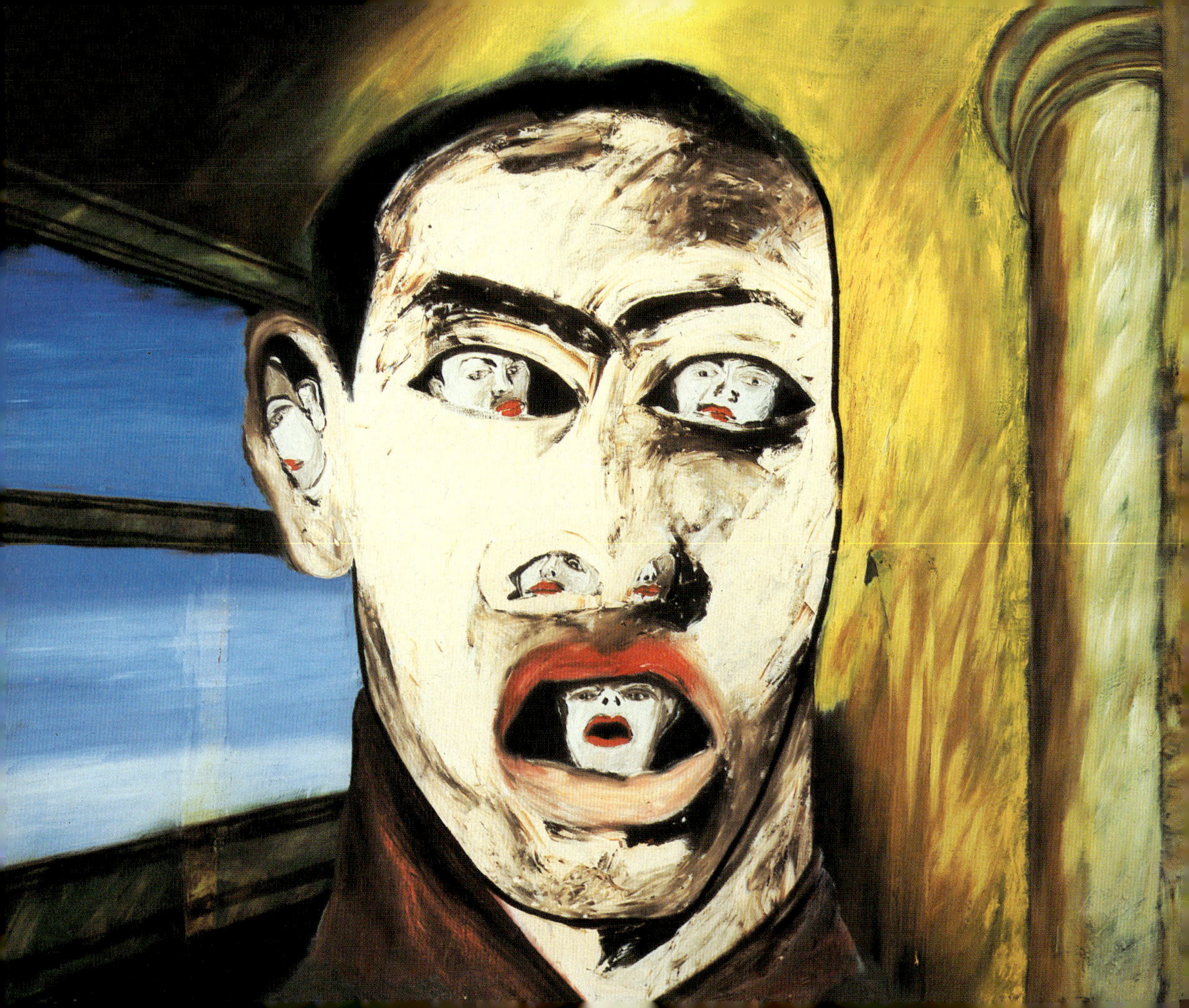

6
Neo-Expressionism

"You know, there is a landscape of the world and there is also an inner landscape of the world. It changes as much as the face of the earth has been changing throughout all these thousands of years. The landscape we see inside us in our own imagination changes also, it is not the same."[1]

—— FRANCESCO CLEMENTE ——

Francesco Clemente
Untitled 1983
Courtesy Thomas Ammann, Zürich

The Return
of Narrative Painting

Neo-Expressionism marked a significant turning point in contemporary art, one that the Pluralism of the 1970s only hinted at. Realism, Photo-Realism, and Pattern and Decoration indicated a shift toward populism, away from the elitism and hermeticism of Minimalism, Conceptual Art, Earthworks, site-specific sculpture, Video, Film, and Performance Art. Realism and Photo-Realism with their traditional illusionistic craftsmanship, and Pattern and Decoration with its decorative beauty, were easily comprehensible to the new, novice audience that was becoming interested in contemporary art in large numbers. In retrospect, they seem almost like reactionary styles, especially Photo-Realism. The shift that Neo-Expressionism marked was much more significant.

The contemporary art tendencies that have been discussed prior to Pluralism all emphasized perceptual experience above everything else, focusing on the perceptual relationship between the viewer or participant and the artwork. Experimentation with ideas about what an artwork could consist of—the constant expansion of the realm of art—typified the earlier movements. Often, the subject of the earlier artworks was art itself, not only the expanded definition of art, but also such formal issues as dematerialization, horizontality, duration. What seemed most radical about Neo-Expressionism when it first became evident that it was a widely-practiced international aesthetic was its traditionalism.

With the exception of the work by Jonathan Borofsky, Neo-Expressionism was primarily a painting development. Throughout the late 1960s and 1970s the pronouncement that painting was dead was often heard. Andy Warhol's 1966 exhibition at the Leo Castelli Gallery featured hot pink and yellow wallpaper with large images of a cow's head, along with helium-filled silver pillows. It was as though Warhol were saying that the painting was expensive wallpaper and the sculpture party decorations, so light and insubstantial that they could float out of the window or deflate the next day. "Andy killed painting," was the popular conventional wisdom. This recalled Warhol's dealer, Leo Castelli's, response to the accusation that he had killed second generation Abstract Expressionism by ushering in Pop Art: "But they were dead already. I just helped remove the bodies."[2]

But painting was not dead. A handful of courageous painters kept it alive with stunning conviction despite the dominance of many untraditional art-making approaches. Brice Marden, Agnes Martin, and Robert Ryman are but three artists who produced paintings of the highest caliber during the late 1960s and 1970s, maybe the three best. Their pared-down simplified geometry and smooth surfaces paralleled the concerns of the Minimalists, though Minimalism was primarily a sculpture style. And then there was one who, looking back, may have been the grandfather and father of Neo-Expressionism in the United States: Philip Guston.

It was not only that painting is a traditional art medium that made Neo-Expressionism such an important turning point, although it is impossible to feel again how intoxicating it was to go into galleries and smell the rich odor of drying oil paint. Certain Photo-Realists and Pattern and Decoration artists claimed that realism and decoration were shockingly radical ideas at the time, and perhaps they were in a conservative way, like the use of painting—a conservative and traditional art medium—by the Neo-Expressionists. Being "shockingly radical" does not in itself make great art, as most of Photo-Realism and Pattern and Decoration artworks proved. Neo-Expressionism's transformational impact on contemporary art extended far beyond a single idea.

The personal, autobiographical, sensuous, erotic, emotional, spontaneous, narrative, intuitive, and historical, along with myth, literature, and music inform Neo-Expressionism. The content of art opened up to a fuller range of human experience from its former more narrow focus on perceptual issues and on concepts of art itself. From hermeticism to gregariousness is another way to characterize the change of mood, or from reductivism to expansiveness.

But if one had to choose the single most transformational idea that Neo-Expressionism brought into being, it would have perhaps to be the reversal of the strongest current of continuity running throughout Modernist Art, the notion of aesthetic unity that informs Minimalist reductivism, the idea that every element should be subordinated to unity.[3] In Minimalism the notion took the most extreme form with the insistence that the artwork's content be a single perceptual phenomenon. Following that direction, what was the next step for artists to take without entering into hair-splitting? And once the art object has been dematerialized by Conceptual Art, Earthworks, Video, Film, and Performance Art—dematerialization being the aesthetic unity—what future direction is indicated? Nearly every future direction indicated by new developments in the 1970s proved specious, mere hair-splitting, except one: New Image Painting (see pages 160–63).

Parallels exist between New Image Painting and Neo-Expressionism—the interest in narrative content is paramount—but the New Image painters retained the Modernist ban on illusionism, while the Neo-Expressionists abandoned even that.

In overturning the main concerns of Modernism, Neo-Expressionism ushered in new ideas about the possibilities of content and form. This led to the Post-Modernists' critique of cultural signs and images with embedded cultural meanings, such as in the work of Barbara Kruger (see pages 193–95), which in turn led to the current critique of art as a commodity in the marketplace, as in Jeff Koons's art (see pages 237–38), and the preoccupation with the impossibility of making a truly original visual statement within those confines that characterizes both of these latter developments. Neo-Expressionism is in this sense the beginning of Post-Modernism. And so, this book is divided into essentially two halves, each half resting on different basic premises: one, a continuation of the hermeticism of Modernism and the avant-garde (up to Pluralism), the other, a tendency to refer to the less hermetic, more mainstream imagery of mass media, popular culture, literature, music, and myth—in short, to address a broader, more populist audience.

PHILIP GUSTON

Philip Guston (1913–80) had a long and very distinguished career as an Abstract Expressionist painter before he began making in 1967, at the age of 54, cartoon-like representational paintings with richly brushed surfaces. When he first showed his new art at the Marlborough Gallery in 1970 the art world was baffled. Not a single painting sold. Art critic Peter Schjeldahl, who had long admired Guston's sensitive abstractions, recalls: "I was scared of the abject psychic content he had unclenched, and I was scared *for* an idealistic sense of art, as a refuge from life's disorder, which I had absorbed without examining."[4]

"I got sick and tired of all that Purity! Wanted to tell Stories," Guston explained.[5] The paintings came in a flood. "From 1967–69 I painted like mad. The pictures came so fast I had to make memoes to myself, at a table drinking coffee. 'Paint *them*.' I felt like a movie director. Like opening a Pandora's box, and all those images came out."[6]

Regarding his motivation for making such a radical shift in his art Guston said:

So when the 1960s came along I was feeling split, schizophrenic. The war, what was happening to America, the brutality of the world. What kind of man am I, sitting at home, reading magazines, going into a frustrated fury about everything—and then going into my studio to adjust a red to a blue.

I thought there must be some way I could do something about it. I knew ahead of me a road was laying. A very crude, inchoate road. I wanted to be complete again, as I was when I was a kid … Wanted to be whole between what I thought and what I felt.[7]

The year was 1977 when Guston made the above observations about his work of the late 1960s. Four years later, in 1981, the first of two major international exhibitions within two years announced an international array of artists working in a mode that be-

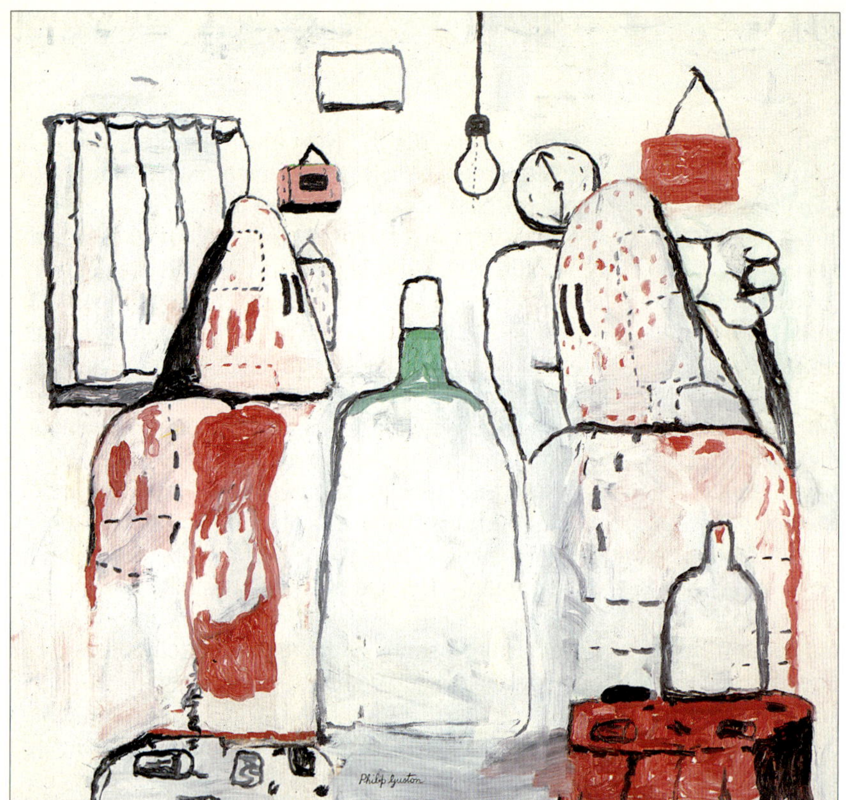

6.1 PHILIP GUSTON
Bad Habits 1970
Oil on canvas
73 × 78ins
(185.5 × 198.2cm)
Courtesy Australian National
Gallery, Canberra

came known as Neo-Expressionism. Guston's art was included in *A New Spirit of Painting* at the Royal Academy of Arts in London in 1981, but not in *Zeitgeist* at the Internationale Kunstausstellung in Berlin in 1982. Writing in the catalogue for *A New Spirit of Painting*, one of the show's organizers, Christos M. Joachimides, stated:

The optimistic belief, so widespread in the 1960s, that the ills of society could be quickly rectified through sufficiently active personal commitment, did not last long into the 1970s; the oil crisis and the threat to material well-being it ushered in led to widespread feelings of resignation and mistrust. The more insecure one's material future seemed, the more inviting became the comforts of the imagination. A period of insight gave way to a period of self-examination.[8]

Guston anticipated the shifting sensibility by years. Against the background of the political assassinations and racial violence of the 1960s, against the Vietnam war, the immoral Nixon presidency, inflation, and the Arab oil embargo, Guston painted cartoonish, hooded, Ku Klux Klan-like figures in the sensuous, creamy oil paint surfaces he perfected as an Abstract Expressionist. "The paint handling is beautiful, with a beauty that in the comfortless con-

text is heartbreaking," wrote Peter Schjeldahl.[9]

At the center of the dense and disjointed world Guston painted was the artist himself, frequently depicted as a figure with one large, staring eye in profile. At other times as in *Bad Habits* (Fig. **6.1**), he was symbolically present in the form of tobacco or alcohol. "The whips, bottles, and cigarette butts that litter his studio in *Bad Habits* ... are the stimulants upon which the artist depends for release from his catatonic distress and the emblems of his often masochistic vocation. Painting itself is both a gesture of hope and another 'bad habit,' a routine of heightened sensation and self-punishment that promises escape from anxiety yet all too frequently exacerbates it," wrote the art critic Robert Storr.[10] Strong emotions, these. One of the anonymous, hooded figures threatens the impassive other, both of them spotted with the "hemorrhoidal" color Guston so frequently used, to quote one of the painter's favorite authors, Nikolai Gogol, master of the grotesque. A huge liquor bottle on a table littered with cigarette butts stands between the two figures and points to a dangling bare light bulb, symbol of tawdry lodgings. Altogether, *Bad Habits* characterizes a mood of high anxiety that pervades Guston's late paintings and much of Neo-Expressionism.

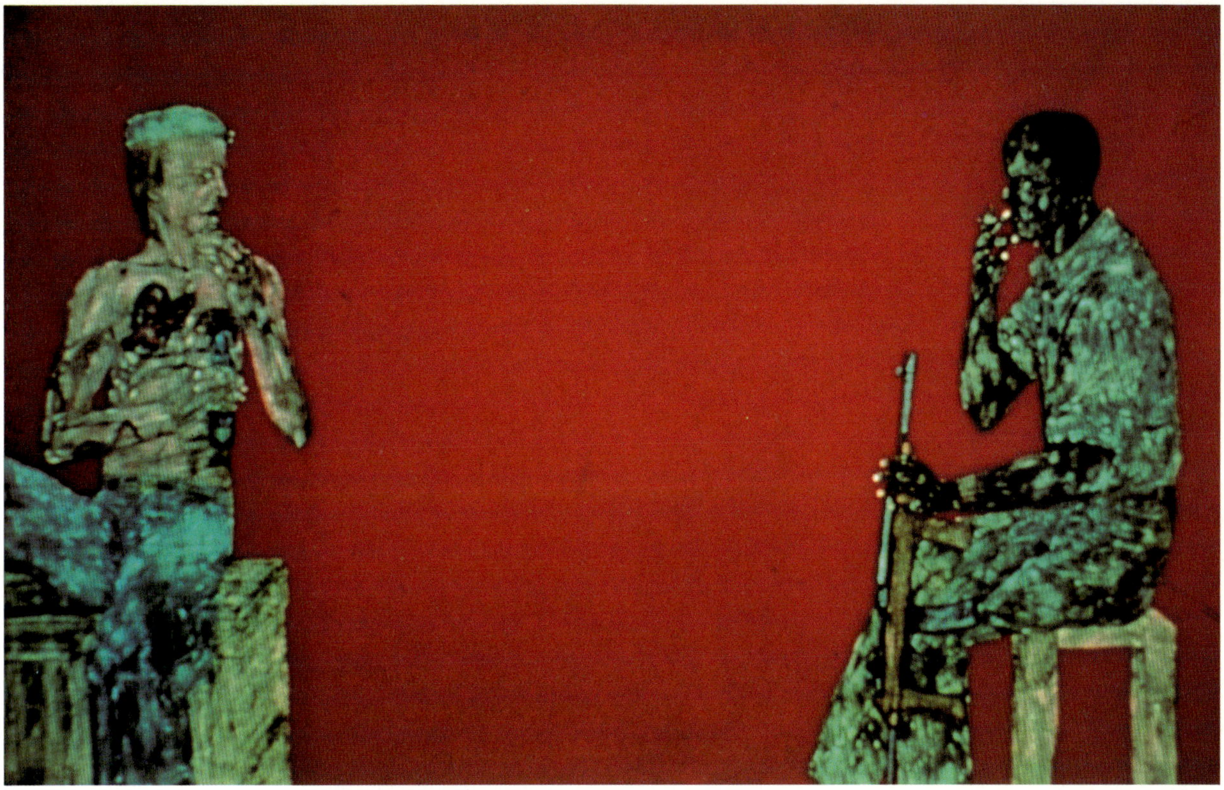

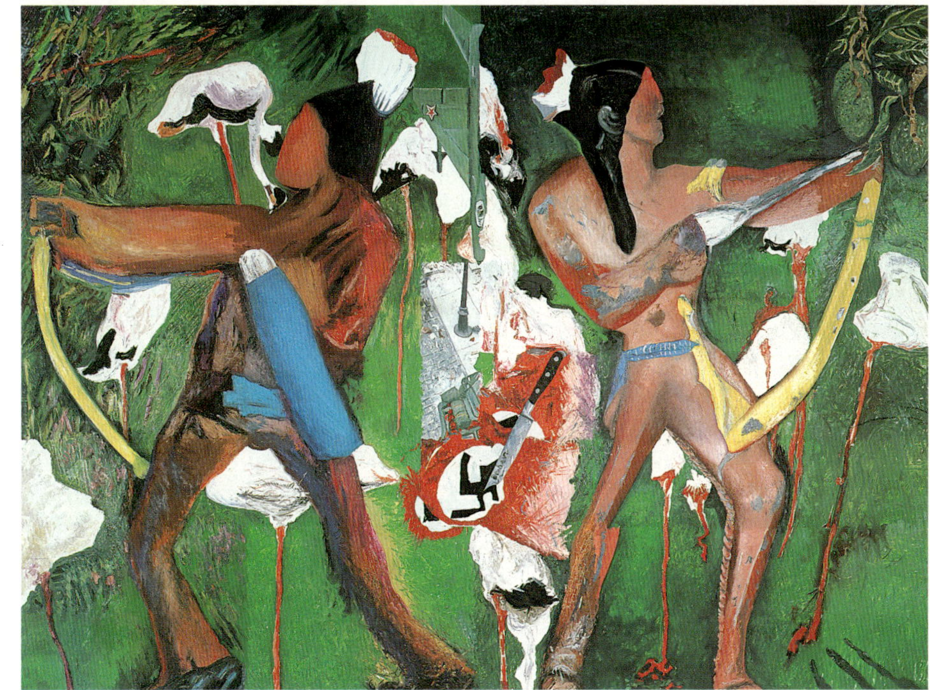

6.2 LEON GOLUB
Mercenaries III 1980
Acrylic on canvas
120 × 198ins
(304.8 × 502.9cm)
Collection of The Eli Broad
Family Foundation
*"I would like to think that
these paintings have a sense
of that immediacy, that
contemporaneity of events.
They are poised to be almost
physically palpable, a tactile
tension of events."*[11]

6.3 MALCOLM MORLEY
Out Dark Spot 1978
Oil on canvas
72⅝ × 98¾ins
(185.3 × 250.8cm)
Courtesy Saatchi Collection,
London

LEON GOLUB

If Philip Guston is the grandfather and father of Neo-Expressionism, Leon Golub (born 1922) and Malcolm Morley are its uncles. Golub painted figurative images of power and vulnerability from the beginning of his career in the 1950s. In 1972, following Richard Nixon's landslide presidential victory over George McGovern's anti-war campaign, the mining of Haiphong harbor, the bombing of Cambodia, and the Watergate break-in, Golub decided to become more specific with his subject matter. Formerly, he had used photographs of athletes and antique sculpture as his models; now, he began using news photographs of the Vietnam war.

In the spring of 1979, the mercenaries who are so much a part of third-world politics—of power and vulnerability—became Golub's subjects, in a series of huge unstretched canvases attached directly to the walls with nails through grommets. Not stretching them solved the technical problem of how to move the oversized canvases (by rolling them up) but also represented a public declaration, like a banner. *Mer-cenaries III* (Fig. **6.2**, see page 171) measures 10 × 16½ feet (3 × 5 m); not living room scale.

Golub uses more than one news photo for each of the figures in the Mercenaries series, making a composite out of the multiple sources. He usually emphasizes the mercenaries' brutality by placing the viewer in a precarious relationship to the scene.

In *Mercenaries III*, two menacing mercenaries scowl at each other across an expanse of raw-flesh red space that has the visual effect of inserting the viewer between them. Though they are smoking cigarettes and drinking beer—maybe on their time off—they seem tightly coiled, as if the slightest provocation would make them spring into brutal action. Golub works the painted surface by constantly building up layers of paint, then scraping them down to the canvas with a meat cleaver. The result is a feeling of nerves rubbed bare. If it could make a sound, the dry, rubbed surface would sound like fingernails on a blackboard. If you could feel it, it would be like splinters under the fingernails.

MALCOLM MORLEY

In 1984 the art critic Gary Indiana astutely observed that: "In retrospect, Morley's early paintings seem like parodies of Photo-Realism before the fact."[12] Morley's *S. S. Amsterdam in front of Rotterdam*, 1966, (see page 152) anticipated Photo-Realism yet markedly differed from the later Photo-Realists' work, as we have seen (see page 151). Morley anticipated Neo-Expressionism, too; his art has never fitted neatly into styles or movements.

Beginning in 1969, Morley began charging his surfaces with a painterly treatment, at a time when the Photo-Realists adhered to a very smooth, photo-like finish. Morley continued to paint from photographic reproductions, but in some cases he began to superimpose elements from various sources into collage-like art works. He continued to use a grid, and to paint one square at a time, with his canvas upside down to avoid becoming overly preoccupied with the image. The painted surface eventually emerged as at least an equal player, at first with methodical, patterned brushwork, but gradually with more freedom and variety in his gestures. By the mid-1970s, Morley painted from toys and other non-photographic sources as models, sometimes combining them with sources from photographic reproductions, sometimes not.

"I build my paintings from disconnected parts," Morley said. "They are put together and create their own architecture—an architecture of images—like a de Chirico. The painting assembles itself around a specific set of objects."[13] Increasingly since the early- to mid-1970s, the objects may have personal significance for Morley, may represent a specific historical period (usually distorted through contemporary perceptions), or may represent what the art critic Klaus Kertess called "the eroticism of seeing,"[14] sometimes all three. Morley carefully balances the symbolic or mythical with the naturalistic, based on observation of the subject before him and translated into lusciously painted sensuous surfaces. (He abandoned acrylics in favor of oil paint, which can achieve a much wider variety of effects.) "I take painting very literally to be a thing to do with seeing. I want to know what perception is in terms of painting. The idea is to try to develop a painterly sense of the world and to create a dialogue between the painterly seeing and its resolution on the flat plane of the canvas. I want the eyes to float and bob like buoys on the wetness of the painted surface."[15]

Out Dark Spot (Fig. **6.3**, see page 171) represents two native American archers in a humid green landscape with exotic cranes. What appears to be a rent divides the canvas, revealing part of an airplane with a bomb falling on a city (seen from above) and a knife stabbed into overlapping swastika flags. The flags are the same colors as the cranes and the native Americans' hair and headdresses, thus establishing visual analogies between them and setting up a poetics of seeing. Born in 1931, Morley was an adolescent in wartime London (he moved to New York City in 1958). He remembers the Nazi air-raids, the bombs falling, and his concern, after an explosion came close to his home, for the toy model he was building (the native Americans are painted from toys). The painting's title refers to the swastikas, prominently placed in the center of the lower third of the rectangular canvas, where they cannot escape our attention. The lush tropical landscape, depicting the Edenic myth of Morley's adopted country, contrasts his former one under the Nazi scourge. Autobiography, history, myth, and the erotics of seeing merge.

The art critic Hilton Kramer wrote that what Morley's paintings "boast an abundance of is a kind of heated feeling and visceral intensity that we hardly expected to find in pictorial art in the days when it was so completely dominated by the ideas of clarity, irony, and orderly form."[16]

JONATHAN BOROFSKY

The main subject of the art of Jonathan Borofsky (born 1942) is the artist himself, represented in painting and sculpture as a *Running Man, Hammering Man, Man with a Briefcase, Flying Figure,* and *Chattering Man,* among other manifestations. By extension, these figures represent Everyman. They symbolize the artist's—and our—spiritual lives, enacted at a particular political moment. A maker of individual objects as well as site-specific installations and drawings directly on walls, floors, ceilings, columns, and air-conditioning ducts, Borofsky works in painting, sculpture, drawing, video, audio and light.

As an aid to meditation, Borofsky began obsessively counting on sheets of paper in 1969, after having given up making art. Eventually, he began making drawings of his dreams on the counting pages, drawing them as crudely and directly as possible. Dream drawings are the sources of many of his images. For an installation at the Paula Cooper Gallery in 1976, Borofsky painted his drawings directly on the walls and stood a 3 feet (91.5 cm) high stack of papers on which he had counted to over two million in the center of the room. The drawings were both of his own inner life and images taken from printed sources, like an encyclopedia or newspaper. He numbers every artwork with the number he has reached in his counting.

Borofsky usually reuses images in various permutations, as though they are archetypal symbols taken from a dream-world visual vocabulary. As in dreams, Borofsky's symbols have multiple meanings. A drawing of a shoemaker taken from an encyclopedia for the 1976 Paula Cooper Gallery show later metamorphosed into an 11 feet (3.4 m) high motorized sculpture of a *Hammering Man* which grew even bigger in subsequent versions. The *Hammering Man* symbolizes the artist (Borofsky) as worker and all workers in general, as well as the striking Solidarity workers in Poland at that time. The dual connotation of "strike"—to work (as in hammering) or not to work—pleased Borofsky.

The 1980 Paula Cooper Gallery installation where the *Hammering Man* debuted included wall drawings, paintings, and sculptures positioned throughout the space to create an environment (Fig. **6.4**). Individual objects meshed with the whole scheme. Run-

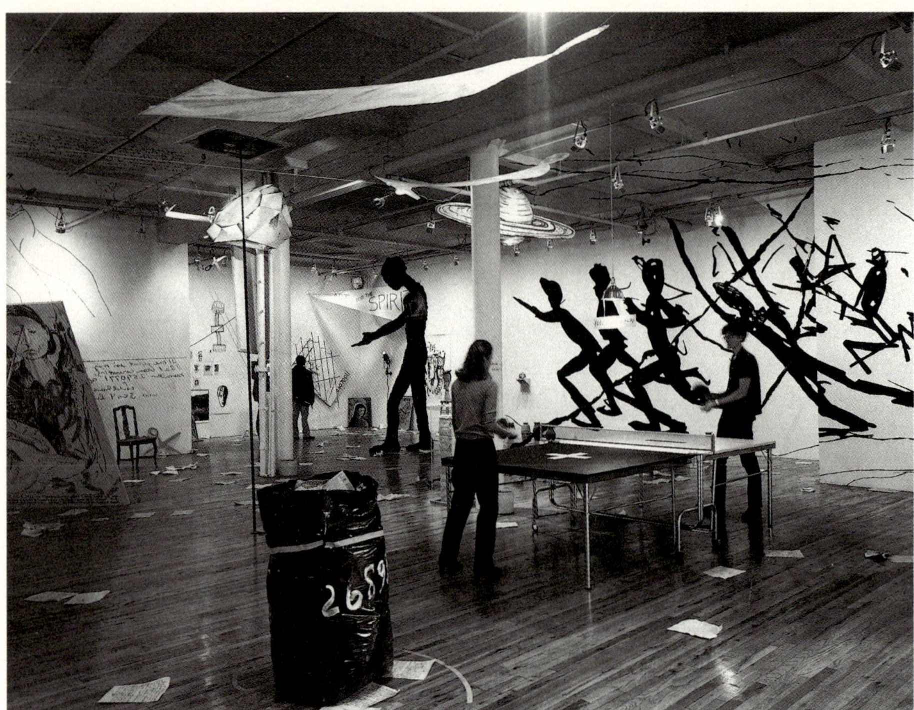

6.4 **JONATHAN BOROFSKY**
Paula Cooper Gallery
Installation 1980
Mixed media, dimensions variable
Courtesy Paula Cooper Gallery, New York

ning figures painted directly on two walls and around a corner turned toward the *Hammering Man*; black streamers coming from them and attaching to the floor made the drawing's lines sculptural. The running figures originated in the same drawing as the *Hammering Man* in 1977. Borofsky first used them in an installation at the Portland Center for the Visual Arts in 1979; also in 1979, a single, freestanding, 7½ feet (2.3 m) high running figure representing Borofsky himself appeared in another Paula Cooper Gallery installation. Borofsky painted this latter image directly on walls many times, once directly on the Berlin wall as part of his contribution to *Zeitgeist* in 1982, this time symbolizing not only Borofsky but also East Berliners and their desire to escape. Also for this show, Borofsky painted red rubies on the walls of a room overlooking East Berlin and the site of the former Nazi Gestapo torture chambers, the rubies symbolizing hearts and by implication, compassion. A *Flying Figure* was suspended outside the window, symbolizing the desire for freedom. Various hammering men have appeared in installations in Los Angeles, Basel, Rotterdam, Ghent, and Kassel.

Borofsky typically deals with political issues and themes of violence, oppression, and anxiety in his works. The Nazis are his most often-used image of evil, appearing as Hitler, as ovens, and as other symbols of oppression. A wall drawing made in 1979 and titled *I dreamed that some Hitler-type person was not allowing everyone to roller skate in public places at 2,566,499*, and the placement of a barbecue numbered *2,673,115* in his 1980 Paula Cooper installation both use this image of evil. Nazism represents oppression of the spirit, which for Borofsky is the greatest evil. Sometimes he uses exemplars of political freedom, such as superimposing the face of Lech Walesa over his own forehead in *Self-Portrait at 2,783,685 and 2,686,889*, 1981–82. A former shipyard worker, Walesa led an illegal strike in Communist Poland that eventually led to reforms and his election as the President of Poland. In a wall drawing for the 1979 Whitney Biennial Borofsky refers to Steve Biko, a slain leader of the black anti-apartheid movement in South Africa. In this installation, Borofsky also depicts the Ayatollah Khomeini, Iran's revolutionary Muslim who led the overthrow of the Shah and the taking of American hostages.

Painted directly on walls and frequently bending around corners or onto the floor, ceiling, columns, or air-conditioning ducts, Borofsky's drawings have the intensity of visions. They hover in space. The installations surround viewers, engaging us as no single traditional object can. Borofsky said:

I wish I could come up with a better word than "installation." For me, it has to do with an awareness of space, and making other people

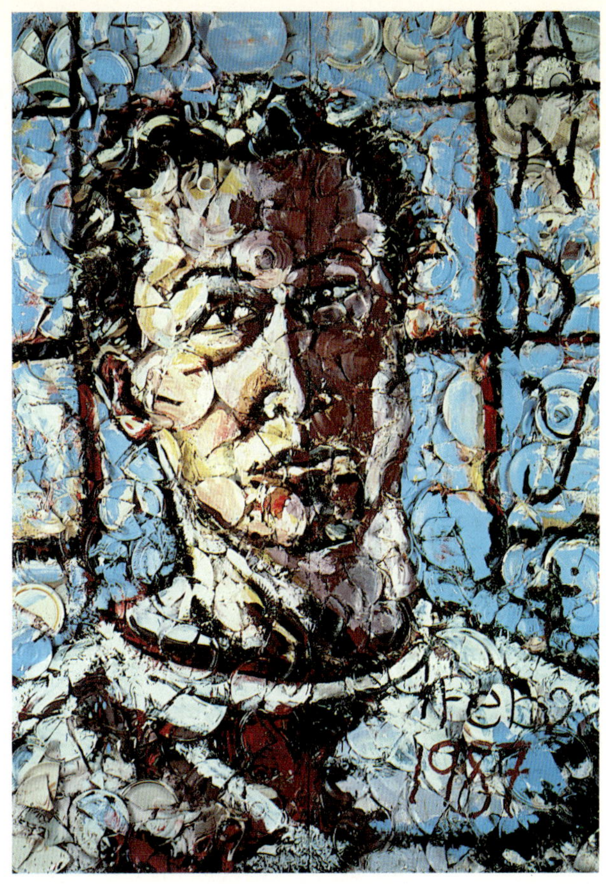

6.5 JULIAN SCHNABEL
Self-Portrait in Andy's Shadow 1987
Oil, Bondo, and plates on wood
103 × 72ins
(261.6 × 182.9cm)
Courtesy The Eli and Edythe L. Broad Collection

6.6 JULIAN SCHNABEL
Bob's Worlds 1980
Oil, wax, crockery on wood and canvas
97½ × 146ins
(243.8 × 365.7cm)
Courtesy Saatchi Collection, London

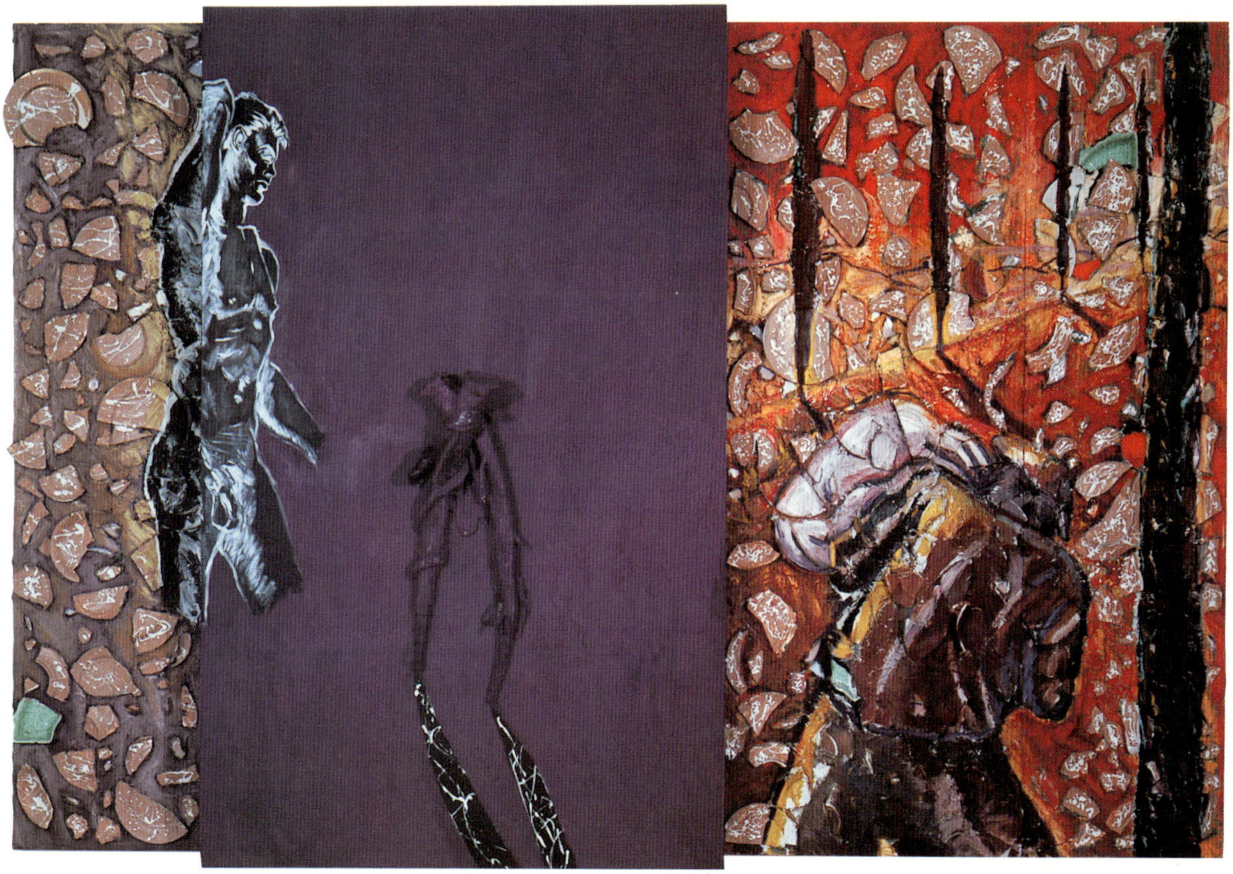

conscious of the entire space they are in, not just the space that the object occupies on the wall. I think of these as walk-in three-dimensional paintings—a stage set, only in this case the viewer is allowed on the stage to participate.[17]

The wall drawings in particular, but also the installations, are difficult to own and to sell—an intentional evasion of the commodification of art that links Borofsky to Conceptual Art and other efforts toward dematerialization. (Although the market for Borofsky's art is very brisk.) Owning the wall drawings and installations requires a different commitment than owning a painting, which can be more easily transported, installed, or exchanged.

Borofsky's art anticipated Neo-Expressionism; he began producing mature work before Neo-Expressionism, or even New Image Painting, became identifiable tendencies. Art critic Mark Rosenthal wrote that: "His art was on one hand a hybrid between avant-garde ideology and traditional values, and on the other hand a look into the future, wherein was found an art variously known as Primary Image, New Image, and Neo-Expressionism."[18]

New Image painters retained the Modernist ban on spatial illusionism. Borofsky's themes, his inclusiveness, and the breakdown of Modernist unity that typifies his art affiliate him with Neo-Expressionism. If he is a Neo-Expressionist—if his art belongs in any category—he is the only one who works in installations and wall drawings, though he also makes paintings, sculptures, drawings, prints, videos, and audio works.

With its emphasis on individuality, its wide-ranging subject matter, and its lack of a philosophical position shared by all of the artists, Neo-Expressionism is an elusive category, especially for American art (in European art the distinctions are more clear). Categories are not ultimately as important as artists are; they only help us to understand individuals within a larger context. If Borofsky's work is, in effect, on the cusp of Conceptual Art and Neo-Expressionism, Julian Schnabel's and David Salle's art is on the cusp between Neo-Expressionism and Post-Modernism.

JULIAN SCHNABEL

From the moment of his first exhibition in 1979, the career of Julian Schnabel (born 1951) became as widely discussed as his art, maybe more so. Reviewing the show in *Art in America*, the art critic Rene Ricard compared Schnabel to Jackson Pollock, citing the similarities of:

The simultaneous juggling of surface and image, the brush-extending application of paint, the inner pressure to make something more than a picture, a nightmare, and more importantly the taurine energy than can be felt in Schnabel's work, at home on the grand scale and the high-priestly mission to be the keeper of the flame, of the Zeitgeist of the big tradition.[19]

The paintings were audacious, physically overbearing enough to feel momentous, to supply the large new inexperienced art audience of ahistorical neophites with a celebrity genius. (There hadn't been a new one since Andy Warhol.) Gluing broken crockery to the surfaces of his huge constructions, Schnabel painted crudely-drawn imagery over it, projecting the surface into the viewer's space with overbearing bombast. Ricard wrote that the plates were "metaphoric to the brushstroke" and that they were to painting what "a prosthesis is to a leg."[20] The "plate paintings," as they came to be known, were widely celebrated, reviled, and publicized. When one of the 1979 plate paintings, *Notre Dame*, came up for auction at Sotheby Parke Bernet in 1983—only four years later, an unusually fast turnover, especially for a 31-year-old artist at the beginning of his career –it sold for $93,500.[21]

By 1980, a great deal of money was being spent—and made—on contemporary art, much more than ever before. New audiences were attracted by the greater accessibility of Pluralism in the 1970s and the recognizable imagery of Neo-Expressionism—"you can see something in it without a doctoral degree," said Schnabel's dealer at the time, Mary Boone[22]—and they had disposable income thanks to Reagonomics and the stock market boom which began on August 13, 1982. The conditions of the art market changed, and with it the mechanisms of how an artist, or at least how some artists, become known changed too.

The art world is not isolated from the rest of the world, particularly with the new audiences coming from a much larger cross-section of the populace than previously. With many more art school graduates producing art than ever before, the market had to expand to support them. To create a market, some galleries became as aggressive with promotion and publicity as more traditionally commercial enterprises. And so the hue and cry of hype and publicity was heard in SoHo and in the press. But the supporters questioned why the art world should be any different than the rest of the world? Hype and publicity are communication techniques in a consumerist, mass-media society.

Because of his sheer conspicuousness, Schnabel became a symbol of the new socio-economic realities of the art world. His art does not critique the art system, as Post-Modernism does, but the phenomenon of his instant success and notoriety focused many important issues. One was the changing role and status of artists; another, the means by which artists become recognized and known; and a third, the question of controversy. All of these issues tie into the over-riding one: the current status of the avant-garde, a subject discussed more thoroughly in Chapter 7: Post-Modernism.

Schnabel's art has been controversial from the beginning, provoking as many strongly divergent opinions for as against it. A few examples follow.

"The art looked 'radical' without being so; it was merely novel, a quality that soon outwears itself," and "They [the paintings] are just bombast and texture—a fresh 'look' that found its temporary spot in the Academy of the Briefly New, and promptly became a cliche."[23]

"When I saw the first plate painting at his studio I knew immediately that no matter what I thought, I was looking at one picture that would reinvent everything, that a point had been made in history and that the art world was finally back," and "Julian has reinvented the art world."[24]

Schnabel is obsessed with surface (Fig. **6.5**, see page 175). The plate paintings violently shatter Modernism's unitary surface and thrust it into the viewer's space. Images painted on the broken crockery hover

in space in front of the surface. (Schnabel painted on velvet, too, a "low" culture material, with the same effect of the paint floating toward the viewer.) The surfaces are blustering, bombastic, and bluntly stated. These adjectives have been used to praise and to condemn them.

But what about the images? Schnabel borrows images from sources other than nature—from literature, films, photographs, religious symbols, and other paintings. "I arrive at making paintings by using a personal selection of images and a cross-referencing of things that seem to have the same kinds of emotional weight. The subject matter is not just what is depicted but the psychological resonance caused by these things and these images," Schnabel said.[25] Though he borrows images like the Post-Modernists do, he does so without intending any critique of their common meanings, instead emphasizing their personal psychological and emotional connotations, an attitude consistent with Neo-Expressionism. "It [a painting] need not be accessible to everyone, and certainly not to everyone's understanding, for although my work is about meaning, it is not necessarily your meaning."[26]

The images never come together into visual coherence; they always seem fragmented and incomplete. Some writers claim this to be an aspect of Schnabel's elegiac, melancholy mood, an expression of fragmentation, alienation, and despair. I agree with those who see the disparity between Schnabel's surfaces and his images, and the failure of the images to cohere, as a major shortcoming, measuring his success high in decibel levels but low in content.

Bob's Worlds (Fig. **6.6**, see page 175) carries the assertive shard-covered surfaces and floating images typical of Schnabel's paintings while demonstrating the absence of a discernible reason for the images to appear in that context. It also shows a marked deficiency that Schnabel is sometimes able to conceal. The male nude is a rare example of Schnabel attempting anything beyond a crudely distorted likeness, and now we know why: because he cannot draw. The ability to render a classical, academic figure is not the measurement of good drawing; the ability to render a convincing image is. As overbearing and dramatic as this male nude is, convincing it is not.

I agree with the art critic Hilton Kramer when he wrote about Schnabel's surfaces: "This has yielded him some striking results at times, yet the question of exactly which images are necessary to his art and which are merely an added-on component of it remains unresolved."[27]

The use of visual cliches typifies Post-Modernism, but in Schnabel we find the last—or maybe only the most recent—cliche of the embattled avant-garde artist.

DAVID SALLE

The art of David Salle (born 1952) first came into prominence at the same time as that of his friend, Julian Schnabel. Salle's art has been nearly as controversial as Schnabel's, though he has not attracted as much personal publicity, perhaps partly because he and his art are not as gregarious and self-assertive. (Both Salle and his art are elusive and wary.) Neither did Salle attract as much market attention as Schnabel's auction debut.

Rob Him of Pleasure, 1979, was Salle's first painting to overlay transparent images, a device he often repeated in his subsequent work. Salle borrows images from art history, from magazines, newspapers and other mass-media sources, and from photographs, some of which he poses. Sometimes rendered in hesitant, sketchily painted lines; sometimes in a tentative-looking grisaille; or in provisional empasto, Salle's figures have an unresolved air, as if something has been withheld.

When Salle moved to New York City from California in 1975, the absence of significant new styles originating in the 1970s, plus the economic slump that dipped the art market, left few options open. Minimalism, Conceptual Art, and their predecessors had already been underway for so long that they rep-represented the possibilities of an earlier generation. Salle was not alone in this predicament—most of the artists he knew shared the same dilemma—but he felt it very acutely nonetheless.

In California, Salle earned a BFA and an MFA from the California Institute of the Arts, or Cal Arts, in 1973 and 1975. His most influential teacher was the Conceptual artist John Baldessari whose teaching has affected a whole generation of American artists, and from whom Salle learned the attitude to regard a wide range of imagery with almost equal interest, taking a studiedly distanced and neutral stance. Salle had been making abstract paintings when he entered Cal

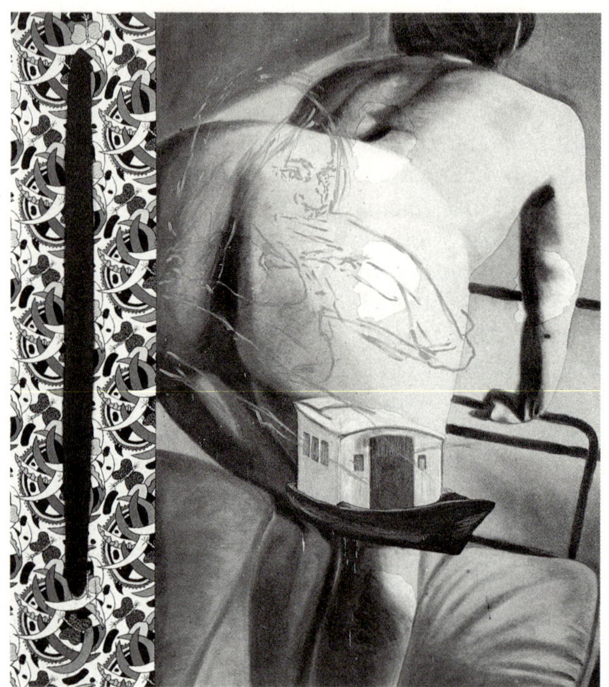

6.7 DAVID SALLE
His Brain 1984
Oil and acrylic on canvas
117 × 108ins
(297.2 × 274.3cm)
Courtesy Gerald S. Eliot,
Chicago

Arts; while there, he began working in Conceptual Art modes.

Both his Conceptual Art background and the widespread sense of painting's depletion must have contributed to the provisional feeling of Salle's mature work. "He makes paintings, but they are dead, inert representations of the impossibility of passion in a culture that has institutionalized self-expression.

They take the most compelling sign for personal authenticity that our culture can provide [in other words, the medium of painting], and attempt to stop it, to reveal its falseness," wrote the art critic Thomas Lawson.[28] The paintings have a 1980s kind of melancholy, a disillusionment with unfulfilled promises, an intellectually controlled and highly self-aware attempt to make significant paintings despite the inhospitable moment. "His is an esthetic of discontent, disclosed through a method of contradiction; it is an art of total disillusionment," wrote the art critic Donald Kuspit.[29]

In 1975, in the absence of new painting to stimulate him, Salle turned to movies, especially those of the 1940s and 1950s directors Preston Sturges and Douglas Sirk. Speaking about the impact of Sirk's films on his art, Salle said:

The films are almost always shot in a very high key in terms of light and color. And there is deep space and strong use of verticals in the composition of the picture; these give a sense of the sugary surface of the reality of American life, and the structure of the drama, the text, is the underside of that same world. The way he was able to make one manifest through the other I thought was quite brilliant and really unparalleled.[30]

From filmic fade-ins and fade-outs Salle also found a precedent for layering images. The layered images in *His Brain* (Fig. **6.7**) are like flashback memories in a daydream sequence. Lincoln's head recalls his likeness on pennies; the placement of one on the bent-over nude's rump implies a smutty tone. But there is nothing nasty happening here. The nude is barely erotic—it's so clinical, and anyway the camera-angle isn't right for pornography. The withholding of eroticism, theatricalizing it instead, parallels Salle's withholding of clear meanings. Overlaying the bent-over nude is a sketchy line painting of another female nude apparently under the covers, implying a before or after scene but not specifying which, if either. The motel curtain fabric that frames the painting's left half enhances the peep-show air. The painted boat almost exactly replicates a Monet painting of his boat-studio. Salle slows down our perception and makes us take time to look, to find the different layers and to connect them. Their meanings are not ones which can be reduced to words, but their overall feeling is one of malaise.

Though he uses found imagery and presents it in a detached and provisional way, Salle recombines the images to create weirdly affecting emotions. It is because of his art's emotional malaise, despite its borrowed images, that it can be called Neo-Expressionist rather than Post-Modern.

ANSELM KIEFER

Anselm Kiefer was born in West Germany in 1945, the last year of World War II, and grew up in the shadow of Nazi Germany's humiliation and shame. In Düsseldorf between 1970 and 1972, he studied art with Joseph Beuys, who said regarding his own decision to become an artist in the late 1940s: "The whole thing is a therapeutic process. For me it was a time when I realized the part the artist can play in indicating the traumas of a time and initiating a healing process."[31]

Kiefer believes in art as an agent of spiritual healing, as a means of remembering historical rupture and continuity, destruction and regeneration. He draws from the events of civilization's past, creating richly encrusted artworks layered with history, myth, art, music, poetry, and folklore, making epic elegies to the human condition.

Surfaces of Kiefer's works are like archeological strata revealing each successive layer in their fissures. He sometimes paints on huge landscape photographs, building up layers of paint, straw, lead, and applied objects. Every material Kiefer uses possesses symbolic meaning, every subject evokes a multitude of references and associations. Huge and heavy—physically affecting—though they are, Kiefer's paintings require reading and knowledge of his themes for a complete understanding.

Nuremberg (Fig. **6.8**) layers acrylic, emulsion, and straw onto a whirling, tilted-up landscape seen from a bird's-eye view, Kiefer's favorite perspective. His frequent landscapes evoke the Germans' deep romantic attachment to the homeland, to the celebra-

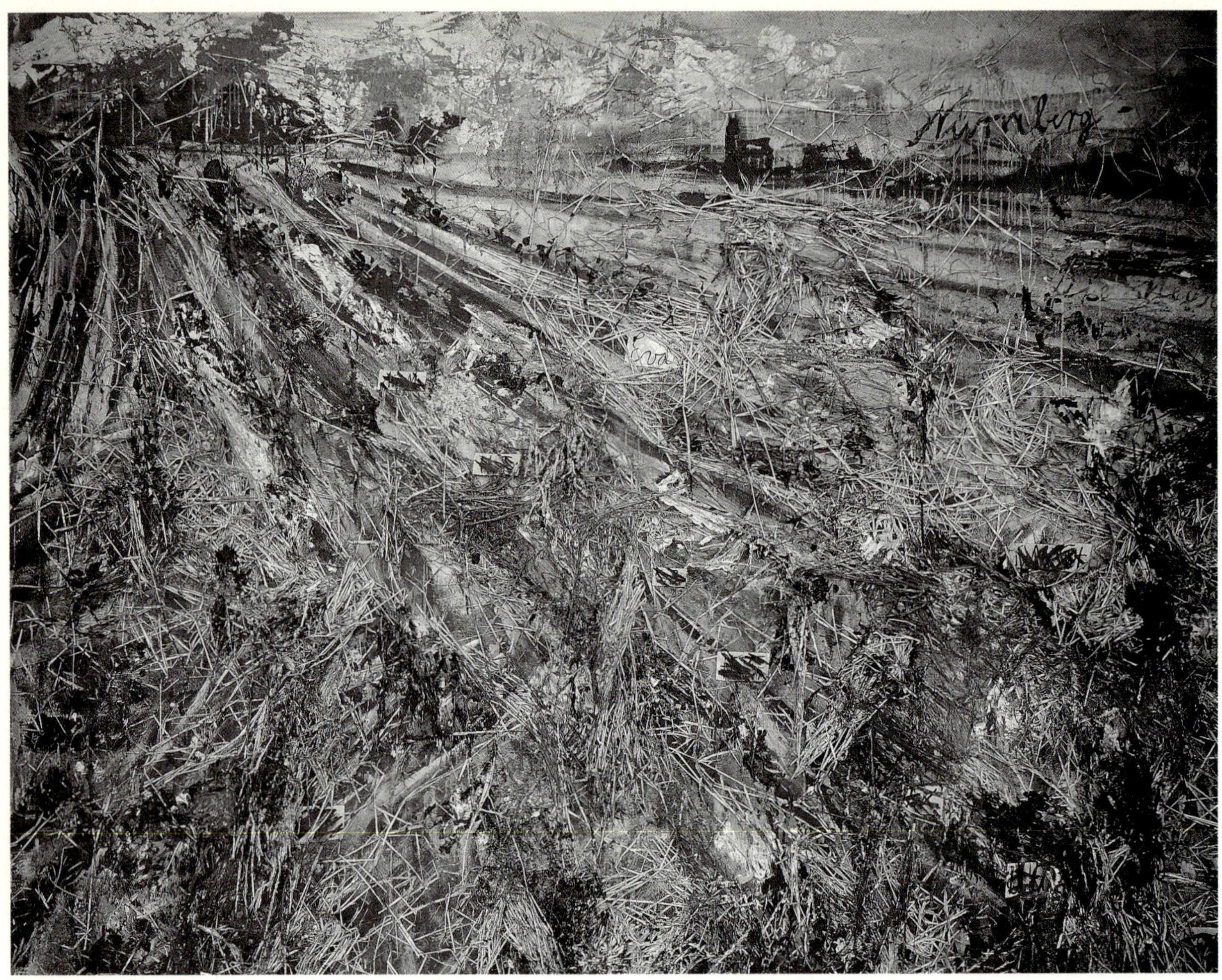

6.8 ANSELM KIEFER
Nürnberg (Nuremberg)
1982
Acrylic emulsion and straw
on canvas
110¼ × 149⅝ins
(280 × 380cm)
Courtesy The Eli and Edythe
L. Broad Collection

tion of blood and soil that marks German myth and runs in a steady current throughout all of German culture, a myth that in its most perverted form became the concept of the super race. The landscape often appears as a former battlefield which, to translate a quote from Victor Hugo which Kiefer has used, "still quakes from the footsteps of fleeing giants."[32] Kiefer traces his themes back to their origins, not to forget but to remember. Like that of Beuys, Kiefer's art regenerates German culture; it rises out of the ashes.

Fire figures prominently as a symbol of destruction and regeneration. The ashen soil depicted in *Nuremberg* evokes the practice of burning fields to clear them, to make way for the new crops. It also suggests invading armies' practice of burning the enemy's crops. From the ashes new crops grow. Nuremberg was the site of a great flowering of German culture in the Middle Ages, of the Renaissance painter Albrecht Dürer's birth, and later of Hitler's rallies and the Nazi war crime trials. Fire figures in alchemy, the medieval belief that fire can transform base materials into gold, desirable not only for its monetary value but also for its believed healing properties, itself a symbol of regeneration. The golden straw evokes alchemy. Golden straw grows from the ashes in *Nuremberg*. Straw and gold are multi-layered symbols in Kiefer's art.

In the popular German folk tale of Rumplestiltskin, the king tells a miller's daughter that he will marry her if she can spin straw into gold. She then finds a dwarf who tells her he will do it for her in exchange for her first child. She agrees, but after the

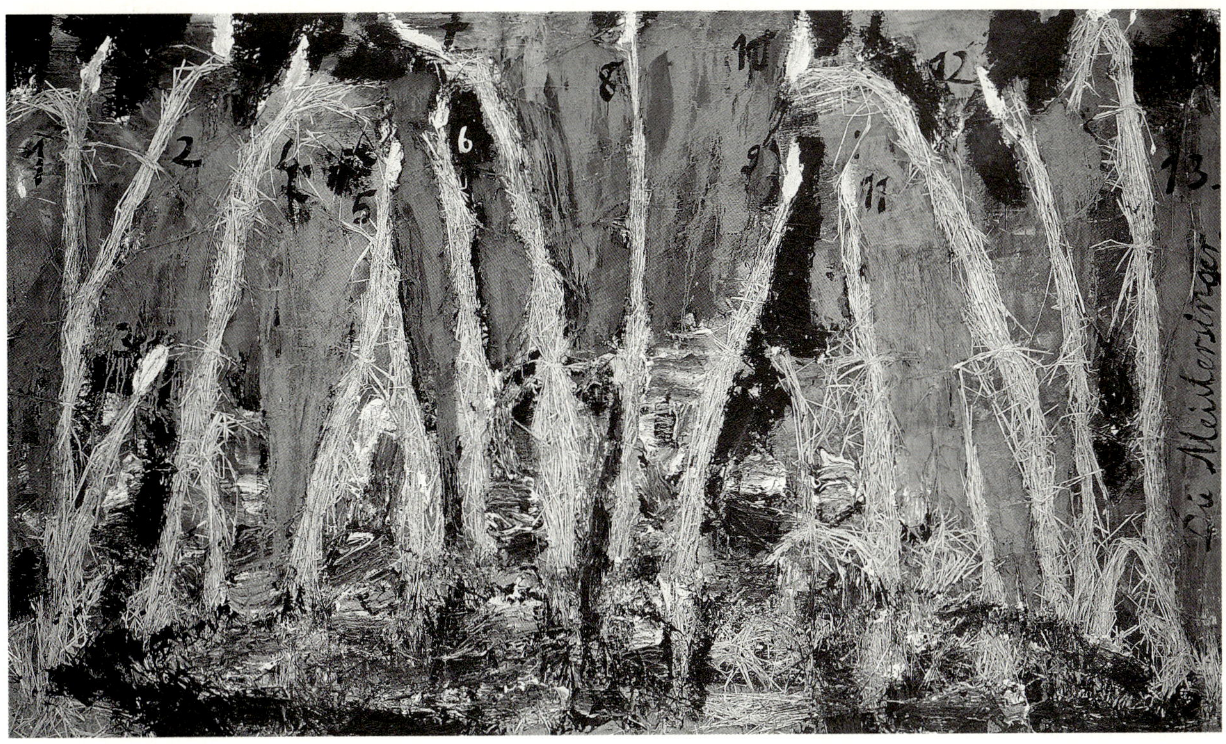

**6.9 ANSELM KIEFER
Die Meistersinger (The
Mastersinger)** 1981
Oil, acrylic, emulsion and
straw on canvas

72½ × 130ins
(184 × 330cm)
Collection Linda and Harry
Macklowe, New York

king's first child is born she regrets the agreement.
The dwarf promises that he will relent if she can
guess his name. One of the queen's servants over-
hears the dwarf's name—Rumplestiltskin—and the
child is saved.

Straw also symbolizes German womanhood. The
post World War II German poet Paul Celan, who
wrote in disconnected images, metaphors, and sentences about the merging of moral and aesthetic
values, composed his poem about the Holocaust—
titled "Death Fugue"—in a concentration camp in
1945. It was published in 1952. His poetry is characterized by rhythmic coherence and the association of
impressions and ideas rather than by a logical and
syntactical sequence, like Kiefer's art. In "Death
Fugue" Celan makes a reference to Margarete in
Goethe's *Faust* in the following lines: "Your golden

hair Margarete/ Your ashen hair Sulamith." Margarete
is a symbol of Aryan womanhood; Sulamith, of
Jewish womanhood. Straw equals the golden hair;
ashes represent the Jews of the Holocaust. Out of
the ashes of the Jews of the Holocaust, Germany is
regenerated.

This horrible thought is nonetheless true. Germany has revived following its downfall; German culture has revived largely because of Beuys and Kiefer.
But their remembering Nazism and daring to suggest
that Germany can transcend Nazism's horrors has led
some to accuse Kiefer of being a Neo-Fascist. Art
critic Peter Schjeldahl best addresses this issue:

*… His great theme of German culture and its
debacle in the Third Reich constitutes just a central
fissure and ruined site, a master metaphor, of his
vision. Its importance as an independent issue
must not be denied, but Kiefer has been viciously
misunderstood by those who have allowed it to
blind them to the fullness of his art. For it is art as
a civilising, redemptive force that is Kiefer's
ultimate theme. In confronting the century's largest
horror, he puts his hope and his ambition to the
test. If, without evasion, art can deal with the Nazi*

catastrophe, he reasonably suggests, it can deal with anything.[33]

Straw, gold, and fire are symbols in Kiefer's *The Mastersingers* (Fig. **6.9**). "The Meistersinger of Nuremberg," a German opera by Richard Wagner, expresses nostalgia for the flowering of Medieval German culture. In Kiefer's painting, burning straw again evokes destruction and regeneration. Fire and gold hold magical powers in Wagner's four-opera cycle, "The Ring of the Nibelungen," a great epic of German culture to which Kiefer makes frequent reference. Gold possessing magic powers is taken from the Rhine Maidens and forged into a ring, making the wearer the master of the world. Wotan obtains the ring. Wotan fathers nine warrior daughter Valkyries and Siegmund, who fathers Siegfried. Wotan's favorite Valkyrie, Brünnhilde, is punished for a misdeed by being put to sleep on a rock circled by a magic fire through which a hero will come to claim her. The magical properties of gold and fire play prominent roles throughout the four opera cycles.

"The Ring of the Nibelungen" is a very long and complicated cycle of operas that this synopsis only briefly sketches in reference to two things: the magic powers of gold and fire. These two potent symbols permeate German culture through Wagner's epic operas, through myth, folklore, poetry, and history. Kiefer utilizes this full range of subject-matter, evoking the biggest issues of our time—of racism, nationalism, war—forging themes of transcendent renewal and regeneration. "It may be possible to overestimate Kiefer's importance to world culture in the late twentieth century," Peter Schjeldahl wrote, "but at this point I don't quite see how."[34]

GEORG BASELITZ

The upside-down figures of Georg Baselitz (born 1938) metaphorically represent two sides of Germany, split into East and West (Communist and democratic) by World War II until they were reunified in 1990, the West divided by conflicts between its Fascist past and its current status as a Republic. Moving from East to West Germany in 1957 at the age of 19, Baselitz keenly felt the division. His aesthetic sensibility links him with the German Expressionism of the Die Brücke painters who worked in Dresden in the early part of the twentieth century, especially Nolde and Kirchner—with their seismically-charged autographic brushwork and themes of alienation and suffering.

Baselitz regards himself as an abstract painter, believing that the effect of turning his figures upsidedown is to discharge them of their traditional subject matter, instead forcing our attention to his aggressive painterliness. But he is both an abstract and a figure painter: another dichotomy.

The art critic Robert Pincus-Witten has observed the formal parallel between Baselitz's upside-downness and the Russian painter, Kandinsky (working in Munich with the Expressionist group Der Blaue Reiter in the early part of the twentieth century) seeing his canvas on its side and being moved by its shapes and colors alone.[35] Kandinsky's conclusions led him to the first abstract paintings. Baselitz rotates his canvases another 90 degrees, acknowledging Kandinsky but turning the precedent into expressive content.

The Crown of Thorns (*Die Dornenkronung*, Fig. **6.10**) depicts two upside-down figures, one placing a crown of thorns on the other. The crowned figure is divided into two different colored halves, and the painting is divided approximately equally between space and figures. Baselitz's woeful figures do not so much exist in space as *through* space, the whipped strokes that comprise them shuddering from space to figures. The figures seem suspended in inaction, frozen into an alien condition, yet caught in the flux of brushwork; movement ripples across the surface but no one moves. They have a tenuous, pained existence, alienated and insecure.

The Nazis termed Expressionist Art "degenerate" and persecuted it, recognizing that the best expressionist images are anti-authoritarian, that they assert the individual over the body politic. Alienation, disorientation, suffering, or despair are individual responses which weaken authoritarianism's claim to total control. Thus, reviving German Expressionism in itself constitutes an anti-Fascist statement, a repudiation of Nazism as well as an acknowledgment of it.

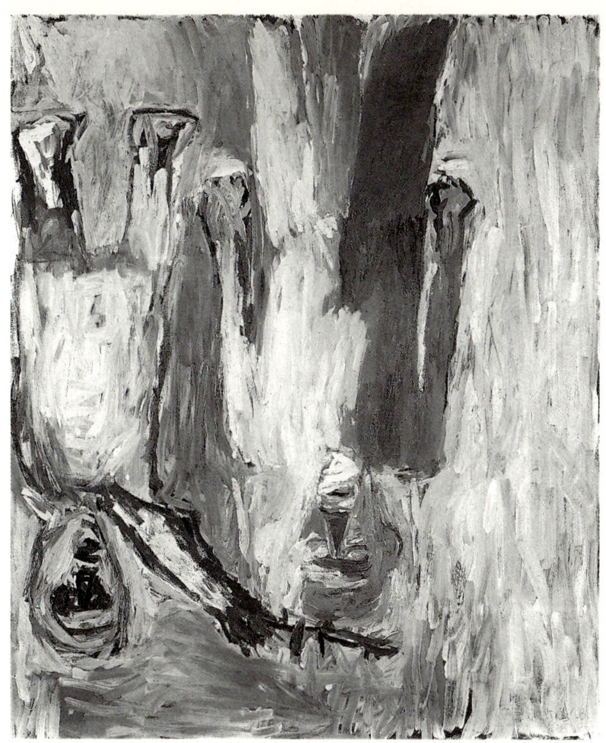

The Nazi's "could not imagine that their own authoritarianism, with its insistence upon petrifying conformity, was the real madness—the real enemy of life, an indication of serious disorientation to life. Baselitz shows us the inauthentic madness of authoritarianism—with its repressive conformity, symbolized by respect for 'normal' appearances and 'normal' orientation in space and 'normal' feelings—and the genuine madness of existence," wrote the art critic Donald B. Kuspit.[36] Baselitz renews the German Expressionist tradition.

6.10 GEORG BASELITZ
Die Dornenkronung
(The Crown of Thorns)
1983
Oil on canvas
117 × 97½ins
(297.2 × 247.7cm)
Courtesy Saatchi Collection,
London

SIGMAR POLKE

Sigmar Polke's temperament is very different from Baselitz's or Kiefer's. He borrows many different found images from diverse sources, including magazines, newspapers, advertising, and art books. In the 1960s his art was thought in America to be a German equivalent to American Pop Art, depicting common images and objects. But Polke (born 1941) interpreted his sources differently from American artists' ironic quotations; Polke's art has a disjunctive, edgy air. It doesn't celebrate the glut of goods of consumer culture's mass production, but reshuffles the found images into discordant transparent overlays. Salle saw Polke's work when he traveled to Europe in 1978, but Polke's work has none of the self-conscious studiedness of Salle's layerings. Polke takes a more spontaneous, expressionistic approach, like free association.

For the *Prayerbook of Maximillian* (Fig. **6.11**)

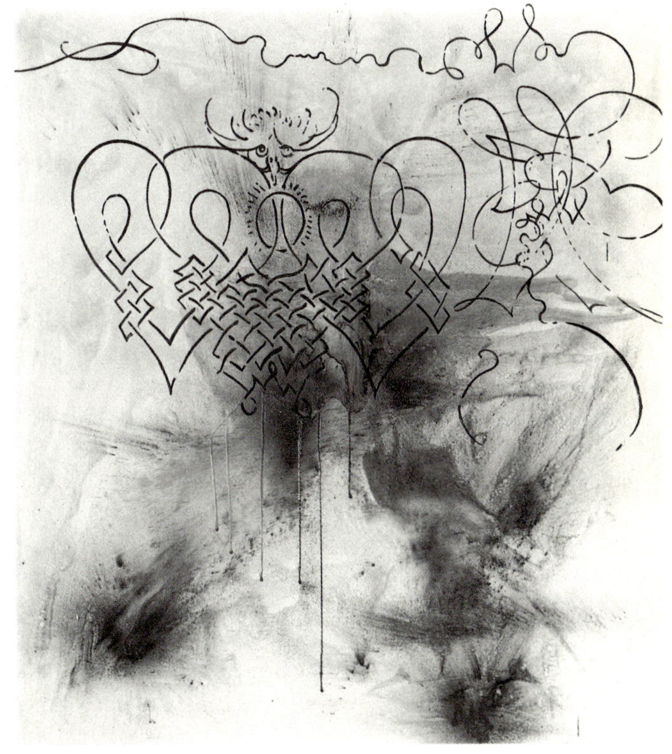

6.11 SIGMAR POLKE
Prayerbook of
Maximillian 1986
Oil and lacquer on canvas

78¾ × 70¾ins
(200 × 180cm)
Courtesy Mary Boone Gallery,
New York

Polke borrowed linear designs by the great German Renaissance painter Albrecht Dürer, literally copying them in large scale over an abstract, painterly, modern pattern. Dürer's prayerbook was printed to look like a hand-drawn manuscript, printed so it would be as up-to-date as possible by using the most advanced image-making concept of the time. (The printing press was invented in the fifteenth century.) Yet Dürer's book also refers to the older tradition of illuminated manuscripts by so closely resembling one. Polke borrows Dürer's dual reference to the future and the past: he seems to say that this is a better symbol of Germany than the swastika. Polke makes Dürer into a symbol of the current renaissance in German art.

FRANCESCO CLEMENTE

The Italian Neo-Expressionist Francesco Clemente was born in 1952 and grew up in Naples, an ancient city with a confluence of Egyptian, Greek, Roman, and Christian influences. He received a classical academic education and began writing poetry and making paintings at an early age. In 1970 he moved to Rome to study architecture, where his exposure to contemporary art heightened; Cy Twombly (an American artist of the generation of Johns and Rauschenberg), Aleghiero Boetti (an Italian artist who is Clemente's contemporary), and Joseph Beuys particularly affected him. *Arte Povera*, a parallel to Conceptual Art with its emphasis on dematerialization, was the most dominant Italian contemporary art at the time.

In 1973 Clemente traveled to India, the first of many trips; the artist, along with his wife and two daughters, now divides his time between their apartment in Rome, a house in Madras, India, and a studio in New York. In 1974 he traveled to Afghanistan with Boetti, and in 1982 he established his studio in New York. Clemente's art ranges widely over materials and imagery as diverse as his locales; movement and dislocation characterize his life and his art, along with his interest in various metaphysical systems, such as Christianity, alchemy, astrology, mythology, Hinduism, and the Tarot. "Style is the weight of what you are," Clemente said. "I didn't want my work to be. I wanted it to become."[37]

A clue to the attraction that India holds for Clemente lies in his following remark: "In six hundred million, or however many people there are in India, there is nobody who, for one second, thinks of the whole as something that you can explain. I mean, there is nobody there who tries to get an image of the whole thing. This means that there are no totalitarian ideas."[38] Fragmentation is a strategy Clemente uses to construct his sensual images; fragmentation expresses both personal and political goals. Rather than symbolizing disjunction and rupture, Clemente's fragmentation stands for spiritual individualism, the opposite of totalitarianism (lingering Fascism is still a strong presence in Italy). Expressing personal goals, Clemente says of fragmentation that "... you cannot trust any part of the self as the one that has to be in charge, so you have to give up techniques of integration."[39] On a political level:

Well, the technique of fragmentation is on the other hand a political stand, since all parties are working toward destruction of the earth, the destruction of animal life, the destruction of the diversity of cultures, destruction of the diversity of sexes, destruction of all diversities.... Maybe one can try the opposite, just let it go to pieces. So the model of fragmentation might be a strategy for survival, for freedom.[40]

Minimalism never held any attraction to Clemente; his is a deeply sensual art. Clemente situates himself in the world through his senses and his imagination, including his memories—"The first memories are images, aren't they?," the artist said[41]—rather than through reason, which he says is a product of the imagination, anyway. Many of Clemente's images depict his own emotions and sensate experiences in the form of self-portraits. *Untitled* (Fig. **6.12**) depicts an interior with the artist's head seen in close-up; smaller self-portrait heads appear in each of the head's orifices. Clemente is obsessed with body orifices and processes, and with skin. Skin is the point of contact between the inside and the outside of the body, between the self and what is outside it. The senses, along with the ori-

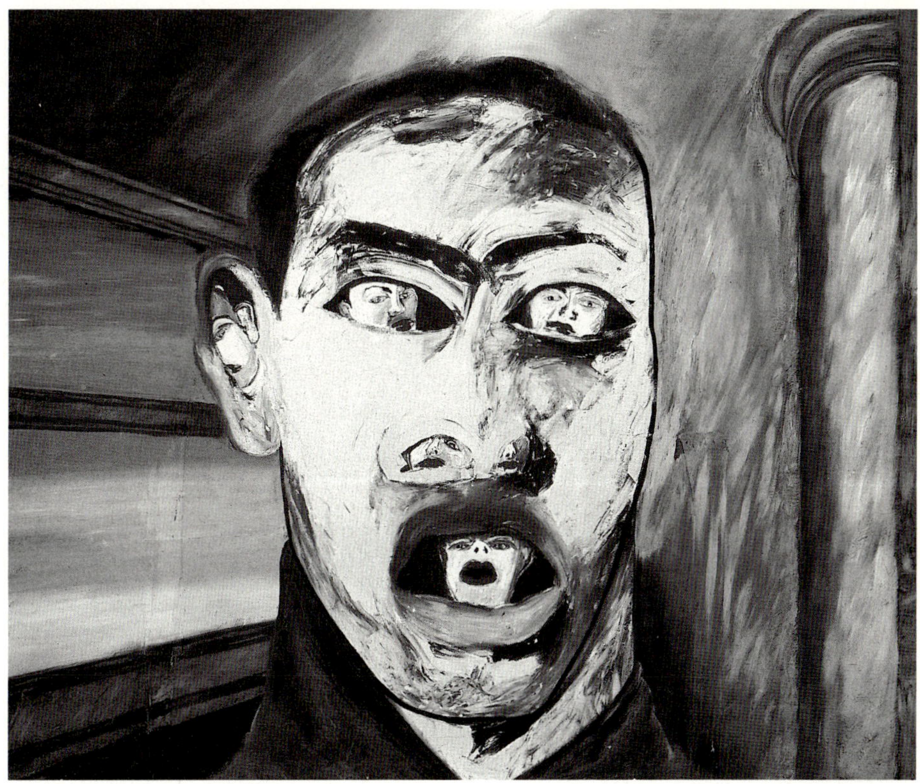

6.12 FRANCESCO CLEMENTE
Untitled 1983
Oil on canvas
78 × 93ins
(198 × 236cm)
Courtesy Thomas Ammann,
Zürich

fices, connect the inside to the outside, as well as substances that enter and exit the body. Placing heads within the orifices magnifies the contact. Maximizing the confluence of the artist's—and our—spiritual and sensate interior with the world outside underlies all of Clemente's art. Clemente said:

So what is the most immediate commonplace of all if not the body? It is something everyone has, and no one can figure out what it is like.... You know, one edge of the room is the perimeter, the walls, and the other edge is the skin, isn't it? ... What I say is that the skin is the commonplace between the space inside the body and the space outside the body.... Here we are touching on one of the most dominant elements of the work: the interest in these two spaces, the space inside and the space outside, and the weights those two spaces have. You know, there is a landscape of the world and there is also an inner landscape of the world. It changes as much as the face of the earth has been changing throughout all these thousands of years. The landscape we see inside us in our imagination changes also, it is not the same.[42]

SANDRO CHIA

Sandro Chia (born 1946) rejects both the precedents of postwar American art and Italian contemporary art, instead favoring early twentieth century Italian Futurism, German Expressionism, and French Fauvism as models, along with Italian Baroque and Renaissance painting. Not surprisingly, the Italian models take precedence. This nationalistic stance and rejection of the hegemony of American art politicizes Chia's art. His strong affiliation with Futurism politicizes it, too, for Futurism was an anarchistic art movement. Endorsing anarchism is another way of undermining authoritarianism.

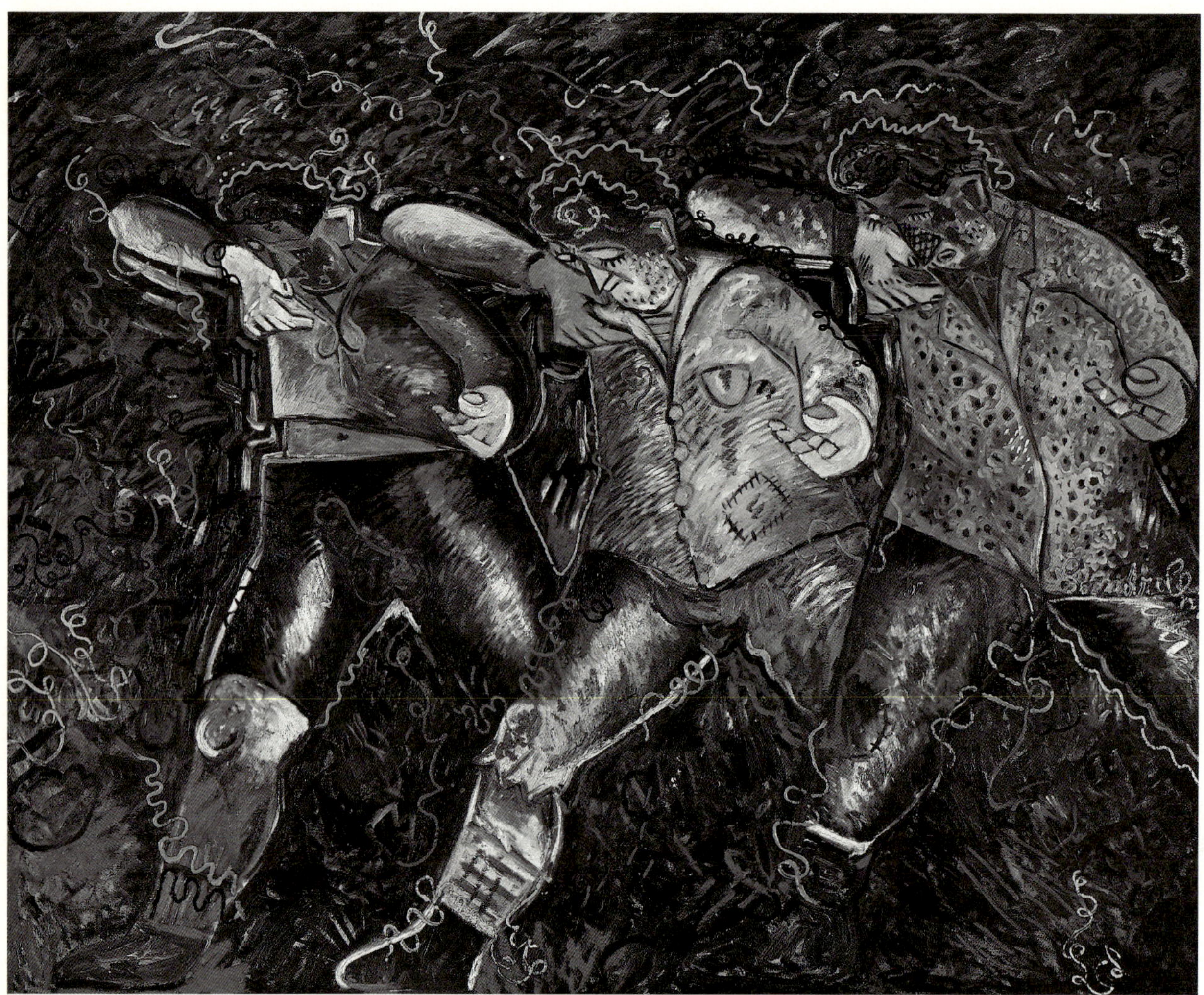

6.13 SANDRO CHIA
Brutes as Protagonists of
a Monkey's Erotic Fantasy
1979–80
Oil on canvas

67⅝ × 84ins
(171.7 × 213.4cm)
Courtesy The Rivendell
Collection, New York

Chia's *Brutes as Protagonists of a Monkey's Erotic Fantasy* (Fig. **6.13**) poses three husky tough guys on the canvas's lower edge, making them look like they have almost stepped into the viewer's space. Their vigorous stride suggests the Futurist Umberto Boccioni's bronze sculpture of 1913, *Unique Forms of Continuity in Space*, while their mask-like faces evoke the African sculpture which the Cubists and Fauvists so admired. Futurists were obsessed with movement and speed; these figures charge toward us as though possessed. Their ragged clothes and gender details, along with the grafitti-like background, accentuate their rudeness. The color, a blend of Futurism, Fauvism, and Expressionism, suggests a sour taste and smell.

The bulky male figures that dominate Chia's art are sometimes accompanied by iconographic references, though their meanings are never exactly clear. "The conventions of iconography are bearable in our era so long as the artist retains his privilege of confounding them," Carter Ratcliff wrote. "This leaves each member of the audience alone with his responsibility to speculate, to see what he can see."[43]

ENZO CUCCHI

Enzo Cucchi (born 1950) lives on the Adriatic Sea in the Italian town of Ancona, built on a rocky peninsula from which one can see the sun rise and set in the sea. Romans founded Ancona in the fourth century BC, and during the Middle Ages and the Renaissance it was an independent maritime republic. Today it serves as an embarkation point for Yugoslavia and Greece. Living in a town so connected to the sea and to history feeds Cucchi's imagination. His subjects are elemental states and primordial myths painted with a melancholic, poetic urgency. Musty smelling decay, and death, frequently recur.

Legends are the only real things that exist, that will keep on existing. The rest is history, but history, as you know, is false. History leaves us with the facts about an event but not the spirit of it. Legend gives us the spirit as well, the smell of the events.[44]

The theatricalized, distorted space of Baroque painting serves Cucchi as a source, especially that of El Greco and Caravaggio. *Closer to the Gods* (Fig. **6.14**) depicts a hilltop city—perhaps Ancora—encircled by the sea in flames. Dramatic backlighting and strong light and dark contrast emotionalize the city in the Baroque manner. El Greco made his space ripple and churn with mottled light and brushwork, a lesson Cucchi learned well. Emotionalizing the space gives Cucchi's painting a primitive, primordial power.

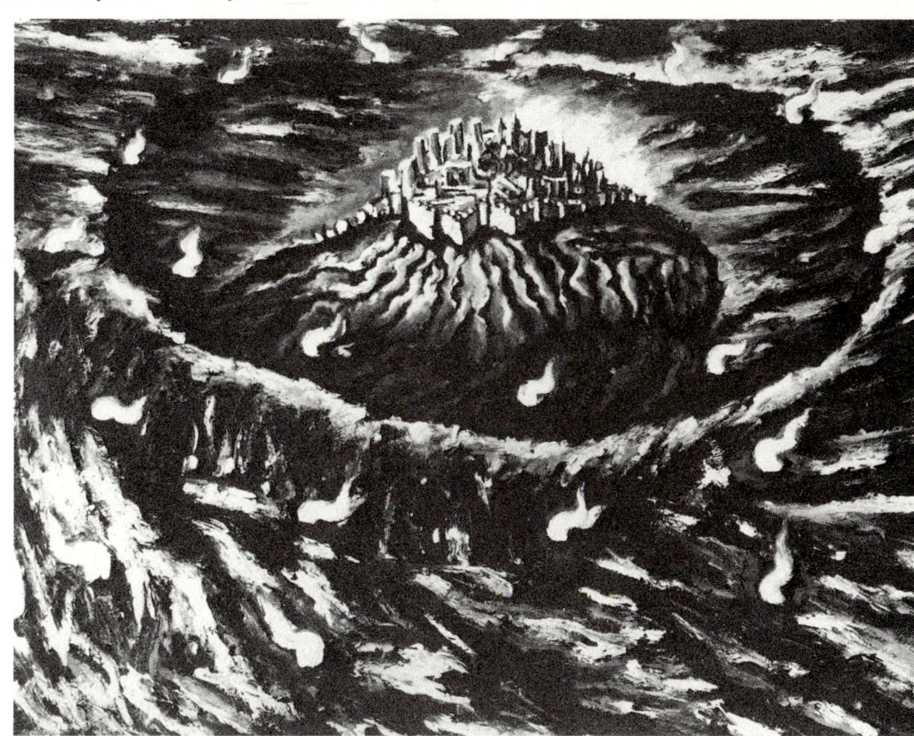

6.14 ENZO CUCCHI
Closer to the Gods 1983
Oil on canvas
110¼ × 141¾ins
(280 × 360cm)
Private Collection, Zürich
Courtesy Galerie Bruno
Bischofberger, Zürich

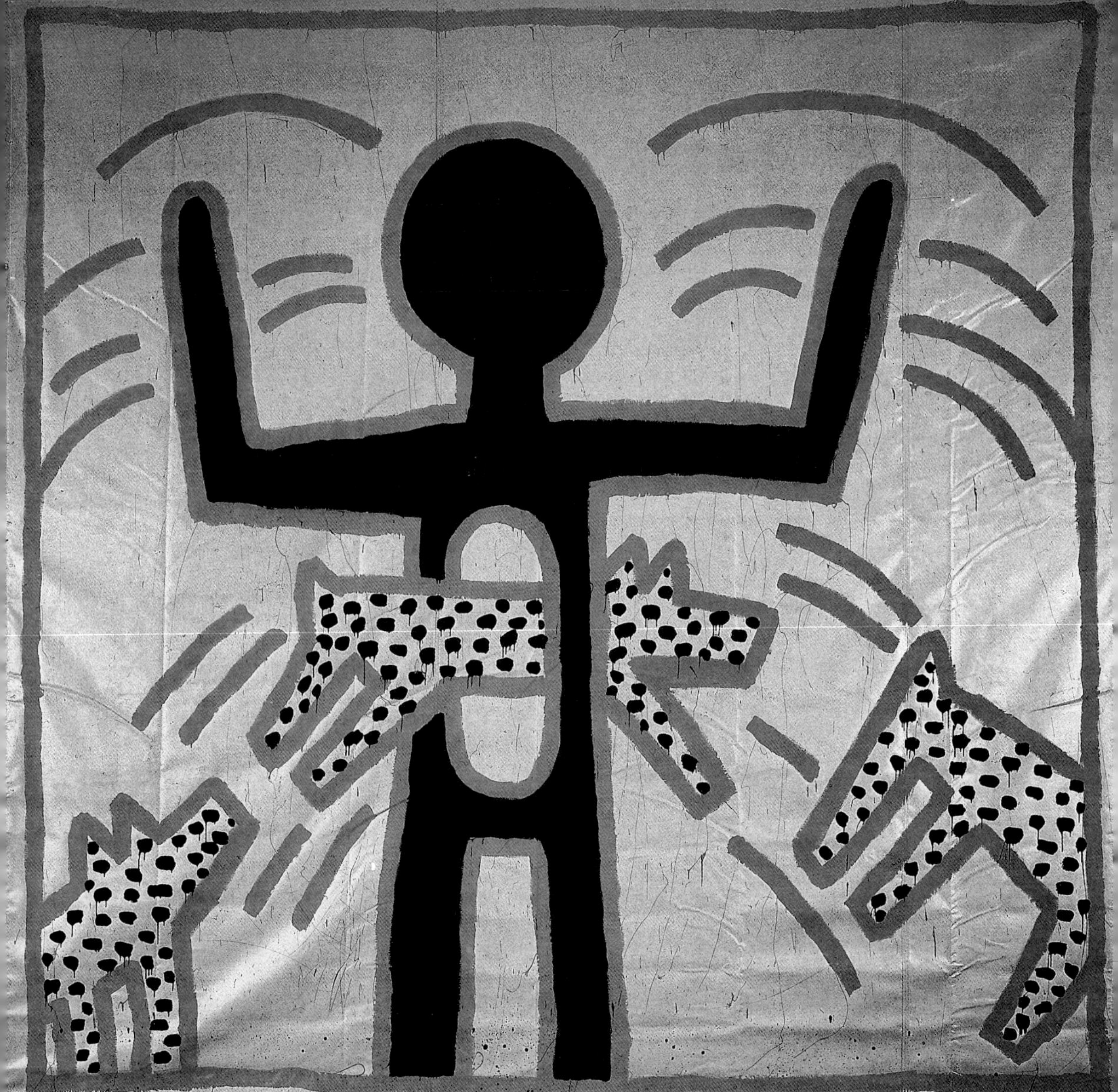

7
Post-Modernism

"*I'm not trying to compete with television or media as much as use them.*"[1]

—— KEITH HARING ——

Keith Haring
Untitled 1982
Courtesy Tony Shafrazi Gallery, New York

Ideas about Post-Modernism have evolved gradually over a period of many years. Various uses of the term maintain so many different meanings that a succinct description evades us; it is likely to always do so.

The first widespread use of the term Post-Modernism originated in the mid-1970s when the architect Charles Jencks termed architecture which overturns the principles of Modernism as "Post-Modern." Late Modernism in architecture took the form of the International Style beginning in the 1920s and featuring steel skeleton structures and glass walls. With its notions of formal clarity and structural unity, Post-Modernism is a kind of architectural parallel to the reductivism of Minimalism and of Modernism in general. Post-Modern architects, Jencks stated, feel free to borrow from prior architectural styles and to recombine them eclectically, as well as to submerge a building's structural logic within its decorative and symbolic elements. To draw a parallel to painting and sculpture, the subject of a Post-Modern building need not be a formal statement about modern architecture itself, but could be symbolic, expressive, narrative, historical, decorative, or could possess any number of qualities deemed by Modernists to no longer be within the province of architecture.

One of the earliest uses of the term Post-Modern in reference to visual art occurs in the art historian Leo Steinberg's work, *Other Criteria*, first given as a lecture at The Museum of Modern Art in New York City in 1968 and published in 1972. Steinberg stated that the proto-Pop Art paintings of Robert Rauschenberg transform space into a "flatbed," significantly referring to a printing press. Rauschenberg made montages out of photographic images of paintings by the Renaissance artists Botticelli, Michelangelo, and Titian and the Baroque artists Velazquez and Rubens, placed alongside photographic images of helicopters, a Coca Cola sign, and other common objects, such as street signs, an army truck and the Statue of Liberty. Steinberg characterized this change to montage-like artworks as expressive of "the most radical shift in the subject matter of art, the shift from nature to culture."[2] Steinberg could not have known in 1968 how prophetic his observation was.

Pop Art provided the precedent for subsequent contemporary artists' borrowings from mass-produced printed imagery, though the Cubists, Dadaists, and Surrealists had similarly borrowed before them. Pop Art's borrowings of pre-existing man-made images are much more direct, less altered, than the earlier precedents. Their directness parallels the immediacy and impact of the electronic communications whose effects on the populace were first becoming widely manifested in the 1960s. The first generation that came of age with television matured in the 1960s. This was a generation that obtained more of its information about the world from television and other mass-media than it did from school, parents, other family members, and nature combined. No wonder this generation shifted the subject matter of art from "nature" to "culture", or at least to an expanded concept of culture which includes television and other mass media, the most pervasive imagery of our time.

Andy Warhol's translation of mass-media photographs into paintings in the 1960s implied a status elevation of the lowly art of photography into the higher one of painting. At the same time, he elevated lower-class subjects, like Elvis Presley (who began his career singing in a lowly-regarded "negro" style) and the abandoned orphan Marilyn Monroe, into The King and a sex goddess, respectively.[3] Warhol used a photographic process to transfer his "found" photographs (which he literally "took") onto photo silkscreens which functioned as crude negatives. He then used the "negatives" to reproduce the appropriated photographs in his multiple-image paintings. John Baldessari coated canvases with photographic emulsion in the 1960s, projected negatives through an enlarger upon them, and developed them into paintings made from photographs, another example of elevating photography's status.

Implicit in their translation of photography into painting is the hierarchy of mediums that has been assumed since the invention of photography. Photography was not even considered a creative art during most of the nineteenth century, but a scientific method of reproduction, a debate that, believe it or not, continues even to this day. Essentially, the debate is between whether photography is an art of creation or of reproduction.

Many Post-Modern female artists—Sherrie Levine, Cindy Sherman, and Barbara Kruger, for example—use photography and its implied second-class status in part as a commentary about the second-class status of women. In short, according to the conventional wisdom, men create while women, like cameras, reproduce. Sherrie Levine's appropriations of only-male artists' imagery, Cindy Sherman's enactments of stereotyped women's roles, and Barbara Kruger's photographic appropriations from mass-media images all reverse photography's—and women's—formerly lowly status.

Post-Modern artists adopt mass-media images and communication strategies and comment upon their effects—not only on perception but on an array of subjects—unlike the Pop artists whose interpretations were mostly limited to irony. Those effects evade easy characterization. The French philosopher Jean Baudrillard described the condition of Post-Modernists as follows: "We are here at the controls of a micro-satelite, in orbit, living no longer as an actor or dramaturge but as a terminal of multiple receptors."[4] Baudrillard's Post-Modern beings are passive receptors, not active initiators. "He can no longer produce the limits of his own being, can no longer play nor stage himself, can no longer produce himself as a mirror. He is now only a pure screen, a switching center for all the networks of influence."[5] According to Baudrillard, our private sphere itself, the source of Modernist alienation and individuality, has passed out of existence. Post-Modern beings are like blank television screens, subject to receive electronic transmissions over which they have no control but which determine their view of the world.

Post-Modernism is not a style in the sense that formal attributes can be clearly identified. As a philosophy or a cultural phenomenon it also defies clear articulation and consensus. Much of the writing is so obscure and speculative that its meanings are unclear. Philosophers, architectural and social historians, and art critics writing about visual art, literature, music, and dance assign different attributes to Post-Modernism and state dates for its inception that sometimes differ by many decades.

Writers whose influence has been most keenly felt in the visual arts are Jean Baudrillard, Georges Bataille, Jean-Francois Lyotard, Michel Foucault, Jacques Derrida, and Roland Barthes. Among their few points of agreement are that Post-Modernism coincides with the post-industrial age, that it represents a rupture with Modernism, that it possesses a dislocation of space and time, and that it represents the fall of the modern myths of progress and mastery.

The post-industrial age is the electronic era, when instead of durable goods the dominant production is of processed information, short-lived imagery, and services. The short-lived nature of electronic information and imagery makes them difficult to analyze. Their content is not so much the "news" they carry as it is how the way they structure what they transmit affects our view of the world; their most lingering manifestation are their effects. Post-Modern artists and philosophers "deconstruct" pre-existing images by taking them out of their usual context and examining them, and "recontextualize" them by placing them in a new context, as a means to understand their meanings and regain a role less as a passive receptor and more as an active free agent.

The concept of pastiche applies to most Post-Modern Art. Pastiche in Post-Modernism involves borrowing from pre-existing images, either imitating them outright or making selections from various ones and combining them. Sometimes not an identifiable image itself but the feeling or aura of a classification of pre-existing visual images is evoked, as in Cindy Sherman's *Untitled Film Stills* or Jenny Holzer's signboards. Post-Modernists sometimes use the film-editing technique of montage—as when Barbara Kruger overlays text with appropriated images. Montage sets a mood more than conveying specific information; it is often used in advertising.

Pastiche differs from parody. Imitations made in parody carry sarcastic connotations; parody is a form of subtle humor or ridicule. Pop artists employ parody toward a humorous end. Andy Warhol's *Campbell Soup Can* paintings humorously parody advertising and mass production as well as serial imagery, such as Monet's *Haystacks*. By placing aesthetically discredited imagery in a fine art context, it is as though Warhol were saying, "Commercial art is art. It is not what it appears to be." Irony typifies Pop Art. Pop artists seem to say that mass-media imagery is, or at least can be seen as, art.

Post-Modernists rarely use parody or irony. They do not establish a hierarchy of "high" and "low" art—all imagery is equal to them. This sanguine attitude could not have occurred without the precedent of Pop Art. Post-Modernists accept the breakdown of former categories of "high" and "low" art and believe that what makes an image important is not the old-fashioned genre distinctions of fine art, popular art, and folk art, but an image's communicative power. Post-Modernists borrow whatever images have achieved the status of cultural signs—images that communicate meaning because of their commonness, their recognizability—and hence, Post-Modernists often use cliches. Cliche is a printing term, from the French *clicher*, which refers to a metal stereotype of a wood engraving. In visual art, a cliche is a commonly reproduced image which communicates commonly understood meaning. Post-Modernists communicate in the language of images with commonly understood meanings.

As such, Post-Modernist imagery is comprehensible to the same audience as television and advertising. Post-Modernism is not oppositional to the majority culture; it is oppositional to Modernism. With Post-Modernism, the adversarial relationship between artists and the general populace that typified modern art since the 1860s comes to an end. Post-Modernists accept post-industrial capitalism and the hegemony of its imagery of advertising and persuasion, thereby annexing its reach. But in deconstructing the language of post-industrial capitalism Post-Modernists assert some degree of dissent. Post-Modern visual artists oppose the reactionary notion of a return to normality that characterizes post-modern politics and social reforms. The return to traditional values like the family, religion, nationalism, and to pre-modern artistic values—or to eclecticism—are not part of their agenda.

Post-Modernists' adoption of the visual language of the majority culture without parody marks the end of the avant-garde—or at least its temporary suspension—for central to the avant-garde was the notion of opposition to the majority culture. In ending modern art's adversarial relationship to the majority culture, Post-Modernism changes the elitist concept of art that it exists on a higher plane than the rest of life itself.

CINDY SHERMAN

Cindy Sherman (born 1954) makes photographs of herself posed in various costumes, wigs, make-up, and settings that evoke unspecified film scenes. (Most of her characters are women, though she sometimes portrays men.) They are not self-portraits or impersonations, but evocations of mass-culture stereotypes using the visual conventions of mass-media, including compositional framing that recalls wide-screened movies. Sherman watched a lot of movies on television as a child growing up in New Jersey; she also played at dress-up. Her assimilation of roles is so complete that she can evoke them without appearing theatrical. Sherman's art does not portray a particular film or actress, rather, it conjures up the authority and power of movie stereotypes.

Between 1977 and 1980, Sherman made a series of black and white *Untitled Film Stills* based mostly on foreign movies. She usually used a remote control shutter release cable to make the exposure herself after setting up the situation and carefully framing it. A few times friends or her father released the shutter. The images compress the extended time of a movie into a single instant suggesting a whole complex of sequences beyond the frame, while remaining completely self-contained. Most of the film stills derive from 1950s prototypes, depicting women whose emotional vulnerability is not meant to signal physical availability. Neither narcissism, exhibitionism, nor voyeurism pertain, though Sherman herself appears in all of the photographs. At the time they were first seen in the late 1970s they seemed brilliantly astute, but they began to seem more strained and artificial as the 1950s revival spread.

A series of large horizontal color images begun in 1981 transcends the period look. These are close-up interior views where Sherman has more control on the lighting and set-up. She exposes an instant print of each scene, adjusts costume, make-up, or setting as required, then makes the final images. Sherman is director, costumer, lighting technician, make-up artist, scenarist, and cinematographer all in one. The nearly life-size images have a scale and color like painting. *Untitled #96* (Fig. **7.1**) shows a young woman dressed in orange reclining on an orange vinyl floor while clutching a scrap of newspaper. Her lack of eye contact and introspective mood focus attention away from her face and divide it equally to all parts of the composition. Everything becomes ex-

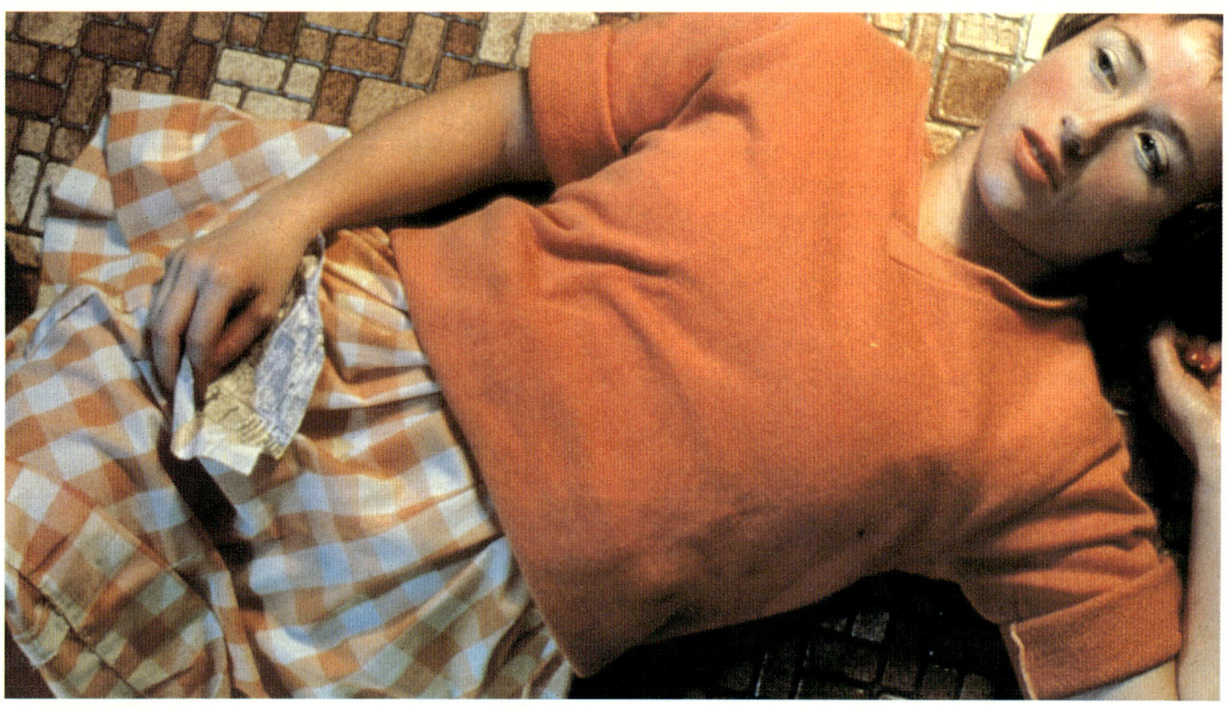

7.1 CINDY SHERMAN
Untitled #96 1981
Color photograph
24 × 48ins
(61 × 122cm)
Courtesy Metro Pictures
I was thinking of a young girl who may have been cleaning the kitchen for her mother and who ripped something out of the newspaper, something asking 'Are you lonely?' or 'Do you want to be friends?' or 'Do you want to go on a vacation?' She's cleaning the floor, she rips this out, and she's thinking about it."[6]

pressive. We cannot tell her thoughts, but we know from the language of movies that she is in a thoughtful state. Sherman meshes the sign system—or semiotics—of film with the pictorial and psychological dynamics of her image.

"I like the idea that people who don't know anything about art can look at [my art] and appreciate it without having to know the history of painting and photography," Sherman said.[7] Her art is not about painting or photography, though it pertains to both, but about movies and stereotypes. For her color images, Sherman makes 35mm slides and sends them to the lab for printing; she is not a photographer in any traditional sense. John Baldessari, Gilbert and George, and William Wegman are her predecessors more than straight photographers, but Sherman is not a Conceptual artist, either. Though her costumed images suggest fashion photographs they have none of their forced gregariousness or exaggerated suggestiveness.

BARBARA KRUGER

Born in Newark, New Jersey in 1945, Barbara Kruger studied at Syracuse University in Syracuse, New York, and Parsons School of Design in New York City. Kruger appropriates black and white photographic images from mass-media sources, crops and blows them up, and overlays them with words which refer both to the images' original subliminal message and Kruger's subversion of it. *You Invest in the Divinity of the Masterpiece* (1981–83) shows a close-up of the hands of God and Adam from the painting of the

Creation of Adam in Michelangelo's Sistine Chapel ceiling overlaid with the words of the title. Michelangelo's masterpiece has been used countless times by advertisers to confer the status of the masterpiece on whatever product or enterprise is being advertised—Kruger debunks their appropriation.

Kruger employs linguistic manipulation like advertising: her language carries hidden gender messages. "You" is always masculine, representing the white male power structure; "I" and "we" are feminine, representing the subjugated victims of the "yous." In a statement she made for an international art exhibition catalogue in 1982, Kruger wrote: "We loiter outside of trade and speech and are obliged to steal language. We are very good mimics. We replicate certain words and pictures and watch them stray from or coincide with your notions of fact and fiction."[8]

Working to expose what Roland Barthes calls "the rhetoric of image," Kruger reveals the hidden ideologies which are the sources of power of mass-media images.[9] *I Am Your Almost Nothing* shows two masculine hands entwined in thin, long blonde hair. In every case, Kruger montages words over the images. She appropriates the images from pre-existing studio photographs but changes them by cropping and enlargement to the scale of paintings. Kruger writes the words and chooses their size, typeface, and placement, then surrounds the image with a red frame. (More than ten years ago Kruger worked as a graphic designer, where she learned the visual language of the mass-media.)

Stereotypes are the language of mass-media. They suspend animation and transform action into gesture, immobilizing their subjects. Stereotypes are instruments of subjection; they produce ideologically identical subjects that can easily be inserted into social slots. Stereotypes promote passivity, receptivity, inactivity. They do not persuade but they act through deterence, what Jean Baudrillard calls "disuasion."[10] Stereotypes enact semiotic coercion; Kruger uses the sign systems of stereotypes to undermine their coercive effects. (Semiotics is the study of signs or signifiers.) Kruger turns a mirror to stereotypes' rhetoric of intimidation, reversing their reversed images and denaturing them.

The technique of montage is an allegorical confiscation, superimposition, and fragmentation. Mon-

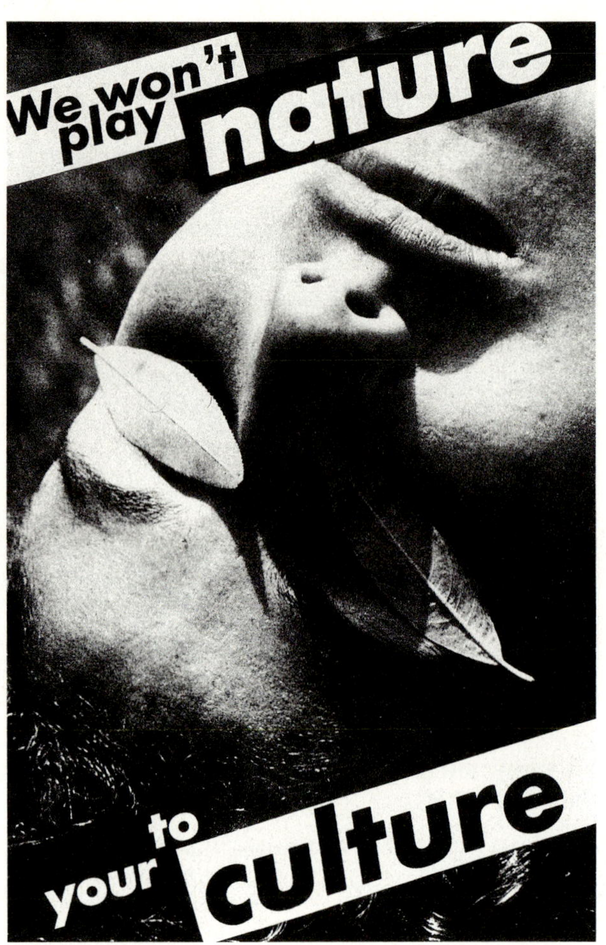

7.2 BARBARA KRUGER
Untitled (We won't play nature to your culture)
1984
Photograph
72 × 48ins
(182.9 × 122cm)
Courtesy Mary Boone Gallery,
New York

tage separates the signifier from the signified—the image from the thing it originally represented in nature. "The procedure of montage is one in which all allegorical principles are executed: appropriation and depletion of meaning, fragmentation and dialectical juxtaposition of fragments, and separation of signifier and signified."[11] Advertising creates persuasive fictions using the techniques of montage. Kruger's *I Will Not Become What I Mean to You* shows a close-up of a woman's face montaged with a tiger's and the words of the title: she uses the language of advertising to regain possession of the image of a woman which advertising has confiscated.

Untitled (*We Won't Play Nature to Your Culture*) (Fig. **7.2**) refuses a passive role but takes a combative stand, using advertising's personal address. Roland Barthes observed that advertising tends "to personal-ize all information, to make every utterance a direct challenge, not directed at the entire mass of readers, but at each reader in particular."[12] Kruger challenges every viewer, not only the admen's stereotypes, but our own as well. She refuses to play the female nature/nurture role to the male culture role just as she refuses to accept the domination of mass-media's false culture over her nature.

JENNY HOLZER

Jenny Holzer (born 1950) works in words made into arresting verbal cliches. Cliches stereotype the particular, making the experience of an individual instantly comprehensible to a larger audience. Cliches typify advertising and other public utterances. Holzer addresses a public audience with posters, official-looking bronze and aluminum plaques, electronic signboards, and carved stone benches.

Holzer first occupied a public sphere with posters printed in plain, declarative typeface with her *Truisms* (1971–79), often contradictory "great thoughts" reduced to cliches. Holzer explains:

The 'Truisms' series is partially a response to a wonderful reading list in the Whitney program [Holzer was a student in the Whitney Museum's internship program at the time]. It included numberless books, all of which were heavies, so just the prospect of wading through them was enough to make me do Jenny Holzer's Reader's Digest *version of Western and Eastern thought. I loved all these great thoughts on Western culture, but I figured I was reasonably bright and reasonably well-educated, and if I couldn't plow through it, certainly a lot of other people couldn't either. I realized the stuff was important and profound, so I thought maybe I could translate these things into a language that was accessible. The result was the 'Truisms'.*[13]

From a crazy man who plastered posters warning about leprosy all over midtown Manhattan, Holzer got the idea to paste her posters on public walls in her SoHo neighborhood. She left no clue what their intention was or who wrote them. Spontaneous comments written in their margins began appearing from her readers. Later, Holzer alphabetized the tru-isms to give them some semblance of order or logic, though many of them are contradictory, for example "A Strong Sense of Duty Imprisons You," and "Absolute Submission Can Be a Form of Freedom," or "A Relaxed Man is Not Necessarily a Better Man," and "Calm is More Conducive to Creativity Than is Anxiety." The ideas are not Holzer's; she only reduced them to cliches.

Context and content are inseparable in Holzer's art. Holzer intended that the *Truisms* be discovered by unwitting viewers in the same context as commercial messages and advertising posters. Set outside the context of art or of literature, side-by-side with commercial messages, the *Truisms* demonstrate that cliches can carry powerful meanings. (Holzer was born and raised in the Midwest, where she says her plain and direct speech pattern was the norm. Advertising's succinctness informs her art, too.)

Holzer followed the *Truisms* series with *Essays* (1979–82) and the *Living Series* (1980–82). *Essays* features paragraph-long discourses set in italics in the New York Times typeface, as though they are quotes from a speaker. The *Living Series* is not italicized; it proffers homespun survival advice such as "WHEN YOU'VE BEEN SOMEWHERE FOR AWHILE, YOU ACQUIRE THE ABILITY TO BE PRACTICALLY INVISIBLE. THIS LETS YOU OPERATE WITH A MINIMUM OF INTERFERENCE," and "MORE THAN ONCE I'VE WAKENED WITH TEARS RUNNING DOWN MY CHEEKS. I HAVE HAD TO THINK WHETHER I WAS CRYING OR WHETHER IT WAS INVOLUNTARY LIKE DROOLING." Holzer preserves a neutral, genderless voice and takes the tone of an objective observer recording observations.

Holzer posted the *Essays* like the *Truisms*, but the *Living Series* was also made into bronze and aluminum official-looking plaques and programmed into electronic signboards. (Later, *Essays* and *Truisms* also appeared on electronic signboards.) Holzer uses contexts of public address: electronic signboards usually carry public service announcements or advertising. Placed on walls outside an art context, the official-looking plaques blandly state Holzer's subversive messages. The *Survival Series* (1983–85) took the form of posters and of metallic stickers which showed up on parking meters, pay phones, rest rooms, and other public places (Fig. **7.2**).

In 1982 the *Truisms* appeared on the electronic signboard at New York's Times Square, on the old New York Times building from which the electronic apple is dropped every New Year's Eve. The signboard faces a large open space filled with pedestrians and traffic, electronic advertising signs, and Broadway marquees. Holzer's pithy statements had to compete with many strong distractions, but they succeeded because they were designed with that context in mind.

Two forms continue to preoccupy Holzer to this day: the series *Under A Rock*, begun in 1986, which has appeared on signboards and carved into stone benches using the same script as the National Cemeteries; and various electronic signboards using earlier writings. In 1986 Holzer programmed the Las Vegas Caesar's Palace electronic signboard with her pithy messages, along with signboards at the University of Nevada's sports center, two shopping centers, and at the Las Vegas airport's baggage and handling area. Her main interest seems to be in utilizing the electronic signboard format: "High technologies do seem to be the media of authority, especially in

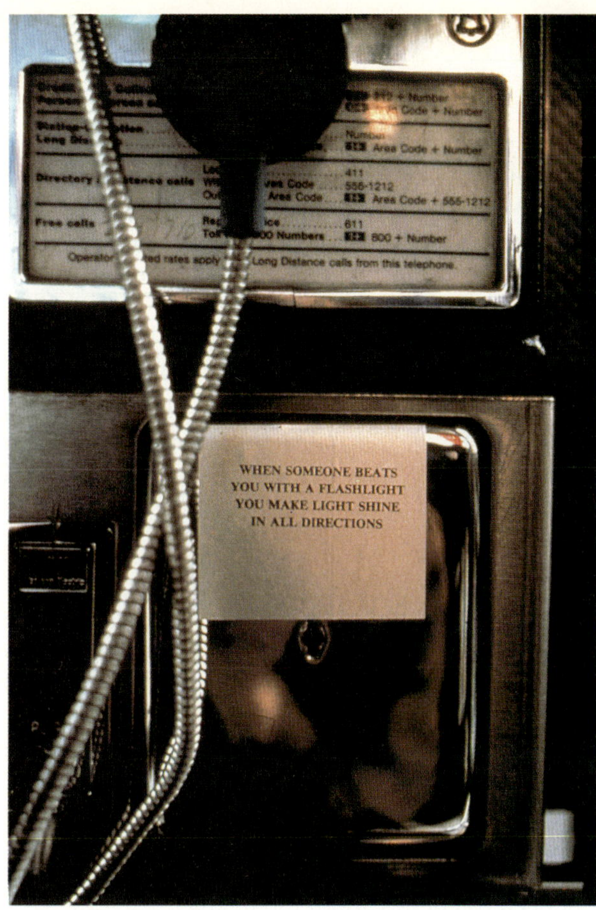

7.3 JENNY HOLZER
Survival 1984
Street installation

Courtesy Barbara Gladstone
Gallery, New York

the '80s," Holzer said. "If you're considered radical, you're either shot or ignored, so I think I can be trickier and possibly more effective if the message seems to come from on high, rather than from beneath."[14]

SHERRIE LEVINE

Sherrie Levine (born 1947) has appropriated images since the late 1970s, first making collages, then photographic copies of photographs of photographs in art books, then photographic copies of photographs of paintings in art books, followed by watercolors of photographs of paintings in art books, then paintings on sheets of plywood covering their knots with gold, followed by current work taken from George Harriman's *Krazy Kat* comics. In every case, Levine does not alter her source in any way. If the reproduction she copies differs from the original artwork, she faithfully copies the reproduction.

Levine's art investigates the idea of originality. The notions of originality and individualism adhere to Modernism and its myth of progress. According to the Modernist myth—in the contemporary period most strongly championed by the art critic Clement Greenberg—painting progresses inevitably toward

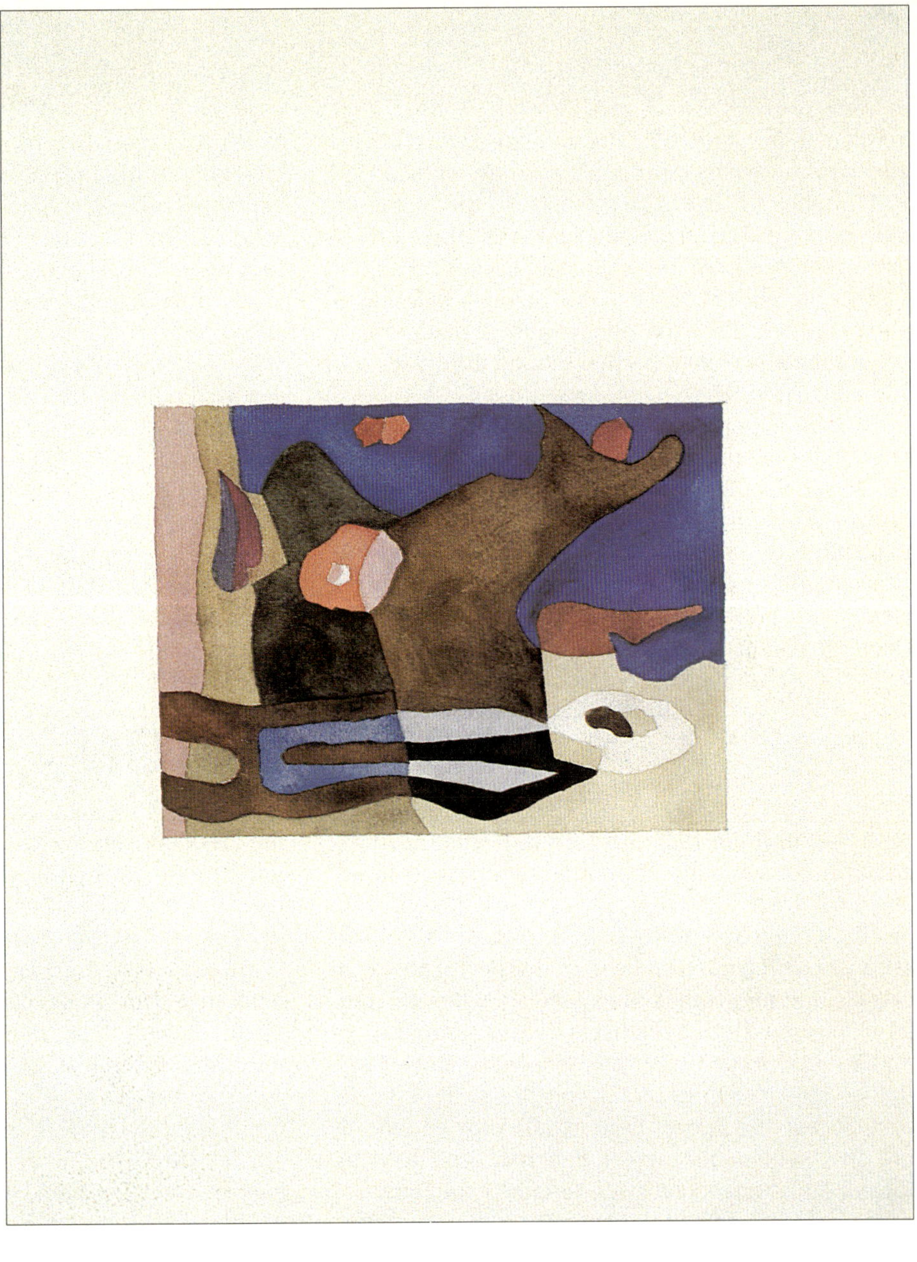

differentiating itself from other mediums by more thoroughly entrenching itself in its area of competence. In other words, painting should be about visual—and only visual—sensations which can only be embodied in painting. Originality consists of finding new ways to further that dialogue. For Levine, that Modernist dialogue no longer exists. Neither does originality in Modernist terms.

Speaking of painting before the modern period, Levine said: "Originality was not an issue. I think that's where Modernism was a real break." Later in the same interview she said, "It's not that I don't think that the word originality means anything or has no meaning. I just think it's gotten a very narrow meaning lately. What I think about in terms of my work is broadening the definitions of the word 'original.'"[15]

All of the works Levine confiscates were made by male artists. "A lot of what my work has been about since the beginning has been realizing the difficulties of situating myself in the art world as a woman, because the art world is so much an arena for the celebration of male desire," Levine said.[16] Levine appropriates "his" art to make this explicit.

After Arthur Dove (Fig. **7.4**) is a watercolor made

from an art book reproduction of Dove's work. Levine traces or draws the reproduction on her standard 11 × 14 inches (27.9 × 35.6 cm) format, then carefully reproduces it. The images she makes are three or four times removed from the originals—Levine calls them "ghosts of ghosts."[17] First the original painting is photographed, then the photograph is made into a color separation, then printed into an art book, then copied by Levine.

"Levine's apparently radical denial of authorship might fail to recognize the socially acceptable, if not desirable, feature it implies: a reaffirmation of the dismantling of the individual ..." wrote the art critic Benjamin H. D. Buchloh.[18] According to Buchloh, mass-media dismantled individualism in favor of stereotypes and cliches; Levine refuses to deny this. Buchloh claims that the medium of painting "pro-vides an experience of reconciliation" with the dismantling of the individual because in paintings "the ultimate subject is always a centralized author," whereas in montage "the subject is the reader/viewer."[19] This is because in montage there are multiple subjects and viewpoints and, consequently, more various interpretations are possible. Levine's fragmentation differs from the "phallocratic" tendency which uses "broken saucers, burnt wood, and crumpled straw," according to Buchloh.[20] He calls these tendencies "phallocratic" because they are practiced by men, a distinction I find strained. Buchloh thus perceives a gender-specific content in Levine's confiscations which, whether one agrees that it is present in Buchloh's sense or not, is certainly present in the power roles that the genders play, within and outside of the art world.

SCOTT BURTON

Scott Burton (born 1939) made objects that blend the functions of sculpture and furniture; they are simultaneously both, and more. Burton, who died of AIDS in 1989, perceived himself as a "public artist," an artist whose intended audience consisted of all social classes and all degrees of experience with art. (Gallery and museum audiences consist primarily of middle- to upper-class, highly educated people.) Rather than designing for self-expressive or solely aesthetic goals, Burton gave equal consideration to his art's setting, placement, function, and psychological and social contexts. The artist explained:

I want to get some social meaning back into art. And I'd like to help change art into some kind of design. I think that the moral, the ethical dimension of art is mostly gone, and only in a newly significant relationship with a non-art audience can any ethical dimension come back into art.... I want to get to not only an ethical, but also some kind of social component as well.... I feel that the autonomy of the studio artist is a trivial thing by now, in our society. Who cares if you paint it blue instead of red?[21]

Burton drew upon the precedents of early twentieth-century Russian Constructivism and the Dutch movement of de Stijl, both of which expressed the desire to integrate artistic issues into everyday life in their functional designs. The Constructivists believed that their objects must "combine 'external decorativeness' with truth to physical materials and functional service in a social context."[22] Burton collaborated with architects, corporations, and private clients, taking their needs into account and designing installations that satisfy those needs while transcending the merely functional. He also designed furniture/sculpture that is not site-specific.

For the Equitable Center in New York, Burton designed a seating area, planter, and floor paving in sumptuous Verde Larisa Greek marble, granite, and bronze. Even though it goes beyond providing seating, many visitors never realize that the installation is art. Yet the high-caliber tone it sets subtly enhances the corporate image. Art in the intended service of a corporation would have been unthinkable earlier in the contemporary period, but Post-Modernists deliberately annex the broadest social sphere. Burton clarified the nature of the majority culture, creating a communal center to the corporation, one that has a formal, ceremonial aspect to it. The lobby is a democratic meeting place but one that nonetheless impresses visitors with its grandeur, opulence, and implied economic and thus social and political power.

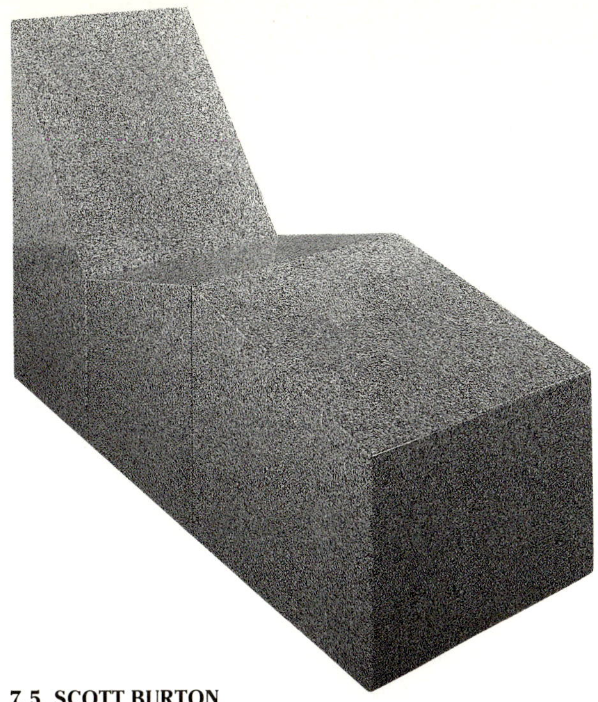

7.5 SCOTT BURTON
Chaise Longue 1983–84
Polished granite
41½ × 24 × 67ins
(105.4 × 61 × 170.2cm)
Collection Lockhart

Minimalism and Conceptual Art were the established artistic norms when Burton first started making his furniture works in the early 1970s. First, he made tableaux by placing pre-existing furniture in different settings, then altered a "found" chair by painting it bronze in 1972, later casting it in bronze in 1975. By the late 1970s, he was fabricating (or having fabricated) furniture of his own design, much of which mimicked established designs, such as his *Lawn Chairs (A Pair)* (1976–79) which alter the classic Adirondack chair (a rustic chair design widely used in New York State's Adirondack mountains). By the early 1980s, most of Burton's designs were unique, though some evidence his fondness for classic furniture design. Many reveal Burton's homage to Minimalism's precedent.

Though Minimalists did not make functional designs, a successful installation of their sculpture interacts with interior architectural spaces, a feature governing most furniture. Burton's *Chaise Longue* (Fig. **7.5**) invests minimalistic geometric shapes with utilitarian function. Made of polished granite, it is not a chaise that one would lounge in for very long, yet it is a piece of furniture. Its mass and enormous weight give it a sculptural and ceremonial presence greater than ordinary furniture. Affiliated with centuries of stone garden furniture, placed in a landscape it could go unnoticed by the art novice as art, and so it seemlessly combines its utilitarian with its artistic function, appealing to a multi-level social and educational spectrum.

KEITH HARING

Keith Haring's dual heroes were Andy Warhol and Walt Disney; he situated his art somewhere between theirs, between fine art and popular art. A series of "Andy Mouse" paintings, drawings, and prints that Haring made in the late 1980s features Warhol with Mickey Mouse ears. The image could be a self-portrait. Haring (1958–1990) drew in a boldly graphic declarative style that is instantly legible, like visual Esperanto. He combined influences from the Belgian painter Pierre Alechinsky and the French artist Jean Dubuffet (both of whom used childlike images and graffiti-like marks) with subway graffiti "writers" and Hanna/Barberra television cartoons.

Throughout his school years, Haring's skill as a cartoonist won him popularity among his schoolmates. By his mid-teen years, the small, blue collar town of Kutztown, Pennsylvania where he grew up seemed a limited horizon, and Haring sought a larger context. By his early twenties, he was in New York City where he enrolled at the School of Visual Arts to meet people. In 1980 he began making white chalk drawings in subway stations on the black paper that was pasted over expired advertisements. The context required quick execution and a quick "read." An image dubbed by the art critic Rene Ricard a "radiant child," a barking dog, a dog jumping through a hole in a man's stomach, a pyramid, and animated faceless figures comprised his visual vocabulary. The New York police had mounted a campaign against the spray-painted graffiti that riddled the subways, so Haring had to work fast to avoid arrest. He went from "blackboard" to "blackboard," covering both sides of

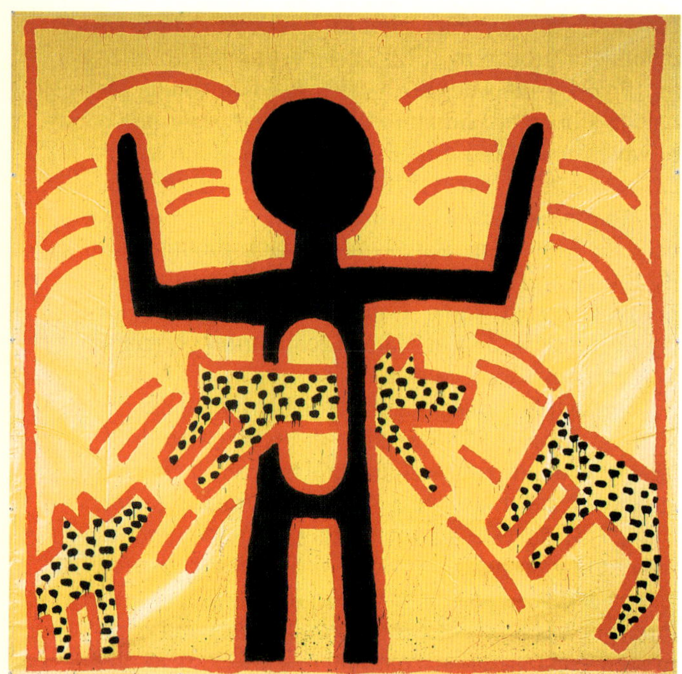

7.6 KEITH HARING
Untitled 1982
Vinyl ink on vinyl tarp
12 × 12ft
(144 × 144ins; 365.7 ×
365.7cm)
Courtesy Tony Shafrazi
Gallery, New York

ing was a political act made by the socially disenfranchized—it is a way of expressing pride and saying "I exist." The minority political agenda along with the cartoonish youth orientation of graffiti meshed with Haring's interests.

Haring also made paintings, at first on vinyl industrial tarpaulins, later on the more traditional format of stretched canvas. An *Untitled* (Fig. **7.6**) work from 1982 shows dogs jumping through a hole in a man's stomach, meant to represent the fatal shooting of John Lennon. His pictographs usually engage topical subject matter: a black figure with a rope around its neck symbolizes "free South Africa," figures with a cross and a rod symbolize Poland's Solidarity strike, the radiant child and barking dog symbolize the artist himself. Typically, Haring sides with ordinary people's social issues and symbolizes them in a visual language anyone can understand. He avoids much reference to the art world and its inbred politics.

Homoerotic themes that were always present in Haring's art became more pronounced toward the end of his life. (Haring died of AIDS on February 16, 1990.) Urgings toward safe sex and warnings about AIDS appear in his prints and paintings as well as posters and more public art forms. Haring's 1989 exhibition at the Tony Shafrazi Gallery featured a giant 12 feet (3.7 m) high phallus-shaped canvas. He worked quickly and prolifically produced drawings, prints, paintings, and sculptures. The paintings became more complex and painterly than they were in the early 1980s.

Yet, although Haring did place his work in fine art galleries and museums, he also continued to make it available to a larger audience. His Pop Shop in New York's SoHo still sells Haring-designed T-shirts, posters, stickers, refrigerator magnets, radios, pins, buttons, Swatch watches, and an inflatable version of the radiant child. Opportunities for Haring to design commercial art projects were endless, but he carefully chose which ones to do. At first Haring was somewhat wary of entering the commercial art realm, but when Haring's designs began appearing in ripped-off versions he felt he had to exercise control. The ever-populist, gregarious artist liked having his work available for as little as 25 cents, to children and to an audience that would not or could not buy a $25,000 painting.

a subway platform, then got back on the train and went to the next station. Thousands of his drawings appeared as if overnight.

Haring considered his subway drawings and many of his other images—posters, T-shirts, buttons, stickers, murals (he even designed a video for the rock singer Grace Jones)—as free art, art for the people. Haring addressed a broader audience by placing his art directly before them, without the middle-man of an art institution. Admiring the skill and grass-roots authenticity of the prolific graffiti "writers," Haring adopted their public forum for his spontaneous art. In New York at the time, graffiti writ-

ERIC FISCHL

Eric Fischl (born 1948) is an American painter in the tradition of Winslow Homer and Edward Hopper, depicting uniquely American psychological states and the precise conditions of a particular moment in the nation's history. His subjects live in the suburbs of the 1980s where they act out their malaise. Fischl implicates the viewer in narrating their unresolvable conflicts, making their dilemmas the viewer's own. Rites of passage from childhood to adulthood, sexual taboos, emotional crises, the lingering effects of neglect and abuse, hysteria under control, boredom, and the brink of disaster are Fischl's subjects, always brought to a barely endurable pitch but saved by a masterful painting ability that recalls great art of the most traditional kind.

What makes Fischl a Post-Modernist? He pierces Modernist painting's flat space with illusionistic depth, but so do the Neo-Expressionists. A disjunctive sense of space and time typifies Fischl's artworks, placing them in the here and now while simultaneously somewhere else. The mobility of time and space follows an electronic pattern, like switching channels and going from Los Angeles to Des Moines, where the same types act out similar psychological dramas. Only, Fischl switches from one historical period to another.

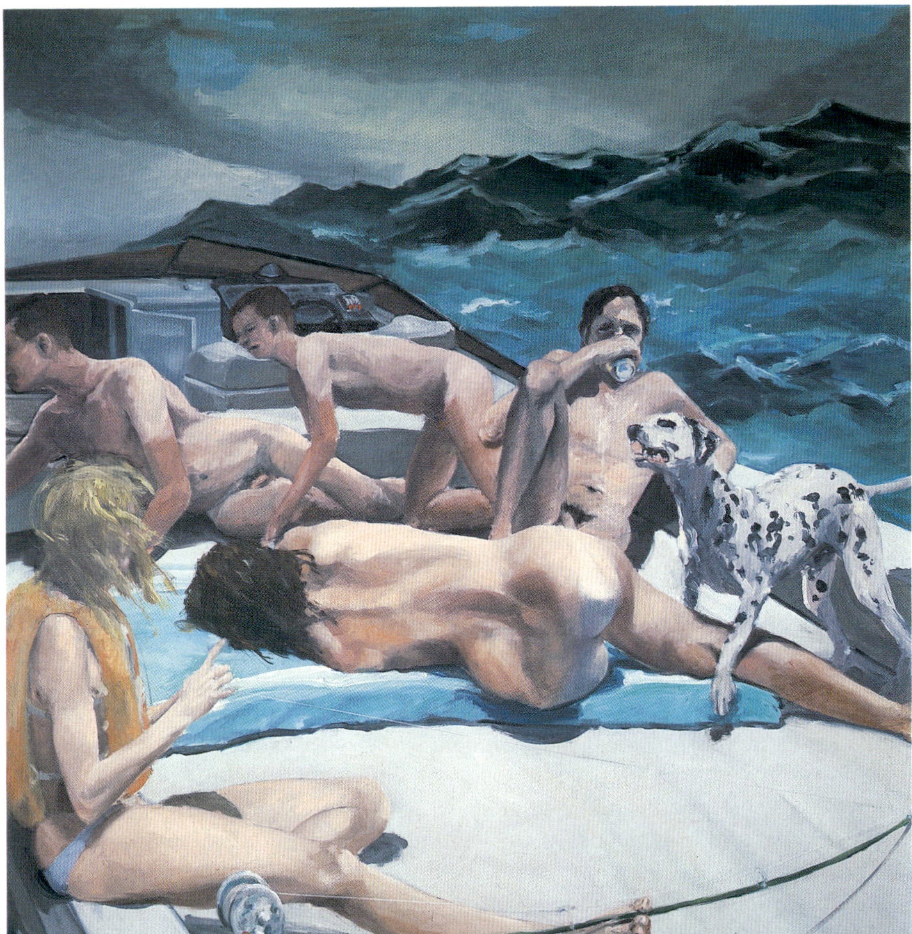

**7.7 ERIC FISCHL
The Old Man's Boat and
the Old Man's Dog** 1982
Oil on canvas
84 × 84ins
(213.4 × 213.4cm)
Courtesy Saatchi Collection,
London

Fischl explains:

The artists of my generation feel that you can borrow freely from any time and place to construct your own image.... My work seems to come out of the nineteenth century, but it also uses twentieth-century primitivism.... All these different styles and philosophies based on different stylistic advances are available for use. It's like the universe has curled back on itself and become full of possibilities that were half-realized but still have a long way to go. In that sense, I think I'm a Post-Modernist...[23]

Nakedness in Fischl's paintings implies making the figures' thoughts and emotions bare. Nakedness in a social setting usually makes us uneasy, like the classic dream of finding yourself naked in a public situation. Naked people seem vulnerable. Naked is not the same as nude: naked people look like they have taken their clothes off, nudes look like they belong that way.

For *The Old Man's Boat and the Old Man's Dog* (Fig. **7.7**), Fischl directly copies a seascape from Winslow Homer's *The Gulf Stream*, and thematically alludes to Géricault's *Raft of the Medusa* and Goya's *Ridiculous Folly*, two nineteenth century (French and Spanish) Romantic prototypes. Yet the mood is 1980s malaise. Only just starting to catch on to the approaching disaster—the dog senses that something is about to go wrong, or is he threatening the girl in the life vest?—the four naked and one clothed figures lounge obliviously on the boat's deck, enjoying the upper-middle-class American perks which typify Fischl's dramas. The two boys notice something in the water—a shark? The beer guzzler is too far gone to care, and the dozing woman (has she passed out?) hasn't even noticed yet. Is this a family? Where is the old man?

Géricault depicted his shipwreck survivors at the moment that they sighted a ship, leaving viewers uncertain about the outcome of their rescue to heighten the drama. His painting is a Romantic metaphor for man's fate, cast adrift on the sea of life with no mooring or rescue assured. Fischl renews that by-now-cliched Romantic notion with a strangely contemporary bite. He squeezes out the sentimental melodrama and makes it credible again. Despite the soap opera and movie connotations, perhaps because of the art references, our emotions hang on the edge. Goya's *Ridiculous Folly* (an etching from the *Disparates* series [ca. 1813–20]) depicts his contemporaries sitting on a rotting tree limb cantilevered over space, oblivious to their imminent doom. Fischl's mood has none of Goya's cynicism or moralizing—it has a strangely contemporary moral detachment and unease.

In effect *The Old Man's Boat and the Old Man's Dog* is a pastiche of art historical themes and images along with soap opera and movie material, of masterpieces mixed with stereotypes and cliches, yet Fischl makes seemless emotional sense. His art addresses epic themes of human relationships and psychological survival in a perilous time.

ROBERT MORRIS

Robert Morris's art has been discussed in the chapters about Minimalism, Earthworks, and Post-Minimalism; he is a multi-faceted artist whose evolution has spanned three decades. Formal issues anchored his earlier art, but in the 1980s Morris created a series of frankly apocalyptic narrative works—firestorms, maelstroms, nuclear holocausts—made of fragmented body parts and landscapes which refer to the nineteenth-century cult of the sublime. The artist explains:

An emotional weariness with what underlies them [modernist forms] has occurred. I would suggest that the shift has occurred with the growing awareness of the more global threats to the existence of life itself. Whether this takes the form of instant nuclear detonation or a more leisurely extinction from a combination of exhaustion of resources and the pervasive, industrially based trashing of our planet, that sense of doom has gathered on the horizon of our perceptions and grows larger everyday.... In any case the future no longer exists and a numbness in the face of a gigantic failure of imagination has set in. The Decorative is the apt mode for such a sensibility, being a response on the edge of numbness.[24]

Untitled (Fig. **7.8**, see page 204) depicts a huge Turneresque firestorm in pastel on paper, surrounded by a fragmented, sculptural low-relief frame in hydrocal, a modeling material. The overall effect is of an assemblage of fragments that dissonantly hang together. Morris made the frame by pressing his fist and other objects into wet plaster, then carving the plaster and casting it with hydrocal. Bones, skulls, and various body parts appear in the series, not in after-the-blast disarray but carefully arranged into *momento mori* or *vanitas*, traditional reminders of mortality. Morris updates an art historical tradition, making a pastiche of earlier tendencies.

LARI PITTMAN

Lari Pittman was born in 1952 and lives in Los Angeles, where he received his education both at UCLA and Cal Arts, the latter school the same one Eric Fischl, David Salle, and Mike Kelley attended. By the 1980s, Los Angeles had become the second most important contemporary art center in the United States—arguably in the world—with internationally significant artists (like Bruce Nauman, Ed Ruscha, John Baldessari) going back for several generations, major galleries, significant museums, and substantial collectors.

At Cal Arts Pittman persisted in being a painter (like Fischl) although it was not a "hip" thing to do. He also identified with the feminists agenda (a very strong presence at the time) which showed up in his art in the form of decoration. With the feminists he was an outsider, a condition which bothered him only slightly. "It seemed gender-confining," the artist said. "And very arbitrary, because embellishment came just as naturally to me. I'm not advocating a genderless attitude—especially now, in our 'age of new delineations.' I'm advocating a complex gender attitude through my work."[25]

Pittman's embellishment takes the form of shapes, patterns, colors, and techniques derived from the daily visual environment of Los Angeles meshed with a strangely mutagenic quality. Plant forms proliferate, allegories of survival and persistence, sometimes withered, rent, over-ripe to the point of bursting, or insect-eaten. Pittman likes plant life, he says, because:

There's something so incessant about its growth and its dumb life, something so vigorous that it makes human life pale in a certain way. Nature can be completely indifferent to man, but man cannot be indifferent to nature.[26]

The narrative has no particular beginning, middle, and climax; instead, you enter wherever your eye lands and "the path that opens up branches and subdivides and expands like an atomic chain reaction," according to the art critic Christopher Knight.[27]

The Baroque effusiveness of Pittman's embellishment carries complex meanings of labored growth, luminous decay, and tentative renewal. Exhaustion—from the endlessly interdependent parts, the hothouse luxuriance of the color, the surfaces groaning under the weight of visual information—overrides everything. "We're very tired Americans," Pittman said. "I mean, how many times can we reinvent ourselves and our culture?"[28] Pittman's abundance represents the rich diversity of cultures and habits of living in Los Angeles, along with the growth, expansion, and proliferation that typifies the myth and reality of Southern California in the 1980s.

With its persimmon oranges and avocado greens, its leaves and tendrils veined like nerve paths, its decorative shapes derived from 1950s surrealist-inspired fabrics and wallpapers, its delicate crystal and spurting blue phalluses, *End of the Century* (Fig. **7.9**) portrays luxuriant decay and renewal. The phalluses suggest the double prospect of renewal and the threat of AIDS with their ejaculations collected in the crystal goblet like a sacrament. The crowded visual field bristles with nervous impulses like an electronic circuit, pulsating in endlessly repeating variations. Energy and exhaustion, vitality and overcrowding, growth and decay, man-made luxuriance and natural abundance—all these qualities describe Los Angeles in the 1980s. And so does the absence of the melancholy or cynicism that so often emerges in 1980s art produced by artists like Salle and Schnabel in New York.

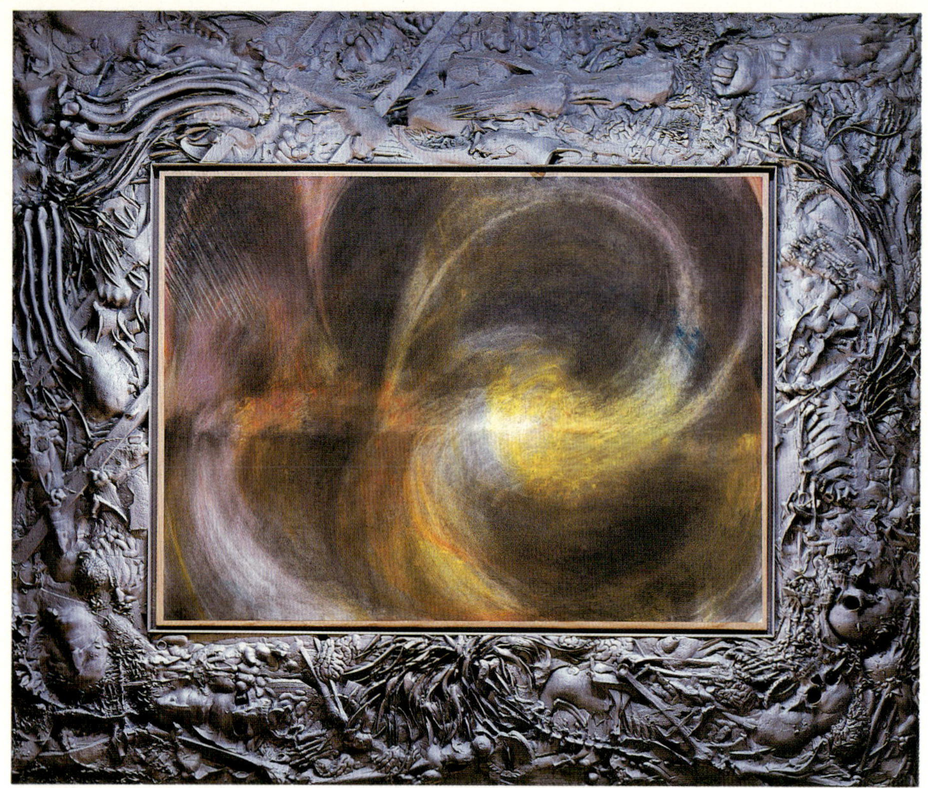

7.8 ROBERT MORRIS
Untitled 1983–84
Painted hydrocal, watercolor,
pastel on paper
6ft 4ins × 7ft 8ins
(193 × 233.7cm)
Courtesy Leo Castelli Gallery,
New York

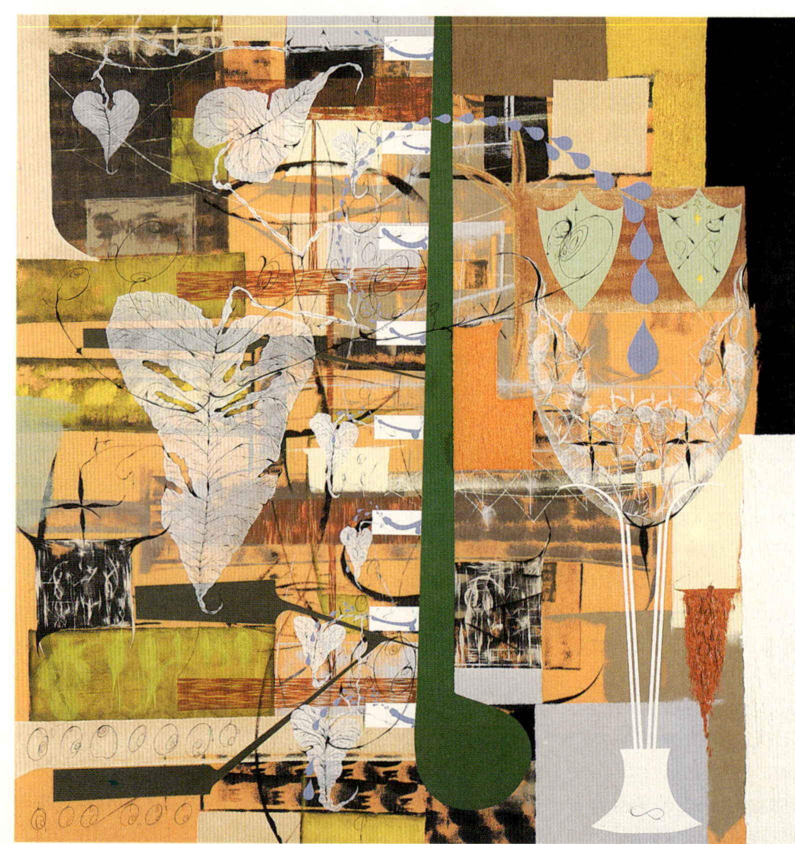

7.9 LARI PITTMAN
End of the Century
1986–87
Oil and acrylic on panel
82 × 80ins
(208.3 × 203.2cm)
Courtesy Phoenix Art
Museum, Arizona
Museum purchase with funds
provided by Regina and G.
Peter Bidstrup

MIKE KELLEY

Mike Kelley (born 1941) describes himself as a blue-collar subversive. (He lives in a working-class neighborhood of Los Angeles, where he moved from Detroit to attend Cal Arts in 1976.) His confrontational art takes the form of performances, banners, assemblages, and drawings; pastiches of popular art forms like posters, greetings cards, cartoons, toys, puppet shows, and other public forms. But Kelley anesthetizes his sources' sweet sentimentalism and makes them blunt and creepy. He explains:

I deal with a lot of dirty issues; the meat of my work is pretty much disagreeable mentalities and subject matter, like right-wing political views and racism. At the same time, I don't like preachy art. I like people to make up their own minds. So my work's not clear; it has a schizophrenic presence in that you can tell what the issues are but not what my stand on them is.[29]

For an installation of *Pay For Your Pleasure* (1988) at Chicago's Renaissance Society Kelley hired a commercial artist to paint portraits of leading historical artists, writers, and intellectuals bearing quotations by them about the outsider role of artists, such as Oscar Wilde's "The fact of a man being a poisoner is nothing against his prose," and William Blake's "Those who restrain desire do so because theirs is weak enough to be contained." Lining a corridor, these floor-to-ceiling images created an environment to which Kelley added a painting by the Chicago-based convicted killer of 33 teenage boys, John Wayne Gacy, a painting of himself as Pogo the clown, a powerful illustration of Wilde's and Blake's notions that artists exist outside conventional notions of morality. Kelley confronted Chicagoans with the filth and creepiness of a dirty issue.

A large felt banner covered with scraps of felt and bearing "first place" through "fifth place" prize ribbons, *No Place* (Fig. **7.10**) encircles a home-made stuffed cloth toy dangling in a hole cut through it. The title refers to the prize the toy did not

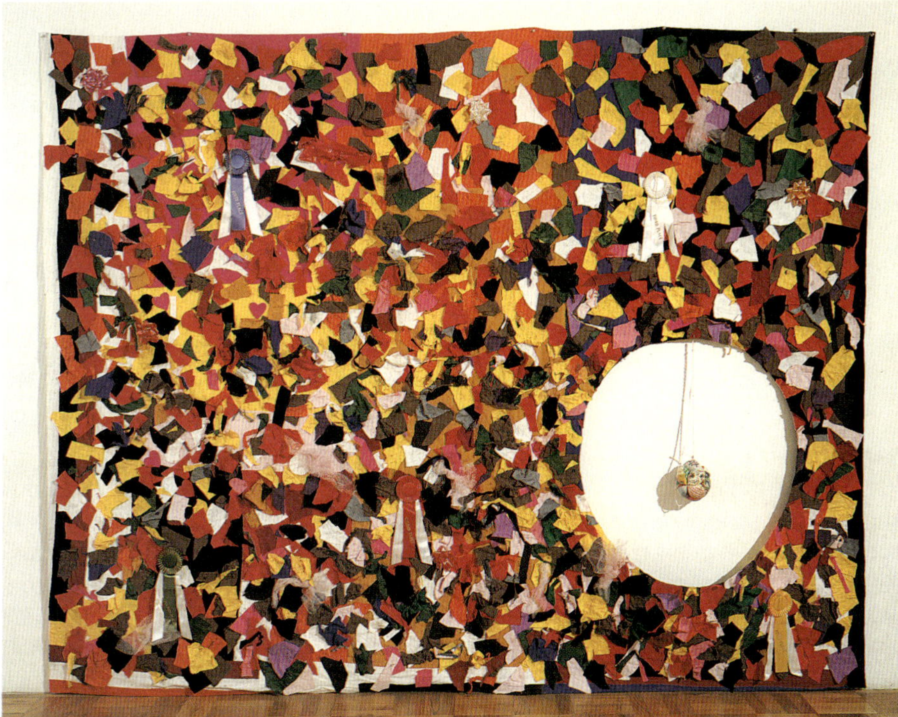

7.10 MIKE KELLEY
No Place 1989
Glued felt, stuffed, sewn
cloth toy with cord
100 × 127 × 6ins
(254 × 322.6 × 15.3cm)
Courtesy Phoenix Art
Museum; Museum Purchase
with funds provided by
Stephane Janssen

get. The toy, a love token signifying hours of useless labor (like a crocheted afghan) comes from a class of objects given as bribes for affection, banal handicrafts representing commonplace sentimentalism, impotent attempts at artistry. The material of the banner—felt—mocks emotion in its punning and conjures up puerile art therapy and cute children's teaching devices.

Kelley also used felt to make a reference to Sister Mary Corita, a nun who in the early 1960s popularized Catholic themes in brightly colored felt banners that became widely known and often imitated. Derived from Matisse, Calder, and other modern artists, her bold felt shapes and decorative colors inspired countless imitations in churches throughout the world. Underneath the scatterings of felt, large blocks of color pay homage to the American Abstract Expressionist painter Hans Hofmann, and to the famous nun whose popularity engendered the short-lived television series starring Sally Field called "The Flying Nun" and a number one hit song titled "Dominique" by "The Singing Nun."

Kelley's felt scraps look vaguely scatalogical (a recurrent theme), like used Kleenex or toilet paper scattered across the ground. The impolite body processes that recur in Kelley's art metaphorically represent things that most people would rather not think about. Another one of Kelley's banners reads "Pants Shitter and Proud. P.S. Jerk Off Too. (and I wear glasses)," while another claims that "I am useless to my culture but God loves me."

Rifts between high and low art, and between the powerful and the powerless underlie Kelley's Post-Modern political art. Couched in "creepy, filthy, dirty" metaphors lie unequal power transactions between authority—in the form of art, the Catholic church, the law, bourgeois notions of propriety—and ordinary people, like you and I.

Post-Modern Performance

Post-Modern performance artists continued to appear in alternate spaces and lofts but also moved into clubs and theaters, venues more commonly associated with entertainers. Like Post-Modern visual artists, performance artists adopted many of the mannerisms, media, subjects, and modes of address of popular culture, especially of mass-media. Post-Modern Performance Art became less rigorously formal, less repetitive, and less cerebral than performance in the 1960s and 1970s. It consequently addresses a broader audience. The two Post-Modern performance artists to be discussed here—Laurie Anderson and Eric Bogosian—made a hit record and a Hollywood movie, respectively.

LAURIE ANDERSON

Beginning in the mid-1970s, Laurie Anderson (born 1942) made audio tapes, records, films, assemblages, photographs, and written anecdotes. From the start her themes have been consistent: technology, urban daily life, alienation, apocalypse, dogs, foreign places, and politics. She combines work in all of her media in her performances, usually unifying them with electric or electronic music (that she or her ensemble plays) and with her voice which she electronically modulates.

Anderson showed her work in galleries, presenting her sound works on records in a juke box, along with visual documentation of performances and written anecdotes she incorporated into her live presentations. *It's Not the Bullet: A Reggae Tune for Chris Burden* (1977) pokes fun at Burden's dead-serious performance work in which he instructed a friend to shoot him in the arm (see page 75). The friend aimed

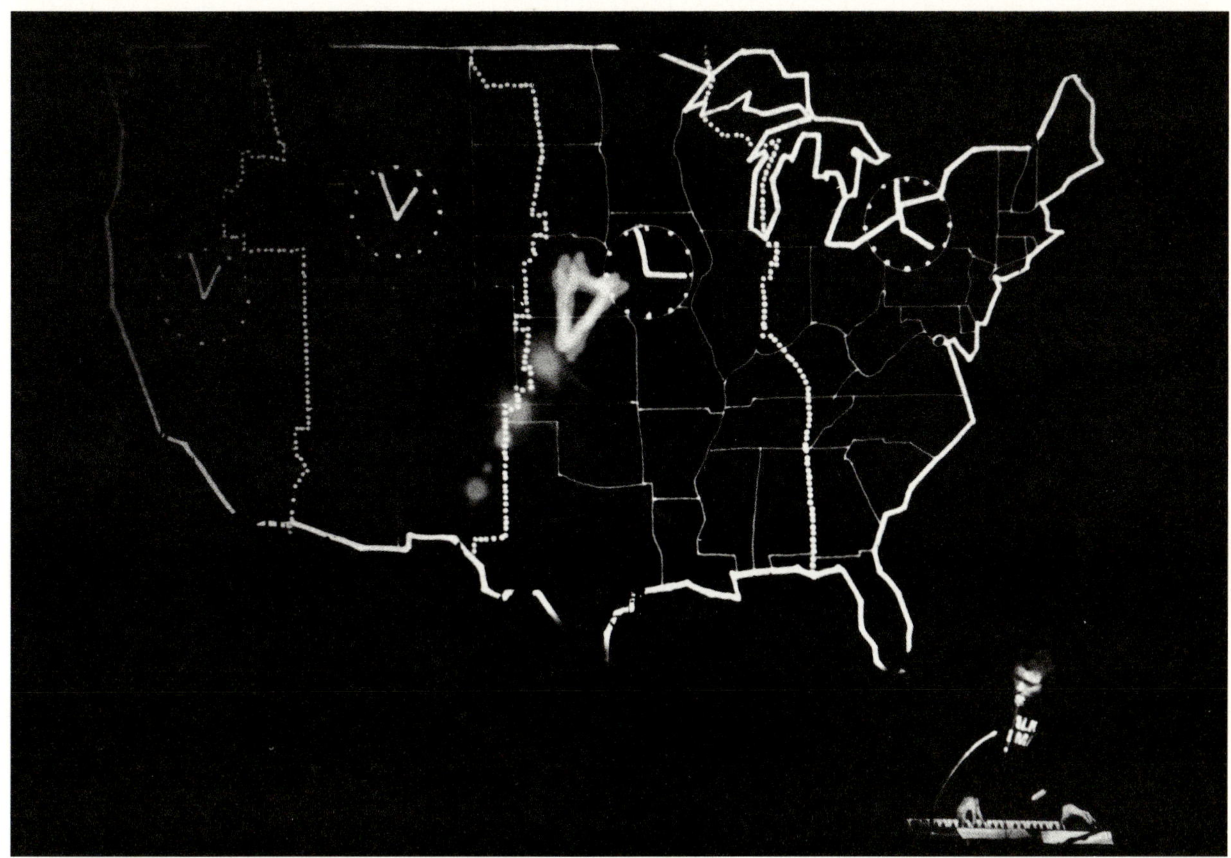

7.11 LAURIE ANDERSON
"Let X = X"
a segment of **United States**
Part II 1980
Performance at Orpheum
Theater, New York
Presented by the Kitchen
Photo courtesy Paula Court
© 1980

poorly and Burden was more seriously wounded than he planned. Anderson intones "It's not the bullet that kills you—oh no/It's the hole, it's the hole, it's the hole, it's the hole."[30] Anderson gave the song a visual form by writing the lyrics out and placing a photograph on the bottom of the page, of a target in a landscape along with her hand holding a violin bow.

In 1981 Anderson had a hit single in England, titled *O Superman*, with incantatory lyrics and an eerie electronic soundtrack. Warner Brothers signed her to a contract and an album with United States distribution followed. The rock music format was an apt one for her art which combines visual art ambitions with rock concert audio-visual entertainment strategies. The album did not make Anderson the Madonna of the early 1980s but it expanded her audience to a much wider one than any postwar performance artist before her.

United States Parts I–IV (Fig. **7.11**) anthologizes 78 performance pieces from a seven-year period of work into a six-hour presentation accompanied by visual projections, slides, films, animated drawings, and both electric and electronic sound instruments. Two years later Anderson incorporated *United States* into a mass-released film anthology of her performance work, titled *Home of the Brave*. Anderson wrote: "There are no plots in *Home of the Brave*. The strategy of this film is to use technology to criticize itself."[31]

In *United States*, Anderson either talks or sings or

there is a musical sequence throughout the entire performance. She plays a white electronic violin with a neon bow; uses her head as a percussion instrument, striking it with her hands while a miniature microphone in her mouth amplifies the sound; places a small light in her mouth and grins like a Cheshire cat in the darkened hall. Anderson treats herself as a medium analogous to the electronic technologies she uses. This "homey" humanization of mass-media technology extends to her littering the stage with electronic equipment such as amplifiers, microphones, and cables that in mass-media presentations is normally behind the scene and unseen. She puts it all center stage and turns it into toys for serious play, a way of intuitively understanding how electronic media work, and work us over.

ERIC BOGOSIAN

Eric Bogosian (born 1953) uses the format of a stand-up comic, acting with spare (if any) props, straightforward street clothes, and monologues. His characters are stock figures from television and movies rendered with stereotypes and cliches. Often he employs the heightened emotionalism and broad theatrical style of soap operas.

7.12 ERIC BOGOSIAN
Drinking in America 1986
Performance at American
Place Theater, New York
Photo courtesy Paula Court
© 1986

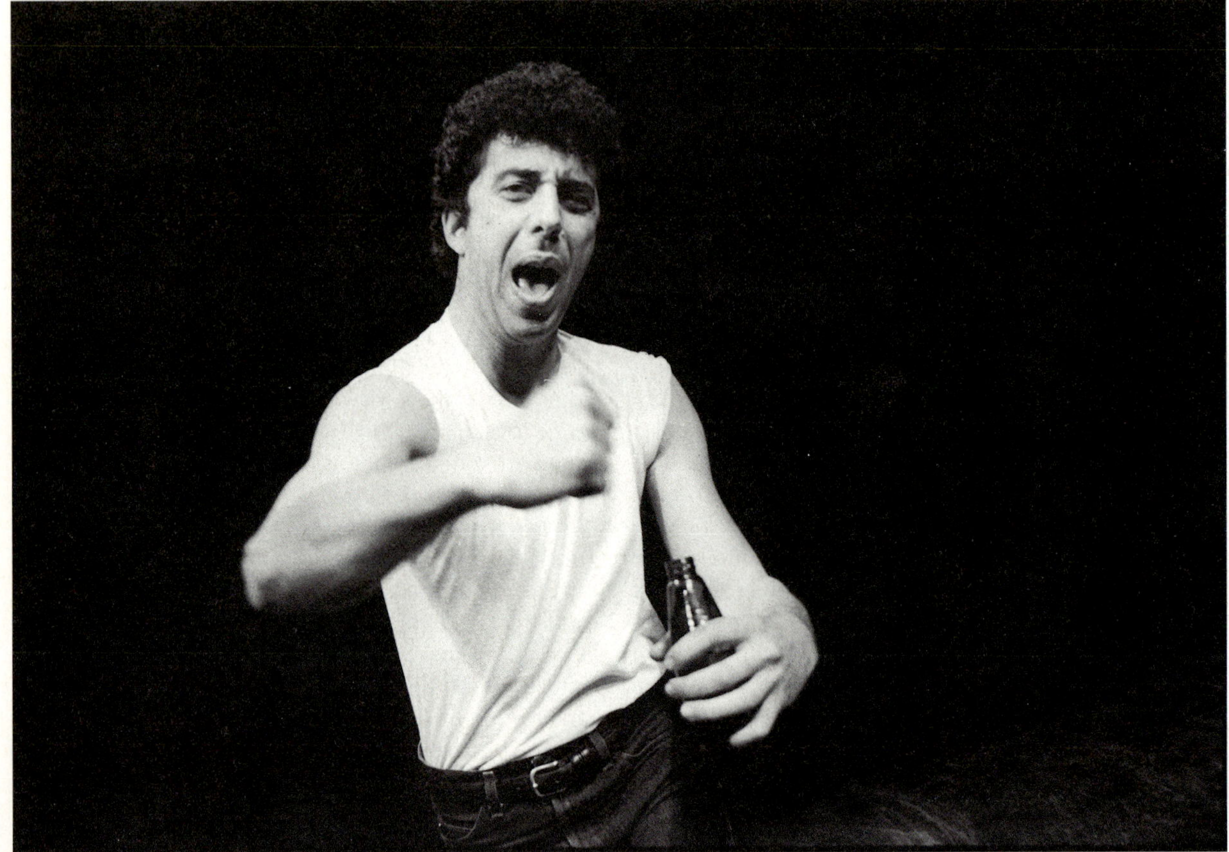

Men Inside (1982–84) is a series of a dozen skits caricaturing male roles in vignettes that are like television commercials. Bogosian does a carnival barker, lounge lizard host, male stripper, Brooklyn street punk, wino, redneck, Italian father, and a preacher. In *Voice of America* (1982–84), Bogosian makes a pastiche of radio and television stereotypes, like commercial announcers, newscasters, evangelists, disc jockeys, and a television science-fiction program narrator type. Bogosian's keen timing, body language, and finely honed acting talent make credible characterizations out of stereotypes. Like Anderson, he appropriates mass-media stereotypes and takes away their numbness, aesthetizes them instead of anesthetizing us.

Drinking in America (Fig. **7.12**) mimics fewer types, concentrating instead on a half-dozen characters intoxicated with real and imagined power. The performance opens with Bogosian reading from his account of an acid trip in a faked journal, proclaiming the truths revealed to him. Then come depictions of a wino, a coke-snorting Hollywood agent, a preacher, a rock star, and a New Jersey thrill-seeking teenager strung out on every drug imaginable. The monologue's subject is the attitudes unleashed by intoxicants, and although the caricatures are as stereotyped as television dramatizations, there is something recognizable in real people in all of them.

Bogosian's format and subjects taken from entertainment modes translate into what his art ostensibly criticizes. Context makes the difference between critique or collusion. Bogosian's commercial film released in 1989, *Talk Radio*, places his art in an entertainment context, crossing over from fine art into popular art. With it, Performance Art becomes undistinguishable from mass entertainment.

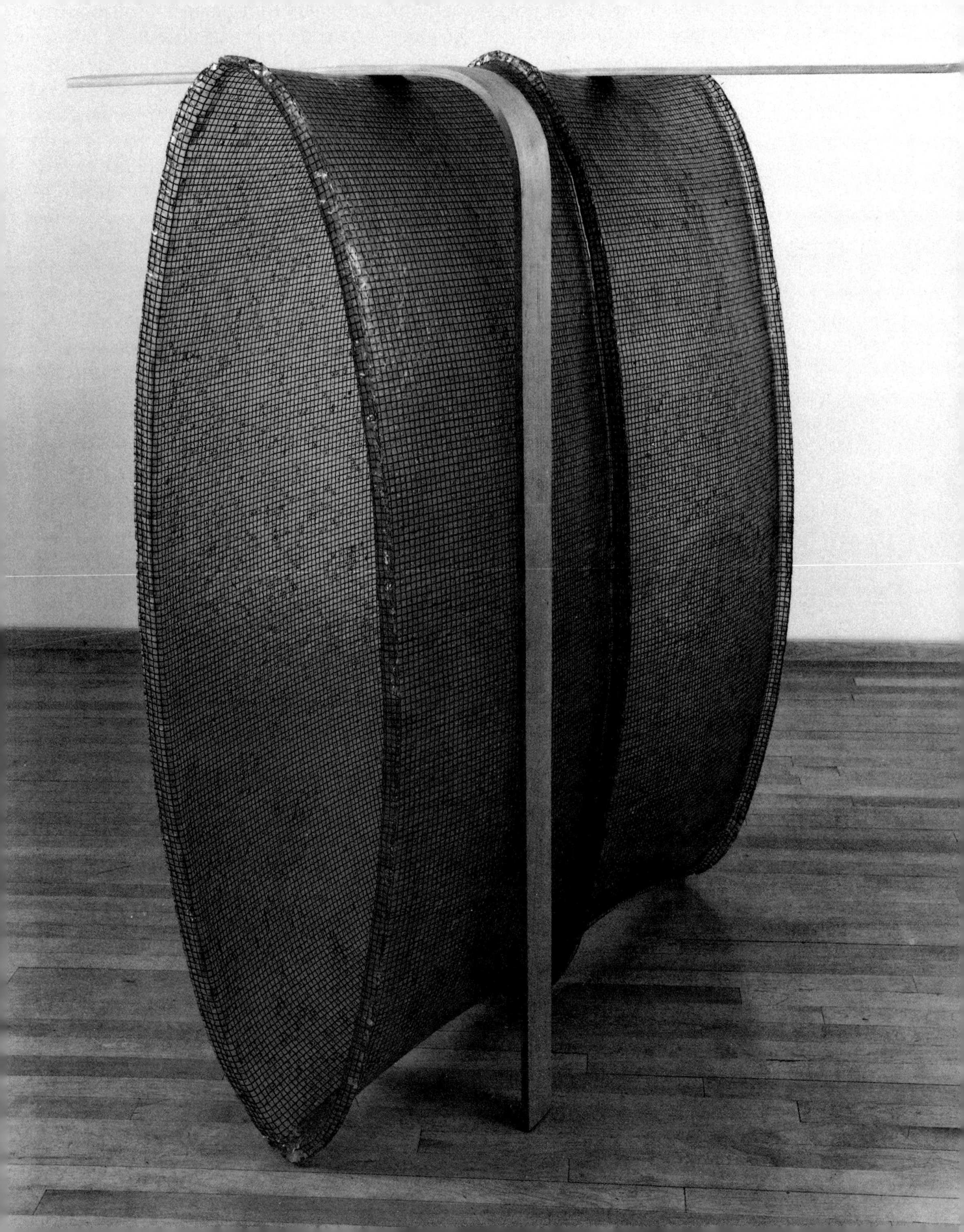

8
Sculpture of the 1980s

"... I want to do everything in my sculpture. I want it to look like it's wet and dry, alive and dead, geometric and organic; I want it to have everything at once."[1]

—— TOM BUTTER ——

Tom Butter
Verge 1988
Courtesy Curt Marcus Gallery, New York

Narration and Metaphor Re-enter Sculpture

Artists throughout the 1970s continued making the Earthworks, site-specific, Conceptual, and Post-Minimal sculpture that they had begun producing in the 1960s. Sculptural forms unique to the decade developed in the 1980s, forms which acknowledged but put aside the antecedents of Minimalism and Post-Minimalism, ending the role of artistic dominance these latter styles had played. Minimalism's geometric purity and structural reductivism along with Post-Minimalism's inflection of Minimalism's precedents and adoption of painterly strategies gave way to the use of more organic forms without artistic derivation from the earlier styles. As they did in painting in the 1980s, narration and metaphor reentered sculpture.

Many sculptors in the 1980s combine various organic forms with associative meanings into novel syntaxes, in effect creating visual sentences out of forms positioned together like words. This analogy to literature carries over into the sculptors' use of multiple parts, often arranged in a relational configuration, rather than the monolithic unity of Minimalism's holistic compositions or the Post-Minimalist's emphasis on a singular, overriding strategy. Relational compositions position elements in relation to other elements, setting up visual hierarchies and dynamic dramas.

Many of the forms the sculptures incorporate are hollow, a condition made evident either by transparent materials, small openings connecting a void to the outside, or linear structures enclosing large volumes of space; in any case, the membrane or skeleton analogy evokes living organisms. References to living entities rather than to the human-made world or human operations had been largely absent from sculpture since the beginning of Minimalism's dominance in the 1960s. The new visual tropes (meaning figures of speech) reintroduce metaphysical metaphors, references to a neglected realm of experience that was ripe for exploration.

Europe was an important arena of sculptural activity in the 1980s, particularly England and Germany. The selection in this chapter includes Richard Deacon and Alison Wilding from England and Tony Cragg, a British sculptor working in Germany. Other artists in this chapter come from various parts of the United States. This selection is meant to represent a range of sculptural forms that are most unique to the 1980s.

RICHARD DEACON

Richard Deacon was born in Wales in 1949 and received his art education in London, both at the St. Martin's School of Art (1969–72) and the Royal College of Art (1974–77), where Tony Cragg was his classmate. He experimented with conceptually-based performances in which he manipulated various materials rather than his own body (most English Performance Art at that time focused on the artist's body, such as that of Gilbert and George, page 75). This led to making sculptures which evidence the operations that brought them into being. As the art critic

Peter Schjeldahl states: "The sensuous and ethical beauty of purposeful labor is his basic compact with the viewer, something to agree on that stimulates an appetite for further agreements."[2]

In December of 1978 Deacon went to the United States for a year, where he read Rilke's *Sonnets to Orpheus* and made a series of drawings based on them. Like his later, related sculptures, the drawings feature bulging loops delineating swelling forms with orifice-like openings. His later sculpture, *For Those Who Have Ears No. 2* (Fig. **8.1**) makes reference

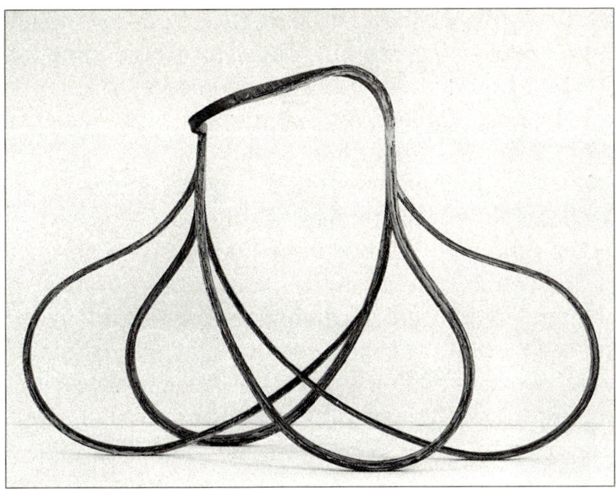

8.1 RICHARD DEACON
For Those Who Have Ears
No. 2 1983
Laminated wood

108 × 144 × 60ins
(274.3 × 365.75 × 152.4cm)
Courtesy The Tate Gallery,
London

to Rilke's *Sonnets to Orpheus* in Deacon's typically oblique way; he constructs metaphors in many layers of laminated meanings, much like the glued wooden strips of this sculpture. As Deacon stated:

> *... the kinds of meaning which I wish to derive and the relationships which I wish to build up between artist and material are not susceptible of precise statement (at least I am not capable of precisely stating them). I am, therefore, left in the position of laying interpretations and description on top of each other in the hope of eventually building up what I require, much as an oyster builds a pearl.*[3]

A poet and musician with magical powers—Orpheus—sings, and those who have ears hear his music. The looping shapes of *For Those Who Have Ears No. 2* suggest ears, harps (the national instrument of Wales), and a lyre (Orpheus's instrument and the Romantic symbol of creativity). These associations are not literally evident but must be "seen" by the viewer, must be "heard" by "those who have ears." Even then the sculpture's meaning evades easy explanation, being a metaphor for a condition of being more than a specific symbol.

Deacon's sculptures associate the sense organs with conditions of being. References to seeing and hearing recur in such works as *For Those Who Have Eyes* (1983), *The Eye Has It* (1983–84), *Other Men's*

Eyes No. 1 (1986), and *Listening to Reason* (1986). This huge latter work features ear-like voids articulated by wooden strips laminated with such a surplus of glue that it oozes out. The ear-like voids are big enough to walk through; attached by tendrils implying nerves, they allow viewers to walk under the whole structure.

Deacon's sculptures are immediately striking and unforgettable. Though composed of many parts and made with painstakingly excessive manual operations—far more joinery and fastening than necessary—they make a unitary impression, but an impression different in effect from Minimalism's unelaborated, holistic paradigm. Deacon's joinings and

8.2 RICHARD DEACON
More Light 1987–88
Plywood and aluminum
106 × 132 × 79ins
(269.2 × 335.9 × 200.7cm)
Courtesy The Saint Louis Art
Museum, Missouri. Purchase:

Funds given by Mr. and Mrs.
James E. Schneithorst, the
Siteman Contemporary Art
Fund, Aurelia and George
Schlapp, and the
Contemporary Art Society

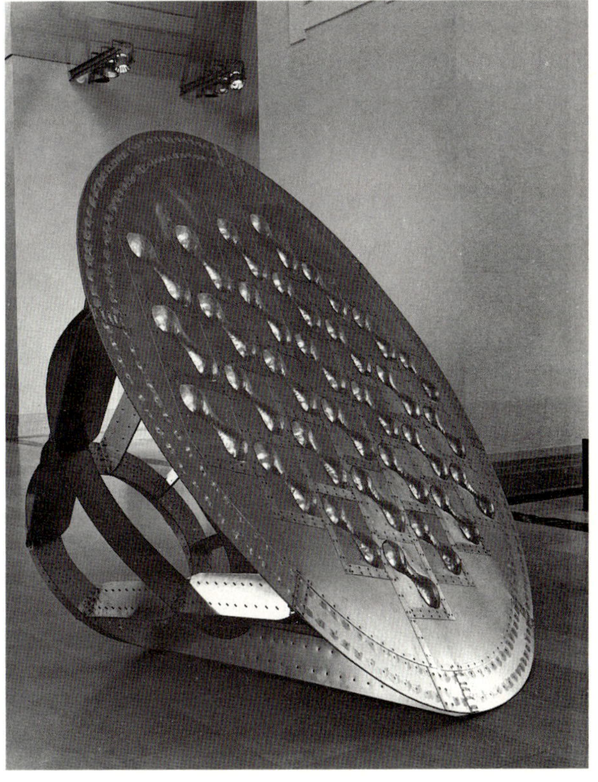

fastenings elaborate the whole, they emphasize its deliberateness with endearing insistence. His intricate handwork enamors the viewer by leading him or her into visual participation in the work's fabrication.

For an open-ended series of small sculptures begun in 1982 titled *Art for Other People*, Deacon employs commonplace materials like linoleum, canvas, plastic, galvanized steel, and imitation leather along with more elitist materials like marble, bronze, brass, and stainless steel, sometimes combining the commonplace and elitist in the same piece. Who are the "other people" this art is for? Presumably not you and I. Is it for people who do not have eyes, or people who do not have ears? Perhaps these more explicit works function as aesthetic training devices for people unaccustomed to looking at more ambitious sculpture.

The title of *More Light* (Fig. **8.2**) is taken from Goethe's last words. Like all of Deacon's meanings it is not intended to be taken literally but constructs a multi-layered metaphor. The huge plywood and aluminum structure suggests a satelite dish or a telescope; in either case, some sort of scientific instrument. The telescope refers to the eye and the satelite dish to the ear; ear shapes articulate the mid-point between the telescope-like eyepiece and the dish. The eyepiece suggests that we see the whole through its aperture, as though everything beyond it is both our visual projection and reception. Thus the whole structure becomes an analogy to visual perception.

Deacon grew up surrounded by science textbooks—his father was a pilot and his mother a doctor, both of them involved in occupations where, as Deacon typically understates the case, "procedure is all-important."[4] Procedural interest shows through in his work in the obsessive abundance of fasteners—many more screws than necessary—and in the insistent clarity of each structural part. The whole resembles an aircraft in its precision, recalling Deacon's assertion that his sculptures are "built all over" like a plane rather than "from the ground up" like a car.[5]

Metaphors in Deacon's work exist both in relation to individual sculptures and to his art as a whole. Eye and ear references abound from one artwork to another, suggesting scientific apparatus, Orphic allusions, and a rich array of meanings. References to literature, science, engineering, and construction exist alongside formal explorations of dualisms like inside and outside, container and contained, skin and skeleton. Deacon refers to himself as a "fabricator,"[6] an apt title with its double meaning of "one who builds" and "one who makes up (a story, reason, lie)."

TONY CRAGG

In the mid-1970s, Tony Cragg (born 1949) began making relief sculptures out of plastic fragments that had been discarded but that, because they are not biodegradable, failed to decompose. The potsherd of the mid-twentieth century—plastic fragments—signal a certain state of civilization. Cragg configured them into facsimiles of Michelangelo's *David*, the British flag, and other easily-recognizable subjects taken from art and popular culture, contemporizing widely known myths (Fig. **8.3**).

Cragg studied sciences in college and once had ambitions for a career in a science field—maybe in geology. He worked for a year as an assistant in a biochemistry laboratory after leaving college. The pureness of scientific and philosophical inquiry appeals to Cragg to this day; he believes that sculpture can maintain a parallel pureness, that it can improve the quality of visual metaphors and syntax.

Familiar objects like beakers, bottles, or a shell, enlarged and translated into bronze, iron, glass, or plaster occur in Cragg's art. Hollow forms with orifices, that suggest living organisms. Cragg's themes include the language and meaning of the objects we have already populated our lives with, and the borderline between the natural and the man-made. The idea of finding a new content for an old form or giving an old content new meaning appeals to Cragg, a conceptual analogy to recycling non-biodegradable materials.

Bronze is almost as non-biodegradable as plastic. Greek bronze sculptures lost for 2,000 years beneath the sea have been reclaimed and restored almost to perfect condition. Bronze, the hallowed fine art material, carries old content with it. An *Untitled*

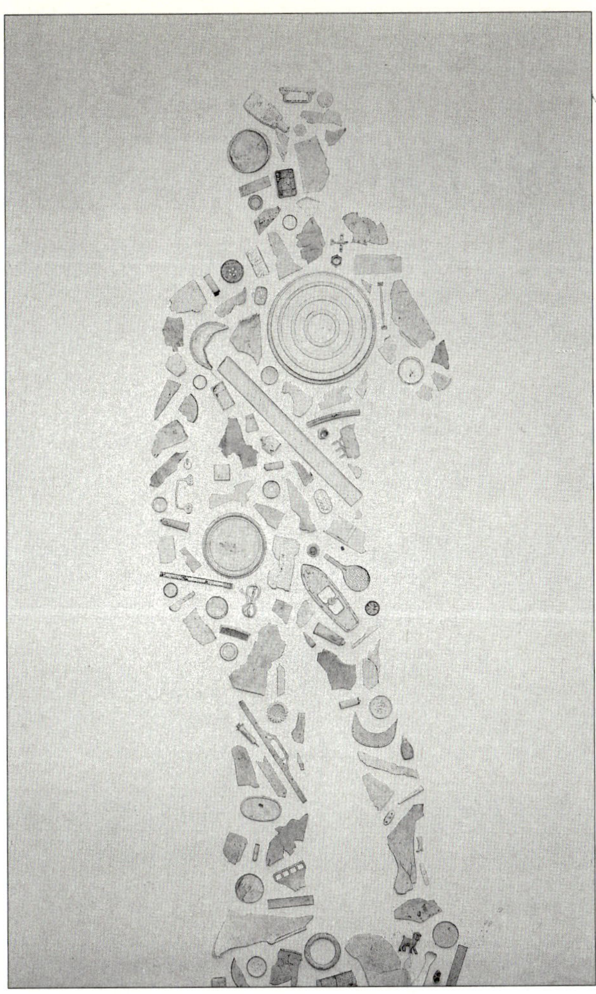

8.3 TONY CRAGG
David 1984
Plastic fragments
126 × 44ins
(320 × 111.8cm)
Courtesy Rivendell
Collection, New York

plications make a rich metaphor. "'Metaphysical' is a very pretentious word, but I do think that even the most ordinary things have a more than merely physical existence," Cragg said.[7]

Cragg's large sculptures are monumental without being pompous, a difficult quality to achieve, especially following the dominance of Henry Moore's sculpture in England, with titles like *Mother and Child* or *Man and Woman*, a precedent Cragg commented upon when he said:

> *When I began making things, in the late 1960s, I was very much influenced by ... people like Donald Judd, Sol LeWitt, Carl André, and Richard Long.... a lot of the work of that time was simply gestural; it denied the possibility of art having a content.... But the most valuable thing they did was clear the air of all that namby-pamby, postwar, somewhat humanitarian wishy-washiness.*[8]

Judd's purging art of "content" gave Cragg the *tabula rasa* he needed to reinvest sculpture with allusions and metaphors. Judd's art served a similar function for Martin Puryear.

8.4 TONY CRAGG
Untitled (Large Bronze)
1988. Bronze
82¾ × 82¾ × 112ins
(210 × 210 × 285cm)
Courtesy Marian Goodman
Gallery, New York
"*I think they can also be quite menacing, and for a very simple reason. Those forms are very useful forms, and sculpture is supremely useless, so there's a menace that results from the contrast. There's something very threatening from the contrast. There's something very threatening about anything that disrupts our useful world, anything that refuses to subjugate itself to function.*"[9]

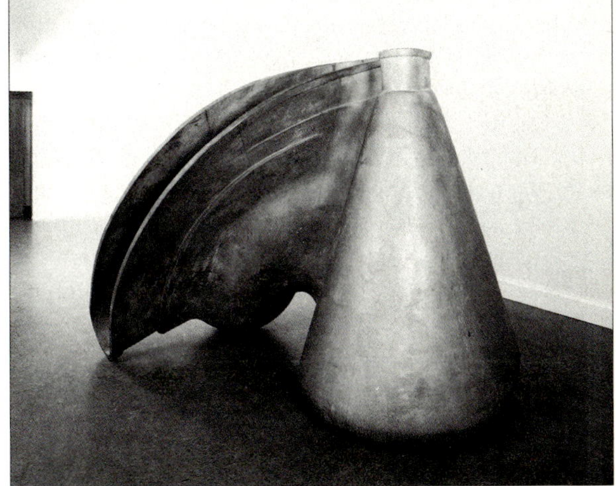

(Fig. **8.4**) bronze sculpture from 1988 grafts together what appear to be two cone-shaped laboratory flasks the height of a normal adult, one standing upright and one on its side. The connecting shapes suggest movement, as though the upright flask tipped over and was caught by the sculptural equivalent to a time-lapse photograph. But as the viewer moves around the sculpture, it becomes clear that the tipped-over flask is not identical to the upright one. From the side and back, their shapes suggest gorgeous breasts, a reading that encourages the vaginal suggestiveness of the frontal open slit. Anthropomorphic, sensual, geometric, scientific—these complex and contradictory im-

MARTIN PURYEAR

"When I first saw Donald Judd's work," Martin Puryear (born 1941) said, "it cleared the air for me to do whatever I wanted. And I wanted purity and simplicity. But I couldn't be as distant as Judd—the working process is essential to me. After Minimalism, there wasn't much to continue with. You can only rarefy something so much before you have nothing left. And I'm really committed to objects, not to dogma."[10]

Puryear subscribes to the hand-made tradition of sculpture. Born in Washington, D.C., in his early twenties he traveled to West Africa where he was exposed to traditional crafts like basketry and weaving. Further study took him from Africa to Stockholm's Royal Academy of Art where he learned woodworking and Swedish craft techniques. From there he went to Yale for an MFA, and since 1978 has lived in Chicago.

Just as it did for Cragg, Minimalism "cleared the air" for Puryear. Cragg subsequently emphasized *content*; Puryear, *objects*. Of course, neither is exclusive of the other, but Puryear's emphasis reveals his devotion to the hand processes of traditional object making. A black artist, Puryear associates handwork with the manual labor that blacks historically performed in the United States; other than that, he disclaims any racial content in his art.

Puryear's forms are nearly always biomorphic or organic, but they usually result more from their materials and the processes involved in forming them than from any preconceived metaphoric intent. Before beginning to fabricate them, Puryear thoroughly plans his sculptures to fully exploit the sensual quality of the materials.

Seer (Fig. **8.5**) features an animal horn-like form rising out of a wire cage resembling a huge hoop skirt. A hollow form like many of Cragg's and Deacon's, *Seer* implies enclosure while allowing the viewer to see clear through it, unlike many of Puryear's other sculptures which only give glimpses of interior voids. *Seer's* horn-like shape enhances the ceremonial feeling, as though some special being or spirit were enclosed in this position of honor. Given this ceremonial connotation, a primitive or shamanistic reading is inevitable, yet the horn-like form derives

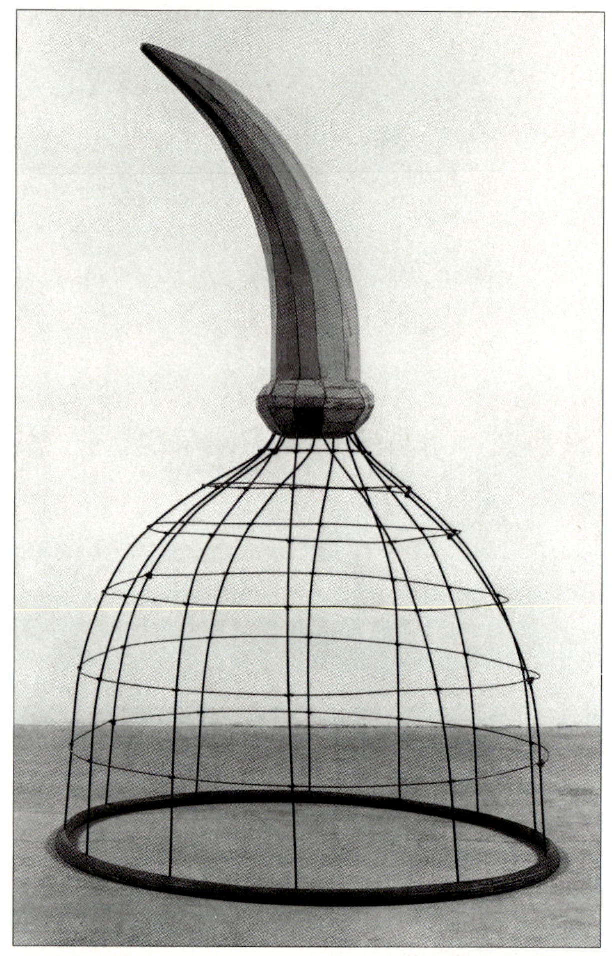

8.5 MARTIN PURYEAR
Seer 1984
Water-based paint on wood and wire
78 × 52¼ × 45ins
(198.2 × 132.6 × 114.3cm)
FN 85.3276

Purchase with Funds Contributed by the Louis and Bessie Adler Foundation, Seymour M. Klein, President Solomon R. Guggenheim Museum, New York
Photo Douglas M. Parker

more from Giacometti's *Disagreeable Object* (1931) than directly from primitive sculpture, more from twentieth-century sculpture's adaptations than from the primary source. The elegance of Puryear's pristine craftsmanship makes *Seer* a hallowed, treasured object in a privileged realm of sculpture.

JOHN DUFF

John Duff was born in Indiana in 1943 and received a BFA degree from the San Francisco Art Institute in 1967. In 1968 he moved to New York where he still lives and works. Duff's work appeared in the 1969 Whitney Museum's *Anti-Illusion* show that was so important a watershed for Post-Minimalism. His skeletal, joined wood and wire structures, with their looping rhythms and articulated voids only partially anticipated his later fiberglass works. Dispensing with the skeleton parallel, transluscent fiberglass more resembles cartilage than either flesh or bone.

Duff's organic forms look as though they grew naturally according to an inevitable, pre-ordained plan. Their slow unfolding, billowing, and twisting suggests plant life growing in a slow motion, time lapse film. Yet their transluscent cartilage-like character retains an animal connotation. Some of them, like *Serrated Wedge (Open) II* (Fig. **8.6**), float off the wall like an inchworm feeling its way down a tree branch, or a seed pod twisting as it tenses toward popping open and propelling its seeds.

Awkward and vulnerable, *Serrated Wedge (Open) II* opposes the procedural, conceptual, or philosophical self-evidence of most sculpture since 1960, instead favoring an allusive, multi-leveled tone. Nonetheless, a structural logic as simple as any there could be leads to the complicated form. Duff alternates a wedge shape from facing the viewer to facing the wall, each alternation connected to the other in an undulating, serrated rhythm. While the structural logic (or its subversion) would have taken center stage in sculpture from the 1960s and 1970s—Bruce Nauman's and Eva Hesse's works in fiberglass or latex are important precedents (see pages 34 and 120)—here it goes almost unnoticed as a taken-for-granted sub-theme. Logic yields the form, but the form does not yield logical content. Duff takes the formal homework as a given condition and goes on from there.

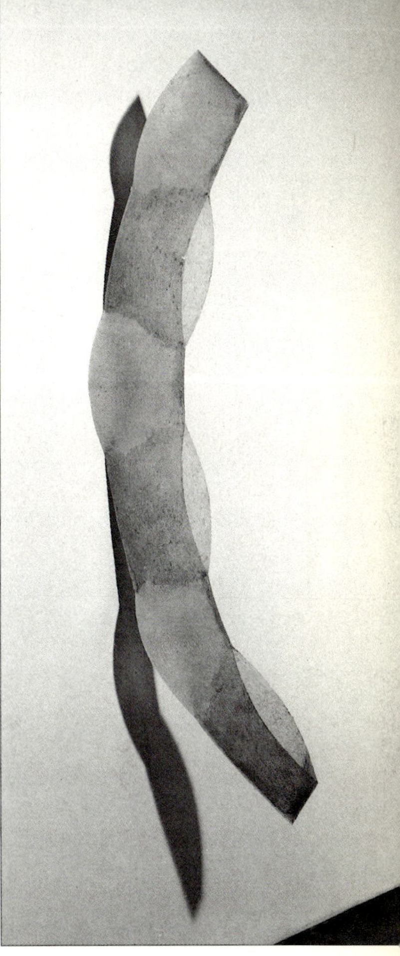

8.6 JOHN DUFF
Serrated Wedge (Open) II
1986
Fiberglass, enamel paint, shellac
80 × 5½ × 26ins
(203.2 × 13.9 × 66cm)
Courtesy Blum Helman Gallery

ALISON WILDING

The English sculptor Alison Wilding (born 1948) makes mysterious metaphors that are either abstract representations or analogies. *Fedora* (1985), for example, abstractly resembles the well-known man's hat that was popular in the 1940s, thus evoking a whole era, but it also conjures up the Russian Constructivist sculpture of Naum Gabo and Anton Pevsner (among the first to use voids in sculpture) and, with the hole through which one can see light, the sculpture of the twentieth-century English artist, Barbara Hepworth. The Hepworth reference is a pointed one, because she may be the only truly renowned English female sculptor in the modern period. The fedora is a man's hat; here, it is pierced with a hole which makes reference to both a female artist and to female genitals. Wilding's feminist content in effect alters the dominant phallocentrism of art history, a condition pertaining even more to sculpture than to two-dimensional visual arts. She turns a man's hat— with a woman's name—into an evocative metaphor

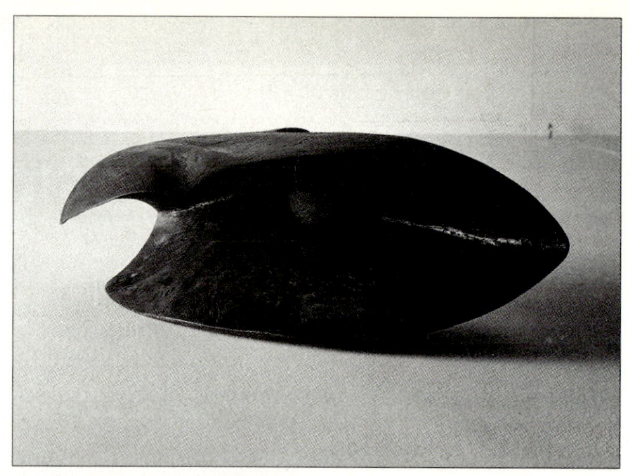

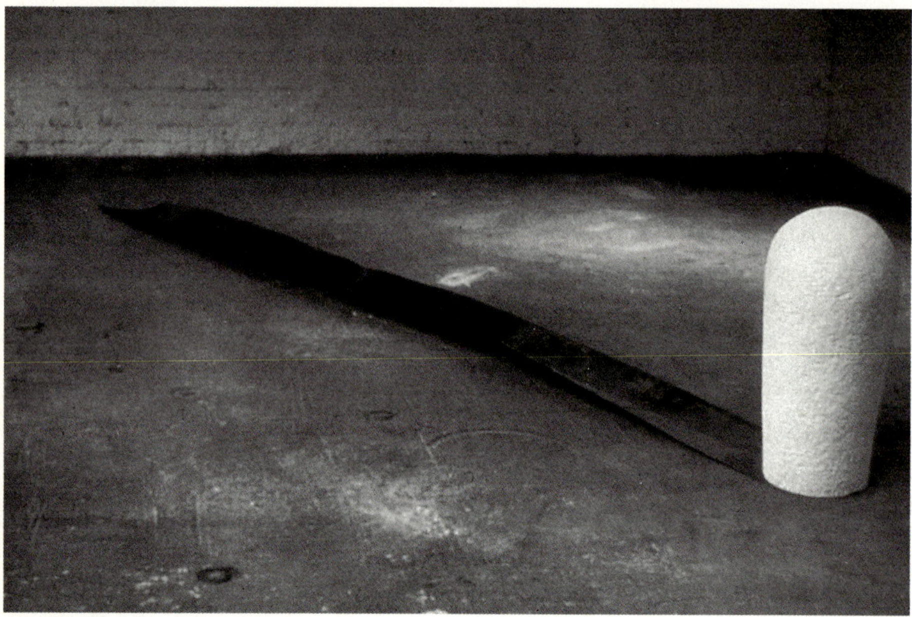

8.7 ALISON WILDING
Into the Dark 1985
Pigments and lead on limewood
12½ × 19 × 6ins
(31.8 × 48.3 × 15.2cm)
Courtesy Salvatore Ala Gallery, New York

8.8 ALISON WILDING
Into the Heart 1984
Portland stone, patinated copper, lead
23 × 9 × 145ins
(58.4 × 22.9 × 368.3cm)
Courtesy Salvatore Ala Gallery, New York

for the recognition of women artists.

Into the Dark (Fig. **8.7**) abstractly represents a neckless, truncated wooden torso hung high on a wall so viewers can see into the hollow core. Deep in the upper torso where the throat would enter the chest cavity, Wilding inserted a cast lead form which terminates in a rounded knob inside the hollow, visible from below. It evokes cliches like "lump in the throat" or "heavy heart." Here, the opening like that in *Fedora* has been blocked with a suffocating effect.

The Romanian sculptor Constantin Brancusi's art is referred to more than once by sculptors in the 1980s who pay homage to him while invoking his authority for distilling metaphysical meanings to their essences. Brancusi's highly simplified forms are re-

dolent of spiritual life, unlike the more formal explorations of the Cubists and Constructivists which dominated twentieth-century sculpture. Wilding's *Into the Heart* (Fig. **8.8**), with its elemental Portland stone form, evokes Brancusi's essentialized stone carvings. The lead trough and patinated copper disc of *Into the Heart* resemble cast shadows at the same time that they suggest a sculptural base. Brancusi integrated his bases into his sculptures, thus eliminating the pedestal and furthering Rodin's assertion of what became the dominant formal issue of twentieth-century sculpture: the relationship between sculpture and its base, or the horizon. Here, Wilding returns to the twentieth century source of the sculptural dialogue that has continued from Carl André's metal plate "rugs" to the present.

PETER SHELTON

Peter Shelton was born in Troy, Ohio in 1951 and received a BA degree from Pomona College in Clermont, California in 1973. He lives and works in California. His art refers to the human body, either in abstract representations or by the way in which he physically engages the viewer's body. He works in discrete objects, aggregates of objects, installations that direct the viewer's perceptions, or combinations of these options. Being educated in California in the 1970s where, he says, "The tablets read, 'Thou shalt make art in this fashion'"[11] pushed him to the point where "multiplicity was always a moral imperative. It was a lie to make a work of art that didn't recognize that for every posture or hypothesis there was an opposite."[12]

Shelton's installation *floatinghouse, DEADMAN* (1985) features a cedar and paper house with a floor plan shaped like a spread-eagle man, suspended by cables attached to counterweights (deadmen) of similar shape. When visitors enter the house the floor wavers as the weights shift, momentarily upsetting their balance. Every step makes the house rise and fall, sway or shift. The house becomes an organic entity: architecture, like all human tools, is an exten-

**8.9 PETER SHELTON
SWEATHOUSE and little
principals** 1977–82
At Contemporary Arts Forum,
Santa Barbara, California
Steel
Gallery dimensions 12 × 25
× 36ft

(3.7 × 7.6 × 11m)
Sweathouse 7 × 7 × 7ft
(2.1 × 2.1 × 2.1m)
Photo Peter Shelton
Courtesy of L.A. Louver
Gallery, Venice, California

**8.10 PETER SHELTON
Eyesballs** 1983
Cast iron, steel
35½ × 4½ × 2½ins
(90.2 × 11.4 × 6.4cm)
Photo Tom Vinetz
Courtesy of L.A. Louver
Gallery, Venice, California

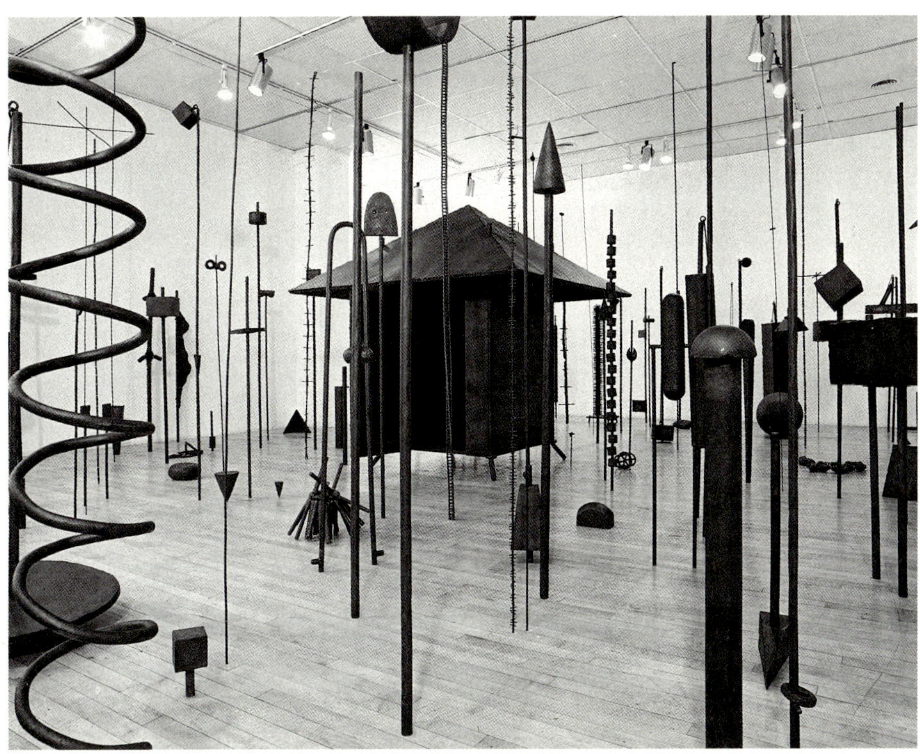

sion of the human body, an analogy that is carried out in the floor plan and in the counterweights.

An earlier installation, made in 1977–82, *SWEAT-HOUSE and little principals* (Fig. **8.9**) includes a small architectural enclosure surrounded by dozens of abstract representations of body parts. One of these, *Eyesballs* (Fig. **8.10**), was also made as a discrete sculpture. Suspended from the ceiling on an iron rod, two sets of orbs approximately the size of eyeballs and testicles hang at appropriate heights. Suspending objects from the ceiling links them to architecture as their means of rising up from the horizon. Their engagement with gravity is not lessened by their not standing on the ground plane, only the conditions of their verticality are elaborated. Architectural structure and space become determining factors, and these are man-made elements made to human proportions.

JACKIE WINSOR

Jackie Winsor made her first penetrated cube in 1976, out of 18 layers of sheetrock with small squares cut through the face of each piece. Winsor explains:

Initially, I was trying to quiet the space—to approach my own inner self. Sheetrock was used to make a space that was as quiet and private as the experience of closing your eyes. The glimmerings of light that could be seen through the holes were the passages inward.[13]

The association of interiorization with emotional resonances typifies sculptors of the 1980s who have created the hollow forms that have become emblematic of the decade.

Winsor's sculptures of the 1980s depart from her earlier Post-Minimalist work which was more concerned with process (see page 135), but continue her interest in interiorization and in finding quiet places for contemplation. *Blue Hemisphere* (Fig. **8.11**) is a large blue concrete shell, open at the top, with a deep blue hollow interior. The blue creates a mysterious, immeasurable space, as deep as the night sky and as rich in associations. The thin shell's mundane exterior of burnished concrete measurably circumscribes the enclosed space, but the blue opens it up to illogical dimensions. The deep space and celestial allusions of *Blue Hemisphere* create a moving medita-

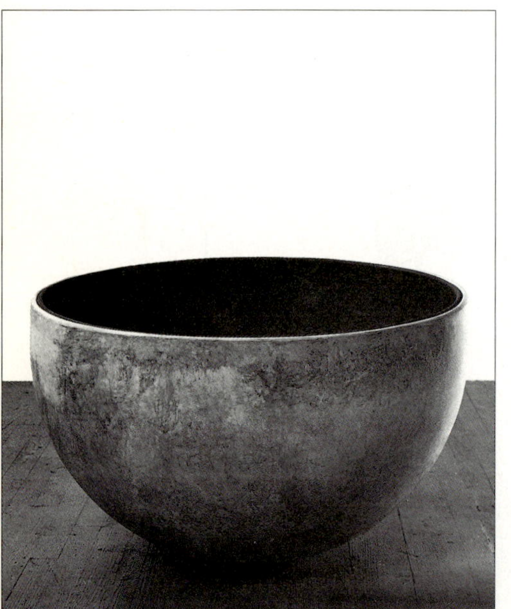

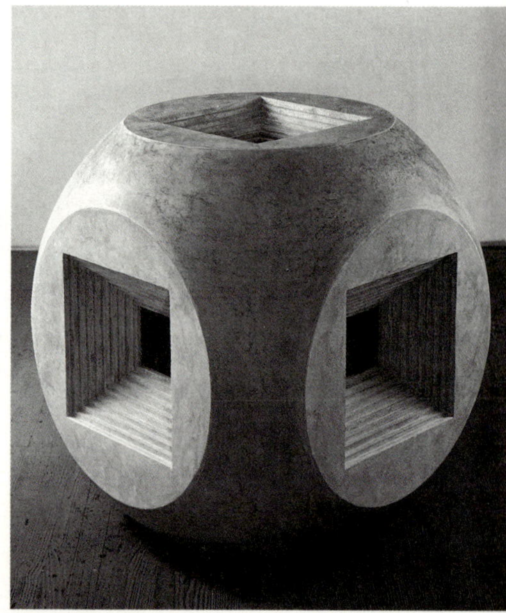

8.11 JACKIE WINSOR
Blue Hemisphere 1987
Concrete, pigment
34 × 34 × 34ins
(86.4 × 86.4 × 86.4cm)
Courtesy The Rivendell
Collection, New York
"I wanted the inner to become outer, the concealed to become revealed and the silence to be bigger than the piece. There is strength hidden in the willingness to be vulnerable."[14]

8.12 JACKIE WINSOR
Circle/Square 1987
Concrete, pigment
34 × 34 × 34ins
(86.4 × 86.4 × 86.4cm)
Courtesy Margo Leavin
Gallery, Los Angeles

tive experience.

Circle/Square (Fig. **8.12**) is a burnished concrete sphere with six circular faces "sliced" into it suggesting a cube. Each face is indented with a negative step pyramid, narrowing to a small square opening into an orange interior void. The 34 inch (86.4 cm) cubic form requires viewers to bend over to look into the void, but despite the large exterior openings, they narrow so much that one cannot visually penetrate the entire interior. It seems bigger than it actually is, immeasurable, and unattainable. *Circle/Square* acquires a presence that is much larger than its physical bulk or its actual enclosed space. What it withholds enlarges it.

RONI HORN

Employing spare geometric forms, Roni Horn's work at first glance appears to be Minimalist. But on a second glance it is not even Minimalistic; it does not even use the forms of Minimalism. Though Horn's forms require the neutral spaces and careful placements of Minimal sculpture, they do not conform to Minimalism's self-evident structural clarity. *Asphere* I (Fig. **8.13**) is not a perfect sphere, but a slight elipse measuring 12¼ × 12¾ inches (31.1 × 32.4 cm), requiring viewers to look and look before figuring it out. Something appears not quite right, not quite according to our preconceptions based on our experiences with Minimalism, so we have to keep looking until we finally see the form for what it is. Horn slows down our perception and makes us refine the quality of our seeing.

Like other sculptors of the 1980s, Horn (born 1955) takes Minimalism and Post-Minimalism for granted and goes on from there. Her art does not so much comment upon Minimalism as build upon it, accepting it as an artistic given. Horn dates from a generation whose early or pre-teen years, not their twenties, coincided with the advent of Minimalism. "I never felt a strong connection to Minimalism," Horn said, "either from an art-critical point of view or a purely artistic one. Minimalist Art is, in a sense, antidialectical: things are self-contained almost to the exclusion of non-ideal relationships."[15] In Horn's work, "The object is not the end; what I'm interested in is the experience it provides for—how it incites and animates dialogue."[16]

Horn's art requires viewers to become active participants rather than passive receptors, resisting easy perception. "My work is in part a critique of the ways, so pervasive in the television and entertainment industries, of placing the viewer in a passive relationship to the world."[17] "In the end I keep coming back to this desire to circumvent things which interface between actual experience and perceptions of it."[18]

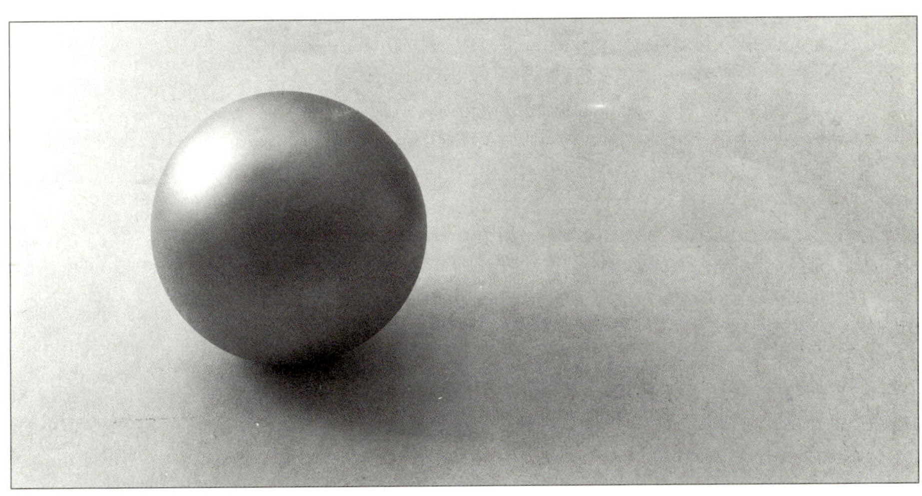

8.13 RONI HORN
Asphere I 1988
Solid forged copper
12¼ × 12¾ins
(31.1 × 32.4cm) diameter
300lbs (136.1kg)
Courtesy Mary Boone Gallery,
New York

LIZ LARNER

Liz Larner's petri dish "portraits," such as *Margo Leavin: Three Breaths and an Inoculation* (1987) or *John Dogg Culture* (1988) made of "spit, cough, and bottom of shoe sole," poke irreverent fun at Post-Minimalism's process art. In the neutral scientific culture medium of the petri dish, the named substances grow molds. Larner (born 1960) says about another petri dish work, titled *Whipped Cream, Heroin, Salmon Eggs*, "The meaning you get from your association with the words and the meaning you get from the object when you're near it are sometimes two different things."[19]

Larner subverts meaning by associating discrepant sensory experiences with narrative information, the latter either in titles or identifiable forms. *Lead Cornucopia* (1987), for example, is a small 10 × 10 × 22 inches (25.4 × 25.4 × 55.9 cm) form resembling a cornucopia basket or pastry, yet it weighs 300 pounds (136.08 kg). *Lash Mat* (1989) is a 10 feet × 11 inches (3.1 m × 27.9 cm) scarf-like form made of human eyelashes and leather.

Wall Scratcher (Fig. **8.14**), on the other hand, looks and acts like its title sounds. A small motorized mechanism, its pointed arm rhythmically moves like a pumping oil well. Placed so the point scratches the wall at its furthest extension, it gradually digs a pencil-thin groove in the wall. Moving it a few inches every day it is exhibited results in a whole series of digs in the wall, biting the hand that feeds it. The oil well analogy is an apt one, considering the catastrophic coastal oil spills like the *Exxon Valdez* in 1989, during which an estimated 240,000 barrels of oil were spilled off the coast of Alaska. Oil washed up on beaches and coves, nearly 40,000 birds and otters died, and Exxon spent two billion dollars on the cleanup. Larner spent her teenage years in California, the land of car culture, during the Iranian oil embargo, and Iraq invaded oil-rich Kuwait in 1990.

Larner's multi-leveled works share a deadpan humorous parody of scientific procedures, whose neutral and dispassionate methods ideally yield objective data. Instead, Larner skews the experiments to achieve preordained results, results which unmask our faith in objectivity and cause us to doubt, to look again. Her art requires a complete engagement of all our senses, an integration of all our sensory data, and a questioning of our preconceived conclusions.

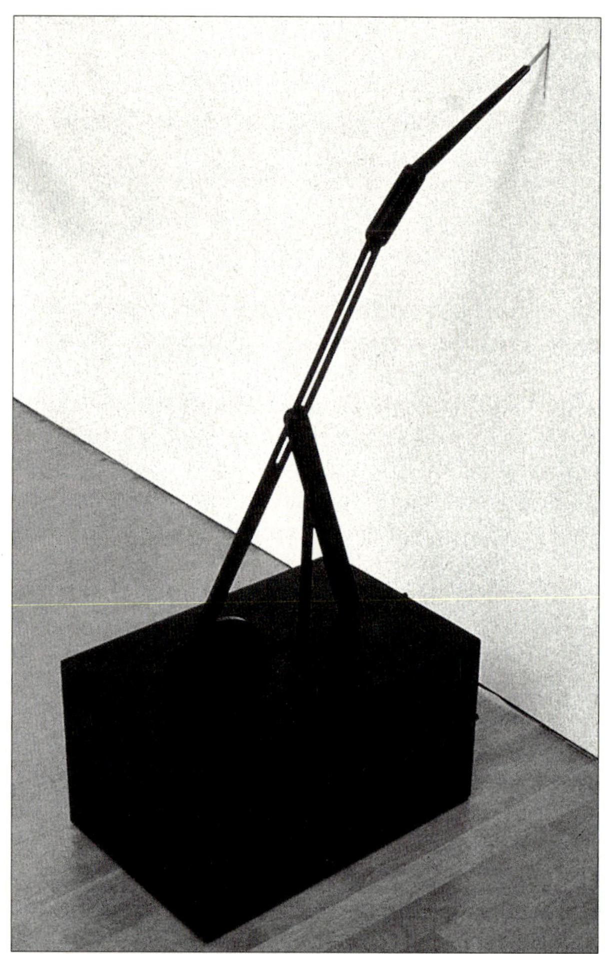

8.14 LIZ LARNER
Wall Scratcher 1988
Anodized aluminum, 12 volt
gear motor and battery,
spring steel
47 × 18½ × 12¼ ins
(119.4 × 47 × 31.1 cm)
Courtesy 303 Gallery, New
York

PHOEBE ADAMS

Phoebe Adams (born 1953) has lived and worked in Philadelphia since she moved there to attend the Philadelphia College of Art (she received a BFA in 1976). Adams' bronze sculptures lean against or hang from walls, sometimes intersecting two walls in a corner, sometimes connecting walls with floors. To the formal question "Where does sculpture occur?," Minimalists and Post-Minimalists would answer "On the horizon," while Earthwork artists might say, "Below the horizon." Whichever the case, they assume the floor or the ground to be sculpture's place. Not so for Adams.

Symbols, metaphors, analogies—richly allusive subject matter derived from suggestions of decay and growth, deterioration and regeneration, pollution and cleansing, tension and compression: these are Adams' subjects. Adams' *Measure by Measure* (1988) joins two corner walls with a tapered, elbow-jointed, spring-like form alluding to organic growth. Balancing its elbow on the floor, it appears to arm-wrestle the walls into place with metaphoric weight and tension.

Adams' forms seem to grow and transform themselves before our eyes. "I like things that can be something else, things that hold inside of themselves motion and change," Adams says.[20] Though cast in bronze, many of her forms seem deceptively light. *The Waste That is Ours* (Fig. **8.15**) includes a cast bronze billowing drape and flowing liquid that look fleeting, though they are fixed in hard metal. Their tenuous, fragile, and ephemeral quality typifies Adams' art.

Growth and metamorphosis are metaphors for the psychic process, for thought and its transforma-

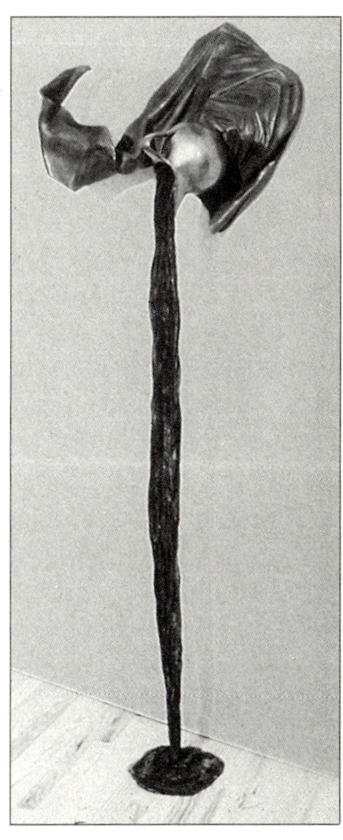

8.15 PHOEBE ADAMS
The Waste That Is Ours
1986
Bronze with patina
78 × 30 × 13ins
(198.1 × 76.2 × 33cm)
Courtesy The Anderson
Collection, California

tion into new thoughts. A tenuous thread might connect one idea to another through an illogical association that nonetheless makes sense. An awkward flow of thoughts or a jump from one subject area to another might unexpectedly lead to a revelation. Fleeting thoughts might recur because they are fixed in the memory, as though psychologically permanent like bronze is physically permanent. Or a thought might transform itself over time into a different idea. Forms that represent thoughts are Adams' vocabulary, that she transforms and translates into constantly evolving meanings.

TOM BUTTER

The purity of the Minimalist idea and the purity of their solutions made it very difficult to follow. It was an endgame that was very interesting, but one that you couldn't move any further. The Minimalists narrowed and reduced, so I felt I had to open things up again; it was just too narrow for me to operate in. . . . I want to do everything in my sculpture. I want it to look like it's wet and dry, alive and dead, geometric and organic; I want it to have everything at once.[21]

Bruce Nauman's and Eva Hesse's eccentric abstract fiberglass sculptures from the 1960s and 1970s (see pages 34 and 120) precede Tom Butter's glistening translucent forms; the artist acknowledges both sources. Butter (born 1952) started working in fiberglass in 1979, a material that suits him for its lightness, pliability, transluscence, and merging of dualities like wet and dry, hard and soft, geometric and organic. Many of his early forms look plant-like, like hollow pods or shafts suggesting growth. While Nauman's and Hesse's fiberglass sculptures look manmade, Butter's early works look like they could have grown from genetically mutated seeds.

Butter also acknowledges John Duff, the Japanese-American sculptor Isamu Noguchi's organic forms and the American sculptor Barbara Zucker's use of folded and pleated planes as sources for his art, but his "hip" visual wit distinguishes him as an artist with his own approach. Using only a few elements, Butter stages comical sculptural events full of surprises and audaciousness. *Verge* (Fig. **8.16**) teeters on its spindly legs. The fiberglass and wire mesh hollow suggests a sleek fish form (a homage to Brancusi). But why is it on legs? Does *Verge* symbolically represent life forms crawling from the sea up onto land?

The interior of *Verge* is like the body cavity of a gutted fish. Proportioned so that viewers must bend down to look through it, the void implies containment, like a horizontal body bag. Its ovoid shape neither expands nor contracts but rests in a fixed position. Teetering on its legs and ribs, *Verge* pokes witty fun at the act of raising sculpture up from the floor, as though one can do so only with trepidation and tentativeness.

Many of Butter's sculptures have a public and a private side, a front and a back, that give dual impressions of a simultaneously gregarious and retiring

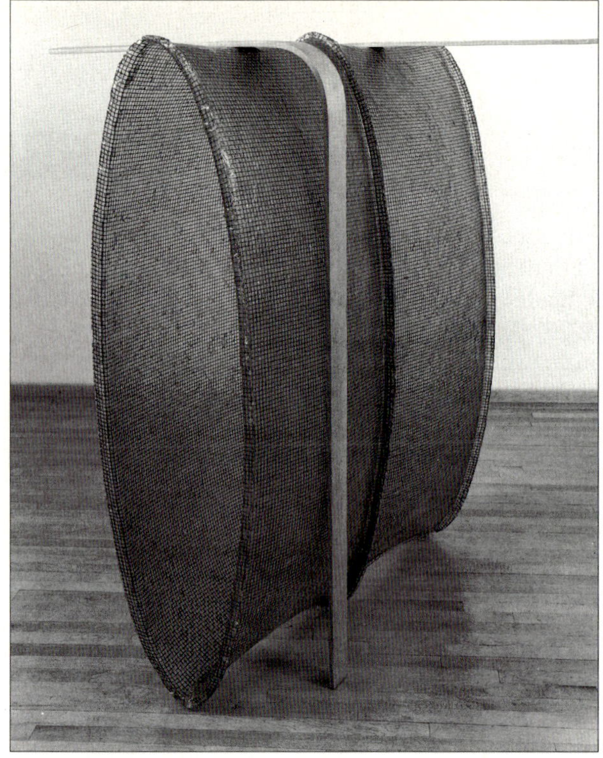

8.16 TOM BUTTER
Verge 1988
Fiberglass, wire mesh, maple
56 × 45 × 40ins
(142.2 × 114.3 × 101.6cm)
Courtesy Curt Marcus
Gallery, New York

personality. *Levity* (see page 239) floats a gently arced wooded plane cantilevered from a mottled black fiberglass curve. The wooden arc dominates the front view, from behind the curving fiberglass plane is all there is to see. With these two spare elements, Butter creates an elegant, subtle sculpture that both comments upon Minimalism and transcends it.

CAROL HEPPER

Carol Hepper (born 1953) grew up on her parents' ranch in South Dakota next to the Standing Rock Sioux Reservation, where she witnessed Indian pow-wows and rituals. Her schoolmates had colorful names like Virgil Taken Alive, Selby Noisy Hawk, and Tracita Red Legs, and the nearest settlement was the town of McLaughlin, population 1,500. Visual culture was the endless plains landscape, native American traditions—like burial mounds and rituals—and whatever the artist made from local materials. Her first exposure to contemporary visual art took place at the age of 18 when she visited the Walker Art Center and saw works by the American sculptors Lee Bontecou and Louise Nevelson, Jean Dubuffet (see page

110), the early Minimalists, and Joseph Beuys (see page 118), whose use of his personal history deeply moved Hepper. "I suddenly realized," Hepper said, "that you don't have to stop building things just because you reach a certain age."[22]

Hepper makes hand-crafted open forms out of materials native to South Dakota. Living in New York now, she has willow branches shipped to her by her rancher father (she also uses woods from upstate New York and New England). Soaking the branches to make them pliable, she bends or weaves them into embracing, rhythmic forms. Some, like *Two Stroke Roll* (Fig. **8.17**), suggest baskets or cages, meticulously hand-crafted with labor-intensive operations, evoking a lyrical connection to landscape and to centuries-old native traditions. *Two Stroke Roll* suggests the shamanistic quality of Joseph Beuys's references to his own personal history, but in a less *Angst*-ridden, more celebratory way. It pays homage to the endless prairie plains where the native willow grows along creek beds.

Crossbend (Fig. **8.18**) is a more recent work that may reflect Hepper's move to New York (she still frequently returns to South Dakota). It reveals a more man-made uniformity than the multi-leveled variations of *Two Stroke Roll*. The steel joints come from a huge hardware store Hepper found in Long Island City, Queens. Her found materials now include ones from a congested urban milieu. Combining the bent willow branches from her native South Dakota, the new works synthesize her rural and urban experiences. If they feel more strained and contained, so must the artist. Hepper's autobiographical, lyrical, and hand-crafted art typifies sculpture in the 1980s.

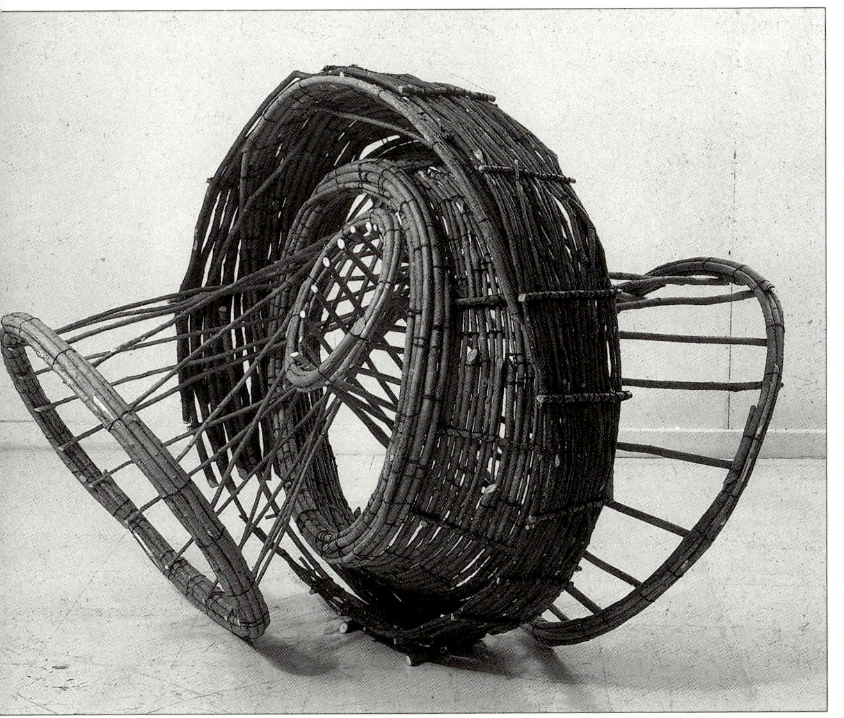

8.17 CAROL HEPPER
Two Stroke Roll 1987–88
Wood, wire, pigment
48 × 59 × 48ins
(122 × 150 × 122cm)
The Metropolitan Museum of Art
Gift of Kempf Hogan, in memory of Lydia Winston Malbin and in honor of her daughter and son-in-law, Sally and Eliot Robinson, 1990 (1990.301). Photograph from Rosa Esman Gallery, New York

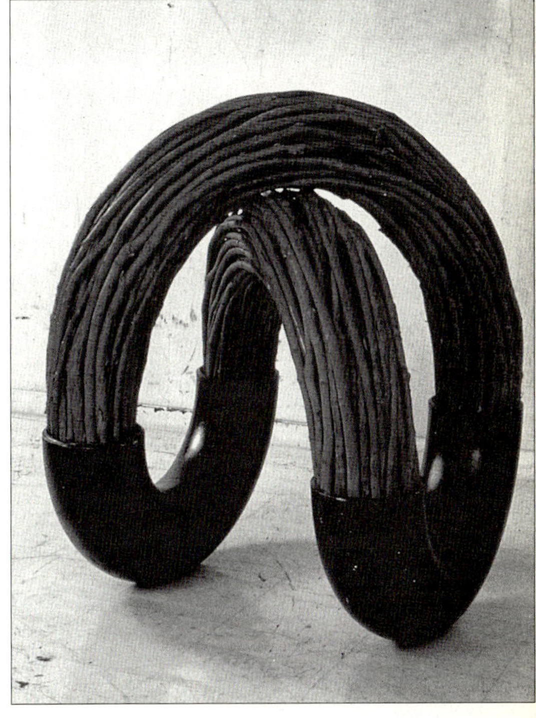

8.18 CAROL HEPPER
Crossbend 1989
Wood and steel
44 × 35 × 33ins
(111.8 × 88.9 × 83.8cm)
Collection Martin Margulies
Courtesy Rosa Esman Gallery, New York

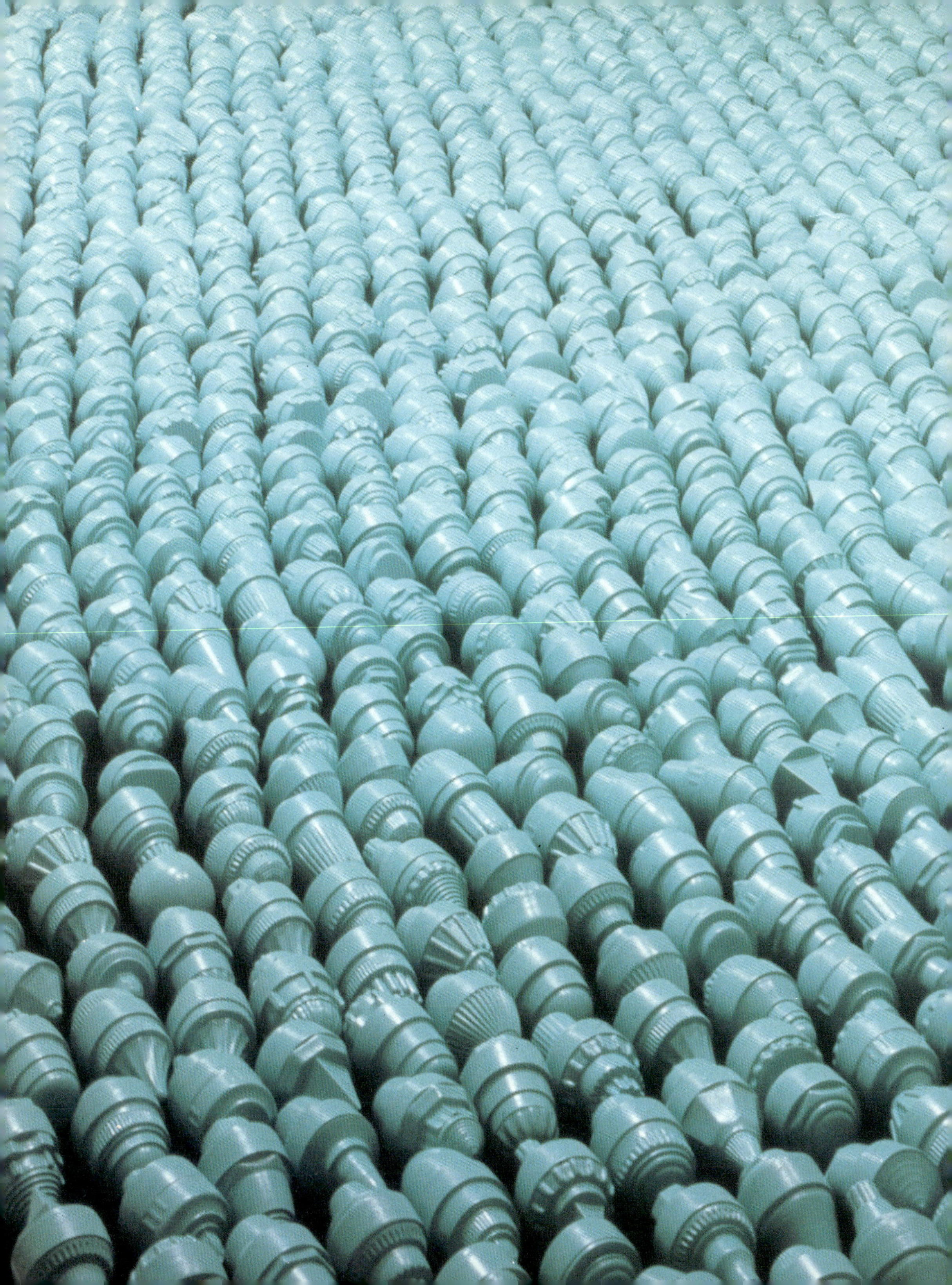

9
Simulationism

"The real sense of imaginary freedom we seek out through art comes through our wishful identification with the forces of money and power which we associate as supporting it, or underwriting it."[1]

—— ALLAN McCOLLUM ——

Allan McCollum
Individual Works (detail)   1987–88
Courtesy John Weber Gallery, New York

Simulacra and Art's Status as Commodities

Simulationism is currently the most often-used term for a tendency that first began attracting attention around 1985 and has also been called Neo-Geo (meaning "new geometric art"), Smart Art, Neo-Futurism, Neo-Pop, Neo-Conceptualism, and New Abstraction. The term Simulationism comes from the post-structuralist French philosopher Jean Baudrillard's term "simulacra."

Baudrillard believes that we live in a world in which more meaning is attached to appearances than to tangible reality. Appearances—or simulacra—have become a reality of their own. For example, we vote for a political candidate based on his or her "image" rather than record, or we buy a product for its professed enhancement of our self-image rather than its tangible benefits. Our motivations have less to do with tangible reality than with mass-media images over which we have no control. We are passive receptors—mere consumers—in the late capitalist, post-industrial commodity culture.

In this soulless society our selection of consumer products is about as self-expressive as we get. If we still believe that we have control over our destiny, that we have free will, or that art embodies the metaphysical values of self-determination and the full exercise of the imagination, we are deluding ourselves. As the art critic Robert Pincus-Witten stated regarding Simulationist Jeff Koons, "Once, sculpture was about carving, then modelling. With Modernism it became construction. Today it's shopping."[2]

Simulacra are simulations of reality, not imitations. They are substitutes rather than equivalents. They have a language and a meaning all their own. We are led by merchandisers into believing that simulacra are equivalents, that chemical sweeteners, for example, equate with sugar, when they only do so in their effect. We are junkies for effects. We do not question what is giving us the desired effects as long as we get our fix. Because the substitutes are so unsatisfying, we keep wanting more, and newer, effects.

Consumers equate newness with goodness. In the Sumulationist's view, this equation is part of the myth of Modernism and its belief in the heroic individual capable of bringing new realities into being. Art critic Roberta Smith wrote:

In all his works comprising 'The New' [a series], Koons equated consumerism's object-lust with Modernism's compulsive pursuit of the newest in art innovations, and compared the semi-esthetic (if not semi-religious) aura of a brand-new household appliance with the 'presence' of the art object. Newness for Koons seemed to be a state of perfection, of completely uncorrupted integrity; for him, a thing is most powerful when it is new.[3]

In post-industrial consumer culture, art is just another commodity.

In post-structuralist and neo-Marxist theory, art is a symbol of power and social prestige. Those who own it signal that they have enough discretionary income to afford it and enough education to understand and appreciate it. For the Simulationists, those who make it are managers manipulating and interpreting information about the existing world, not people who make unique objects symbolizing experiences that never existed before. Art becomes a management tool, no longer primarily a means of personal exploration. Those who believe in this latter concept of art are trapped in the romantic past of Modernism and its belief in heroic individualism.

Probably more art is being produced in the 1990s than at any other time in history. More artists are working than at any other time. (Estimates of the number of artists working in the United States vary from 200,000 to 1,000,000.) More contemporary art galleries exist now than ever before. Galleries compete for sales with larger numbers of galleries. As in other kinds of merchandising, they employ advertising and public relations techniques similar to those used to promote other products. For this large a number of artists and galleries to reach audiences they must address a broader spectrum of the public than when fewer artists and galleries existed. Publicity, hype, and public relations extend to all realms of the post-industrial commodity culture.

The dominant managerial class is Simulationism's target audience, the lawyers, stockbrokers, psychoanalysts, dentists, accountants, business executives, computer programmers, telecasters, writers, and others who make up the information and service industries and who have larger amounts of discretionary income—and, because of their numbers, greater need for self-image enhancement—than ever before. The managerial class that formerly existed in smaller numbers and hardly ever bought art before now exists in large numbers and buys it with regularity.

Allan McCollum's generic paintings called *Surrogates*, Haim Steinbach's formica shelves laden with consumer products, and Jeff Koons's cast stainless-steel commemorative whiskey decanters express nostalgia for the American middle-class home as fictionalized on network television in programs like "The Brady Bunch." Many of the Simulationists' artworks intentionally resemble the furnishings of an average middle-class home. The artists do not disdain kitsch taste but celebrate it. Their harking back to the taste of the vanishing bourgeois home parallels the newly dominant bourgeoisie's imitation of aristocratic taste in the mid-nineteenth century. The managerial class—Koons was once a stockbroker—waxes nostalgic over a cliché-ridden vision of the past.

If the Simulationists' view seems cynical, it is also naïve. For underlying it is an unquestioning full subscription to the values of our late capitalist, post-industrial commodity culture. Artworks are bought and sold as emblems of power and prestige, facts that Simulationists endorse and subscribe to. "What choice do we have?," they seem to say. Their works confirm that these are the conditions under which art is currently presented to the public, the conditions under which artists make their livings. Simulationists want to buy into these conditions and to succeed according to them. To deny the conditions would be to live a fiction, they seem to say. To confirm them is to live in the real world. If the Simulationists' views seem cynical to us, perhaps we still subscribe to the outmoded Modernist view of art as a series of heroic individual triumphs over an oppressive majority culture.

The appropriations of the Post-Modernists are the most recent precedent to the Simulationists' use of pre-existing objects and images. Duchamp's "readymades" and Pop artists' imitations of mass-media imagery are also important prototypes. But Sherrie Levine's direct copying of reproductions of artworks (see page 195) and her process of questioning the concept of originality that Modernism fostered form the indispensible link between Simulationism and previous art. The prior concept of originality that Levine's, and to a lesser extent other Post-Modernists', art call into question made Simulationism possible.

Simulationism carries forward ideas proposed by earlier artists without really adding much more than increased emphasis and new effects. For the most part, it is a shallow art, "dead on arrival" to quote the art critic Donald Kuspit.[4] "Meanwhile, the intense peculiarity of this moment must not be despised," wrote the art critic Peter Schjeldahl.[5] "Simulationism being a fiesta of unchanges."[6] In corroborating and celebrating the most commodity-driven interpretation of art's role in contemporary society, Simulationism may be attending its own funeral. "If only art could accomplish the magic act of its own disappearance!" Jean Baudrillard said, "But it continues to make believe it is disappearing when it is already gone."[7]

TIM EBNER

The Californian artist Tim Ebner (born 1953) is possibly one of the best Simulationists. He focuses the issues without being too self-consciously serious, and without beating us over the head with his cleverness, like Jeff Koons. Ebner approaches the art end-game with good-natured wit and lighthearted humor that softens the art-critical content and makes the artworks the primary artifacts, not the explanation. Maybe his being outside the frenzied hype of Manhattan in the late 1980s, in Los Angeles, has something

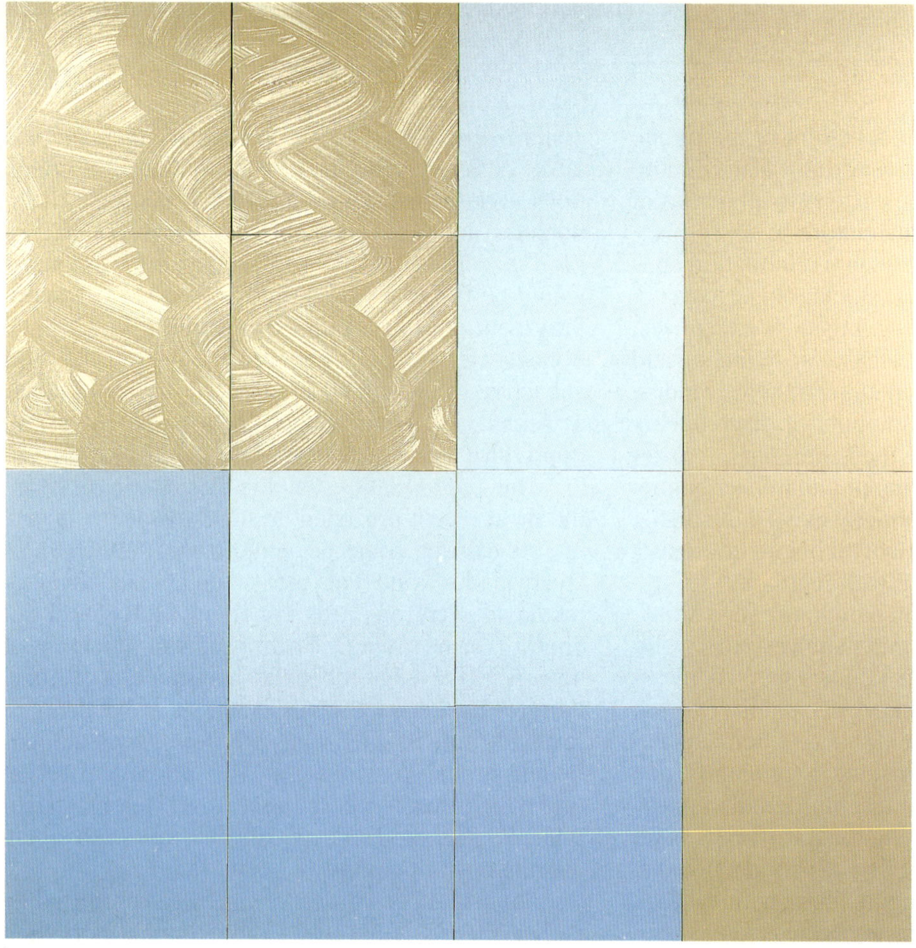

to do with his more mellow approach. I suspect his tactful equal billing of Minimalist, Conceptual Art, and Post-Modernist ideas, along with Expressionist and Color Field painting precedents, accounts for his non-confrontational tone.

Ebner produces paintings in series based on Conceptual Art-derived strategies, uses Minimalistic images, references Color Field and Abstract Expressionist painting, and, in his appropriations, borrows a Post-Modernist strategy. His art comments upon the art market system by acknowledging galleries, museums, private collectors, interior decorators, corporations, art critics, art shippers, and art storage companies.

The *Color Cue* series (Fig. **9.1**), begun in 1986, derives from the paint company Dunn-Edwards' color chips recommending color combinations for interior decorating. Each chip features a hue in light and darker values along with a third complementary color. Dunn-Edwards produces paints in those colors that year and offers carpets, counter-top coverings,

and other interior decorator items in the same palette, thus legislating home and office decor in one democratic fell swoop. Ebner adopts the generic color combinations, relegating the role of selecting the colors of his paintings to an anonymous decorator and assuring that his paintings will fit in everybody's decor.

Each painting in the series features 16 2-feet square (0.61 m sq) canvas panels, four each of the two different tones, four of the complementary color, and four of the complementary color brushed over a contrasting background. For the 12 solid-colored panels, Ebner sprays up to 25 coats of paint, sanding and burnishing between coats, to produce an enamel-like, factory finish. For the brushed panels, he uses a monoprint technique. Attaching two roofing tar brushes together by the handles, he swoops the brushes across a 4 × 4 feet (1.22 × 1.22 m) sheet of glass in gestures emblematic of Expressionist painting but lacking their seismic connotations. Then he places each panel face down on the glass, printing the brushes' tracks. In both cases—spraying or printing—the artist's hand does not directly apply the paint.

Ebner builds intricately crafted pine crates to hold the panels, eight to a crate. The crates serve as shipping and storage vessels and, if they travel very much, soon acquire tags and labels that make them look like old-fashioned steamer trunks. Each painting is accompanied by an installation manual diagramming all of the possible combinations and arrangements of the panels. Attached to the wall by velcro, the panels can be installed in any number or configuration. Some variations resemble Color Field painting, some Expressionist painting, some Minimalism, and so on; here's an Elsworth Kelly, there's a Brice Marden, and so forth. And the grid, of course, is the most indelible Minimalist figure of speech.

The crates and diagrams resemble furniture and decorators' plans, like sectional sofas, thus commenting on the destiny of so much serious art as corporate or home decor. In post-structuralist language, Ebner deconstructs the corporate appropriation of art. The furniture analogy also makes reference to Richard Artschwager, Scott Burton, and other Post-Modernists who cross over from fine art into popular art forms. Working in series and following a production line pattern, Ebner negates standard conventions of originality and self-expression in favor of a more commodity-oriented method. Yet despite all of his distancing mechanisms Ebner makes art that is distinctly his own and unlike anyone else's.

Using the archetypes of pure abstraction, Ebner's paintings are emblematic—representational—of the heroic periods of Abstract painting, when it was possible for a square of flat color or a brushstroke to represent nothing but itself and the visual possibilities it embodied. His paintings represent a time when it was possible for an artist to deny the conventional visual world in favor of a uniquely personal vision. The early twentieth-century Dutch Abstract painter Piet Mondrian, the early twentieth-century Russian Abstract painter Kasimir Malevich, and the American Abstract Expressionists Franz Kline and Ad Reinhardt are all conjured up by Ebner's emblematic abstract representations, as well as the impossibility of reliving their lone, fraught denials. The post-Post-Modern artist lives in a different, less individualistic, less heroically risky, time.

PETER HALLEY

Peter Halley (born 1953) is an accomplished and persuasive speaker and writer about his and other artists' work. His theoretical treatises and eloquent commentaries underpin his art. For example:

I don't think of my work as abstract at all; instead of using the word abstract I always use the word diagrammatic. The issue to me is that at a certain point when all these artificial systems of communication and transportation were being laid out, that was the age of abstract art. So in a Mondrian or even in a Frank Stella, what you have is an ideal depiction of what circulation and the flow of information or transportation would be like if this goal of circulation were completed. But I

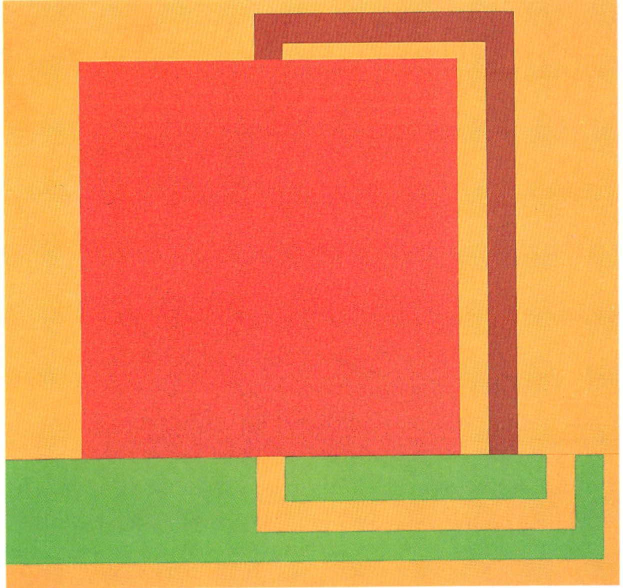

9.2 PETER HALLEY
Magenta Cell 1989
Day-Glo acrylic, acrylic, Roll-A-Tex on canvas

100½ × 90ins
(255.3 × 228.6cm)
Courtesy Sonnabend Gallery,
New York

think in the contemporary world this has been completed and the geometric has become the real in terms of what's out there in the world. Geometry is backtracking and enclosing the old idea of the natural in the diagrammatic. I think the videogame is very important in this regard, as are computer graphics. In a video game you might have a little geometric man walking across the screen and you have a situation in which these ideal geometric elements are being deployed to represent an old kind of organic natural reality.[8]

For Halley, geometry is diagrammatically representational, not only representational of buildings, streets, and circuitry, but also representational of systems of power and control. As he sees it, in the industrial period (roughly, the late-nineteenth to mid-twentieth centuries) cities, factories, hospitals, prisons, apartment blocks were laid out in configurations that allowed authorities to see into all of their spaces at once. Industrial geometry with its panoptic organization signifies authoritarian power, the power of capital over labor. The universal, utopian evocations of Mondrian and other geometric Abstractionists —even the Minimalists—derived from the overriding clarity of such a unified view.

During the post-industrial era, geometry signifies microchips and circuitry with their flow of electronic information, as well as pipes carrying heat, electricity, air conditioning, telephone messages, and other services into architectural spaces. Halley calls the elements of his geometric paintings "cells" and "conduits" which he makes out of day-glo colors—

simulacra of colors that appear in nature—and fake stucco-textured backgrounds. His generation is not so much one of industrial production as post-industrial consumption. The post-structuralists Michel Foucault and Jean Baudrillard provide the indispensible texts.

Simulacra in the form of nostalgic references to previous abstract geometric painting recur in Halley's art, references to Barnet Newman, Ad Reinhardt, Frank Stella, Russian Constructivism, and Dutch de Stijl. Some of the references are pointed, some oblique. Knowing the references enriches one's experience of the paintings, but not knowing them does not make the paintings devoid of meaning. They still evoke geometric abstraction and the hallowed, heroic days of Modernist painting. Halley mocks the treasured Modernist role of art as privileged experience, and the belief that art could have a transformative effect on society.

He intends nothing transcendent. Halley's paintings (Fig. **9.2**) look more like managerial flow charts than metaphysical metaphors. They employ the signs and symbols of corporate visual language, recalling international signage and "you are here" directional locators. Yet many of them are so big that they possess strong presence and suggest the mural tradition of emphatic public gestures. Resembling revered art conventions and being, after all, paintings—anomalies of the handmade pre-industrial craft tradition—Halley's paintings seem barely (if at all) within the boundaries of his elaborately circumscribed polemic.

ALLAN McCOLLUM

Allan McCollum (born 1944) has made over 2,000 nearly identical painting-like objects which he calls "surrogates," substitutes for art. They consist of a black frame, a white mat, and a black center. From 1978 to 1982 he made them out of wood; thereafter, he has cast them in plaster from rubber molds which emphasize their mass production. Lately, McCollum has painted some of the objects in candy colors. He always installs groups of them to emphasize that they are identical and interchangeable in meaning. The surrogates are intentionally devoid of aesthetic in-

terest but instead function as signs of paintings—simulacra—rather than paintings themselves. They do not focus on the unique subject matter of an individual painting, but on the subject of artworks in general as signifiers of power and wealth. The artist said:

The real sense of imaginary freedom we seek out through art comes through our wishful identification with the forces of money and power which we associate as supporting it, or underwriting it. We identify with the art's patronage and we find a feeling of safety and security by imagining that we belong to an elite group of some kind: a group whose tastes we share and who will protect us from harm. If one has money and power on one's side, we believe, we are free from all significant anxiety.[9]

McCollum believes that art functions to alleviate anxiety about powerlessness, both for artists, the art audience, and for collectors and patrons. Participating in art means consorting with power and wealth. Individual artworks are artifacts that facilitate "our imaginary identification with those who dominate us."[10] Participating in art tells the powerful people we fear and who dominate us that we are engaged in a harmless activity. Powerful people use art to dominate us. We use art to identify with powerful people and to alleviate our fears of them.

Placing artworks in the same category as other commodities, McCollum examines them as embodiments of values other than aesthetic ones. He takes artworks out of their mystified, privileged realm as conveyors of metaphysical meanings and instead considers the roles they play in society. None of his surrogates embodies a separate, unique idea: they all mean the same thing, "like an advertisement or a logo," the artist says.

My first impulse was to make only one painting, and exhibit it over and over again, to create a sort of archival object—like the government's Bureau of Standards maintains the standard "inch" in platinum. But this solution eliminated the possibility of exchange transactions—and how could a thing represent an art object if it couldn't be bought and sold?[11]

The device of repetition emphasizes McCollum's notion of power. Repetition is used by religions and by the military to create the impression of power, ubiquity, and spectacle. Repetition is hypnotic and conveys meaning in itself. Repeating the same surrogates over and over emphasizes their generic meaning and devalues the notion of unique objects. The aura of the unique art object gives way to the aura of mass production.

Individual Works (Fig. **9.3**) consists of 10,000 handgrenade-like objects McCollum made from 150 different elements originally cast from cat toys, candy molds, drawer pulls, and bottle caps. Each object is made from up to eight parts. No two are alike, but

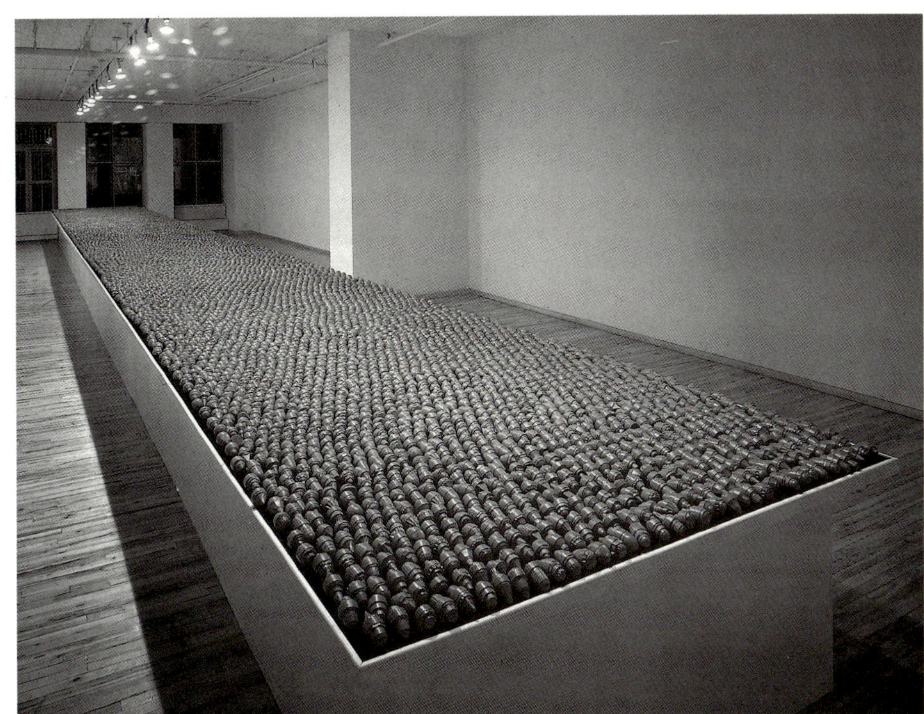

9.3 ALLAN McCOLLUM
Individual Works 1987–88
Enamel on hydrocal,
10,000 pieces approximately
Dimensions variable
Courtesy John Weber Gallery,
New York

it is impossible for viewers to determine that for themselves because there are simply too many to compare. The work is a parody of how an excess of consumer goods has a paralyzing effect on consumers' ability to make a selection. The differences between each object are superficial, existing only to allow the possibility that each one could claim to be "new and improved." Altogether, they function the same as the surrogates, as generic commodities.

If McCollum takes a side, it is in favor of freeing art from being a tool of power, control, and the enforcement of social class boundaries. He sees his art as functioning to call attention to the forces that legislate art's meaning. But the very people whose usurpation of art McCollum abhors—wealthy collectors—buy his art. In buying it, do they negate his criticism of them, or does their buying it negate their usurpation of art? Ultimately, money is the greatest value in a capitalist consumers' society. McCollum's work calls attention to this fact while mutely acknowledging that art cannot change the world. One admires him for

crying wolf, but ultimately his is an impotent outcry, for he buys into the system by participating in it.

The artist reveals his underlying psychology in relating the following incident:

When I was a child, both of my parents worked on the assembly line of a large aircraft factory in Southern California. One Christmas, the company invited all of the employees of this huge industrial complex to bring their children to an enormous party in one of their larger warehouses, and all of us were given exactly identical Christmas gifts.... There must have been hundreds and hundreds of them, maybe thousands, and we all had to stand in line for maybe half an hour to get one—handed to us by Santa Claus, of course.... I found the whole experience really frightening, as I recall, but, naturally, I wanted the gift. This is the sort of nightmarishly ambiguous atmosphere I try to create with my installations, sometimes.... As I've said, so much of art is about fear-in-the-face-of-power.[12]

ASHLEY BICKERTON

Ashley Bickerton was born in 1959 in Barbados, West Indies, received a BFA degree from the California Institute of the Arts in 1982, and completed the Whitney Museum Independent Studies Program in 1985. He lives and works in New York.

Tormented Self-Portrait (Susie at Arles) #2 (Fig. **9.4**) is covered with the corporate logos of the products the artist uses, defining him as a consumer whose being is both expressed and determined by the products he chooses. Marlboro, Fruit of the Loom, Renault, US Sprint, Tylenol, Nike, Trojan, Citibank, TV Guide, The Village Voice, Surfer Magazine, and Cusano Rojo Muscal appear alongside Integral Yoga/Natural Foods, New York Rainforest Alliance, Greenpeace, and CalArts. You are what you consume. That, and the clubs you belong to.

Like most of Bickerton's art, *Tormented Self-Portrait (Susie at Arles) #2* comes equipped with a padded vinyl cover (rolled up at the bottom) to protect it in shipping, and installation instructions (printed on the upper left). "In the process of wanting to say exactly what it was, I realized that art is moved

and shipped, and it gets damaged," the artist said[13]. Other works include padded handles to make it easier to carry them, levels to facilitate installing them, and digital counters designating their approximate current value.

Tormented Self-Portrait (Susie at Arles) #2 includes three logos of Bickerton's alter ego, Susie Culturelux, promising "The best in sensory and intellectual experiences." Why did he choose a female name? Artists are usually catalogued according to the father's surname, according to Bickerton's logic, so he chose a casual female first name to throw that whole process into doubt. The artist's name becomes a name brand, like a logo, as in referring to "a Picasso" the same way one refers to "a Ferrari." If art functions as a sign of commodity status, then why not design art with that function in mind?

Bickerton's current plans include making objects to parachute into a rainforest or to set adrift on ocean currents, taking them out of the art context and putting them into a natural setting like exquisite, dislocated cultural artifacts, perhaps creating weird cargo

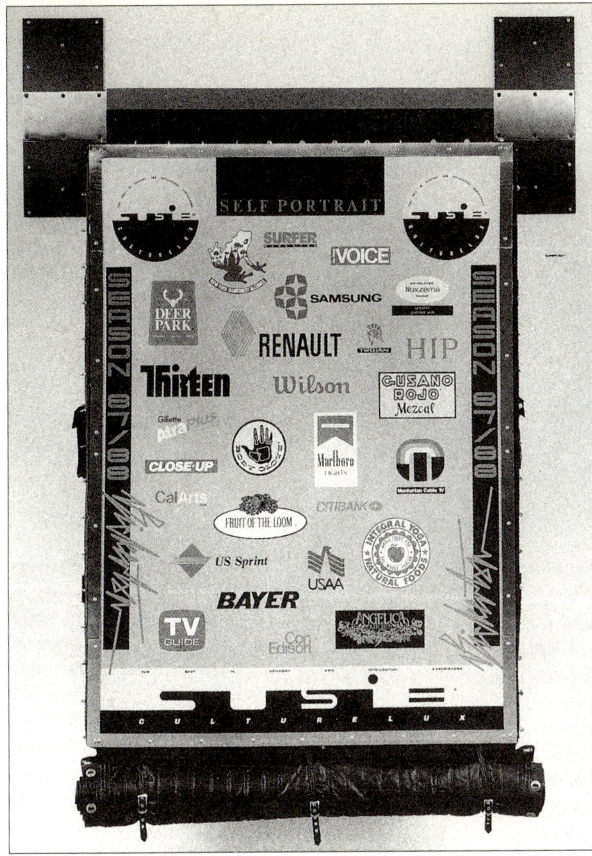

9.4 ASHLEY BICKERTON Tormented Self-Portrait (Susie at Arles) #2 1988 Mixed media construction with padded black leather 90 × 69 × 18ins (228.6 × 175.3 × 45.7cm) Courtesy Sonnabend Gallery, New York

"I wanted to build art that was exactly what it was and what it was for. I've said before that these are the sporting goods that operate on the race track of art. They were designed for that circuit."[14]

cults. "Smithson posited his project in the fluid and entropic site of the space between the cultural and the natural," the artist said, "between reclamation and disintegration in the situationist theater of abandoned quarries and eroding strip mines. In so much

as I have inverted much of this thinking in the production of an archly cultural artifact, a paradigm in culture's relentless plastic profile against nature, it seemed perverse to suddenly rip this thing out of that context and dump it awkwardly in this otherworldly terrain."[15]

References to Robert Smithson recur in Simulationists' remarks. Bickerton also said, "I've always said that if you keep your spiral jetty somewhere at the edge of your own horizon, you'll keep working toward it."[16] Peter Halley paid homage to Smithson in his essay, "Beat, Minimalism, New Wave and Robert Smithson"[17] in which he quoted from a published conversation I had with Smithson in 1972, as follows:

See, what I'm talking about are relationships. Art has tended to be viewed in terms of isolation, neutralization, separation, and this is encouraged. Art is supposed to be on some eternal plane, free from the experiences of the world, and I'm more interested in those experiences, not as a refutation of art, but as a part of that experience, or interwoven, in other words, all these factors come into it.[18]

Smithson continued, "So I'm just saying that it would be nice if the artist could maintain a certain involvement with his production, and this is the great issue, I think it will be the growing issue, of the seventies: the investigation of the apparatus the artist is threaded through."[19] Smithson could not have known how long it would take for his prophetic remark to take hold, or how much his intentions would become deflected by the Simulationists. For, while Smithson provided the grounding idea for art that investigates the apparatus it is threaded through, judging from how well I knew him and from his art, I think he would have enjoyed the perversity of Bickerton's and others' subversions, but regretted their naïvity.

HAIM STEINBACH

Since the mid-1980s, Haim Steinbach (born 1944) has been making wedge-shaped, formica-covered shelves laden with various consumer products (Fig. **9.5**). Steinbach shops for the products, selecting them for their design qualities and juxtaposing them, usually in quantities of more than one of each product, to

resemble a graphically arresting store display. He does not affix the products to the shelves but provides collectors with diagrams of their placement along with instructions for their care, such as dusting, polishing, and oiling. The values of good merchandising are implicit in his works: merchandise as art,

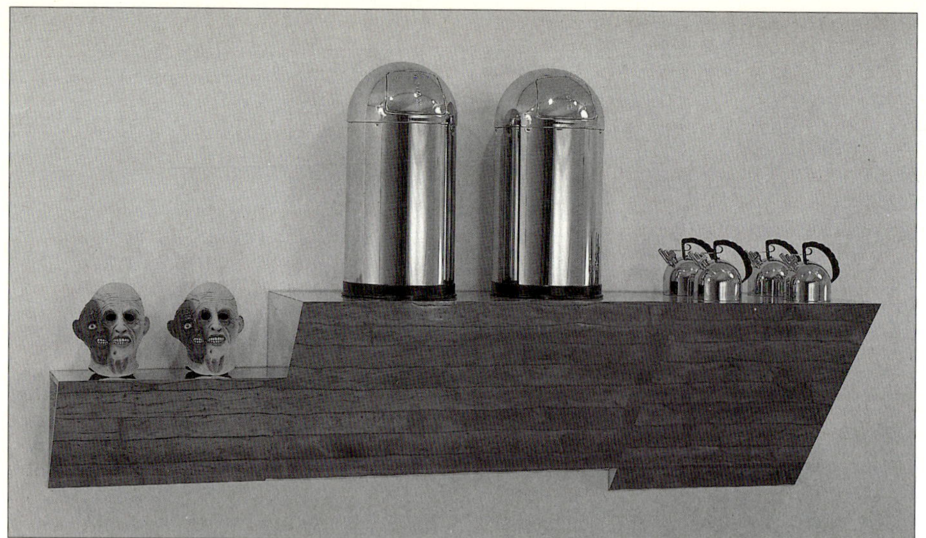

art as merchandise.

The products vary from modernistic toilet-bowl brushes to sparkle lamps, lava lamps, bullet-shaped chrome trash cans, art deco-style water pitchers, Bold detergent boxes, Nike tennis shoes, women's shoes, cooking pots, and LED digital clocks. (While Jeff Koons usually chooses more macho products to celebrate, Steinbach crosses over traditional gender roles and buys kitchen implements and other "women's" products. The central role of shopping—traditionally thought of as women's work—in Steinbach's art is another example of gender blur.) His work seems to universally say that the commodities we buy define who we are in our post-industrial consumer culture.

Steinbach's process of selecting pre-existing consumer products differs from Marcel Duchamp's selection of his "readymades," unaltered mass-produced items. Duchamp approached his task with "aesthetic anesthesia," devoid of interest in their aesthetic qualities. *Au contraire* for Steinbach, who takes great interest in their appearance. Yet he does not intend any comment upon the taste culture his objects represent: though the lava lamps and many of his other objects may be kitsch, Steinbach does not mean to ridicule the low level of taste they appeal to.

"Steinbach maintains ... that verdicts of innocence or culpability are not his concern," wrote the art critic Holland Cotter. "... that his work exists precisely on that thin line of 'extreme ambivalence' between criticism and celebration: a state of fascination, you might say, both with the enticement of the objects and with the values they create and preserve."[20] This morally neutral stance is like that of television, advertising, merchandising, and other mass-media: give the public what they want, without taking responsibility for the values represented. The individualism of Modernism and its opposition to the majority consumer culture gives way to a total adoption of its morality and sales techniques. Skeptics could say that this is the way the current art market works in the first place, so don't be naïve and deny it, and they would be at least partially correct. This is what is most shocking about Steinbach's art.

Now that his art is selling well and he can shop in higher price categories, Steinbach plans to begin including more upmarket products, including fine art wares like ancient pottery. Anything that is for sale, any consumer product, is a potential commodity for his art. His pricing structure is designed to accommodate whatever value commodities he selects: he has standard prices for each different size of shelf; to that he adds the cost of the products on display.

In the world of simulacra, the image other people have of us affects our own self-image. Other people judge us by our taste, and our taste is nowhere more evident than in the products we buy: our clothes, furniture, dishes, jewelry, decorative items, clocks, briefcases, art, and so on. We proudly display the emblems of our taste and economic status on shelves in our homes and our visitors judge whether our taste is kitsch, bourgeois, upmarket, or outdated according to the commodities by which we have defined ourselves. Steinbach mimics this phenomenon in his art. In Steinbach's hands, art has become just another commodity by which consumers define themselves and are judged.

JEFF KOONS

Jeff Koons (born 1955) began working in his current vein as early as 1979, though he did not have a solo show until 1985, when he first started attracting critical attention. To date he has worked in five series: in chronological order, "The New," "Equilibrium," "Luxury and Degradation," "Statuary," and his most recent series of larger-than-life-sized carved wood and porcelain knickknacks.

"The New" consisted of new vacuum cleaners and rug shampooers placed in plexiglass boxes lit by flourescent tubes, celebrating the desirable state of newness of consumer products, a condition which, for a human being, "is unachievable; the individual can't be while the machine can," according to the artist. "I always knew it was about birth and immortality."[21] "Equilibrium" included scuba equipment cast in bronze, paintings of advertisements featuring sports stars, and new basketballs hovering in the middle of full or half-filled aquarium-like tanks of water. These latter objects symbolize the balance of desires—or equilibrium—of new consumer prod-

ucts, a condition unobtainable by human beings. "Luxury and Degradation" consisted of stainless steel (which Koons refers to as "proletariat silver") casts of Jim Beam limited-edition whiskey decanters shaped like trains, along with stainless-steel casts of other implements of alcohol consumption like Baccarat crystal, and paintings of liquor advertisements. Koons's 1987 series, "Statuary," included inflatable toys, dolls, figurines, and plaster portrait busts—all cast in stainless steel—focusing on the middle-class art object.

In 1989 Koons simultaneously exhibited at three galleries in three cities and ran full-page advertisements featuring images of himself in four art magazines. "With hysterical deadpan earnestness, these ads let us know that the product and its promotion are inextricably bound; but their tongue-in-cheek-hand-on-wallet glitz might as readily be selling breath freshener as an art balm," wrote the art critic Klaus Kertess.[22] The same critic wrote: "For his new line of sculptures, Jeff Koons has ordered up an outrage-

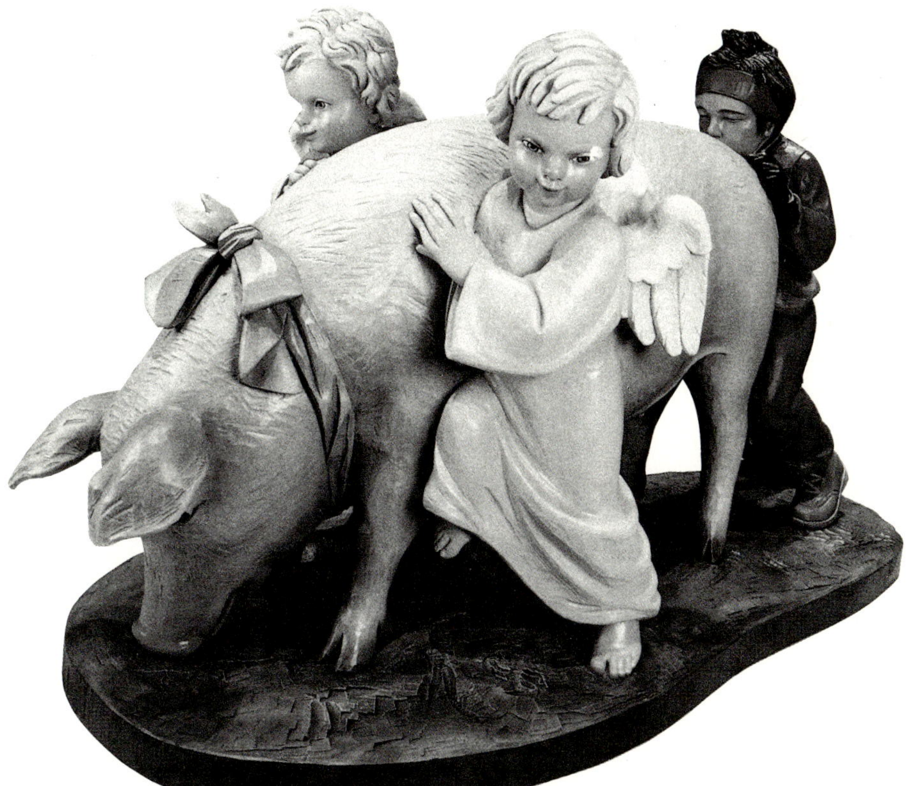

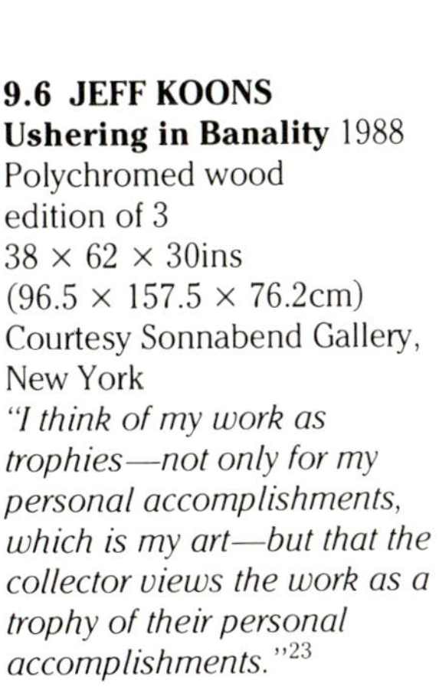

9.6 JEFF KOONS
Ushering in Banality 1988
Polychromed wood
edition of 3
38 × 62 × 30ins
(96.5 × 157.5 × 76.2cm)
Courtesy Sonnabend Gallery,
New York
"I think of my work as trophies—not only for my personal accomplishments, which is my art—but that the collector views the work as a trophy of their personal accomplishments."[23]

ously fragrant and flagrant bouquet of dazed and debased figures of speechlessness plucked from the aisles of a delirious, shopping-mall arcadia."[24] Koons hired wood-carvers and porcelain-makers in Germany and Italy to make life-sized or nearly as large knickknacks featuring, for example, a German pin-up hugging the Pink Panther (taken from two separate photographs); a recumbent white porcelain Michael Jackson with his arm around his pet chimp, Bubbles; a 7 feet (2.1 m) tall toy bear confiding in a London policeman; Buster Keaton with a bird perched on his shoulder astride a donkey (taken from a photograph); and a beribboned life-sized pig being pushed by two angels and a little boy (from behind) titled *Ushering in Banality* (Fig. **9.6**). The master craftsmen signed each piece, and Koons signed each one on the bottom.

None of the Simulationists has manufactured such an image of novelty and provocation as Koons has. Koons created knickknacks for the managerial class whose taste was formed in bourgeois homes chock-a-block with Hummel figurines and cuckoo clocks. Thus he created an instant market as brilliantly as though he had performed market research (or had he?), as well as guaranteed that he would have a hot press. "His extravagant confections wallow in a sticky-fingered baseness and sentimentality endemic to disenfranchised craft and franchised pulp but seldom seen in high art since the Pre-Raphaelites and Bouguereau," wrote Klaus Kertess.[25] In his babe-in-the-woods, innocent and naïve way, Koons is as effective a media manipulator as Andy Warhol, and more suited to this age when culture watching has become a mass-media spectator sport.

We might suspect Koons of being ironic, of intending a put-down of the taste his art mimics, but he has no ironic intent at all. "I don't find any ironic quality in the work at all. What it does have for me is a sense of the tragic. My objects aren't cute. The vacuum, 'The New,' has a sense of tragedy because you only reflect on your own mortality. The equilibrium tanks are a reflection on the unachievable psychological and sociological states of being."[26] Koons is completely sincere in addressing his chosen audience, and aboveboard about his intentions.

My work will use everything that it can to communicate. It will use any trick; it'll do anything—absolutely anything—to communicate and to win the viewer over.... What you have to do is exploit yourself and take the responsibility to victimize others. It's time that we regain everything that we had—all our powers—and exploit that.[27]

What I find most exasperating about Koons is his simultaneous cynicism and naïvity. He embraces the segment of the current art world that is overstimulated and hyped-up as though it were an absolute given with no options, as though no alternative ever existed, could exist, or will exist. His, and most of the Simulationists', art (except Ebner's), places artworks in the same realm as other commodities and reduces them to emblems of rank, power, and authority, which is one realm in which art has always functioned, but only one. I find this one-dimensional reading of art incredibly naïve. And the wholehearted swallowing of post-structuralist simulacra reeks to me of superficial sloganism. For most Simulationists, novelty passes for newness. Simulationism is not Bouguereau and the Pre-Raphaelites recapitulated, it's the Photo-Realism of the 1980s.

Epilogue

From the necessary organization of this book into succeeding chapters it might appear that the only contemporary art being made at this moment is Simulationism, but most of the artists discussed in this book are still making art in the 1990s. Some are no longer living—Andy Warhol, Joseph Beuys, Scott Burton, and Keith Haring, for example—but most continue to make the same quality of art which originally made their reputations.

Because of the brevity of this book, I have emphasized art produced at the time of each artist's first significant recognition. I would have preferred to have been able to deal with each artist's career more in its entirety—for example, to have brought the art of Sol LeWitt, Bruce Nauman, John Baldessari, William Wegman, Richard Serra, and Jonathan Borofsky up to date. But I will have to reserve that pleasure for another, longer treatment.

The closer we come to the present, the more opinions appear in my discussion. No consensus has yet been reached about the art of the most recent past. Differences of opinions, endemic to contemporary art, particularly abound regarding the most recent art. The opinions I have expressed are not unique to me—they are held by at least as many influential art critics and historians as are the opposing views—but I have stated them as opinions to make it clear that a consensus has not yet been reached.

Even if a consensus had been reached—as in the majority of the views expressed in this book—opinions are all there are in making judgments about art, particularly contemporary art; there is no empirical way to measure quality. This is one of the reasons why contemporary art continues to fascinate me: there is always an opportunity to see something new that changes one's views.

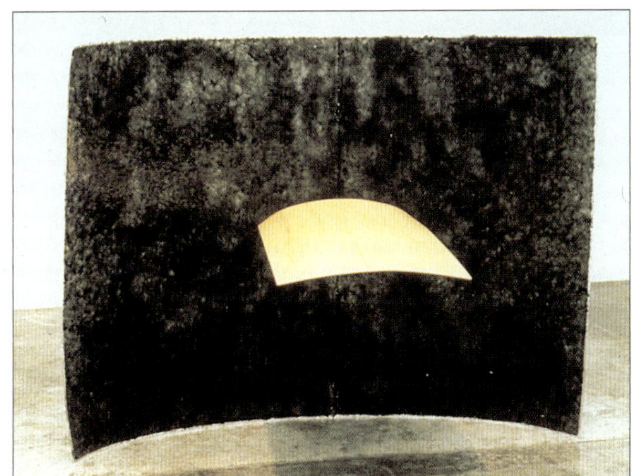

TOM BUTTER
Levity 1988
Wood on fiberglass
48 × 69 × 31ins
(122 × 175.3 × 78.7cm)
Courtesy Curt Marcus
Gallery, New York

Notes

INTRODUCTION

1 Brydon Smith, *Donald Judd*. Ottawa: National Gallery of Canada, exhibition catalogue, May 24–July 6, 1975, plus catalogue raisonne, 1960–1974, p. 25.

2 RoseLee Goldberg, *Performance: Live Art 1909 to the Present*. New York: Harry N. Abrams, Inc., 1979, p. 80.

3 Ibid., p. 82.

4 Calvin Tomkins, *Off the Wall: The Art World of Our Time*. Garden City, New York: Doubleday and Company, 1980, p. 149.

5 Ibid., p. 152.

6 Claes Oldenburg, *Store Days*, New York: Something Else Press, 1967, p. 39.

7 Goldberg, op. cit., p. 85.

8 Tomkins, op. cit., p. 154.

9 Barbara Haskell, *BLAM! The Explosion of Pop, Minimalism, and Performance: 1958–1964*. New York: Whitney Museum of American Art in association with W. W. Norton and Company, 1984, p. 49.

10 Ibid.

11 Ibid.

12 Ibid., p. 59.

13 Goldberg, op. cit., p. 90.

14 Ibid., p. 92.

15 Altogether, there are thirteen examples of the *Bottle Rack*. The 1914 version was "lost;" the second version dates from 1921 and is in the Robert Lebel collection; the third version dates from 1961 and was owned by the late Man Ray; the fourth version dates from 1961 and is owned by Robert Rauschenberg; the fifth version dates from 1963 and belongs to Ulf Linde in Stockholm; the sixth through thirteenth versions are in an edition of eight issued by the Galeria Schwarz, Milan, in 1964. Anne D'Harnoncourt and Kynastan McShine, eds, *Marcel Duchamp*.

New York and Philadelphia: The Museum of Modern Art and the Philadelphia Museum of Art, 1973, p. 275.

16 David Bourdon, "The Razed Sites of Carl Andre," *Artforum*, Volume V, No. 2 (October 1966), p. 17.

17 Peter Schjeldahl, *Art of Our Time: The Saatchi Collection*, Volume I, London: Lund Humphries (in association with Rizzoli, New York), p. 11.

18 Rosalind E. Krauss, *The Originality of the Avant-Garde and Other Modernist Myths*. Cambridge, Mass.: MIT Press, 1985, pp. 280–82.

19 Carl Andre, in *Carl Andre*. New York: The Solomon R. Guggenheim Museum, exhibition catalogue, 1970. p. 6.

20 Smith, op. cit., p. 25.

21 Ibid., p. 11.

22 Ibid., p. 28.

23 Ibid., p. 30.

24 Lucy R. Lippard stated, "Since his work is characterized by content and dynamic change rather than by perceptual stasis and neutralization, he has also subverted the canons of the 'minimal' art with which it has been associated." Alicia Legg, ed., *Sol LeWitt*, The Museum of Modern Art, New York, 1978, p. 23. Peter Schjeldahl wrote, "If Sol LeWitt, my own favourite Minimalist, had never created anything but his wall-drawing ideas—sets of written instructions capable of being executed by anyone almost anywhere—his eminence would be assured." Peter Schjeldahl, *Art of Our Time: The Saatchi Collection*, Volume I. London: Lund Humphries (in association with Rizzoli, New York), 1984, p. 20.

25 Legg, ed., *Sol LeWitt*, op. cit., p. 166.

26 Ibid., Robert Rosenblum, "Notes on Sol LeWitt," p. 18.

Chapter 1: CONCEPTUAL ART

1 Sol LeWitt, "Sentences on Conceptual Art," *Art Language*, May, 1969, reprinted in Alicia Legg, ed., *Sol LeWitt*. New York: The Museum of Modern Art, exhibition catalogue, 1978, p. 168.

2 Andy Grundberg and Kathleen McCarthy Gauss, *Photography and Art: Interactions Since 1946*. New York: Abbeville Press, 1987, pp. 135–36.

3 Ursula Meyer, *Conceptual Art*. New York: E. P. Dutton and Co., Inc., 1972, p. ix, quoting Marcel Duchamp's statement at a conference during the "Assemblage" Exhibition, The Museum of Modern Art, 1961.

4 John Coplans, "Concerning 'Various Small Fires': Ed Ruscha Discusses His Perplexing Publications,"*Artforum*, February, 1965, p. 25.

5 Ibid.

6 Douglas Davis, "From Common Sense, Mr. Ruscha Evokes Art," *National Observer*, July 28, 1969, quoted in Meyer, op. cit., p. XIV.

7 Bruce Nauman took a master's degree in art at the University of California at Davis (1965–66), studying under William T. Wiley whose penchant for punning apparently influenced him. In the summer of 1966 Nauman moved to San Francisco where he taught a course at the San Francisco Art Institute. In 1968 he had his first show at the Leo Castelli Gallery in New York City, and in 1969 he moved to Pasadena, California (near Los Angeles). From 1979 until 1990 he lived in Pecos, New Mexico. Currently, he lives in Galisteo, New Mexico.

8 Jane Livingston and Marcia Tucker, *Bruce Nauman*. Los Angeles: Los Angeles County Museum of Art, exhibition catalogue, 1972, p. 11.

9 Joe Raffaele and Elizabeth Baker, "The Way Out West: Interviews with 4 San Francisco Artists," *Art News*, Summer 1967, p. 75.

10 Livingston, op. cit., p. 15.

11 Grundberg, op. cit., p. 137.

12 John Baldessari, *John Baldessari*, with essays by Marcia Tucker and Robert Pincus-Witten and an interview by Nancy Drew. New York: The New Museum, exhibition catalogue, 1981, p. 65.

13 Ibid., p. 8.

14 Ibid., p. 10.

15 Ibid., p. 15, and Abraham Moses, *Information Theory and Esthetic Perception*. Chicago: University of Illinois Press, 1968, p. 128.

16 Ibid., p. 17.

17 Ibid., p. 37.

18 Grundberg, op. cit., p. 137.

19 Carl Andre, "A Note on Bernhard and Hilla Becher," *Artforum*, December, 1972, p. 59.

20 Brenda Richardson, *Gilbert and George*. Baltimore: The Baltimore Museum of Art, 1984, p. 8.

21 Ibid., p. 38.

22 April Kingsley, ed., "Concept Vs. Art Object: A Conversation between Douglas Huebler and Budd Hopkins," *Arts Magazine*, April, 1972, p. 50.

23 April Kingsley, "Douglas Huebler," *Artforum*, May, 1972, p. 78.

24 Kingsley, ed., op. cit., p. 53.

25 Ibid., p. 52.

26 Ibid., p. 51.

27 Meyer, op. cit., p. 137.

28 Jeanne Siegel, "An Interview with Hans Haacke," *Arts Magazine*, May, 1971, p. 20.

29 Thomas M. Messer, "Guest Editorial," *Arts Magazine*, June, 1971, pp. 4–5.

30 Lisa Lyons and Kim Levin, *Wegman's World*. Minneapolis: Walker Art Center, exhibition catalogue, 1983, p. 10.

31 Ibid., pp. 25–27.

32 David L. Shirey, "Impossible Art: What It Is," ("Thinkworks"), *Art in America*, May, 1969, p. 41.

33 Jack Burnham, "Alice's Head: Reflections on Conceptual Art," *Artforum*, February, 1970, p. 43.

34 Bruce Kurtz, "Interview with Guiseppe Panza di Biumo," *Arts Magazine*, March, 1972, pp. 42–43.

35 Robert Pincus-Witten, "Mel Bochner: The Constant as Variable," *Artforum*, December, 1972, p. 32.

36 Ibid., pp. 32–34.

37 Bruce Kurtz, "Documenta V: A Critical Preview," *Arts Magazine*, Summer 1972, p. 38.

38 Sol LeWitt, "Wall Drawings," reprinted from *Arts Magazine*, April 1970, in Alicia Legg, ed., essays by Lucy R. Lippard, Bernice Rose, and Robert Rosenblum, *Sol LeWitt*. New York: The Museum of Modern Art, exhibition catalogue, 1978, p. 169.

39 Sol LeWitt, "On Wall Drawings," *Sol LeWitt*. The Hague, Netherlands: Haags Gemeentemuseum, exhibition catalogue, 1970, p. 61.

40 Sol LeWitt, "All Wall Drawings," *Arts Magazine*, February, 1972, p. 44.

41 Ibid.

42 Lawrence Alloway, "Sol LeWitt: Modules, Walls, Books," *Artforum*, April, 1975, p. 39.

43 Sol LeWitt, *Sol LeWitt Wall Drawings 1968–1984*. Amsterdam: the Stedelijk Museum; Eindhoven, Holland: Van Abbemuseum; and Hartford, Connecticut: the Wadsworth Atheneum, 1984, p. 101.

44 Sol LeWitt, "Sentences on Conceptual Art," *Art-Language*, May, 1969, reprinted in Legg, ed., op. cit., p. 168.

45 Legg, op. cit., "Notes on Sol LeWitt," by Robert Rosenblum, p. 19.

46 Ibid., p. 15.

Chapter 2: VIDEO, FILM AND PERFORMANCE ART

1 Douglas Davis and Allison Simmons, eds, *The New Television: A Public/Private Art*. Cambridge, Mass.: The MIT Press, 1977, p. 110.

2 Marshall McLuhan, *Understanding Media: The Extensions of Man*. New York: Signet, 1964, p. 23.

3 Though our ears are in fixed positions on our heads, our heads are normally in constant motion. In fact, our eyes are also normally in constant motion, perceiving the world in a series of glimpses that our brain synthesizes into composite images, a fact that the Cubist painters took into account when they broke down the fixed point of view of Renaissance linear perspective. The sequential movement of our eyes in a one-thing-at-a-time linear pattern is actually a trained, unnatural perceptual pattern requiring learning and concentration. People more accustomed to perceiving auditory and tactile sensations find it difficult—even impossible—to structure their perceptual patterns in the linear sequences that reading requires. For many people who watched television and listened to music long before they learned to read, and thus established contrary perceptual patterns, print with its linear sequentiality is not their favored medium.

4 Barbara Haskell, *BLAM! The Explosion of Pop, Minimalism, and Performance 1958–64*. New York: Whitney Museum of American Art in association with W. W. Norton and Company, exhibition catalogue, 1984, p. 134.

5 Stephen Koch, *Stargazer: Andy Warhol's World and His Films*. New York: Praeger, 1973, p. 60.

6 Ibid., p. 23.

7 RoseLee Goldberg, *Performance Art: Live Art 1909 to the Present*. New York: Harry N. Abrams, 1979, p. 96.

8 Much of the discussion of Nam June Paik is excerpted from the author's essay, "PaikVision," *Artforum*, October, 1982, pp. 52–55.

9 John G. Hanhardt, *Nam June Paik*, with essays by Dieter Ronte, Michael Nyman, John G. Hanhardt, and David A. Ross. New York: Whitney Museum of American Art in association with W. W. Norton & Company, exhibition catalogue, 1982, p. 102.

10 Some of the discussion of Joan Jonas is excerpted from two of the author's earlier essays: "The Present Tense," in Ira Schneider and Beryl Korot, eds, *Video Art: An Anthology*, copyright © 1976 by The Raindance Foundation, Inc., reprinted by permission of Harcourt Brace Jovanovich, Inc., pp. 234–43; and "Video is Being Invented," *Arts Magazine*, December/January, 1973, pp. 37–44.

11 Joan Jonas (with Rosalind Krauss), "Seven Years," *The Drama Review*, March, 1975, p. 13.

12 Kurtz, "The Present Tense," in Schneider/Korot, op. cit., pp. 239–40.

13 Davis/Simmons, op. cit., p. 110.

14 Lizzie Borden, videotape descriptions in *Castelli-Sonnabend Videotapes and Films*. New York: Castelli-Sonnabend Tapes and Films, Inc., 1974, p. 26.

15 Some of this discussion of Wegman is excerpted from the author's "Video is Being Invented," *Arts Magazine*, December/January, 1973, pp. 37–44.

16 Some of the discussion of Peter Campus is excerpted from the author's "Fields," *Arts Magazine*, May/June, 1973, pp. 25–29.

17 Ibid., p. 26.

18 Bruce Nauman, "Bruce Nauman: Interview," *Avalanche*, Winter, 1971, p. 25.

19 Annette Michelson, "Toward Snow," *Artforum*, June, 1971, p. 31.

20 Ibid., p. 33.

21 Richard Serra, "Richard Serra: Interview," *Avalanche*, Winter, 1971, p. 20.

22 Richard Serra, *Castelli-Sonnabend Videotapes and Films*, 1976–77 Supplement. New York: Castelli-Sonnabend Videotapes and Films, Inc., 1977, p. SS 40.

23 RoseLee Goldberg, *Performance: Live Art 1909 to the Present*. New York: Harry N. Abrams, 1979, p. 100.

24 Ibid.

25 Ursula Meyer, *Conceptual Art*. New York: E. P. Dutton and Co., Inc., 1972, p. 3.

26 Brenda Richardson, *Gilbert and George*. Baltimore, Maryland: The Baltimore Museum of Art, exhibition catalogue, 1984, p. 18.

27 Robert Horwitz, "Chris Burden," *Artforum*, May, 1976, p. 27.

28 Bruce Kurtz, "Artists' Video at the Crossroads," *Art in America*, January/February, 1977, p. 37.

29 Ibid., p. 39.

Chapter 3: EARTHWORKS AND SITE-SPECIFIC SCULPTURE

1 Robert Hobbs, *Robert Smithson: Sculpture*. Ithaca and London: Cornell University Press, 1981, p. 45.

2 Michael Heizer, "The Art of Michael Heizer," *Artforum*, December 1969, p. 34.

3 Nancy Holt, ed., *The Writings of Robert Smithson*. New York: New York University Press, 1979. "Conversation with Robert Smithson on April 22nd 1972," edited by Bruce Kurtz, p. 200.

4 Heizer, op. cit., p. 36.

5 Holt, ed., op. cit., p. 203.

6 Ibid.

7 Bruce Kurtz, "Last Call at Max's," *Artforum*, April, 1981, p. 28.

8 Holt, ed., op. cit., "Interview with Robert Smithson for the Archives of American Art/Smithsonian Institute," interview conducted by Paul Cummings on July 14 and 19, 1972, p. 153.

9 Holt, ed., op. cit., "The Spiral Jetty," by Robert Smithson, p. 113.

10 Hobbs, op. cit., "The Monuments of Passaic," by Robert Smithson, p. 94, reprinted from *Artforum*, December, 1967.

11 Holt, ed., op. cit., "The Spiral Jetty," by Robert Smithson, p. 111.

12 Hobbs, op. cit., "Robert Smithson, The *Amarillo Ramp*," by John Coplans, p. 54.

13 Holt, ed., op. cit., p. 115.

14 Ibid., "The Monuments of Passaic," by Robert Smithson, p. 90, reprinted from *Artforum*, December, 1967,

15 Hobbs, op. cit., p. 43.

16 Ibid., p. 193.

17 Ibid., p. 45.

18 Ibid., p. 48.

19 Michael Heizer, *Michael Heizer: Sculpture in Reverse*. Los Angeles: The Museum of Contemporary Art, 1984, p. 26.

20 Ibid., pp. 26–27.

21 Ibid.

22 Ibid., p. 36.

23 Ibid., pp. 36–37.

24 Ibid., p. 10.

25 Ibid., p. 16.

26 Ibid., p. 79.

27 Ibid., pp. 36–37.

28 Ibid., p. 33.

29 Elizabeth C. Baker, "Artworks on the Land," *Art in America*, January, 1976, p. 95.

30 Hobbs, op. cit., p. 54.

31 Walter De Maria, "The Lightning Field," *Artforum*, April, 1980, p. 58.

32 Cornell University, *Earth Art*. Ithaca, New York: Andrew Dickson White Museum of Art, exhibition catalogue, 1970, unpaginated.

33 Robert Morris, "Three Extra-Visual Artists: Works in Progress," *Artforum*, January, 1971, p. 28.

34 Robert Morris, "Aligned with Nazca," *Artforum*, October, 1975, p. 33.

35 Ibid.

36 Richard Serra, "Shift," edited by Rosalind Krauss, *Arts Magazine*, April, 1973, p. 50.

37 Ibid.

38 Ibid., p. 51.

39 Nancy Holt, "Sun Tunnels," *Artforum*, April, 1977, p. 35.

40 Ibid.

41 Hugh M. Davies and Ronald J. Onorato, *Sitings: Alice Aycock, Richard Fleischner, Mary Miss, George Trakas*. La Jolla, California: La Jolla Museum of Contemporary Art, 1986, p. 110.

42 Ibid., pp. 39–40.

43 Christo, *The Running Fence Project: Christo*. New York: Harry N. Abrams, Inc., 1980, unpaginated.

44 Laurence Weschler, *Seeing is Forgetting the Name of the Thing One Sees: A Life of Contemporary Artist Robert Irwin*. Berkeley: University of California Press, 1982, p. 101.

45 Ibid., p. 106.

46 Ibid., p. 99.

47 Laurence Weschler, "Profiles: Taking Art to Point Zero—II," *New*

Yorker, March 15, 1982, p. 80.
48 Robert Irwin, *Being and Circumstance: Notes Toward a Conditional Art*. Larkspur Landing, California: The Lapis Press, 1985, pp. 26–27.
49 Ibid., p. 95.
50 Ibid., p. 96.
51 Julia Brown, ed., *Occluded Front: James Turrell*. Los Angeles: Museum of Contemporary Art and The Lapis Press, 1985, p. 14.
52 Ibid., p. 43.
53 Ibid., p. 22.
54 Ibid., p. 42.

Chapter 4: POST-MINIMALISM

1 Lucy Lippard, *Eva Hesse*. New York: New York University Press, 1976, p. 56.
2 Robert Pincus-Witten, *Post Minimalism*. London: Out of London Press, 1977, pp. 15–16.
3 Lippard, op. cit., p. 70.
4 Richard Armstrong, *Artschwager, Richard*. New York: Whitney Museum of American Art in Association with W. W. Norton and Company, 1988, p. 17.
5 Ibid., quoting from Jan DeVitt, "The Object: Still Life. Interviews with New Object Makers, Richard Artschwager and Claes Oldenburg, on Craftsmanship, Art, and Function," *Craft Horizons*, September–October, 1965, p. 54.
6 Ibid.
7 Armstrong, op. cit., p. 45.
8 Coosje van Bruggen, "Richard Artschwager," *Artforum*, September, 1983, p. 45.
9 Lucas Samaras, *Lucas Samaras*. New York: Whitney Museum of American Art, exhibition catalogue, 1972, unpaginated.
10 Kim Levin, *Lucas Samaras*. New York: Harry N. Abrams, Inc., 1975, p. 51.
11 Ibid., p. 15.
12 Samaras, op. cit., unpaginated.
13 Levin, op. cit., p. 37.
14 Ibid., pp. 19–20.
15 Ibid., p. 20.
16 Ibid., pp. 45–46.
17 Ibid., p. 27.
18 Samaras, op. cit., unpaginated.
19 Lippard, op. cit., p. 197.
20 Robert Pincus-Witten and Linda Shearer, *Eva Hesse: A Memorial Exhibition*. New York: Solomon R. Guggenheim Museum, exhibition catalogue, 1972, "Eva Hesse: Last Works," by Linda Shearer, unpaginated.
21 Lippard, op. cit., p. 86.
22 Ibid., p. 56.
23 Ibid., p. 83.
24 Pincus-Witten and Shearer, op. cit., unpaginated.
25 Lippard, op. cit., p. 56.
26 Ibid., p. 56.
27 Pincus-Witten and Shearer, op. cit., unpaginated.
28 Ibid.
29 Lippard, op. cit., p. 96.
30 Pincus-Witten and Shearer, op. cit., unpaginated.
31 Ibid.
32 Ibid.
33 Robert Pincus-Witten, "Keith Sonnier: Materials and Pictorialism," *Artforum*, October, 1969, p. 44; reprinted in Pincus-Witten, *Post-Minimalism*, op. cit., p. 39.
34 Ibid., p. 40 (p. 35 in *Post-Minimalism*).
35 Ibid., p. 40 (quoted from Lippard's essay about the 1966 Fishbach Gallery *Eccentric Abstraction* show she organized) (p. 35 in *Post-Minimalism*).
36 Emily Wasserman, "Group Show, Bykert Gallery," (review), *Artforum*, September, 1969, p. 59.
37 Ibid.
38 Pincus-Witten, *Post-Minimalism*, op. cit., p. 153.
39 Ibid., p. 151.
40 Richard Serra, *Richard Serra: Interviews, Etc., 1970–1980*, written and compiled in collaboration with Clara Weyergraf. Yonkers, New York: The Hudson River Museum, 1980, "Interview: Richard Serra and Bernard Lamarche-Vadel, New York City, May, 1980," p. 138.
41 Ibid., "Play it Again, Sam," first published in *Arts Magazine*, February, 1970, pp. 15–16.
42 Pincus-Witten, *Post-Minimalism*, op. cit., p. 30.
43 Robert Morris, "Anti-Form," *Artforum*, April, 1968, p. 35.
44 Ibid., p. 34.
45 Pincus-Witten, *Post-Minimalism*, op. cit., p. 122.
46 Jane Livingston, "Barry Le Va: Distributional Sculpture," *Artforum*, November, 1968, p. 54.
47 Emily Wasserman, "Alan Saret, Bykert Gallery," (review), *Artforum*, January, 1969, p. 59.
48 Richard Armstrong, "Alan Saret, Daniel Weinberg Gallery," (review), *Artforum*, February, 1980, p. 106.
49 John Gruen, "Jackie Winsor: Eloquence of a 'Yankee Pioneer'," *Art News*, March, 1979, p. 58.
50 Robert Pincus-Witten, "Winsor Knots: The Sculpture of Jackie Winsor," *Arts Magazine*, June, 1977, p. 131.
51 Gruen, op. cit., p. 58.
52 Pincus-Witten, op. cit., p. 130.
53 Emily Wasserman, "Richard Tuttle, Betty Parsons Gallery," (review), *Artforum*, March, 1968, p. 57.
54 Roberta Smith, "Richard Tuttle, Whitney Museum of American Art," (review), *Artforum*, January, 1976, p. 61.
55 Richard Marshall and Roberta Smith, *Joel Shapiro*. New York: Whitney Museum of American Art, exhibition catalogue, 1982, p. 19.
56 Ibid., pp. 17–18.
57 Ibid., p. 96.
58 Ibid., p. 19.
59 Ibid., p. 96.
60 Ibid., p. 101.

Chapter 5: PLURALISM

1 Richard Marshall, *New Image Painting*. New York: Whitney Museum of American Art, exhibition catalogue, 1978, p. 14.
2 *Philip Pearlstein: Paintings and Watercolors*, John and Mabel Ringling Museum of Art, essay by Michael Auping, p. 3.
3 Frank H. Goodyear, Jr., *Contemporary American Realism Since 1960*. Boston: New York Graphic Society, 1981, p. 72.
4 Kirk Varnedoe, *Duane Hanson*. New York: Harry N. Abrams, Inc., 1985, p. 24.
5 Gregory Battcock, ed., *Super Realism: A Critical Anthology*. New York: E. P. Dutton, Inc., 1975, "Reality Again," by Harold Rosenberg, p. 138.

6 Varnedoe, op. cit., p. 25.
7 Battcock, ed., op. cit., Kim Levin, "Post-Style Illusionism," p. 177.
8 Lisa Lyons and Robert Storr, *Chuck Close*. New York: Rizzoli, 1987, p. 28.
9 Ibid.
10 Ibid.
11 Battcock, op. cit., William Dykes, "The Photo as Subject: The Paintings and Drawings of Chuck Close," p. 161.
12 Louis K. Meisel, *Richard Estes: The Complete Paintings 1966–85*. New York: Harry N. Abrams, Inc., 1986, p. 19.
13 Ibid., p. 17.
14 Cindy Nemser, "Conversation with Audrey Flack," *Arts Magazine*, February, 1974, p. 37.
15 Corinne Robins, *The Pluralist Era: American Art 1968–81*. New York: Harper and Row, 1984, p. 140.
16 John Perreault, "Issues in Pattern Painting," *Artforum*, November, 1977, p. 33.
17 *Judy Pfaff: Autonomous Objects*. Charlotte, South Carolina: Knight Gallery, exhibition catalogue, essay by Robert Smith, p. 2.
18 Robins, op. cit., p. 142.
19 Ibid.
20 Marshall, op. cit., p. 14.
21 Dupuy Warrick Reed, "Nicholas Africano: Responsible Relevance," *Arts Magazine*, June, 1969, p. 158.
22 Mark Rosenthal, "The Ascendance of Subject Matter and a 1960s Sensibility," *Arts Magazine*, June, 1982, p. 92.
23 Marshall, op. cit., p. 38.
24 Lisbet Nilson, "Susan Rothenberg: Every Brushstroke Is a Surprise," *Art News*, February, 1984, p. 51.
25 Ibid., pp. 50–51.
26 Susan Rothenberg, "Susan Rothenberg," (artist's statement), *Art in America*, December, 1982, p. 65.

Chapter 6: NEO-EXPRESSIONISM

1 Francesco Clemente, *Clemente*, "An Interview with Francesco Clemente," by Rainer Crone and Georgia Marsh. New York: Vintage Books, 1987, pp. 46–47.
2 Calvin Tomkins, "Profiles: A Good Eye and a Good Ear," *The New Yorker*, May 26, 1980, p. 40.
3 Peter Schjeldahl's essay about Philip Guston in *Art of Our Time: The Saatchi Collection*, Volume 3 (London: Lund Humphries, 1984) is the source of this idea. For example: "I could not take seriously Guston's reversal of the modernist's priority—the subordination of every element to an aesthetic unity—so I got his work backward, failing to see the purposes of its disunity." p. 13. And, "The fundamental question Guston addressed was not how or what to paint, but *why*: the need for a reason sufficient to each painting and inescapably evident in each painting. Nothing else could recover conviction for an art gutted by the burn-out of modernist ideals." p. 14.
4 Ibid., p. 12.
5 Robert Storr, *Philip Guston*. New York: Abbeville Press, 1986, p. 52.
6 Ibid.
7 Ibid., p. 53.
8 *A New Spirit in Painting*, essay by Christos M. Jaochimides. London: Royal Academy of Arts, exhibition catalogue, 1981, p. 14.
9 Schjeldahl, op. cit., p. 13.
10 Storr, op. cit., p. 81.
11 Lynn Gumpert and Ned Rifkin, *Golub*, New York: The New Museum of Contemporary Art, exhibition catalogue, 1984, p. 57.
12 Gary Indiana, "Disasters in the Sandbox," *Art in America*, May, 1984, p. 114.
13 Michael R. Klein, "Traveling in Styles," *Art News*, March, 1983, p. 90.
14 Klaus Kertess, "Malcolm Morley: Talking about Seeing," *Artforum*, Summer, 1980, p. 48.
15 Ibid.
16 Hilton Kramer, "Malcolm Morley," in *Art of Our Time: The Saatchi Collection*, Volume 3, p. 21.
17 Mark Rosenthal and Richard Marshall, *Jonathan Borofsky*. Philadelphia and New York: Philadelphia Museum of Art in association with the Whitney Museum of American Art, exhibition catalogue, 1984, p. 105.
18 Ibid., p. 28.
19 Rene Ricard, "Julian Schnabel's Plate Painting at Mary Boone," *Art in America*, November, 1979, p. 126.
20 Ibid., p. 125.
21 Lisbet Nilson, "Making it Neo," *Art News*, September, 1983, p. 62.
22 Ibid., p. 67.
23 Robert Hughes, "Rip-Off Artist," *The New Republic*, December 14, 1987, pp. 28 and 30.
24 Rene Ricard, "Not About Julian Schnabel," *Artforum*, Summer, 1981, pp. 80 and 79.
25 Gerald Marzorati, "Julian Schnabel: Plate It as It Lays," *Art News*, April, 1985, p. 66.
26 Julian Schnabel, "The Patients and the Doctors," *Artforum*, February, 1984, p. 56.
27 Hilton Kramer, "Julian Schnabel," *Art of Our Time: The Saatchi Collection*, Volume 3, p. 28.
28 Thomas Lawson, "Last Exit: Painting," *Artforum*, October, 1981, p. 42.
29 Donald Kuspit, "David Salle at Mary Boone Gallery," *Artforum*, November, 1985, p. 103.
30 David Salle, *Salle* (an interview with David Salle by Peter Schjeldahl). New York: Vintage Books, 1987, p. 22.
31 Kim Levin, "Joseph Beuys: The New Order," *Arts Magazine*, April, 1980, pp. 154–55.
32 Peter Schjeldahl, "Anselm Kiefer," in *Art of Our Time: The Saatchi Collection*, Volume 3, p. 15.
33 Ibid.
34 Ibid., p. 17.
35 Robert Pincus-Witten, "Georg Baselitz: From Nolde to Kandinsky to Matisse, A Speculative History of Recent German Painting," *Arts Magazine*, June, 1986, p. 34.
36 Donald B. Kuspit, "Pandemonium: The Root of Georg Baselitz's Imagery," *Arts Magazine*, June, 1986, p. 25.
37 Clemente, op. cit., p. 26.
38 Michael Auping, *Francesco Clemente*. New York: The John and

Mable Ringling Museum of Art in association with Harry N. Abrams, Inc., 1985, p. 20.

39 Clemente, op. cit., p. 60.

40 Ibid.

41 Ibid., p. 7.

42 Ibid., pp. 46–47.

43 Carter Ratcliff, "On Iconography and Some Italians," *Art in America*, September, 1982, p. 153.

44 Eleanor Heartney, "Apocalyptic Visions, Arcadian Dreams," *Art News*, January, 1986, p. 89.

Chapter 7: POST-MODERNISM

1 Keith Haring (interview).

2 Leo Steinberg, *Other Criteria: Confrontations with Twentieth Century Art*. London, Oxford, and New York: Oxford University Press, 1972, p. 84.

3 Christopher Knight "Ruscha in Context: In the Beginning Was the Word," in Lannan Museum, *Edward Ruscha*. Lake Worth, Florida: distributed by Harry N. Abrams, Inc., New York, 1987, pp. 43–59, and Christopher Knight, "Censorship and Photography's 150th," *Los Angeles Times*, December 17, 1989.

4 Jean Baudrillard, "The Ecstasy of Communication," in *The Anti-Aesthetic: Essays on Postmodern Culture*, edited by Hal Foster. Port Townsend, Washington: Bay Press, 1983, p. 128.

5 Ibid., p. 133.

6 Cindy Sherman, *Cindy Sherman*, with an introduction by Peter Schjeldahl and an afterword by I. Michael Danoff. New York: Pantheon Books, 1984, p. 10.

7 Ibid., p. 195.

8 Barbara Kruger, *We won't play nature to your culture*, with essays by Craig Owens and Jane Weinstock. London and Basel: Institute of Contemporary Art and Kunsthalle, 1983, exhibition catalogue, p. 13.

9 Ibid., p. 5.

10 Ibid., these ideas about stereotypes are from Craig Owens' essay, "The Medusa Effect or, The Spectacular Ruse," pp. 5–11.

11 Benjamin H. D. Buchloh, "Allegorical Procedures: Appropriation and Montage in Contemporary Art," *Artforum*, September, 1982, p. 44.

12 Roland Barthes, *The Fashion System*, translated by M. Ward and R. Howard, New York: Hill and Wang, 1983, p. 266.

13 Jenny Holzer, *Jenny Holzer: Signs*. Des Moines, Iowa: Des Moines Art Center, 1986, exhibition catalogue, with essay by Joan Simon, p. 67.

14 Ibid., p. 75.

15 Jeanne Siegel, "After Sherrie Levine," *Arts Magazine*, June, 1985, p. 141.

16 Ibid., p. 142.

17 Ibid., p. 141.

18 Benjamin H. D. Buchloh, "Allegorical Procedures: Appropriation and Montage in Contemporary Art," *Artforum*, September, 1982, p. 52.

19 Ibid.

20 Ibid.

21 Brenda Richardson, *Scott Burton*. Baltimore: The Baltimore Museum of Art, exhibition catalogue, 1986, p. 10.

22 Ibid., p. 49.

23 Eric Fischl, *Eric Fischl*, an interview conducted by Donald Kuspit. New York: Vintage Books, 1987, p. 46.

24 Robert Morris, *Robert Morris: Works of the Eighties*, with essays by Edward F. Fry and Donald P. Kuspit and contributions by I. Michael Danoff, Mary Jane Jacob and Paul Schimmel. Chicago and Newport Beach, California: Museum of Contemporary Art and Newport Harbor Art Museum, 1986, p. 14.

25 Christopher Knight, "L.A. Art Star Has a Stroke of Ingenious Reinvention," *Los Angeles Herald Examiner*, February 22, 1987, p. E 6.

26 Ibid.

27 Ibid.

28 Ibid., p. E 1.

29 Mike Kelley, "Mike Kelley," (interview), *Art in America*, May, 1987, p. 197.

30 Gregory Battcock, ed., *The Art of Performance: A Critical Anthology*. New York: E. P. Dutton, 1984, Bob La Frenais, "An Interview with Laurie Anderson," p. 257.

31 Tony Cokes, "Laurie Anderson at the 57th Street Playhouse," *Art in America*, July, 1986, p. 120.

Chapter 8: SCULPTURE OF THE 1980s

1 "Sculptors' Interviews: Tom Butter," *Art in America*, November, 1985, p. 112.

2 John Caldwell, *Richard Deacon*, with essays by Lynne Cook, Richard Deacon, Michael Newman, and Peter Schjeldahl. Pittsburgh, Pennsylvania: The Carnegie Museum of Art, exhibition catalogue, 1988, p. 59.

3 Ibid., "Silence, Exile, Cunning," by Richard Deacon, p. 11.

4 Ibid., "The Tone of Labor," by Peter Schjeldahl, p. 60.

5 Ibid., p. 63.

6 Ibid., p. 61.

7 Andrew Graham-Dixon, "Cragg's Way," *Art News*, March, 1989, p. 137.

8 Ibid., p. 136.

9 Ibid., p. 137.

10 Steven Henry Madoff, "Sculpture Unbound," *Art News*, November, 1986, pp. 104–5.

11 Peter Clothier, "Peter Shelton: Dwellings in the Abstract," *Art News*, September, 1987, p. 83.

12 Ibid., p. 84.

13 *Enclosing the Void: Eight Contemporary Sculptors*, essay by Susan Lubowsky. Whitney Museum of American Art at Equitable Center, exhibition catalogue, 1989, p. 3.

14 Ibid., p. 4.

15 "Sculptors' Interviews: Roni Horn," *Art in America*, November, 1985, p. 120.

16 Ibid.

17 Ibid.

18 Ibid.

19 Ralph Rugoff, "An Impressive Group of Emerging Talents Extends the Limits of 'L.A. Art': The Wry Stuff," *L.A. Style*, March, 1988, p. 78.

20 *Sculpture Inside Outside*, introduction by Martin Friedman, essays by Douglas Dreishpoon, Nancy Princenthal, Carter Ratcliff,

and Joan Simon. Minneapolis and New York: Walker Art Center and Rizzoli, exhibition catalogue, 1988, p. 77.
21 "Sculptors' Interviews: Tom Butter," *Art in America*, November, 1985, p. 112.
22 George Melrod, "Carol Hepper Sheds Her Skin," *Sculpture Magazine*, May/June, 1989, p. 26.

Chapter 9: SIMULATIONISM
1 A. Robbins, "An Interview with Allan McCollum," *Arts Magazine*, October, 1985, p. 40.
2 Robert Pincus-Witten, "Entries: Concentrated Juice and Kitschy Kitschy Koons," *Arts Magazine*, February, 1989, p. 38.
3 Roberta Smith, "Rituals of Consumption," *Art in America*, May, 1988, p. 167.
4 Eleanor Heartney, "The Hot New Cool Art: Simulationism," *Art News*, January, 1987, p. 132.
5 Peter Schjeldahl, "A Visit to the Salon of Autumn 1986," *Art in America*, December, 1986, p. 20.
6 Ibid.
7 Catherine Francblin, "Interview with Jean Beaudrillard," *Flash Art*, October/November, 1986, p. 55.
8 Jeanne Siegel, "The Artist/Critic of the Eighties, Part One: Peter Halley and Stephen Westfall," *Arts Magazine*, September, 1985, p. 73.
9 Robbins, op. cit., p. 40.
10 Ibid., p. 43.
11 Ibid., p. 41.
12 Ibid., p. 44.
13 Shaun Caley, "Ashley Bickerton: A Revealing Expose of the Application of Art," *Flash Art*, November/December, 1988, p. 81.
14 Ibid.
15 "Fluid Mechanics: A Conversation Between Ashley Bickerton and Aimee Rankin (An Artist's Dialogue)," *Arts Magazine*, December, 1987, p. 82.
16 Caley, op. cit.
17 Peter Halley, *Collected Essays: 1981–87*. Zürich, Switzerland: Bruno Bischofberger, 1988, pp. 12–21.
18 Nancy Holt, ed., *The Writings of Robert Smithson*, "Conversation with Robert Smithson on April 22nd, 1972," edited by Bruce Kurtz. New York: New York University Press, 1979, p. 200.
19 Ibid.
20 Holland Cotter, "Haim Steinbach: Shelf Life," *Art in America*, May, 1988, p. 160.
21 Jeanne Siegel, "Jeff Koons: Unachievable States of Being," *Arts Magazine*, October, 1986, p. 68.
22 Klaus Kertess, "Bad," *Parkett*, Volume 19, 1989, p. 30.
23 Siegel, op. cit.
24 Kertess, op. cit.
25 Ibid., p. 34.
26 Siegel, op. cit., p. 71.
27 Jeff Koons, "From Full Fathom Five," *Parkett*, Volume 19, 1989, pp. 44–47.

CREDITS

The author, publishers and John Calmann and King Ltd wish to thank the artists, museums, galleries, collectors, and other owners who have kindly allowed works to be reproduced in this book. In general sources have been given on the captions but credits for photographers and other copyright holders are listed below.

0.1 Photo: Reunion des musees nationaux, Paris; 0.5 © Saatchi Collection, London; 0.6 Photo: Douglas M. Parker Studio, Margo Leavin Gallery, Los Angeles; 0.7, 0.10, 0.11, 0.13 Photos: Giorgio Colombo, Milan; page 28 Hulton Picture Library; page 29 Popperfoto; 1.1 Courtesy Ed Ruscha; 1.2, 1.4, 1.5, 1.6, 1.7 Copyright 1991 Bruce Nauman/ARS N.Y.; 1.5 © Saatchi Collection, London. Photo: Prudence Cuming Associates Ltd, London; 1.6 © Saatchi Collection, London; 1.10 Sonnabend Gallery, New York; 1.16 Holly and Horace Solomon, New York; 1.20 Photo: Giorgio Colombo, Milan; 1.23 Photographed by Robert E. Mates and Paul Katz; 2.1, 2.2 Copyright 1991 The Estate and Foundation of Andy Warhol/ARS N.Y.; 2.16 Photo: Giorgio Colombo, Milan. Copyright 1991 Bruce Nauman/ARS N.Y.; 2.17 Copyright 1991 Bruce Nauman/ARS N.Y.; 3.7 Photo: Gianfranco Gorgoni/Contact; 3.14, 3.16 Photo: John Cliett; 3.27 Photo: Danny Bersotti–Tim Fox; 3.28 Photo: Giorgio Colombo, Milan; 3.29 Photo by and copyright of, Dick Wiser; 4.3 Copyright 1991 Pollock-Krasner Foundation/ARS N.Y.; 4.4 © Saatchi Collection, London; 4.6 Photo: Kim Levin; 4.7 Photo: Bill Jacobson Studio; 4.8 Photo: Walter J. Russell; 4.13 Courtesy The Estate of Eva Hesse and Robert Miller Gallery; 4.20 Photo: David Heald; 4.21, 4.32 Photo: Giorgio Colombo, Milan; 4.26 Photo: Courtesy Paula Cooper Gallery, New York. Collection High Museum of Art, Atlanta, Georgia; purchase with funds from the National Endowment for the Arts and the Mekibero Guild; 4.29 Courtesy of the Greenberg Gallery, St. Louis; 4.30 Photo: Geoffrey Clements, New York. Installation photograph from the exhibition Richard Tuttle held at the Whitney Museum of American Art, 1975; page 142 Popperfoto; page 143 Hulton Picture Library; 5.2 Photo: Eeva-Inkeri; 5.3 Photo: Eric Pollitzer, New York; 5.4, 5.15 © Saatchi Collection, London; 5.13 Photo: Private Collection; page 164 Topham Picture Library; page 165 (top) Topham Picture Library, (bottom) Popperfoto; 6.3, 6.10 © Saatchi Collection, London; 6.13 Provenance: Sperone Westwater; 7.5 Courtesy Doris Saatchi, London; 7.7 © Saatchi Collection, London; 7.9 Photo: Craig Smith; 7.10 Photo: Rosamund Felsen Gallery; 8.6 Photo: Earl Pipling; 8.11 Photo: Eeva-Inkeri; 8.13 Photo: Bill Jacobson Studio.

Glossary

ABSTRACT The absence of visual resemblance to things in the physical world, often characterized by referring to the essence rather than the appearance of the subject.

ABSTRACT EXPRESSIONISM A style of painting that emerged in the United States in the late 1940s that is characterized by large-scale canvases, vast depicted space, and sweeping gestural brushwork. Jackson Pollock, Willem de Kooning, Franz Kline, and Hans Hoffman typified the style, while Barnett Newman and Mark Rothko were less gestural artists.

ACTION PAINTING A term used to describe the art of the more gestural Abstract Expressionists. It was said that the act of painting was their subject. The feeling of movement and rhythm in their brushwork described their actions as they painted. Jackson Pollock's "drip" paintings, in which he poured or flicked skeins of paint on a canvas laid on the floor, are a seismic record of his physical actions.

AESTHETIC Pertaining to a sense of the beautiful.

ANTHROPOMORPHISM The visual reference to, or representation of, the human body, no matter how abstract.

AVANT-GARDE Originating in France in the mid-nineteenth century, the concept that art opposes the majority culture. Instead, artists forge into uncharted artistic territories ahead of their audience's ability to understand their ideas. The term is French for a military scout.

BAROQUE The period in Europe from about 1600 to 1800, during which artists tended toward realism, ornateness, dramatization, strong light-and-dark contrasts, and vivid colors.

CLASSICISM Movements, periods, and impulses in Western art that prized qualities of harmony and formal restraint and claimed direct inspiration from Classical models. Traditionally contrasted with Romanticism.

COLLAGE A two-dimensional technique in which materials are attached to a flat surface.

COLOR FIELD PAINTING An abstract style of painting that emerged in the United States in the late 1950s that is characterized by large scale canvases with expanses of bright colors and the absence of spatial illusionism.

CONCEPTUAL ART An art style which emerged in the mid-1960s in which ideas are more important than visual appearances. Many Conceptual artists worked with the idea of making the artwork impermanent, thus dematerializing it.

CONSTRUCTIVISM An art movement that emerged in Russia in the 1910s and 1920s that is characterized by geometric abstraction and the practice of making sculptures by adding (or constructing) various materials together rather than carving, modeling, or casting.

CUBISM A style of painting originated by Pablo Picasso and Georges Braque in Paris in the 1910s that is characterized by the depiction of many different views of a subject simultaneously, combining them into one flat image. Three-dimensional forms were rendered in interlocking and overlapping flat planes, thereby creating a flat, grid-like surface.

EARTHWORKS Originating in the late 1960s, Earthworks are large-scale outdoor sculptures in which the surface of the earth is part of the medium.

FAUVISM An art movement led by Henri Matisse that originated in Paris in the first decade of the twentieth century and that was characterized by the use of bold colors and simplified shapes to visually locate things in space and to express their inner qualities rather than their superficial appearance.

FINE ARTS Painting, sculpture, drawing, printmaking, and certain uses of photography, as opposed to commercial art like advertising, movies, television, posters, package and product design.

FORMAL/FORMALIST A critical tendency in painting and sculpture to isolate purely visual phenomena as the sole subject or means that the artist uses, apart from any reference to things outside the artwork.

FOUND OBJECT An object that is presented as a work of art or as part of one, but which was not originally intended as art; also called an *objet trouvé*. It is an object that the artist finds rather than makes.

FUTURISM A movement initiated in Italy in 1909 to sweep aside all artistic conventions and capture the qualities of modern industrial life. The Futurists used the overlapping and interlocking planes of Cubism but added dynamic movement and bright colors.

GESSO In painting, a mixture of very fine plaster or chalk and glue that is applied to the canvas or other support. The purpose is to prevent the support from chemically reacting with the paint.

GESTALT The overall form of an artwork apart from its individual parts; or the overall, singular formal impression that an artwork conveys.

GESTURAL A style of painting or drawing in which the artist's arm and hand movements are apparent in the finished artwork.

GRAPHIC DESIGN The arts involved in creating two-dimensional images for commercial purposes. Graphic designers often work with type as well as illustrations; the printed surface may range from paper to fabrics.

GRISAILLE A style of painting using only greys usually characterized by sculptural modeling in light and dark.

HAPPENINGS A type of performance art that originated in the 1950s and that often combines visual art with music, dance, theater, literature, and innovative actions that defy categorization. They were often at least partially improvisational in nature, hence they just "happened."

IDEALIZED Art in which images conform more to ideal aesthetic standards than to real life.

IMPASTO The thickly built-up surface of a painting.

IMPRESSIONISM An art movement that developed in France in the 1860s and 1870s by artists who sought to capture the way light falls momentarily and fleetingly across contemporary subjects. Many Impressionists set their easels up out of doors and painted directly from nature. The surfaces of their paintings are often fragmented into dots and dashes of bright colors. Some of the major artists were Claude Monet, Edgar Degas, Auguste Renoir, and Camille Pissarro.

INSTALLATION PIECE Artworks in which the setting where they are seen is made by the artist to be an integral part of the work. Or, a three-dimensional designed environment set up (often temporarily) as a work of art.

INTERNATIONAL STYLE An architectural style, originating in Europe after World War I, characterized by rectangular forms, white walls, large windows, flat roofs, and the absence of ornamentation.

MANNERISM An artistic style in Italy from approximately 1525 to 1600 in which artists developed a more subjective, emotional, theatrical approach than in the preceding High Renaissance period.

MEDIUM 1. The material or means of expression with which the artist works. 2. The liquid solvent, such as water or linseed oil, in which pigment is suspended to make paint fluid and workable.

MINIMALISM An art movement of the 1960s and 1970s that emphasized repetitions of basic geometric forms such as cubes, rectangles, and triangles along with their relationship to both interior architectural spaces and the viewers' movement in space.

MIXED MEDIA The combined use of several different techniques—such as drawing, painting, and printmaking—in a single artwork.

MODERNISM Linked with the avant-garde, Modernism is the notion that artists and artworks are obliged to venture into unknown and singular artistic territories. The ideas of high risk along with lone achievement lend Modernism an heroic connotation.

MONTAGE A composite image produced by assembling various images and/or words together. Or, in cinematography, the compositional technique of splicing together short shots of related meaning to create an overall feeling.

NAIVE ART Art created by artists with no formal training.

NARRATIVE Art with storytelling subject matter.

NATURALISM A style of art that seeks to represent accurately and faithfully the actual appearance of things.

NEGATIVE SPACE Space formed between painted, drawn, sculpted, or otherwise-rendered positive shapes.

NEOCLASSICISM The late eighteenth and early nineteenth century return to classical aesthetics in Europe.

NEW IMAGE PAINTING The reemergence of narrative, representational painting in the late 1970s after several decades of abstraction's dominance.

PATTERN AND DECORATION An art style characterized by the use of elaborate patterns and decorative colors and configurations that emerged in the 1970s, partially as a reaction against Minimalism's spare geometry.

PERFORMANCE ART Art in which the subject is the performer's own body, actions, coverings, props, and the setting that the artist creates.

PHOTOREALISM Art that is as representational as a photograph and that is made from looking at a photograph or photographic reproduction rather than at the original subject.

PICTURE PLANE The actual, two-dimensional plane of a painting, drawing, or print, rather than the space depicted within it.

PLURALISM The simultaneous presence of many conflicting styles of art without any single style dominating.

POP ART The style that began in the early 1960s characterized by the imitation of commercial art such as advertising, movies, posters, television, comics, billboards, magazines, and consumer products as well as the mass-production of these items.

POSITIVE SPACE Filled areas in an artwork or those intended to be seen as objects.

POST-IMPRESSIONISM Mid-nineteenth to early twentieth century artists who extended the freedom of color and brushwork of the Impressionists into more emotional and analytical painting than the primarily descriptive Impressionism. The analytical Post-Impressionists were Georges Seurat and Paul Cezanne; the emotional ones, Vincent van Gogh and Paul Gauguin.

POST-MINIMALISM A style that emerged

in the late 1960s that employed some of the artistic assumptions of Minimalism but that reacted against them, adding gesture, movement, process, autobiography, narrative, and anthropomorphism to Minimalism's spare and static geometry, formalism, and emphasis on purely perceptual phenomena.

POST-MODERNISM A style that emerged in the 1980s that reversed the Modernists' opposition to the majority culture by embracing and using commonly understood images, symbols, and signs from popular culture and fine art alike, often combining many sources in one artwork. Post-Modernists aimed to reach a wider audience than the narrow, elitist one of the Modernists.

POST-PAINTERLY ABSTRACTION A term used by the American art critic Clement Greenberg to designate the smoothly-painted abstract paintings that chronologically followed Abstract Expressionism. Color Field Painting became the preferred term.

PROCESS ART Art in which the process of its making is the primary subject of the artwork. Processes such as pouring, melting, splashing, tearing, or scattering typify process art, an aspect of Post-Minimalism.

PROTO POP ART Art which chronologically preceded Pop Art but which contained some of its ingredients. Robert Rauschenberg and Jasper Johns are the primary proto Pop artists. Rauschenberg's use of photographic images taken from newspapers and magazines plus his incorporation of manufactured objects into his artworks prefigured Pop artists' borrowing from mass media and commerce. Jasper Johns's paintings of targets, flags, alphabets, maps, and other printed, person-made subjects rather than of the natural world prefigured Pop artists borrowing from commercial art graphics. Both artists, however, carried over a handmade appearance of their painted surfaces rather than employing the slick, machine made appearance favored by the later Pop artists.

REALISM In mid-nineteenth century France, an artistic movement that concentrated on subjects of everyday, and often working-class, life captured in a straightforward style that avoided stylization, emotionalism, or idealization.

REDUCTIVE GEOMETRY The most spare and essential manifestation a geometric shape or form can be made into, devoid of any unnecessary connotation, surface, color, or other element.

REGIONALIST An artist whose art is about experiences or artistic issues that are unique to a particular region but which may lack larger scope.

RENAISSANCE The period in Europe from about 1400 to 1600 during which interest in the physical world awakened, and the dignity and worth of the individual came to be emphasized. In art, the harmony, symmetry, and rationality of Classical works were revived.

REPRESENTATIONAL Referring to artworks that aim to present likenesses of known subjects.

ROMANTICISM A nineteenth-century art style that formed in reaction to Neoclassicism. Romanticists were concerned with individuality, subjectivity, and self-expression and their paintings emphasized changing color, atmosphere, light, and subjective, sensual effects. Romanticism in the more general art historical sense is often seen in opposition to or in succession with Classicism. For example, the Renaissance is seen as a Classical period, whereas the Baroque period is seen as a Romantic one.

SERIAL IMAGERY The practice of using the same basic forms, colors, or syntax, without major variation, within each example in a series of artworks. The slight variations from one artwork to another in the series thus become more distinct than if they were made as individual works. Serial imagery is different from theme and variation in the degree of difference between each artwork in the series.

SIGNATURE MATERIAL An odd material—such as flocking, lead, rubber, or neon—which an artist uses frequently and with which he or she becomes identified, as with a signature.

SITE-SPECIFIC SCULPTURE Sculpture that is so integrated with its site that it could not be moved or made at a different site without significantly altering its aesthetic or destroying it.

SPACE The area occupied, activated, or suggested by an artwork.

SPATIAL ILLUSIONISM The illusion of three-dimensional space on a two-dimensional surface.

SURREALISM An early twentieth-century art movement that was concerned with portraying the workings of the subconscious mind as revealed in dreams or in irrational behavior. Surrealists expressed irrationality and dream logic by arranging incongruous images that defy common-sense interpretations. Some Surrealists also employed automatism, or the use of accidents, as in blotting or doodling, believing that they were thereby tapping the unconscious. This was an important precedent to the Abstract Expressionists' use of automatism.

THREE-DIMENSIONAL Possessing the dimensions of height, width, and depth.

TWO-DIMENSIONAL Possessing the dimensions of height and width.

TYPOGRAPHY The art of designing, sizing, and combining letterforms or type faces on a printed page.

VIDEO An electronic process of creating moving pictures by laying down images and sound as tracks on magnetic tape.

Bibliography

INTRODUCTION

Battcock, Gregory, ed., *Minimalism: A Critical Anthology*. New York: E. P. Dutton & Company, Inc., 1968.

Bourdon, David, *Carl Andre*. New York: Jaap Rietman, Inc., 1978.

Compton, Michael and Sylvester, David, *Robert Morris*. London: The Tate Gallery, exhibition catalogue, 1971.

D'Harnoncourt, Anne and McShine, Kynastan, eds., *Marcel Duchamp*. New York and Philadelphia: The Museum of Modern Art and the Philadelphia Museum of Art, 1973.

Geist, Sidney, *Constantin Brancusi: 1876–1957*. New York: Solomon R. Guggenheim Museum, exhibition catalogue, 1969.

Goldberg, RoseLee, *Performance: Live Art 1909 to the Present*. New York: Harry N. Abrams, Inc., 1979.

Haskell, Barbara. *BLAM!: The Explosion of Pop, Minimalism, and Performance 1958–1964*. New York: Whitney Museum of American Art, exhibition catalogue, in association with W. W. Norton and Company, New York and London, 1984.

Judd, Donald, *Complete Writings 1959–1975*. Halifax, Nova Scotia: The Press of the Nova Scotia College of Art and Design and New York: New York University Press, 1975.

Schjeldahl, Peter, *Art of Our Time: The Saatchi Collection*, Volume 1. London: Lund Humphries in association with Rizzoli, New York, 1984.

Smith, Brydon, *Donald Judd*. Ottawa, Canada: National Gallery of Canada, Ottawa, exhibition catalogue, 1975.

Tomkins, Calvin, *Off the Wall: The Art World of Our Time*. Garden City, New York: Doubleday and Company, 1980.

Waldman, Diane, *Carl Andre*. New York: Solomon R. Guggenheim Museum, exhibition catalogue, 1970.

Chapter 1: CONCEPTUAL ART

Baldessari, John, *John Baldessari*. New York: The New Museum, exhibition catalogue, 1981.

Battcock, Gregory, ed., *Idea Art: A Critical Anthology*. New York: E. P. Dutton and Company, Inc., 1973.

Burden, Chris, *Chris Burden: A Twenty-Year Survey*. Newport Beach, California: Newport Harbor Art Museum, exhibition catalogue, 1988.

Grundberg, Andy and Gauss, Kathleen McCarthy, *Photography and Art: Interactions Since 1946*. New York: Abbeville Press, 1987.

Legg, Alicia, ed., essays by Lucy R. Lippard, Bernice Rose, and Robert Rosenblum, *Sol LeWitt*. New York: The Museum of Modern Art, exhibition catalogue, 1978.

LeWitt, Sol, *Sol LeWitt Drawings 1968–1984*. Amsterdam: the Stedelijk Museum; Eindhoven, Holland: Van Abbemuseum; and Hartford, Connecticut: the Wadsworth Atheneum, 1984.

Livingston, Jane and Tucker, Marcia, *Bruce Nauman*. Los Angeles: Los Angeles County Museum of Art, exhibition catalogue, 1972.

Lyons, Lisa and Levin, Kim, *Wegman's World*. Minneapolis: Walker Art Center, exhibition catalogue, 1983.

Meyer, Ursula, *Conceptual Art*. New York: E. P. Dutton and Company, Inc., 1972.

Richardson, Brenda, *Gilbert and George*. Baltimore, Maryland: The Baltimore Museum of Art, exhibition catalogue, 1984.

van Bruggin, Coosje, *John Baldessari*. New York: Rizzoli, 1990.

Chapter 2: VIDEO, FILM, AND PERFORMANCE ART

Borden, Lizzie, et al, *Castelli-Sonnabend Videotapes and Films*. New York: Castelli-Sonnabend Tapes and Films, Inc., 1974.

Coplans, John, *Andy Warhol*. Pasadena, California: Pasadena Art Museum, exhibition catalogue, 1970.

Davis, Douglas and Simmons, Allison, eds., *The New Television: A Public/Private Art*. Cambridge, Massachusetts: The MIT Press, 1977.

Frascina, Francis and Harrison, Charles, eds., *Modern Art and Modernism: A Critical Anthology*. New York: Harper and Row, 1982.

Goldberg, RoseLee, *Performance: Live Art 1909 to the Present*. New York: Harry N. Abrams, Inc., 1979.

Hanhardt, John G., ed., with essays by Dieter Ronte, Michael Nyman, John G. Hanhardt, and David A. Ross, *Nam June Paik*. New York: Whitney Museum of American Art in association with W. W. Norton and Company, exhibition catalogue, 1982.

Hanhardt, John G., ed., *Video Culture: A Critical Investigation*. Rochester, New York: Gibbs M. Smith, Inc., Peregrine Smith Books in association with Visual Studies Workshop Press, 1986.

Haskell, Barbara, *BLAM!: The*

Explosion of Pop, Minimalism, and Performance: 1958–1964. New York: Whitney Museum of American Art, in association with W. W. Norton and Company, exhibition catalogue, 1984.

Kaprow, Allan, *Assemblage, Environments & Happenings*. New York: Harry N. Abrams, Inc., undated.

Koch, Stephen, *Stargazer: Andy Warhol's World and His Films*. New York: Praeger, 1973.

McLuhan, Marshall, *The Medium is the Massage: An Inventory of Effects*. New York: Bantam Books, 1967.

McLuhan, Marshall, *Understanding Media: The Extensions of Man*. New York: Signet, 1964.

Oldenburg, Claes, *Store Days*. New York: Something Else Press, 1967.

Richardson, Brenda, *Gilbert and George*. Baltimore, Maryland: The Baltimore Museum of Art, exhibition catalogue, 1984.

Schneider, Ira and Korot, Beryl, eds., *Video Art: An Anthology*. New York: Harcourt Brace Jovanovich, 1976.

Snow, Michael, *Michael Snow/A Survey*. Toronto, Ontario, Canada: The Art Gallery of Ontario in collaboration with the Isaacs Gallery, 1970.

Tomkins, Calvin, *Off the Wall: The Art World of Our Time*. Garden City, New York: Doubleday and Company, 1980.

Tomkin, Calvin, *The Bride and the Bachelors*. New York: Viking, 1968.

Chapter 3: EARTHWORKS AND SITE-SPECIFIC SCULPTURE

Adcock, Craig and Russell, John, *James Turrell: The Roden Crater Project*. Tucson, Arizona: The University of Arizona Museum of Art, exhibition catalogue, 1986.

Armstrong, Richard and Marshall, Richard, *The New Sculpture: 1965–1975*. New York: Whitney Museum of American Art, 1990.

Baker, Elizabeth, "Artworks on the Land," *Art in America*, January, 1976.

Brown, Julia, ed., *Michael Heizer: Sculpture in Reverse*. Los Angeles: The Museum of Contemporary Art, 1984.

Brown, Julia, ed., *Occluded Front: James Turrell*. Los Angeles: The Museum of Contemporary Art and The Lapis Press, 1985.

Heizer, Michael, "The Art of Michael Heizer," *Artforum*, December, 1969.

Hobbs, Robert, *Robert Smithson: Sculpture*. Ithaca and London: Cornell University Press, 1981.

Holt, Nancy, ed., *The Writings of Robert Smithson*. New York: New York University Press, 1979.

Kurtz, Bruce, "Last Call at Max's," *Artforum*, April, 1981.

Chapter 4: POST-MINIMALISM

Armstrong, Richard, *Artschwager, Richard*. New York: Whitney Museum of American Art, exhibition catalogue, 1988.

Krauss, Rosalind, *Richard Serra/Sculpture*. New York: The Museum of Modern Art, exhibition catalogue, 1986.

Levin, Kim, *Lucas Samaras*. New York: Harry N. Abrams, Inc., 1975.

Lippard, Lucy, *Eva Hesse*. New York: New York University Press, 1976.

Marshall, Richard and Smith, Roberta, *Joel Shapiro*. New York: Whitney Museum of American Art, exhibition catalogue, 1982.

Monte, James and Tucker, Marcia, *Anti-Illusion: Procedures/Materials*. New York: Whitney Museum of American Art, exhibition catalogue, 1969.

Pincus-Witten, Robert, *Post-Minimalism*. London: Out of London Press, 1977.

Pincus-Witten, Robert and Shearer, Linda, *Eva Hesse: A Memorial Exhibition*. New York: Solomon R. Guggenheim Museum, exhibition catalogue, 1972.

Samaras, Lucas, *Lucas Samaras*. New York: Whitney Museum of American Art, exhibition catalogue, 1972.

Serra, Richard and Weyergraf, Clara, *Richard Serra: Interviews, Etc., 1970–1980*. Yonkers, New York: The Hudson River Museum, 1980.

Szeeman, Harald, *When Attitudes Become Form*. Berne, Switzerland and London: Kunsthalle Berne and The Institute of Contemporary Arts, exhibition catalogue, 1969.

Tucker, Marcia, *Richard Tuttle*. New York: Whitney Museum of American Art, exhibition catalogue, 1975.

Chapter 5: PLURALISM

Battcock, Gregory, ed., *Super Realism: A Critical Anthology*. New York: E. P. Dutton and Company, Inc., 1975.

Goodyear, Frank H., Jr., *Contemporary American Realism Since 1960*. Boston: New York Graphic Society, 1981.

Lyons, Lisa and Storr, Robert, *Chuck Close*. New York: Rizzoli, 1987.

Marshall, Richard, *New Image Painting*. New York: Whitney Museum of American Art, exhibition catalogue, 1978.

Meisel, Louis K., *Photorealism*. New York: Harry N. Abrams, Inc., 1980.

Meisel, Louis K., *Richard Estes: The Complete Paintings 1966–1985*, essay by John Perreault. New York: Harry N. Abrams, Inc., 1986.

Pearlstein, Philip, *Philip Pearlstein: Paintings and Watercolours*, with essay by Michael Auping. Florida: The John and Mable Ringling Museum of Art, exhibition catalogue, 1981.

Robbins, Corinne, *The Pluralist Era: American Art, 1968–1981*. New York: Harper and Row, 1984.

Varnedoe, Kirk, *Duane Hanson*. New York: Harry N. Abrams, Inc., 1985.

Chapter 6: NEO-EXPRESSIONISM

A New Spirit in Painting, essay by Christos M. Jaochimides. London: Royal Academy of Arts, exhibition catalogue, 1981.

Art of Our Time: The Saatchi Collection, Volumes 3 and 4. London and New York: Lund Humphries in association with Rizzoli, 1984.

Auping, Michael, *Francesco Clemente*. New York: Harry N. Abrams, Inc., 1985.

Clemente, Francesco, *Clemente*, interview with Rainer Crone and Georgia Marsh. New York: Vintage Books, 1987.

Gumpert, Lynn and Rifkin, Ned, *Golub*. New York: The New Museum of Contemporary Art, exhibition catalogue, 1984.

Kardon, Janet, *David Salle*, with an essay by Lisa Phillips. Philadelphia: Institute of Contemporary Art, University of Pennsylvania, 1986.

Oliva, Achille Bonito, *The Italian Trans-avantgarde*. Milan: Giancarlo Politi Editore, 1981.

Polke, Sigmar, *Sigmar Polke*. Cologne: Joseph Haubrich Kunsthalle, exhibition catalogue, 1984.

Rosenthal, Mark, *Anselm Kiefer*. Chicago and Philadelphia: The Art Institute of Chicago and the Philadelphia Museum of Art, exhibition catalogue, 1987.

Rosenthal, Mark, and Marshall, Richard, *Jonathan Borofsky*. Philadelphia: Philadelphia Museum of Art in association with the Whitney Museum of American Art, 1984.

Salle, David, *Salle*, interview with Peter Schjeldahl. New York: Vintage Books, 1987.

Storr, Robert, *Philip Guston*. New York: Abbeville Press, 1986.

Zeitgeist, various essayists. Berlin: Internationale Kunstausstellung, exhibition catalogue, 1982.

Chapter 7: POST-MODERNISM

Battcock, Gregory, ed., *The Art of Performance: A Critical Anthology* New York: E. P. Dutton and Company, Inc.

Felshin, Nina and McEvilley, Thomas, *Focus on the Image: The Rivendell Collection*. New York: ITA Ciroiratuibm 1985.

Fischl, Eric, *Eric Fischl*, essay by Peter Schjeldahl. New York: Stewart, Tabori and Chang, 1988.

Foster, Hal, ed., *The Anti-Aesthetic: Essays on Postmodern Culture*. Port Townsend, Washington: Bay Press, 1983.

Haring, Keith, *Keith Haring*, essays by Robert Pincus-Witten and Jeffrey Deitch. New York: Tony Shafrazi Gallery, exhibition catalogue, 1982.

Holzer, Jenny, *Jenny Holzer*. Des Moines, Iowa: Des Moines Art Center, exhibition catalogue, 1986.

Kruger, Barbara, *We won't play nature to your culture*, essays by Craig Owens and Jane Weinstock. London: Institute of Contemporary Arts, exhibition catalogue, 1983.

Morris, Robert, *Robert Morris: Works of the Eighties*, essays by Robert F. Fry and Donald Kuspit and contributions by I. Michael Danoff, Mary Jane Jacob, and Paul Schimmel. Chicago and Newport Beach, California: Museum of Contemporary Art and Newport Harbor Art Museum, exhibition catalogue, 1986.

Richardson, Brenda, *Scott Burton*. Baltimore: The Baltimore Museum of Art, exhibition catalogue, 1989.

Sherman, Cindy, *Cindy Sherman*, essays by Peter Schjeldahl and I. Michael Danoff. New York: Pantheon Books, 1984.

Waldman, Diane, *Enzo Cucchi*. New York: Solomon R. Guggenheim Museum and Rizzoli, 1986.

Chapter 8: SCULPTURE OF THE 1980s

Caldwell, John, *Richard Deacon*, with essays by Lynne Cook, Richard Deacon, Michael Newman, and Peter Schjeldahl. Pittsburgh, Pennsylvania: The Carnegie Museum of Art, 1988.

Clothier, Peter, "Peter Shelton: Dwellings in the Abstract," *Art News*, September, 1987.

Graham-Dixon, Andrew, "Cragg's Way," *Art News*, March, 1989.

Madoff, Steven Henry, "Sculpture Unbound," *Art News*, Nov., 1986.

Melrod, George, "Carol Hepper Sheds Her Skin," *Sculpture Magazine*, May/June, 1989.

Rugoff, Ralph, "An Impressive Group of Emerging Talents Extends the Limits of 'L.A. Art': The Wry Stuff," *L.A. Style*, March, 1988.

"Sculptors' Interviews: Tom Butter," *Art in America*, November, 1985.

"Sculptors' Interviews: Roni Horn," *Art in America*, November, 1985.

Walker Art Center, Minneapolis, *Sculpture Inside/Outside*, exhibition catalogue, introduction by Martin Friedman, essays by Douglas Dreishpoon, Nancy Princenthal, Carter Ratcliff, and Joan Simon. New York: Rizzoli, 1988.

Whitney Museum of American Art at Equitable Center, *Enclosing the Void: Eight Contemporary Sculptors*, essay by Susan Lubowsky, exhibition catalogue, 1989.

Chapter 9: SIMULATIONISM

Bickerton, Ashley, and Rankin, Aimee, "Fluid Mechanics: A Conversation Between Ashley Bickerton and Aimee Rankin (An Artists' Dialogue)," *Arts Magazine*, December, 1987.

Calley, Shaun, "Ashley Bickerton: A Revealing Exposé of the Application of Art," *Flash Art*, November/December, 1988.

Cotter, Holland, "Haim Steinbach: Shelf Life," *Art in America*, May, 1988.

Francblin, Catherine, "Interview with Jean Baudrillard," *Flash Art*, October/November, 1986.

Halley, Peter, *Collected Essays: 1981–87*. Zürich, Switzerland: Bruno Bischofberger, 1988.

Heartney, Eleanor, "The Hot New Cool Art: Simulationism," *Art News*, January, 1987.

Holt, Nancy, ed., *The Writings of Robert Smithson*, "Conversation with Robert Smithson on April 22, 1972," edited by Bruce Kurtz. New York: New York University Press, 1979.

Kertess, Klaus, "Bad," *Parkett*, Volume 19, 1989.

Koons, Jeff, "From Full Fathom Five," *Parkett*, Volume 19, 1989.

Pincus-Witten, Robert, "Entries: Concentrated Juice and Kitschy Kitschy Koons," *Arts Magazine*, February, 1989.

Robbins, A., "An Interview with Allan McCollum," *Arts Magazine*, October, 1985.

Schjeldahl, Peter, "A Visit to the Salon of Autumn 1986," *Art in America*, December, 1986.

Siegel, Jeanne, "Jeff Koons: Unachievable States of Being," *Arts Magazine*, October, 1986.

Siegel, Jeanne, "The Artist/Critic of the Eighties, Part One: Peter Halley and Stephen Westfall," *Arts Magazine*, September, 1985.

Smith, Roberta, "Rituals of Consumption," *Art in America*, May, 1988.

Index

Numbers in bold refer to illustrations